RUSSIA'S WAR ON UKRAINE

Understanding why Russia invaded Ukraine requires preparing for what may come next. This book is the first to provide an interdisciplinary study of the first full-scale war in Europe since 1945, which is having global ramifications on interstate relations, international law, international organisations, energy questions and economies. Written by two leading scholars of Ukrainian and Russian politics and history, and based on extensive fieldwork and primary sources, the book moves beyond established Western ideas about Russia to show that Russian military aggression against Ukraine is domestically, not externally, driven. The authors analyse the statements and policies of the Russian leadership under Vladimir Putin, Russia's post-communist political culture and Russia's understanding of itself as a civilisation without borders. Imperial nationalism, nostalgia, Russia's divergent identity and political system to Ukraine's and Kremlin anti-Western xenophobia are the key elements underlying Russian war against Ukraine.

TARAS KUZIO is Professor at the National University of Kyiv, Mohyla Academy (Ukraine). He has written and edited twenty-four books and seven think tank monographs, including, most recently, *Russia and Modern Fascism: New Perspectives on the Kremlin's War Against Ukraine* (2025), *Crimea: Where Russia's War Started and Where Ukraine Will Win* (2024), *Russian Disinformation and Western Scholarship* (2023) and *Russian Nationalism and the Russian-Ukrainian War* (2022).

MICHAŁ WAWRZONEK is Professor at the Ignatianum University in Cracow (Poland). He is the author or co author of four monographs: *Memory, Politics and Legacy of Metropolitan Andrey Sheptytsky* (2023), *Orthodoxy Versus Post-Communism? Belarus, Serbia, Ukraine and the Russkiy Mir* (2016), *Religion and Politics in Ukraine: The Orthodox and Greek Catholic Churches as Elements of Ukraine's Political System* (2014) and *Ecumenical Activity of Metropolitan Sheptytsky in Ukraine and Russia* (2006 in Ukrainian).

RUSSIA'S WAR ON UKRAINE

The Four Roots of Putin's Invasion

TARAS KUZIO
National University of Kyiv, Mohyla Academy

MICHAŁ WAWRZONEK
Ignatianum University in Cracow

Shaftesbury Road, Cambridge CB2 8EA, United Kingdom

One Liberty Plaza, 20th Floor, New York, NY 10006, USA

477 Williamstown Road, Port Melbourne, VIC 3207, Australia

314–321, 3rd Floor, Plot 3, Splendor Forum, Jasola District Centre, New Delhi – 110025, India

103 Penang Road, #05-06/07, Visioncrest Commercial, Singapore 238467

Cambridge University Press is part of Cambridge University Press & Assessment, a department of the University of Cambridge.

We share the University's mission to contribute to society through the pursuit of education, learning and research at the highest international levels of excellence.

www.cambridge.org
Information on this title: www.cambridge.org/9781009645539

DOI: 10.1017/9781009645553

© Taras Kuzio and Michał Wawrzonek 2026

This publication is in copyright. Subject to statutory exception and to the provisions of relevant collective licensing agreements, no reproduction of any part may take place without the written permission of Cambridge University Press & Assessment.

When citing this work, please include a reference to the DOI 10.1017/9781009645553

First published 2026

Cover image: Images and design inspiration: Yuriy Savinov.

A catalogue record for this publication is available from the British Library

A Cataloging-in-Publication data record for this book is available from the Library of Congress

ISBN 978-1-009-64550-8 Hardback
ISBN 978-1-009-64553-9 Paperback

Cambridge University Press & Assessment has no responsibility for the persistence or accuracy of URLs for external or third-party internet websites referred to in this publication and does not guarantee that any content on such websites is, or will remain, accurate or appropriate.

For EU product safety concerns, contact us at Calle de José Abascal, 56, 1º, 28003 Madrid, Spain, or email eugpsr@cambridge.org

Since the declared goals of the SVO ['special military operation'] are in principle incompatible with the continued existence of a terrorist organisation called Ukraine, it is absolutely clear that we must liquidate it completely.

Russian State Duma and A Just Russia Party deputy Anatoly Wasserman

(*Moskovski Komsomolets*, 2 August 2025 https://www.mk.ru/politics/2025/08/02/na-trampa-davyat-vasserman-soobshhil-kogda-zavershitsya-svo-na-ukraine.html)

CONTENTS

Acknowledgements   *page* viii

Introduction: Russia's War on Ukraine – The Four Roots of Putin's Invasion   1

PART I   Imperialism and Nationalism

1. Imperial Nationalism   21
2. Pan-Russian World and Ukraine   57
3. Russian Orthodox Church and Ukraine   91

PART II   Nostalgia

4. Great Patriotic War and Cult of Stalin   127
5. Ukrainian 'Nationalists/Fascists/Nazis'   172

PART III   Divergence

6. Diverging Identities in Russia and Ukraine   217
7. Diverging Political Systems in Russia and Ukraine   260

PART IV   International Dimension

8. Messianism, Imperialism and Anti-Colonialism   297
9. Xenophobia   342

Index   382

ACKNOWLEDGEMENTS

We would like to thank Paul D'Aniei (University of California at Riverside) for strategic advice during the initial stages of developing the framework for our book. We would also like to thank Roman Małecki (Ignatianum University in Cracow), Alicja Curanović (University of Warsaw) and Marcin Składanowski (Catholic University of Lublin) for their invaluable assistance in the preparation of our manuscript for publication.

Introduction

Russia's War on Ukraine – The Four Roots of Putin's Invasion

After 1991, an orientalist image of central-eastern Europe and Eurasia among scholars and political elites in the West persisted, especially towards countries that emerged from the former Soviet Union. Orientalist prejudices were manifested in descriptions of Eurasia as a region where ethnic nationalism, separatism, and extremism was widespread. While Ukrainians demanded to be classified as Europeans, they were relegated to Eurasia and viewed through a Russian lens until the 2003–2004 Orange Revolution, although we believe it took until Russia's 2022 full-scale invasion for the West to view Ukraine as a state fully independent of Russia.

Hans Kohn's framework for understanding 'good civic nationalism' to exist in the West and 'bad ethnic nationalism' to be predominant in the East continued to influence this orientalist paradigm (for a contemporary example see Onuch and Hale, 2022; for critiques see Kuzio, 2002; Shevel, 2024). This prevented an understanding of nation and state building processes in Ukraine and the roots of problem areas in Ukrainian-Russian relations after 1991. Meanwhile, scholars and policymakers exaggerated regional and linguistic divisions in Ukraine, leading most to believe Russian-speakers in southeastern Ukraine would sympathise with a Russian invasion force (Kuzyk, 2019).

Jakob Hauter (2023, p. 29) writes that most of the Western academic writing in 2014–2021 on the causes of the conflict in the Donbas region of eastern Ukraine was closer to the Russian 'civil war narrative' than the Ukrainian 'invasion narrative'. Dominique Arel and Jesse Driscoll (2023) were late in defining the Russian-Ukrainian war in 2014–2021 as a 'civil war' in their study published after the full-scale invasion (for a different perspective see Hauter, 2023; Larys, 2025). Hauter (2023, p. 31) argued that a 'civil war narrative' is unable to explain the strength and success of Ukrainian resistance and resilience after 2022 if we are supposed to believe Ukrainians were unable to contain a 'civil war' in the preceding eight years. Ukraine's resistance and resilience after 2022 is only explainable by viewing it as a response to the acceleration of an existing Russian-Ukrainian war that became full-scale. Hauter (2023) analyses six 'critical junctures' between April and August 2014 and finds Russian intervention in four of them with the two where there is no evidence of Russian intervention experiencing the least amount of violence. Greater violence and evolution of the conflict into a Russian-Ukrainian war from 2014 was a product of Russian escalation at every stage of these six 'critical junctures'.

Western scholars, think tank experts and policymakers who had bought into the 'civil war narrative' viewed Ukraine as a weak and divided state. Western leaders vetoed the supply of military assistance to Ukraine while leading US academics and think tank experts on Russia and Eurasia opposed the sending of military aid to Ukraine.[1] Western policymakers treated the DNR (Donetsk Peoples Republic) and LNR (Luhansk Peoples Republic) as 'independent actors' (rather than Russian proxy entities) and Russia as not a party to the conflict and a peace mediator (Hauter, 2023). The West continued business as usual with Russia (e.g., building Nord Stream II) and imposed weak sanctions against Russia. It is not surprising that in 2022, there was therefore general agreement among Western scholars, think tank experts and policymakers that Ukraine would be quickly defeated and occupied by Russia (Cohen and O'Brien, 2024). In other words, they held similar views to the Kremlin's stereotypes of Ukraine that propelled belief in the 'special military operation' quickly defeating and conquering Ukraine.

The Western orientalist paradigm would look to Russia playing the role of an actor that resolved 'deep-seated problems' in central-eastern Europe, but especially in Eurasia. A good example of this Western approach was President George H. W. Bush's infamous 'chicken Kyiv' speech to the Ukrainian parliament on 1 August 1991 warning about the dangers of 'suicidal nationalism'. In the post-Soviet era, the West did not challenge the Kremlin's hegemonic claim to a Eurasian sphere of influence or seek to resolve frozen conflicts manufactured by Russia in Moldova, Georgia, and Azerbaijan.

In many ways the persistence of a Western orientalist paradigm is unsurprising. After 1991, most Soviet scholars of the Soviet Union and Kremlinologists became Russianists who nevertheless claimed an expertise on Ukraine and all of Eurasia. Most Western journalists continue to write from Moscow about the countries which emerged from the Soviet Union. It is therefore not surprising that research on countries that emerged from the Soviet Union remains dominated by Russianists who,

---

[1] www.foreignaffairs.com/ask-the-experts/2015-02-24/should-united-states-arm-ukraine

in the main use primary sources from Russia and thereby practise what we call academic orientalism (Kuzio, 2020, pp. 66–81). Social processes taking place in the non-Russian successor states of the former Soviet Union remained on the margin of 'mainstream' research until decades after 1991. This was especially true in the case of Ukraine until the Orange and 2013–2014 Euromaidan Revolutions, and in many cases even later. For example, Western art galleries and museums ignored requests to change the description of exhibited painters from Ukraine to 'Ukrainian', rather than 'Russian', until after the 2022 full-scale invasion.[2] Ukrainians were only viewed as European by Brussels after Russia's full-scale invasion when the EU offered Ukraine candidate status in June 2022.

Russia's first invasion of Ukraine in 2014 produced some good studies but also several highly Russophile and even pro-Vladimir Putin studies (for a survey see Kuzio, 2023, pp. 87–122). The 2022 full-scale invasion led to a second round of books by scholars without expertise on Ukraine, Russian-Ukrainian relations and the roots of Russian imperial nationalist and chauvinistic attitudes towards Ukraine and Ukrainians. Western scholars barely noticed the de-humanisation of Ukrainians in the Russian media and official discourse and dissemination of White Russian émigré thinking and writing, which had been taking place for nearly two decades before Russia's full-scale invasion. Some scholars have provided original studies of the full-scale war and the roots of Russia's military aggression and genocidal goals (D'Anieri, 2019, 2023; Kuzio, 2022; Koval and Tereshchenko, 2023; Hauter, 2023; Popova and Shevel, 2024; Garner, 2023; McGlynn, 2023; Plokhy, 2023; Karatnycky, 2024; Davis, 2024; Ash, 2024; Finkel, 2024; Larys, 2025). Nevertheless, scholars of Russia writing about the war have continued to practice academic orientalism (for two examples see Arutunyan, 2022; Ramani, 2023) or have written about the full-scale war using a Russophile lens or without a deep understanding of the roots of the war (for an overview see Kuzio, 2023).

There has been an absence of scholarly study of White Russian émigrés in Western academic journals and books. The one scholar who has studied the rehabilitation of White Russian émigrés is Marlene Laruelle (see Laruelle and Karnysheva, 2022). Laruelle and Margarita Karnysheva (2002, p. 98), though, have downplayed their influence on Putin's regime, writing that the influence of Ivan Ilyin on the Kremlin's

---

[2] See the interview with Creative Director of the Ukrainian Institute (https://ui.org.ua/) Tetyana Filevska and co-founder of the civic organisation Ukraine WOW (https://ukrainewow.org/) Julia Solovey on 'Ukraine: The Latest,' *The Telegraph*, 21 February 2025. www.youtube.com/watch?v=6glrov7Z5eU

ideology 'still awaits verification' while those claiming Putin's vision of Russia is based on Ilyin have yet to show 'any direct connection between the two [which] remain to be traced'. Putin is 'much more cautious' towards the rehabilitation of White Russian emigres, Ilyin and General Anton Denikin, and they therefore do not 'inspire the Kremlin's vision of Russia' (Laruelle, 2025, pp. 8, 37).

Scholars are therefore faced with a conundrum as to the paucity of academic research about two important 'roots' of the Russian-Ukrainian war. The first is the transition from the Soviet recognition of the existence of a separate Ukrainian people to the Tsarist and White Russian émigré denial Ukrainians exist and claim Ukrainians and Russians are 'one people' and Ukrainians are the Little Russian branch of a pan-Russian people (*obshcherusskij narod*). Scholars of Russian nationalism, including Laruelle (2022, 2025), do not provide an explanation as to when this happened and why this took place. The second is when and why did Putin's obsession with Ukraine and Ukrainians radicalise and lead to his decision to launch a 'special military operation' on 24 February 2022?

The deterioration in Ukrainian-Russian relations came about because of two interrelated factors taking place at a similar time after 2012–2014. Firstly, because of Ukrainian nation-building policies under Presidents Poroshenko and Volodymyr Zelenskyy (2019) and the marginalisation of pro-Russian political forces. This important transformation of Ukrainian identity has largely been ignored in studies of Russian nationalism and ideology in Putin's regime; Laruelle (2025, pp. 67–68, 106) provides only brief comments on the receipt of autocephaly for the Orthodox Church of Ukraine, forbidding of Soviet symbols, Ukrainian language becoming 'compulsory' and the 'banning' of pro-Russian TV channels. In fact, Ukraine adopted these, and many more identity policies after 2014 that angered Moscow, which we discuss in Chapters 6 and 7. Secondly, these developments in Ukraine were taking place at the same time as imperial nationalism was growing in Russia after Putin returned to the presidency in 2012.

We therefore argue that White Russian emigres have been a major influence on how Putin, the Kremlin and the Russian people came to view Ukraine as an artificial construct and Ukrainians as not constituting a separate people. Viewed from Kyiv, therefore, memory politics in Putin's Russia did not resemble a 'centrist and moderate force that refuses all "extremes"' (Laruelle, 2025, p. 8). Russia's new school textbooks, introduced in September 2023, a project led by Vladimir Medinsky, chairman of the Russian Military Historical Society and head of Russia's delegation in peace talks with Ukraine, Moscow State Institute of International

Relations (MGIMO) Rector Anatoly Torkunov and head of the Institute of General History of the Russian Academy of Sciences Alexander Chubaryan, present Ukraine as an artificial, accidental and hostile formation towards Russia and justify Russian military aggression against Ukraine. From the vantage point of Kyiv, Putin's Russia did not resemble a regime that was 'centrist' and negative towards ethnonationalism (Laruelle, 2025, p. 192) but was turbo charged by imperial nationalism.

This book's eight chapters analyse four roots lying behind Russia's full-scale invasion of Ukraine: Imperialism and Nationalism; Nostalgia; Divergence, and Xenophobia. Although revanchism is a better definition of Russia's policies of reclaiming lost territory and supporting co-ethnics in Ukraine, this book conflates imperialism and nationalism into the term imperial nationalism.

As this book will show, these four roots are closely linked. For example, a strengthened Ukrainian identity fuels anti-Western xenophobia among Russian imperial nationalists because they view 'Ukrainianism' as a Western-supported and artificial construct aimed at dividing the 'Russian people'. Russia and Ukraine's increasing divergence, with the former following an authoritarian path within Eurasia and the latter a democratic path within Europe, has led to Russian feelings of 'betrayal' by Ukrainians and nostalgia for the Tsarist Empire and Soviet Union when Russia was recognised as a great power and Russians and Ukrainians were united as 'fraternal peoples' in an idealised world. As one Russian media outlet declared: 'Liberal globalists fight Russia with the hands of Ukrainian Nazis'.[3]

Russia's obsession with Ukraine was not invented by Putin but goes back centuries. The Muscovite kingdom became the Russian Empire in 1721, twelve years after the defeat of Ukrainian Cossack Hetman Ivan Mazepa and his Swedish allies at the Battle of Poltava. Russia has since then associated a union with Ukraine as enabling Russia to become a great power, or empire. Zbigniew Brzezinski famously wrote that 'Without Ukraine, Russia ceases to be an empire, but with Ukraine suborned and then subordinated, Russia automatically becomes an empire'. Putin (2020) said Russia could regain its status as 'a global rival' to Western powers by uniting with Ukraine. 'Some like dividing Ukraine and Russia. They believe it's a very important goal', Putin complained, 'Since any integration of Russia and Ukraine, along with their capacities and competitive advantages, would spell the emergence of a rival – a global rival for both Europe and the world'.

---

[3] https://euvsdisinfo.eu/report/liberal-globalists-fight-russia-with-the-hands-of-ukrainian-nazis/

The Tsarist Empire sought to block and repress the re-emergence of a Ukrainian identity distinct from Russian. These policies have been condemned by Ukraine but ignored by Putin and Russian imperial nationalists. The Ukrainian language was banned in the Tsarist Empire in July 1863 when Minister of Interior Petr Valuev prohibited public education and religious texts in Ukrainian. In May 1876, Tsar Alexander II issued the Ems Edict, which was far more severe and intended to destroy the development of Ukrainian literature and culture. The Tsarist Empire banned the import of Ukrainian language publications; printing of religious and grammar books in Ukrainian; and the publishing of books in Ukrainian for 'common people' and intellectual elites. Ukrainian-language publications were removed from libraries. Theatre performances, songs, poetry, and readings in Ukrainian were banned.

The Tsarist Empire – like contemporary Russia – claimed there had never been a Ukrainian state or language and culture, Ukrainians had no history, and they were Little Russians, one of three branches of a mythical pan-Russian people. Ukrainian identity distinct from Russian is a challenge to the foundational myth of a 'thousand-year Russian statehood'. Without Ukraine accepting its status as Little Russia, Russia's claim to Kyiv Rus as the cradle of the Russian state and a thousand-year history is challenged by Ukrainian national history. Moscow is 600 years younger than Kyiv and was a small village at the time of the Mongol destruction of Kyiv Rus in 1240. Ukrainian historians and Ukrainian identity views Kyiv Rus as the first Ukrainian state, as most of its territory lay within the borders of contemporary Ukraine. After 1240 the legacy of Kyiv Rus went to the Galician-Volhynian Kingdom. Russian historians and imperial nationalists view 'Kievan Russia' as the first Russian state, which after 1240 transferred to Vladimir-Suzdal, Muscovy, the Russian Empire, Soviet Union, and Russian Federation.

The doyen of Ukrainian history Mykhaylo Hrushevsky had to relocate from Kyiv to the Austro-Hungarian Empire, where he was appointed in 1894 to the chair of Ukrainian history at Lemberg (Lviv) University. In 1898 he began publishing his ten volume *History of Ukraine-Rus*, with the final volume published in 1937. Hrushevsky developed a framework which separated Russian and Ukrainian histories, thereby reinforcing a Ukrainian identity distinct from Russian. As we show in this book, contest between Ukrainian and pan-Russian identities and competing views of history lies at the heart of the Kremlin's war against Ukraine. Tsarist Russian policies – in a similar manner to Russian military aggression since 2014 – backfired. In both instances, repression of Ukrainian identity produced the opposite effect of speeding up its flowering and crystallisation.

The Soviet Union officially recognised a separate Ukrainian identity. However, at the same time, the USSR promoted eastern Slavic unity with Ukrainians and Russians described as having been born together and remaining forever united. Throughout the Soviet era, a Ukrainian identity distinct from Russian continued to compete with an eastern Slavic (pan-Russian) identity whose three peoples – Russians, Ukrainian, Belarusians – were to merge into a Russian-speaking Soviet people (*Homo Sovieticus*).

National communists, popular in Ukraine but not in Russia, were influential during three periods of liberalisation of the Soviet system: in the 1920s during the policies of indigenisation (Ukrainisation); in the 1960s under Soviet Ukrainian Communist Party of Ukraine (KPU) leader Petro Shelest, and from 1985 under Communist Party of the Soviet Union leader Mikhail Gorbachev. During periods of Soviet conservatism, a pan-Russian identity and Soviet Russian nationalism was accompanied by greater bouts of political repression and Russification: in 1934–1953 under dictator Joseph Stalin and between 1972 and 1989 under Soviet Ukrainian Communist Party leader Volodymyr Shcherbytsky. In post-Stalin USSR, Ukrainians represented the largest proportional to their population size group of political prisoners.

The two extremes of Ukraine's political spectrum, national communists and integral nationalists, both upheld a Ukrainian identity distinct from Russian. Ukrainian integral nationalist ideologue Dmytro Dontsov's influenced the KPZU (Communist Party of Western Ukraine) and leading national communists such as Mykola Khvylovy in Soviet Ukraine. Dontsov found a 'kindred spirit' in national communist Khvylovy, and they both called upon Ukraine to turn its back on Russia and turn towards Europe. Khvylovy and Dontsov both believed the removal of Russian influences would create an independent Ukrainian culture. Khvylovy, like other leading national communists, committed suicide in 1933, the year Stalin unleashed the *Holodomor*, which murdered four to five million Ukrainians and was followed by the Executed Renaissance and great terror. Shelest was removed in 1971 and was accused of 'national deviationism', because in his writings and statements about Ukrainian history, he analysed Ukraine's past separately from the history of Russia.

Russian Presidents Boris Yeltsin and Putin both viewed Eurasia as Russia's exclusive sphere of influence. They built Russia's post-Soviet relations with its neighbours, especially Ukraine and Belarus, upon the Soviet model of relations between Moscow and the Soviet republics where Russians are the leaders, and the Kremlin dominates and dictates to republics without real sovereignty. In the Kremlin's world view, the three eastern Slavs constituted the core of the Soviet Union, where

Russians, Ukrainians, and Belarusians had dominated the Soviet political, economic, military, and security elites. In the post-Soviet era, the Pan-Russian World (*Russkij mir*) would unite the three eastern Slavs through a pan-Russian identity and constitute the core of Russia's 'state-civilisation' and Eurasia (Wawrzonek, 2014).

We translate *Russkij mir* when used by Russian officials, religious leaders and others as the Pan-Russian World. When we are referring to the official organisation, we use the Russian World Foundation. *Russkij mir* is commonly translated as the Russian World, but we believe this leads to confusion, as it suggests the concept only refers to people who consider themselves Russians. But Putin, the Kremlin, and Russian imperial nationalists define the concept of *Russkij mir* as broader to include Russians, Ukrainians and Belarusians in an imagined eastern Slavic civilisational community whose political and spiritual centre is in Moscow, and whose identity is grounded in nostalgia for the Tsarist Empire and the Soviet Union, and which is xenophobic towards liberal values, the 'collective West' and the US-led unipolar world. We therefore use both the Pan-Russian World and *Russkij mir* because the concept incorporates all four roots of the war that are analysed in the nine chapters in this book.

As Paul D'Anieri has shown (2019), since the disintegration of the Soviet Union in 1991, Russia has had a long-term inability to come to terms with an independent Ukraine outside the Pan-Russian World, and therefore Russia's demands towards Ukraine have remained constant. In 2009, Russian President Dmitri Medvedev (2009; Kuzio, 2015, pp. 438–439) issued demands to President Viktor Yushchenko that were the same as those made by President Putin to President Volodymyr Zelenskyy thirteen years later after Russia launched its full-scale invasion of Ukraine. On both occasions, Medvedev and Putin demanded similar changes in Ukrainian memory politics, language, culture, religion and Euro-Atlantic integration. In the Spring 2022 peace talks, Russia demanded the repeal of an old law on TV and Radio (1994), law on Culture (2011), four de-communisation laws (2015), laws on the state service and judiciary (2016), education law (2017), language law (2019), and law on titular nations in Ukraine (2021), as well as a halt to alleged 'discrimination' against the Russian Orthodox Church in Ukraine and insisted Ukraine never joins NATO (Kuzio, 2024). Russia is disingenuous about not being opposed to Ukraine joining the European Union; in 2013, the Kremlin successfully pressured President Viktor Yanukovych to drop its integration into the EU, which is likely to mean it would oppose Ukraine's future membership. The Kremlin has derailed Georgia's path to EU membership.

The Kremlin's goal of 'de-nazification' and demands for Ukraine's capitulation include the removal of the Ukrainian president and government and its replacement with pro-Russian proxies. Russia falsely claims Zelenskyy is the illegitimate president of Ukraine and that any governmental body formed under his presidency is by extension illegitimate. The Kremlin is using a false reading of the Ukrainian constitution and Ukrainian legislation to delegitimise Ukraine's government and sovereignty because elections in 2024 could not have been held under martial law. In addition, the Kremlin continues a long-standing claim the Ukrainian government has been illegitimate since the Euromaidan Revolution 'illegal putsch'.

The revival and promotion of White Russian émigré writings deepened Russian belief they and Ukrainians are 'one people', the Ukrainian language is a Russian dialect, and Ukraine is an artificial construct and Western puppet state. The Kremlin's demands, whether Medvedev's in 2009 or Putin's in 2022, lie in how Russian imperial nationalists could only view Ukraine as a Little Russian puppet state, like Alexander Lukashenka's White Russia (Belarus) (Wawrzonek, 2014), and not as an independent state with its own agency. Until 2013, the Kremlin used soft power, energy, and the weaponisation of corruption to influence Ukrainian domestic and foreign policies and the country's trajectory. In 2014, after the second failure to use Yanukovych to achieve its goals in Ukraine (the first being during the Orange Revolution), the Kremlin reverted to military aggression. Russia invaded and annexed Crimea and supported pro-Russian uprisings in southeast Ukraine.

Russian territorial claims towards Ukraine have existed throughout the post-Soviet era. Russia annexed Crimea in 2014 and declared its fate decided and not open to future negotiations. From 2014, Putin and other Russian leaders declared southeastern Ukraine to be the 'historical Russian land' of *Novorossiya* (New Russia), and in 2022, four Ukrainian *oblasts* (Donetsk, Luhansk, Zaporizhzhya, Kherson) were annexed. If the 'special military operation' had gone to plan, Ukraine would have been reduced to a Little Russian puppet state based around its central regions. The Kremlin is offering Western Ukraine, which Russian imperial nationalists have never seen as part of the Pan-Russian World, to Poland, Hungary, and Romania.

The two Minsk Accords to end the Russian-Ukrainian war, signed in 2014 and 2015, were viewed by the Kremlin as a means to transform Ukraine, through its Donetsk and Luhansk Peoples Republics acting as Trojan Horses, into a Little Russian puppet state. The refusal of Presidents Petro Poroshenko and Zelenskyy to implement the Kremlin's interpretation of the Minsk Accords, coupled with the widening divergence of Ukraine from Russia after 2014, led to the decision in 2022 to launch a 'special military operation' to effectively teach Kyiv a lesson by quickly subjugating Ukraine and replacing Zelenskyy with a pro-Russian puppet regime led by leader of the Russian Opposition Platform-For Life Party Viktor Medvedchuk or Yanukovych. As this book shows, the 'special military operation' failed because it was premised on a Russian imperial nationalist myth of Ukraine inhabited primarily by Little Russians eager to be 'liberated' from their Nazi yoke.

Therefore, throughout the post-Soviet era, the Kremlin grappled with two interrelated questions. Firstly, whether a Ukrainian *or* (Russia's preference) a pan-Russian identity would dominate Ukraine (Kuzio, 2024). Secondly, whether Ukraine would be part of Europe *or* (the Kremlin's preference) the Pan-Russian World and Eurasia (Wawrzonek, 2014). Between 1991 and 2013, Ukraine found itself in what Michał Wawrzonek (2014) described as the 'grey zone' where two identities and foreign policy orientations competed, with conflict especially acute between the Orange and Euromaidan Revolutions (2004–2014). The Kremlin's hopes were pinned on Yanukovych, Ukraine's pro-Russian presidential candidate in the 2004 elections and who as president in 2010–2014 had implemented Medvedev's demands. The Kremlin pressured Yanukovych to reject European integration, which he did in November 2013, and following this support, Ukraine joining the Eurasian Economic Union, after his re-election in 2015, during his second presidential term. The Kremlin's plans collapsed after Ukrainians mobilised the Euromaidan Revolution and, following four months of violence and the killing of one hundred protestors, Yanukovych fled from office. In 2014, with Euromaidan Revolutionaries coming to power, the pendulum swung in favour of Ukrainian identity and Ukraine's European orientation, which widened Ukraine's divergence from Russia. To the Kremlin's chagrin, Ukrainians had escaped from the 'grey zone' and were rapidly moving away from Russia and Eurasia. Growing Russian-Ukrainian divergence after 2014 was an important factor in the Kremlin's decision to launch the 'special military operation'.

If the 'special military operation' had gone to plan, its goals of 'de-nazification' and 'de-militarisation' would have led to Ukraine's Little Russianisation; that is, Belarusianisation. The Institute for the Study of War has analysed Russia's demands for ending the war in the Spring 2022 peace talks and ever since as Ukraine's capitulation (Institute for the Study of War, 2024a, 2024b, 2025). Medvedev's demands in 2009 and Putin's since 2022 towards Ukraine bring together the four roots of Russia's war against Ukraine that are analysed in this book: *Imperialism and Nationalism, Nostalgia, Divergence,* and the *International Dimension*.

Imperial Nationalism: the first root, is an extreme form of nationalism fused with imperialism and revanchism. Since the mid 2000s, the revival and promotion of White Russian émigré ideas, writings, and ideologues, spread among the Russian elites and Russian people a denial of the existence of a Ukrainian people distinct from Russians and a belief that Ukraine was an artificial construct and puppet state of the West. This, in turn, reinforced a long-held Russian view of treating Ukrainians as a Little Russian branch of the pan-Russian people, alongside Belarusians (White Russians) and Russians (Great Russians). White Russian émigré writers and generals have been officially reburied in Russia, and their books have been republished in mass editions and circulated in schools, the armed forces, and among state officials and politicians. Fascist and anti-Semitic White Russian émigré writer Ivan Ilyin, who denied the existence of a Ukrainian people, became Putin's favourite author nearly two decades ago. Ilyin's writings were republished in large editions and assigned to provincial governors and military leaders to study. Two decades ago in 2005, Putin supervised the reburial of Ilyin's remains in Moscow's Donskoy cemetery.

With Belarusians brought back within the pan-Russian people as early as 1994, when Alexander Lukashenka was elected Belarusian president, and especially after the 2020 fraudulent elections, the Kremlin's main target has long been Ukraine (Barros, 2025). The closest the Kremlin came to reintegrating Ukraine came with the election of Ukraine's only pro-Russian president, Yanukovych (2010–2014). His removal from power by the Euromaidan Revolution prevented Russia's goal of Ukraine turning its back on Europe and joining Russia and Belarus as the Pan-Russian World core of Eurasia. Russia's revenge was the annexation of Crimea and first invasion of Ukraine.

History is central to Russia's war against Ukraine and Putin's desire to enter Russian history in the footsteps of earlier great leaders. Returning to the Russian presidency in 2012, Putin believed his destiny was to enter Russian history as the gatherer of the pan-Russian people. Speaking to the World Russian Peoples Council, Putin lamented how in 1917 and 1991 there had been 'artificial' and 'violent divisions' of the great Russian people, 'a *triune* (tripartite) of Russians, Belarusians, and Ukrainians'. The reunification of the three eastern Slavic peoples in the Pan-Russian World and 'Holy Rus' would go some way towards overcoming the trauma felt by Putin and most Russians of the 'major geopolitical disaster of the (20th) century', as Putin described the disintegration of the USSR. On the 350th anniversary of Peter the Great's birth in June 2022, Putin denied Russia had conquered land controlled by Sweden in the Great Northern War: 'He [Peter the Great] was not taking away anything, he was returning'.

The Russian Orthodox Church, which was revived after a period of persecution by the Bolsheviks in 1943, institutionalised Russian imperial nationalism in the Soviet and Russian political systems, sacralising the concept of 'Holy Rus' discourse as one of the core identities of the Soviet Union. Throughout the Soviet era, Ukrainian Churches were banned, and the Russian Orthodox Church held a privileged position as the only canonical Orthodox Church in Ukraine. The Moscow Patriarchate lost this status only in 2018–2019, when Patriarch Bartholomew I of Constantinople removed Ukraine from Russian canonical territory and granted the Orthodox Church of Ukraine autocephaly (independence) from the Russian Orthodox Church. Ukrainian Orthodox autocephaly added to the accelerating dynamic since 2014 of Ukraine's divergence from Russia. Russia's capitulation demands to Ukraine include the reversal of Ukraine's Orthodox autocephaly and the reinstatement of the primacy of the Russian Orthodox Church.

The Russian Orthodox Church's promotion of the quasi-religious cult of the Great Patriotic War and Russian-Ukrainian unity in the Pan-Russian World legitimised anti-Western xenophobia in public discourse under the guise of defending conservative moral values against Western liberalism and secularism. The Russian Orthodox Church was the key institution given the task of institutionalising and legitimising eternal Russian-Ukrainian unity. Russian Orthodox Church structures in Ukraine served as a support base for pro-Russian forces during the Orange and Euromaidan Revolutions and for pro-Russian political parties and presidential candidates during election campaigns. The Moscow Patriarchate actively promotes a narrative that sacralises Russia's war against Ukraine by presenting it as a fight between a superior pan-Russian civilisation against satanic Ukrainian Nazis and their puppet masters, the 'collective West'.

The imperial nationalism is very evident in the tone and arrogance of Russia's approach towards Ukraine, which have remained the same as during the Spring 2022 peace talks; that is, a demand for Ukraine's capitulation. The Russian delegation was led by former Minister of Culture and Chairman of the Russian Military Society Vladimir Medinsky, who insisted (but Ukraine refused) the talks be held for symbolic reasons in

Belovezhskaya Pushcha, the hunting lodge in Belarus where Russian, Ukrainian and Belarusians leaders met in December 1991 to dismantle the USSR. Medinsky has been a major influence over the rewriting of new Russian school textbooks and published a 'gatherers of Russian land' book series where Putin is following in the footsteps of Alexander Nevsky, Ivan III, Peter I, Catherine I, Alexander I, Alexander III and Joseph Stalin (Zygar, 2023). Medinsky was the ghostwriter of Putin's (2021) long essay, which was distributed throughout Russia's armed forces and provided ideological justification for Russia's full-scale invasion.

Nostalgia: the second root is analysed through the quasi-religious promotion of the Great Patriotic War, personality cult of dictator Stalin and revival of Soviet era propaganda against 'Ukrainian nationalists' and 'Nazis'. The main Soviet anniversary during Putin's youth became the Great Patriotic War on 9 May, overtaking the Bolshevik Revolution on 7 November. As president, Putin militarised the Great Patriotic War by returning military parades and transforming the anniversary into a celebration of military victory, rather than commemoration of human suffering. Russia moved from 'Never Again!' to 'We Can Do It Again!' Linked to the quasi-religious Great Patriotic War has been a cult of Stalin through a denial, downplaying and marginalisation of his massive crimes against humanity, including against Russians, and playing up the leader's military victory, and building of a new empire and nuclear superpower. While most Russians hold a positive view of Stalin, most Ukrainians view him as a tyrant. Russia was angered by Ukraine's movement away from celebrating the Great Patriotic War (1941–1945) to the Second World War (1939–1945) and denouncing communism and Nazism as twin evils.

The term – Nazis – was frequently used by the Soviet regime and continues to be used by Russia as a derogatory label applied to all those, irrespective of their political views, who did not see Ukraine's future in the USSR and who do not see Ukraine's future in the Pan-Russian World and Eurasia. Of all the countries, Ukraine leads in being condemned as 'Nazi' by Russian propaganda. Russian war atrocities and war crimes are justified because Ukraine is a 'Nazi' state. A lack of introspection of Russian and Soviet crimes against humanity, cult of Stalin and de-humanisation of Ukrainians prepared the ground for the committing of war crimes and genocide by Russian forces against Ukrainians. Ukrainians fighting against Russia are allegedly not representative of most Ukrainians who desire to live within the Pan-Russian World.

Throughout Putin's quarter of a century in power, directly and indirectly, the Kremlin has always been hostile towards Ukraine's de-Stalinisation and de-communisation and, as part of its wide-scale demands for Ukraine's capitulation, is insisting on a reversal of Ukrainian memory politics. Throughout the post-Soviet era, Russia and Ukraine have especially diverged in their memory politics. Russia's Tsarist and Soviet nostalgia and Ukraine's denunciation of Tsarist and Soviet rule placed the two countries on a collision course. Medinsky's new school textbooks praise Stalin 'as a wise and effective leader thanks to whom the Soviet Union won the war and ordinary people began to live much better' leaving the reader 'feeling that Stalin's victims were guilty and suffered a well-deserved punishment' (Zygar, 2023). The new school textbook's twenty-eight pages on the war in Ukraine 'contain, of course, no history and only outright propaganda – a set of clichés recycled from Russian television' (Zygar, 2023). Soviet propaganda campaigns against Ukrainian 'nationalists/fascists/Nazis' underpin Russia's demand for Ukraine's 'de-nazification'.

Divergence: the third root lies in Russia and Ukraine's divergence in identity and political systems since the early 1990s, and especially since the Orange and Euromaidan Revolutions. Since 1991 Russia repeatedly intervened in domestic Ukrainian politics in support of pro-Russian forces, a catch-all term that included support for Russian memory politics, the Russian language as a state language, primacy of the Russian Orthodox Church, and integration into the Pan-Russian World and Eurasia. Support for these policies was always weaker in Ukraine than in Belarus; for example, only one of six Ukrainian presidents – Yanukovych – was pro-Russian.

Russian military aggression in 2014 had the unintended consequences of marginalising pro-Russian forces in Ukraine by removing 16 per cent of voters in Russian-occupied Ukraine who traditionally voted for these forces. If in the two decades prior to 2014, divergence had been gradual, after 2014, Ukrainian memory politics began to radically move away from Tsarist, Soviet and Russian views and perceptions. This was taking place alongside the removal of the influence of Russian soft power in the media, language, and religion. The election of Zelenskyy did not change this trend, as he not only continued the memory politics, religious, and media policies of his predecessor, Poroshenko, but radicalised them further by banning five pro-Russian television channels and criminally charging pro-Russian politicians. Russia's full-scale invasion made the same mistake as in 2014: military aggression, this time even more brutal, eviscerated what remained linked to Russia by leading to the banning of twelve pro-Russian political parties and legislation circumscribing the Russian Orthodox Church's ties to Moscow.

Since 1991, Russia and Ukraine have diverged politically into an authoritarian dictatorship and democracy, respectively. The Kremlin's military aggression against Ukraine is an outgrowth of a cult of war; for example, surrounding commemoration of the Great Patriotic War and cult of Stalin; nature of Russia's regime which transformed from authoritarianism into a fascist dictatorship after constitutional changes in 2020 made Putin de facto president for life, and widespread political repression. Ukraine's democratisation naturally took it on a path to Europe.

Xenophobia: the fourth root has been fanned by Russia since the mid 2000s but became particularly shrill after 2014 when the Kremlin's xenophobia is linked it to Ukrainian identity and Kyiv's desire to break free from Russian control. After 2014, Ukraine's conflict with Russia and the West's increasingly confrontational relationship with Moscow were now tightly bound together. Denying the existence of a Ukrainian people distinct from Russians, Russia must attribute Ukraine's resilience and determination by describing the 'special military operation' as a war against the West and NATO.

Russia has expanded its war goals to destroying the US-led unipolar world by replacing it with a multipolar world. Russia has expanded its holy war against Ukraine through military alliances with countries who hold similar anti-Western goals – China, Iran, and North Korea. Russia is a revolutionary power pushing back against the US-led unipolar world, no longer accepting the international order which emerged after the Cold War.

Russian messianism about the 'liberation' of *Novorossiya* (New Russia) and imperialism towards Ukraine is evident in the Kremlin's capitulation demands for Ukrainian forces to completely withdraw from Ukrainian-controlled territory in Donetsk, Luhansk, Zaporizhzhya, and Kherson *oblasts* (which Russia illegally annexed in September 2022), none of which it fully controls. The Kremlin is demanding Ukraine, and the West recognise the four illegally annexed *oblasts* as part of Russia.

The Kremlin's capitulation demands include Ukraine must officially abandon its goal of ever joining NATO before Russia can agree to a ceasefire and peace negotiations; Russia is in effect demanding a veto over the addition of new members of NATO. The Kremlin demand for Ukraine's capitulation includes the proviso it signs a peace treaty independently and not on the orders of its 'Western masters', reiterating a long standing and false Russian imperial nationalist claim Ukraine is a US and Western puppet state. Putin seeks a summit with US President Donald Trump, which would agree on a second Yalta agreement which, as on the first occasion in 1945, would recognise Western and Russian spheres of influence; Ukraine and Eurasia would, of course belong to Russia's exclusive domain. The Kremlin's capitulation demand for Ukraine's full 'de-militarisation' limiting the Ukrainian armed forces to 85,000 soldiers (down from their current number of 980,000) and destruction of Western military equipment would complete the transformation of Ukraine into a Little Russian puppet state.

These four roots of Russia's war against Ukraine – Imperialism and Nationalism; Nostalgia; Divergence, and Xenophobia – came together on the eve of the full-scale invasion on 24 February 2022. Russian imperial nationalists had come to the realisation Ukraine was being 'lost' forever and had to be forcibly returned to the Pan-Russian World through a 'special military operation'. Putin echoed Stalin in fearing the 'loss' of Ukraine. Believing – wrongly – that most Ukrainians would act as Little Russians by welcoming the Russian army, the Kremlin was convinced 'artificial' Ukraine would be defeated quickly, Kyiv captured in a few days and Zelenskyy replaced by a Russia-friendly puppet ruler. Ukraine would come to resemble the Russian puppet state of Belarus (Barros, 2025). The Russian army and security forces would implement 'de-nazification' to destroy Ukrainian identity and return Ukrainians to their Little Russian roots.

As we have witnessed from three years of full-scale war, Russian imperial nationalist myths of Ukraine and Ukrainians had nothing to do with reality. The Kremlin's plans for a rapid 'special military operation' became a long-drawn-out full-scale war with Ukraine and its Western allies that has expanded into a global war between the West and the anti-Western Axis of Upheaval.

References

Arel, D. and Driscoll, J. (2023). *Ukraine's Unnamed War: Before the Russian Invasion of 2022*. Cambridge: Cambridge University Press.

Arutunyan, A. (2022). *Hybrid Warriors, Proxies, Freelancers and Moscow's Struggle for Ukraine*. London: Hurst and Co.

Ash, L. (2024). *The Baton and the Cross: Russia's Church from Pagans to Putin*. London: Icon Books.

Barros, G. (2025). *Russia's Quiet Conquest: Belarus*, Institute for the Study of War, 14 January. www.understandingwar.org/sites/default/files/Russia%27s%20Quiet%20Conquest%20Belarus.pdf

Cohen, E. A. and O'Brien, P. (2024). 'The Russia-Ukraine War: A Study in Analytic Failure,' Center for Strategic and International Studies, 24 September. www.csis.org/analysis/russia-ukraine-war-study-analytic-failure

D'Anieri, P. (2019, 2023). *Ukraine and Russia: From Civilized Divorce to Uncivil War*. Cambridge: Cambridge University Press.

Davis, J. (2024). *In Their Own Words: How Russian Propagandists Reveal Putin's Intentions*. Stuttgart: Ibidem; New York: Columbia University Press.

Finkel, E. (2024). *Intent to Destroy: Russia's Two-Hundred-Year Quest to Dominate Ukraine*. London: Basic Books.

Garner, I. (2023). *Z Generation: Into the Heart of Russia's Fascist Youth*. London: Hurst and Co.

Hauter, J. (2023). *Russia's Overlooked Invasion: The Causes of the 2014 Outbreak of War in Ukraine's Donbas*. Stuttgart: Ibidem; New York: Columbia University Press.

Institute for the Study of War. (2024a). 'Russian Offensive Campaign Assessment', 14 June. www.understandingwar.org/backgrounder/russian-offensive-campaign-assessment-june-14-2024

Institute for the Study of War. (2024b). 'Russian Offensive Campaign Assessment', 19 December. https://understandingwar.org/backgrounder/russian-offensive-campaign-assessment-december-19-2024

Institute for the Study of War. (2025). 'Russian Offensive Campaign Assessment', 11 January. www.understandingwar.org/backgrounder/russian-offensive-campaign-assessment-january-11-2025

Karatnycky, A. (2024). *Battleground Ukraine: From Independence to the War with Russia*. New Haven, CT: Yale University Press.

Koval, N. and Tereshchenko, D. (2023). *Russian Cultural Diplomacy Under Putin*. Stuttgart: Ibidem; New York: Columbia University Press.

Kuzio, T. (2002). 'The Myth of the Civic State: A Critical Survey of Hans Kohn's Framework for Understanding Nationalism,' *Ethnic and Racial Studies*, 25 (1): 20–39.

Kuzio, T. (2015). *Ukraine: Democratization, Corruption, and the New Russian Imperialism*. Santa Barbara, CA: Praeger.

Kuzio, T. (2020). *Crisis in Russian Studies? Nationalism (Imperialism), Racism, and War*. Bristol: E-International Relations. www.e-ir.info/publication/crisis-in-russian-studies-nationalism-imperialism-racism-and-war/

Kuzio, T. (2022). *Russian Nationalism and the Russian-Ukrainian War: Autocracy-Orthodoxy-Nationality*. London: Routledge.

Kuzio, T. (ed.). (2023). *Russian Disinformation and Western Scholarship*. Stuttgart: Ibidem; New York: Columbia University Press.

Kuzio, T. (2024). 'Ukrainian versus Pan-Russian Identities: The Roots of Russia's Invasion of Ukraine,' *Studies in Ethnicities and Nationalism*, 24 (3): 233–402.

Kuzyk, P. (2019). 'Ukraine's National Integration Before and After 2014. Shifting "East–West" Polarization Line and Strengthening Political Community,' *Eurasian Economics and Geography*, 60 (6): 709–735.

Laruelle, M. and Karnysheva, M. (2022). *Memory Politics and the Russian Civil War*. London: Bloomsbury Academic.

Laruelle, M. (2025). *Ideology and Meaning-Making Under the Putin Regime*. Stanford: Standford University Press.

Larys, M. (2025). *Rebel Militias in Eastern Ukraine: From Leaderless Groups to Proxy Army*. London: Routledge.

McGlynn, J. (2023). *Russia's War*. London: Bloomsbury.
Medvedev, D. (2009). 'Message to the President of Ukraine Viktor Yushchenko,' 11 August. http://special.kremlin.ru/catalog/countries/UA/events/5158
Onuch, O. and Hale, H. (2022). *The Zelensky Effect*. London: Hurst and Co.
Plokhy, S. (2023). *The Russo-Ukrainian War: The Return of History*. London: Penguin Books.
Popova, M. and Shevel, O. (2024). *Russia and Ukraine: Entangled Histories. Diverging States*. Cambridge and Hoboken, NJ: Polity Press.
Putin, V. (2020). 'Interview with Tass News Agency,' 21 February. www.en.kremlin.ru/events/president/transcripts/62835
Putin, V. (2021). 'On the Historical Unity of Russians and Ukrainians,' 12 July. https://kremlin.ru/events/president/news/66181
Ramani, S. (2023). *Putin's War on Ukraine: Russia's Campaign for Global Counter-Revolution*. London: Hurst and Co.
Shevel, O. (2024). 'Some Lessons from the Post-Soviet Era and the Russo-Ukrainian War for the Study of Nationalism,' *Ethics and International Affairs*, 38 (3): 333–353.
Wawrzonek, M. (2014). 'Ukraine in the "Gray Zone": Between the "Russkiy Mir" and Europe,' *East European Politics and Societies*, 28 (4): 758–780.
Zygar, M. (2023). 'The Man Behind Putin's Warped View of History,' *New York Times*, 19 September. www.nytimes.com/2023/09/19/opinion/putin-russia-medinsky.html

PART I

Imperialism and Nationalism

1

Imperial Nationalism

Russian President Putin said to the President of the European Commission Jose Manuel Barroso:
 'Why are you defending Ukraine? It's the creation of the CIA and the European Commission.'[1]

Russia's 'Ukrainian question' has very deep roots and is shot through with contradictions between 'good' Little Russians, who accept they are part of a Pan-Russian people and forever belong to the Pan-Russian World, and 'bad' Ukrainians, who believe they are a people distinct from Russians with their own agency and future in Europe. Russians view Ukrainians as an 'organic part of Russia, sometimes as different and exotic' and Ukraine as the cradle of Russian culture and statehood (Edenborg, 2017, p. 298). At the same time, Ukrainians are backward, uncivilised, inferior, sly and chaotic. Former director of the *Pivdenmash* Soviet military plant and Ukrainian President Leonid Kuchma (2023, p.11) believes Russians 'don't understand us' and 'they very much hate our statehood and will do everything to destroy it (or at the very least weaken it)'.

Ukrainians as Russia's 'Other' is common in colonial settings. As I wrote, 'Ukrainians and Irish were therefore both alien and kindred, wild and mild, dangerous and idyllic, subversive troublemakers and empire loyalists' (Kuzio, 2020, p. 93). 'Good' Ukrainians and Irish were those who assimilated, understood their low status and accepted they needed a guiding hand from an 'elder brother'. 'Bad' Ukrainians and Irish were those who rejected these three steps and believed they were distinct peoples from Russians and the British (Shkandrij, 2001, pp. 215–216, 2019). Portending future territorial claims, former Ukrainian President Kuchma (2023, p. 22) writes that Russians had little understanding of where Ukraine ends and Russia begins and were convinced Kyiv is the 'Mother of Russian

---

[1] Episode 1, 'My Backyard,' *BBC* series, *Putin vs. the West*, 30 January 2023. www.bbc.co.uk/iplayer/episode/p0dlz7tz/putin-vs-the-west-series-1-1-my-backyard

Cities' (by misconstruing Rus as Russian). Russians viewed Ukrainians as 'sympathetic family members from the village who like to sing, have food specialities, their own sense of humour and a comical rural dialect'.

Putin is a product of the Soviet era, but he lives in the nineteenth century (Soldatov and Borogan, 2019, p. 218). In the Tsarist Empire, Ukrainians did not exist, they were described as Little Russians, one of three branches of a mythical pan-Russian people (the other two being great and white Russians). In the Soviet Union, Russia accepted Ukraine's junior status as a Soviet republic. Russian imperial nationalists will only accept a Little Russia (i.e., Ukraine resembling the Russian puppet state of Belarus). Eugene Finkel (2024, pp. 212, 223) defines Russia's goal of transforming Ukraine into a Little Russia as 'genocide' (see We Had No Choice, 2022; Sergeytsev, 2022; Ibrahim, 2023; Russia's Systematic Program for the Re-Education and Adoption of Ukraine's Children, 2023).

The full-scale invasion goals of 'de-nazification' and 'de-militarisation' are being implemented in occupied Ukraine, which the Kremlin seeks to apply to the remainder of the country. Russia's new 'Strategy to Counter Extremism' (Putin, 2024b) points to Ukraine as the main extremist threat to Russia and promoter of neo-Nazi ideas and Russophobic policies towards Russians and Russian speakers.

Russian imperial nationalists demand Ukrainians accept they are a Little Russian branch of the Pan-Russian people and will never accept a Ukraine independent of Russia which is led by a president who believes Ukrainians are a people distinct from Russians and which believes it has a right to decide its own memory politics, language and foreign and security policies. The Levada Centre (2024a) showed Russians only held positive views of Ukraine when it was led by President Yanukovych in 2010–2014, who of six Ukrainian presidents was the only one who was pro-Russian. Russians held negative views of Ukraine during the Orange and Euromaidan Revolutions and during the Yushchenko, Poroshenko and Zelenskyy presidencies. A brief positive view of Ukraine in 2019, when Zelenskyy was elected, changed when he did not become a Ukrainian version of Belarusian self-declared President Alexander Lukashenka. Russian views of Ukraine became negative from 2020 until the full-scale invasion and since 2022, Russian negative views of Ukraine have increased, showing most of the Russian people support the so-called 'special military operation'.

Since 1991, Russia has found it very difficult to accept an independent Ukraine (D'Anieri, 2019). In 1995, over half of Russians and two-thirds of Russian elites believed Russia and Ukraine should be unified. Less than a fifth of Russians (17 per cent) were convinced that Russians and Ukrainians were different peoples (Finkel, 2024, p. 168). Imperial restoration and conquest were not official policies under Yeltsin; nevertheless, the Russian president was unhappy with Ukrainian independence and threatened Ukraine's borders. An adviser to Gorbachev described southeast Ukraine and Crimea as 'historical parts of Russia' two decades before Putin (Finkel, 2024, p. 157). Ultimately, the biggest mistake of Russian liberals was they failed to articulate an alternative, post-imperial and civic Russian identity, leaving the field open for Russian imperial nationalists (Finkel, 2024, p. 167).

Russian imperial nationalists were frustrated about the loss of Ukraine, a place they viewed as the cradle of 'Russian' culture and identity. Walter Laqueur (1993, p. 276) wrote that the Russian nationalist alternative of invading Ukraine was 'hardly a practical proposition', a prediction that unfortunately did not stand the test of time. The Soviet Union included a Ukrainian republic and recognised Ukrainians as a separate people, although forever bonded with Russians. Under Putin, history had come full circle with him reverting to the Tsarist denial of the existence of Ukraine and Ukrainians (Plokhy, 2023b, pp. 283–298; From Accepting NATO Aspirations to 'Denazifying': 20+ Years of Putin's Changing Views on Ukraine, 2022).

Since 1991, Russia has pressured Ukraine to follow the path of Lukashenka's Belarus, a Russian satellite state resembling in many ways the Soviet Belarusian republic. Lukashenka's Belarus implements Russian memory politics (for example, the Great Patriotic War), pays homage to the leadership of the Russian people, upholds the primacy of the Russian Orthodox Church and does not seek European integration. Belarus accepts it is Russia's younger brother. For Russia, a Belarusian-style status is the only satisfactory option for Ukraine. This would be where Ukrainians are the 'eternal younger brother who has no right to mature and is consigned to perpetual mediocrity. He has no right to an independent existence; he must forever be attached to his older Russian brother' (Pritsak, 1992, p. XII).

Throughout the period since 1991, Russia has used threats, energy pressure, soft power, blatant interference in elections and assassinations to make Ukraine resemble Belarus. After failed attempts in 2004 to elect and in 2015 to maintain Yanukovych in power, Ukraine's only pro-Russian president, Russia opted to use military means in 2014. The goals of the two Minsk accords were to transform Ukraine into a dysfunctional Russian puppet state and were never implemented. The failure of the Minsk accords, coupled with Ukraine's rapid divergence from Russia under Presidents Poroshenko after 2014 and Zelenskyy after 2019, led to the Kremlin's decision to launch a 'special military operation' which they expected would quickly conquer Ukraine. The so-called 'special military operation' became a full-scale war.

The 'gathering of Russian lands' is a constant in Tsarist, Soviet, and since 1991, Russian history. Russians view the 1654 Treaty of Pereyaslav between Cossack Ukraine and Muscovy as the 'reunion of Russia and Ukraine'; that is, one episode in the 'gathering of Russian lands'. Cossack Ukraine viewed the treaty as a military alliance against Poland; Muscovy viewed the treaty as Ukraine's subjugation. The 350th anniversary of the treaty was celebrated by the Soviet regime in 1954 with the transfer of Crimea from the Soviet Russian to the Soviet Ukrainian republics. In 1979, the 325th anniversary was also celebrated by the Soviet regime. Ukrainians viewed the treaty as a military alliance of equals against Poland and viewed the oath to the Muscovite tsar as conditional on him respecting Ukraine's rights (which he did not). Russia, on the other hand, viewed – and continues to view – the treaty as Ukraine's 'eternal subjection' (Plokhy, 2023b, p. 53).

Stalin's annexation of Western Ukraine and Western Belarus during World War Two continued the 'gathering of [Southern] Russian lands' begun by Tsar Ivan III (Tolz, 2001, pp. 209–234; Plokhy, 2017, pp. 179, 185). Putin returned to the presidency in 2012 with the goal of becoming the contemporary 'gatherer of Russian lands' by targeting Ukraine (Kuzio, 2022, pp. 156–176). Russia had gone through two major traumas, the disintegration of the Soviet Union and the break-up of Russian-Ukrainian unity; Putin was determined to reverse the latter and restore Ukraine as a Little Russian branch of the Pan-Russian people (Troianovski, 2021). Russian imperial nationalists understand the 'gathering of Russian lands' as the three eastern Slavs being forever bound together.

Russian President Putin's military aggression against Ukraine in 2014 was buttressed by an 'unprecedented appeal to Russian nationalism' (Plokhy, 2023a, p. 119). Russia's annexation of Crimea 'made imperialism and nationalism key elements and driving forces of Russian foreign policy' (Plokhy, 2023a, p. 120; McGlynn, 2023). Donbas Russian nationalist Alexander Zhuchkovsky (n.d., p. 205) described Putin's speech in the Kremlin which officially annexed Crimea as a 'Russian nationalist manifesto'. During the decade between Russia's two invasions of Ukraine, from 2014 to 2022, Russian imperial nationalism became a dominant force in Putin's Russia, providing ideological justification for the Kremlin's plan to destroy the Ukrainian state and Ukrainian identity. With echoes of

Stalin's murder of Polish elites in 1940 and deportations and war crimes in the three Baltic states and Western Ukraine in the 1940s, Russia's army invaded Ukraine with prepared lists of Ukrainians to be imprisoned, deported, and killed (Applebaum and Gumenyuk, 2023). Russia's 'kill lists' included Ukrainian state officials, political leaders, journalists, teachers, intellectuals, clergy, and civil society activists (Kinetz, 2022; Kozerova, 2023; Chovgan, 2023). As Andrei Soldatov and Irina Borogan (2022) have written, Putin's FSB (Federal Security Service) has become a contemporary version of Stalin's secret police, the NKVD (People's Commissariat for Internal Affairs) and has embraced some of Stalin's methods.

The Soviet concept of 'three brotherly Slavic people' had 'acknowledged a greater degree of separateness between Ukrainians, Belarusians, and Russians' (Tolz, 2002, p. 239), but of course under Russian leadership. The myth of Russian primacy, coupled with the right to rule the peoples of the USSR, was central to Soviet nationalities policies and historiography from the mid 1930s to the mid 1980s (Farmer, 1980, p. 207).

The Soviet regime also promoted eternal Russian-Ukrainian unity (Wojnowski, 2017). From the mid 2000s, that is, for nearly two decades before Russia's full-scale invasion of Ukraine, Putin's regime promoted the revival and rehabilitation of historical myths and stereotypes from the Tsarist Empire and White Russian émigrés who had supported the anti-Bolshevik Whites and, after their defeat in 1920–1921, had fled to Europe. The republication of White Russian émigré literature influenced Russian leaders' discourse and media in their ridiculing of Ukraine as an artificial construct. The Kremlin's claims that Russians and Ukrainians constitute 'one people' are 'one of the oldest and most deeply ingrained myths used against Ukraine' (Disinformation about the Current Russian-Ukrainian Conflict, 2022; see also Minchenia; Kuzio, 2022; Kremlin Hate Speech Incites War Crimes in Ukraine, 2022; When Words Kill – From Moscow to Mariupol, 2022; Applebaum, 2022).

These pre-Soviet and Soviet myths of Ukraine and Ukrainians came together in Putin's (2021b) essay, which was made mandatory reading at military academies prior to Russia's full-scale invasion of Ukraine (Harding, 2022, p. 107). Russian imperial nationalists imagine 'Russia' as a 'state-civilisation' empire whose inner core is a Pan-Russian people composed of Great, Little, and White Russians (Russians, Ukrainians and Belarusians, respectively) (Lewis, 2023, p. 384).

This chapter is divided into six sections. The first discusses Russian nationalists who have been first and foremost imperial nationalists because they supported and continue to support Russia as an empire rather than a nation state (Motyl, 1990; Rowley, 2000; Hosking, 1998). The second analyses why Russian imperial nationalists view 'Russia' as a 'state-civilisation' empire. The third analyses Putin's obsession with Russian identity, Ukraine and Ukrainians. The fourth section investigates the revival and rehabilitation of White Russian émigrés and their return to Russia. The fifth section analyses how the de-humanisation of Ukraine and Ukrainians provided the ideological justification for Russia's full-scale invasion of Ukraine and war crimes (Kremlin Hate Speech Incites War Crimes in Ukraine, 2022; When Words Kill – From Moscow to Mariupol, 2022; Sergeytsev, 2022; We Had No Choice, 2022; Ibrahim, 2023; Russia's Systematic Program for the Re-Education and Adoption of Ukraine's Children, 2023; Hate Speech and Calls for Genocide in Putin's Russia, 2024). The final section investigates two ideological justifications used by the Kremlin for its 'special military operation'. The first was the depiction of Ukraine as a puppet, failed and artificial state that is controlled by the US. The second was how the US had transformed Ukraine after the 2014 Euromaidan 'putsch' into an 'Anti-Russia' that was taking the country on an irrevocable divergence from Russia (see Oliinyk and Kuzio, 2021; Kelly and Kovalchuk, 2024). A lack of historical statehood led Ukraine, Putin (2022) claimed, into 'emulating foreign models'. Ukraine since the 2014 Euromaidan putsch has been under 'external control' and had become a 'colony with a puppet regime' where all state appointments are made by the US, Ukraine's armed forces are under NATO's control and NATO training missions are 'in fact, foreign military bases' (Putin, 2022).

Understanding Russian Nationalism and Identity

There are many types of nationalism, and the term has therefore been confusingly used, including when discussing Russian nationalism. Civic forms of nationalism are akin to patriotism in their appeal to a territorially bound polity. There are of course exceptions; Germany used an ethnic definition of citizenship in 1945–1990, and Estonia and Latvia adopted ethnic criteria for citizenship when they renewed their independence in 1991. Ethnic definitions limit citizenship to those who hold the same ethnicity, in this case Germans, Estonians and Latvians, while civic citizenship is open to anybody, irrespective of ethnicity. The full inclusivity of civic nationalism is a relatively recent phenomenon. Women, for example, did not receive the vote until the twentieth century; in France, the home of the 1789 revolutionary slogan 'Liberty-Equality-Fraternity', women received the franchise as late as 1945.

Nationalism is a term that usually has negative connotations because of its association with ethnic conflicts and extremist political movements. In fact, nationalists can be found on the left (e.g., Scotland, Wales, Ireland, Quebec, Cuba and Ukraine) as well as on the right. Many separatist nationalist movements in the West have been leftist. Ukrainians and the Irish have a historical tradition of left-wing nationalism (Velychenko, Ruane, and Hrynevych, 2022). More confusing still is the link between nationalism and imperialism. The UK and France were both democratic states and multinational empires; civic nationalism and imperialism were not incompatible.

Russian nationalism is commonly used by scholars, often without an understanding of its many threads. As Vera Tolz (1998) has explained, post-imperial civic forms of nationalism proved to be unpopular in Russia in the 1990s because most Russians understand 'Russia' to be bigger than the Russian Federation. In the mid 1990s, less than a third of Russians (29 per cent) were satisfied with the borders of the Russian Federation (Finkel, 2024, p. 168). Indeed, this was also the case in the Soviet Union, which most Russians understood as the same as 'Russia'; Putin has called the Soviet Union 'Historical Russia' (Osborn and Ostroukh, 2021). The Russian SFSR (Soviet Federative Socialist Republic) was the only republic of fifteen which did not possess republican institutions, such as a Communist Party and Academy of Sciences, closely integrating Soviet and Russian identities.

This chapter uses imperial nationalism, which is more dominant among Russians than the unpopular civic nationalism that denotes the fusion of Russian imperialism and nationalism. Andrei Kolesnikov (2023b) describes the fusion of Tsarist and Soviet nostalgia in Putin's Russia as 'Stalinist nationalist imperialism', which has become the 'de facto ideology' of Putin's regime. Head of the Russian World Foundation, Viacheslav Nikonov, grandson of Stalin's Foreign Minister Viacheslav Molotov, is not surprising sentimentally inclined towards Stalin (Koval and Tereshchenko, 2023, pp. 116–117). Maria Snegovaya, Michael Kimmage and Jade McGlynn (2023) prefer to use the term 'imperial nationalist statism'. Roger Cohen (2022) uses 'autocratic nationalism' to describe Russia from 2012, the year Putin returned to the presidency.

Cohen (2022) believes the influence of Russian exceptionalism propounded by White Russian émigré writers, such as Ivan Ilyin, created a 'macho embodiment of conservative Orthodox Christian values'. Yuri Kovalchuk, a close adviser to Putin since the 1990s, is fascinated by Ilyin, which was used in the writing of Putin's (2021b) essay, which provided the 'intellectual justification' for the full-scale invasion (Ash, 2024, p. 164).

Sergei Medvedev (2023), Kolesnikov (2023b) and Snegovaya, Kimmage and McGlynn (2023) define 'Stalinist nationalist imperialism' and 'imperial nationalist statism' as nostalgia for Russia's imperial and Soviet past, belief in Russian superiority, exceptionalism, imperial traditions, traditional and conservative Christian values, the Russian and Soviet states understood as civilisation empires, and hostility to the West and Western liberalism. Russia should be restored to the centre of a unique and superior Eurasian civilisation with an exclusive sphere of influence, like Russia's place in the Soviet Union, in an existential battle with an immoral and hypocritical West that seeks to marginalise and destroy Russia, as in the 1990s (Langdon and Tismaneanu, 2020, pp. 120–122). Robyn Dixon (2024) describes 'scientific Putinism' as having created an 'orthodox Sharia' which combines xenophobia, paranoia, anti-Semitism and misogynism. Russia has had a 'Putin doctrine' since 2007–2008, when the Russian World Foundation and *Rossotrudnichestvo* (Federal Agency for the Commonwealth of Independent States, Compatriots Living Abroad) were founded, whose core is the 'Holy Rus' of Russia, Ukraine and Belarus (Koval and Tereshchenko, 2023, pp. 11, 106–107). Both organisations have provided 'open ideological support' for Russian military aggression against Ukraine (Koval and Tereshchenko, 2023, pp. 63, 101). In the same year, the domestic and émigré Russian Orthodox Churches were re-united. The émigré Russian Orthodox Church did not condemn the annexation of Crimea or Russia's 2014 and 2022 invasions of Ukraine (Ash, 2024, pp. 172, 174). The influence of the Russian Orthodox Church dramatically expanded after 2007–2009, following the election of Kirill as patriarch, with the Church becoming an ally of Putin's 'gathering of Russian lands', leading to the merger of 'ethno-religious chauvinism and militaristic neo-imperialist expansionism' (Stoyanov, 2024).

Alexander J. Motyl (1990) wrote that Russian nationalism was a myth if we understand nationalism as a force that seeks to build an independent state. David G. Rowley (2000, p. 23) wrote: 'The term "Russian nationalism" has been carelessly used to apply to a style of thought that is in fact "imperialism", thus obscuring the profound differences between European and Russian national consciousness'. Russian political forces and ideologists did not articulate demands for an independent Russian state outside the Tsarist Empire or the Soviet Union. This is not so unusual; after all, the English have not created nationalist parties seeking independence from the UK. Russian liberal dissidents did not articulate calls for self-determination and instead sought to transform the USSR into a looser confederation of states. Russian imperial nationalists sought to transform the USSR into a new Russian Empire (Rowley, 2000; Motyl, 1990, p. 165). Rowley (2000, p. 23) continued: 'That Russians expressed their national consciousness through the discourse of imperialism rather than the discourse of nationalism has far reaching implications for both Russian history and nationalism theory'. The Russian SFSR did not declare independence from the Soviet Union in 1991; Russia Day is held on 12 June, the day the Russian SFSR declared sovereignty in 1990.

In the 1990s, Russian civic nationalism was, as Tolz (1998) wrote, weak with imperial nationalists on the extreme right as well as extreme left being more popular. The 1991 and 1993 coups failed to remove Gorbachev and Yeltsin, respectively, but its extreme left and right backers eventually became mainstream under Putin (Laqueur, 1993; Clover, 2016). Since 2000, when Putin was first elected president, he has embraced imperial nationalism and united its different strands. The 1993 coup united Stalinists, Soviet restorationists and fascists, who were committed to 'A greater Russia' (Bohlen, 1993; see Laqueur, 1993). The 'red (pro-Soviet)-brown (fascist)' coalition that had led the 1991 and 1993 coup d'états was broadened from the mid 2000s into a 'red-brown-white' coalition uniting nostalgia for the Soviet Union (red), Russian Orthodox fundamentalists and nostalgists for Tsarist Russia (whites) and fascists (brown) (Laruelle, 2016). In 2012, the 'red-white-brown' coalition led by Alexander Dugin, Alexander Prokhanov and Sergei Kurginyan created the Izborsk Club.

The dominance of imperial nationalism in Russia was especially important for Belarusians and Ukrainians, who were viewed not as peoples distinct from Russians but as two branches of a Pan-Russian people. The re-unification of Belarus was to all intents and purposes resolved after Sovietophile Alexander Lukashenka took power in 1994, and especially after fraudulent elections in 2020. Ukraine was always more recalcitrant and difficult for Russian imperial nationalists to subdue which, as this book shows, became Putin's obsession. Putin believes the loss of Ukraine would be a 'mutilation' of the Russian body and soul. Stalin said, 'we may lose Ukraine' and Putin similarly said, 'We must deal with Ukraine, or we'll lose it' (Zygar, 2023a, pp. 106, 217).

After the disintegration of the Soviet Union, the four most popular Russian identities (numbered from one to four) denied the existence of a Ukrainian people distinct from Russians and believe Ukraine is an unquestionable part of a Pan-Russian people. These four identities represent different strands of Russian imperial nationalism and together provided the ideological justification behind Russia's two invasions of Ukraine in 2014 and 2022.

1. *Imperial Identity*: 'The Russians are defined as an imperial people or through their mission to create a supranational state', (i.e., Tsarist Empire, USSR, Eurasian Union). 'Decades and sometimes centuries of existence within one state (common history) are supposed to be the basis for the continuation of a multi-ethnic state within the borders of the former USSR' (Tolz, 1998, p. 995). 'Historic Russia' and the Soviet Union were the same, Putin reminded us (Osborn and Ostroukh, 2021), a viewpoint which has its roots in Stalin giving the Soviet Union a 'Russian national face' with an official history that was 'Russocentric, statist, and de facto coterminous with the history of Russia' (Velychenko, 1993, p. 22).
2. *Pan-Russian People Identity*: 'The Russians as a nation of all eastern Slavs, united by common origin and culture. Ethno-cultural similarities and a common past are viewed as the main markers of national identity' (Tolz, 1998, p. 995). A Little Russian identity within a Pan-Russian people would uphold the superiority of the Russian language, monopolisation of the Russian Orthodox Church, centrality of the cult of the Great Patriotic War and Soviet nostalgia. Russian dissident Alexander Solzhenitsyn's proposal for a Russian Union (1991) to replace the Soviet Union aimed to maintain unity of the Pan-Russian people (see Michel, 2024).
3. *Russian-Speaking Compatriot Identity*: 'The Russians as a community of Russian speakers, regardless of their ethnic origin. Language is the main marker of national identity' (Tolz, 1998, pp. 995–996). 'Those viewing the Russians as a community of eastern Slavs or Russian speakers also place a particular emphasis on Orthodoxy as a marker of Russian national identity' (Tolz, 1998, p. 996). Throughout the post-Soviet era, the Russian nation defined as a community of Russian speakers has been popular among Russian politicians.

    Russian-speaking compatriots are assumed to be pro-Russian (Shulman, 2005). Pro-Russian should be understood as holding a nostalgia for the achievements of the USSR, supporting a pro-Russian geopolitical orientation, voting for pro-Russian political forces, backing the elevation of Russian to a second state language, and adopting a critical view of the West; for example, viewing the Orange and Euromaidan Revolutions as CIA organised conspiracies against Russia. Tolz (2001, p. 232) writes that Russians have traditionally viewed Ukrainian nationalism 'as the result of intrigues by European powers and/or the United States (i.e., the West)'. In Ukraine, the assumption that speaking Russian leads to the prioritisation of support for Russia and the Pan-Russian World over Ukraine was shown to be misplaced.

In 2014, Russian leaders believed Ukraine's Russian speakers would support the detachment of New Russia (*Novorossiya*, the Tsarist term for southeastern Ukraine) from Ukraine (Kuzio, 2019). Ending 'the genocide' of Russian speakers in the Donbas was the official justification used by Putin for launching his so-called 'special military operation' against Ukraine in 2022. Only 2 per cent of Ukrainians believed Russia's justification for invading Ukraine was to protect Russian speakers (The Sixth National Poll: The Language Issue in Ukraine, 2022). The Kremlin had believed their own propaganda about Little Russians waiting to greet the Russian army as 'liberators' and therefore the initial invasion force of 175,000 was relatively small; in 1968, the Warsaw Pact invaded Czechoslovakia, with only a quarter of Ukraine's population, using a quarter of a million troops.

In 2014 and since 2022, Russian speakers have shown a greater loyalty to Ukraine than to the Pan-Russian World. A major reason why is because Russian-speaking Ukrainians are thoroughly integrated into Ukrainian society. The 2001 Ukrainian census recorded that Russians had declined from 22 to 17 per cent of Ukraine's population since the 1989 Soviet census. Public opinion surveys since the 2014 crisis have recorded a decline in the population of Ukraine declaring their identity as 'ethnic Russian' to only 2 per cent (Kulyk, 2023), a ten-fold decrease in just over three decades. Meanwhile, the proportion of Ukrainians who declare their identity as 'ethnic Ukrainian' has grown from 78 per cent of the population in the 1989 Soviet census to between 92 per cent (Tenth National Survey: Ideological Markers of the War 2022) and 95 per cent of Ukraine's population (Kulyk, 2023). Many of these self-declared 'ethnic Ukrainians' are of course, Russian speakers.

4. *Racial Identity*: 'The Russians defined racially (i.e., blood ties constitute the basis of common identity')' (Tolz, 1998, p. 996). A racially defined 'Russian' identity would, as in the previous three, include Ukrainians and Belarusians.
5. *Civic Identity*: A civic Russian (*Rossiiskaia*) nation whose members are the inhabitants of the Russian Federation would recognise Ukrainians as a different people living in an independent state (Tolz, 1998, p. 996). A Russian civic identity has been the most unpopular of these five identities. There are no pure civic states because democracies are grounded within nation-states that are built on ethno-cultural cores (Kuzio, 2002).

Russia as a 'State-Civilisation' Empire

The embracing of imperial, pan-Russian, Russian-speaking, and racial identities by Russian imperial nationalists rules out equating Russian identity with a nation-state, in this case the Russian Federation. Only a civic identity would guarantee Russia's adherence to the principle of the territorial integrity of states. Roman Szporluk (1985) writes that Russia having created an empire before a nation-state meant that Russians were never sure what 'Russia' is.

Since 2012, Russia has been defined as a unique 'state-civilisation' which is a 'revanchist conservative ideology' (Koval and Tereshchenko, 2023, p. 19). At its core lies the Pan-Russian World as a cultural and civilisation community. A 'state-civilisation' blurs the borders between the Russian Federation and Eurasia (Lewis, 2023). Medvedev (2023, p. 107) believes Russia cannot see itself as anything but an empire. Snegovaya, Kimmage, and McGlynn (2023) write that a messianic vision of Russia as a 'state-civilisation' empire borrows 'heavily from fascist theories' that emphasise 'civilisation and even a racial aspect of Russian identity'. Putin's favourite author – White Russian émigré writer Ilyin – praised the rise to power of the Nazis and was the most radical thinker of Russian imperialism in the twentieth century (Schneider-Deters, 2024, pp. 137–138). Russian cultural messianism feeds on nostalgia and resentment for the pre 1991 world when the USSR was a respected superpower in a multipolar world. Kolesnikov (2023b) views Russian exceptionalism and militarism as providing ideological justification for the Kremlin's war against Ukraine to defeat the US-led unipolar world, leading to the reassertion of Russia as a great power in a multipolar world.

Russian imperial nationalists believe the world is divided into civilisation centres, each with their 'natural' spheres of influence. Russia lies at the centre of Eurasian civilisation which Russian imperial nationalists view as Russia's exclusive sphere of influence. Russia has disrespected the sovereignty of fourteen successor states from the USSR, demanding none of the fourteen successor states join NATO and the EU or invite UN peacekeepers to police their (Russian manufactured) ethnic conflicts.

Russian imperial nationalists believe Russia is fighting a war on Ukrainian territory against the US-NATO 'civilisation bloc', which is often described by the Kremlin as 'Anglo Saxon' (What do the pro-Kremlin media mean by "Anglo-Saxons"? 2020). NATO is allegedly a 'military-civilisation' bloc hostile to Russia, a viewpoint which is an 'article of faith' and 'central to Putin's conception of the state' (Sherr and Gretskiy, 2023). Russian imperial nationalists view the war as a conflict between two civilisation blocs over whether Ukraine will be part of Eurasia or the West. Russian Foreign Minister Sergei Lavrov said, 'if Ukraine joins NATO either Ukraine disappears, or NATO does'.[2]

The roots of Russian anti-Western xenophobia, which has grown to alarming heights since the mid 2000s, lies in resentment and anger at the perception as to how the West allegedly mistreated Russia in the 1990s and threatened the country's statehood. Russian martyrdom and resurrection in the war against Ukraine and its Western sponsors will be one way to overcome the trauma of the 1990s (Garner, 2023, pp. 33, 48). Resentment has cultivated a Russian victim narrative; an allegation the West is always out to humiliate Russia and not respect it as a great power. Leon Aron (2023, p. 36) writes that, 'a perennial war with the American-led West' has become 'integral to the regime's legitimacy'.

The influence of messianism over Soviet and Russian foreign policy grew after Putin returned to the presidency in 2012, when Russia became a *revolutionary power* (see Trenin, 2024). Russian imperial nationalists began to define Russia as the world's shield against apocalyptic chaos fanned by the West (Kolesnikov, 2023a). Russia was a bulwark against liberalism, globalisation, and US-orchestrated colour revolutions, and defined itself as a defender of Christian, spiritual and traditional values (Lewis, 2023, p. 379). A powerful Russian state, strong in its sovereignty and confident in its identity, could become a bulwark against Western expansionism and the US imposing its values on Russia (Lewis, 2023, pp. 380–381). Russia is the only true Christian state in Europe and protector of the world from the Ukrainian and Western Anti-Christ, Russians are the chosen people, and Moscow is once again the Third Rome. Russia is the restrainer in Syria, Ukraine and elsewhere where it is fighting the forces of evil (Engstrom, 2014). Russia is saved by the Russian 'Jesus Christ' (Putin), who is defending Russian values, culture, traditions and history in the *sviashchennaia voina* ('holy war') to liberate Russian lands the Soviet Union wrongly included within Ukraine (Grylls, 2024). In fact, the Kremlin believes 'Russia has a legal, moral, and religious obligation to extirpate these supposed threats and restore Ukraine to its rightful place as a historically Russian land' (Kagan, Barros, Mikkelsen, Mealie, 2023).

---

[2] https://x.com/BRICSinfo/status/1811401242251530373

In 2022, Russia transitioned into a *revolutionary power* with the goal of fighting the West in Ukraine and destroying the US-led unipolar world which has existed since the end of the Cold War. A poll by the Levada Centre (2023), Russia's last remaining independent polling organisation, found nearly a third of Russians believing Russia's 'special military operation' was launched to prevent an attack on Russia by the NATO and US-controlled Ukrainian puppet state (Levada Centre, 2023). Lavrov (2024) made the spurious claim the 'special military operation' was not directed against Ukrainians, with whom Russians 'are still bound by fraternal ties', but the 'criminal regime' operating on behalf of its 'Western curators'. It was not Russia's military aggression against Ukraine that was destroying Russian-Ukrainian 'brotherhood' because 'The process of destroying this ideology of brotherhood and unity began in Ukraine' (Lavrov, 2024). In the dystopian world of Russian imperial nationalism, Ukrainians are themselves to blame for being militarily attacked and it was the West that started the war (Thirteen Myths about Russia's War against Ukraine exposed, 2024). Nearly two-thirds of Russians blame NATO for the war igniting in Ukraine (Levada Centre, 2024b).

Putin's Obsession with Russian Identity and Ukraine

Lawrence Freedman (2024) describes Putin as a 'strategic fanatic' because of his 'deeply reactionary and obsessive views' of Ukraine and the 'ideological underpinnings of Putinism'. Luke Harding (2023a) described Putin's obsession of destroying Ukraine as a 'competitive alternative to Russia' as 'a kind of mania or mental disorder'. Then head of Russia's Security Council Nikolai Patrushev rarely raised his voice except about Ukraine which 'was very emotional and uncharacteristic of him', US National Security Adviser John Bolton recalled (Grove, Cullison, and Pancevski, 2023). Russian Deputy Foreign Minister Sergei Ryabkov shouted during negotiations in Geneva, 'We need Ukraine! We won't go anywhere without Ukraine!' (Goryashko, Fokht, and Samokhina, 2023).

Mikhail Zygar (2022) describes Putin as also obsessed with history. Andrei Kolesnikov (2023a) believes Putin is obsessed with his mission as the 'gatherer of Russian lands' (Manipulating Memory: Rewriting School History Books, 2024). Ukraine is central to this 'gathering' (Laruelle, 2024, p. 15); after all, Muscovy became the Russian Empire in 1721, twelve years after the defeat of Ukrainian Hetman Ivan Mazepa at the Battle of Poltava.

The Kremlin's claims to a single stream of Russian history from Grand Prince Vladimir (Volodymyr) to Putin aimed to create an 'unbroken continuity between past and present' (McGlynn, 2023, p. 34). The Russian nation was born in Kyiv Rus, which was the first Russian state (Tolz, 2002). Kyiv Rus launched the 'foundation of the enormous Russian state', Putin (2013b) said, with Russia and Ukraine henceforth sharing 'common traditions, common mentality, common history and common culture'. Metropolitan Tikhon (Shevkhunov) conflated Grand Prince Vladimir (Volodymyr) with Putin and declared Kyiv to be the spiritual home of Russian Orthodoxy which after Ukraine and Russia were reunited, would be cleansed of its Ukrainian identity (Ash, 2024, p. 124).

The claim of a 'thousand years of Russian' statehood (Snegovaya, Kimmage, and McGlynn, 2023) challenged Ukrainian claims to Kyiv Rus being the first Ukrainian state; in effect, Russia and Ukraine were both claiming their origins lay exclusively in Kyiv Rus (Garner, 2023, p. 193). In 2008, on the 1020th anniversary of the adoption of Christianity, Ukraine launched a new annual holiday. Two years later, Russia introduced a new holiday for Kyiv Rus as the foundation of Russian statehood (Kuzio, 2022, pp. 161–162). In 2021, President Zelenskyy expanded the anniversary of Kyiv Rus adopting Christianity to become the 'Day of Ukrainian Statehood', saying 'We [Ukrainians] are the heirs of statehood that existed more than a thousand years ago'. 'Orthodoxy originated here, the old Slavonic language originated here, and its successor is the modern-day Ukrainian language' (Zelenskyy, 2021b). Three quarters of Ukrainians believe they are descendants of Kyiv Rus and only 8 per cent feel Russia is also a descendant (Rating Sociological Group, 2021). Zelenskyy (2021a) warned 'And cousins and very distant relatives [Russians] should not encroach on her legacy. They should not try to prove their involvement in the history of thousands of years and thousands of events, being from the places where they took place thousands of kilometres away'. On the eve of Russia's full-scale invasion, Ukraine and Russia were laying exclusive claim to Kyiv Rus as the birthplace of their statehoods.

Speaking to the World Russian Peoples Council, Putin (2023a) defined the Pan-Russian World as originating in 'Ancient Rus, the Muscovite Kingdom, the Russian Empire, the Soviet Union, this is modern Russia'. Russian leaders no longer describe the medieval kingdom as Kyiv Rus but as Rus to monopolise its history as 'Russian' (Garner, 2023, p. 193). Cohen (2022) writes how Putin 'spun himself into a historical mythology' by thinking of a '1000-year empire'. Ukraine's appropriation of Kyiv Rus as the first Ukrainian state undermined the myth of a 'thousand years of Russian statehood' (Zygar, 2023b, p. 331).

After 2012, Putin frequently sat in archives and 'began to immerse himself much more in the texts of authors with similar views to Ilyin' (Zhegulev, 2023). A year later, Putin and Patriarch Kirill's visit to Ukraine on the 1025th anniversary of the adoption of Christianity by Kyiv Rus included speaking at a conference on 'Orthodox-Slavic Values', praying at an evening service at the Kyiv *Pecherska Lavra* (Monastery of the Caves) and attending a parade of the Black Sea Fleet in Sevastopol. Putin (2013a) emphasised the 'common roots' of Russians and Ukrainians who had benefitted from living in a 'common Fatherland'. Patriarch Kirill (2013) said that the Russian Orthodox Church had played a 'decisive contribution to the preservation of the spiritual unity' and a 'common spiritual basis that unites our people'. It is these 'common spiritual values that make us a single people', Kirill (2013) added.

Their visit to Kyiv was a step towards Putin's goal of the 'gathering of Russian lands' by lobbying President Yanukovych to turn away from Europe and reorientate towards Eurasia. During their visit, Putin spent a lengthy period in the Kyiv Pechersk Lavra, which became a 'mystical experience' for Putin and convinced him of the need to fight for Ukraine because Russians and Ukrainians are 'one people' with common spiritual values (Zygar, 2023a, p. 276). Russian TV presenter Vladimir Solovyov said, 'Russian holy sites have to be liberated' in Kyiv (Apt, 2024).

Russian traditional spiritual and moral values were approved in a presidential decree in 2021 on the eve of Russia's full-scale invasion of Ukraine (Putin, 2022b). The Russian Orthodox Church outlined its commitment to reuniting the *triune* Pan-Russian people and the Pan-Russian World (World Russian Peoples Council, 2024).

White Russian Émigrés Return to Russia

Ilyin became Putin's favourite author during the rehabilitation and popularisation of White Russian émigré writings which began in the mid 2000s. White Russian émigrés were reburied in Russia; the Russian president supervised the return of Ilyin's remains to Russia and his reburial in Moscow's Donskoi cemetery. Their writings were republished and promoted by the Russian state. Ilyin's works were circulated to provincial governors, schools, and the armed forces. Medvedev (2023, p. 95) describes Putin as an 'orthodox chekist, carrying a book by Ivan Ilyin'.

Dugin, a fascist and Russia's leading ideologist of Eurasianism (Shekhovtsov, 2008), said that since 2014, Russia is 'fighting so it [Ukraine] doesn't exist anymore' (Apt, 2024). In 2014, Dugin said, 'We should clean up Ukraine from the idiots. The genocide of these cretins is due and inevitable', adding 'I think we should kill, kill, kill [Ukrainians], there can't be any other talk' (Sauer, 2022). In 2022, Dugin's desire to 'kill, kill, kill Ukrainians' came true and he said, 'Ukraine no longer exists for us' (Apt, 2024; see Sergeytsev, 2022). His writings were so extreme and influential the Ukrainian security services planned to assassinate him, but instead they mistakenly killed his daughter Daria in August 2022. The infamous Dugin was appointed in December 2023 to head the Ivan Ilyin Higher Political School at the Russian State University for Humanities in Moscow to 'fill the ideological vacuum with Russian content' of 'Russian civilisation, identity and traditional Russian spiritual and moral values'.

Putin's (2021b) archival work and rehabilitation of White Russian émigrés came to fruition in his long essay on Russian-Ukrainian unity published in July 2021 which was a 'manifesto for war' (Sherr and Gretskiy, 2023). Eugene Finkel (2024, p. 162) described the essay as a modern incarnation of the literature published by the extreme Club of Russian Nationalists in Kyiv in the early twentieth century. The essay was read out to members of Russia's armed forces who would invade Ukraine eight months later (Trofimov, 2024, p. 21). Putin's essay, drafted by former minister of culture and head of the Russian Military History Society Vladimir Medinsky, left no room for an independent Ukraine or Ukrainian identity and was an ultimatum to the West to surrender Ukraine to Russia's sphere of influence (Zygar, 2023a, p. 358; Bugayova, Stepanenko, and Kagan, 2023; Kirillova, 2023). Two years later these ideas influenced the publication of an 800-page collection of 242 documents, *On the Historical Unity of Russia and Ukraine* (Arahcheev, et al., 2023).

Putin's (2024a) obsession with Ukraine was visible in his rant during an 'interview' with US journalist Tucker Carlson, during which he gave the American journalist a history of the 'southern Russian lands' and Ukrainian 'artificial state' and how Austrians, Poles and the Soviet regime had deceived Little Russians into believing they are Ukrainians (Thirteen Myths about Russia's War against Ukraine exposed, 2024). Pyotr Tolstoy, a descendant of the writer Leo Tolstoy and deputy chairman of the State Duma, described Ukrainian independence as 'just a legend that was made up by the Bolsheviks and by Ukrainian nationalists' (Apt, 2024). Ukrainians are simply Russians who refuse to admit this fact (Davis, 2024, p. 184).

Ilyin's influence on Putin can be found in his disdain for democracy, denial of Ukrainians as a people distinct from Russians, and anti-Western xenophobia.

1. *Disdain for Democracy*: Ilyin believed that liberal democracy is not suited to Russia as it would corrupt Russian cultural traditions and undermine its spiritual unity. Russia should not blindly copy Western political systems because it possessed a national character that is fundamentally different from that found in the West. Russia should push back against an 'aggressive' West seeking to impose its 'alien' liberal values on to it. Putin's Russia describes Europe as spiritually decadent because of its loss of national sovereignty to globalisation and the EU superstate, multiculturalism, and LGBTQ+. Russian 'sovereign democracy', coined by the Kremlin's political technologist Vladislav Surkov in 2005, reflects Russia taking its own 'special path' (McGlynn, 2023, p. 12)
2. *Denial of a Ukrainian People*: Ilyin denied the existence of a Ukrainian people distinct from Russians, believing they had been hoodwinked by Western conspiracies into believing they are not Little Russians.[3] Kremlin spokesman Dmitri Peskov said the Ukrainian authorities 'may try to fool the people, instil hatred for Russia' and deprive them of the Russian media 'But two fraternal peoples cannot lose each other' because they remain 'brotherly peoples'.[4]

   Ukraine is an artificial failed, puppet state (The Idea of Ukraine is Based on a Mythologised Lie, 2019). Denial of the existence of a separate Ukrainian people are widespread in Russia (Apt, 2024). Deputy head of the Russian Security Council Medvedev has taken these claims to an absurd extreme with his discourse that Ukrainians have no 'stable self-identification', Ukraine is 'artificial', has 'no civilisation content', and is a 'lie' and 'fiction' that has never existed because 'Ukraine is undoubtedly Russia!' (Apt, 2024; The Idea of Ukraine is Based on a Mythologised Lie, 2019).

   On the eve of Russia's invasion of Crimea, senior Russian officials and governors were sent copies of *Nashi Zadachi* (*Our Tasks*) by Ilyin, (1883–1954) *Opravdanie dobra* (*The Justification of the Good*) by Vladimir Solovyov (1853–1900), and *Filosofiia neravenstva* (*The Philosophy of Inequality*) by Nikolai Berdyaev (1874–1948) (Langdon

---

[3] https://euvsdisinfo.eu/report/ukrainians-are-russians-brainwashed-by-the-west/
[4] D. Peskov, Russian Television, Channel 1, 17 December 2021.

and Tismaneanu, 2020, pp. 83–112). Timothy Snyder (2018) believes: 'Since 2012, Russian policy towards Ukraine has been made on the basis of first principles, and those policies have been Ilyin's'.
3. *Anti-Western Xenophobia*: Ilyin distrusted the West, believing it to be hostile towards Russia. He believed it was paramount to preserve Russia's distinctive identity as 'not merely a nation but a 'state-civilisation'' (Aron, 2023, p. 40). The West seeks to replace Russian values with 'pseudo-values' and alien ideals that are a threat to its cultural sovereignty (Aron, 2023, pp. 41–42).

In 2014, White Russian émigrés rallied in support of Russian imperialism towards Ukraine (Belton, 2020, p. 422). In the 2014 crisis, one hundred 'princes, counts, and others whose names ranked among the most storied in tsarist Russia – Tolstoy, Pushkin, Sheremetev' signed a 'Solidarity with Russia' open letter officially penned by Prince Dmitry Shakhovskoi (Feifer, 2015). The open letter, which condemned 'pro-Nazi military groups' for killing eastern Ukrainians, heavily drew on Kremlin disinformation (Feifer, 2015). The Russian newspaper *Komsomolskaya Pravda* published an article with the headline 'White Russian Émigrés Support Mother Russia Again', writing: 'For the first time since 1941–1945, White Russia and Red Russia, past Russia and God willing, future Russia have met' (Feifer, 2015).

Russian Orthodox oligarch Konstantin Malofeev and his imperial nationalist allies strongly supported denials of Ukrainians as a people distinct from Russians. Malofeev said 'Ukraine is part of Russia. It is an artificial creation on the ruins of the empire' (Belton, 2020, 427). Malofeev added that the inhabitants of southeastern Ukraine (i.e., New Russia) have 'always been Russian. They've been Russian forever' (Belton, 2020, p. 427).

Ideological Justification for Russia's Invasion of Ukraine

Russia's full-scale invasion of Ukraine came about because Russian leaders no longer believed it was possible to use soft power to ensure pan-Russian identity would remain in place or become dominant in Ukraine. With the marginalisation of pro-Russian political forces after 2014, the Kremlin attempted to pressure Kyiv to implement the Russian definition of the Minsk accords, which would have transformed Ukraine into a loose confederation within Russia's sphere of influence. The Kremlin viewed the Minsk Accords as the last chance to influence Ukraine's trajectory, but by 2020–2021, it had become evident that Zelenskyy, like his predecessor Poroshenko, would not implement the Russian interpretation of what had been signed.

The Kremlin viewed the Minsk accords as a mechanism to transform Ukraine into a Little Russian protectorate, controlling Kyiv through the Donetsk Peoples Republic (DNR) and Luhansk Peoples Republics (LNR). Popova and Shevel (2023, p. 216) write that the Kremlin viewed the Minsk accords as a means to 'vassalize' Ukraine. Both Poroshenko and Zelenskyy refused to implement the Minsk Accords because they would have transformed the Russian-controlled DNR and LNR into a de facto Trojan Horse inside a federalised Ukraine. Just as the Kremlin was becoming exasperated by Kyiv's unwillingness to implement the Russian interpretation of the Minsk Accords, Poroshenko and Zelenskyy were implementing domestic and foreign policies that cemented the dominance of Ukrainian identity and marginalisation of pan-Russian identity.

After the Euromaidan Revolution, the pace of Ukraine's and Russia's divergence which, as Chapter 8 shows, had been gradually taking place since 1991, accelerated. Russia felt that time was slipping away, and Ukraine would soon be forever lost. The Kremlin described the divergence of 'Anti-Russia' Ukraine from Russia as a threat to Russian security. Medvedev described the Ukrainian state after 2014 as a 'constant, direct and clear threat to Russia' which required 'Ukraine's political regime' to be 'completely dismantled' (Rosenberg, 2022).

In 2020–2021, Putin and the Kremlin concluded the only manner a pan-Russian identity could become dominant in Ukraine would be through a swiftly executed military operation. The 'special military operation' would undertake regime change, destroy Ukrainian identity ('de-nazification'), and create a 'neutral' truncated puppet state ('de-militarisation'). A successful 'special military operation' would provide the Kremlin with the ability to forcefully impose a pan-Russian identity upon a Little Russian puppet state. Russian Deputy Minister of Foreign Affairs Mikhail Galuzin (2023) reiterated Russia's goals as a 'neutral, non-aligned, and nuclear-free status for Ukraine', its 'de-militarisation' and 'de-nazification', 'recognition of new territorial realities' (i.e., Kyiv accepting the loss of Crimea and four southeastern *oblasts*) and 'ensuring the rights of Russian-speaking citizens'. These demands, which were similar to those made by Medvedev to Yushchenko (Medvedev, 2009; Kuzio, 2015, pp. 458–459), were made by Russia to the Ukrainian delegation at the spring 2022 and 2025 peace talks. Russia's delegation was headed by Medinsky who, as an aide to the president, had penned Putin's (2021b) pseudo-historical article and managed the publication of Russia's new school textbooks (Zygar, 2023b).

The Kremlin provided two ideological justifications for Russia's full-scale invasion of Ukraine. The first was to destroy 'Anti-Russia' Ukraine which the country had allegedly become since the Euromaidan 'putsch'. The second was to reunite 'historical Russian lands' with Russia. This territory, in the eyes of Putin and Russian imperial nationalists, had been wrongly included within Ukraine by Soviet leader Vladimir Lenin.

Destroy 'Anti-Russia' Ukraine

The roots of the Russian view of Ukraine and Ukrainians as Western puppets stretch back to the Tsarist and especially the Soviet era (analysed in Chapter 5). The Soviet regime portrayed Ukrainian nationalists as 'an exclusively foreign problem that corrupted former Soviet citizens' because Ukrainian nationalism was foreign to Ukraine and Ukrainians (Erlacher, 2013, pp. 297, 301). Standing behind Ukrainian 'bourgeois nationalists' were the secret services of 'centres of imperialism' (Erlacher, 2013, p. 311). Ukrainian nationalists implemented the instructions of foreigners (see Key Narratives in Pro-Kremlin Disinformation: "Nazis", 2022).

It is not a long stretch to see how such conspiratorial views influence Russia when the former Soviet secret services are running the country. In the eyes of the Kremlin, the Orange and Euromaidan Revolutions were orchestrated by the West and 'Ordinary Ukrainians are simply used as a bargaining chip, a tool to contain Russia' (Patrushev, 2022a). The bulk of Ukrainians were intrinsically loyal to the Soviet Union and are to Russia but are occasionally manipulated, duped, and led astray by the West (Belton, 2020, pp. 269; Felgenhauer, 2021). Russia views Ukraine as 'where power is exercised by a certain number of political adventurers' since 2014 over the heads of the bulk of Ukrainians who desire to be aligned with Russia (Bordachev, 2021).

In Russia's dystopian world, the so-called 'special military operation' is not an invasion, but intervention to support one side of a 'civil war' by assisting the (loyal to Russia) Ukrainian majority to kick out pro-Western Nazi puppets (Putin, 2022).[5] Head of *RT* Magarita Simonyan said Russia is helping the discriminated against 'Russian people' in Ukraine; understood as Little Russian Ukrainians who are loyal to a pan-Russian identity.[6]

---

[5] https://euvsdisinfo.eu/report/russia-did-not-invade-ukraine/
[6] https://x.com/JuliaDavisNews, 20 June 2022.

Russia's so-called 'special military operation' is 'not at war with the people of Ukraine' who are supposedly loyal to Russia but are 'hostages of the Kyiv regime and its Western handlers, who have in fact occupied that country in the political, military and economic sense' (Putin, 2023a). It is Ukraine's fault that Russia was forced to intervene.[7] Putin, and the Kremlin, ignores the outcome of four elections (two presidential, two parliamentary) held since 2014. Ukrainian leaders have democratic legitimacy and were not imposed on Ukrainians. Nevertheless, Putin is adamant that Russia knows best for Ukrainians, claiming 'The current Ukrainian regime is serving not national interests but the interest of third countries' (Putin, 2023a). Russia is claiming the right to decide how Ukraine should be ruled by an authoritarian dictator, like Lukashenka, and not through democratic elections.

Such thinking rejects the very idea that Ukrainians have agency, either dissidents in the Soviet Union or protestors on the Maidan. Ukraine has no basis in history and never had an independent state; Ukrainian land is an inalienable part of Russia; and Ukrainians lack their own identity, culture, religion, and language (Rumer and Weiss, 2021). Russian leaders are convinced Ukraine 'is a territory under external management by foreign forces' (Seddon and Manson, 2021). Ukraine has been placed under 'external control', run by 'Western capitals' and turned into a 'political or economic protectorate' and a 'colony with a puppet regime' (Putin, 2022).

In Russia's dystopian world, Ukraine in the Soviet Union had 'true sovereignty' and although article 72 of the 1977 constitution permitted self-determination there was no need for Ukrainians to take this step. Belarus is not a Russian puppet state but a 'sovereign country' while Ukraine is a Western 'protectorate' (Patrushev, 2021). The West is promoting 'Anti-Russia' because the West does not want to see a powerful Russia-Ukraine axis that would pose a challenge to the US-led unipolar world.

Russia is angry because 'from time immemorial' Russians had lived in what is called Ukraine whose identity is discriminated against by Ukrainian 'far-right nationalists' Putin (2021a). Ukrainian nationalists and Russophobes built a Ukrainian state 'emulating foreign models' based 'on the negation of everything that united us' (Putin, 2022). Since 2014, 'Ukraine is slowly but surely turning into some kind of polar opposite of Russia, some kind of anti-Russia' (Osborn and Marrow, 2021).

---

[7] https://euvsdisinfo.eu/report/ukraine-itself-is-to-blame-for-the-russian-invasion-of-ukraine/

'Anti-Russia' divides 'an essentially single people' because the US is 'instilling in Ukrainians the exclusivity of their nation and hatred for everything Russian' (Patrushev, 2022a). 'Westerners know that Russia and Ukraine have always been a single and inseparable people with a common culture and destiny' (Patrushev, 2022a). The West is using 'Anti-Russia' Ukraine to pressure Russia and to create conditions for the 'further fragmentation of the Russian ethnic group' (Patrushev, 2022b).

Since 2014, a Western conspiracy had transformed Ukraine into 'Anti-Russia'. Russian Foreign Minister Lavrov (2024) blamed the West for transforming Ukraine into 'Anti-Russia', claiming that without its 'meddling' Russians and Ukrainians would be 'brotherly' peoples – as they allegedly were in the Soviet Union. The claim, analysed in Chapter 8, that Russians and Ukrainians always had 'brotherly' relations and Ukrainians can only prosper when in union with Russia is propounded by Soviet and Russian history writing; meanwhile, Ukrainian historiography critically scrutinises the suppression of Ukrainian identity, culture, and language (see Wynar, 1988). Since the early 1990s, Russia has repeatedly complained that Ukrainian history writing and school textbooks was inculcating an 'entire generation of youth in hostility and hatred of Russia',[8] with Tsarist Russian and Soviet rule over Ukraine described as being that of 'enslavers' and 'colonisers'[9] (Thirteen Myths about Russia's War against Ukraine exposed, 2024; see Wynar, 1988).

Declaring Ukraine to be 'Anti-Russia' opened the path for Russian imperial nationalists to inflame their Ukrainophobia discourse. Medvedev attacked 'bastards and geeks' (Ukrainians) who want death for Russians (Apt, 2024). Russians concluded that one of the invasion goals of 'de-nazification' had to be more thoroughly implemented over a longer period because Ukrainians had been more indoctrinated by 'nationalist/fascist/nazi' propaganda than the Kremlin had initially believed (Harding, 2023b, pp. 31, 42, 45, 47, 67, 78–79, 89; see Key Narratives in Pro-Kremlin Disinformation: "Nazis", 2022). Russian imperial nationalist propagandists adjusted their propaganda in two ways. The first was to blame dogged resistance because Russia was fighting not only Ukraine but the 'collective West'. The second, was to allege that the 'indoctrination' of Ukrainians with anti-Russian nationalism and 'Nazism' had been taking

---

[8] https://tass.kribrum.ru/nazism; https://rvio.histrf.ru/activities/news/eksperty-obsudili-korni-ukrainskogo-nacizma
[9] Ibid.

place throughout the post-Soviet era (and not just since 2014) and was therefore more deeply entrenched.

How could the Kremlin defeat 'Anti-Russia' Ukraine? Believing Ukraine to be an American colony meant that Russia needed to talk directly to the US over the heads of Ukrainians. Medvedev (2021) said there was no sense for Russia 'to deal with vassals. Business must be done with the overlord'. These Russian views have deepened since the Spring 2022 peace talks. The Kremlin viewed the election of Donald Trump as the possibility of Russia again being recognised as an equal and a great power by the US, with whom it would sign a new Yalta agreement dividing the world into spheres of influence. Ukraine, and Eurasia, would be recognised by the US as Russia's exclusive sphere of influence – a demand made by two Russian presidents and most Russian politicians since the early 1990s. (Seddon, 2024).

New York Times correspondent Hedrick Smith (1976, p. 567) had written half a century ago that the US is 'the one country against which Russians feel compelled to measure themselves, the one worthy standard in the world'. Russia's historical inferiority complex has always demanded the US recognise Russia as an equal, which they believed existed in the Cold War when the US treated the Soviet Union with respect. Chapter 9 analyses how Russia views its war against Ukraine as a broader struggle to reshape the international order by changing the since 1991 US-led unipolar for the Cold War multipolar world.

Reunite 'Historical Russian Lands' with Russia That Were Wrongly Included in Ukraine

Throughout the post-Soviet era, Russia has harboured territorial claims towards Crimea (Levada Centre, 2019) and since 2008, towards southeastern Ukraine. Russia's irredentism towards southeastern Ukraine first became evident in Putin's speech to the April 2008 NATO-Russia Council when he described Ukraine as a 'fragile' country (Putin, 2008). Sergei Karaganov, director of the Institute of Europe at the Russian Academy of Sciences, described Ukraine as a failed state without the ability to produce ruling elites, and called for Russia to restore justice by taking back 'Russian lands' included in Ukraine (Kulakov, 2009). In 2011, Putin told former US President Bill Clinton, 'that he did not agree with the [Budapest] agreement I made with Yeltsin' (Chaffin, 2023). Putin said, 'I don't agree with it. And I do not support it. And I am not bound by it' (Chaffin, 2023). Putin was referring to what Ukraine understood to be security guarantees in the 1994 Budapest Memorandum given by the US, UK, and Russian Federation to respect Ukraine's sovereignty and territorial integrity in exchange for Ukraine giving up the world's third largest nuclear weapons arsenal it had inherited from the USSR.

In 2014, Putin took three steps in laying territorial claims towards Ukraine. The first was to occupy and annex Crimea. A high majority of Russians supported the annexation of Crimea; with 84 per cent believing the referendum was free and fair and 89 per cent of the opinion that Ukrainians should accept the results (Pew Research Centre, 2014). The Kremlin can only lay claim to Crimea as 'always being Russian' by monopolising Kyiv Rus history as the beginning of a 'thousand-years of Russian statehood'. Russia's claims to ownership of Crimea 'is one of the key narratives of the Kremlin's view of history' (Back to school in Russia – more revision of history, 2024).

The second was to revive the term New Russia (*Novorossiya*) to lay territorial claim to 'Russian historical lands' in southeast Ukraine. As Olivia I. Durand (2022) writes, Putin's claims to New Russia are based on untruths and distortions of history. Southeast Ukraine had a long history before Russia's annexation in 1783, and it was not, as Putin alleged, empty 'wild fields'. Ukrainians had been settling in the region since the seventeenth century and became most of the region's inhabitants. 'Claiming Southern Ukraine as historically and uniquely Russia is not only factually inaccurate, but also a completely modern assertion that serves recolonising purposes', Durand (2022, p. 75) writes.

The third was to describe Ukraine as an 'artificial' construct and support the dismemberment of Ukraine – contrary to agreements and treaties signed by Russia with Ukraine. Russian propaganda convinced Russians this was perfectly reasonable, with nearly two-thirds (61 per cent) agreeing that territories within Russia's neighbours could belong to Russia (Despite Concerns about Governance, Ukrainians Want to Remain One Country, 2014). During the eight years between Russia's two invasions in 2014 and 2022, Putin's (2020) rhetoric laying claim to Ukrainian territory grew, with him claiming Ukraine 'received an enormous amount of Russian lands' and arguing that in 1991, Ukraine should not have 'carried away these gifts from the Russian people'.

Since 2012–2014, Putin (2021a) has repeatedly described southeast Ukraine as 'historical Russian lands'. Ukraine included 'historical Russian territories' in its southeast which Soviet leaders wrongly included in the Soviet Ukrainian republic. In 2014, Putin revived the Tsarist term 'New Russia' to lay territorial claim towards Ukraine's southeast, calling the region 'Russian Western lands' and 'ancestral Russian lands', adding *Prichernomorie* (Black Sea coast lands) 'never had anything to do with Ukraine' (Socor, 2020). Putin (2023b) said, 'The southeastern part of Ukraine has always been pro-Russian because it is historically a Russian territory', adding 'that the entire Black Sea region was incorporated into Russia as the result of Russo-Turkish wars. What does Ukraine have to do with that? Neither Crimea nor the Black Sea region has any connection to Ukraine. Odesa is a Russian city. We know this. Everyone knows this. But they [Ukrainians] have concocted some historical nonsense'.

Since the full-scale invasion, Russian officials have expanded their claims beyond southeastern Ukraine to most of the remainder of Ukraine'; the exception being the western *oblasts*, which Russian imperial nationalists believe were never part of the Pan-Russian World. Kyiv, Kharkiv, Odesa, and Dnipro are described as 'Russian' cities by Russian politicians and journalists. Kyiv is defined as the birthplace of the Russian people and Russian orthodoxy. 'Kyiv is the mother of Russian cities' Putin (2014) said in his speech after the annexation of Crimea, where Kyiv Rus laid 'the civilisation foundation which unites the peoples of Russia, Ukraine, and Belarus'. Kyiv, Dnipro, Kharkiv, Dnipro, Odesa, Mykolayiv, and Zaporizhzhya are 'Russian cities', Medvedev said (Apt, 2024). Journalist Sergei Mardan described Ukraine as the 'territory of Russia' and Kyiv as always having been a 'Russian city' (Apt, 2024).

Conclusion

The term Russian imperial nationalism used in this chapter combines imperialism and nationalism in support of 'state-civilisation' empires (Motyl, 1990; Rowley, 2000). Throughout the post-Soviet era, civic Russian identity was always weaker than imperial nationalism because most Russians imagined 'Russia' to be bigger than the Russian SFSR and after 1991 bigger than the Russian Federation. Russian nationalists never supported the secession of Russia from the Russian Empire or the Russian SFSR from the Soviet Union and did not declare independence from the USSR.

Russian imperial nationalists have been obsessed with Ukraine and Ukrainians throughout the post-Soviet era. They found it difficult to accept Ukrainian independence outside the Russian World. The revival and rehabilitation of White Russian émigrés and their return to Russia during the nearly two decades prior to the full-scale invasion prepared the ground for the de-humanisation of Ukraine and Ukrainians

(Sergeytsev, 2022; Ibrahim, 2023; Hate Speech and Calls for Genocide in Putin's Russia, 2024). The roots of the brutality of Russian military aggression against civilians and war crimes committed by the Russian army and security forces, as evidenced by six arrest warrants issued by the ICC (International Criminal Court) (Kremlin Hate Speech Incites War Crimes in Ukraine, 2022; When Words Kill – From Moscow to Mariupol, 2022; Applebaum, 2022), are to be found in the Soviet legacy of disrespect for human rights and nearly two decades of post-Soviet dehumanisation of Ukrainians (Sergeytsev, 2022; Troianovski, 2022; Hate Speech and Calls for Genocide in Putin's Russia, 2024). After returning to the presidency in 2012, Putin set about implementing the 'gathering of Russian lands', the reunion of the Pan-Russian people and 'liberating' 'historical Russian lands' wrongly included by Soviet leaders in Ukraine. Putin's destiny, he believes, is to enter Russian history alongside his heroes – Peter I, Catherine I, and Stalin – three leaders he told former Polish President Alexander Kwasniewski he admired (Dixon, 2024; see Kuzio, 2017). Historical preparation and ideological justification for Russia's invasions of Ukraine in 2014 and 2022 are to be found in Ukraine depicted as an artificial, failed, and puppet state and Russians and Ukrainians described as 'one people'. US control over Ukraine since the Euromaidan 'putsch' transformed Ukraine into an 'Anti-Russia' which the so-called 'special military operation' had to destroy before Ukraine was forever lost to Russia.

References

Applebaum, A. (2022). 'Ukraine and the Words That Lead to Mass Murder. First Comes the Dehumanization. Then Comes the Killing,' *The Atlantic*, 25 April. www.theatlantic.com/magazine/archive/2022/06/ukraine-mass-murder-hate-speech-soviet/629629/

Applebaum, A. and Gumenyuk, N. (2023). 'They Didn't Understand Anything, but Just Spoiled People's Lives,' *The Atlantic*, 14 February. www.theatlantic.com/ideas/archive/2023/02/russia-ukraine-war-potemkin-occupation-murder-torture/672841/

Apt, C. (2024). 'Russia's Elimination Rhetoric against Ukraine: A Collection.' Washington, DC: Just Security, 18 April. www.justsecurity.org/81789/russias-eliminationist-rhetoric-against-ukraine-a-collection.

Arahcheev, V. A., Bezyev, D. A., Grigoriev, E. M., et al. (2023). *Sbornyk dokumentov "Ob istorycheskom iedynstve russkykh i ukraintsev*. Moscow: Communication of Epochs Foundation. https://rusarchives.ru/novosti-rosarhiva/23-06-2023-sbornik-dokumentov-ob-istoricheskom-edinstve-russkih-i-ukraincev

Aron, L. (2023). *Riding the Tiger: Vladimir Putin's Russia and the Uses of War.* Washington, DC: American Enterprise Institute.

Ash, L. (2024). *The Baton and Cross: Russia's Church from Pagans to Putin.* London: Icon Books.

Back to school in Russia – more revision of history. (2024). *EUvsDisinfo,* 6 September. https://euvsdisinfo.eu/back-to-school-in-russia-more-revision-of-history/

Belton, C. (2020). *Putin's People. How the KGB Took Back Russia and Then Took on the West.* London: William Collins.

Bohlen, C. (1993). 'Cradle of Russian Revolution a Hotbed of Disgust,' *New York Times,* 22 June. www.nytimes.com/1993/06/22/world/cradle-of-russian-revolution-a-hotbed-of-disgust.html

Bordachev, T. (2021). 'Pochemu Rossiia i SSha ne mogut reshyt ukrainskyi vopros,' *Vzgliad,* 4 November. https://vz.ru/opinions/2021/11/4/1127593.html

Bugayova, N., Stepanenko, K., and Kagan, F. W. (2023). *Weakness is Lethal: Why Putin Invaded Ukraine and How the War Must End.* Washington, DC: Institute for the Study of War, 1 October. https://understandingwar.org/backgrounder/weakness-lethal-why-putin-invaded-ukraine-and-how-war-must-end

Chaffin, J. (2023). 'Bill Clinton Saw Vladimir Putin's Ukraine Campaign As 'Just a Matter of Time,' *Financial Times,* 5 May. www.ft.com/content/404af8ef-d073-4edc-ab25-384442864342

Chovgan, V., Romanov, M. and Melnychuk, V. (2023). *Nine Circles of Hell. Places of Detention in Ukraine Under the Russian Occupation, March 2022-December 2022* Copenhagen: DIGNITY [Danish Institute Against Torture]. www.dignity.dk/wp-content/uploads/42-Nine-circles-of-hell.pdf

Clover, C. (2016). *Black Wind, White Snow. The Rise of Russia's New Nationalism.* New Haven, CT: Yale University Press.

Cohen, R. (2022). 'The Making of Vladimir Putin. Tracing Putin's 22-year Slide from Statesman to Tyrant,' *New York Times,* 26 February. www.nytimes.com/2022/03/26/world/europe/vladimir-putin-russia.html

D'Anieri, P. (2019). *Ukraine and Russia: From Civilized Divorce to Uncivil War.* Cambridge: Cambridge University Press.

Davis, J. (2024). *In Their Own Words. How Russian Propagandists Reveal Putin's Intentions.* Stuttgart: Ibidem; New York: Columbia University Press.

Disinformation About the Current Russian-Ukrainian Conflict. (2022). *EUvsDisinfo,* 24 January. https://euvsdisinfo.eu/disinformation-about-the-current-russia-ukraine-conflict-seven-myths-debunked/

Dixon, R. (2024). 'Under Putin, a Militarized New Russia Rises to Challenge US and the West,' *The Washington Post,* 6 May. www.washingtonpost.com/world/interactive/2024/putin-values-russian-society-conservatism/

Durand, O. I. (2022). 'New Russia' and the Legacies of Settler Colonialism in Southern Ukraine,' *Journal of Applied History,* 4: 58–75.

Edenborg, E. (2017). 'Creativity, Geopolitics and Antological Security: Satire on Russia and the War in Ukraine,' *Postcolonial Studies,* 20 (3): 294–316.

Engström, M. (2014). 'Contemporary Russian Messianism and New Russian Foreign Policy,' *Contemporary Security Policy*, 35 (3): 356–379.

Erlacher, T. (2013). 'Denationalizing Treachery: The Ukrainian Insurgent Army and the Organization of Ukrainian Nationalists in Late Soviet Discourse, 1945–1985,' *REGION: Regional Studies of Russia, Eastern Europe and Central Asia*, 2 (2): 289–316.

Farmer, K. C. (1980). *Ukrainian Nationalism in the Post-Stalin Era. Myths, Symbols and Ideology in Soviet Nationalities Policies*. The Hague: Martinus Nijhoff Publishers.

Feifer, G. (2015). 'Putin's White Guard. Why Russia's Former Nobility is Supporting the Kremlin,' *Foreign Affairs*, 23 March. www.foreignaffairs.com/articles/russian-federation/2015-03-23/putins-white-guard

Felgenhauer, P. (2021). 'Escalating Russian-Western Tensions Are Reflected in Confrontation in Donbas,' *Eurasia Daily Monitor*, 18 (28), 18 February. https://jamestown.org/program/escalating-russian-western-tensions-are-reflected-in-confrontation-in-donbas/

Finkel, E. (2024). *Intent to Destroy. Russia's Two-Hundred-Year Quest to Dominate Ukraine*. London: Basic Books.

Freedman, L. (2024). 'Putin the Fanatic,' *Substack*, 2 April. https://samf.substack.com/p/putin-the-fanatic

From Accepting NATO Aspirations to 'Denazifying': 20+ Years of Putin's Changing Views on Ukraine. (2022). *Russia Matters*, 16 June. www.russiamatters.org/analysis/accepting-nato-aspirations-denazifying-20-years-putins-changing-views-ukraine

Galuzin, M. (2023). 'Interview,' *RIA Novosti*, 30 December. https://ria.ru/20231230/galuzin-1919056047.html

Garner, I. (2023). *Generation Z. Into the Heart of Russia's Fascist Youth*. London: Hurst.

Goryashko, S., Fokht, E. and Samokhina, S. (2023). 'Threats, Insults and Kremlin 'robots': How Russia Diplomacy Died under Putin,' *BBC Russian Service*, 3 September. www.bbc.co.uk/news/world-europe-66509180

Grove, T., Cullison, A., and Pancevski, B. (2023). 'How Putin's Right-Hand Man Took Out Prigozhin,' *Wall Street Journal*, 22 December. www.wsj.com/world/russia/putin-patrushev-plan-prigozhin-assassination-428d5ed8

Grylls, G. (2024). 'Putin Compares Himself to Jesus Christ in His Battle to Uphold Tradition,' *The Times*, 10 April. www.thetimes.com/world/russia-ukraine-war/article/vladimir-putin-jesus-christ-comparison-russia-7720bgz7w

Harding, L. (2022). *Invasion: Russia's Bloody War and Ukraine's Fight for Survival*. London: Guardian and Faber.

Harding, A. (2023a). *A Small Stubborn Town. Life, Death and Defiance in Ukraine*. London: Ithaka Press.

Harding, L. (2023b). 'US Will 'Lose Face before World' If It Abandons Kyiv, Says ex-Ukraine President,' *The Guardian*, 11 December. www.theguardian.com/world/2023/dec/11/us-will-lose-face-before-world-if-it-abandons-kyiv-says-ex-ukraine-president

Hate Speech and Calls for Genocide in Putin's Russia. (2024). *EUvsDisinfo*, 19 February. https://euvsdisinfo.eu/hate-speech-and-calls-for-genocide-in-putins-russia/

Hosking, G. (1998). 'Can Russia Become a Nation-state?' *Nations and Nationalism*, 4 (4): 449–462.

Ibrahim, A. (2023). 'Russia is Attempting Genocide in Ukraine,' *Foreign Policy*, 3 August. https://foreignpolicy.com/2023/08/03/russia-ukraine-war-genocide-bucha-izium-icc-war-crimes/

Kagan, F. W., Barros, G., Mikkelsen, N. and Mealie, D. (2023). *The Lands Ukraine Must Liberate*, The Institute for the Study of War, 31 December. www.understandingwar.org/backgrounder/lands-ukraine-must-liberate

Kelly, A. and Kovalchuk, I. (2024). 'Ukrainian Education and Russian Literature: Curriculum Change in a Time of War,' *Slavonic and East European Review*, 102 (3): 526–557.

Key Narratives in Pro-Kremlin Disinformation: "Nazis". (2022). *EUvsDisinfo*, 20 September. https://euvsdisinfo.eu/key-narratives-in-pro-kremlin-disinformation-nazis/

Kinetz, E. (2022). ''We will find you:' Russians Hunt Down Ukrainians on Lists,' *Associated Press*, 21 December. https://apnews.com/article/russia-ukraine-europe-3ae1bccfb0ef34dbe363f7c289ce7934

Kirill. P. (2013). 'Speech by His Holiness Patriarch Kirill after the Prayer Service on Vladimir Hill in Kyiv,' www.patriarchia.ru/db/text/3128846.html

Kirillova, K. (2023). 'Aggressive Nuclear Propaganda Sets Trap for the Kremlin,' *Eurasia Daily Monitor*, 20 (135), 5 September. https://jamestown.org/program/aggressive-nuclear-propaganda-sets-trap-for-the-kremlin/

Kolesnikov, A. (2023a). 'The Plot Against Russia. How Putin Revived Stalinist Anti-Americanism to Justify a Botched War,' *Foreign Affairs*, 25 March. www.foreignaffairs.com/russian-federation/plot-against-russia#:~:text=By%20fixating%20on%20the%20United,%2C%20if%20not%20destroy%2C%20us.

Kolesnikov, A. (2023b). 'The End of the Russian Idea,' *Foreign Affairs*, 22 August. www.foreignaffairs.com/russian-federation/vladimir-putin-end-russian-idea

Koval, N. and Tereshchenko, D. (2023). *Russian Cultural Diplomacy under Putin*. Stuttgart: Ibidem; New York: Columbia University Press.

Kozerova, V. (2023). 'Calculated Evil. How Putin's Forces Use War Crimes and Torture to Erase Ukrainian Identity,' *Politico*, 3 March. www.politico.eu/article/ukraine-war-putin-forces-use-war-crimes-and-torture-to-erase-ukrainian-identity/

Kremlin Hate Speech Incites War Crimes in Ukraine. (2022). *EUvsDisinfo*, 9 June. https://euvsdisinfo.eu/kremlin-hate-speech-incites-war-crimes-in-ukraine/

Kuchma, L. (2023). *Ukrayina – Ne Rosiya. Dvatsyat Rokiv Potomu*. Kyiv: Adef-Ukrayina.

Kulakov, A. (2009). 'Failed state, abo Ukrayina ochyma Rosii,' *Ukrayinska Pravda*, 23 March. www.pravda.com.ua/articles/2009/03/23/3823825/

Kulyk, V. (2023). 'Mova ta identychnist v Ukrayini na kinets 2022-ho,' *Zbruch*, 7 January. https://zbruc.eu/node/114247?fbclid=IwAR399VVX7y4EDXgVe dqvA2o1B1nIEUGylLtBIEBotJ16hxjItDQ0L-cOvJM

Kuzio, T. (2002). 'The Myth of the Civic State: A Critical Survey of Hans Kohn's Framework for Understanding Nationalism,' *Ethnic and Racial Studies*, 25 (1): 20–39.

Kuzio, T. (2015). *Ukraine: Democratization, Corruption, and the New Russian Imperialism*. Santa Barbara, CA: Praeger.

Kuzio, T. (2017). 'Stalinism and Russian and Ukrainian National Identities,' *Communist and Post-Communist Studies*, 50 (4): 289–302.

Kuzio, T. (2019). 'Russian Stereotypes and Myths of Ukraine and Ukrainians and Why Novorossiya Failed,' *Communist and Post-Communist Studies*, 52 (4), 297–309.

Kuzio, T. (2020). 'Empire Loyalism and Nationalism in Ukraine and Ireland. Comparing the Sources of Conflict in the Donbas and Ulster,' *Communist and Post-Communist Studies*, 53 (3): 88–106.

Kuzio, T. (2022). *Russian Nationalism and the Russian-Ukrainian War: Autocracy-Orthodoxy-Nationality*. London: Routledge.

Langdon, K. C. and Tismaneanu, V. (2020). *Putin's Totalitarian Democracy. Ideology, Myth, and Violence in the Twenty-First Century*. Cham: Imprint Springer International Publishing.

Laqueur, W. (1993). *Black Hundred. The Rise of the Extreme Right in Russia*. New York: Harper Collins.

Laruelle, M. (2016). 'The Three Colors of Novorossiya, or the Russian Nationalist Mythmaking of the Ukrainian Crisis,' *Post-Soviet Affairs*, 32 (1): 55–74.

Laruelle, M. (2024). *Russia's Ideological Construction in the Context of the War in Ukraine*, Report No. 46. Paris: French Institute of International Relations. www.ifri.org/en/publications/etudes-de-lifri/russieeurasiereports/russias-ideological-construction-context-war

Lavrov, S. (2024). Speech to the United Nations Security Council, 22 January. https://mid.ru/en/foreign_policy/news/1927070/

Levada Centre. (2019). 'Crimea: five years', 11 April. www.levada.ru/en/2019/04/11/crimea-five-years/

Levada Centre. (2023). 'Conflict with Ukraine: February 2023', March. www.levada.ru/2023/03/02/konflikt-s-ukrainoj-otsenki-fevralya-2023-goda/

Levada Centre. (2024a). 'Attitudes towards China, Brazil, Turkey, Iran, France, Ukraine, USA, EU, and UN', 15 October. www.levada.ru/2024/10/15/otnoshenie-k-kitayu-brazilii-turtsii-iranu-frantsii-ukraine-ssha-es-i-oon/

Levada Centre. (2024b). 'Lesser Evil: Why Interest in the US Presidential Election Has Increased Again in Russia', 5 November. www.levada.ru/2024/11/05/menshee-iz-zol-pochemu-v-rossii-vnov-vyros-interes-k-vyboram-prezidenta-ssha/

Lewis, D. (2023). 'The Role of Ideology in Russian Foreign Policy' In: J. M. Leader and M. L. Haas (eds.), *The Routledge Handbook of Ideology and International Relations*. London: Routledge: 374–390.

Manipulating Memory: Rewriting School History Books. (2024). *EU vs Disinfo*, 16 February. https://euvsdisinfo.eu/manipulating-memory-rewriting-school-history-books/

McGlynn, J. (2023). *Memory Makers. The Politics of the Past in Putin's Russia*. London: Bloomsbury.

Medvedev, D. (2009). 'Message to the President of Ukraine Viktor Yushchenko,' 11 August. http://kremlin.ru/events/president/news/5158

Medvedev, D. (2021). 'Pochemu bessmyslennyi kontaktyi s nyneshnym ukrainskym rukovodstom,' *Komersant*, 11 October. www.kommersant.ru/doc/5028300?from=glavnoe_1#id2123318

Medvedev, S. (2023). *A War Made in Russia*. London: Polity.

Michel, C. (2024). 'How Aleksandr Solzhenitsyn Became Putin's Spiritual Guru,' *Foreign Policy*, 7 April. https://foreignpolicy.com/2024/04/07/putin-russia-nationalism-solzhenitsyn-became-putins-spiritual-guru-ukraine/

Minchenia, A., Tornquist-Plewa, B. and Yurchuk, Y. (2018). 'Humour as a Mode of Hegemonic Control: Comic Representations of Belarusian and Ukrainian Leaders in Official Russian Media' In: N. Bernsand and B. Tornquist-Plewa (eds.), *Cultural and Political Imaginaries in Putin's Russia*. Leiden: Brill Academic Publishers: 211–231.

Motyl, A. J. (1990). 'The Myth of Russian Nationalism' In: A. J. Motyl (ed.), *Sovietology, Rationality, Nationality. Coming to Grips with Nationalism in the USSR*. New York: Columbia University Press: 161–173.

Oliinyk, A. and Kuzio, T. (2021). 'The Euromaidan Revolution of Dignity, Reforms and De-Communisation in Ukraine,' *Europe-Asia Studies*, 73 (5): 807–836.

Osborn, A. and Ostroukh, A. (2021). 'Putin Rues Soviet Collapse as Demise of "Historical Russia",' *Reuters*, 12 December. www.reuters.com/world/europe/putin-rues-soviet-collapse-demise-historical-russia-2021-12-12/#:~:text=%22It%20was%20a%20disintegration%20of,into%20a%20completely%20different%20country

Osborn, A. and Marrow, A. (2021). 'Putin Says Ukraine Is Becoming an "anti-Russia," Pledges Response,' *Reuters*, 14 May. www.reuters.com/world/europe/putin-says-russia-will-respond-ukraines-cleansing-political-space-2021-05-14/

Patrushev, N. (2021). Interview, *Argumenty i Fakty*, 23 November. https://aif.ru/politics/world/zapad_i_ego_zalozhniki_nikolay_patrushev_o_prichinah_krizisa_s_migrantami

Patrushev, N. (2022a). Interview, *Rosiiskaya Gazeta*, 26 April. https://rg.ru/2022/04/26/patrushev-zapad-sozdal-imperiiu-lzhi-predpolagaiushchuiu-unichtozhenie-rossii.html

Patrushev, N. (2022b). Interview, *RIA Novosti*, 3 November. https://ria.ru/20221103/ukraina-1828862220.html

Pew Research Centre. (2014). 'Despite Concerns about Governance, Ukrainians Want to Remain One Country', 8 May. www.pewresearch.org/global/2014/05/08/despite-concerns-about-governance-ukrainians-want-to-remain-one-country/

Plokhy, S. (2017). *Lost Kingdom. A History of Russian Nationalism from Ivan the Great to Vladimir Putin*. London: Penguin Books.
Plokhy, S. (2023a). *The Russo-Ukrainian War*. Dublin: Penguin Books.
Plokhy, S. (2023b). *The Frontline. Essays on Ukraine's Past and Present*. Cambridge, MA: Harvard University Press.
Pritsak, O. (1992). 'The Problem of a Ukrainian-Russian Dialogue' In: P. J. Potichnyj, M. Raeff, J. Pelenski and G. N. Zekulin (eds.), *Ukraine and Russia in Their Historical Encounter*. Edmonton: Canadian Institute of Ukrainian Studies: ix–xiv.
Popova, M. and Shevel, O. (2023). *Russia and Ukraine. Entangled Histories. Diverging States*. Cambridge and Hoboken, NJ: Polity Press.
Putin, V. (2008). 'Speech to the NATO Summit in Bucharest,' 2 April. www.unian.info/world/111033-text-of-putin-s-speech-at-nato-summit-bucharest-april-2-2008.html
Putin, V. (2013a). 'Conference "Orthodox-Slavic Values – the Basis of Ukraine's Civilizational Choice",' 27 July. http://kremlin.ru/events/president/news/18961
Putin, V. (2013b). 'Meeting of the Valdai International Discussion Club,' 19 September. http://en.kremlin.ru/events/president/news/19243
Putin, V. (2014). 'Address by the President of the Russian Federation,' 18 March. http://en.special.kremlin.ru/events/president/news/20603
Putin, V. (2020). 'Russia, Kremlin, Putin,' Interview on Rossiia-1 TV channel, 21 June. https://smotrim.ru/video/2198622
Putin, V. (2021a). Direct Line Forum, 30 June. http://en.kremlin.ru/events/president/news/65973
Putin, V. (2021b). 'On the Historical Unity of Russians and Ukrainians,' 12 July. http://en.kremlin.ru/events/president/news/66181
Putin, V. (2022a). 'Address by the President of the Russian Federation,' 21 February. http://en.kremlin.ru/events/president/news/67828
Putin, V. (2022b). 'On approving the Fundamentals of State Policy to Preserve and Strengthen Traditional Russian Spiritual and Moral Values,' 9 November. http://en.kremlin.ru/acts/news/69810
Putin, V. (2023b). 'Speech to World Russian Peoples Council,' 28 November. http://en.kremlin.ru/events/president/news/72863
Putin, V. (2023b). 'Direct Line Forum,' 14 December. http://en.kremlin.ru/events/president/transcripts/72994
Putin, V. (2024a). 'Interview with Tucker Carlson,' 8 February. http://en.kremlin.ru/events/president/news/73411
Putin, V. (2024b). 'Decree on 'Strategy to Counter Extremism in Russia,' 28 December. http://kremlin.ru/acts/news/76020
Rating Sociological Group. (2021). 'Suspilno-politychni nastroii naselennya,' 6 July. https://ratinggroup.ua/research/ukraine/obschestvenno-politicheskie_nastroeniya_naseleniya_30_iyunya-3_iyulya_2021.html
Rating Sociological Group. (2022a). 'Tenth National Survey: Ideological Markers of the War,' 3 May. https://ratinggroup.ua/en/research/ukraine/desyatyy_obschenacionalnyy_opros_ideologicheskie_markery_voyny_27_aprelya_2022.html

Rating Sociological Group. (2022b). 'The Sixth National Poll: The Language Issue in Ukraine,' 25 March. https://ratinggroup.ua/en/research/ukraine/language_issue_in_ukraine_march_19th_2022.html

Rosenberg, S. (2022). 'What Is Vladimir Putin Thinking and Planning?' *BBC News*, 12 October. www.bbc.co.uk/news/world-europe-63231823

Rowley, D. G. (2000). 'Imperial versus National Discourse: The Case of Russia,' *Nations and Nationalism*, 6 (1): 23–42.

Rumer, E. and Weiss, A. S. (2021). 'Ukraine: Putin's Unfinished Business,' Carnegie Endowment for International Peace, 12 November. https://carnegieendowment.org/research/2021/11/ukraine-putins-unfinished-business?lang=en

Russia's Systematic Program for the Re-education and Adoption of Ukraine's Children. (2023). Conflict Observatory 14 February. https://hub.conflictobservatory.org/portal/sharing/rest/content/items/97f919ccfe524d31a241b53ca44076b8/data

Sauer, A. (2022). 'Dugin: Who Is Putin Ally and Apparent Car Bombing Target?' *The Guardian*, 21 August. www.theguardian.com/world/2022/aug/21/alexander-dugin-who-putin-ally-apparent-car-bombing-target

Schneider-Deters, W. (2024). *Russia's War in Ukraine. Debates on Peace, Fascism, and War Crimes, 2022–2023*. Stuttgart: Ibidem; New York: Columbia University Press.

Seddon, M. and Manson, K. (2021). 'Troops Build-up Shows Putin Views Ukraine as "Unfinished Business",' *Financial Times*, 15 November. www.ft.com/content/b4bc9313-3a69-4140-bd36-d06df9925e61

Seddon, M. (2024). 'Vladimir Putin to Reject Donald Trump's Opening Peace Offer, Says Russian Tycoon,' *Financial Times*, 2 December 2024. www.ft.com/content/ac39b604-ef6d-41cb-bb8c-0eb76e002176

Sergeytsev, T. (2022). 'What Should Russia Do with Ukraine?' *RIA Novosti*, 3 April. https://ria.ru/20220403/ukraina-1781469605.html

Shekhovtsov, A. (2008). 'The Palingenetic Thrust of Russian Neo-Eurasianism: Ideas of Rebirth in Aleksandr Dugin's Worldview,' *Totalitarian Movements and Political Religions*, 9 (4): 491–506.

Sherr, J. and Gretskiy, I. (2023). *Why Russia Went to War. A Three-Dimensional Perspective*, January. Tallinn: International Centre for Defence and Security. https://icds.ee/en/why-russia-went-to-war-a-three-dimensional-perspective/

Shkandrij, M. (2001). *Russia and Ukraine. Literature and the Discourse of Empire from Napoleonic to Postcolonial Times*. Montreal-Kingston: McGill-Queens University Press.

Shulman, S. (2005). 'National Identity and Public Support for Political and Economic Reform in Ukraine,' *Slavic Review*, 64 (1): 59–87.

Smith, H. (1976). *The Russians*. London: Sphere Books.

Snegovaya, M., Kimmage, M. and McGlynn, J. (2023). 'Putin the Ideologue. The Kremlin's Potent Mix of Nationalism, Grievance, and Mythmaking,' *Foreign Affairs*, 16 November. www.foreignaffairs.com/russian-federation/putin-ideologue

Snyder, T. (2018). 'Ivan Ilyin, Putin's Philosopher of Russian Fascism,' *New York Review of Books*, 5 April. www.nybooks.com/daily/2018/03/16/ivan-ilyin-putins-philosopher-of-russian-fascism

Socor, V. (2020). 'Putin and Ukraine's Black Sea Lands: Another Iteration of New Russia?' *Eurasia Daily Monitor*, 17 (2), 14 January. https://jamestown.org/program/putin-and-ukraines-black-sea-lands-another-iteration-of-novorossiya/

Soldatov, A. and Borogan, I. (2019). *Compatriots. The Brutal and Chaotic History of Russian Exiles, Emigres and Agents Abroad*. New York: Public Affairs.

Soldatov, A. and Borogan, I. (2022). 'Putin's New Police State. In the Shadow of War, the FSB Embraces Stalin's Methods,' *Foreign Affairs*, 27 July. www.foreignaffairs.com/russian-federation/putins-new-police-state

Solzhenitsyn, A. (1991). *Rebuilding Russia: Reflections and Tentative Proposals*. New York: Farrar, Straus, and Giroux.

Stoyanov, Y. (2024). 'The War in Ukraine: Challenges to Just War Doctrines in Eastern Orthodoxy,' *Studies in Christian Ethics*, 37 (3): 669–692.

Szporluk, R. (1985). 'National History as a Political Background: The Case of Ukraine and Belarus' In: M. S. Pap (ed.), *Russian Empire: Some Aspects of Tsarist and Soviet Colonia Practices*. Cleveland, OH: John Carroll University and Ukrainian Historical Association: 131–182.

The Idea of Ukraine is Based on a Mythologised Lie. (2019). *EUvsDisinfo*, 17 June. https://euvsdisinfo.eu/report/the-idea-of-ukraine-is-based-on-a-mythologised-lie

Thirteen Myths about Russia's War against Ukraine Exposed. (2024). *EUvsDisinfo*, 21 February. https://euvsdisinfo.eu/thirteen-myths-about-russias-war-against-ukraine-exposed/

Tolz, V. (1998). 'Forging the Nation: National Identity and Nation Building in Post-Communist Russia,' *Europe-Asia Studies*, 50 (6): 993–1022.

Tolz, V. (2001). *Inventing the Nation. Russia*. London: Arnold.

Tolz, V. (2002). 'Rethinking Russian-Ukrainian Relations: A New Trend in Nation-building in Post-Communist Russia?' *Nations and Nationalism*, 8 (2): 235–253.

Trenin, D. (2024). 'Russia Is Undergoing a New, Invisible Revolution,' *RT*, 2 April. www.rt.com/russia/595266-ukraine-west-pushed-russia/

Trofimov, Y. (2024). *The Russian Invasion and Ukraine's War of Independence. Our Enemies Will Vanish*. London: Penguin Michael Joseph.

Troianovski, A. (2021). 'What's Driving Putin's Ukrainian Brinkmanship?' *New York Times*, 5 December 2021. www.nytimes.com/2021/12/05/world/europe/putin-russia-ukraine-troops.html

Troianovski, A. (2022). 'Atrocities in Ukraine Have Deep Roots in Russian Military,' *New York Times*, 17 April 2022. www.nytimes.com/2022/04/17/world/europe/ukraine-war-russia-atrocities.html

Velychenko, S. (1993). *Shaping Identity in Eastern Europe and Russia. Soviet Russian and Polish Accounts of Ukrainian History, 1914–1991*. New York: St. Martin's Press.

Velychenko, S., Ruane, J. and Hrynevych, L. (2022). *Ireland and Ukraine. Essays in Comparative History and Politics*. Stuttgart: Ibidem; New York: Columbia University Press.

What do the pro-Kremlin media mean by "Anglo-Saxons"? (2020). *EUvsDisinfo*, 10 January. https://euvsdisinfo.eu/what-do-the-pro-kremlin-media-mean-by-anglo-saxons/

We Had No Choice. (2022). '"Filtration" and the Crime of Forcibly Transferring Ukrainian Civilians to Russia,' *Human Rights Watch*, 1 September. www.hrw.org/report/2022/09/01/we-had-no-choice/filtration-and-crime-forcibly-transferring-ukrainian-civilians

When Words Kill – From Moscow to Mariupol. (2022). *EUvsDisinfo*, 17 June. https://euvsdisinfo.eu/when-words-kill-from-moscow-to-mariupol/

Wojnowski, Z. (2017). *The Near Abroad. Eastern Europe and Soviet Patriotism in Ukraine, 1956–1985*. Toronto: University of Toronto Press.

World Russian Peoples Council. (2024). Russian Orthodox Church, Congress, Moscow, 27 March. https://pravoslavie.ru/159347.html

Wynar, L. R. (1988). *Mykhailo Hrushevsky. Ukrainian-Russian Confrontation in Historiography*. Toronto-New York-Munich: Ukrainian Historical Association, 55–64.

Zelenskyy, V. (2021a). '"Ukraine. Kyivan Rus". 1033" Address by President Volodymyr Zelenskyy on the occasion of the Day of Christianisation of Kyivan Rus' – Ukraine,' 28 July. www.president.gov.ua/en/news/ukrayina-kiyivska-rus-1033-zvernennya-prezidenta-volodimira-69757

Zelenskyy, V. (2021b). 'Speech by President Volodymyr Zelenskyy on the Occasion of the 30th Anniversary of Ukraine's Independence,' 24 August. www.president.gov.ua/en/news/promova-prezidenta-volodimira-zelenskogo-z-nagodi-30-yi-rich-70333

Zhegulev, I. (2023). 'Kak Putin voznenavydel Ukrainu,' *Verstka*, 25 April. https://verstka.media/kak-putin-pridumal-voynu

Zhuchkovsky, A. (n.d.). *85 Days in Slavyansk*. London: Amazon.

Zygar, M. (2022). 'How Vladimir Putin Lost Interest in the Present,' *New York Times*, 10 March. www.nytimes.com/2022/03/10/opinion/putin-russia-ukraine.html

Zygar, M. (2023a). 'The Man behind Putin's Warped View of History,' *New York Times*, 19 September. www.nytimes.com/2023/09/19/opinion/putin-russia-medinsky.html

Zygar, M. (2023b). *War and Punishment. The Story of Russian Oppression and Ukrainian Resistance*. London: Weidenfeld and Nicolson.

2

Pan-Russian World and Ukraine

Pan-Russian identity is the way Putin and the Kremlin define and perceive Russia's place and role in international relations (Wawrzonek, 2024). Its conceptual framework is found in the ideology of the Pan-Russian World (*Russkij mir*), which came into being in the 2000s during Putin's first two terms in office during what we define as the first critical juncture following the Georgian Rose and Ukrainian Orange Revolutions. The Pan-Russian World unites the three eastern Slavs, or 'Holy Rus' in the language of the Russian Orthodox Church (see Chapter 3), who represented the core of the Soviet Union and who should continue to constitute the core of Eurasia and Russia as a 'state-civilisation'.

This chapter consists of three main parts. The first part analyses the process of shaping the institutional base for the Pan-Russian World as symbolic space. The second part of the chapter describes the evolution of the Pan-Russian World ideology from the early 1990s to the full-scale invasion and since. The third part analyses the Ukrainian question in the ideology of the Pan-Russian World. Together the analysis in the three sections will reconstruct the ideological legitimisation of the Kremlin's policies towards Ukraine.

The ideology of the Pan-Russian World combines anti-Westernism, aspirations to be recognised as a great power and changing the unipolar to a multipolar world. The Pan-Russian World is an ideology drawing on arbitrarily interpreted cultural and theoretical ideas selectively borrowed from the West, such as multiple modernities, clash of civilisations, postmodernism, and globalisation combined with traditional Russian imperialism, cultural pan-Russian chauvinism, the heritage of Orthodox culture, Soviet nostalgia and a cult of Stalin. These were adapted to the needs of Putin's authoritarian regime and dictatorship.

The Pan-Russian World is not only a set of abstract ideas. It also includes structures that emerged because of the institutionalisation of this ideology. Andrzej Kozicki (2019, p. 19) assumes that 'symbolic institutionalisation is the formalisation of rituals, signs and other manifestations of national identity as external evidence of the history of the nation and the state'. The process of symbolic institutionalisation is crucial for the functioning of the entire political system 'which is always in interaction with the symbolic – or cultural – system of a given society' (Kozicki, 2019, p. 18). The subjectivity of actors operating in the political field is closely related to their subjectivity within the symbolic field (Zarycki, 2010). The real strength and stability of a political regime also depends on its symbolic capital and the discourse shaped through it intended to legitimise the regime and its actors.

The Institutionalisation of the Pan-Russian World Ideology

In the early post-Soviet era, the Russian authorities were unable to implement any effective and coordinated policy in the management of symbolic space which was bottom-up. On the one hand, there were initiatives on the rehabilitation of victims of Soviet repression, commemoration of the crimes of totalitarianism and the construction of a broadly understood civil society, such as the Memorial Association. However, quite quickly the process of symbolic institutionalisation was dominated by circles that promoted imperial nationalist narratives drawing on the resuscitation of the legacy of White Russian émigrés, Soviet nostalgia and grievances surrounding Russia's cultural and spiritual supremacy in the post-Soviet space. The World Russian People's Council (WRPC) played a key role in these developments.

In the early 1990s, an environment was institutionalised that would later provide Putin's imperial nationalism with specific content, such as defining the enemies and allies of post-Soviet Russia and reconstructing 'mental maps' that would determine the Kremlin's policy in subsequent years.

WRPC was created by representatives of various communities and social organisations in the early 1990s as a discussion platform. Its mission was:

> To analyse losses and gains in the most important areas of life, to determine the most important goals and values of Russian national existence, to declare Russian understanding of their role in world history, outline ways to strengthen the unity of the Russian people, protect the rights and interests of compatriots, and establish civil peace and interethnic peace on Russian soil and intranational harmony.[1]

---

[1] 'Rossiiskaia sobornaia mysl 26–28 maia 1993 goda.' https://vrns.ru/documents/stenogramma-i-vsemirnogo-russkogo-narodnogo-sobora/

The political identity of the creators of the WRPC, at least judging by the declarations adopted by them and especially during the first congress in 1993, can be described as eclectic in nature. According to the official version, the 'Inspirer and spiritual leader of the Council' was then Metropolitan of Smolensk and Kaliningrad, and since 2009, Patriarch Kirill.[2] However, according to other sources, the initiative initially came from secular circles, and only then did Russian Orthodox Church representatives become involved.[3]

In its early years the WRPC was a non-governmental organisation in the textbook sense of the word, which is evidenced by its first meeting. The initiators included several organisations and none of them were – at least officially – political in nature. The organisers of the first congress deliberately wished to avoid 'the opportunistic and political nature of the speeches and documents adopted at the Council' and therefore the participation of 'political parties and organisations' was excluded from the deliberations.

The next congress took place in February 1995 when it remained non-governmental in nature, only changing from the third congress held in December of the same year. Then, Prime Minister Viktor Chernomyrdin, Chairman of the State Duma Ivan Rybkin and the Chairman of the Federation Council Vladimir Shumeiko sent letters of support to the participants of the congress. The deliberations were attended by the leaders of all the most important political parties at that time, from the leader of the Communist Party of the Russian Federation (KPRF) Gennadiy Zyuganov to Democratic Choice leader Yegor Gaidar (Stenographic record, 1995). From then, the guests attending all subsequent congresses would be senior representatives of Russian state authorities, with the minister of foreign affairs a regular guest. The sending of letters of support to congress participants by the Russian president also became a ritual, and he has often attended WRPC meetings in person. Over time, the WRPC became a forum that crafted a new ideology that would legitimise Russia's political system and leaders.

Just after Putin was elected for his first term, the Kremlin began to take control over the process of symbolic institutionalisation in post-Soviet Russia of which Pan-Russian World ideology was central. Putin achieved this goal with the assistance of five important tools. These

---

[2] 'Vsiemirnyi Russkij Narodnyi Sobor (VRNS). Spravka.' www.ria.ru/20100525/238031233.html
[3] Ibid.

included establishing an alliance with the Russian Orthodox Church (this is covered in Chapter 3), capturing the movement in defence of compatriot's (Russian speakers outside the Russian Federation), taking control over the WRPC, launching the Russian World Foundation, and manufacturing historical memory through a network of Kremlin-based institutions.

Compatriots

In 2000 a doctrine of 'spiritual security' was included in Russia's National Security Concept. Over time, 'spiritual-moral values and legacy' occupied greater space in Russian security concepts (Veres and Palotai, 2024). What gives the first National Security Concept significance is that unlike in the US where similar documents serve as only a temporary political guidance, Russia's version was signed into law and therefore became a legally binding document (Veres and Palotai, 2024). The Kremlin took the first steps to institutionalise the doctrine of 'spiritual security' while seeking to coordinate its policy towards compatriots. As a rule, 'in the early 1990s, the problem of compatriots as part of the "Russian problem" was exclusively the topic of the so-called Russian patriotic movement, in which, as in other segments of public consciousness, one could find the widest range of views and ways of expression' (Omarova, 2008, p. 37).

The state took the initiative in outlining policies towards compatriots immediately after Putin first took office in 2000. During the First Congress of Compatriots in 2001, Putin used the term the Pan-Russian World, perhaps for the first time in a wide public forum. He associated this concept with 'spiritual self-determination' and underlined that 'after all, the concept of the Pan-Russian World from time immemorial went far beyond the geographical borders of Russia and even far beyond the borders of the Russian ethnic group'.[4] As Chapter 1 showed, Russian identity through the Pan-Russian World and later 'state-civilisation' is bigger than the Russian Federation.

The concept of the Pan-Russian World was widely used during the next congress in 2003 and subsequently. At the 2006 congress of compatriots, Putin presented a vision of a coordinated state policy towards compatriots within the successor states of the former Soviet Union who would support the development of the Russian language 'as our common heritage from

---

[4] 'Vystuplieniie na otkrytii Kongriessa sootechestviennikov,' http://special.kremlin.ru/events/president/transcripts/21359

the times of the Soviet Union' as a 'basis for cooperation' and 'friendship'.[5] Referring to the concept of the Pan-Russian World, Putin stated: 'We are truly united, and no borders or barriers will interfere with this unity. We have only one common goal – to make this unity even stronger'.[6]

The culmination of the process of etatisation of policy towards compatriots was the creation of the government agency *Rossotrudnichestvo* (Federal Agency for the Commonwealth of Independent States Affairs, Compatriots Living Abroad, and International Humanitarian Cooperation) in 2008 to promote the Russian language and culture and build and maintain ties with people identifying with Russia and living beyond its borders. *Rossotrudnichestvo*, headed by the grandson of the former Chairman of the SVR (Foreign Intelligence Service) and Foreign Minister Yevgeny Primakov, is built on the former Soviet All-Union Society for Cultural Relations with Foreign Countries, thus continuing in the tradition of Soviet 'cultural diplomacy' (Koval, Irysova, Tytiuk, and Tereshchenko, 2023).

The Russian World Foundation

The Russian World Foundation, established in 2007 continued the process of institutionalisation of the symbolic concept of a unique and superior 'state-civilisation' community with Russia at the centre. In its early format its official statutory objectives included the promotion of the Russian language and culture throughout the world, maintaining ties with Russian diasporas, 'creating a favorable public opinion for Russia' and 'universalising knowledge' about Russia (Wawrzonek, 2014, p. 760). The creation of the Russian World Foundation should be interpreted as an attempt to develop Russian soft power.

The original definition of the Pan-Russian World concept promoted the Russian language as an instrument of influencing public space in Eurasia. Other forms of influence were also planned, such as the creation of a homogenous media space and cooperation with the Russian Orthodox Church, which 'was the first one to realise not only the possibility but also the necessity of rebuilding the Pan-Russian World civilisation' (Russkij mir, 2010, p. 28).

---

[5] 'Vstupitielnoie slovo Priezidienta Rossii V. V. Putina na vsiemirnom kongresie sootiechestvienniekov prozhivaiushchikh za rubiezhom,' St. Petersburg, 24 October 2006. www.mid.ru/ru/foreign_policy/compatriots/vsemirnyy_kongress_sootechestvennikov/2006_vsemirnyy_kongress_sootechestvennikov/1713257/

[6] Ibid.

For many years, the head of the Russian World Foundation was Viacheslav Nikonov, grandson of Stalin's Foreign Minister Viacheslav Molotov. Nikonov described the background to the Russian World Foundation's creation by citing Putin, who said in 2007

> In this year which has been declared the 'Year of the Russian Language,' there is every reason to remind us that Russian is the language of the historic brotherhood of peoples, the language of true international communication. It not only carries a whole stratum of global achievements, but it is also the living space of the many millions of people that make up the Pan-Russian World which is, naturally, much larger than Russia itself.

Valerii Tishkov, an anthropologist and former chairman of the State Committee of the RSFSR on Nationalities, said after hearing this: 'Well, this is very important, we need to think this through' (Russkij mir, 2010, p. 70). Putin's rhetoric was completely drawn from Soviet Communist Party propaganda and Soviet nationalities policy.

Putin had already used the term 'Pan-Russian World' and it has been present in public discourse in Russia since the early 1990s; however, the term ceased to henceforth be a figure of speech and became a part of Russian reality. Nikonov's foundational myth about the origins of the concept of the Pan-Russian World illustrates Bourdieu's (2000, p. 186) idea that:

> the state is the site par excellence of the imposition of the *nomos*, the official and effective principle of constructing the world, with, for example all the acts of consecration and accreditation which ratify, legalise, legitimise 'regularise' situations or acts of union (marriage, various contracts, etc.) or separation (divorce, breach of contract) which are thus raised from the status of pure contingent fact, unofficial or even disguised (a 'relationship') to the status of official fact, know and recognized by all, published and public.

The establishment of the Russian World Foundation was an 'act of consecration and accreditation' of the dogma of the existence of a Pan-Russian identity at the centre of a unique and superior 'state-civilisation'. This was also the moment when this dogma would be built into the structure of the Russian political system. Political actors, led by Putin, would increasingly strive to monopolise selected resources of symbolic capital, such as the Russian language, Russian-speaking culture, compatriots, Russian Orthodox Christianity, and historical memory, all of which became encapsulated within Pan-Russian World ideology.

Russian Centres

One of the goals of the Russian World Foundation was to spread influence and soft power abroad through Russian centres. According to the last available report on Russian World Foundation activities, there were 119 Russian Centres operating in fifty-two countries around the world (Report, 2021, p. 2). By 2024, this number had declined to fifty Russian Centres,[7] probably because of the full-scale invasion of Ukraine. It could be assumed that some Russian World Foundation's branches abroad existed on paper only, and the numbers given in annual reports should therefore be treated as exaggerated propaganda, rather than reliable reporting.

There are also indications that the Russian World Foundation does not exercise actual control over the activities of all its Russian Centres. For example, the Russian World Foundation's *Deutsch-Russische Kulturinstitut* in Dresden is listed as one of the few Russian Centres in Western Europe. On 9 March 2024, on the anniversary of the birth of the Ukrainian bard Taras Shevchenko, this branch organised a meeting dedicated to him.[8] The tradition of holding 'Shevchenko evenings' dates to the nineteenth century and have always been an important element of Ukrainian cultural life. The symbolic capital that is associated with them, especially after Russia invaded Ukraine, is difficult to reconcile with the mission of the Russian World Foundation about the historical and cultural unity of Russians and Ukrainians. Another Russian Centre in Germany is the Phoenix Association in Mainz, which published a protest on 6 March 2022 against the war in Ukraine[9] and organised the transportation of humanitarian aid to Ukraine.[10] These statements and activities contradicted Russian World Foundation support for the 'special military operation'.

WRPC as the Main Institution Promoting the Ideology of the Pan-Russian World

The very visual setting and scale of the 2023 WRPC congress showed it is becoming the key institution in the Russian symbolic space. The congress

---

[7] https://russkiymir.ru/rucenter/catalogue.php
[8] 'Frauengestalten im Leben und Schaffen des ukrainischen Dichters Taras Schewtschenko.' https://drki.de/event/frauengestalten-im-leben-und-schaffen-des-ukrainischen-dichters-taras-schewchenko/
[9] https://phoenix-mainz.de/unsere-statement/
[10] 'Phoenix Mainzer organsiert Hilfetransport für Ukraine.' https://phoenix-mainz.de/помощь-для-украины-copy

took place at the prestigious Kremlin State Palace and was financially supported by the Presidential Fund for Cultural Initiatives. The congress began with Putin's speech, where he referred to the war in Ukraine as a struggle of a 'national liberation nature' with Russia 'in the vanguard of the fight for a better, just world' against the 'colonial' West. Putin referred to the Great Patriotic War several times and emphasised that both then and now, the source of strength that allows Russia to fulfill its messianic mission is the Russian Orthodox Church.[11]

The speeches of WRPC participants promoted imperial nationalist megalomania and vitriolic discourse about the moral and spiritual superiority of Russia over the West. The key importance of the WRPC in the structure of the symbolic space to which Pan-Russian World ideology belongs is also evidenced by the 2023 congress establishing the Ivan Ilyin Higher Political School as a new department in the Russian State Humanitarian University. Eurasianist and fascist Alexander Dugin, who has been a leading participant in the WRPC from the very beginning, was appointed as its dean. The Ivan Ilyin Higher Political School is to develop and implement a 'new paradigm' of teaching in the field of humanities and social sciences which will be 'oriented at shaping students' worldview based on Russian 'state-civilisation' identity and traditional Russian spiritual values'.[12] The emergence of this new 'political school' proves that the process of symbolic institutionalisation of the Pan-Russian World ideology continues to be undertaken.

The goals of the Ivan Ilyin Higher Political School were presented during a special WRPC panel by the dean of the Russian State Humanitarian University, Aleksandr Bezborodov who emphasised that it would focus on the analysis of the genesis, course and heroes of the 'special military operation' in Ukraine. Its studies are to be used by other research centres and department's that teach the modern history of Russia.

The Ivan Ilyin Higher Political School will also work on 'improving the professional qualifications of lecturers'. In turn, Deputy Minister of Science and Higher Education of the Russian Federation, Konstantin Mogilevskii, spoke on the same panel about the need to shape 'patriotic attitudes among young people based on traditional national values'. Russian state authorities intend to achieve this goal by introducing

---

[11] 'Plienarnoie zasiedaniie XXV Vsiemirnogo Russkogo Narodnogo sobora v Gosudarstviennom Kriemlievskom dvortsie.' www.youtube.com/watch?v=QGvJJ5WFUS0

[12] 'Polozhieniie ob. Uchebno-nauchnom tsientrie "Vysshaia politicheskaia sokola imieni Ivana Ilina."' www.rsuh.ru/upload/main/vpsh/Положение%20ВПШ.pdf

special courses on Russian history and 'Russian statehood' for students.[13] Dugin, mentioned many times by speakers, stated that Russia must 'save its humanities' and thanks to this it will also 'save the world's humanities'. The newly appointed director of the Ivan Ilyin Higher Political School explained that the most important task that needs to be accomplished is to 'correct the mistakes made by the West',[14] a euphemism for removing Western influence.

From the overall context in which the establishment of the Ivan Ilyin Higher Political School was announced, it can be concluded that the Kremlin is intensifying its propagation of the Pan-Russian World ideology through a coordinated and institutionalised indoctrination system. One of its pillars is the WRPC, showing how a radical outsider in the early 1990's could move to the ideological mainstream under Putin.

Institutionalisation of State Controlled Manufacturing of Memory of the Past

Another phenomenon related to the process of symbolic institutionalisation of the Pan-Russian World ideology is manufacturing Russian history in defence of Russian imperialism. In 2012, not coincidentally the year Putin returns to the presidency, the Russian Historical Society (RHS) was established as another institution that, over time, began to play an important role in organising the Pan-Russian World symbolic space. The founding members included the Russian World Foundation and SVR Chairman Sergei Naryshkin. Officially, the RHS aims to provide 'an objective and honest study of history on a national scale'.[15] The RHS conducts publishing and educational activities whose aim is to 'scientifically' legitimise the Pan-Russian World propaganda in Russian-occupied Ukraine and elsewhere. Naryshkin reported that 'landing forces with leading Russian historians' who regularly visit 'regional universities in *Novorossiya* [New Russia]' were sent to the 'new entities of the Russian Federation'. Among many who visit Russian-occupied Ukraine, Viktor Kondrashyn made students in Melitopol aware of 'the basic facts that refute the anti-scientific concept of the *Holodomor* as a genocide'.[16]

---

[13] 'XXV Vsiemirnyi Russkij Narodnyi Sobor: Obrazovatielnaia sektsiia.' https://vrns.ru/documents/xxv-vsemirnyy-russkiy-narodnyy-sobor-obrazovatelnaya-sektsiya/
[14] Ibid.
[15] https://historyrussia.org/sergey-naryshkin.html
[16] Sergei Naryshkin, 'Nieobkhodimo posliedovatielno otstaivat istoricheskuiu pravdu Novorosii.' https://historyrussia.org/sobytiya/sergej-naryshkin-neobkhodimo-posledovatelno-otstaivat-istoricheskuyu-pravdu-novorossii.html

The RHS shows how the process of symbolic institutionalisation in Russia is influenced by the weaponisation of memory of the past. A few months after the full-scale invasion of Ukraine, Naryshkin stated: 'Today, in the context of unprecedented hybrid aggression by the totalitarian-liberal regimes of the West, the history of our country is necessarily turning into a battlefield. Our geopolitical opponents deliberately distort and manipulate facts to deprive our people of a sense of common historical destiny and undermine our self-confidence'.[17] Putin's (2021) long essay reflected the de-humanisation of Ukrainians found in the weaponisation of Russian history.

Informal Patterns of Institutionalisation of the Pan-Russian World

Putin established the activities for institutions that shape symbolic space in the Pan-Russian World and management of symbolic capital, which was particularly true for the RHS. One such activity was the round table organised by the RHS, which took place in January 2022[18] on the anniversary of the 1654 Pereyaslav Agreement. The event was opened by Naryshkin, who emphasised that 'over a thousand-year history, Russians, Ukrainians and Belarusians have been and remain one nation', noting 'this is explicitly mentioned' in Putin's essay. Naryshkin expressed his belief that the 'overwhelming majority' of people in Russia, Ukraine and Belarus support this thesis. At the end of his speech, Naryshkin noted that 'Modern Russia has done a lot to make Ukraine an independent state. And of course, we are interested in good neighbourly and as close and mutually beneficial mutual relations as possible between the two parts of one nation'.[19] This declaration was made just prior to the full-scale invasion.

Interestingly, among the participants of the 'deliberations' inaugurated by Naryshkin were two Ukrainian historians – Petro Tolochko and Georgiy Kasianov. Despite Russian military aggression taking place since 2014, and the ostracisation of Russian academics by Ukrainian scholars, Tolochko and Kasianov continued to believe in the possibilities and prospects of cooperation between historians of both countries. Both presented themselves as outsiders and nonconformists who opposed the official

---

[17] Ibid.
[18] 'Onlain translatsiia kruglogo stola, posviashchionnogo osnovnym tendientsiam v istorii Ukrainy.' www.youtube.com/watch?v=60MIQfLh2Y8
[19] Ibid.

'nationalist' historical narrative imposed by the Ukrainian authorities, and for this reason they faced a torrent of criticism in Ukraine and abroad. Tolochko complained that in Ukraine we 'cannot do anything' claiming he was subject to state restrictions.[20] Kasianov's said that an obstacle to the development of cooperation in Ukrainian-Russian dialogue over their historical past is the extreme politicisation of academic activities in Ukraine. Kasianov also suggested that contacts between Russian and Ukrainian historians should be developed with the help of 'so-called NGOs', a rather strange proposal, as in Putin's Russia they no longer functioned as independent structures.[21]

To best interpret the meaning of this event, it is necessary to consider that the process of symbolic institutionalisation takes place according to the rules imposed by Putin's regime in the formal and informal dimensions. Considering the context in which the above-mentioned quasi-scientific event took place, it should be interpreted as a test of the loyalty of its Ukrainian participants and a test of their readiness to dialogue within the parameters of Putin's essay. These informal rules could be additionally observed during the next event organised by Naryshkin and the Russian Historical Society in November 2022. At its conclusion, the Russian president addressed Naryshkin with the words: 'I would like to thank you for the work you are doing through the Russian Historical Society', adding 'I have always concluded that the service you lead today is close to that of the Russian Geographical Society'.[22] Naryshkin, responding to Putin, emphasised that 'many graduates of history faculties of our universities work in our [SVR] service'.[23]

The round table showed how the 'culture of the state leadership' works in practice. Networks of insiders are tied together by following an unwritten code and subject to strict control. The main elements of the narrative about the historical past are imposed by the president, and the coherence of the narrative about the past is directly supervised by the chairman of the SVR. Putin's essay showed how state power is the highest authority in determining historical truth in Russia, replicating the Soviet Union where the Communist Party controlled history writing. The version of 'historical truth' in Putin's Russia has ontological significance for his regime.

---

[20] Ibid.
[21] Ibid.
[22] 'Vstriecha Vladimira Putina s istorikami i predstavitieliami tradutsionnykh religii Rossii.' http://komitet.info/about/activities-of-the-committees/22264
[23] Ibid.

Following Putin's essay came the publication by the Federal Archives Agency of 242 documents that were intended to illustrate and confirm Putin's theses of Russians and Ukrainians as 'one people'. Andrei Artyzov, director of the Federal Archives Agency and member of the RHS presidium, stated that these documents confirm that the Soviet period was the time of greatest economic development for Ukraine. As a result, Artyzov believes Ukraine 'left the Soviet Union as an economically strengthened state with a higher standard of living than in neighbouring Poland'.[24]

Evolution of the Pan-Russian World Ideology

After the disintegration of the USSR, the Kremlin was unable to formulate clear and coherent answers to fundamental questions related to the ideological basis of the new social and political order in post-Soviet Russia. The question of who the enemy was and who was Russia's ally remained unclear. There was no strategy for attracting allies and dealing with enemies, as well as an internally coherent narrative that would define Russia's place in the system of international relations. This vacuum was filled by the ideology of the Pan-Russian World.

In Russian-occupied Ukraine the process of 'de-nazification' (de-Ukrainisation) includes the spreading and institutionalisation of Pan-Russian World ideology. The Russian-occupation authorities have introduced a free satellite package called 'Russian World' that is 'directly imposed on residents by installation brigades overseen by Russian Deputy Prime Minister Dmitry Chernyshenko' and which provides access to twenty Russian channels and ten local channels (McGlynn, 2023).

According to Marlene Laruelle (2015, p. 3) 'the "Russian World" has several fathers: a biological one, Petr Shchedrovitsky, and a spiritual father, Gleb Pavlovsky, who nurtured and inspired it'. However, the Pan-Russian World was rather synonymous with a specific strategy for building a new image of Russia and was primarily associated with 'the idea of a domestic and international brand for Russia' (Laruelle, 2015, p. 5). Shchedrovitsky stated that the 'Russian World is the means, the instrument to make Russia and the Russian Federation adapt to globalisation. Small countries adapt themselves by bringing globalisation into themselves; large ones do

---

[24] 'A. N. Artyzov, 'My nie dolzhny dopuskat, choby lozhnaia istoriia stanovilas nastavnitsiei polityki.' https://historyrussia.org/polemika/intervyu-s-istorikami/andrej-artizov-my-ne-dolzhny-dopuskat-chtoby-lozhnaya-istoriya-stanovilas-nastavnitsej-lozhnoj-politiki.html

so by entering the space of globalisation' (Laruelle, 2015, p. 5). In this sense the Pan-Russian World should be treated as a political marketing tool to shape Russia's image, not to provide answers to key questions about the real basis of the state's ideology.

However, when it comes to shaping and sharing the Pan-Russian World ideology among the post-Soviet Russian elites, one cannot limit oneself only to the narrative created by the Kremlin's political technologists. The concept has become a permanent element of the discourse created by other actors shaping the symbolic space of Russia after 1991, such as the WRPC or groups championing the protection of compatriots. When the process of the institutionalisation of the Pan-Russian World ideology gained momentum after 2007, various representatives of Russian intellectual elites joined the discussions about the concept of Russia as a 'state-civilisation'. It was clearly visible that the concept of the Pan-Russian World was a means to validate neo-Soviet resentments, Russian chauvinism and White Russian *émigré* imperial nationalism and Eurasianism.

During these discussions, Nikonov raised the 'reconstruction of the tissue of the Pan-Russian World' which included 'bringing the ashes of our great ancestors, such as the philosopher Ivan Ilyin and General Anton Denikin, home' (Russkij mir, 2010, p. 13). Another participant in the discussion, Maksym Shevchenko, described Ilyin as 'a penetrating philosopher, one of the few who created a technological project for the establishment and development of the Pan-Russian World' (Russkij mir, 2010, p. 81). Shevchenko also defined the 'Russian essence, the Russian nature' as based on 'expansion in all forms, not just military'. Shevchenko emphasised, 'Thank God, no one needs war anymore. But the military position, the military principle, and military honour remained the most important component of Russian self-awareness for centuries' (Russkij mir, 2010, p. 82). Alexei Kozyrev also expressed a similar imperialist spirit, underlining that 'The essence of Russian culture is not only military or political expansion. The primary task of the Pan-Russian World is the expansion of Russian culture, the Russian presence in various countries and in various linguistic spaces' (Russkij mir, 2010, p. 85).

During this discussion about the concept of the Pan-Russian World, Vladimir Malakhov emphasised that 'Chauvinism in general and cultural chauvinism in particular are unacceptable here. Neither is the reduction of Russian culture to its folklore manifestations acceptable, as we need to work with a living, actual culture and not the reduction of Russianness to Orthodoxy, that is, the clericalisation of Russian culture. There is no need for Russia to be associated with the Moscow Patriarchate, with people in robes and hoods, because this is perceived as an anti-modernist project' (Russkij mir, 2010, p. 102). Malakhov also warned against reducing the Russian language to the role of a tool for implementing state policy (Russkij mir, 2010, p. 101). Sergei Nikolskii criticised the understanding of the Pan-Russian World as imperialism stating, 'Expansion is a terrible thing'. He cited as examples the suppression of the January Uprising by Tsarist Russia in 1863–1864, the Soviet invasion of Hungary in 1956 and the Warsaw Pact invasion of Czechoslovakia in 1968. 'In this positive capacity, Russia should still be a country of culture, a country of creation, and not destruction. (…) Until we deal with our own predatory consciousness, no world will need us. The world does not need expansionism' Nikolskii concluded (Russkij mir, 2010, p. 97).

During the discussion, the issue of Russia and the Pan-Russian World relations with the world was also raised. Georgii Bovt wondered, for example, whether 'We are able and are we ready now to determine the meaning of so-called universal values, of pan-European civilisation, which in our country appear precisely as 'so-called'? Does this mean that they do not exist or that we should not be defined in relation to what has become the result of the entire human experience and the development of its culture, to that of globalisation? Or should we insist on some archaic self-identity'(Russkij mir, 2010, p. 83). Socialist Boris Kagarlitskii predicted that 'if the strategy of self-isolation and opposing oneself to the surrounding world begins to dominate the development of the Pan-Russian World, this will be a disaster for it. By entering a dead end, it will eliminate the most powerful potential that exists in Russian culture and in Russian tradition' (Russkij mir, 2010, p. 100). In turn, Aleksei Kara-Murza called for the 'rehabilitation' of 'Russian enlightened liberalism'. In his opinion, it 'has long become an element of the Russian 'national soil'". Kara-Murza argued Russia needs a 'nationwide dialogue' in search of its 'state-civilisation' identity. He also predicted that 'Without this dialogue and without taking into account the liberal vision of the world, the Russian World is unlikely to become a reality' (Russkij mir, 2010, p. 19).

During the discussion participants presented different opinions on the importance of symbolic capital related to the Soviet period for the concept of the Pan-Russian World. On the one hand, there were advocates for its rehabilitation which proposed to harmonise Soviet and pre-Soviet heritages and reshape them to contemporary needs. Sergii Nikolskii held a different opinion, stating that 'Generalissimo Stalin and Marshal Beria' were indeed 'part of our history'. However, he opposed the inclusion of this legacy as 'value in our history' asking 'Is this what we want? Or do we admit that there was such a terrible thing, there was no escape, but we need to do something about it and somehow overcome it?' Nikolskii referred to Germany, which 'renounced its terrible past, the damage she caused to humanity. In this situation, we still pretend that nothing terrible happened in the Soviet past, that everything was normal'. Nikolskii criticised the use of the Pan-Russian World as an opportunity to uncritically rehabilitate the Soviet legacy (Russkij mir, 2010, pp. 97–98).

The issue of loyalty to the regime in Russia was also raised as a criterion for belonging to the Pan-Russian World. Vladimir Malakhov said that 'he was puzzled' by an idea 'to consider political loyalty as a criterion of Russianness'. Malakhov argued that 'There are different objects of loyalty. There is loyalty to culture, loyalty addressed to culture; there is loyalty addressed to the state as an idea, loyalty to statehood; and finally, there is loyalty to the political regime. And if I am loyal not only to Russian culture, but also to Russian statehood, to Russia as a certain political body, this does not mean that I am a priori loyal to the regime that has been established in my country' (Russkij mir, 2010, p. 102).

Putin's Pan-Russian World

Prior to Putin returning to the presidency in 2012, there remained some autonomy in Putin's regime in the field of ideology and history writing. After 2012, the Kremlin took control of the ideological discussions surrounding and direction of the WRPC, and the Pan-Russian World became an ideology of Russian expansionism, 'gathering of Russian lands' and struggle with the West.

Since 2012, Putin's regime has developed three key components of the Pan-Russian World. These are the quasi-religious cult and myth of the Great Patriotic War (this is analysed in Chapter 4); the concept of a 'divided [pan-Russian] nation; and superior to Western 'spiritual-moral values' found within Russia's 'state-civilisation'.

A Divided (Pan-) Russian Nation

The notion of a 'divided [pan-Russian] nation' already appeared during the first congress of the WRPC in 1993, where its participants demanded that the Russian state pursue a coordinated policy of 'assistance to all Russians who have become victims of the illegal dismemberment of the united Russian people' following the disintegration of the USSR (Stenographic record, 1993). WRPC declarations blamed the disintegration of the USSR for resulting in a 'divided [pan-Russian] nation'. This was mentioned, for example, in the Address of the First World Russian Peoples Council 'On understanding the national interests of Russia and the Russian people' which called for 'careful and conscious' restoration of the unity of the nation that found itself in foreign 'states and parts of the historical Russian state'. The resolution 'On the *Russkij* [Russian] nation' wrote about the 'total disintegration of the state into nationally owned principalities'. Given this new situation, it was necessary to search for 'new flexible universal structures that would allow Russians to maintain their unity' (Stenographic record, 1993).

Another document from the first meeting stated that 'We should strive to establish dual citizenship status for Russians living in the countries of the CIS (Commonwealth of Independent States). The Russian people should be recognised as a dismembered nation and their right to unification should be proclaimed' (Resolution, 1993). The participants of the 1993 WRPC congress ruled out the use of 'force and military methods' for the goal of uniting the 'divided [pan-Russian] nation' (Address, 1993). At the same time, however, they emphasised 'Russia has not only a moral, but a legal basis for the Russian principled policy of protecting the interests of both Russians and other peoples whose rights have been violated and who are fighting for their historical choice'. Moreover, members of the WRPC demanded that 'principles of respecting the rights of Russian and Russian-speaking residents and granting dual citizenship' should become a condition for the 'normal development of relations with the new states' (Address, 1993).

Participants at the second WRPC congress held in February 1995 made a special appeal to the *Russkij* [Russian] nation. They emphasised that a 'divided [pan-Russian] nation' has 'the right to re-unification in a single state body' and demanded the Russian authorities take active steps to implement this 'right' (Address, 1995). Although the authors of the appeal emphasised this should be undertaken in a 'peaceful and non-violent' manner it was clear such attempts would lead to conflict, as they did after 2014. In the mid 1990s, 'The Russian leadership clearly demonstrated its refusal to take active steps to resolve the problem of the status of Russian speakers in the post-Soviet space', Emil Pain, deputy head of the Analytical Department of the Russian president's office, stated, adding that 'in state foreign policy, the idea of the disunity of the people is always used to re-unite lands. Russia does not have such a policy' (Barash, 2012, p. 178). In other words, the then Russian authorities did not at that time question the sovereignty of post-Soviet states under the pretext of uniting the 'divided [pan-Russian] nation'. This would change after Putin came to power in 2000. Meanwhile, throughout its existence the WRPC has been a forum where the idea of rebuilding the unity of the 'divided [pan-Russian] nation' was consistently promoted, especially with regard to Ukraine and Belarus.

A separate element that appeared in the participants' speeches was the question of the 'natural' unity of the Russian supra-ethnic community, which had been shaped by Russian statehood, according to then Metropolitan of Smolensk and Kaliningrad Kirill, since the fifteenth century. Metropolitan Kirill stated that 'the core and support of the principle of universalism was Russian mentality developed by Orthodoxy which permeated and consolidated the state into a single organism' (Stenographic record, 1993). This concept of 'universalism' is a synonym for attachment to *sobornost* (unity) as the most frequently repeated notion within the discourse of the Pan-Russian World. Andrei Kazantsev (2008, p. 3) argued that *sobornaia kultura* (culture of unity) 'rejects partisanship and fragmentation in favour of demonstrating inner unity through unanimous acceptance of decisions taken by ruling elites. It also principally rejects procedural or legal constraints. This is the actual meaning of the concept of a "divided [pan-Russian] nation" within the Pan-Russian World'.

Spiritual-Moral Values

The place and meaning of the concept of spiritual-moral values in public debates in post-Soviet Russia has evolved since the 1990s when it was a marginal element of discourse outside the Russian political mainstream. In the 2000s, 'the concept of spiritual-moral values migrated to the very centre of the Russian public security debate' (Østbø, 2017, p. 212; Stoeckl, 2022). Jardar Østbø (2017, p. 212) writes that the KPRF played a pioneering role in this respect. However, it is worth noting that from the very beginning they were in competition with the WRPC, the Russian Orthodox Church, and circles that built their anti-liberal agenda on the traditions of pre-revolutionary Russian conservatism and imperial nationalism. The KPRF and its leader Gennadiy Zyuganov were co-opted into the WRPC.

This seemingly strange coalition of the Russian Orthodox Church, Orthodox conservatives, and communists within the WRPC cemented the 'red (pro-Soviet)-white (Orthodox fundamentalist, imperial nationalist)-brown (fascist)' alliance that became mainstream under Putin as well as consolidating a critical approach towards liberal democracy and the 'collective West'. WRPC members criticised the 1990s for the imposition of 'alien' Western values and rise of oligarchs as leading to a crisis in material and spiritual spheres. Natalia Narochnitskaya, who in later years would be one of the most important propagandists of the Pan-Russian World propaganda, said during the 1993 WRPC congress that 'the false prophets, dressed in the beautiful clothes of democracy, have already made a monstrous substitution before the eyes of the beautiful Russian liberal; that is, the idea of transforming the disappointed regime with the idea of destroying the state as such' (Stenographic record, 1993).

Over the coming years, cooperation between the WRPC and Russian political leaders would tighten and develop the discourse of 'spiritual-moral values', especially after 2012. The main topic of the 2011 WRPC congress was 'Basic values as the foundation of national unity' (Basic values, 2011; Curanović, 2015, p. 9). Putin sent a message of support which congratulated the WRPC for having made 'a significant contribution' 'to strengthening the enduring spiritual, moral and family traditions, preserving the rich historical heritage of our people' and to 'restoring the spiritual, national and cultural integrity of the *Russkij mir*'.[25] Shortly thereafter, presidential candidate Putin (2012) published an article which was dedicated to the national question' where he emphasized 'the task of integrating organically different ethnic groups and confessions' using 'basic, common ethical, moral, spiritual values' such as 'charity, mutual aid, truth, justice, respect for elders, ideals of family and work'. Thus, Putin repeated the most important values that had been adopted by the WRPC.

A decade later, after the full-scale invasion in October 2022, the WRPC congress adopted a resolution related to 'spiritual-moral values'. On this occasion it gained the status of not only a 'programme document' but also a 'recommendation addressed to the legislative and executive bodies of Russia'. In fact, the document repeated virtually all the theses that were officially published for public discussion in January 2022.[26] The WRPC was imitating a 'public discussion' to legitimise the Kremlin's conservative ideological revolution.

The anonymous authors of the resolution alleged the West is waging a 'total hybrid war' against Russia using the 'aggressive ideology of neo-liberalism, secularism and Russophobia' (Resolution, 2022). The

---

[25] https://vrns.ru/documents/privetstvie-predsedatelya-pravitelstva-rossii-v-v-putina-uchastnikam-xv-vrns/
[26] www.memri.org/reports/russia-publishes-draft-decree-public-policy-preserve-and-strengthen-traditional-spiritual

document included a demand to remove 'human dignity, rights and freedoms' from Russian 'spiritual-moral values' because 'they were shaped under the influence of the ideas of the Enlightenment and in the context of the development of European Catholic and Protestant thought'. They recommended that this 'strategic' set include values without which 'it is difficult to imagine the history of Russia', such as 'faith in God, love for the Homeland, readiness to make sacrifices' and 'fidelity, duty and honour'. Moreover, the resolution contained a recommendation to provide 'traditional spiritual and moral ideals and values' with 'effective legal protection'.

A few days later, Putin issued a decree entitled 'The basics of state policy to preserve and strengthen traditional Russian spiritual and moral values' which would become part of the national security concept of the Russian Federation. Russia faced 'a global civilisation and value crisis leading to the loss of traditional spiritual and moral guidelines and moral principles by humanity'. The document also indicated specific sources of these threats that included 'activities of the United States of America and other unfriendly foreign states, several transnational corporations and foreign non-profit organisations' seeking to 'impose a system of ideas and values that are alien to the Russian people and destructive to Russian society'.[27]

As Østbø (2017, p. 201) pointed out, 'first and foremost, it must be said about the content of the spiritual and moral value concept that its definition is less important than its connotation as an emotionally charged term that conveys a deep sense of *ressentiment* against the West'. Østbø (2017, p. 211) highlighted 'the highly confrontational vocabulary and the outright 'war-talk' employed within the discourse around 'spiritual-moral values'. Following Russia's full-scale invasion, this discourse was further radicalised, undoubtedly, with the assistance of the WRPC. This is clearly seen in the resolution adopted at the end of the WRPC forum which took place in May 2023 in Luhansk, which defined the international identity and mission of Russia by referring to the biblical concept of *Katechon* (Restrainer). Carl Schmidt introduced the concept of *Katechon* to the field of political philosophy and Dugin, who called himself a follower of Schmidt, to the fields of political and geopolitical discourse (Engström, 2014, p. 367). The post-Soviet concept of *Katechon* is 'an eclectic postmodernist mixture of all previous interpretations' (Engström, 2014, p. 368).

---

[27] 'Osnovy gosurdastviennoi polityki po sokhranjieniiu i ukrieplieniiu traditsionnykh rossiiskikh dukhovno-nravstviennykh tsiennostei.' www.consultant.ru/document/cons_doc_LAW_430906/c595db4951fa2b3967c0a1bcc5e5bbf7332e9c38/

Yegor Kholmogorov, who has been actively promoting the concept of the Pan-Russian World since the mid 2000s most succinctly expressed the *Katechon* essence of Russia's mission in the world by saying 'Russians always 'defend', even when it might seem that they attack' (Engström, 2014, p. 365). As seen in the Luhansk Declaration, Russia's full-scale invasion of Ukraine is described as a 'national liberation war', 'anti-colonialism' and a 'holy war' in which 'Russia and its people are protecting the spiritual space of Holy Rus', fulfilling the mission of *Katechon*, and saving the world from the onset of global evil and the victory of the West which has fallen into Satanism'.[28] This misuse of *Katechon* is deeply infused with traditional Russian messianism.

Less than a year later, the main theses of the Luhansk declaration were solemnly repeated in the 'order' adopted during the extraordinary meeting of the WRPC held in Moscow in March 2024 and chaired by Patriarch Kirill. Moreover, the authors of the document postulated a return to the 'doctrine of *triune* [tripartite] Russian nation, which has existed for three centuries', according to which Great Russians, Little Russians and White Russians are 'sub-ethnie' of one nation that 'includes all Eastern Slavs who are descendants of historical Russia'. Moreover, according to the content of the 'order', the 'doctrine of the *triune* nation' should receive 'legal protection' by becoming a Russian spiritual-moral value that is officially regulated.[29]

Pan-Russian World and Ukraine

Russian imperial nationalists deny the existence of a Ukrainian people distinct from Russians (Putin, 2021). They were assisted in the promotion of an artificial Ukrainian identity by the Bolsheviks, who divided the territory of 'historical Russia' by including parts of it within the borders of Ukraine. In this respect, Putin declared that 'modern Ukraine is entirely the product of the Soviet era' (Putin, 2021). Ukrainian aspirations to secede from the *triune* nation result not only from the influence of external factors (i.e., the West) but are also the result of disastrous Soviet policies.

---

[28] 'Riezolutsiia Vserossiiskogo foruma Miezhdunarodnoi obshchestviennoi organizatsii 'Vsiemirnyi Russkij Narodnyi Sobor' 'Russkij mir' v Luganskie.' https://vrns.ru/forumy/rezolyutsiya-vserossiyskogo-foruma-moo-vsemirnyy-russkiy-narodnyy-sobor-russkiy-mir-v-luganske/

[29] 'Nakaz XXV Vsiemirnogo Russkogo Narodnogo Sobora 'Nastoiashchie i budushcheie russkogo mira.' https://vrns.ru/news/nakaz-xxv-vsemirnogo-russkogo-narodnogo-sobora-nastoyashchee-i-budushchee-russkogo-mira/

Already in 1995, during the third WRPC meeting, Nikolai Sergieiev stated that 'The most important and gravest crime of Bolshevism is the crime against the Russian people, when the single Russian nation was artificially and forcibly divided into three parts; albeit related ones, as it was presented to us throughout the entire Soviet era' (Stenographic record, 1995).

Thus, the Russian president and Kremlin propaganda are articulating WRPC discourse that has been in existence since the early 1990s, and which was strengthened by the dissemination of White Russian émigré thinkers and writers from the mid 2000s. In the early 1990s, Natalia Narochnitskaya argued that 'Ukraine is subject to the strongest pressure from the Vatican-inspired anti-Orthodox forces of Galicia, which are about to completely poison us using Russophobic ideas of Ukrainians and Muscovites being racially different. Kyiv is the mother of Russian cities… Germany following the footsteps of its Kaiser's, is directing these initiatives in Ukraine' (Sektsiia, 1993).

The goal of returning to the 'artificially' lost unity of Ukraine and Russia also appeared in the speeches of other participants of the WRPC congress in December 1995. For example, LDPRF (Liberal Democrat Party of the Russian Federation) leader Vladimir Zhirinovskii announced that 'If Ukraine does not want to join Russia, then Russia will join Ukraine. We have three capitals: Moscow, Kyiv, and Petrograd' (Stenographic record, 1995). In turn, in 1999, Sergei Baburin, during one of the subsequent meetings of the WRPC, expressed hope that the 'forces gravitating towards Russia' in Ukraine would receive 'support and additional resources' and thanks to this, 'historical Russia will be reborn within its real borders' (Stenographic record, 1999). Russian imperial nationalists confusingly defined 'Historic Russia' with both the pan-Russian nation and, in the case of Putin, the Soviet Union.

The 'unity of the peoples of Ukraine and Russia' postulated during the WRPC congress was quite closely linked to the problem of the 'unity' of the Russian Orthodox Church. This meant that any attempt to create an autocephalous Orthodox Church in Ukraine would not only lead to the disintegration of the Russian Orthodox Church itself but also undermine the dogma of the alleged unity of the Russian-Ukrainian civilisation community. It is no coincidence that in 2001, Konstantin Zatulin, assessing the then state of Russian-Ukrainian relations, stated at the WRPC congress that 'you can sign any new agreements with Ukraine, forgive debts, but the rupture of the single Church space, the split into two separate, independent Churches, ultimately means there is no future guarantee of the friendship of the Russian and Ukrainian peoples' (Plenary session, 2001).

Representatives of pro-Russian groups from Ukraine that 'gravitated towards Russia' also took part in WRPC congresses. They also emphasised that the possible loss of the Moscow Patriarchate's monopoly over Ukraine would bring far-reaching political consequences.

A first challenge for supporters of pan-Russian unity was the 2003-2004 Orange Revolution which was brought about by election fraud to bring Yanukovych to power. The greater mobilisation skills of Ukrainians who held an identity distinct to Russians prevailed and the Supreme Court overthrew his election and in a re-run of the second round Viktor Yushchenko was elected president (Kuzio, 2010). The Orange Revolution and Yushchenko's presidency increased democratisation and new developments in memory politics that solidified Ukrainian identity.

Nevertheless, the Kremlin continued to propagate Russian soft power, especially through so-called political orthodoxy (Hovorun, 2018) which was a marginal but at the same time a vocal informal movement within the Russian Orthodox Church in Ukraine. Its activists spread anti-Western hysteria in the Ukrainian public space and discredited the importance of the Orange Revolution through politicisation and weaponisation of religion. In 2007, representatives of this political orthodoxy also participated in the WRPC congress where Valerii Kaurov warned that 'the problem of the separation of the Ukrainian Orthodox Church from the Moscow Patriarchate is as threatening a question as Ukraine's entry into NATO. This is the red line that cannot be crossed' (Sektsiia, 2007). Kaurov continued: 'The separation of the Orthodox Church in Ukraine (from Russia) would represent the breaking of the last connection between Kyivan and Muscovite Rus after which Ukraine would become an anti-Russian state' (Sektsiia, 2007). Although written in the 2000s, Kaurov accurately predicted how Ukraine's Orthodox autocephaly in 2018–2019 was an important development in the transformation of Ukraine into what the Kremlin described as 'Anti-Russia'. In turn, Yurii Yegorov warned 'the separation of Ukrainians from the (Russian) Orthodox Church is also a civilisation project. To prepare Ukrainians for joining NATO and the EU, they need to be torn away from Russian civilisation, they need to be separated from the Russian Orthodox Church' (Sektsiia, 2007).

Yanukovych won the 2010 presidential elections. The Kremlin quickly began to pressure Yanukovych to adopt the demands raised by President Dmitri Medvedev in his 2009 'address' to the Ukrainian president and the ideological tenets of the Pan-Russian World. Yushchenko had supported autocephaly for Ukrainian Orthodox. Yanukovych clearly favoured the Russian Orthodox Church, freezing relations with other religious confessions while strengthening his relationship with the Moscow Patriarchate.[30] This could be seen during his presidential inauguration, which was attended by Patriarch Kirill as a special guest, giving credence to the concept of the integration of Ukraine and Russia within the Pan-Russian World (Ukrayina-2013, 2013, p. 3).

Patriarch Kirill promoted Yanukovych as leader of a country belonging to the Pan-Russian World civilisation. During one of his three visits to Ukraine in 2010, Kirill (2010) described Yanukovych as a 'deeply religious man' who based his political activity on the 'Orthodox worldview' and who serves the 'spiritual enlightenment of his people'. Patriarch Kirill awarded President Yanukovych the Medal of the Holy Prince Vladimir (first class) and praised him 'as a politician who was undertaking the spiritual task of awakening the nation' (Wołowski, 2010). In January 2011, Patriarch Kirill awarded Yanukovych the Patriarch Alexei II Award 'for outstanding achievements in strengthening the unity of Orthodox nations' and for 'the strengthening and implementation of Christian values in the life of society'. The prize was awarded by the International Social Unity of Orthodox Nations Fund at the request of one of the leading Communist Party of Ukraine (KPU) activists, Yekaterina Samoylyuk who sits on its board.[31] These awards were rather odd as Yanukovych had never been very religious and he was linked since the 1990s to Donetsk organised crime and corrupt oligarchs (Kuzio, 2014).

Patriarch Kirill, during his visits to Ukraine, appealed for the building of 'the world of old Rus' and of an 'Orthodox civilisation' which would 'unite those Slavic peoples who trace their origin back to the tradition of 'Holy Rus' – namely the Russian, Ukrainian and Belarusian peoples' (Wołowski, 2010). Paweł Wołowski (2010) pointed out that Kirill's agenda 'fitted into the Kremlin's wider plans for integration by returning to the de facto political, economic and cultural domination of Ukraine by Russia'. Kirill has been promoting pan-Russian identity since being 'elected' Russian Orthodox Church patriarch and, looking to the concept of 'Holy Rus', has been influential in encouraging Putin to view himself as the 'gatherer of Russian lands'.

However, Kirill's promotion of pan-Russian identity was considered a threat to the business interests of some Ukrainian oligarchs in the Party of

---

[30] 'Tserkovno-relihiina sytuatsiia u kraiini.' www.irs.in.ua/index.php?option=com_content&view=article&id=941%3A1&catid=37%3Aart&Itemid=64&lang=uk

[31] 'Yanukovych otrymaie 50 tysiach dolariv premii vid Kyryla.' www.unian.net/ukr/news/news-417043.html

Regions. The Ukrainian authorities supported pan-Russian identity and Orthodox civilisation at the same time as supposedly seeking to sign an Association Agreement with the EU. The time for balancing, or multi-vector foreign policy, was over as the Kremlin increasingly pressured Yanukovych to choose the Pan-Russian World and Eurasia over Europe, which he did in November 2013. Ukrainian Foreign Minister Konstantin Hryshchenko (2011) stressed, in the spirit of multi-vectorism, that Ukraine could not turn either exclusively to the West or to the East, as both vectors were 'important each in themselves, and not as an instrument used for pursuing these and other geopolitical plans'. From 2012, the Kremlin applied extensive pressure on Yanukovych to make a 'civilisation choice' for Ukraine by wholeheartedly supporting pan-Russian identity and turning away from Europe.

After Putin returned to the presidency in 2012 as the 'gatherer of Russian lands', the Kremlin ruled out multi-vectorism as an option for Ukraine. This was clearly visible during the celebrations of the 1,025th anniversary of the baptism of Kyivan Rus in Kyiv in 2013. Katarzyna Chawryło and Tadeusz Iwański (2013) write that although the celebrations took place in Kyiv, 'the key role' in their organisation 'was played by the Russian government, which took advantage of the religious ceremony to symbolically emphasise its pursuit of Ukraine's subordination'. It is no accident that Putin was the central figure at the celebration, visiting Kyiv to attend the 'Slavic-Orthodox Values – the Basis for Ukraine's Civilisational Choice' conference organised by the most pro-Russian political force in Ukraine, Ukrainian Choice, led by Viktor Medvedchuk, where he stated that Ukraine's place was in the Pan-Russian World and Eurasia. Armenia, which was also placed under pressure at the same time, backed away from signing an Association Agreement with the EU and instead joined the CIS Customs Union (which became the Eurasian Economic Union). Putin stressed 'the common spiritual and cultural roots of Ukraine and Russia, and of a centuries-old "community of destiny"' (Chawryło and Iwański, 2013).

Four months later, Yanukovych refused to sign the Association Agreement between Ukraine and the EU and thus made the 'civilisation choice' in line with Putin's demand. His decision led to a major political crisis, the Euromaidan Revolution of Dignity and, after four months of violent protest, Yanukovych fleeing from power and the coming to power of Euromaidan revolutionaries.

The Kremlin's disinformation, propaganda and rhetoric have always described Yanukovych as having been overthrown in a 'putsch' by 'nationalists, neo-Nazis, Russophobes, and anti-Semites'. They are nothing but puppets in the hands of Western enemies who 'aimed' this action 'against Ukraine, Russia and Eurasian integration' (Putin, 2014). These Nazis managed to seize power by resorting 'to terror, murder, and riots' (Putin, 2014). As is repeatedly the case, the Kremlin believes it knows better than Ukrainians how they think and feel. Euromaidan revolutionaries have gained support in Ukraine only because they do not understand their own history and have lost the sense of belonging to the pan-Russian nation. Patriarch Kirill (2014a, 2014b) explained at the WRPC congress in that year that 'Unity and tradition as a force that transmits, among other things, the values and cultural codes of the nation, are an indispensable condition for society to maintain its integrity and unity in any historical period'. Its antithesis was the Euromaidan Revolution which, according to Patriarch Kirill, highlighted the 'tragic division' within Ukrainian society between those who preserved and understood the 'cultural code of the (*triune*) nation' and those who have lost it. Eight years later, the 'special military operation' goal of 'de-nazification' aimed to return Little Russian identity to Ukrainians who had been deluded into believing they were a different people to Russians.

The dwindling number of Ukrainians who preserved this 'cultural code' certainly included the Ukrainian historian Tolochko (2018) who during his speech to the WRPC congress in 2018 declared that he 'considers himself part of the Pan-Russian World' because it 'was born on the banks of the Dnipro in the former Kyivan Rus'. Tolochko (2018) emphasised that the civilisation community that was born at that time was the 'East Slavic Orthodox world', which basically means 'the same' as Pan-Russian World but sounds 'more neutral'. Tolochko (2018) also said he 'doesn't know what we should do in Brussels or Washington' because he feels 'foreign' there, while 'in Moscow and St. Petersburg' he knows he is 'at home'. The Ukrainian historian disingenuously claimed, 'there are millions of people like him in Ukraine' (Tolochko, 2018).

However, despite such exaggerated claims, advocates of the Pan-Russian World in Ukraine have grappled with low levels of interest in the idea of Ukraine and Russia as belonging to a single civilisation community or viewing this concept as an agenda for Ukraine's future trajectory. Therefore, after Yanukovych fled from office in February 2014, new 'silent adherents' appeared within the narrative on the Pan-Russian World. According to them, after 2014, the authorities in Ukraine launched mass persecution of 'millions' of the Pan-Russian World supporters. As a result, those who were brave enough to support Ukraine within the Pan-Russian

World were killed, while those who were 'not strong enough' were intimidated and 'are either silent or say something that their persecutors would like to hear' (Kirill, 2014a). Such discourse was used by the Kremlin to claim it launched its 'special military operation' to end the 'genocide' of Russian speakers in Ukraine.

The question of 'silent adherents' is of particular importance to our understanding of Russia's policies towards Ukraine after 2014. Patriarch Kirill's discourse sketches an image of Ukraine, where brave individuals express the will of the terrorised part of Ukrainian society, and are part of a large silent majority of the Pan-Russian World constituency in post-2014 Ukraine. This fallacy ignored how Russia's military aggression in 2014 had led to an even greater divergence between Ukraine and Russia (discussed in Chapters 6 and 7). Kirill's and Putin's myths about a Little Russian majority waiting to be liberated by Russia ultimately underpinned belief in the 'special military operation' bringing a quick military victory. Expecting Little Russians to be greeting Russian troops with bread and salt as 'liberators' explained the small size of Russia's invasion force of only 175,000 troops.

Holy War Against Satanic Ukraine and the West

The discourse about Ukraine within the Pan-Russian World ideology has clearly become radicalised after the full-scale invasion, as witnessed in the May 2023 Luhansk declaration of the WRPC that repeated the negative rhetoric found in Russian propaganda and disinformation. The crux of this imperial nationalist discourse is the allegation that 'modern Ukraine' as a sovereign and independent political community constitutes an 'existential threat to Russia'. Therefore, after the victory of the 'special military operation' the entire territory of present-day Ukraine should lie 'within Russia's zone of exclusive influence'.[32] Deputy Head of the Russian Security Council Medvedev (2024) said that 'Ukraine is, of course, Russia' and that the concept of a sovereign Ukrainian state and a Ukrainian identity distinct to Russian must 'disappear forever'.

Karolina Hird (2024, p. 8) wrote: 'The war in Ukraine is primarily a war for control of people, not land'. This was confirmed by Medvedev (2024) who stated during the above-mentioned speech that 'Russia is more interested in subjugating Ukraine's people than taking its territory'. He

---

[32] 'Rezolutsiia Vserossiiskogo foruma…'

underlined that 'the main value that Russia seeks from its occupation of Ukraine is through controlling its people'. Hird (2024, p. 8) emphasised that 'Putin's project (…) is the destruction of Ukraine's distinctive political, social, linguistic, and religious identity. Putin seeks to make real his false ideological conviction that Ukrainians are simply confused Russians with an invented identity, language, and history that a small, Western-backed minority is seeking to impose on most of the inhabitants'.

Adherents of the Pan-Russian World believe Ukraine was created because of the artificial division of the pan-Russian nation after the disintegration of the Soviet Union. They ignore the fact that while the USSR promoted eastern Slavic unity it also recognised a Ukrainian identity and language separate to Russian. Defining the geopolitical space of the former USSR as 'post-Soviet' sanctioned and institutionalised this division. Therefore, in the Pan-Russian World ideology, instead of the term 'post-Soviet' they use 'Historical Russia' and 'Holy Rus'. In Patriarch Kirill's narrative, the notion of 'Holy Rus' refers to a spiritual-mythical entity which comprises the territories of today's Russian Federation, Ukraine, and Belarus and is viewed as a constant throughout history since the tenth century, 'apparently essentially unchanged by changing political circumstances' (Horsfjord, 2024, p. 6). Moreover, the understanding of the Pan-Russian World increasingly included a dystopian Ukraine experiencing conflict between 'holy' Russian civilisation and 'evil' (and satanic) West.[33]

During the 24th WRPC congress in October 2023, Dugin (2023) explained that 'Today, two ideas, two armies are colliding, those of the angels and those of demons'. Dugin (2023) claimed Ukraine is the site of a battlefield between (Russian) angels and (Western) demons. Russia as 'Holy Rus' is facing and fighting the 'forces of absolute, world historical evil' who 'are opposed to us' (Dugin, 2023). One of the leading propagandists of a pan-Russian civilisation community, Konstantin Malofeev (2022), dubbed the 'Orthodox oligarch', believes the Russian language and Russian culture no longer lie at the core of the Pan-Russian World; instead, there is a 'belief in the imperial mission and idea'. Malofeev (2022) told the WRPC congress that a 'holy war between good and evil' is taking place in the Donbas. The evil is represented by soldiers fighting on the Ukrainian side who speak Russian who, Malofeev (2022) claimed, were responsible

---

[33] Op cit., 'Nakaz XXV Vsiemirnogo Russkogo…; 'Kremlin evokes Satan in support of the war.' https://euvsdisinfo.eu/kremlin-evokes-satan-in-support-of-the-war/; 'The followers of Satan have seized power in Kyiv.' https://euvsdisinfo.eu/report/the-followers-of-satan-have-seized-power-in-kyiv/

for the worst war crimes and on the other side was Russia 'fighting for the salvation of their souls and for the future of their children'. He described them as 'not people' (Malofeev, 2022).

Malofeev is not a unique example of a Russian Orthodox fundamentalist who supports the revival of traditional Christian values and promotes an eliminationist rhetoric against Ukrainians. In August 2023 Yevgienii Nikiforov, who was a cocreator of the Radonezh Orthodox brotherhood and a head of a radio channel with the same name, stated on the Russian television channel *Spas*:

> [Ukrainians are] godless, it's all about godlessness… The main problem is our own faint-heartedness! From the very start, we've been trying to negotiate! You can't make deals with demons! There's nothing to negotiate… They have no laws; they are a lawless people! They are the offspring of lawlessness… The illness in Ukraine is so far gone that you can't convince them or negotiate with them. You can't cure them this way! Only surgery will work there. The only response to these statements by the Nazis is a Solntsepyok [heavy thermobaric rocket launcher]. It must be burned out! (Apt, 2024, p. 61).

Conclusion

In Russia, 'political power is strongly concentrated in a narrow circle of the elite' (Zarycki, 2010, p. 55) and is legitimised by an imposed 'discourse in the symbolic sphere' imbued with the Pan-Russian World ideology. The concept of the Pan-Russian World emerged from Solzhenitsyn's Russian Union (1990–1991) and the Russian Orthodox Church and WRPC's 'Holy Rus' in the first half of the 1990s. Then this discourse was relatively marginal but in the 2000s it became mainstream under Putin, evolving in the second decade of the twenty first century into the concept of a Russian 'state-civilisation' without borders, the slogan of Putin's 2024 election campaign. As Chapter 1 showed, Russian identity was always bigger than the Russian SFSR and Russian Federation with 'Historic Russia' being identified with 'Holy Rus', the Pan-Russian World and the Soviet Union.

Kozicki (2019, pp. 18–19) wrote that the disintegration of the USSR left an ideological void which was filled by the Pan-Russian World ideology and Russian imperial nationalism, rather than democracy. As Tolz (2001) showed, a civic, post-imperial Russian identity was the weakest of five Russian identities in the 1990s. Ultimately, the capturing of Russia's mainstream came about through the resuscitation of symbolic capital associated with Russian imperial nationalism, chauvinism and messianism, along with the simultaneous re-Sovietisation of Russia, religious dogma of the Great Patriotic War and cult of Stalin. The Pan-Russian World and pan-Russian identity provides the ideological roots for how the Kremlin understands Russia's place as a great power in the world, reinforcing its denial of Ukraine as a separate and sovereign state, providing xenophobia towards the 'collective West' and buttressing the goal of overturning the US-led unipolar world. These ideological roots outline Russia's main existential enemy as the 'collective West' which controls the Ukrainian 'puppet' state, defines Russia's 'natural' state to be an empire, and reinforces its claim of Eurasia as its exclusive sphere of influence.

The Pan-Russian World concept outlines the desired institutional order which should be organised in Eurasia with ready-made ideological templates and definitions of the rules by which countries like Ukraine are expected to operate. The Pan-Russian World functions within a neo-patrimonial framework of patron, client, and loyalty. The primary role of the state and the structures of hard power are to govern all spheres of social life, including the cultural and scientific. It is consequently no coincidence that SVR Chairman Naryshkin plays a leading role in Russian historical policy. Within this neo-patrimonial framework, Russia lies at the centre of a unique and superior 'state-civilisation' whose core is the Pan-Russian World and 'Holy Rus' uniting the pan-Russian nation through the Russian Orthodox Church and the Russian language.

The Pan-Russian World ideology has evolved since 1991. Initially, it was a tool for consolidating the grassroots movement of non-governmental organisations who contested the Westernising transformation of Russia in the 1990s. The Pan-Russian World was also founded to coordinate Russian state policy towards compatriots living outside the Russian Federation in Eurasia. The Kremlin used the Pan-Russian World as soft power inside and outside Eurasia. After Putin first was first elected in 2000, the Russian state quickly took control over the process of symbolic institutionalisation and symbolic capital of the Pan-Russian World.

The Pan-Russian World institutions 'have been for a long time spinning the narratives that were taken at face value, promoting the current Russian regime's understanding of the world order and supporting Russian-centred versions of history and politics throughout the Eastern European region, influencing indirectly or directly the decision-making processes in different countries' (Koval and Tereshchenko, 2023, p. 200). This especially referred to the 'ideas and narratives in Russian and Eastern European studies' (Koval, Tereshchenko 2023, p. 200; see Kuzio 2020, pp. 9–35). Ultimately, the Pan-Russian World failed to win many adherents or improve Russia's image because it was always an imperial nationalist ideology legitimising the authoritarian and dictatorial nature of Putin's Russia's and supporting Russian military aggression. After Russia's first invasion of Ukraine in 2014, the Pan-Russian World as a concept became radicalised as aggressive propaganda in an extremely primitive manner. A new 'symphony' between the secular and clerical authorities was formed between the Kremlin and the Russian Orthodox Church. Both sides of the 'symphony' refer to eschatological phraseology and 'traditional views and attitudes;' in fact, however, the entire discourse 'is foremost about authority, hierarchy, legitimisation, and national identity' (Curanović, 2015, p. 10). As Alicja Curanović (2015, p. 10) wrote, 'from the perspective of the Kremlin, religion is important as an integrative element of tradition and as a source of moral norms' while 'the transcendent aspect of religion is deliberately dismissed by the authorities'.

One of the key elements of the ideology of the Pan-Russian World is the assumption that Ukrainians as a people distinct from Russians do not exist and they are a Little Russian branch of the pan-Russian people. Ukrainians who defend their cultural and political distinctiveness allegedly have a distorted image of their own past, and they don't understand they are fighting against 'brotherly' Russians. The Kremlin used soft power to support the unity of Ukrainians and Russians prior to 2014, through invasion and hybrid warfare from 2014 to 2021 and by launching a 'special military operation' in 2022. The Pan-Russian World ideology has been central to Putin's belief in himself as the 'gatherer of Russia lands' since 2012 to the present. However, the essential elements of the Pan-Russian World ideology were articulated and institutionalised as far back as the early 1990s, immediately following the disintegration of 'Historical Russia'; that is, the USSR.

References

Address. (1993). 'Obrashcheniie I Vsiemirnogo Russkogo Sobora 'O ponimanii natsionalnykh intieriesov Rossii i russkogo Naroda.' https://vrns.ru/documents/obrashchenie-i-vsemirnogo-russkogo-sobora-o-ponimanii-natsionalnykh-interesov-rossii-i-russkogo-naro/

Address. (1995). 'Obrashcheniie I Vsiemirnogo Russkogo Sobora k russkomu narodu.' https://vrns.ru/documents/obrashcheniya-ii-vsemirnogo-russkogo-sobora/

Apt, C. (2024). Russia's Eliminationist Rhetoric against Ukraine: A Collection, Just Security, 18 April. www.justsecurity.org/81789/russias-eliminationist-rhetoric-against-ukraine-a-collection/

religious confessions while strengthening his relationship with the Moscow Patriarchate.[30] This could be seen during his presidential inauguration, which was attended by Patriarch Kirill as a special guest, giving credence to the concept of the integration of Ukraine and Russia within the Pan-Russian World (Ukrayina-2013, 2013, p. 3).

Patriarch Kirill promoted Yanukovych as leader of a country belonging to the Pan-Russian World civilisation. During one of his three visits to Ukraine in 2010, Kirill (2010) described Yanukovych as a 'deeply religious man' who based his political activity on the 'Orthodox worldview' and who serves the 'spiritual enlightenment of his people'. Patriarch Kirill awarded President Yanukovych the Medal of the Holy Prince Vladimir (first class) and praised him 'as a politician who was undertaking the spiritual task of awakening the nation' (Wołowski, 2010). In January 2011, Patriarch Kirill awarded Yanukovych the Patriarch Alexei II Award 'for outstanding achievements in strengthening the unity of Orthodox nations' and for 'the strengthening and implementation of Christian values in the life of society'. The prize was awarded by the International Social Unity of Orthodox Nations Fund at the request of one of the leading Communist Party of Ukraine (KPU) activists, Yekaterina Samoylyuk who sits on its board.[31] These awards were rather odd as Yanukovych had never been very religious and he was linked since the 1990s to Donetsk organised crime and corrupt oligarchs (Kuzio, 2014).

Patriarch Kirill, during his visits to Ukraine, appealed for the building of 'the world of old Rus' and of an 'Orthodox civilisation' which would 'unite those Slavic peoples who trace their origin back to the tradition of 'Holy Rus' – namely the Russian, Ukrainian and Belarusian peoples' (Wołowski, 2010). Paweł Wołowski (2010) pointed out that Kirill's agenda 'fitted into the Kremlin's wider plans for integration by returning to the de facto political, economic and cultural domination of Ukraine by Russia'. Kirill has been promoting pan-Russian identity since being 'elected' Russian Orthodox Church patriarch and, looking to the concept of 'Holy Rus', has been influential in encouraging Putin to view himself as the 'gatherer of Russian lands'.

However, Kirill's promotion of pan-Russian identity was considered a threat to the business interests of some Ukrainian oligarchs in the Party of

---

[30] 'Tserkovno-relihiina sytuatsiia u kraiini.' www.irs.in.ua/index.php?option=com_content&view=article&id=941%3A1&catid=37%3Aart&Itemid=64&lang=uk

[31] 'Yanukovych otrymaie 50 tysiach dolariv premii vid Kyryla.' www.unian.net/ukr/news/news-417043.html

Regions. The Ukrainian authorities supported pan-Russian identity and Orthodox civilisation at the same time as supposedly seeking to sign an Association Agreement with the EU. The time for balancing, or multi-vector foreign policy, was over as the Kremlin increasingly pressured Yanukovych to choose the Pan-Russian World and Eurasia over Europe, which he did in November 2013. Ukrainian Foreign Minister Konstantin Hryshchenko (2011) stressed, in the spirit of multi-vectorism, that Ukraine could not turn either exclusively to the West or to the East, as both vectors were 'important each in themselves, and not as an instrument used for pursuing these and other geopolitical plans'. From 2012, the Kremlin applied extensive pressure on Yanukovych to make a 'civilisation choice' for Ukraine by wholeheartedly supporting pan-Russian identity and turning away from Europe.

After Putin returned to the presidency in 2012 as the 'gatherer of Russian lands', the Kremlin ruled out multi-vectorism as an option for Ukraine. This was clearly visible during the celebrations of the 1,025th anniversary of the baptism of Kyivan Rus in Kyiv in 2013. Katarzyna Chawryło and Tadeusz Iwański (2013) write that although the celebrations took place in Kyiv, 'the key role' in their organisation 'was played by the Russian government, which took advantage of the religious ceremony to symbolically emphasise its pursuit of Ukraine's subordination'. It is no accident that Putin was the central figure at the celebration, visiting Kyiv to attend the 'Slavic-Orthodox Values – the Basis for Ukraine's Civilisational Choice' conference organised by the most pro-Russian political force in Ukraine, Ukrainian Choice, led by Viktor Medvedchuk, where he stated that Ukraine's place was in the Pan-Russian World and Eurasia. Armenia, which was also placed under pressure at the same time, backed away from signing an Association Agreement with the EU and instead joined the CIS Customs Union (which became the Eurasian Economic Union). Putin stressed 'the common spiritual and cultural roots of Ukraine and Russia, and of a centuries-old "community of destiny"' (Chawryło and Iwański, 2013).

Four months later, Yanukovych refused to sign the Association Agreement between Ukraine and the EU and thus made the 'civilisation choice' in line with Putin's demand. His decision led to a major political crisis, the Euromaidan Revolution of Dignity and, after four months of violent protest, Yanukovych fleeing from power and the coming to power of Euromaidan revolutionaries.

The Kremlin's disinformation, propaganda and rhetoric have always described Yanukovych as having been overthrown in a 'putsch' by 'nationalists, neo-Nazis, Russophobes, and anti-Semites'. They are nothing but puppets in the hands of Western enemies who 'aimed' this action 'against Ukraine, Russia and Eurasian integration' (Putin, 2014). These Nazis managed to seize power by resorting 'to terror, murder, and riots' (Putin, 2014). As is repeatedly the case, the Kremlin believes it knows better than Ukrainians how they think and feel. Euromaidan revolutionaries have gained support in Ukraine only because they do not understand their own history and have lost the sense of belonging to the pan-Russian nation. Patriarch Kirill (2014a, 2014b) explained at the WRPC congress in that year that 'Unity and tradition as a force that transmits, among other things, the values and cultural codes of the nation, are an indispensable condition for society to maintain its integrity and unity in any historical period'. Its antithesis was the Euromaidan Revolution which, according to Patriarch Kirill, highlighted the 'tragic division' within Ukrainian society between those who preserved and understood the 'cultural code of the (*triune*) nation' and those who have lost it. Eight years later, the 'special military operation' goal of 'de-nazification' aimed to return Little Russian identity to Ukrainians who had been deluded into believing they were a different people to Russians.

The dwindling number of Ukrainians who preserved this 'cultural code' certainly included the Ukrainian historian Tolochko (2018) who during his speech to the WRPC congress in 2018 declared that he 'considers himself part of the Pan-Russian World' because it 'was born on the banks of the Dnipro in the former Kyivan Rus'. Tolochko (2018) emphasised that the civilisation community that was born at that time was the 'East Slavic Orthodox world', which basically means 'the same' as Pan-Russian World but sounds 'more neutral'. Tolochko (2018) also said he 'doesn't know what we should do in Brussels or Washington' because he feels 'foreign' there, while 'in Moscow and St. Petersburg' he knows he is 'at home'. The Ukrainian historian disingenuously claimed, 'there are millions of people like him in Ukraine' (Tolochko, 2018).

However, despite such exaggerated claims, advocates of the Pan-Russian World in Ukraine have grappled with low levels of interest in the idea of Ukraine and Russia as belonging to a single civilisation community or viewing this concept as an agenda for Ukraine's future trajectory. Therefore, after Yanukovych fled from office in February 2014, new 'silent adherents' appeared within the narrative on the Pan-Russian World. According to them, after 2014, the authorities in Ukraine launched mass persecution of 'millions' of the Pan-Russian World supporters. As a result, those who were brave enough to support Ukraine within the Pan-Russian

World were killed, while those who were 'not strong enough' were intimidated and 'are either silent or say something that their persecutors would like to hear' (Kirill, 2014a). Such discourse was used by the Kremlin to claim it launched its 'special military operation' to end the 'genocide' of Russian speakers in Ukraine.

The question of 'silent adherents' is of particular importance to our understanding of Russia's policies towards Ukraine after 2014. Patriarch Kirill's discourse sketches an image of Ukraine, where brave individuals express the will of the terrorised part of Ukrainian society, and are part of a large silent majority of the Pan-Russian World constituency in post-2014 Ukraine. This fallacy ignored how Russia's military aggression in 2014 had led to an even greater divergence between Ukraine and Russia (discussed in Chapters 6 and 7). Kirill's and Putin's myths about a Little Russian majority waiting to be liberated by Russia ultimately underpinned belief in the 'special military operation' bringing a quick military victory. Expecting Little Russians to be greeting Russian troops with bread and salt as 'liberators' explained the small size of Russia's invasion force of only 175,000 troops.

Holy War Against Satanic Ukraine and the West

The discourse about Ukraine within the Pan-Russian World ideology has clearly become radicalised after the full-scale invasion, as witnessed in the May 2023 Luhansk declaration of the WRPC that repeated the negative rhetoric found in Russian propaganda and disinformation. The crux of this imperial nationalist discourse is the allegation that 'modern Ukraine' as a sovereign and independent political community constitutes an 'existential threat to Russia'. Therefore, after the victory of the 'special military operation' the entire territory of present-day Ukraine should lie 'within Russia's zone of exclusive influence'.[32] Deputy Head of the Russian Security Council Medvedev (2024) said that 'Ukraine is, of course, Russia' and that the concept of a sovereign Ukrainian state and a Ukrainian identity distinct to Russian must 'disappear forever'.

Karolina Hird (2024, p. 8) wrote: 'The war in Ukraine is primarily a war for control of people, not land'. This was confirmed by Medvedev (2024) who stated during the above-mentioned speech that 'Russia is more interested in subjugating Ukraine's people than taking its territory'. He

---

[32] 'Rezolutsiia Vserossiiskogo foruma…'

or improve Russia's image because it was always an imperial nationalist ideology legitimising the authoritarian and dictatorial nature of Putin's Russia's and supporting Russian military aggression. After Russia's first invasion of Ukraine in 2014, the Pan-Russian World as a concept became radicalised as aggressive propaganda in an extremely primitive manner. A new 'symphony' between the secular and clerical authorities was formed between the Kremlin and the Russian Orthodox Church. Both sides of the 'symphony' refer to eschatological phraseology and 'traditional views and attitudes;' in fact, however, the entire discourse 'is foremost about authority, hierarchy, legitimisation, and national identity' (Curanović, 2015, p. 10). As Alicja Curanović (2015, p. 10) wrote, 'from the perspective of the Kremlin, religion is important as an integrative element of tradition and as a source of moral norms' while 'the transcendent aspect of religion is deliberately dismissed by the authorities'.

One of the key elements of the ideology of the Pan-Russian World is the assumption that Ukrainians as a people distinct from Russians do not exist and they are a Little Russian branch of the pan-Russian people. Ukrainians who defend their cultural and political distinctiveness allegedly have a distorted image of their own past, and they don't understand they are fighting against 'brotherly' Russians. The Kremlin used soft power to support the unity of Ukrainians and Russians prior to 2014, through invasion and hybrid warfare from 2014 to 2021 and by launching a 'special military operation' in 2022. The Pan-Russian World ideology has been central to Putin's belief in himself as the 'gatherer of Russia lands' since 2012 to the present. However, the essential elements of the Pan-Russian World ideology were articulated and institutionalised as far back as the early 1990s, immediately following the disintegration of 'Historical Russia'; that is, the USSR.

References

Address. (1993). 'Obrashcheniie I Vsiemirnogo Russkogo Sobora 'O ponimanii natsionalnykh intieriesov Rossii i russkogo Naroda.' https://vrns.ru/documents/obrashchenie-i-vsemirnogo-russkogo-sobora-o-ponimanii-natsionalnykh-interesov-rossii-i-russkogo-naro/

Address. (1995). 'Obrashcheniie I Vsiemirnogo Russkogo Sobora k russkomu narodu.' https://vrns.ru/documents/obrashcheniya-ii-vsemirnogo-russkogo-sobora/

Apt, C. (2024). Russia's Eliminationist Rhetoric against Ukraine: A Collection, Just Security, 18 April. www.justsecurity.org/81789/russias-eliminationist-rhetoric-against-ukraine-a-collection/

along with the simultaneous re-Sovietisation of Russia, religious dogma of the Great Patriotic War and cult of Stalin. The Pan-Russian World and pan-Russian identity provides the ideological roots for how the Kremlin understands Russia's place as a great power in the world, reinforcing its denial of Ukraine as a separate and sovereign state, providing xenophobia towards the 'collective West' and buttressing the goal of overturning the US-led unipolar world. These ideological roots outline Russia's main existential enemy as the 'collective West' which controls the Ukrainian 'puppet' state, defines Russia's 'natural' state to be an empire, and reinforces its claim of Eurasia as its exclusive sphere of influence.

The Pan-Russian World concept outlines the desired institutional order which should be organised in Eurasia with ready-made ideological templates and definitions of the rules by which countries like Ukraine are expected to operate. The Pan-Russian World functions within a neo-patrimonial framework of patron, client, and loyalty. The primary role of the state and the structures of hard power are to govern all spheres of social life, including the cultural and scientific. It is consequently no coincidence that SVR Chairman Naryshkin plays a leading role in Russian historical policy. Within this neo-patrimonial framework, Russia lies at the centre of a unique and superior 'state-civilisation' whose core is the Pan-Russian World and 'Holy Rus' uniting the pan-Russian nation through the Russian Orthodox Church and the Russian language.

The Pan-Russian World ideology has evolved since 1991. Initially, it was a tool for consolidating the grassroots movement of non-governmental organisations who contested the Westernising transformation of Russia in the 1990s. The Pan-Russian World was also founded to coordinate Russian state policy towards compatriots living outside the Russian Federation in Eurasia. The Kremlin used the Pan-Russian World as soft power inside and outside Eurasia. After Putin first was first elected in 2000, the Russian state quickly took control over the process of symbolic institutionalisation and symbolic capital of the Pan-Russian World.

The Pan-Russian World institutions 'have been for a long time spinning the narratives that were taken at face value, promoting the current Russian regime's understanding of the world order and supporting Russian-centred versions of history and politics throughout the Eastern European region, influencing indirectly or directly the decision-making processes in different countries' (Koval and Tereshchenko, 2023, p. 200). This especially referred to the 'ideas and narratives in Russian and Eastern European studies' (Koval, Tereshchenko 2023, p. 200; see Kuzio 2020, pp. 9–35). Ultimately, the Pan-Russian World failed to win many adherents for the worst war crimes and on the other side was Russia 'fighting for the salvation of their souls and for the future of their children'. He described them as 'not people' (Malofeev, 2022).

Malofeev is not a unique example of a Russian Orthodox fundamentalist who supports the revival of traditional Christian values and promotes an eliminationist rhetoric against Ukrainians. In August 2023 Yevgienii Nikiforov, who was a cocreator of the Radonezh Orthodox brotherhood and a head of a radio channel with the same name, stated on the Russian television channel *Spas*:

> [Ukrainians are] godless, it's all about godlessness... The main problem is our own faint-heartedness! From the very start, we've been trying to negotiate! You can't make deals with demons! There's nothing to negotiate... They have no laws; they are a lawless people! They are the offspring of lawlessness... The illness in Ukraine is so far gone that you can't convince them or negotiate with them. You can't cure them this way! Only surgery will work there. The only response to these statements by the Nazis is a Solntsepyok [heavy thermobaric rocket launcher]. It must be burned out! (Apt, 2024, p. 61).

Conclusion

In Russia, 'political power is strongly concentrated in a narrow circle of the elite' (Zarycki, 2010, p. 55) and is legitimised by an imposed 'discourse in the symbolic sphere' imbued with the Pan-Russian World ideology. The concept of the Pan-Russian World emerged from Solzhenitsyn's Russian Union (1990–1991) and the Russian Orthodox Church and WRPC's 'Holy Rus' in the first half of the 1990s. Then this discourse was relatively marginal but in the 2000s it became mainstream under Putin, evolving in the second decade of the twenty first century into the concept of a Russian 'state-civilisation' without borders, the slogan of Putin's 2024 election campaign. As Chapter 1 showed, Russian identity was always bigger than the Russian SFSR and Russian Federation with 'Historic Russia' being identified with 'Holy Rus', the Pan-Russian World and the Soviet Union.

Kozicki (2019, pp. 18–19) wrote that the disintegration of the USSR left an ideological void which was filled by the Pan-Russian World ideology and Russian imperial nationalism, rather than democracy. As Tolz (2001) showed, a civic, post-imperial Russian identity was the weakest of five Russian identities in the 1990s. Ultimately, the capturing of Russia's mainstream came about through the resuscitation of symbolic capital associated with Russian imperial nationalism, chauvinism and messianism, underlined that 'the main value that Russia seeks from its occupation of Ukraine is through controlling its people'. Hird (2024, p. 8) emphasised that 'Putin's project (…) is the destruction of Ukraine's distinctive political, social, linguistic, and religious identity. Putin seeks to make real his false ideological conviction that Ukrainians are simply confused Russians with an invented identity, language, and history that a small, Western-backed minority is seeking to impose on most of the inhabitants'.

Adherents of the Pan-Russian World believe Ukraine was created because of the artificial division of the pan-Russian nation after the disintegration of the Soviet Union. They ignore the fact that while the USSR promoted eastern Slavic unity it also recognised a Ukrainian identity and language separate to Russian. Defining the geopolitical space of the former USSR as 'post-Soviet' sanctioned and institutionalised this division. Therefore, in the Pan-Russian World ideology, instead of the term 'post-Soviet' they use 'Historical Russia' and 'Holy Rus'. In Patriarch Kirill's narrative, the notion of 'Holy Rus' refers to a spiritual-mythical entity which comprises the territories of today's Russian Federation, Ukraine, and Belarus and is viewed as a constant throughout history since the tenth century, 'apparently essentially unchanged by changing political circumstances' (Horsfjord, 2024, p. 6). Moreover, the understanding of the Pan-Russian World increasingly included a dystopian Ukraine experiencing conflict between 'holy' Russian civilisation and 'evil' (and satanic) West.[33]

During the 24th WRPC congress in October 2023, Dugin (2023) explained that 'Today, two ideas, two armies are colliding, those of the angels and those of demons'. Dugin (2023) claimed Ukraine is the site of a battlefield between (Russian) angels and (Western) demons. Russia as 'Holy Rus' is facing and fighting the 'forces of absolute, world historical evil' who 'are opposed to us' (Dugin, 2023). One of the leading propagandists of a pan-Russian civilisation community, Konstantin Malofeev (2022), dubbed the 'Orthodox oligarch', believes the Russian language and Russian culture no longer lie at the core of the Pan-Russian World; instead, there is a 'belief in the imperial mission and idea'. Malofeev (2022) told the WRPC congress that a 'holy war between good and evil' is taking place in the Donbas. The evil is represented by soldiers fighting on the Ukrainian side who speak Russian who, Malofeev (2022) claimed, were responsible

---

[33] Op cit., 'Nakaz XXV Vsiemirnogo Russkogo…; 'Kremlin evokes Satan in support of the war.' https://euvsdisinfo.eu/kremlin-evokes-satan-in-support-of-the-war/; 'The followers of Satan have seized power in Kyiv.' https://euvsdisinfo.eu/report/the-followers-of-satan-have-seized-power-in-kyiv/

Barash, R. (2012). 'Razdieliennyi russkij narod ili razdieliennaia sovietskaia natsia?' In: *Forum novieishei vostochnoievropieiskoi istorii i kultury- Russkoie izdaniie*. 1. www1.ku.de/ZIMOS/forum/inhaltruss17.html
Basic values. (2011). 'Bazysnyie tsennosti – osnova obshchienatsionalnoi identychnosti.' https://vrns.ru/documents/bazisnye-tsennosti-osnova-obshchenatsionalnoy-identichnosti/
Bourdieu, P. (2000). *Pascalian Meditations*. Stanford, CA: Stanford University Press.
Chawryło K. and Iwański T. (2013). 'Russian-Ukrainian Tensions with the Anniversary of the Christianisation of Kyivan Rus in the Background,' Centre for Eastern Studies, 7 August. www.osw.waw.pl/en/publikacje/analyses/2013-08-07/russian-ukrainian-tensions-anniversary-christianisation-kyivan-rus
Curanović, A. (2015). 'The Guardians of Traditional Values Russia and the Russian Orthodox Church in the Quest for Status,' *Transatlantic Academy Paper Series*, 1.
Dugin, A. (2023). 'Vystuplieniie rossiiskogo filosofa, doktora politicheskikh i sotsiologicheskikh nauk, kandydata filosofskikh nauk, professora A. G. Dugina.' https://vrns.ru/documents/vystuplenie-rossiyskogo-filosofa-doktora-politicheskikh-i-sotsiologicheskikh-nauk-kandidata-filosofs/
Engström, M. (2014). 'Contemporary Russian Messianism and New Russian Foreign Policy,' *Contemporary Security Policy*, 35 (3): 356–379.
Hird, K. (2024). *The Kremlin's Occupation Playbook: Coerced Russification and Ethnic Cleansing in Occupied Ukraine*. Washington DC: Institute for the Study of War. www.understandingwar.org/backgrounder/kremlins-occupation-playbook-coerced-russification-and-ethnic-cleansing-occupied
Horsfjord, V. L. (2024). 'Patriarch and Patriot: History in Patriarch Kirill's Sermons in the First Year of the Full-Scale War in Ukraine,' *Religion, State & Society*, 52 (4): 367–382.
Hovorun, C. (2018). *Political orthodoxies*. Minneapolis: Fortress Press.
Hryshchenko, K. (2011). 'Glava MID Konstantin Grishchenko: Ukrainie nie podkhodit shablon 'russkogo mira' u nieie otlichnyi ot Rossii put v budushchieie.' www.religion.in.ua/news/vazhlivo/7828-glava-mid-konstantin-grishhenko-ukraine-ne-podxodit-shablon-russkogo-mira-u-nee-otlichnyj-ot-rossii-put-v-budushhee.html
Kazantsev, A. (2008). 'Suivieriennaia diemokratiia' v sovriemiennoi Rossii: struktura, kontseptsiia i ideologiemy' In: *Publichnoie prostranstvo, grazhdanskoie obshchiestvo i vlast.: opyt razvitiia i vzaiemodieistviia*. Moskva: Izdatielstvo ROSSPIEN.
Kirill. (2010). 'Kyrylo: Yanukovych sluzhyt spravi dukhovnoii prosvity svoho narodu.' https://ua.korrespondent.net/amp/1100995-kirilo-yanukovich-sluzhit-spravi-duhovnoyi-prosviti-svogo-narodu
Kirill. (2014a). 'Slovo pastyria.' www.patriarchia.ru/ua/db/text/3728244.html
Kirill. (2014b). 'Slovo Glavy VRNS, Sviatieishego Partiarkha Moskovskogo i Vsieia Rusi Kirilla na XVIII Vsiemirnom Russkom Narodom Soborie.'

https://vrns.ru/documents/slovo-glavy-vrns-svyateyshego-patriarkha-moskovskogo-i-vseya-rusi-kirilla-na-xviii-vsemirnom-russkom/

Koval, N., Irysova, M., Tytiuk, S. and Tereshchenko, D. (2023) 'Rossotrudnichestvo: The Unbearable Harshness of Soft Power' In: N. Koval and D. Tereshchenko (eds.), *Russian Cultural Diplomacy under Putin. Rossotrudnichestvo, the "Russkiy Mir" Foundation, and the Gorchakov Fund in 2007–2022*. Stuttgart: Ibidem; New York: Columbia University Press: 23–98.

Koval N. and Tereshchenko D. (2023). 'Conclusions: Russian Cultural Diplomacy after 2022' In: N. Koval and D. Tereshchenko (eds.), *Russian Cultural Diplomacy under Putin. Rossotrudnichestvo, the "Russkiy Mir" Foundation, and the Gorchakov Fund in 2007–2022*. Stuttgart: Ibidem; New York: Columbia University Press: 199–204.

Kozicki, A. (2019). *Instytucjonalizacja symboliczna w Izraelu*. Warszawa: Fundacja na rzecz Warsztatów Analiz Socjologicznych.

Kuzio, T. (2010). 'Nationalism, Identity and Civil Society in Ukraine: Understanding the Orange Revolution,' *Communist and Post-Communist Studies*, 43 (3): 285–296.

Kuzio, T. (2014). 'Crime, Politics and Business in 1990s Ukraine,' *Communist and Post-Communist Politics*, 47 (2): 195–210.

Kuzio, T. (2020). *Crisis in Russian Studies? Nationalism (Imperialism), Racism, and War*. Bristol: E-International Relations. www.e-ir.info/publication/crisis-in-russian-studies-nationalism-imperialism-racism-and-war/

Laruelle, M. (2015). *The "Russian World": Russia's Soft Power and Geopolitical Imagination*. Washington: Center on Global Interests. www.ponarseurasia.org/the-russian-world-russia-s-soft-power-and-geopolitical-imagination/

Malofeev, K. (2022). Interview, 12 December. https://smotrim.ru/video/2528818

McGlynn, J. (2023). 'How Russian Propaganda Built an Alternate Reality in Occupied Ukraine,' *Moscow Times*, 27 October. www.themoscowtimes.com/2023/10/27/how-russian-propaganda-built-an-alternate-reality-in-occupied-ukraine-a82900

Medvedev, D. (2024). 'Gieograficheskiie i stratiegicheskiie granicy Rossii. Dmitrii Miedviediev na festivalie molodiozhy 4 marta 2024.' www.youtube.com/watch?v=42l1woXzHsw

Omarova, Z. (2008). 'K voprosu ob opriedielienii poniatiia "sootiechiestvienniki za rubiezhom,"' *Vlast*, 3: 34–41.

Østbø, J. (2017). 'Securitizing 'Spiritual-Moral Values' in Russia,' *Post-Soviet Affairs*, 33 (3): 200–216.

Plenary Session. (2001). 'Plienarnyie zasiedannia v Khramie Khrysta Spasitielia.' https://vrns.ru/documents/plenarnye-zasedaniya-v-khrame-khrista-spasitelya/

Putin, V. (2012). 'Rossiia: natsionalnyi vopros,' *Nezavisimaya Gazeta*, 23 January. www.ng.ru/politics/2012-01-23/1_national.html?print=Y

Putin, V. (2014). 'Vladimir Putin Addressed State Duma Deputies, Federation Council Members, Heads of Russian Regions and Civil Society Representatives in the Kremlin,' 18 March. http://en.kremlin.ru/events/president/news/20603

Putin, V. (2021). 'On the Historical Unity of Russians and Ukrainians,' 12 July. http://en.kremlin.ru/events/president/news/66181

Report. (2021). 'Rezolutsiia siektsii 'O russkoi natsii,' 1993. Otchet o dieiatielnosti fonda 'Russkij mir' v 2020 godu. https://vrns.ru/documents/rezolyutsiya-sektsii-o-russkoy-natsii/

Resolution. (1993). 'Riezolutsia tiematicheskoi gruppy "Russkaia kultura, vospitaniie i obrazovaniie"', https://vrns.ru/documents/stenogramma-i-vsemirnogo-russkogo-narodnogo-sobora/

Resolution. (2022). 'Nakaz XXIV Vsiemirnogo Russkogo Narodnogo Sobora.' https://vrns.ru/documents/nakaz-xxiv-vsemirnogo-russkogo-narodnogo-sobora/

Russkij mir. (2010). 'Smysly i tsiennosti Russkogo mira' In: Viacheslav Nikonov (ed.), *Sbornik stattiei i materialov kruglykh stolov, organizovannykh fondom 'Russkij mir*. Moskva: Fond Russkiy Mir. https://russkiymir.ru/events/docs/Смыслы%20и%20ценности%20Русского%20мира%202010.pdf

Sektsiia. (1993) 'Siektsiia 'Rossiia v sovriemeinnom mirie.' https://vrns.ru/documents/stenogramma-i-vsemirnogo-russkogo-narodnogo-sobora/

Sektsiia. (2007). 'Siektsiia 'Pravoslaviie-stierzhen sovmiestnogo bytiia narodom Rossii i vostochnykh slavian. Vzaimodieistviie religii i etnosov – usloviie sushchestvovaniia i protsvietaniia russkoi tsivilizatsii.' https://vrns.ru/documents/sektsiya-pravoslavie-sterzhen-sovmestnogo-bytiya-narodov-rossii-i-vostochnykh-slavyan-vzaimodeystvie/

Stenographic Record. (1993). 'Stienogramma i Vsiemirnogo Russkogo Narodnogo Sobora.' https://vrns.ru/documents/stenogramma-i-vsemirnogo-russkogo-narodnogo-sobora/

Stenographic Record. (1995). 'Stienogramma III VRNS.' https://vrns.ru/documents/stenogramma-iii-vrns/

Stenographic Record. (1999). 'Stienogramma pervogo dnia zasiedaniia V VRNS, Rossiia nakanunie 2000-letiia Khristianstva. Viera. Narod. Vlast.' https://vrns.ru/documents/stenogramma-pervogo-dnya-zasedaniya-v-vrns-rossiya-nakanune-2000-letiya-khristianstva-vera-narod-vla/

Stoeckl, K. (2022). 'Russia's Spiritual Security Doctrine as a Challenge to European Comprehensive Security Approaches,' *The Review of Faith & International Affairs*, 20 (4): 37–44.

Tolochko, P. (2018). 'Akadiemik NAN Ukrainy P. P. Tolochko: Bieznravstvienno otkazatsia ot nashiei obshiei istorii.' https://vrns.ru/documents/akademik-nan-ukrainy-p-p-tolochko-beznravstvenno-otkazyvatsya-ot-nashey-obshchey-istorii/

Tolz, V. (2001). *Inventing the Nation. Russia*. London: Arnold and Hodder.

Ukrayina-2013. (2013). 'Derzhavno-konfesiini vidnosyny,' Razumkov Centre, *Natsionalna Bezpeka i Oborona*, 138 (1): 3–14. https://razumkov.org.ua/uploads/journal/ukr/NSD138_2013_ukr.pdf

Veres, K. G. and Palotai, M. (2024). 'Russia: Orthodox by Culture, Imperialist by Nature', *Providence Magazine*, 23 January. https://providencemag.com/2024/01/russia-orthodox-by-culture-imperialist-by-nature/

Wołowski, P. (2010). 'Patriarch Kirill in Ukraine – the Servant of God in the Service of Politics.' www.osw.waw.pl/en/publikacje/analyses/2010-08-04/patriarch-kirill-ukraine-servant-god-service-politics

Wawrzonek, M. (2014). 'Ukraine in the 'Gray Zone': Between the 'Russkiy Mir' and Europe,' *East European Politics and Societies and Cultures*, 28 (4): 758–780.

Wawrzonek, M. (2024). 'The Concept of the Russkiy Mir: The Ideological Foundation of Ruscism' In: Y. Avvakumov and O. Turiy (eds.), *The Churches and the War. Religion, Religious Diplomacy, and Russia's Aggression against Ukraine*. Lviv: Ukrainian Catholic University Press: 35–57.

Zarycki, T. (2010). 'Podmiotowość w sferze symbolicznej' In: J. Szomburg (ed.), *Jaka podmiotowość Polski w XXI wieku?* Gdańsk: Instytut Badań nad Gospodarką Rynkową: 55–63.

3

Russian Orthodox Church and Ukraine

The Russian Orthodox Church has been an ally of Putin's imperial nationalism throughout most of his quarter of a century of ruling Russia. This alliance became especially prominent after Kirill was 'elected' patriarch of the Russian Orthodox Church in 2009, during two invasions of Ukraine in 2014 and 2022 and during the crisis over the loss of canonical control over Ukraine and autocephaly for the Orthodox Church of Ukraine (OCU) in 2018–2019. In its embracing of war, the Russian Orthodox Church is fuelled by nationalism, a heresy of ethnophyletism condemned by the Ecumenical Patriarch in 1872 (Ash, 2024, p. 293). Kirill's support for Russia's war against Ukraine 'puts him close to jihadist preachers of hate' (Schneider-Deters, 2024, p. 149).

This chapter consists of four sections. The first describes the origins of the Russian Orthodox Church and the Moscow Patriarchate in their contemporary institutional form. The second analyses the mythical and real size of the Russian Orthodox Church. The third analyses the way in which Russian Orthodox Church structures operated during critical junctures in Ukrainian social and political life, such as the Sovietisation of Western Ukraine after 1945, the disintegration of the USSR and the emergence of an independent Ukrainian state; the consolidation of a pluralistic model of society which manifested itself in events such as John Paul II's pilgrimage to Ukraine in 2001, Orange Revolution, Euromaidan Revolution and Russian military aggression after 2014. The fourth describes the phenomenon of 'confessional diplomacy' as a specific dimension of Russian Orthodox Church activity.

The Emergence of the Moscow Patriarchate

The patriarchate in Moscow was formally established in 1587. However, during the reign of Peter I, the patriarchate was replaced by a collegial body – the Most Holy Synod. Formally, the institution of the Moscow Patriarch as the single head of the Russian Orthodox Church was restored in 1917. This was one of the key decisions made by the Russian Orthodox Church Council of Moscow (Destivelle, 2006). The convening and deliberations of this Council could have become the beginning of the spiritual and institutional rebirth of the Russian Orthodox Church. However, this did not happen, because the Bolshevik revolution began at the same time. From its outbreak until the Nazi invasion in 1941, the Soviet state eliminated religion and destroyed the Russian Orthodox Church. According to data collected by Anna Dickinson 'by 1940 97.6 per cent of the churches open in 1916 were closed' in Russia. (Dickinson, 2000b, p. 330). Moreover, in 1939 the number of Russian Orthodox Church clergy was less than 10 per cent of its pre-revolutionary figure (Dickinson, 2000b, p. 332). Only four hierarchs remained alive.

In 1927, Metropolitan Sergius (Stargoroskii), who performed the duties of the Moscow Patriarch as locum tenens, sent a message to the faithful in which he stated that the route to a normalisation of relations between the Russian Orthodox Church and the state in the USSR was blocked by some of the clergy's anti-Soviet sentiments. Moreover, he stated that belonging to Christianity does not preclude acceptance of the Soviet Union as 'his civil country, whose joys and successes are our joys and successes, and failures – our failures'. The Soviet system should be accepted as a fact, a manifestation of the Divine Will, opposing it would be unwise. Sergius invited all those who shared this view to cooperate (Pospielovskii, 1995, p. 117). As noted by Alexander Mazyrin, 'On behalf of the Patriarchal Synod, complete political solidarity with the Soviet regime was expressed. The enemies of the Soviet regime were declared enemies of the Church. (…) This, in fact, meant a rejection of the principle of church apoliticality, which had previously been carried out by the leadership of the Patriarchal Church'. Sergius' declaration sparked conflict within the Russian Orthodox Church and determined the way of understanding the relationship between the hierarchy of the Orthodox Church and the state.

Dmitry Pospielovskii states that Sergius had no choice. Pospielovskii asserts, that at least metropolitan Sergius was able to save the 'core of the higher administration of the Orthodox Church' (Pospielovskii, 1995, p. 118). It should be added, however, that this survival strategy did not protect the Russian Orthodox Church clergy and faithful from further repression. Moreover, it meant acceptance of a state of permanent humiliation. The Sergius Declaration of 1927 would become a constitution for relations between the Russian Orthodox Church and the Soviet state in the following decades and determine the internal rules according to which the Russian Orthodox Church would function. Ultimately, they would become structured in 1943, when Stalin 'unfroze' the institution of patriarchy.

In September 1943, the four Russian Orthodox Church bishops who remained were summoned to the Kremlin for a meeting with Stalin, Molotov, and former NKVD officer Georgii Karpov, who became the first chairman of the Council for the Affairs of the Russian Orthodox Church. Orthodox bishops learnt about the conditions upon which the Russian Orthodox Church's future cooperation with the Soviet state was to be based. When the institution of patriarchy was restored in 1917, the head of the Russian Orthodox Church was titled Patriarch of Moscow and all Russia (*Patriarkh Moskovskii i vseia Rossii*). During the meeting, Metropolitan Sergii proposed to change the title to Patriarch of Moscow and all Rus (*Patriarkh Moskovskii i vsieia Rusi*), to which Stalin agreed. Under the new Russian Orthodox Church, 'Russia' referred only to part of the territory over which the Moscow Patriarch originally had jurisdiction. However, 'the word Rus recalled the Kyiv era, when the ancestors of the Great Russians (Russians), Little Russians (Ukrainians) and White Russians (Belarusians) – three Orthodox nations, constituted one Russian nation' (Tsypin, 2012, p. 462). The meeting with the metropolitans was part of the Soviet institutional preparations that would facilitate regaining control over the 'recovered" territories of Western Ukraine, and 'It combined a return to official "top-down" cultural policy with a recognition of the power and potential usefulness of the Russian Orthodox Church' (Dickinson, 2000a, p. 338). Henceforth, the election of the Moscow Patriarch depended on the consent of the Bolshevik authorities, and Sergius unsuccessfully waited for this consent for eighteen years. The year 1943 was a 'historic moment' in the history of the Russian Orthodox Church (Tsypin, 2012, p. 464). However, the 'rebirth' of the Russian Orthodox Church was not a return to the pre-revolutionary era but the establishment of a new institution.

The Size of the Russian Orthodox Church: Myths and Realities

The Russian Orthodox Church claims to be the largest Orthodox Church in the world, and the Moscow Patriarchate aspires to play the role of the contemporary centre of Eastern Christianity based on the number of parishes and symbolic capital (a place of worship that is particularly important from the historical, spiritual, and cultural point of view). The importance of the Russian Orthodox Church is based primarily on statistical data; however, as Paul Goble (2024) noted these statistics, 'focus on structures rather than identification and church attendance and, therefore, are misleading. They overstate the size of the Russian church'. The size of the Russian Orthodox Church declined after the OCU received autocephaly in 2019; 40 per cent of Russian Orthodox Church parishes were in Ukraine.

Patriarch Kirill reported in 2015 that the number of 'actual parishes' was 35,496.[1] Some of the parishes were virtual while many were mere 'temples and other rooms where liturgy is celebrated'.[2] These numbers include Russian Orthodox Church parishes in the Russian Federation and outside, including in Ukraine. There were 14,960 Russian Orthodox Church parishes in the Russian Federation in 2015;[3] at the same time, in Ukraine, the Ukrainian Orthodox Church ([UOC] coming under the jurisdiction of the Russian Orthodox Church)[4] had 12,241 parishes.[5] In 2019, on the eve of Ukrainian autocephaly, the Russian Orthodox Church had 17,231 parishes in the Russian Federation[6] and 12,437 in Ukraine.[7] These figures showed how Ukraine, a country with a third of Russia's population, was more religious than Russia and whose territory accounted for a large proportion of Russian Orthodox Church parishes.

In addition, in the historical, cultural, and spiritual dimensions, Ukraine is of fundamental importance. Patriarch Kirill and President Putin have repeatedly stated 'Kyiv is the mother of Rus' towns', 'Kyivan cradle', and 'baptism in the Dnipro River'. The myth of Kyivan Rus as the birthplace of the *triune* (tripartite) pan-Russian people is a permanent facet of the discourse of the Pan-Russian World (*Russkij mir*). There are sanctuaries and places in Ukraine that are of fundamental importance for the Eastern

---

[1] 'Doklad Patriarkha Moskovskogo i vseia Rusi Kirilla na Arkhiiereiskomu soveshchanii.' www.patriarchia.ru/db/text/3979067

[2] 'Doklad Sviatieishego Patriarkha Moskovskogo i vseia Rusi Kirilla na Arkhiiereiskomu Soborie Russkoi Pravoslavnoi Tserkvi 2 fievralia 2016 goda.' www.patriarchia.ru/db/text/4366063.html

[3] 'Chislo religioznykh organizatsii zaregistrirovannykh v Rjssiiskoi Fiederatsii na 1 ianvaria 2015 g.' https://rosstat.gov.ru/bgd/regl/b15_11/IssWWW.exe/Stg/d01/11-03.htm

[4] In this chapter, the Ukrainian Orthodox Church (UOC), 'Russian Orthodox Church structures in Ukraine' and 'structures of the Moscow Patriarchate in Ukraine' are used synonymously.

[5] 'Relihiini orhanizatsii v Ukraiini (stanom na 1 sichnia 2015 r.).' https://risu.ua/religiyni-organizaciji-v-ukrajini-stanom-na-1-sichnya-2015-r_n74529

[6] 'Chislo religioznykh organizatsii zaregistrirovannykh v Rossiiskoi Fiederatsii na koniets 2018 g.' https://rosstat.gov.ru/storage/mediabank/02-11.docx

[7] 'Relihiini orhanizatsii v Ukraiini (stanom na 1 sichnia 2019 r.).' www.risu.ua/religiyni-organizaciji-v-ukrajini-stanom-na-1-sichnya-2019-r_n97463

European Orthodox tradition, such as the Kyiv-Pechersk Monastery and Pochayv Monastery.

In 2018–2019, the Patriarch of Constantinople Bartholomew I removed Ukraine from under Russian Orthodox Church's usurped canonical control, took the Metropolis of Kyiv under his jurisdiction, and issued a *Tomos* granting the OCU autocephaly. These developments caused an earthquake in the Kremlin because they undermined the concept of a *triune* pan-Russian people (*obshcherusskij narod*); after all, a Pan-Russian World is impossible without Kyiv and Ukraine. After Russia's full-scale invasion of Ukraine, the status of the Russian Orthodox Church in Ukraine became particularly important.

Structures of Russian Orthodox Church in Ukraine

Russian Orthodox Church and Ukraine in the USSR

Alexei I was formally elected Patriarch of Moscow in early 1945. At that time, all Western Ukraine was occupied by Soviet troops. The process of Sovietisation of the newly incorporated areas of Soviet Ukraine, which were within the borders of Poland before the Second World War, would begin. In the case of Galicia, one of the key elements of this process would be the liquidation of the Ukrainian Greek Catholic Church (UGCC) using the revived Russian Orthodox Church. The UGCC was to 'self-dissolve' and its clergy were to 'return' to unity with the Russian Orthodox Church. An 'initiative group' was established inside the UGCC, headed by Greek Catholic priest Havryil Kostelnyk, who was to carry out the work of 'unification' under the inspiration and strict supervision of the NKVD.

On 3 October 1945, Kostelnyk prepared a report for Patriarch Alexei I on the progress in preparations for the planned 'unification', stating to date, over 800 priests have joined the 'initiative group' and predicted the rest of the clergy would join in the coming months (Likvidatsiia, 2006b, p. 286). However, later in his report, Kostelnyk 'honestly' confessed that only a few had joined out of their own conviction. The leader of the 'initiative group' admitted that 'if there were no pressure from the state, in the current conditions there would probably not be even 50 clergy who would be willing to destroy the Greek Catholic Church in order to transform it into an Orthodox one' (Likvidatsiia, 2006b, p. 287). 'Most of our priests' Kostelnyk concluded, 'do not believe in a better future for the Church in the Soviet Union' (Likvidatsiia, 2006b, p. 287).

A few weeks later, in early December 1945, Patriarch Alexei I raised the issue of 'unification of Uniate's with the Orthodox Church' in a letter to the chairman of the Council for the Affairs of the Russian Orthodox Church Karpov. Citing Kostelnyk's report, he assured him that 'the matter of unification is moving forward' and it is expected that by the end of the year the remaining clergy will join the 'initiative group' 'except for a small number of reluctant ones' (Pisma 2009, p. 92). The NKVD developed extensive operational activities among the Greek Catholic clergy, and the Soviet authorities were aware of their moods. Moreover, since August 1945, the NKVD had taken under their surveillance the members of the 'initiative group' and Kostelnyk himself (Likvidatsiia, 2006, p. 26).

The Russian Orthodox Church assumed that the population in areas annexed by the USSR would voluntarily accept the Soviet order, as had the Russian Orthodox Church. Over the next few decades, the official narrative about the alleged self-dissolution of the UGCC and 'return' of its clergy to the Russian Orthodox Church would become a founding myth to legitimise Soviet power in Galicia. The Russian Orthodox Church took control of the UGCC network of parishes with their material and human resources. In 1950, in Galicia, the Russian Orthodox Church controlled 2,594 former UGCC parishes, or approximately 18 per cent of registered Russian Orthodox Church parishes (Lahodych 2012, p. 131). Of the 14,477 Russian Orthodox Church parishes in the USSR, as many as 9,383 were in Ukraine with a high proportion in the western *oblasts* (Lahodych, 2012, p. 131). In mid 1985, approximately two-thirds of Russian Orthodox Church parishes were in Ukraine.[8] The Russian Orthodox Church was reliant on the high number of parishes it controlled in Ukraine to claim its power and influence in the Orthodox world.

The UGCC ceased to exist only formally. It was deregistered and banned, but some of the faithful and clergy went 'underground' and created the 'catacomb church'. Those who functioned within Russian Orthodox Church parishes 'reunited' but remained loyal to the UGCC. Nataliia Shlikhta wrote, 'converted Greek Catholics constructed a lived identity that allowed them to preserve their religious and national distinctiveness and thus form a certain "community of the formally converted."' They existed in two worlds, the UGCC and imposed Russian Orthodox Church. They were 'Russian Orthodox Church' who signed reunification pledges, but also at the same time underground UGCC (Shlikhta, 2004, p. 268).

Local officials from the Council for the Affairs of the Russian Orthodox Church (later the Council for Religious Affairs) 'clearly distinguished

---

[8] Viktor Yelenskyi, 'Religiia i pieriestroika v Ukrainie.' www.religare.ru/2_7596.html

between proper "Orthodox" and those who had "reunited" with Orthodoxy' (Shlikhta, 2004, p. 268). The Russian Orthodox Church hierarchy may have realised that the conversion of Greek Catholics to the Russian Orthodox Church was only superficial. However, as Shlikhta noted, the distinction between 'proper' and 'reunited' Russian Orthodox Church was only used within the Soviet power apparatus, while outside the official narrative it was described as the historic return of Uniates to unity with the Russian Orthodox Church. Maintaining this myth was existential to the Moscow Patriarchate and they clung to it until the end of the USSR.

Its highest representative, and at the same time one of the most important hierarchs in the Russian Orthodox Church, Metropolitan Filaret (Denysenko) of Kyiv and Halych, claimed in an interview as late as June 1989: 'As you know, at the Church Council held in Lviv in March 1946, a decision was made on the self-liquidation of the Greek Catholic (Uniate) Church in Ukraine and its return to the bosom of Russian Orthodoxy'.[9] Metropolitan Filaret also emphasised that the 1946 council was 'fully canonical' and enjoyed universal support among the clergy and faithful.[10]

However, by 1989, the strategy developed over the previous decades, which had created a façade of reality using Stalinist rhetoric, stopped working because Soviet repressive organs, which were key to supporting Russian Orthodox Church control over Ukrainian religious life, was ineffectual. At the beginning of 1985, the leading activist of the 'Catacomb Church', Yosyp Terelia, was sentenced to seven years in prison for publicly publicising the persecuted Greek Catholic Church,[11] only four years before the legalisation of the UGCC. In December 1989, Soviet leader Mikhail Gorbachev, after visiting the Vatican and meeting with Pope John Paul II, agreed to the UGCC's exit 'from the catacombs'.

As Jane Ellis (1990, p. 316) wrote: 'Orthodox hierarchs reacted to the legalisation of the Ukrainian Greek Catholic Church with statements in December 1989 and January 1990 which suggested something close to panic', a state of mind which resembled their reaction to Ukrainian Orthodox receiving autocephaly nearly three decades later. Legalisation of the UGCC, and Ukrainian Autocephalous Orthodox Church, spelled disaster for the Russian Orthodox Church in Galicia.

---

[9] 'Interviu z mytropolytom Filaretom (1989).' https://risu.ua/interv-yu-z-mitropolitom-filaretom-1989_n35526
[10] Ibid.
[11] Op cit., Viktor Yelenskyi, 'Religiia…'

The Russian Orthodox Church tried to fight back but were swimming against the tide. Metropolitan Filaret (Denysenko) appealed to the Communist Ukrainian authorities using discourse in place since the late 1940s: 'Throughout the entire period, we stood on patriotic positions, always did everything for the benefit of our Fatherland, did everything to bring benefit in the most difficult moments (...) It seems that we served faithfully, and for the fact that we served faithfully, we now turned out to be unnecessary. Catholics of the Eastern Rite are becoming more needed'.[12] This discourse reflected Russian Orthodox Church hierarchs having become slaves of the Stalinist narrative they had been repeating for nearly five decades. Instead of searching for a compromise, they tried to adapt reality once again to the image that was encoded in this narrative. It had been the Soviet apparatus of coercion and repression which had allowed the Russian Orthodox Church to control religious life in Ukraine. The Moscow Patriarchate attempted to save their control over religious life in Ukraine by creating the UOC.

The Russian Orthodox Church and Independent Ukraine

In June 1990, during the Russian Orthodox Church bishops' council, elections were held for a new head of the Russian Orthodox Church to replace Patriarch Pimen (Izviekov). One of the contenders was Metropolitan Filaret (Denysenko), but his candidacy was defeated, and Alexei II (Ridiger) became the new patriarch. A little over a year later, in August 1991, the Ukrainian parliament adopted a Declaration of Independence. At the beginning of November, the UOC synod, chaired by Metropolitan Filaret, requested autonomy from the Moscow Patriarchate.

There were two main drivers of this decision. Firstly, the personal ambitions of Filaret who failed to become Russian Orthodox Church Patriarch. Secondly, Ukraine's independence; President Leonid Kravchuk supported independence for Ukrainian Orthodox (Kuzio, 1997, p. 395). Filaret said the UOC should be adjusted to 'the status of the state'.[13] In other words, from the perspective of the Metropolitan of Kyiv, in 1991 a potential new patron – independent Ukraine. The Moscow Patriarchate removed Filaret from his position in April 1992, and he finally left the

---

[12] 'Stenohrama zustrichi Kosmy arkhyiereiiv RPTs z holovoiu VR SRSR A. Lukianovym z pytan peredilennia tserkovnoii vlscnosti v Halychyni.' www.risu.ua/stenograma-zustrichi-vosmi-arhiyerejiv-rpc-z-golovoyu-vr-srsr-a-luk-yanovim-z-pitan-peredilennya-cerkovnoji-vlasnosti-v-galichini_n33951

[13] 'Patriarkh Filaret (Denysenko). Vospominaniia o 1990-1992 godakh.' http://religion.in.ua/

Russian Orthodox Church. Practically all Russian Orthodox Church bishops who had been under his jurisdiction declined to support Filaret, replacing him as Metropolitan with Volodymyr (Sabodan).

Filaret lost his position in the hierarchy of the Russian Orthodox Church, but he gained new patronage by becoming part of the elites of the newly established Ukrainian state. Although this was not powerful enough to defeat competition from the Moscow Patriarchate, Kravchuk and the new Ukrainian state's apparatus supported the creation of an Orthodox Church independent from the Moscow Patriarchate. The process of institutionalising the idea of Ukrainian autocephaly was very complicated and full of dramatic twists, especially in 1990s (Wawrzonek, 2014, pp. 159–164; Kuzio, 1997).

In March 1992, the Russian Orthodox Church and President Yeltsin's advisor Sergei Stankevich, laid out its conception of the territory of the former USSR as an exclusive Russian sphere of influence (Nizioł, 2004, p. 159). By the end of that year, the term 'Near Abroad' entered the official dictionary of Russian diplomacy as the way to differentiate former Soviet republics from the 'Far Abroad' (Curanović, 2012, 133) Alicja Curanović (2012, p. 134) points out the interconnection between Kremlin's 'Near Abroad' and Russian Orthodox Church's 'canonical territory', both of which aimed to maintain 'the post-Soviet space within the Russian sphere of influence' (Curanović, 2012, p. 134). Russian Orthodox Church clergy in Ukraine attending the 'Kharkiv Council' could count on support from Moscow from both the Kremlin and the Russian Orthodox Church. In May 1993, the World Russian National Council stated that 'in the new countries, privileged support from Russia' will be enjoyed by 'these forces which see their future together with Russia'.[14]

Two Models for Orthodoxy Identity in Ukraine: Pan-Russian and Ukrainian

As Myroslaw Tataryn (2001, p. 155) aptly noted, even though Russia and Ukraine 'have shared much common historical, political and religious experience over the past 300 years' in the late 1990s both countries developed 'two models of religious liberty and two models for orthodoxy'.

---

[14] 'Obrashcheniie i Vsiemirnogo Russkogo Sobora "O ponimanii natsionalnykh intiereiesov Rossii i russkogo naroda".' https://vrns.ru/documents/obrashchenie-i-vsemirnogo-russkogo-sobora-o-ponimanii-natsionalnykh-interesov-rossii-i-russkogo-naro/

Throughout this book we have defined these competing identities as pan-Russian and Ukrainian distinct from Russian. They differed in their understanding of the relationship between the state and religious institutions. The Russian Orthodox Church in Russia achieved a privileged position over other religions in Russia. Moreover, as Svetlana Filonova stated in early 1997, 'the fact that Orthodoxy as a religious teaching has become host to politicians and that xenophobia and nationalism are gathering strength under the cover of Orthodoxy is only half the trouble. The real problem is that an imperial ideology cloaked in priestly vestments has acquired the status of inviolability and become an ideology without an opposition or opponents (Tataryn, 2001, p. 157). In contrast, 'the Ukrainian situation, unlike that of Russia, was from its outset characterised by pluralism' (Tataryn, 2001, p. 161).

John Paul II's pilgrimage to Ukraine in 2001 was an example of religious pluralism in Ukraine (Yelenskyi, 2001). The Moscow Patriarchate was loudly, aggressively, and hysterically against the papal pilgrimage (Yelenskyi, 2001, pp. 26–27). The Kremlin also treated the Pope's visit to Ukraine as a political provocation (Yelenskyi, 2001, p. 28).

Patriarch Alexei II stated the Catholic Church 'should take into account the position of Orthodox believers in Ukraine', who represent the majority of the country's inhabitants, and 'cancel the visit'. Thus, Alexei II claimed to speak on behalf of Ukrainians; in fact, most Ukrainians were positive about the Pope's visit, and opponents were a small minority (Stricker, 2001, p. 219). The UOC boycotted the Pope's visit to Ukraine. The Russian Orthodox Church and its Ukrainian branch, UOC, assumed it possessed a monopoly on deciding who is Orthodox and who is not (the privilege of canonicity), organisation of exclusive spheres of influence (canonical territory) and privileged relations with the structures of state power (patronage in exchange for legitimisation).

John Paul II celebrated mass in Lviv attended by 1.5 million believers, which was by far the largest public gathering in the history of Ukraine. A few days earlier the Pope celebrated a similar mass at Chaika airport in Kyiv attended by 50,000 believers.[15] Although it was not an impressive result for such an important and symbolic event with the participation of John Paul II, it is worth paying attention to one important detail: no members of the Russian Orthodox Church hierarchy had ever gathered

---

[15] 'Pilgrimage of John Paul II to Ukraine – 2001. Dimensions of Unit.' https://jp2online.pl/en/publication/oficijnij-vizit-ivana-pavla-ii-v-ukrayinu-2001-r-proyavi-yednosti;UHVibGljYXRpb246MTEy

so many believers in Kyiv nor in any other place in Ukraine. This example shows very clearly that the number of officially registered Russian Orthodox Church parishes says little about the actual influence of a given church or a spiritual leader in Ukraine.

Andrii Yurash identified this phenomenon while analysing events related to the Orange Revolution. Yurash noted that 'when we look at the map of Ukraine after the 2004 presidential elections, we can see that the UOC is the largest Church in fourteen of the seventeen regions where Yushchenko won, with the exception being the three Galician *oblasts*' (Yurash, 2005, p. 382). Both the Moscow Patriarchate and the UOC were very actively involved in the promotion of Yushchenko's opponent – Yanukovych – through the blessing given to Yanukovych by Metropolitan Volodymyr (Sabodan) of Kyiv, or their journey together to Mount Athos and the Holy Land (Yurash, 2005, p. 375). Even on 9 November 2004, after serious allegations were raised about election fraud in the first round of voting, Metropolitan Volodymyr stressed in an interview that from among all the candidates, he only blessed Yanukovych who, in the eyes of the UOC, was 'an Orthodox president', 'God's candidate' or he 'deserves the attention of God and men'.[16]

On the day before the second round of voting, Yanukovych and his 'family circle' visited the Kyiv-Pochayv Lavra to 'talk to the people and pray that everything would turn out well in the country'.[17] At the end of the campaign, before a repeat of the second round on St. Nicholas day, Yanukovych visited another important monastery – the Assumption of the Blessed Virgin Mary in Svyatohorsk in Donetsk *oblast*. He assured journalists that on St. Nicholas' day, he 'traditionally goes to Church with his family'. He revealed that he prayed for 'peace, justice, order and the rebirth of Ukraine' and that 'the elections be carried out fairly and transparently'.[18] Throughout the campaign, Yanukovych appeared to be the only legitimate candidate and defender of the only true and 'canonical' Orthodox Church in Ukraine, which he made clear during a televised debate on 15 November 2004.

---

[16] Oleh Turii, 'Tserkva i vybory: uroky 2004 roku.' https://risu.ua/cerkva-i-vibori-uroki-2004-roku_n34283

[17] 'Pieried vyborami Viktor Yanukovich posietit Kiievo-Pecherskuiu Lavru.' http://pravoslavye.org.ua/2004/11/19112004_kiev_pered_viborami_viktor_yanukovich_posetit_kievo-pecherskuyu_lavru/

[18] 'V dien cviatogo Nicolaia Viktor Yanukovich posietil Cviato-Uspiensku Cviatohorskuiu lavru.' http://pravoslavye.org.ua/2004/12/20122004_svyatogorsk_v_den_svyatogo_nikolaya_viktor_yanukovich_posetil_svyato-uspenskuyu_svyatogorskuyu_lavru/

Yanukovych was supported by the Russian Orthodox Church and UOC because he and the Party of Regions, and their Communist Party of Ukraine ally, upheld a pan-Russian identity. Transcripts of the proceedings of the Council of Archbishops of the Russian Orthodox Church, which took place between 3 and 8 October 2004, includes an interesting record of the meeting where Metropolitan Volodymyr (Sabodan) thanked Putin for 'financial assistance' for 'the city-centre's of the diocese which the schismatics took over and now hold the Cathedral in their hands'.[19] In response, President Putin stressed: 'He cannot and does not have the right to participate in solving some of the problems of the Ukrainian Orthodox Church'. President Kuchma and he have established 'concrete steps to support the different objects of the Russian Orthodox Church in Ukraine'. Putin invited to his official birthday event Kuchma and Yanukovych 'under such informal circumstances' to discuss concrete support for the Russian Orthodox Church in Ukraine.[20]

Patriarch Alexei II expressed the belief 'most citizens' wanted 'to deepen brotherly mutual ties with Russia' and that the political crisis related to the Orange Revolution would be resolved without the participation of 'destructive external forces'.[21] Whereas Metropolitan Volodymyr said the UOC would not legitimise power gained through bloodshed. On 30 November 2004, the UOC Holy Synod declared that 'for the Orthodox Church, there is not just orange or white-blue, but all are our brothers and sisters in Christ'.[22] The Orange Revolution opened up divisions in the Russian Orthodox Church in Ukraine between two models for Orthodoxy – Ukrainian 'pluralistic' and civic on the one hand, and pan-Russian 'exclusivist' and anti-Western on the other.

Even before the Orange Revolution within the UOC, religious-political groups associating themselves with the Russian Orthodox Church, and with the fundamentalist and anti-hierarchical tendency within it,

---

[19] 'Dokumenty Arkhyiereiskoho Soboru 2004 r. Rosiiskoii Pravoslavnoii Tserkvy shchodo Ukraiiny.' https://risu.ua/dokumenti-arhiyereyskogo-soboru-2004-r-rosiyskoji-pravoslavnoji-cerkvi-shchodo-ukrajini_n35539

[20] Ibid.

[21] 'Patriarkh Aleksii II napravil tieliegrammu so slovami poddierzhki Prezidentu Ukrainy Leonidu Kuchmie.' http://pravoslavye.org.ua/2004/11/25112004_moskva_patriarh_aleksiy_ii_napravil_telegrammu_so_slovami_podderzhki_prezidentu_ukraini_leonidu_kuchme/

[22] 'Vid imeni Sviashchennoho Synodu Ukraiinskoii Pravoslavnoii Tserkvy Blazhennishyi Mytropolyt Volodymyr zvernuvsia do narodu Ukraiiny.' http://pravoslavye.org.ua/2004/11/30112004_kiyiv_vd_men_svyashchennogo_sinodu_ukrainskoi_pravoslavnoi_tserkvi_blazhenniishiy_mitropolit_volodimir_zvernuvsya_do_narodu_ukraini/

appeared. Over time, this phenomenon began to be identified in Ukraine as 'political orthodoxy'. Its representatives condemned the wing of the episcopate that was inclined towards the Ukrainian pluralistic and civic model for Orthodoxy. Nikolay Mitrokhin wrote that 'political Orthodoxy' was 'secretly or openly supported by dozens of bishops and numerous priests as well as by active laymen and laywomen' who believed that 'the episcopate has "sold out"' the Church to the secular leadership in the post-Soviet states and to the 'satanic' Western powers that stand behind them' (Mitrokhin, 2010, p. 241). Conflict between the pan-Russian exclusivist and Ukrainian pluralistic models for Orthodoxy within UOC intensified after the Orange Revolution and from 2007, exclusivist circles would espouse the Pan-Russian World ideology.

During and after the Orange Revolution part of the UOC began steps to provide the UOC with real 'independence'. This was never about questioning the UOC's canonical subordination to the Moscow Patriarchate. However, within the UOC, there were attempts to find a place for an 'independent' Ukrainian, Kyiv variety of Orthodox identity. Metropolitan Volodymyr (Sabodan) highlighted three factors. Firstly, specific organisational culture of the Kyiv metropolis, which was formed when it was subordinated to the Patriarchate of Constantinople. The Kyiv metropolis under the jurisdiction of the Patriarchate of Constantinople was organisationally self-sufficient.[23] Secondly, cultural pluralism and openness to interactions with Western cultural circles. Thirdly, Ukraine's integration into the EU.

Volodymyr (Sabodan) believed in 1990 the Kyiv metropolis regained its former, 'natural' place and status in terms of its place in the hierarchy of Orthodox church structures. Metropolitan Volodymyr carefully formulated the UOC as achieving 'independence' without formalisation in the form of autocephaly. The Moscow Patriarchate also referred to centuries-old symbolic capital, but its organisational culture and 'mission' was formulated in 1943 and completely shaped during the Soviet era. Therefore, although Volodymyr (Sabodan) and the Russian Orthodox Church leadership used the same concepts as 'sobornost', 'unity', and 'independence' they understood them completely differently. For the UOC they expanded the scope of the 'organisational independence' while for the Russian Orthodox Church they were intended to ensure the preservation

---

[23] 'K 20-letiiu Blagocloviennoi Gramoty Sviatieishego Patriarcha Moskovskogo i vsieia Rusi Alieksieia II o darovanii Ukrainskoi Pravoslavnoi Tserkvi samostoiatielnosti v upravlienii.' www.patriarchia.ru/db/text/1302845.html

of the existing centralised and vertical structure which had been shaped in the Stalinist era. The UOC and the Russian Orthodox Church Abroad (ROCA) had the same status within the Russian Orthodox Church. However, in the case of the UOC a 'self-governing Church' would lead to its organisational independence, while ROCA received this status because of its unification with the Russian Orthodox Church in 2007.

In June 2008, at the Russian Orthodox Church Archbishop's Council in Moscow, Metropolitan Volodymyr (Sabodan) said the key determinant in Ukraine of the UOC's existence is diversity. The spiritual identity of left-bank Ukraine was determined by 'creative interaction' with Russia, while the cultural landscape of the regions of right bank Ukraine was determined by Ukrainian-Polish, Romanian, Austrian, Hungarian, and Lithuanian relations. Metropolitan Volodymyr (Sabodan) said the two parts of Ukraine are different but at the same time 'inseparable' because they have much in common, above all Christianity, inherited from Kyiv Rus Grand Prince Volodymyr the Great.[24] The UOC should support processes by which antagonisms between the Eastern and Western elements of culture in Ukraine are creatively transformed 'in the synthetic whole based on Orthodox tradition'.[25] Ukrainian lands are a 'self-sufficient social and cultural space', Metropolitan Volodymyr (Sabodan) said.

Metropolitan Volodymyr (Sabodan) publicly formulated his 'European creed' during a lecture he gave in Warsaw in February 2008 when he was awarded the title of 'doctor honoris causa' by the Academy of Christian Theology. He praised the positive results of the process of European integration, which he believed are the source of political stability, and noted that 'the complex distribution of power between national and supranational institutions reduces the temptation to rule as such'. The Metropolitan admitted that perhaps the EU's decision-making process is not as efficient 'as one would wish', but on the other hand, decisions undertaken by them 'are the result of a complex compromise and do not depend on the will of one man, who by nature may be wrong'.[26] He positively assessed the EU as not possessing a 'messianic paradigm of power', which, 'in fact, often turns out to be false messianism'.[27] Metropolitan Volodymyr (Sabodan) indirectly criticised the political

---

[24] 'Ukrainskoie Pravoslaviie na rubiezhie epokh. Vyzovy sovriemennosti, tiendientsii razvitiia.' www.patriarchia.ru/db/text/427267.html
[25] Ibid.
[26] Ibid.
[27] Ibid.

culture of the post-Soviet area that had become sanctified within the Pan-Russian World concept. On 30 September 2013, Metropolitan Volodymyr (Sabodan) signed with representatives of other Ukrainian religious communities an appeal 'on the discussion concerning European values in Ukraine'[28] just prior to the Eastern Partnership summit in Vilnius during which Yanukovych was to sign EU-Ukraine Association Agreement. It stressed the importance of European roots in Ukraine's identity. The appeal stated that 'our social and state life' was formed 'in a relationship with Europe and its spiritual, cultural, educational and legal tradition'.[29] The appeal made it clear that only one option is compatible with Ukraine's 'historical roots;' that is, becoming an independent state 'within the circle of free European nations'.[30] The Kremlin's competing project, promoted through the Pan-Russian World propaganda, claimed Ukraine culturally and in terms of civilisation is part of the Russian Orthodox world. Adding his signature to the appeal Metropolitan Volodymyr (Sabodan) unleashed protests from pro-Russian organisations supporting pan-Russian 'political Orthodoxy'. They held a large religious procession on 4 November 2013 in the centre of Kyiv with Russian imperial flags, icons, and images of the last Russian Tsar Nicholas II.[31] Pan-Russian identity showed its allegiance to both the 'red' Russian Orthodox Church, formed during the Stalin era, and the 'white' Russian Orthodox Church, which was dominated by White Russian émigrés.

Thus, after the Orange Revolution the UOC sought to reform its status within the Moscow Patriarchate which required a re-evaluation of the understanding of the Russian Orthodox Church and its place and role in social life and at least partially agree with a pluralistic model for Orthodoxy. This would not happen, as in December 2008 the Moscow Patriarch changed from Alexei II to Kirill (Gundiaiev). Patriarch Kirill was a supporter of strict centralisation of power, with which he agreed with Putin, and under him Russian Orthodox Church social doctrine rejected the concept of political freedom and civil rights (Pravoslavnaia tserkov, 2012, p. 17). Sergei Filatov, summarising the first two years of Kirill's rule, stated 'The Russian Orthodox Church is in fact the only large and influential

[28] 'Zvernennia Tserkov i relihiinykh orhanizatsii do ukraiinskoho narodu shodo dyskusji pro yevropeiski tsinnosti v Ukraiini.' https://docs.ugcc.ua/1310/
[29] Ibid.
[30] Ibid.
[31] 'Representatives of Political Orthodoxy Hold Procession against EU Association Agreement.' www.risu.ua/en/representatives-of-political-orthodoxy-hold-procession-against-eu-association-agreement_n65644

Christian church in the world that is alien to the principles of democracy and human rights' (Pravoslavnaia tserkov, 2012, p. 17). Kirill transformed the Russian Orthodox Church into 'something like a powerful business corporation or, if you like, a vertical of power, similar to what the secular government in Russia is now' (Pravoslavnaia tserkov, 2012, p. 22).

The organisational culture of the Russian Orthodox Church under Kirill was adapted to its mission in its 'canonical territory' which showed a growing alignment of his pan-Russian imperial nationalistic views with those of Putin that were crystalising from 2007, when the Russian World Foundation was founded and the Russian Orthodox Church was unified, and 2012, when he returned to the presidency with Kirill supporting him as the 'gatherer of Russian lands'. In this message 'the central place is occupied by faith in Russia, in its highest destiny, in its holiness. (…) Regardless of personal faith in God, Kirill and his like-minded people do not preach faith in God, but a neo-Slavophile ideology of national revival, which is essentially secular' (Pravoslavnaia tserkov, 2012, p. 34).

Patriarch Kirill, allied to the Kremlin, immediately began an intense crusade to consolidate Ukraine's ties with the Pan-Russian World civilisation community. As Filatov noted, the geopolitical situation in Ukraine after the Orange Revolution contributed to 'ideological consolidation' of the Russian Orthodox Church and the Kremlin around the ideals of Russian (*Russkaia*) civilisation, and the Russian (*Russkaia*) path of development (Pravoslavnaia tserkov 2012, 20). Russian imperial nationalism upheld an exclusivist model for Orthodoxy and the ideology of a pan-Russian nation of great, little, and white Russians (Russians, Ukrainians, and Belarusians respectively). Defining *Russkaia* civilisation in this manner necessitated Ukraine was defined as the Russian Orthodox Church's canonical territory.

Andrei Okara (Pravoslavnaia tserkov, 2012, pp. 311–312) noted that the 'Ukrainian' question' included several interconnected components:

1. The creation of a local Orthodox Church in Ukraine.
2. The limits given for the autonomy of the UOC within the Moscow Patriarchate.
3. The relationship of the UOC with the Ukrainian state.
4. Relations with other Eastern Christian Ukrainian jurisdictions.
5. The return to Ukraine of the jurisdiction of the Ecumenical (Constantinople) Patriarchate.
6. The annulling of anathemas against Cossack Hetman Ivan Mazepa who, in an alliance with Sweden, led a Ukrainian uprising against Muscovy in 1709.

7. Change in the jurisdiction of Ukrainian Orthodoxy from under Constantinople to Moscow in 1686.
8. The use of the Ukrainian literary language in church life.

A pluralistic model for Orthodoxy, which Metropolitan Volodymyr (Sabodan) moderately supported, could not be reconciled with how the Russian Orthodox Church perceived the UOC's place within the Pan-Russian World. After 2009, Patriarch Kirill undertook a 'pastoral offensive' through repeated visits to Ukraine to demonstrate the leadership of the Moscow Patriarch within 'canonical Orthodoxy' in Ukraine. Kirill's visits provoked increasing calls for the 'organisational independence' of the UOC. In February 2008 in Warsaw, Metropolitan Volodymyr (Sabodan) argued that 'a comparative analysis of the canonical rights of the Ukrainian Church, which today is a self-governing Church within the Moscow Patriarchate, and the canonical rights of the autocephalous Greek Orthodox Church shows that our real rights are even greater than those of the autocephalous Church of Greece'.[32] The UOC 'independently resolves most church issues, and its canonical dependence on the Russian (Orthodox Church) is expressed only in the prayerful commemoration of the Patriarch of Moscow during divine service, as well as in the Patriarchal blessing of the Primate elected by the Council of the UOC'.[33] Kirill ignored these moderate demands and behaved like an arrogant host, not a guest, during his visits, showing he did not consider Ukraine to be a real country, again like Putin. During his first visit Kirill convened the Holy Synod of the Russian Orthodox Church at the Kyiv Pechersk Monastery, where he described Kyiv as 'a capital of southern Russian Orthodoxy',[34] a reflection of his (and the Kremlin's) support for pan-Russian identity. In 2010–2013, Patriarch Kirill visited Ukraine every year on the anniversary of the baptism of Kyivan Rus when he convened meetings of the Holy Synod of the Russian Orthodox Church at the Kyiv-Pechersk Monastery. The UOC should have acted as the host, but in practice Patriarch Kirill treated the Kyiv-Pechersk Monastery as an additional residence.

The monastery area and buildings, including the *Sviato Uspenska* Kyiv-Pechersk Monastery headed by Metropolitan Pavlo (Lebid), were leased by the Ukrainian state to the UOC from the early 1990s; after the full-scale

---

[32] 'Ukraiinska Pravoslavna Tserkva: sohodennia…'
[33] Ibid.
[34] 'V Kiievo-Piecherskoi lavrie prokhodit zasiedaniie Sviashchennogo Sinoda Russkoi Pravoslavnoi Tserkvi.' www.patriarchia.ru/db/text/703863.html

invasion the lease was not renewed in 2023. The UOC used the monastery area as its own property, building new buildings and modifying existing ones, even though the entire area was formally under state protection as an architectural monument.[35] *Sviato Uspenska* Kyiv-Pechersk Monastery, as a corporate entity, received financial support directly from the Kremlin. Metropolitan Pavlo (Lebid) admitted in interviews he received 'large sums' from President Putin for renovation works in the monastery and did not hide the fact he intended to continue to ask for such support from the Kremlin because, as he emphasised, 'our authorities are not in a great hurry to assist the monastery'.[36] This meant that the 'religious organisation' operating in the monastery was under the Kremlin's special protection and there would be periodic clashes with the Ukrainian authorities, especially after 2022.

For three decades of Ukrainian independence, the Kyiv-Pechersk Monastery was allowed to act as a diffuser of Russian imperial nationalism and pan-Russian identity. Control over the Kyiv-Pechersk Monastery, due to its unique symbolic capital, became an important tool for legitimising the Pan-Russian World ideology. This explains why Kirill's pilgrimages to Ukraine always included visits to the Kyiv-Pechersk Monastery which he used to challenge Metropolitan Volodymyr's (Sabodan) assessments about the 'independence' of the UOC. The autonomous status of the UOC was reduced in 2011 when the statute of the Russian Orthodox Church centralised the management of its structures and limited the self-government of 'autonomous Orthodox Churches', bringing them more closely under the 'central bodies' of the Russian Orthodox Church (Pravoslavnaia tserkov, 2012, p. 319).

Kirill and the UOC's opposing views of exclusivism and pluralism respectively increasingly clashed in the run up to Russia's first invasion in 2014. In July 2013, a conference on Pan-Slavic unity was held at the Kyiv-Pechersk Monastery with Putin's and Yanukovych's participation and Viktor Medvedchuk playing a key organisational role behind the scenes. From 2012 to 2013, the Kremlin and its Russian Orthodox Church ally imposed huge pressure on Yanukovych to back away from European integration and turn towards the Pan-Russian World and Eurasia. This

---

[35] 'Yak Moskovskyy patriarkhat pryvatyzovuvav Kyievo-Pechersku lavru.' https://texty .org.ua/articles/108873/yak-moskovskyj-patriarhat-pryvatyzovuvav-kyyevo-pechersku- lavru-vid-radyanskoho-soyuzu-do-yanukovycha/

[36] 'U Kyievo-Pecherskii lavri rozrakhovuiut na metsenatstvo Putina.' https://risu .ua/u-kiyevo-pecherskiy-lavri-rozrahovuyut-na-mecenatstvo-putina_n55135

brought dividends; in November 2013 Yanukovych refused to sign the Association Agreement with the EU sparking the Euromaidan Revolution.

During the Euromaidan Revolution, exclusivist and pluralist models of Orthodoxy were on display. On 1 January 2014 Patriarch Kirill expressed his belief protests would not affect 'our common spiritual unity'.[37] On 22 January 2014, Yanukovych, and his political allies, took part in a prayer service in Kyiv-Pechersk Lavra for the commemoration of the Ukrainian Day of Unity and Freedom (a holiday commemorating the unification of Eastern and Western Ukraine in an independent state in January 1919); on the same day five protestors were killed by snipers. The UOC Superior of Kyiv-Pechersk Lavra, Metropolitan Pavlo (Lebid), compared Yanukovych to Christ carrying the cross to Golgotha and assured the president that the Russian Orthodox Church would stand by his side 'to the very end' (Maidan i Tserkva, 2014, p. 429).

On 1 March 2014, shortly after Russia's annexation of Crimea and a month before Russian-backed armed conflict in Eastern Ukraine, the chairman of the Synodal Department for Church-Society Relations, Vsevolod Chaplin, spoke about 'Russia's peace mission', invoking the 'divided (pan) Russian nation' which has the right to 'reunify into one state body'.[38] Chaplin described the 'mission' of Russian soldiers as to 'defend freedom and independence' when making decisions about this 'unification'.[39] After thousands of civilian and military casualties and two million IDP's (Internally Displaced Persons) and refugees, Patriarch Kirill continued to talk about the 'spiritual unity' of the nations of 'historical Russia' (i.e., encompassing great, little, and white Russians).[40]

In turn, Georgy Kovalenko, a spokesman for the UOC, said 'we survived the years 2004–2005 and we learned certain conclusions [from that period]' (Maidan i Tserkva, 2014, p. 663). In October 2014, Kovalenko said: 'The Moscow Patriarchate was not at the Maidan. The Ukrainian Orthodox Church was at the Maidan. This is because the UOC is the

---

[37] 'Patriarkh Kirill: Yevromaidan nie pokoliebliet dukhovnogo yedinstva Rusi.' https://gazeta.ua/ru/articles/life/_patriarh-kirill-evromajdan-ne-pokoleblet-duhovnogo-edinstva-rusi/534848

[38] 'V Tserkvi vidiat mirotvorcheskoi missiiu Rossii na Ukrainie.' www.interfax-russia.ru/south-and-north-caucasus/main/v-cerkvi-vidyat-mirotvorcheskoy-missiyu-rossii-na-ukraine

[39] Ibid.

[40] 'Slovo Sviatieishego Patriarkha Kirilla na torzhestviennom priiemie v Kriemlie po sluchaiu 1000-lietiia predstavleniia pavnoapostolnogo kniazia Vladimira.' www.patriarchia.ru/db/text/4178879.html

Orthodox Church of the people of Ukraine, and unfortunately the Moscow Patriarchate remains as the Orthodox Church of the Soviet Union'.[41] Kovalenko emphasised that 'Today, it is the Soviet Union that is fighting against Ukraine. *Homo Sovieticus* (*Sovok*) is trying to be revived not only on the territory of the Russian Federation, but there are also many *sovoks* in our Ukrainian state and in our Ukrainian church'.

The Euromaidan Revolution shaped a new social and political reality in Ukraine. At the same time, it highlighted serious differences between the Moscow Patriarchate and part of the UOC regarding how the Russian Orthodox Church would act in this new reality. Would it continue to promote exclusivist 'unity' in mythical 'Historical Russia' or accept Ukraine was a pluralistic society? The Moscow Patriarchate continued to control the UOC and after his death, Volodymyr (Sabodan) was replaced by Onufrii (Berezovskyy) who was 'considered by the leadership of the Moscow Patriarchate as a faithful supporter of the united Russian Orthodox Church' (Firsov, 2015, p. 367).

Patriarch Kirill could count on the loyalty of nearly the entire UOC episcopate during the crisis in 2018–2019 when Patriarch Bartholomew I issued a *Tomos* granting autocephaly to the OCU placing it under the canonical jurisdiction of Constantinople. As a result, the Moscow Patriarchate is losing Ukraine, which is a pivotal part of the Pan-Russian World.

The *Tomos* put the loyalty of the UOC MP episcopate towards the Moscow Patriarchate to the test and they remained loyal. Only one hierarch of the UOC joined the OCU. Lower-ranking clergy, who since the Orange Revolution were the intellectual leaders of the transformation of the UOC towards a pluralistic model for Orthodoxy, left the Russian Orthodox Church. Kovalenko joined OCU in 2019. The UOC did not reflect on its status within the Russian Orthodox Church in response to the full-scale invasion of Ukraine. Although the Moscow Patriarchate legitimises Russian military aggression and war crimes through an increasingly radical and xenophobic form of the Pan-Russian World and pan-Russian ideology, no crisis materialised. Since 2022, there has been a dramatic decline in Ukrainian public trust in the UOC, a high number of defections to the OCU (Kyiv International Institute of Sociology, 2024), and criminal cases against UOC clergy who support

---

[41] 'Eks-spikier UPTs: „Moskovskii Patriarchat, k cozhalieniiu, ostaietsia Tserkvoiu Sovietskogo Soiuza.' https://risu.ua/ru/eks-spiker-upc-moskovskiy-patriarhat-k-sozhaleniyu-ostaetsya-cerkovyu-sovetskogo-soyuza_n71313

Russian military aggression. As a result, the percentage of respondents declaring they belonged to the UOC among those who consider themselves Orthodox dropped from 21.9 per cent in 2021 to 9.2 per cent in 2023 (Razumkov Centre, 2024, p. 38). In August 2024, the Ukrainian parliament amended legislation to pressure the UOC to cut its ties to the Russian Orthodox Church and in July 2025 UOC Metropolitan Onufriy lost his Ukrainian citizenship because of his Russian citizenship; a law adopted the month before allowed dual citizenship but excluded this from 'aggressor countries' Russia and Belarus. According to opinion polls from 2023 'the total ban on the activities of the UOC-MP in Ukraine is supported by the vast majority of respondents in the West (74 per cent) and the Centre (57 per cent), as well as by a relative majority in the East (40 per cent) and the South (34 per cent)' (Ukrainian Society, State and Church in War 2024, p. 21). The UOC had 12,190 officially registered 'religious organisations' in 2015, and in each subsequent year, their number decreased. By January 2024, the UOC had 10,586 parishes (at least on paper) compared to 8,075 parishes for the OCU.[42]

On 27 May 2022, the UOC council introduced changes to its statute to 'prove' it had become truly independent from the Russian Orthodox Church.[43] In September 2022, Metropolitan Onufrii (Berezovskyy) explained the UOC remains bound to the Russian Orthodox Church in terms of decisions that concern 'dogmas of faith and holy canons'.[44] However, in organisational and administrative terms, the UOC is allegedly 'independent', and is able to 'independently create dioceses and monasteries, and elect and ordain bishops'.[45] However, the reality is very different. After 2014, the Russian Orthodox Church established a Crimean metropolis and became the state church in the DNR (Donetsk Peoples Republic) and LNR (Luhansk Peoples Republic). The Moscow Patriarchate began to remove the UOC and thereby increase its control over Russian-occupied Ukraine. Since 2022, the Russian Orthodox Church took control of 1,619 former UOC parishes, excluding them from the jurisdiction of the metropolitan of Kyiv. The Russian Orthodox Church created a new diocese

---

[42] 'Zvit pro mrezhu relihiinykh orhanizatsii v Ukraiini stanom na 1 sichnia 2024 roku.' https://docs.google.com/spreadsheets/d/1vcq1ulAaH8jEOY6HcJyq0GTmDo3SEW6F/edit#gid=39530429

[43] 'Vysnnovok relihiieznavchoii ekspertyzy Statutu pro upravlinnia Ukraiinskoii Pravoslavnoii Tserkvy.' https://dess.gov.ua/vysnovok-relihiieznavchoi-ekspertyzy-statutu-pro-upravlinnia-ukrainskoi-pravoslavnoi-tserkvy/

[44] https://dess.gov.ua/wp-content/uploads/2022/12/4-Vidpovid-UPTS.pdf

[45] Ibid.

in Russian-occupied Kherson *oblast*.[46] The Russian Orthodox Church worked hand in glove with the Russian occupying civilian and military authorities using the Stalinist template after the Second World War when the Soviet regime forcibly liquidated the UGCC and 'united' it with the Russian Orthodox Church.

The Moscow Patriarchate's exclusivist model for Orthodoxy allows no competition from Ukrainian denominations, whether the OCU, UGCC, or Protestant and evangelical Churches; all of which are banned in Russian occupied Ukraine. In these areas, the Russian Orthodox Church is working with the Russian occupying civilian and military structure to de-Ukrainianise and Russify the population and region towards the goal of destroying Ukrainian identity and replacing it with a Little Russian. As in 1939–1945, so since 2014 and 2022, the Pan-Russian World and pan-Russian people was brought to Ukraine through external Soviet and Russian military aggression.

The Russian Orthodox Church and Diplomacy

In 1943, Stalin's decision to revive the Russian Orthodox Church gave the USSR an additional tool 'that would influence other Orthodox and Slavic peoples in Eastern Europe' (Dickinson 2000a, 338). The Moscow Patriarchate was revived as the central element of the 'system of Orthodox unity' based on a network of contacts and international connections that had been built 'with the active support of the state's Council for the Russian Orthodox Church'. Soviet institutions responsible for the control of the religious sphere gained greater influence on Orthodox Churches in Poland, Czechoslovakia, Bulgaria, and Albania (Bolotov, 2011, p. 286).

A good example is Poland. In 1946, the Polish Orthodox Church renounced the autocephaly it had obtained in 1924 from the Patriarch of Constantinople, describing it as 'non-canonical' and returned to the jurisdiction of the Moscow Patriarchate (Mironowicz 2005, p. 244). In communist Poland, the Orthodox Church in Poland would be controlled by the Kremlin. In 1981, the Orthodox Church in Poland condemned Solidarity and 'all those who try to undermine the foundations of the socialist system' (Mironowicz, 2005, p. 288). The Orthodox Church in Poland has not recognised the autocephaly of the OCU and since Russia's full-scale

---

[46] 'Alhorytm zakhoplennia Moskvoiu yeparkhii UPTs na tymchasovo okupovanykh terytoriiakh.' https://lb.ua/news/2023/12/30/591348_algoritmi_zahoplennya_moskvoyu.ht

invasion, Polish Orthodox Church Metropolitan Sava made scandalous statements which repeated Kremlin propaganda.[47]

The restoration of the Moscow Patriarchate and 'codification of the freedoms of the Russian Orthodox Church', which took place during Stalin's meeting with three selected Russian Orthodox Church hierarchs in September 1943, were intended to build the image of the USSR as a reliable partner in building a new peaceful order at the end of the Second World War. As Sergei Bolotov (2011, p. 285) emphasised, the Russian Orthodox Church's activities in the international arena were directly coordinated by the Soviet authorities, and until the end of the 1950s, these were 'anti-fascist agitation, pro-Soviet propaganda and strengthening the bonds between the USSR and its allies'.

Since 1991, the Russian Orthodox Church cooperated with the Russian authorities in 'trying to rebuild the country's distinct geopolitical and historical identity and thereby enhance Russia's position in the globalised world' (Curanović, 2012, p. 141). In this context, Russian Orthodox tradition and the Russian Orthodox Church appeared 'as a particular asset which can be important for the purposes of forming identity, legitimisation, international image and so on' (Curanović, 2012, p. 141). This referred to the international identity of Russia and the identity of the former Soviet Union which the Kremlin considered a zone of exclusive Russian influence, and the Moscow Patriarchate treated as its 'canonical territory'. The Russian Orthodox Church aspired to be the leader of a common front of 'traditional religions' who were united with the Russian state in their opposition to and condemnation of 'Western values', globalisation, and the human rights model 'in its liberal interpretation' (Lunkin, 2018, p. 167). Essentially, the Moscow Patriarchy and Russian Orthodox Church were promoting imperial nationalistic and xenophobic views ahead of Putin who embraced them from the mid-2000s.

The partnership between the Russian Orthodox Church and the Russian state, in accordance with established tradition, was asymmetrical. That is, the goals, methods and directions were set by the Russian state, and the Russian Orthodox Church adapted to them. In return, the Russian state ensured that the Russian Orthodox Church's supraregional and global ambitions received material support, including supporting

---

[47] '"Rosyjski Kościół lśni duchowym odrodzeniem i służy przykładem". Szokujący list metropolity polskiej Cerkwi.' www.polskieradio.pl/399/7977/Artykul/3113680,Rosyjski-Kosciol-lsni-duchowym-odrodzeniem-i-sluzy-przykladem-Szokujacy-list-metropolity-polskiej-Cerkwi

the takeover of existing temples (London, Nice) or the building of new ones (Paris). Roman Lunkin (2018, p. 169) writes that the Russian Orthodox Church

> received quite a lot of ideological, administrative, and financial support from the Russian state. Essentially, it was the secular power that helped the Russian Orthodox Church to feel its presence on different continents, and Patriarch Kirill to become a Christian figure on an international scale (this is evidenced by the visits of the head of the Russian Orthodox Church to Japan in 2012, to China in 2013, and a striking visit to Latin America in 2016 after meeting with Pope Francis in Havana).

The process of institutionalising cooperation between the Russian Orthodox Church and the Russian state in the sphere of diplomacy gained new dynamics under Putin. In 2003, Patriarch Alexei II visited the Russian Foreign Minister and an 'experts' group' was established which agreed on joint activities. In 2015, the Committee for international Cooperation within the Council for Cooperation with Religious Institutions at the president's office was established 'to give state diplomacy recommendations regarding international activity, social morality, and traditional values' (Curanović, 2017, p. 103). Cooperation between the Russian Orthodox Church and Russian state institutions responsible for foreign policy was held together by formal agreements and personal relationships between their representatives, including with Foreign Minister Sergei Lavrov. As Alicja Curanović (2017, p. 103) noted, new 'rituals' appeared such as 'a common celebration of Easter holiday by hierarchs and diplomats at the Ministry of Foreign Affairs, or the patriarch's blessing on the National Day of Diplomats. Symbolically, in 2015 Lavrov was awarded the order of Sergius of Radonezh and Patriarch Kirill received an honorary doctorate from the Russian Diplomatic Academy'.

The Russian Orthodox Church and the Russian state held similar imperial nationalistic views towards the former Soviet republics. 'Integration of the post-Soviet space with the participation of the Russian Orthodox Church' became 'one of the first and urgent tasks of the Church, since the unity of its parts, which de facto exist independently in other states, depends on this' (Lunkin, 2018, p. 169). For the Russian Orthodox Church, the key country in the former Soviet Union was Ukraine which Patriarch Kirill visited many times between 2009 and 2013.

The loss of canonical jurisdiction over Ukraine, which was removed by the Constantinople Patriarch in autumn 2018, and autocephaly of the Orthodox Church in Ukraine the following year, has reduced the international influence of the Russian Orthodox Church because it is no longer the largest Orthodox community in the world. The leadership of the Russian Orthodox Church among Orthodox communities and the image of Russia as the leader of a global or continental (European) conservative revolution are both under question. The Russian Orthodox Church and its 'Holy Rus' narrative came together with imperial nationalist propaganda of the *triune* nation, Pan-Russian World and the Kremlin's approach to historical questions. These four factors represented what we in this book describe as a pan-Russian identity in Ukraine that was supported by the Russian Orthodox Church from 1991 and Russian state under Putin from the mid-2000s.

Five of Ukraine's six presidents, the exception being Yanukovych, supported autocephaly for the Orthodox Church in Ukraine. The Russian Orthodox Church, Putin and his allies strongly opposed autocephaly; President Medvedev and Lavrov demanded Yushchenko did 'not interfere in the internal affairs of Churches' (Curanović, 2012, p. 170). As noted by Curanović (2012, p. 170) 'the joint appearance of the Russian president and foreign affairs minister was intended to discipline Kyiv before the second event in Russian-Ukrainian relations following the Orange Revolution in which religion and politics were entangled with one another – the celebration of the 1020th anniversary of the baptism of Rus in 25–27 July 2008'.

Alexei II travelled to Kyiv with the patriarchs of Alexandria, Jerusalem, and Constantinople. The Moscow Patriarchate complained that during Alexei II's celebrations in Kyiv, he was marginalised in the media in favour of the Patriarch of Constantinople. What's more, 'during the course of the celebrations, the Russian Foreign Affairs Ministry officially protested against the lack of respect shown for the head of the Russian Church, while after the celebration's closing, the Foreign Affairs Ministry asked the Ukrainian ambassador in Moscow for an explanation on this matter' (Curanović, 2012, p. 171). This was an example of 'confessional diplomacy' practiced jointly by the Russian state and the Moscow Patriarchate.

Moreover, in cooperation with the Ministry of Foreign Affairs, Russian Orthodox Church structures abroad are to constitute a base for state policy towards compatriots. It is no coincidence that the participants of the 2009 Brussels round-table 'The Russian Orthodox Church and compatriots in European countries: experience and prospects for co-working' concluded that 'for compatriots in many countries of the world, the dioceses and parishes of the Russian Orthodox Church are an active, unique, unifying and consolidating principle'.⁴⁸ They demanded 'participation of representatives of the Moscow Patriarchate and the Russian Church Abroad in country and regional coordination councils of compatriots through building systemic cooperation between parishes and diplomatic missions in host countries'.⁴⁹

In 2010, Lavrov emphasised that

> The traditions of cooperation between the Motherland's diplomacy and the Russian Orthodox Church go back centuries. Even today, working hand in hand, we assist the Russian diaspora abroad and protect the rights of Russians who find themselves far from their homeland. The [Russian Orthodox] Church, in essence, resolves the same questions as diplomacy by carrying out a peacekeeping mission and promoting historical reconciliation in the Commonwealth of Independent States and other regions of the world.⁵⁰

A 2012 presidential decree enhanced cooperation between the Ministry of Foreign Affairs and *Rossotrudnichestvo* through a special 'Fund for the Support and Protection of the Rights of Compatriots Living Abroad'. One place in the supervisory council was granted for the head of the Russian Orthodox Church's External Relations Metropolitan Antonii.⁵¹ This alliance of 'throne and altar' is based not only on officially concluded agreements and formal structures as well as a network of informal connections between Patriarch Kirill and President Putin, and the Russian Orthodox Church and state structures, especially since 2012.

The Russian Orthodox Church was also used in Russian diplomacy as an additional tool to influence international organisations. The Moscow Patriarchate, together with the Russian Ministry of Foreign Affairs proposed numerous initiatives to establish consultative bodies with representatives of religious confessions at the UN, OSCE (Organisation for Security and Cooperation in Europe), Council of Europe and the EU (Curanović 2017, p. 107). These were intended to influence debates on human rights and their observance at international forums. Russian state diplomacy and the Russian Orthodox Church promoted 'traditional values' at the United Nations Human Rights Council and the Parliamentary Assembly of the Council of Europe (Stoeckl and Uzlaner, 2022, pp. 136–151).

---

[48] 'Koomiunikie kruglogo stola „Russia Pravoslavnaia Tserkov i sootechestvenniki v stranakh Yevropy: opyt i perspektivy sorabotniczestva.' www.mid.ru/ru/foreign_policy/compatriots/mezhdunarodnye_tematicheskie_konferentsii/1749882/

[49] Ibid.

[50] 'Vystuplieniie S. V. Lavrova na XIV VRNS.' https://vrns.ru/documents/vystuplenie-s-v-lavrova-na-xiv-vrns/

[51] https://pravfond.ru/about/popechitelskiy-sovet/

The Kremlin is continuing to implement this strategy even after Russia's full-scale invasion of Ukraine. For example, on 17 November 2023, a debate on freedom of religion in Ukraine was held at the UN Security Council, led by Assistant Secretary-General for Human Rights in the Office of the United Nations High Commissioner for Human Rights Ilze Brands Kehris, attended by, among others, the Moscow Patriarchate, Vakhtang Kipshidze, and Permanent Representative of Russia to the UN Vasilii Nebenzia. Kipshidze claimed that 'An analysis of the situation leads us to the assessment that the authorities of the country have an objective of completely annihilating the Ukrainian Orthodox Church'. Moreover, the Moscow Patriarchate asserted that 'the Kyiv regime is trying to justify the purge of the country's religious field and free the hands of radicals to violence and lawlessness'.[52] Nebenzia compared Zelenskyy to 'Roman emperors who persecuted Christians' and 'the only thing missing is a Colosseum with Christians torn to pieces, although the Kyiv regime is moving towards this'.[53] Thankfully, other participants did not support Kipshidze's and Nebenzia's disinformation. French representative Nicolas de Rivière said, 'although the Russian Federation is once again exploiting the Council to wage a campaign of disinformation, it will not succeed in diverting attention from its illegal war of aggression against Ukraine or its countless violations of international human rights law and international humanitarian law'.[54]

The Russian Orthodox Church and Russian state are unable to impose a false narrative of religious persecution of the Russian Orthodox Church in Ukraine. This does not mean, however, that Russian disinformation surrounding this has not proven to be useful. 'The warmongering of the Patriarch of Moscow' seriously damaged 'the trademark of Russia as a stronghold of conservative values'. However, as Kristina Stoeckl and Dmitri Uzlaner pointed out: 'in ultraconservative Christian Right circles, Russia's aggression – and the Western sanctions in response – may also have a galvanizing effect. Actors on the Christian Right both in Russia and in the West will be receptive to the justification of Russia's war against Ukraine in moral conservative terms ("fighting against gay parades")' (Stoeckl and Uzlaner, 2022, p. 155).

---

[52] 'Freedom of Religion Must Prevail in Ukraine, Even as War Drags On, Senior UN Human Rights Official Tells Security Council.' https://press.un.org/en/2023/sc15500.doc.htm
[53] Ibid.
[54] Ibid.

The question of 'religious persecution in Ukraine' is another area of disinformation which has influenced some populist nationalist Republican Party members of the US House of Representatives and the Senate. This was clearly visible during debates surrounding a US military aid package to Ukraine. Senator James D. Vance said, 'when American leaders frame this as a war for democracy and human rights, it would be good if the recipient of the aid was a little bit more careful of human rights, including religious liberties'. Vance cited 'news reports of priests being investigated; Church assets being seized, and priests being arrested'. Firebrand populist Marjorie Taylor Greene claimed that 'the Ukrainian government is attacking Christians … Russia is not doing that. They are not attacking Christianity. As a matter of fact, they seem to be protecting it'.[55] Steven Moore, a former chief of staff in the U.S. House of Representatives, visited about one hundred Republican congressional offices between September 2023 and January 2024 and found about one third 'said they're concerned about Zelenskyy persecuting Ukrainian Christians'.[56]

Relations between the Moscow Patriarchate and the Vatican during the pontificate of the Pope Francis remained good, despite Russia's full-scale invasion of Ukraine. The meeting of Pope Francis and Patriarch Kirill in Havana in 2016 was a success of Russian 'confessional diplomacy' that helped shape the image of the Moscow Patriarch as one of the main leaders of Christianity in the modern world. Their 'Joint Declaration' condemned 'Uniatism' which caused consternation among Ukrainian Greek Catholics. The Vatican, for reasons that are not fully understood, were deceived into becoming involved in a game whose aim is to shape the atmosphere and opinions favourable to Russian foreign policy. This is confirmed by controversial statements by Pope Francis after the full-scale invasion of Ukraine, such as blaming the full-scale invasion on NATO 'barking' at Russia's door. When asked in an interview whether Pope Francis intended to visit Kyiv he replied: 'First I have to travel to Moscow, first I have to meet Putin'.[57] This may indicate Pope Francis was under the illusion he had established a special partnership with the Russian authorities and did not understand how instrumentally the Russian side approaches these relations. Subsequent statements made at key moments in the Russian-Ukrainian war confirm the Vatican remains defenceless

---

[55] https://x.com/AccountableGOP/status/1777363785142964668
[56] Op. cit., 'Is religious liberty…'
[57] 'Pope says NATO may have caused Russia's invasion of Ukraine.' www.politico.eu/article/pope-francis-nato-cause-ukraine-invasion-russia/

against Russian overtures as part of the above-mentioned 'confessional diplomacy'. This is evidenced by Pope Francis' unfortunate appeal in March 2024 to Ukrainians to have the 'courage of raising the white flag' and the statement of the Vatican's Secretary of State, Cardinal Pietro Parolin, who stated in June 2024 that use of military equipment supplied by NATO members against Russia 'could lead to an escalation that no one will be able to control' and that this is 'a disturbing prospect'.[58]

Conclusion

After 1943, in the new formula of the Moscow Patriarchate, the concept of 'canonical continuity' and maintaining administrative continuity were separated from the heritage of the Russian Orthodox Church. They became a tool of symbolic violence intended to legitimise the Moscow Patriarchate after its revival by Stalin. The legalisation of the Russian Orthodox Church in 1943 created a 'red-white-brown' alliance, a symbiosis between imperial Russia and the Soviet Union. Meanwhile the reunion of the domestic and diaspora Russian Orthodox Church in 2007 deepened this 'red-white-brown' alliance of imperial nationalists who claimed Ukraine did not exist and was Little Russia and denied the existence of Ukrainians who are in fact a Little Russian branch of a pan-Russian people.

The Moscow Patriarchate, like any other Church structure, has two dimensions. The first is the conceptual dimension; that is, a certain manner in exercising authority and symbolic capital. In addition, we can also distinguish the practical dimension; that is, the actual mechanisms that determine the functioning of the Russian Orthodox Church and the specific results of this activity. In the Russian Orthodox Church, both dimensions show a very strong dependence on relations with the Russian and Soviet authorities. As a result, the implementation of the fundamental mission of the Russian Orthodox Church of evangelisation and pastoral care became closely linked and subordinated to the fundamental imperative of the need to legitimise secular power under Stalin and subsequent Soviet leaders. The Russian Orthodox Church continued this practice after the disintegration of the Soviet Union, especially under Putin. The Russian Orthodox Church's alliance with the Soviet and Russian authorities

---

[58] 'Vatican's top diplomat calls use of NATO weapons against Russia disturbing.' https://cruxnow.com/vatican/2024/06/vaticans-top-diplomat-calls-use-of-nato-weapons-against-russia-disturbing

reinforced support for imperial nationalism, especially towards Ukraine because of its crucial importance in the pan-Russian nation.

The revival and re-legalisation of the Moscow Patriarchate came with the Russian Orthodox Church being used as another channel through which the Kremlin could exert influence in the Soviet empire. Moreover, the Russian Orthodox Church continues to play since 1991 an additional dimension of the Kremlin's foreign and security policy towards Ukraine and the former USSR, which are seen as Russia's exclusive sphere of influence and Ukraine and Belarus as belonging to the Pan-Russian World, and countries further afield. Its effectiveness as a tool for consolidating the post-Soviet space under Moscow's leadership has been questioned by Ukrainians in the Orange and Euromaidan Revolutions and when defending their country from Russian military aggression.

The Orange and Euromaidan Revolutions showed that limitless and absolute reliance on instructions received from Moscow and on its neo-patrimonial patronage were no longer a decisive advantage neither in religious nor in social life in Ukraine. Neither possible concessions or financial support to the UOC from the Kremlin, nor personal relations with Putin, compensated for the losses the UOC suffered from. After the Orange Revolution two unfavourable processes for the Moscow Patriarchate began in Ukraine. Some representatives of the 'core of the higher administration' of the UOC began to strive to put content into the formal formulations about the 'independence' of their Church. Moreover, some of them were influenced by changes in Ukrainian society and left the hermetic world in which its position and values were determined by the Moscow Patriarchate. The Moscow Patriarchate responded to these trends in two ways. First, there was a formal centralisation of its structures. Secondly, support was obtained from Orthodox exclusivist fundamentalists and pro-Moscow and pro-Russian circles in the UOC. Russian imperial nationalist policy turned out to be surprisingly compatible with the exclusivist model for Orthodoxy, as understood by the Moscow Patriarchate and Russian Orthodox Church. Metropolitan Volodymyr (Sabodan) and supporters of the pluralistic model for Orthodoxy did not have a sufficiently strong position within the Russian Orthodox Church episcopate and sufficiently strong and effective support from political actors to achieve changes in the UOC.

The future of the Russian Orthodox Church as the largest Orthodox Church, aspirations of the Moscow Patriarchate to be the leader of the

Orthodox world and anti-Western 'conservative revolution' largely depend on the fate of the Russian Orthodox Church in Ukraine. These, in turn, depend on three factors. The first is the Russian Orthodox Church will spread, sidelining the UOC, in areas of Ukraine occupied by the Russian army. The second is the level of determination of Orthodox faithful in Ukraine to ensure continued transfers of their parishes from the Russian Orthodox Church to the OCU. The third is the policy of the Ukrainian state; specifically, the strength of political will to take control over religious infrastructure under the Russian Orthodox Church that remains formally state property. The UOC hierarchy is passive in the face of calamitous events since the full-scale invasion. Metropolitan Onufrii and the UOC are waiting in the hope of obtaining a patron for their Church in the new situation.

As cooperation between the Russian Orthodox Church and the Russian state increased in the sphere of diplomacy, there was a significant change in the conceptual complexities of foreign policy. Alicja Curanović (2017, p. 103) described this as a transition 'from declared pragmatism to moralising conservatism'. Russia's wars against Ukraine have resulted in several failures in the international arena, both for the Kremlin (e.g., sanctions, international isolation, NATO enlargement, empowerment of Ukraine in international relations) and the Russian Orthodox Church (e.g., the Patriarchate of Constantinople removing Ukraine from Russian Orthodox Church canonical territory, autocephaly for the OCU, loss of UOC parishes to the OCU). Kristina Stoeckl (2020, p. 54) pointed out that 'for a large part of the post-Soviet period' the Russian Orthodox Church aimed to create an image of a universal and 'a transnational' community. However, with the mentioned above setbacks in Ukraine the Moscow Patriarchate shifted from its hitherto narrative towards 'a nation-state discourse'. Therefore, a certain characteristic pattern can be noticed: the greater the failures in Russian foreign policy, the greater the consolidation there has been of the symbiotic partnership between the Russian imperial nationalist state and the Russian Orthodox Church. Russia's war against Ukraine has cemented the close ties between the Russian Orthodox Church, following the unification of its domestic Stalinist and external White Russian émigré branches, and an imperial nationalist Kremlin, which has promoted Tsarist and Soviet nostalgia and a cult of Stalin. Together they are pursuing the goal of the destruction of the Ukrainian state and Ukrainian identity and creation of a pan-Russian people.

References

Ash, L. (2024). *The Baton and Cross. Russia's Church from Pagans to Putin.* London: Icon Books.

Bolotov, S. (2011). *Russkaia Pravoslavnaiia Tserkov i Miezhdunarodnaia Politika SSSR v 1930-ie-1950-ie gody.* Moskva: Izdatielstvo Krutitskogo podvoria.

Curanović, A. (2012). *The Religious Factor in Russia's Foreign Policy.* London-New York: Routledge.

Curanović, A. (2017). 'Religion and Human Rights in Russia's Foreign Policy' In: *Shifting Power and Human Rights Diplomacy.* Amsterdam: Amnesty International Netherlands: 97–110.

Destivelle, H. (2006). *Le Concile de Moscou (1917-1918). La création des institutions conciliaires de l'Église orthodoxe russe.* Paris: Éditions du Cerf.

Dickinson, A. (2000a). 'A Marriage of Convenience? Domestic and Foreign Policy Reasons for the 1943 Soviet Church-State 'Concordat,' *Religion, State and Society,* 28 (4): 337–346.

Dickinson, A. (2000b). 'Quantifying Religious Oppression: Russian Orthodox Church Closures and Repression of Priests 1917–41,' *Religion, State and Society,* 28 (4): 327–335.

Ellis, J. (1990). 'Hierarchs and Dissidents: Conflict over the Future of the Russian Orthodox Church,' *Religion in Communist Lands,* 18 (4): 307–318.

Firsov, S. (2015). 'Tsierkov, obshchestvo i vlast pri sviatieishem Patriarkhie Moskovskom I vsieia Rusi Kirillie (Gundiaievie) v 2013-2015 gg.' *Viestnik Russkoi khristianskoi gumanitarnoi akademii,* 16 (4): 263–275.

Goble, P. (2024). 'Religious Life on the Rise in Ukraine, with Enormous Consequences for Kyiv and Moscow,' *Eurasia Daily Monitor,* 21 (87), 6 June. https://jamestown.org/program/religious-life-on-the-rise-in-ukraine-with-enormous-consequences-for-kyiv-and-moscow/

Kuzio, T. (1997). 'In Search of Unity and Autocephaly: Ukraine's Orthodox Churches,' *Religion, State and Society,* 25 (4): 393–415.

Kyiv International Institute of Sociology. (2024). 'What Should be the Government's Policy and Trust in the Ukrainian Orthodox Church (Moscow Patriarchate)', 7 May. https://kiis.com.ua/?lang=eng&cat=reports&id=1404&page=1

Lahodych, M. (2012). 'Vidnovlennia Pravoslavnoii Tserkvy v radianskii Halychyni.' Naukovi zapysky Natsionalnoho universytetu 'Ostrozka akademiia,' *Seriia: Istorychne relihiieznavstvo,* 7: 123–138.

Likvidatsiia (2006). *Likvidatsiia UHKTs (1939-1946). Dokumenty radianskykh orhaniv derzhavnoii bezpeky, 1.* Kyiv: PP Serhiichuk M. I.

Lunkin, R. (2018). 'Tserkov i vnieshniaia politika: ot "russkogo mira" k globalizatsii.' *Nauchnyie viedomosti. Sieriia Istoriia. Politologiia,* 54 (1): 165–175.

Maidan i Tserkva (2014). *Khronika podii ta ekspertna otsinka.* Kyiv: Sammit-Knyha.

Mironowicz, A. (2005). *Kościół prawosławny na ziemiach polskich w XIX i XX wieku.* Białystok: Wydawnictwo Uniwersytetu w Białymstoku.

Mitrokhin, N. (2010). 'Orthodoxy in Ukrainian Political Life 2004–2009,' *Religion, State and Society*, 38 (3): 229–251.
Nizioł, M. (2004). *Dylematy kulturowe międzynarodowej roli Rosji*. Lublin: Wydawnictwo UMCS.
Pisma. (2009). *Pisma patriarcha Aleksiia i v Soviet po dielam Russkoi pravoslavnoi tserkvi pri Sovietie narodnykh komissarov – Soviete ministrov SSSR. 1945-1970 gg., 1.* Moskva: ROSSPEN.
Pospielovskii D. (1995). *Russkaya pravoslavnaya tserkov v XX viekie*. Moskva: Respublika.
Pravoslavnaia tserkov. (2012). *Pravoslavnaia tserkov pri novom patriarkhie*. Moskva: Moskovskii Tsentr Karnegi.
Razumkov Centre. (2024). Ukrainian Society, State and Church in War. Church and Religious Situation in Ukraine. https://razumkov.org.ua/en/articles/ukrainian-society-state-and-church-in-war-church-and-religious-situation-in-ukraine-2023
Schneider-Deters, W. (2024). *Russia's War in Ukraine. Debates on Peace, Fascism, and War Crimes, 2022-2023*. Stuttgart: Ibidem; New York: Columbia University Press.
Shlikhta, N. (2004). '"Greek Catholic"–"Orthodox"–"Soviet": A Symbiosis or a Conflict of Identitites?' *Religion, State and Society*, 32 (3): 261–273.
Stricker, G. (2001). 'On a Delicate Mission: Pope John Paul II in Ukraine,' *Religion, State & Society*, 29 (3): 215–225.
Stoeckl, K. (2020). *Russian Orthodoxy and Secularism*. Leiden-Boston: Brill.
Stoeckl, K. and Uzlaner, D. (2022). *The Moralist International Russia in the Global Culture Wars*. New York: Fordham University Press.
Tataryn, M. (2001). 'Russia and Ukraine: Two Models of Religious Liberty and Two Models for Orthodoxy,' *Religion, State and Society*, 29 (3): 155–172.
Tsypin, V. (2012). *Istoriia Russkoi pravoslavnoi tserkvi. Synodalnyi i novieishyi periody 1700-2005*. Moskva: Izdatelstvo Srietienskogo monastyria.
Wawrzonek, M. (2014). *Religion and Politics in Ukraine. The Orthodox and Greek Catholic Churches as Elements of Ukraine's Political System*. Newcastle upon Tyne: Cambridge Scholars Publishing.
Yelenskyi, V. (2001). 'Vizyt papy Yoana Pavla II v Ukraiinu: dyskusii i kontroversii,' *Kolehiia. Almanakh khrystyianskoii tradytsii*, 2 (4): 24–30.
Yurash, A. (2005). 'Orthodoxy and the 2004 Ukrainian Presidential Electoral Campaign,' *Religion, State and Society*, 33 (4): 367–386.

PART II

Nostalgia

4

Great Patriotic War and Cult of Stalin

Fifty of the Soviet Union's sixty-nine years was led by Joseph Stalin (1924–1953) and conservative Communist Party leaders Leonid Brezhnev (1964–1982), Yuri Andropov (1982–1984), and Konstantin Chernenko (1984–1985). The USSR experienced only three short periods of liberalisation in the 1920s under Vladimir Lenin, in 1953–1964 under Nikita Khrushchev and in 1985–1991 under Mikhail Gorbachev. Stalin and Stalinism hold a dominating influence over Soviet history, Putin's socialisation into Soviet life and Soviet and Russian imperial nationalism.

A cult of Stalin is indispensable to Putin's Great Patriotic War religion. Stalin is Putin's hero alongside Peter I and Catherine I, three transformational leaders of Russian history who expanded the Russian and Soviet empires. Stalin defeated the Nazis, extended Soviet territory into the Baltic states, Western Ukraine, and Western Belarus, and built a Soviet empire in central-eastern Europe while industrialisation and modernisation transformed the country into a superpower with nuclear weapons. Importantly, the might of the USSR ensured respect and fear from the US and West. This view provided the USSR with equality to the US in a multipolar world where one of the leading poles was the Soviet Union. It is therefore not coincidental the number of monuments of Stalin in Putin's Russia has grown since the 2014 annexation of Crimea which imperial nationalists and the Russian public viewed as the return of Russia as a great power; indeed, a fifth of the 100 new monuments of Stalin are full-scale in size (Zygar, 2025).

A cult of Stalin, return to pre-Gorbachev denial of his crimes against humanity, and unwillingness to take accountability or undertake an introspection of these crimes have had four important ramifications (see Chapter 8). Firstly, these have been a facilitator of the evolution of Putin's regime from democracy to authoritarianism after 2000 and since 2020–2022, to a dictatorship. Timothy Snyder (2022), Sergei Medvedev (2023), Alexander Etkind (2023), and Mikhail Epstein (2022) describe Putin's Russia as schizophrenic fascist where the Kremlin accuses Ukraine and the West of being 'fascist' and Nazi while itself being more akin to a fascist regime (see Chapters 5 and 7).

Secondly, they have facilitated a continued disrespect for human life at home towards Russians, Chechens and other national minorities, and abroad, towards Georgians, Syrians, and Ukrainians. Thirdly, these have fed a growing cult of war in Russia that fuels a call for sacrifice for the motherland, foreign military interventions, a specific understanding of messianism, and full-scale invasions, a cult of Putin following in the steps of past imperial Russian leaders, territorial expansionism, and belief Russia's natural condition is to be an empire not a nation-state (see Chapters 8 and 9). Putin brought to power the former Soviet KGB and military leadership who transformed Russia into a militocracy, feeding a cult of war, assaults against Russian democracy, military aggression towards Georgia, Syria, and Ukraine, and anti-Western xenophobia (Kryshtanovskaya and White, 2003). Only seven years into Putin's rule over Russia, *The Economist* described Russia as a 'KGB state' (The making of a Neo-KGB state, 2007).

Fourthly, denial of crimes against humanity, such as the *Holodomor*, the murder of Polish military officers in the forest of Katyn,[1] and absence of de-communisation in Russia has led to the continuation of Russian imperial innocence and perpetration of war crimes in Ukraine (Young, 2015). The covering up of Stalin's crimes against humanity is made possible by the closure of Soviet archives (Kohut, 2015; Oliinyk and Kuzio, 2021). Historical revisionism on the scale that is taking place in Putin's Russia 'became the travelling companion to calls for genocide or annihilation' (Historical Revisionism: 'Polish imperialism against Ukraine and Belarus', 2023).

The first and second invasions of Ukraine are depicted in Russian propaganda and disinformation as the continuation of the Great Patriotic War's fight against 'Nazis', this time fighting Ukrainian Nazis and its Western backers (see Chapter 5; Laruelle, 2024, p. 19). Havard Baekken (2023) describes this as 'war merging' where boundaries are blurred between Russia's current war against Ukraine and past wars fought by Russia, especially the Great Patriotic War. Russian soldiers in Ukraine are fighting Nazis and liberating Europe from fascism – as they did in the first half of the 1940s in the Great Patriotic War. Important aspects of this

---

[1] The *EUvsDisinfo* database, which was established in 2015, includes fifteen cases of Russian disinformation on Katyn that return to the pre-Gorbachev era of blaming the Nazis for the murder of Polish officers. See https://euvsdisinfo.eu/disinformation-cases/?text=katyn

mythology are Russian victimhood and messianism which are rooted in Russian exceptionalism (Baekken, 2023). Maria Domańska (2019) believes the Russian 'messianic myth' of the USSR saving the world from evil is a convenient way to reinforce Russia's imperial innocence and cover up the darker side of Russian history. Meanwhile, demands Russia's great power status be recognised by the US are a means to legitimise wars and military interventions.

Putin's Russia's has refashioned memory politics to support a historical revisionism that monopolises the Great Patriotic Warm by, for example, claiming Russian soldiers would have won the Great Patriotic War without Ukrainians and other non-Russian Soviet peoples. Excusing the Molotov–Ribbentrop Pact as having 'made sense', in Putin's words,[2] whitewashes the inconvenient fact it was Stalin (not Ukrainian nationalists) who was the biggest Nazi collaborator. The Kremlin's historical revisionism again conveniently ignores the far larger number of Russians than Ukrainians or other peoples who participated in Nazi military formations (Higgins, 2017). Finally, Putin's Russia downplays the importance of US lend-lease military aid without which the USSR would have been unable to defeat the Nazis.

This chapter is divided into six sections. The first analyses the close ties between the Pan-Russian World and Putin's Great Patriotic War religion. Patriarch Kirill has wholeheartedly supported Russian messianism, imperialism, a cult of war and military aggression against Ukraine. The second discusses two approaches to the Great Patriotic War. Liberalisers Gorbachev and Boris Yeltsin, taking heed of huge human losses, commemorated the Great Patriotic War under the slogan 'Never Again!' Imperial nationalist Putin celebrates military victory in the Great Patriotic War under the slogan 'We Can Do It Again!', becoming political repression at home and military aggression and empire building abroad (Victory Day, 9 May in the past in the USSR and Russia today, 2023). Robert Paxton (2004, pp. 37, 218) reminds us that fascist regimes are preoccupied with decline and rejuvenation, humiliation and victimhood, and blood and death. Roger Griffin believes the driving force of fascism is the utopian goal of a national community's rebirth which Putin's 'palingenetic ultranationalism' understands as the 'gathering of Russian lands' into the Pan-Russian World (Schneider-Deters, 2024, p. 132). The return of annual military parades from 9th May 2008 were to showcase Russia as a great power rising from the ashes after the disintegration of 'Historic Russia'

[2] www.pravda.com.ua/news/2015/05/10/7067409/

(USSR) and threat to Russian statehood in the 1990s (Aron, 2023). The third section analyses stagnation of the interpretation of the Molotov–Ribbentrop Pact from criticism to defence and justification of Stalin's decision to sign an agreement with the Nazis. The fourth section details four aspects of re-Sovietisation and re-Stalinisation in Putin's Russia: hiding Stalin's crimes against humanity; promoting a positive image of Stalin among the Russian public; inculcating Russian and Soviet myths in school textbooks; and fanning a cult of war. The fifth section analyses Ukraine's de-Sovietisation and de-communisation since the late 1980s to the Euromaidan Revolution (Oliinyk and Kuzio, 2021). The final section investigates how Nazi Ukraine became Putin's Russian 'Other' during and since the first invasion of Ukraine in 2014 (for a more in-depth analysis of the sixth section, see Chapter 5).

The Pan-Russian World and Great Patriotic War

In Russia, discussions surrounding the assessment of the Soviet period and Stalinism continued long after the disintegration of the USSR. Ironically, it was the Russian Orthodox Church-dominated World Russian People Council (WRPC) which led the way in reviving the Soviet alternative view of the Great Patriotic War myth and integrating it with the history of Russian statehood, thereby uniting communism, and Russian Orthodoxy into one cultural and civilisation whole. This was the ideological line that Putin has supported throughout his quarter of a century of rule. Russia's source of spiritual strength ensured victory in the Great Patriotic War and 'was a patriotic spiritual impulse of the people, their loyalty to Orthodox domestic traditions and faith in the ideals of goodness and justice'.[3] The Russian Orthodox Church, which had been re-legalised in 1943 (see Chapter 3), 'despite all the horrors experienced by the Russian people before the war' was able to maintain influence over the attitudes of Soviet citizens at that time and mobilise them to fight'.[4] It was a 'great battle between good and evil' in which the 'great Russian nation' deserves the greatest merit.[5] Patriarch Alexei II believed the Great Patriotic War was a time of 'spiritual rebirth' after many years of the 'reign of godless atheism' when 'a believing nation (…) confirmed it wants to be Orthodox'

---

[3] https://vrns.ru/documents/dokumenty-rassmotrennye-na-sektsiyakh-ii-vsemirnogo-russkogo-sobora/
[4] Ibid.
[5] Ibid.

and at the same time it wishes to 'recognise the Soviet Union as its civic homeland' (Russkaja Pravoslavnaja Cerkov i Velikaja otechestvennaja vojna, 2005, p. 4). Stalin granted a 'spiritual rebirth' only to the Russian Orthodox Church which benefitted from the receipt of parishes from the repressed Ukrainian Autocephalous Orthodox and Greek Catholic Churches. The 'spiritual rebirth' of Ukrainian Churches only came about after 1991 when, with the assistance of the Vatican and Constantinople Patriarch Bartholomew I, they were re-legalised, the Russian Orthodox Church lost its canonical control over Ukraine (which Muscovy had usurped in 1686) and received autocephaly for the Orthodox Church of Ukraine. Discourse about the role of the Russian Orthodox Church during the Great Patriotic War was evident in Patriarch Kirill's sermon in September 2013 to the participants of the St. George's youth parade in Moscow, where he presented as models of their willingness to undertake sacrifices for their country – Saint and Grand Prince Alexander Nevsky, Prince Dmitri Donskoy, Marshal Georgy Zhukov, and *Komsomol* (Communist Youth League) war heroes Zoya Kosmodemiańska and Oleksandr Matrossov.[6]

Imperial nationalistic memory politics surrounding the Great Patriotic War consolidated upholders of the concept of the Pan-Russian World who were convinced a superior Russian civilisation was reborn again in a 'new baptism' in the heat of the Great Patriotic War and victory over the Nazi Antichrist. The Great Patriotic War was a clash between evil Nazis and the Russian people, who drew their strength from the 'message of the Gospel and God's commandments that had always been set on building and focused on understanding in terms of the eschatological future'.[7] Russia fought and defeated Nazism and Satanism in the first Great Patriotic War; it will do the same today in the second Great Patriotic War in Ukraine. Traditional Russian messianism feeds into the deeply held view only the Soviet people (not the West) fought for humanity against the Nazis and feeds Russian political and academic discourse which 'unashamedly defends the expansionist policies of the Soviet Union' (Petrov, 2018).

Later, as part of the Pan-Russian World ideology, the Great Patriotic War was redefined as mystically uniting the 'multinational [Soviet] people' with Stalin. Putin's speech to the WRPC congress in 2023 said that after the Nazi invasion of the Soviet Union, Stalin began addressing the

---

[6] http://risu.org.ua/ua/index/all_news/orthodox/moscow_patriarchy/52252/
[7] www.vrns.ru/history/965/#.VUhhOvntmko

'Soviet people' as 'Brothers and Sisters' instead of 'Citizens'. As a result, Putin assured those present, 'God, the Church and our eternal traditions were immediately remembered'.[8] This version of the myth about the Great Patriotic War transformed the USSR into a homeland of the Russian people where 'Russia' and the USSR became the same as 'Historic Russia'. Russians increasingly came to identify themselves not with the Russian SFSR, which alone of the fifteen republics did not possess republican institutions, but with the Soviet Union (see Chapter 1). Russian historian Andrey Fursov believed the Russian people, Soviet regime and the 'Stalinist system as their shield and sword' made history and showed 'our [Russian] greatness' (Apryshchenko, 2020, p. 146).

In the Soviet Union the history of the USSR was co-terminus with Russian history, and Putin described the disintegration of the USSR as the demise of 'Historic Russia;'[9] thus, reversing its disintegration would rejuvenate Great Russia. Three quarters of Russians believe Russia is a great power, up from just under a third in 1999 when Putin first took power as prime minister (Levada Centre, 2017). The Great Patriotic War had recreated a Russian congruence between the Tsarist Empire and the USSR as Historical Russia, thus reinforcing Russian belief in exceptionalism and a special place in history (Tolz and Hutchings, 2023).

The Russian World Foundation was launched in 2007, during what this book views as the first critical juncture in Putin's Russia. The first two critical junctures (mid 2000s and 2012) moved Putin's Russia to more extreme forms of imperial nationalism while the third (2020–2022) moved the Russian regime to a dictatorship (Garner and Kuzio, 2025). 2007 was a major year in the first critical juncture: in February, Putin gave his well-known xenophobic speech to the Munich Security Conference; in April, Russia launched a cyber-attack against Estonia; in May the domestic 'red' and émigré 'white' branches of the Russian Orthodox Church reunited; and in June, the Pan-Russian World Foundation was launched. Vyacheslav Nikonov, grandson of the infamous Foreign Minister Viacheslav Molotov under Stalin, was instrumental in setting up the Russian World Foundation (Zygar, 2016, p. 108). A year later, on 9th May 2008, military parades began to be held on Victory Day – four months before Russia invaded Georgia and, after recognising their 'independence', *de facto* annexed South Ossetia and Abkhazia.

---

[8] https://vrns.ru/news/plenarnoe-zasedanie-khkhv-vsemirnogo-russkogo-narodnogo-sobora/

[9] www.reuters.com/world/europe/putin-rues-soviet-collapse-demise-historical-russia-2021-12-12/

From the mid 2000s, Putin's Russia fanned nostalgia for the Soviet Union and a cult of Stalin and from 2008, held annual military parades on Victory Day (Victory Day, 9 May in the Past in the USSR and Russia Today, 2024). From 2012, when Putin returned to the presidency and our second juncture begins, the Russian president begins to praise the Soviet dictator. In May 2009, the supposedly 'liberal' Russian President Dmitri Medvedev created the Presidential Commission to Counter Attempts to Falsify History to the Detriment of Russia's Interests. Only four months later, Medvedev (2009) sent a highly undiplomatic 'address' to Ukrainian President Viktor Yushchenko demanding changes in his country's domestic (especially memory politics, language, and religion) and foreign policies (Kuzio, 2015, pp. 438–439). Although the Commission was closed in February 2012, its ideology was continued in legislation adopted in April 2014 to counter the 'falsification' of the history of the Second World War. Ukraine's de-communisation laws, one of which replaced celebration of the Great Patriotic War to commemoration of the Second World War (Oliinyk and Kuzio, 2021), became a major target of the Kremlin's pushback against Ukraine's movement away from Soviet and pan-Russian approaches to history.

Two Different Approaches to the Great Patriotic War

The Great Patriotic War has been approached in two different ways. Soviet and Russian liberalisers Gorbachev and Yeltsin refrained from holding military parades on 9th May Victory Day and commemorated the Great Patriotic War in a less bombastic manner. Their slogan, recognising the colossal civilian and military suffering was 'Never Again!' Imperial nationalist Putin fundamentally changed Russia's approach with a bombastic and aggressive 'We Can Do It Again!' slogan with the holding of military parades on 9th May Victory Day. Putin's approach to the Great Patriotic War was accompanied with a broader cult of war inside Russia, political repression at home and military aggression abroad. Gorbachev and Yeltsin condemned Stalinism and eschewed Russian empire building. Putin promoted a cult of Stalin, embraced imperialism and sought to follow in Stalin's footsteps by rebuilding Russia as a great power with a new empire.

Gorbachev, Yeltsin and the Great Patriotic War: 'Never Again!'

From 1985 until the 1990s the Great Patriotic War was portrayed as a people's war with tremendous human suffering. Soviet leader Gorbachev's *glasnost* (openness) ushered in debate about 'blank spots' in Soviet history and Stalin's rule. Recognition of the inhumane character of the Stalinist regime and its crimes against humanity redefined heroism in the Great Patriotic War as being undertaken by the Soviet peoples – not the Communist Party leadership – and despite Stalinist repressions (Fedor, Kangaspuro, Lassila, and Zhurzhenko, 2017, p. 50).

Under Gorbachev, liberal Russian intellectuals asked why there had been so many Soviet casualties, why the USSR was so unprepared for war, and what was the cause of its initial defeats. They complimented all the nations of the Soviet Union for the victory, rather than just the 'great leader' Stalin (Tumarkin, 1994, pp. 187–198). Under Gorbachev the Soviet media talked of the millions who had died under Stalin and discussed whether Stalinism had roots in Leninism or whether it was an aberration. The fundamental question was whether communist ideology was to blame or had communism been poorly implemented by Stalin (Tolz, 1988a, 1988b).

Gorbachev sought to focus criticism upon Stalin as a Soviet leader who had 'distorted' and undertook 'excesses' that made him different to Lenin. Attempts to critically reassess the 'Soviet experiment' by stating 'Lenin was good, Stalin was bad' was not widely accepted and undermined the KPSS's (Communist Party of the Soviet Union) legitimacy. Ukrainian national communists such as Ivan Dzyuba had argued this line in the 1960s but that was superseded by decades of the 'era of stagnation', political repression and Russification that had made the claim redundant. If Stalinism had naturally evolved from Leninism, the entire Soviet system was a criminal enterprise because all the arrested 'enemies of the people' were not guilty and 'the country was not being run by a legal government but by a group of gangsters' (Satter, 2012, p. 118). Discussion of 'blank spots' as 'distortions' of Leninist policies proved to be increasingly untenable because large numbers of eyewitness accounts were published during Gorbachev's glasnost, access to official documents became easier, and the print runs of *samvydav* (in Russian, *samizdat*) literature increased.

Yeltsin continued the Gorbachev era's opening of 'blank spots' in Soviet history where 'the new Russian ruling elite sought to reframe the memory of the war according to the new vision of Russia as a democratic European nation. This memory politics was manifested in the revision of the official commemoration rituals, as evidenced by the public rhetoric employed by President Yeltsin in the quest for new national symbols'(Fedor, Kangaspuro, Lassila, and Zhurzhenko, 2017, p. 50). Yeltsin's continuation of the critical reconceptualisation of Soviet history faced growing opposition from the red (pro-Soviet)-brown (fascist) opposition, the political forces which had launched the failed 1991 and 1993 hardline coups. They organised alternative celebrations of the Great Patriotic War anniversary like those that had been performed in the Soviet Union during the 'era of stagnation'. Thus, commemorative activities became another field of confrontation between Yeltsin and the 'red-brown' alliance dominated Russian parliament (Fedor, Kangaspuro, Lassila, and Zhurzhenko, 2017, p. 51). In the 2000s, whites, who supported White Russian émigré imperial nationalism and Russian Orthodox fundamentalism, joined and broadened the alliance into 'red-white-brown'.

Yeltsin's continuation of Gorbachev's de-Sovietisation of the memory of the Great Patriotic War was too unpopular to compete with the imperial nationalist alternative championed by the 'red-brown' alliance of Soviet nostalgists, imperial nationalists and fascists. In Putin's Russia, the framework of the ideology of the Pan-Russian World was integrated with the heritages of the Soviet Union and Russian civilisation thus reinforcing the 'red-white-brown' alliance which broadened from the mid 2000s with the rehabilitation and dissemination of White Russian émigré thinkers and writers. In the 1990s there had been a hesitancy to praise Stalin in the Pan-Russian World and Great Patriotic War discourse, but this would change under Putin, who transformed the Great Patriotic War from commemoration of human tragedy into celebration of military victory, promoted a cult of Stalin, and monopolised victory in the Great Patriotic War by the Russian (not the 'multi-national' Soviet) people. Putin and Stalin's appeal to Russian history and pride draws upon the same 'great power chauvinism' (Kolesnikov, 2022). On 24 May 1945, Stalin made his famous toast during a banquet celebrating victory over the Nazis, 'I drink, first and foremost, to the health of the Russian people, because it is the most outstanding nation among all the nations that make up the Soviet Union' (Zygar, 2025). The elevation of Russians to the status of 'elder brother' of the eastern Slavs and 'leader' of the Soviet nations was the culmination of the integration of imperial nationalism and Bolshevism (national Bolshevism) that had been taking place during the previous decade and the legalisation of the Russian Orthodox Church in the Great Patriotic War as the Church of 'Holy Rus' (see Chapter 3).

Ukraine has unsurprisingly condemned Putin Russia's monopolisation of the Great Patriotic War for ignoring the large contribution made by Ukrainians to the defeat of Nazism (In New TV Spots, Ukraine Accuses Russia of 'Misappropriating' Victory Day, 2015). 3.2 million Ukrainians were in the Soviet army, including three quarters of a million from western Ukraine. Fifty-seven per cent of Soviet partisans were Ukrainians. In addition, 120,000 Ukrainians served in the Polish army, 80,000 in the US, 45,000 in the armed forces of the British Empire and 40,000 in the Canadian (Olszański, 2017).

Putin and the Great Patriotic War: 'We Can Do It Again!'

Putin was born in 1952, just as the Stalin era was ending and Soviet leader Khrushchev was beginning to introduce de-Stalinisation. Four heroes in Putin's Russia are Stalin, Soviet cosmonaut Yuri Gagarin and singer Vladimir Vysotsky; Gorbachev or Khrushchev are never mentioned (Khrushcheva, 2025). Putin has always held a preference for conservative Soviet leaders – Stalin, Brezhnev, and former KGB Chairman and KPSS First Secretary Andropov. Putin has criticised Lenin for giving Ukrainians their own republic, which allegedly served to create an artificial Ukrainian identity; nevertheless, Lenin cannot be ignored by such a devoted Soviet nostalgist. Putin sovietised Russia in the conservative image of the USSR he had nostalgia for (Kryshtanovskaya and White, 2009). Nina L. Khrushcheva (2025) described the fanning of Soviet nostalgia with triumphant films about the Great Patriotic War, Soviet songs sung by contemporary artists on TV, replaying of Soviet films, advertisements touting Soviet heroism and attacking Western influences, Soviet texts included in school curricula, and art exhibitions linked to Soviet themes.

Since 1964, in Putin's case from the age of twelve, he witnessed the revival of annual parades of the Great Patriotic War and how it became a Soviet religion when 9th May Victory Day joined the 7th of November Bolshevik Revolution as the two main Soviet holidays. The Great Patriotic War was an important Soviet holiday for two decades, from 1964 to Gorbachev becoming first secretary of the KPSS in 1985. The USSR only held four 9th May Victory Day military parades in 1945, 1965, 1985, and 1990.

Just over a decade later, in 1975, Putin joined the KGB. Writing in the 1970s, *New York Times* correspondent in the USSR Hedrick Smith (1976, p. 330) found that Russians viewed Stalin as a great leader who had transformed a peasant country into one that had 'made the rest of the world tremble at Soviet power'. Putin remained a true believer of Soviet communism – unlike most people in the USSR at that time. Putin's nostalgia for the Brezhnev and Andropov eras, the annual 9th of May Victory Day celebrations and his career in the KGB are at odds with how this period of Soviet history became described by Gorbachev as the 'era of stagnation'. Economic efficiency was sacrificed for the status quo and stability in a 'neo-Stalinist system' that eventually exhausted itself (Zaslavsky, 1982, p. 131).

The Great Patriotic War and official Soviet Russian nationalism came to legitimise the Soviet state at a time of a declining belief in communism during the 1970s–1980s (Brudny, 1998, pp. 58–60). The extent of how Ukrainians fell out of love with Soviet communism could be seen in only 150,000 joining the re-legalised KPU (Communist Party of Ukraine) in 1993, a massive drop from the 3.5 million members it had in 1985. The Russian SFSR did not have its own republican communist party until 1990.

The eclipse of belief in communism and concomitant growth of Russian imperial nationalism took place when 'The Soviet media waxed rhapsodic about the Russians having always been the greatest, wisest, bravest, and most virtuous of all nations' (Yekelchyk, 2004, p. 88). Russian dissident Andrei Amalrik (1971, pp. 36–37) wrote how during the Brezhnev era, Soviet Russian nationalism was permitted to promote messianism and 'an extreme scorn and hostility to everything non-Russian'. Putin was socialised into this merger of Soviet communism and Soviet Russian nationalism which has given birth to the 'red-white-brown' alliance that underpins his regime, military aggression against Ukraine, and xenophobia against the West.

Stalin and the three conservative Soviet leaders Putin have nostalgia for allowed Russian nationalism to flower within official Soviet publications, Soviet propaganda campaigns, and historiography. VOOPIK (All-Russian Society for Protection of Historical and Cultural Monuments) and *Otechestvo* (Fatherland) were created as 'independent' societal groups by the KPSS at the same time as the 9th of May Victory Day of the Great Patriotic War became a state holiday. The mobilisation of millions of Russians in official nationalist activities under the overall banner of 'Soviet (in effect Russian) patriotism', in which Putin most likely participated as a youngster, planted the seeds for the growth of Russian imperial nationalism in the post-Soviet era. Lev Kopelev, a colleague of Roy Medvedev's, warned that VOOPIK had 'become in essence a legal association of new Black Hundreds' (Dunlop, 1979, p. 27). Decades of official support for Soviet Russian nationalism by the 'Russian Party' in the KPSS, the KGB and the military provided the ideological roots for the creation of official nationalistic organisations in Gorbachev's USSR. In 1987, the fascist organisation *Pamiat* took control of VOOPIK, declaring its loyalty to Soviet leader Lenin but believing his entourage was dominated by

Jews and Freemasons. In the late 1980s, fascist and Eurasianist Alexander Dugin was a member of *Pamiat* before becoming an adviser to Zyuganov, leader of the KPRF (Communist Party of the Russian Federation), and co-founder of the National Bolshevik and Eurasia Parties in the 1990s. Dugin's ideological affiliations clearly show similarities to Putin of drawing from all three strands of the 'red-white-brown' alliance.

Soviet and Russian commemoration of the Great Patriotic War promoted four interconnected myths. The first myth is only those who fought against the Nazis in the Soviet Army were 'patriots' while all others were 'collaborators' and 'traitors'. Ukrainians were among the biggest 'collaborators' of the former Soviet nations, and Ukrainian nationalists were depicted as 'criminals' and 'fascist minions'. Although the far larger in number of Russians who served in the Nazi forces are not celebrated in Putin's Russia neither are they also condemned in the same obsessive manner as Ukrainian Nazis. Similarly, as Chapter 5 argues, Soviet propaganda attacked Ukrainian while ignoring Russian Nazi collaborators.

The second myth claimed the Great Patriotic War was won by the USSR to which the contemporary Russian Federation is the lawful successor. The USSR was 'Historic Russia'. The third myth is the Russian people played the greatest role in the defeat of the Nazis. All three of the above myths prove the vitality of Soviet propaganda stereotypes in the Russian discourse on the Second World War. The fourth myth, however, is directly related to Putin's motives for unleashing the war against Ukraine and the way in which Russian aggression against Ukraine is legitimised. This myth is related to the period before the Great Patriotic War when the Soviet Union and the Third Reich divided Eastern Europe between them in the Molotov–Ribbentrop Pact.

The Molotov–Ribbentrop Pact

The Nazi–Soviet Pact was signed in Moscow by German Foreign Minister Joachim von Ribbentrop and Soviet Foreign Minister Molotov on 23rd August 1939. The pact consisted of two main components: a public non-aggression agreement and a secret protocol. Under the terms of the secret protocol, Poland would be partitioned between Germany and the Soviet Union with Germany allocated the western regions while the Soviet Union would occupy the eastern part of the country. Additionally, the three Baltic States of Estonia, Latvia, and Lithuania, were assigned to the Soviet sphere of influence, along with Finland and the Bessarabia region of Romania. This arrangement effectively granted the Soviet Union the right to occupy these territories without Nazi interference.[10]

Liberalisers Denounce the Molotov–Ribbentrop Pact

The Molotov–Ribbentrop Pact was one of the key historical events that determined the course of the Second World War in central-eastern Europe in 1939–1941. However, it was a taboo topic in the USSR and the Soviet satellite states, and it was only during Gorbachev's *glasnost* that this topic began to be publicly discussed. In 1989, the Congress of People's Deputies of the Soviet Union adopted a special resolution on this issue that condemned the secret protocols as Stalin's instrument to force ultimatums and pressure on other states, in violation of the legal obligations undertaken to them (Congress of People's Deputies of the USSR, 1989).

This critical view survived the Yeltsin era but was eventually subjected to historical revisionism under Putin. In 2009, during the commemoration in Westerplatte, Gdańsk of the 70th anniversary of the outbreak of the Second World War, Putin (2009) admitted that cooperation with the Nazis was in fact 'a collusion that led to us solving our own problems at the expense of others'. Putin (2009) added that the Molotov–Ribbentrop Pact and all other pacts and agreements with the Nazis concluded in Europe in 1934–1939 'were unacceptable from a moral point of view; in practice they turned out to be senseless and had tragic consequences'.

Conservative Imperial Nationalists Defend Stalin and the Molotov–Ribbentrop Pact

However, since returning to the presidency and during our second critical juncture in 2012, Putin's narrative on this subject has been changing. Putin increasingly claimed the Molotov–Ribbentrop Pact was the correct decision for Stalin to take (Istoricheskaja Pamjat, 2020). Putin (2020b) presented the current narrative on this subject in his mini-treatise published on the 75th anniversary of the end of the Great Patriotic War in which he claimed the Molotov–Ribbentrop Pact resulted from Stalin's proper 'understanding' of the 'nature of external threats'. Stalin and his entourage believed everything was heading towards a confrontation between the Soviet Union and Germany and its allies, and he acted 'to win the precious time needed to strengthen the country's defence' (Putin, 2020b).

---

[10] www.europeremembers.com/pl/stories/428/the-german-soviet-pact

The Molotov–Ribbentrop Pact was, Putin (2020b) now argued, consistent with the security requirements of the Soviet Union, because if the USSR had allowed the Nazis to occupy all of Poland, 'the Wehrmacht would *de facto* have been on the outskirts of Minsk'. The Soviet Union simply 'had no other choice' and had to occupy the eastern regions of inter-war Poland (Putin, 2020b). Moreover, Putin's (2020b) historical revisionism claimed taking control of Lithuania, Latvia and Estonia in 1939 assisted in the implementation of the Soviet Union's 'military-strategic, defensive goals'. Putin was falling back on tried and tested Russian imperial innocence, claiming the USSR had been invited into the three Baltic states (see Chapter 8).

There are two reasons for Putin's (2020b) historical revisionism. Firstly, he instrumentalised memory politics about the Second World War for the purpose of legitimising Russia's invasion of Ukraine which is described as a continuation of the Soviet Union's fight to liberate Europe from Nazism. Meanwhile, the annexation of Ukrainian territories is related to the implementation of Russia's 'military-strategic and defensive goals' – as was the case with the annexation of eastern Poland and the three Baltic states. On 24 February 2022, in his speech launching the 'special military operation', Putin (2022a) emphasised: 'the current events have nothing to do with a desire to infringe on the interests of Ukraine and the Ukrainian people. They relate to defending Russia from those who have taken Ukraine hostage and are trying to use it against our country and our people. I reiterate we are acting to defend ourselves from the threats created for us and from a worse peril than what is happening now'. A few months later, Putin (2022b) explained to journalists during a CIS (Commonwealth of Independent States) summit that the goal of the 'special military operation' was the 'liberation of the Donbas, protection of these people and creation of conditions that would guarantee the security of Russia itself'.

Putin's defence of the Molotov–Ribbentrop Pact demonstrates the same line of argumentation used by his Stalinist predecessors. At the heart of this defence is the key assumption that central-eastern Europe is a geopolitical space the former Soviet Union and Russia can freely shape, depending on their strategic goals, with its fate dependent on the current state of relations between the Soviet Union/Russia and the West. A second reason for Putin's historical revisionism was changes in the paradigm of shared European memory. The transformation of this paradigm began after the accession of central-eastern European countries to NATO and the EU which gained momentum following the Euromaidan Revolution and Russia's full-scale invasion. Until then, myths surrounding the Great Patriotic War were not only intended to legitimise Russia's right to shape the borders of central-eastern Europe, but also to define Russia's role as the guardian of the 'correct' interpretation of the past that this region of Europe should hold. The official and 'correct' Kremlin paradigm claims, as per the historical revisionism we analyse in Chapter 8, that Stalin, the strategic leader, 'liberated' Europe and the world from the plague of fascism and Nazism and brought 'freedom' to central-eastern Europe. It was under Stalin's leadership that a new post-war 'concert of powers' was built in the Yalta agreement that ensured stability within Europe and the world (Putin, 2020b).

Europe and Ukraine Equate Nazi and Communist Totalitarianism

Putin's Russia's is steadfastly opposed to equating Communist and Nazi ideologies and their committing of crimes against humanity. European institutions have equated Nazism and communism in seven resolutions adopted between 2006 and 2019. Ukraine joined Europe's equating of Nazi and communist totalitarianism with the adoption of the 2015 de-communisation laws (Oliinyk and Kuzio, 2021).

The seven resolutions were:

Parliamentary Assembly of the Council of Europe (PACE) 'strongly condemns crimes of totalitarian communist regimes' (Council of Europe, 2006).
EU 'European Public Hearing on Crimes Committed by Totalitarian Regimes' (European Union, 2007).
Czech Senate 'Prague Declaration on European Conscience and Communism' (Czech Parliament, 2008).
European Parliament resolution 'European Day of Remembrance ('Black Ribbon Day') on 23 August for Victims of Stalinism and Nazism' (European Parliament, 2008).
European Parliament resolution 'European Conscience and Totalitarianism' condemned crimes committed by totalitarian regimes and called for the recognition of 'Communism, Nazism and fascism as a shared legacy' (European Parliament, 2009). The resolution broadened common European memory from only Nazism to also include communism, pointing out two totalitarianisms – Nazism and communism – left their negative mark on twentieth century European history. The

Molotov–Ribbentrop Pact became the symbol of this dual legacy, and the anniversary of its signing was proclaimed as 'Europe-wide Day of Remembrance for the victims of all totalitarian and authoritarian regimes'.

Parliamentary Assembly of the Organisation for Security and Cooperation in Europe 'Vilnius Declaration' condemned Soviet and Nazi totalitarianism (Organisation for Security and Cooperation in Europe, 2009).

European Parliament resolution on the 'Importance of European Remembrance for the Future of Europe' (European Parliament, 2019). The resolution described the Molotov–Ribbentrop Pact as one of the main causes of the Second World War because Nazi Germany and the Soviet Union shared 'the goal of world conquest and divided Europe into two zones of influence'. Moreover, the European Parliament called on the European Commission 'to decisively counteract' Russia's efforts 'to distort historical facts and whitewash crimes committed by the Soviet totalitarian regime'.

These seven European parliamentary resolutions, as well as the memory politics of central-eastern European countries, especially Ukraine, are a manifestation of their empowerment surrounding the discourse on Europe's past heritage. As well as a reaction to the weaponisation of memory politics and historical revisionism by Putin's Russia. Shortly after the European parliament adopted the 2019 resolution, a debate on historical policy was held in the editorial office of the journal *Russia in Global Affairs* whose participants concluded that 'historical memory is yet another plane on which political problems are resolved'. Discourse on the Second World War and its consequences for central-eastern Europe is of particular importance for what Dmitri Yefriemenko called 'mnemonic security' (Istoricheskaia Pamiat, 2020). This became the subject of debates among Russian historians, sociologists and political scientists and the Russian Security Council (Sovieshchaniie s Postoiannymi, 2024).

The Kremlin has sought to impose its official paradigm of the memory of the Second World War, especially upon Ukraine and central-eastern Europe. Yefriemenko proposed that 'qualified Russian experts' infiltrate the network of historical memory researchers that have been established in central-eastern Europe in recent years (Istoricheskaia Pamiat, 2020). Putin (2020b), on the other hand, insisted that the 'correct' interpretation of the past is consistent with the 'conclusions of the Nuremberg Tribunal' that should be implemented by the five permanent members of the UN Security Council because they 'bear special responsibility for the preservation of civilisation' (Putin 2020a). Putin (2020a) condemned 'historical revisionism' over the discourse of the memory of the Second World War in the European Parliament and among former Nazi 'accomplices' in central-eastern Europe. One of the main elements of Putin's 'revisionism' are the reassessment of the Kremlin's narrative on the Molotov–Ribbentrop Pact and the root causes of the Second World War.

Re-Sovietisation and Re-Stalinisation of Putin's Russia

Putin, like other former Soviet *siloviki* (security forces), admired Stalin and Andropov (Zygar, 2016 pp. 29–30, 152). The cult of Stalin, which took off in the second decade of Putin's rule over Russia, facilitated a 'Stalinist-type dictatorship' in Russia and 'contributes to the support of Russia's aggressive foreign policy' (Kyiv International Institute of Sociology, 2023). Stalinism 'is becoming a state ideology, almost a religion in Putin's Russia', Mikhail Zygar (2025) wrote adding that since Russia's full-scale invasion 'glorification of Stalinist terror has turned into an orchestrated state policy'. Zygar (2025) writes 'modern Putinism is an exact reincarnation of late Stalinism in all its manifestations: an imperial ideology defined by anti-Westernism, a cult of the leader, repression of dissenters branded as traitors, and the absolute supremacy of the state over the individual in all matters'. Chapters 8 and 9 analyse Russia's continued imperial innocence and lack of scrutiny of its colonialism, genocidal past, two invasions of Ukraine and war crimes against Chechens, Georgians, Ukrainians and Syrians.

Ignoring Crimes against Humanity

In Putin's Russia the Great Patriotic War has become 'sacralised' and 'canonised' through the denial of Stalin's crimes against humanity (Aron, 2023, p. 57). Praise of Stalin has featured prominently in Russian imperial nationalist publications where he is defended by those who have a visceral hatred for Gorbachev who they accused of destroying the 'Russian state' (i.e., the USSR) in league with the West. Russian imperial nationalists defend Stalin by highlighting 'mitigating circumstances for Stalin's misdeeds' and blaming his crimes on foreigners (Laqueur, 1993, p. 158).

Pavel Felgenhauer (2019) writes that, 'Modern Russian state propaganda has for years been promoting Stalin as the main organiser of the victory over Nazi Germany in the Second World War. And this victory is projected with more and more vigour as the defining moment of Russian state history and a popular focal point uniting all loyal citizens around the flag; consequently, annual celebrations of the Great Patriotic War become more and more lavish'. Sanctification of Stalin's role, 'has become the main ideological foundation of Mr. Putin's velvet Stalinism' (Take Care of Russia, 2016). A cult of Stalin was undertaken alongside the promotion of a macho image of Putin (Luhn, 2016; Sperling, 2016).

Putin's Russia could not both praise Stalin and denounce his crimes against humanity; the latter are therefore ignored, downplayed, or excused. A Great Patriotic War religion must 'suppress memory of the Gulag' and the 'sufferings of the victims of the Soviet system' (Khapaeva, 2009, p. 369), creating a 'partial amnesia' where historical memory is 'strangely selective'. Russians with imperial innocence bear no responsibility for Stalin's crimes and are told by Putin they have nothing to be ashamed of; that is, 'The war myth prevents reflection on the responsibility for Soviet crimes' (Khapaeva, 2009, p. 369). A Russian Communist activist said, 'In my opinion, he didn't kill enough people'. Meanwhile, a younger Russian argued 'He wasn't a dictator or a tyrant. He was the greatest leader of our country. He raised it to incredible heights' (For Some Russians, Stalin 'Didn't Kill Enough People', 2016).

The widespread cult of Stalin in Putin's Russia leaves no room for his victims. Russia's only museum of Soviet political repression, housed in the Perm Gulag where many political prisoners died, was remodelled in summer 2014 and no longer emphasises the crimes of the Stalin era (MacKinnon, 2015; Nougayrede, 2015; Peter, 2015; Walker, 2015). At the end of 2024, the Museum of the Gulag in Moscow was closed using the flimsy excuse of 'fire safety violations'.

Myths about Stalin and the Great Patriotic War are intended to generate support for the Kremlin's domestic and foreign policies, especially Russia's war against Ukraine and its anti-Western xenophobia. These myths are a projection of a specific system of 'values' which consists of a belief in 'Russia's status as a great power entitled to claim spheres of influence and determine the fate of the region and the world' through a 'cult of war and brute force' (Domańska and Rogoża, 2021, p. 97). Within the Kremlin's historical discourse promoting Russia as a great power, Stalin is the triumphant victor in the Second World War. This is supposed 'to compensate for Russia's loss of its great power status, while on the social and welfare level Stalin often embodies people's passive longing for a modest, caring and just leader: the truly good tsar' (Domańska and Rogoża, 2021, p. 96).

In this discourse, the issue of Stalinist crimes and the alliance of the USSR with the Third Reich at the beginning of the Second World War was either radically marginalised or instrumentalised. On 18th May 2007, Russian Orthodox Patriarch Alexei II together with the head of the Russian Orthodox Church Abroad Metropolitan Laurus consecrated a stone in the Sanctuary of New Martyrs and Confessors of Russia at the Butovo firing range where the NKVD killed over 20,000 people. The day before, both hierarchs had signed the act of canonical communion, uniting the Stalinist 'red' and Russian émigré 'white' Churches. In this way, as Zuzanna Bogumił and Tatiana Voronina (2023, p. 178) noted, Butovo 'became a symbol of the reconciliation of both Churches and the most important Russian Orthodox Church sanctuary for new martyrs'. Putin visited Butovo in October of the same year on the Day of Remembrance for Victims of Political Repressions; however, 'it was the first and the last time that Putin or any high-ranking state representative' visited this place. Moreover, Bogumił and Voronina (2023, p. 178) believe a few years later Kirill, Russian Orthodox Church Patriarch Alexei II successor, 'also lost deep interest in Butovo and it was clear that the official memory politics of the Moscow Patriarchate towards Soviet repressions had changed' (Bogumił and Voronina, 2023, p. 178). Since the granting of autocephaly to the Orthodox Church of Ukraine in 2018–2019 and full-scale invasion in 2022, the 'Russian Orthodox Church has joined in the revival of Stalin's cult. Icons depicting the Soviet dictator are increasingly appearing in churches' (Zygar, 2025). 'It is difficult to imagine anything more illogical', Zygar (2025) writes, 'after all, under Stalin, thousands of Orthodox priests were executed, churches across the country were destroyed, and believers were persecuted and sent to the Gulag. However, in recent years, an almost alternative biography of Stalin has been invented'.

Within Russian state structures responsible for conducting memory policy, there are two institutions that deal with repression in the USSR. Memorials at the sites of NKVD mass executions in Katyn and Miednoie operate as branches of the State Museum of the Contemporary History of Russia. In both places there are mass graves of Polish officers and state officials who were captured by the Soviets after the Molotov–Ribbentrop Pact and the Soviet invasion of Poland on 17 September 1939 and were then murdered by the NKVD. In the early 1990s, Poland made efforts to commemorate the murder of its citizens in Katyn and Miednoie, prompting the Russian authorities to take care of the memory of Soviet citizens who were buried there. A Russian museum and Orthodox

Church were built in Katyn. In 2017, the memorial was incorporated into the structure of the State Museum of Contemporary History of Russia when 'the message of the site' was 'radically altered' and the Katyn Polish war cemetery 'has become a subject of extreme necro politics' whose condition depends on the state of Polish-Russian relations. This exhibition 'tells a very one sided and in many aspects propagandistic version' of the past (Bogumił and Voronina, 2023, p. 188). However, the sanctuary in Katyn, which was supposed to be a symbol of Polish-Russian reconciliation, is being used 'for nationalistic rituals organised by the Russian Military Historical Society' (Bogumił and Voronina, 2023, p. 189), that is headed by Vladimir Medinsky, an arch imperial nationalist who assisted in the ideological preparation of the full-scale invasion of Ukraine and whose society has published textbooks that are extreme examples of historical revisionism (Zygar, 2023). Domańska and Jadwiga Rogoża (2021, pp. 96–97) pointed out:

> Public sympathy for Stalin rarely translates into genuine, widescale social action or an actual readiness to live in a Stalinist-type state. This is not the purpose for which neo-Stalinism and the 'Great Patriotic War religion' are promoted within the official and unofficial historical discourse in Russia. Rather, it is about cultivating specific 'norms of social life in Russia,' which include 'passivity, inertia, conformism, and citizens' sense of powerlessness towards the state.

Putinism is legitimised through its monopoly on managing the 'correct' discourse of the Soviet past. According to Max Weber's classic definition, the key element of state power is its monopoly on the legal use of physical violence. In Putin's system, it is equally important to maintain a monopoly on symbolic violence, the tool of which is, among others, memory politics. The logic of Putin's memory politics can be clearly seen in the 'Immortal Regiment' whose purpose is to commemorate on the 9th of May Victory Day processions of family members who fought or died during the Great Patriotic War. Initially, it was a local grassroots initiative launched in Tomsk and supported by local independent media; however, very quickly this popular campaign was 'taken over' by the state authorities and in 2015, Putin and Kremlin officials first attended the march, and since then it has resembled state-run, bureaucratic, top-down initiatives (Domańska and Rogoża, 2021, p. 103). The nationalisation of the 'Immortal Regiment' are symbolised by the participation in 2016 of Viacheslav Nikonov, then head of the Russian World Foundation. Nikonov carried a portrait of his grandfather Molotov who signed the Molotov–Ribbentrop Pact (Domańska and Rogoża, 2021, p. 103).

Collecting information about Stalin's crimes leads to political repression – as seen in false criminal charges launched against Yury Dmitriev, a historian, and the head of the Karelia branch of the Russian Memorial Society (Coynash, 2017). In 2016, the Memorial Human Rights Centre, which has undertaken important work documenting Soviet crimes against humanity since 1989, was declared a 'foreign agent' under repressive legislation adopted four years earlier that targeted and sought to halt Western funding of civil society in Russia. The very term 'foreign Agent' was 'once a Stalinist term for traitors, now a legal classification intended to throttle troublesome civil-society groups' (The battle for Russia's history, 2016). The Memorial Human Rights Centre was closed in early 2022, on the eve of Russia's full-scale invasion of Ukraine, and its co-head Oleg Orlov imprisoned two years later for condemning Russia's war against Ukraine.

Popular Views of Stalin in Russia

A 'popular Stalinism' emerged during the 'era of stagnation' that respected and admired his deeds, and which retains a hold on Putin and Russians of all generations. Dina Khapaeva (2009, p. 360) believes a 'positive image of Stalinism has been a stable, persistent representation in mass consciousness'. Ordinary people rehabilitated Stalin by putting his picture in car windshields in the USSR, a practice which has continued in contemporary Russia and the Donetsk People's Republic (DNR) and Luhansk People's Republics (LNR) (Wishnevsky, 1985, 1986; Karmanau, 2015). Smith (1976, p. 314) found in 1970s Russia a 'huge mass of people dreams of Stalin – his strong power'. A DNR separatist with a portrait of Stalin in his windscreen said of the Soviet leader 'I have adored him as a man since my childhood. Because he was a real man' (Ukraine's Fragile Ceasefire, 2015).

In Russia, state-control of the media and education process has led to high levels of positive feelings for Stalin. After thirty-two years in the Soviet and Russian Merchant Navy a sailor who had watched only Russian television on board ship said that Ivan the Terrible and Stalin had been great leaders, and they should have monuments unveiled to them (Shearlaw, 2016). In a vote on Russian television to find the country's most popular historical figure, the producers were at first embarrassed to find the public had voted for Stalin and they rigged the vote in favour of Nevsky (Pomerantsev, 2014, p. 112). However, considering the results of previous public opinion polls, Stalin winning first place should not be a surprise. In a 2012 survey where Russians were asked to name the ten most outstanding

Russians, Stalin also came first ahead of Lenin, Peter I and other historical figures. In two subsequent surveys in 2017 and 2021, Stalin strengthened his position as the leading Russian historical figure (Levada Centre, 2021). It is unlikely that similar polls since the 2014 'embarrassment' that found Stalin to be the most popular leader in Russian history would be again hidden. In 2025, 42 per cent ranked Stalin as first in a poll that asked Russians who they believed were the most outstanding people of all time (Samyie vydaiushiiesia lichnosti v istorii vseh vremjon i narodov, 2025).

Stalin being voted first in TV votes should not be surprising. Levada Centre (2019), Russia's last remaining independent polling organisation, has recorded growing sympathy for Stalin throughout Putin's rule with most Russians holding positive, respectful, and sympathetic views of him. Meanwhile, the proportion of Russians who believe Stalin is a 'criminal' has been in decline. Russians who believe Stalin's repression was justified by the goals of industrialisation and winning the war has continued to grow with 46 per cent of Russians believing Stalin's repressions were less important than the Soviet industrialisation programme to modernise the USSR (Perception of Stalin, 2019). After two decades in office, Putin has succeeded in increasing the number of Russians who hold a positive view of Stalin to 70 per cent with only 19 per cent holding a negative view of him (Perception of Stalin, 2019). Most Russians who hold a positive view of Stalin are not only Communists, but they also come from the *Yedynaia Rossiia* (United Russia) Party, the dominant ruling party, and the pro-regime nationalist LDPRF (Liberal Democratic Party of the Russian Federation).

What is most disturbing is the high number of young Russians born since the USSR disintegrated who also have a positive view of Stalin. These are the same young Russians being sent to die in their hundreds of thousands in Ukraine. When asked what role Stalin played in Russian history, two-thirds of Russians aged 18–24 were entirely or mostly positive, and only 19 per cent were mostly or very negative (Levada Centre, 2019). The Levada Centre (2019) concluded, 'Age does not differentiate respondents by the level of support for negative judgments about the leader – in all age groups the proportion of respondents with a positive attitude dominates over the share of respondents with negative evaluations, and the idea of the positive role of Stalin in the history of the country over the opposite opinion'. Over a third of Russians (35 per cent) aged 18–24 years old ranked Stalin first in a poll of the most outstanding people of all time, only 12 per cent less than Russians aged 55 and over (Levada Centre, 2025).

Better educated and wealthier people and younger respondents identifying with the processes of social modernisation expressed the greatest increase in positive views of Stalin from the second half of the second decade of the twenty-first century (Volkov, 2024). According to the Director of the Levada Centre, Denys Volkov, the myth of the Great Patriotic War, appropriately modelled by state propaganda, contributed to the increase in the popularity of the positive image of Stalin among Russians. Tatiana Stanovaya (2024) writes that these myths resonate with Russia's ruling elites and Russian society. Putin's regime has mobilised Russians into believing the unipolar world system is hostile to Russia and needs transforming. Russian elites support Russia's war against Ukraine. Stanovaya (2024) writes: 'Many Russians see defeating Ukraine as a crucial step in the Kremlin's anti-Western agenda'.

The image of the 'Great Victory' in 1945 was central to this positive image of Stalin, however, without questioning how this success was achieved and its price. As Volkov (2024) noted, 'when we look at the war from this point of view, Stalin's role in it becomes more positive. After all, it was under him that we won, and that is what we are talking about'. Moreover, the increase in the popularity of a positive myth of Stalin should be associated with the first invasion of Ukraine in 2014 which, like the full-scale invasion, was perceived as an extension of long-standing conflict with the West. Crimea was 're-united' with Russia during a second Cold War with Stalin remembered as leading the Soviet Union during the first. At the same time, civil society actors who publicised Stalinist crimes were excluded from Russia's public debate on the past. As Volkov (2024) noted 'their voices have not been heard for several years, and this topic has disappeared from public discourse'.

Jewish victims of the Holocaust are also no longer discussed in Russia's casualties and dead in the Great Patriotic War or included in memorial plaques and museums.[11] Russian historian Konstantin Pakhaliuk, now in exile, believes this is undertaken to present Russians as victims of the West and victims of history. Pakhaliuk argues that the narrative of Russia as a victim has become especially strong since the launch of the full-scale invasion of Ukraine. 'If you are a victim, you cannot bear responsibility', Pakhaliuk said.[12] The root of this victimhood is Russia's mythical imperial innocence.

---

[11] www.bbc.co.uk/news/articles/cwyw0vkzkzdo
[12] Ibid.

School Textbooks and Militarism in Russia

Indoctrinating young Russians, 'lays the foundations for future confrontations and wars between Russia and its alleged "enemies"' (Manipulating Memory. Rewriting School History Books, 2024). Revised school textbooks introduced after Russia's full-scale invasion teach Russian school children to lament the disintegration of the USSR, view the West as evil and always seeking Russia's destruction, and understand the 'special military operation' as defensive to liberate Ukrainians from the hostile 'ultra-nationalist, neo-Nazi [Ukrainian] state' to forestall a US and NATO attack against Russia (Manipulating Memory. Rewriting School History Books, 2024). Throughout Putin's rule over Russia the education system has played a key role in fanning nostalgia for the Soviet Union and a cult of Stalin and transforming the Great Patriotic War into a state-backed religion. Russia's education system presents an upbeat, positive image of Soviet rule and the Stalin era. Russia's Minister of Education Olga Vasilyeva, a 'religious nationalist', praised Stalin for restoring patriotism to the centre of Russian history (The battle for Russia's history. Remember, Remember, 2016).

Since as early as 2008, Russia's school textbooks have whitewashed Stalin as an 'effective manager', praised Stalin as the 'most successful leader of the USSR' and portrayed the USSR as a 'besieged fortress'. The USSR is glorified as an era of Russian greatness and progress and state-driven modernisation where Stalin continued in the tradition of Russian leaders in building strong states. The Great Patriotic War could not have defeated the Nazis without Stalin's industrialisation. In Russian school textbooks, 'The Terror, and the repressions that came before and after it, are minimised', meanwhile, 'Stalin's repressions are portrayed as a pragmatic solution to the difficulties the Soviet Union faced in the pre-war years' (Nelson, 2015, pp. 45 and 47).

Russian first invasion of Ukraine in 2014, and full-scale invasion of Ukraine in 2022 have led to an even greater number of myths and falsehoods being included in school textbooks (Franchetti, 2014; Applebaum, 2023; Ilyushina, 2023; Rumer, 2023; Snegovaya, Kimmage, and McGlynn, 2023; Zygar, 2023). Below are eight myths found in Russian school textbooks:

- Emphasis on Russian military might and victories throughout Russia's 'one-thousand-year history'.
- Positive portrayal of the histories of the Tsarist Empire and the Soviet Union (this is analysed in Chapter 8).

Stalin was a wise and effective leader who made 'mistakes'.

Stalin's victims were guilty, suffered and deserved their punishment. There are no memorials to Tsarist and Soviet crimes against the Russian and non-Russian peoples (Pomerantsev, 2022). Putin's Russia has taken the revival of Stalinism into the realm of dystopia. Between 2022 and 2024, the Russian prosecutor office revoked 4,000 decisions on the rehabilitation of victims of Stalinist repression 'claiming that they had, in fact, been justly punished – allegedly for collaborating with the Nazis' (Zygar, 2025). They have been reclassified as traitors to the motherland.

Show an indifference to Soviet casualties in the Great Patriotic War.

Soviet forces did not commit atrocities during the Second World War. Jade McGlynn (2023) writes that the school textbooks introduced since 2022 'are a narrative of excuses of Russian and Soviet crimes, as well as an exhortation to young readers to accept these crimes past and present – as their own'.

Monopolise the Great Patriotic War by portraying victory over the Nazis as a feat undertaken by the Russian people.

Putin follows in the path of Peter I, Catherine II, Stalin and other great Russian and Soviet leaders in expanding Russian territory and building a new empire, which demonstrates Russia is a great power.

After the Orange Revolution, Soviet-style military 'patriotic education' was revived through 'anti-fascist' groups such as *Nashi* (Ours), *Idushchiie vmyestie* (Walking Together), *Molodaia Gvardiia* (Young Guard), and the Eurasian Youth Movement (Myers, 2007). These groups indoctrinated Russian youth with imperial nationalism and xenophobia towards Ukraine and the West. Indoctrination of young Russians at school, coupled with their militarisation in youth groups such as *Yunarmiia* (The All-Russian Military Patriotic Social Movement 'Young Army') under the Ministry of Defence inculcates a cult of war, imperialism, and a perceived right to deny the human rights of enemy combatants and civilians (Applebaum, 2023). Another new organisation, the Movement of the First youth group, is modelled on the Soviet Pioneers and *Komsomol*. Stalinist era sports parades have also been revived (Revival of the Stalinist Sports Parades in Putin's Russia, 2025).

In Putin's Russia and Russian-occupied Ukraine, children are militarised (Cichowlas, 2017). Children are indoctrinated with Ukrainophobia and anti-Western xenophobia at school and in officially sponsored youth groups. They are forcibly made to participate in Immortal Regiments on

Victory Day parades. At school or in officially sanctioned youth organisations they are made to wear Red Army uniforms, where they play with toy or real weapons.

Lying at the core of these myths, Russian culture obscures and romanticises violence which has been endemic to Tsarist and Soviet history. In 2025, a three-volume Russian military history school textbook, published by Medinsky's Russian Military History Society, depicts the war against Ukraine as a second Great Patriotic War and in the spirit of Russian imperial innocence (see Chapter 8), is being undertaken as a defensive measure to thwart Western aggression against Russia. In line with Russian propaganda narratives of the Ukrainian state having become 'Anti-Russia', Russian school children are taught Ukraine is an 'aggressive anti-Russian bridgehead'.[13]

The Russian Orthodox Church under Kirill is always eager to assist in the integration of Soviet and Russian imperial nationalist memory politics and a cult of war. On 29 May 2019, a special meeting was held between Patriarch Kirill and the children of soldiers whose fathers died during the Russian intervention in the Syrian civil war. The head of the Russian Orthodox Church said: 'Heroism is the highest value of human life, because in heroism the strongest feelings and qualities of a person are manifested, so strong that they overcome even the fear of death (…) the hero is not afraid of death, which means he has a very special power. If there were no heroes, human history would have developed completely differently. (…) You are the children of heroes and must absorb this heroism into your nature with both mind and heart' (Sviatieishyi, 2019).

In a similar vein, a year after the full-scale invasion of Ukraine, Patriarch Kirill hosted a delegation of 'young athletes from Donbas' where he asserted that 'Russia does not abandon its own people. Russia can protect and assist, but the Donbas must also continue its heroic traditions of defending the Motherland – our common united Motherland. And to defend, you need to be supremely confident in the correctness of your case. And I would really like the children and youth of the Donbas to understand that the struggle that is going on now is a just struggle because it is related to the protection of historical heritage' (Slovo Sviatieishevo, 2023).

---

[13] https://rvio.histrf.ru/activities/news/vyshlo-v-svet-novoe-izdanie-uchebnogo-posobiya-voennaya-istoriya-rossii; and www.rbc.ru/politics/27/01/2025/6797914d9a79472922cab394?from=newsfeed

De-Communisation and De-Stalinisation in Ukraine

Russia and Ukraine have been on divergent paths in their memory politics during the entire post-Soviet era. De-sovietisation in Russia took place briefly from the late 1980s to the mid 1990s. Ukraine continued this process from the late 1980s to the present day with a short suspension during Viktor Yanukovych's presidency. As Russia became increasingly defensive and protective of Stalin and the Soviet legacy, Putin argued that 'excessive demonisation of Stalin is one of the means of attacking the Soviet Union and Russia' (Parfitt, 2017).

Ukraine had more to condemn than Russia because, 'Stalin was determined to destroy their culture and traditional way of life' (Naimark, 2010, p. 29; Applebaum, 2017; Martin, 2001, p. 225). In the 1930s and often since then, Ukrainians were perceived as the 'enemy nation' and their submission into a *Homo Sovieticus* would ensure they 'would be completely reliable, trustworthy, and denationalised in all but superficial ways' (Naimark, 2010, p. 78). Soviet leader Khrushchev revealed in his secret speech to the 1956 congress of the KPSS that Stalin had wanted to deport the entire Ukrainian people but 'there were to many of them and there was no place to which to deport them' (Khrushchev, 1976, p. 58). With the Russian invasion goal of 'de-nazification' including torture, executions, rapes, deportations, the kidnapping of children and de-Ukrainisation of occupied territories, it is not surprising Ukrainians see Stalinist echoes of a similar policy of genocide against Ukrainian identity undertaken by Putin's Russia in its current war against Ukraine. The Independent International Commission of Inquiry on Ukraine (IICIU) reported to the United Nations Security Council 'widespread and systematic use of torture by the Russian Federation against civilians and prisoners of war' that was 'a coordinated state policy'. Russian war crimes have taken place throughout Russian-occupied Ukraine that have included 'routine harsh practices designed to scare, break, humiliate, coerce and punish detainees' and 'recurrent beatings in various areas of detention facilities and on various parts of detainees' bodies, intrusive body searches, a prohibition to sit, sleep deprivation, stress positions, forced physical exercise, and prolonged nudity' (de Grieff, 2025). The IICIU added that the 'leadership of detention facilities' and 'higher-ranking Russian authorities have ordered, encouraged, tolerated or taken no action to stop' torture and abuse of human rights. Instead, they have instructed personnel 'to work harshly and with no pity' on Ukrainian detainees and 'directed the doctors not to forget that "prisoners are enemies".' 'Medical care is generally denied in detention facilities, even in situations where detainees had serious, visible, or life-threatening injuries', the UN reported, which 'In some instances, this led to death or severe and irreversible medical complications' (de Grieff, 2025). The UN Human Rights Monitoring Mission in Ukraine expressed alarm at the growing instances of Russian forces executing Ukrainian POW's (Grove, 2025).[14]

For Ukrainians the *Holodomor* has always stood apart as the worst crime against humanity committed by the Soviet regime and is an 'emotional and highly charged' question for Ukrainians (Wanner, 1998, p. 41; Conquest, 1986). The 'complete indifference to human suffering that permeated the Soviet ruling circles in Stalin's time' led to millions of victims in Soviet Ukraine (Snyder, 2010, p. 42). Stalin knew about the *Holodomor* but 'was completely indifferent to the fate of the victims' (Naimark, 2010, p. 77). Millions died in Soviet Ukraine 'in the greatest artificial famine in the history of the world' and 'During the years that both Stalin and Hitler were in power, more people were killed in Ukraine than anywhere else in the bloodlands, or in Europe, or in the world' (Snyder, 2010, p. 20; Kulchytskyy, 2002).

During the conservative Soviet 'era of stagnation' Stalin was praised for his contribution to building an industrialised state and nuclear superpower (Zaslavsky, 1982, pp. 3–9, 20–21). Although a famine happened in 1932–1933 the Kremlin's 'correct' view claims it equally affected Russians, Ukrainians and other Soviet peoples. Ukrainian depictions of the *Holodomor* as a Stalinist genocide against the Ukrainian people have never been accepted in the Kremlin (Young, 2015). Although Presidents Leonid Kravchuk and Leonid Kuchma had described the *Holodomor* as a genocide, it was President Yushchenko who was sent an undiplomatic 'address' by President Medvedev (2009) attacking, amongst other areas, his strong stance that the *Holodomor* was a genocide against the Ukrainian people (Kuzio, 2015, pp. 438–439). In addition to the *Holodomor*, Stalinist terror and repression included the destruction of the Ukrainian Autocephalous Orthodox and Greek-Catholic national churches; murder of the Executed Renaissance intellectuals and national communists; executions of political prisoners in 1941 in western Ukraine (Kiebuzinski and Motyl, 2017); mass deportations from western Ukraine; the 1947 famine; and brutal pacification of western Ukraine during the decade-long war between the Soviet secret police and UPA (Ukrainian Insurgent Army).

[14] https://ukraine.ohchr.org/en/Alarming-Rise-in-Executions-of-Captured-Ukrainian-Military-Personnel

4 GREAT PATRIOTIC WAR AND CULT OF STALIN 155

In the first half of the 1990s, Ukrainian scholars and politicians increasingly redefined the *Holodomor* as genocide. On the 60th anniversary of the famine in September 1993, President Kravchuk said Stalin's goals had been to 'uproot the entire Ukrainian soul' and he described Stalin's policies as 'genocide against one's own people on the basis of instructions issued from outside' (Bilinsky, 1994, p. 79). In November 2001, on the Day of Remembrance (which had replaced annual commemoration of the 1917 Bolshevik Revolution) President Kuchma talked of 'tens of millions of Ukrainians' who had died in war, the *Holodomor* and the Gulag'. Kuchma launched an international campaign on the eve of the 70th anniversary in 2003 of the *Holodomor* to gain support for it to become recognised as a genocide committed against the Ukrainian people.

During Kuchma's presidency the Ukrainian parliament voted on 28 November 2002 for a resolution on the 70th anniversary of the *Holodomor* which described it as an act of genocide against the Ukrainian people (Parliamentary resolution on the 70th Anniversary of the *Holodomor* in Ukraine, 2002). The only parliamentary faction to not support the resolution was the KPU. Two parliamentary factions from the Donbas, Regions of Ukraine and European Choice parliamentary faction voted in favour, as did Viktor Medvedchuk's SDPUo (Social Democratic Party united) (Parliamentary resolution on the 70th Anniversary of the *Holodomor* in Ukraine 2002). Eight years later, President Yanukovych adopted the Kremlin's 'correct' position on the 1932–1933 famine as having affected both Russians and Ukrainians.

Soviet myths about the Great Patriotic War continued to be commemorated in Ukraine under Presidents Kravchuk and Kuchma. Throughout the 1990s, an important element of official memory policy was the celebration of the anniversary of 17 September 1939, when Soviet troops 'liberated' the 'exploited working people of western Ukraine and western Belarus from the yoke of bourgeois Poland'. Although this message had become outdated after the collapse of communism, the cult of the so-called 'Golden September' continued, but in an increasingly 'nationalised' format. According to this updated version, 17 September 1939 was of key importance in the process of state-building in Ukraine because it was then that the historic 're-unification' of ethnic Ukrainian lands into one state had taken place.

In the 1990s, former members of the Soviet *nomenklatura*, such as Kravchuk and Kuchma, continued to celebrate the Soviet myth justifying the 1939 invasion of Poland as 're-unification' in parallel with growing support among national democratic political forces for the re-evaluation of the nationalist drive to independence and unity in 1917–1921. As a result, Kuchma (1999a, 1999b) issued two decrees on 're-unification'. The first decree established an annual holiday on 22 January to celebrate 'The Day of Ukrainian Unity' which took place on that day in 1919 between the UNR (Ukrainian People's Republic) and ZUNR (West Ukrainian People's Republic) (Kuchma, 1999a) while the second decree continued the Soviet commemoration of 're-unification' of Ukrainian lands in 1939 (Kuchma, 1999b). Kuchma (2023, p. 65) continued to hold some positive sentiments about the Soviet 're-unification', writing: 'The Soviet regime did not succeed in Russifying Lviv, but they succeeded in making it Ukrainian, although, of course, this was not the conscious aim of the Kremlin'.

A common misconception among scholars is that it was the 'nationalist' Yushchenko who first defined the *Holodomor* as a genocide and began transforming the memory politics of OUN (Organisation of Ukrainian Nationalists) and UPA; in fact, it was Kuchma (Hrytsenko, 2017, pp. 214–244 on the *Holodomor* and pp. 113–129 on OUN and UPA). Kuchma's memory politics, which has been largely ignored by scholars (for an exception see Kuzio, 1998, pp. 198–229), moved into new areas such as the UNR (Ukrainian Peoples Republic) and war of independence in 1917-1921 against White Russian pro-imperial and Russian Bolshevik forces, the *Holodomor*, and – more tentatively – OUN and UPA. Therefore, Kravchuk and Kuchma should be understood as transitional leaders from the Soviet to a Ukrainian identity distinct from Russian (Kuzio, 1998, pp. 198–229), with Yushchenko, after the Orange Revolution and Petro Poroshenko after the Euromaidan Revolution moving decisively away from a hybrid Soviet and Ukrainian to a Ukrainian identity during the same period as Putin's Russia's regime was becoming imperial nationalist and Ukrainophobic. Kuchma (2000) expanded the 1998 'Day of Memory of the Victims of the *Holodomor*' anniversary to an annual commemoration of the 'Day of Memory of the Victims of the *Holodomor* and Political Repression'. On the seventieth anniversary of the *Holodomor*, Kuchma (2002a, 2002b) issued two decrees while the Ukrainian parliament issued a resolution and appeal (Ukrainian Parliament, 2002; Ukrainian Parliament, 2003); all four documents described the *Holodomor* as a 'genocide'. Nevertheless, in the last years of his second presidential term, Kuchma (2002c) continued to support a hybrid Soviet and Ukrainian identity, issuing a decree on the 350th anniversary of the 1654 Pereyaslav Council, instructing the government to commemorate the 85th anniversary of the birth of Volodymyr Shcherbytsky (Ukrainian Government, 2002; Kuzio, 2015, p.24), and lobbying parliament to commemorate the 85th anniversary of the founding of the *Komsomol* (Ukrainian Parliament, 2004).

The understanding of the significance of the Molotov–Ribbentrop Pact on the part of Ukrainian political elites only began to change under Yushchenko (see Chapters 6 and 7). In 2009, ten years after Kuchma's (1999) decree, a draft parliamentary resolution was prepared by KPU deputy Oleksandr Holub for the celebration of the 70th anniversary of 're-unification' which repeated Soviet propaganda.[15] Now, however, Holub's initiative no longer aroused any interest, and his draft was not put to a vote. Yushchenko (2007, 2010) issued decrees celebrating the one hundredth anniversary of the birth of OUN leader Roman Shukhevych and awarded the title of 'Hero of Ukraine' to OUN leader Stepan Bandera; both had been the subject of antinationalist propaganda in the Soviet era and continue to be condemned by Putin's Russia (see Chapter 5).

The transition from commemoration of hybrid Soviet and Ukrainian to patriotic and nationalist anniversaries began under Kuchma, gathered speed under Yushchenko, temporarily stalled under Yanukovych and went into turbo drive under Poroshenko. Europe did not always welcome these changes in Ukrainian memory politics. The European Parliament condemned Yushchenko's decree on Bandera, writing that OUN had 'collaborated with Nazi Germany' and called upon the Ukrainian authorities to 'reconsider such decisions' to 'maintain its commitment to European values' (in fact, Bandera was imprisoned by the Nazis during the Second World War) (European Parliament, 2010). In 2015, one of four de-communisation laws 'On the Legal Status and Honouring of the Memory of the Fighters for the Independence of Ukraine in the 20th Century' honoured a long list of organisations and dissident movements that had fought for Ukrainian independence, beginning with the UNR and ending with the Popular Movement of Ukraine for Restructuring (*Narodnyi rukh Ukrainy za perebudovu [Rukh]*), established in 1988 (Oliinyk and Kuzio, 2021, pp. 816–817). All these organisations have been condemned as 'nationalist/fascist/Nazi' by 'Historic Russia': the Tsarist Empire, Soviet Union, and Russian Federation.

Ukraine radically diverged from Russia when the Great Patriotic War was replaced by the Second World War in four de-communisation laws adopted after the Euromaidan Revolution. The Ukrainian Institute of National Remembrance developed special guidelines on how to commemorate the Second World War for local government councils and the public. These highlighted the need to use correct historical terminology

---

[15] https://ips.ligazakon.net/document/DF3XD00A?an=3

instead of Soviet and Russian propaganda clichés', such as 'expelling the Nazi occupants' instead of 'liberation from fascist invaders' and 'Second World War' instead of 'Great Patriotic War'. These guidelines explained Ukraine was not liberated after the expulsion of Nazis but was reoccupied by another totalitarian state.[16] The narrative about the 're-unification' of Ukrainian lands finally disappeared from the official discourse of memory in Ukraine. Ukraine joined the European discourse of memory that condemned 'two totalitarianisms' (Nazi and Soviet).

The main holiday changed from 9th May, celebrated by the USSR and Russia, to 8th of May, commemorated by Europe and North America. The 8th of May holiday became the Day of Memory and Reconciliation, signifying a solemn occasion of terrible suffering (Pastushenko, 2020, p. 81). Meanwhile, 9th May remained Victory Day (Yurchuk, 2017). Between 2015 and 2021, monuments to the Great Patriotic War were left in place but their communist symbols were removed. Since 2022, de-russification has led to a drive to remove all Tsarist and Soviet, including Great Patriotic War, monuments and plaques.

At the same time, the discourse of memory politics in Russia is strictly controlled by the Kremlin. The state, through appropriate laws, and provisions in the penal code and constitution, imposes the 'correct' way of interpreting the past. This applies especially to the Great Patriotic War and the Second World War. The current paradigm was presented by Putin (2020a, 2020b, 2021, 2022a, 2022b, 2024), especially dealing on the 75th anniversary of the end of the Great Patriotic War and 'On the Historical Unity of Russians and Ukrainians'. Those brave enough to not follow the 'correct' Kremlin course could be fined or imprisoned for 'publicly identifying the goals, decisions and actions of the USSR authorities, commanders of the armed forces and soldiers of the USSR with the goals, decisions and actions of the Nazis' or 'denying the decisive role of the Soviet nation in the defeat of Nazi Germany and the humanitarian mission of the USSR in liberating Nazi-ruled European countries' (Adamski, 2023, pp. 273–275).

Nazi Ukraine Becomes Russia's 'Other'

Misuse of 'Nazism' in Putin's Russia drew on long-standing Soviet propaganda campaigns against Ukrainian dissidents and nationalists and the Ukrainian diaspora that went as far back as the 1930s (see Chapter 5). After

---

[16] www.memory.gov.ua/news/metodichni-materiali-ukrainskogo-institutu-natsionalnoi-pam-yati-do-70-i-richnitsi-vignannya-na

the Orange and Euromaidan Revolutions the Soviet fascist threat was revived 'as a tool of pro-regime mobilisation in Putin's Russia' (Luxmoore, 2020, p. 824). Russian propaganda and disinformation had three goals: to discredit the Euromaidan Revolution; justify military aggression to protect Russian speakers; and belittle the very idea of Ukrainian statehood (Domańska, 2019; Gaufman, 2015; Pynnöniemi and Rácz, 2016; Nazi east, Nazi west, Nazi over the cuckoo's nest, 2017).

The Kremlin had criticised revised approaches to history writing in Ukraine since the disintegration of the USSR. University of York (Toronto) historian Orest Subtelny's *Ukraine. A History* had been published in the Ukrainian-language in Kyiv as early as 1991 when the USSR still existed; a Russian-language edition appeared three years later. In 1996, during Kuchma's presidency, Ukraine's new *hryvnya* banknotes included Kyiv Rus leaders Grand Prince Volodymyr the Great and Yaroslav the Wise, Cossack Hetman Ivan Mazepa, who together with Swedish allies led a failed independence drive against Muscovy, and historian Mykhaylo Hrushevsky who died in suspicious circumstances in the Soviet Union in 1934 and whose writings were banned in the Soviet Union (Kuzio, 1998, pp. 198–229). The Russian Orthodox Church issued an anathema (excommunication) against Mazepa in 1708 and refuses to revoke it, despite the Ecumenical Patriarch of Constantinople declaring it to be uncanonical.

Ukraine's de-communisation laws were a continuation of a trend that had therefore been taking place since the late 1980s and in fact, came later than similar legislation that had been adopted in the three Baltic states and central-eastern Europe. As Chapter 6 shows, Ukraine's and Russia's histories were going to be impossible to reconcile – irrespective of the de-communisation laws. In the spirit of imperial innocence USSR and Russian history writing praises Tsarist and Soviet rule and, as Putin's (2021) long essay showed, ignored the banning of the Ukrainian language, Russification, de-nationalisation of Ukrainians, and political repression while condemning the description of the 1932–1933 famine as *Holodomor* and genocide (Kuzio, 2002, 2005, 2006). In 2003, the Kremlin ignored President Kuchma's international campaign to obtain support for the recognition of the *Holodomor* as a genocide but, six years later Medvedev (2009) condemned this stance in his 'address' to Yushchenko (Kuzio, 2015, pp. 438–439). Ukraine's stance on the *Holodomor* as a genocide had remained constant since the early 1990s, supported by Presidents Kravchuk, Kuchma and Yushchenko. What had changed was Putin's Russia which had transitioned through its first critical juncture towards imperial nationalism which would become more extreme after two further critical junctures and transition into a fascist dictatorship (Garner and Kuzio, 2025). After the first and second critical junctures, Putin's Russia changed its stance on the *Holodomor*, Katyn, Molotov–Ribbentrop Pact and other important areas of Soviet and Russian history. Putin's Russia has long denied the *Holodomor* was a genocide but, as with claiming the Katyn killings of Polish officers was undertaken by the Nazis, has also regressed to denying a famine took place[17] and accusing historians of the famine, such as Robert Conquest (1986), of being agents of Western secret services.[18]

An independent Ukrainian history is fundamentally incompatible with the Soviet concept of eastern Slavic 'brotherhood' and Russian imperial nationalist concept of pan-Russian unity (see Yermolenko, 2019). Ukraine's de-communisation rehabilitated and commemorated movements and organisations that had fought for independence from foreign powers, of whom the greatest imperialist was Russia. Putin's Russia has continued the Soviet regime's denouncing of Ukrainian nationalist leaders, whether they are Cossack Hetmans (Mazepa), socialists (Symon Petlura) or nationalists (Bandera).

The Kremlin expected Ukraine to pursue history writing like that found in Belarus and Russia, which had little support in Ukraine, except during Yanukovych's presidency. Revision of memory politics in Ukraine since the Euromaidan Revolution were viewed by Russian imperial nationalists as going much further than earlier revisions in history writing and constituting a 'betrayal' of pan-Russian unity. Of all the changes in Ukraine's de-communisation laws, the transition from celebration of military victory in the Great Patriotic War to commemoration of the Second World War, a process that had begun during Yushchenko's presidency, was the most alarming for the Kremlin. The Great Patriotic War had deepened the alleged bond between Russian and Ukrainian 'fraternal brothers' that had existed throughout history and could never be broken. The de-communisation laws also equated communism and Nazism as twin evils, which undermined Putin Russia's Great Patriotic War religion because Victory Day is central to the legitimisation of Putin's regime and 'the nearest thing we have to an official ideology' (Luxmore, 2020). Ukraine's divergence from the Kremlin's 'correct' interpretation of the Second World War 'is seen as a threat to Russia's domination in the post-Soviet space or a direct challenge

---

[17] The *EUvsDisinfo* database has thirty-six cases of Russia denying a famine took place in Ukraine in 1932–1933. See https://euvsdisinfo.eu/disinformation-cases/?text=holodomor%20famine

[18] https://euvsdisinfo.eu/report/holodomor-myth-was-invented-by-the-anglo-saxons/; and https://euvsdisinfo.eu/report/holodomor-was-a-story-invented-by-a-british-spy/

to the very existence of the Russian state' (Apryshchenko, 2020, p. 147). In fact, Ukraine had not cancelled 9th May Victory Day but reinterpreted it and added a new holiday. Ukraine's de-communisation laws maintained the 9th of May as a national holiday, but it would now be for the Second World War in 1939–1945, not the Great Patriotic War in 1941–1945, and a new national holiday The Day of Remembrance and Victory was created on the 8th of May. A decade after the de-communisation laws were adopted, only 11 per cent of Ukrainians viewed 9 May as an important holiday (Kyiv International Institute of Sociology, 2025).

Russia blamed changes in Ukrainian memory politics since the Euromaidan Revolution upon Ukrainian Nazis who had come to power in a putsch and had transformed Ukraine into 'Anti-Russia'. The Kremlin accused the US, and EU, of transforming Ukraine into 'Anti-Russia' and 're-writing' the history of the Second World War (Putin, 2024). In the Kremlin's eyes, it was Ukraine – and Europe – who were the historical revisionists not Putin's Russia who were the only ones who understood and pursued the 'correct' version of Great Patriotic War history.

Conclusion

The myth of the Great Patriotic War occupies a central place in both Russian consciousness and historical propaganda. Myths about the Molotov–Ribbentrop Pact and the Soviet 'liberation' of Europe in 1944–1945 are closely related to it. As Filip Musiał (2023, p. 81) aptly noted, the myth of the Great Patriotic War is supposed to believe 'that in the case of the Soviets we are dealing with victims of unprovoked German aggression who – thanks to their own heroism – defeated the evil that was the Third Reich'. This imperial innocent myth allows us to ignore 'Soviet complicity in causing the global conflict and the earlier German-Soviet cooperation in the interwar period, that is, what led to the Molotov–Ribbentrop Pact and its later effects'. In addition, 'it allows us to remain silent about the crimes committed by the Soviet Union against the nations it conquered in 1939–1941. In its current form, the myth of the Great Patriotic War is intended to legitimise the Soviet Union's seizure of half of the lands of pre-war Poland, as well as the annexation of the territories of the Baltic states and part of Romania' (Musiał, 2023, p. 81).

The Kremlin promotes mythology about the Great Patriotic War using a variety of methods. The most important messages related to discourse around the Second World War, among others, relativise the criminal nature of the Soviet regime. For this purpose, 'they compare the foreign policy of a totalitarian state such as the USSR, whose ideology was based on a communist utopia and whose foreign policy sought to impose this utopia on others, with democratic or authoritarian European states that pose neither a threat to their neighbours nor are committing social experiments and mass crimes against their own citizens' (Adamski, 2023, p. 272).

As Russian historical propaganda, the meaning of concepts is reversed thanks to various semantic procedures. A pact of aggression becomes a pact of non-aggression, enslavement becomes liberation, and attack is called defence. The same language is used by Putin's Russia to legitimise its imperial aspirations, military aggression and war crimes against Ukraine. Russian historical revisionism creates a distorted image of the Second World War in which all those who fought the Red Army or did not support it were Nazi collaborators. Such a paradigm is readapted to conditions in post-Soviet Russia and is primarily about a specific antinomian way of perceiving the surrounding reality (see Chapters 5 and 7).

The myth of the Great Patriotic War lies at the core of discourse about, and belief in, the Russian great power narrative and is targeted at three audiences. The first, the Russian public, has been successful. Russians support the narrative of Russia with a right to be respected as a great power because it is the successor state to the USSR ('Historic Russia'). The second, post-Soviet elites and societies in the former USSR based on the myth of 'brotherhood of arms' has been far less successful. In the Soviet era, dissidents, nationalists, and the Ukrainian diaspora were castigated as 'nationalists/fascists/Nazis'. In Putin's Russia, a far broader definition of Nazis, drawing on Tsarist and White Russian émigré views of a pan-Russian people, is applied to all Ukrainians who hold an identity distinct from Russia and even other nations accused of 'Russophobia'. The third group is the political elites and societies of the West whose crimes have grown to include conspiring to destroy the USSR ('Historic Russia'), instigate colour revolutions in Georgia and Ukraine, organise the putsch that brought Euromaidan Revolutionary Nazis to power in 2014, and transforming Ukraine into 'Anti-Russia'.

Since the Euromaidan Revolution, Ukraine has commemorated the Second World War in the same manner as Europe and North America as a human tragedy. Meanwhile, since 2008, Putin's Russia has celebrated the Great Patriotic War as a military victory through a cult of war that proclaims, 'We Can Do It Again!' (Victory Day, 9 May in the Past in the USSR and Russia Today, 2024) that is coupled with an indifference to human suffering in either the first (1941–1945) or second (since 2014) Great Patriotic Wars. Ukraine's memory politics have shaped Ukrainian democratisation and identity as part of Europe. The Kremlin's memory politics have facilitated Russia's transition to authoritarianism and more recently fascist dictatorship (see Garner and Kuzio, 2025), fanning wars against internal and external enemies through political repression, military aggression and war crimes against the Russian and Chechen peoples at home and Georgians, Syrians, and Ukrainians abroad.

References

Adamski, Ł. (2023). 'Rosyjska polityka historyczna' In: J. Lubecka and M. Zakrzewski (eds.), *Polityka historyczna*. Kraków: Wydawnictwo Naukowe Uniwersytetu Ignatianum w Krakowie, 257–276.
Amalrik, A. (1971). *Will the Soviet Union Survive Until 1984?* London: Allen Lane.
Applebaum, A. (2017). *Red Famine: Stalin's War on Ukraine*. London: Allen Lane.
Applebaum, A. (2023). 'Ukraine and the Words that lead to mass murder,' *The Atlantic*, 25 April. www.theatlantic.com/magazine/archive/2022/06/ukraine-mass-murder-hate-speech-soviet/629629/
Apryshchenko, V. (2020). 'Industry of Retro or Retro-Industry. The Production of Memory in Contemporary Russia,' *Communist and Post-Communist Studies*, 53 (2): 137–152.
Aron, L. (2023). *Riding the Tiger. Vladimir Putin's Russia and the Uses of War*. Washington, DC: American Enterprise Institute.
Baekken, H. (2023). 'Merging the Great Patriotic War and Russian Warfare in Ukraine. A Case- Study of Russian Military Patriotic Clubs in 2022,' *Political Research Exchange*, 5 (1). https://doi.org/10.1080/2474736X.2023.2265135
Bilinsky, Y. (1994). 'Basic Factors in the Foreign Policy of Ukraine. The Impact of the Soviet Experience' In: S. F. Stark (ed.), *The Legacy of History in Russia and the New States of Eurasia*. Armonk, NY: M.E. Sharpe: 171–192.
Bogumił, Z., and Voronina, T. (2023). *More than Alive. The Dead, Orthodoxy and Remembrance in Post-Soviet Russia*. Lausanne-Berlin: Peter Lang.
Brudny, Y. (1998). *Reinventing Russia. Russian Nationalism and the Soviet State, 1953–1991*. Cambridge, MA: Harvard University Press.
Cichowlas, O. (2017). 'How Russian Kids Are Taught World War II,' *Moscow Times*, 8 May. www.themoscowtimes.com/2017/05/08/how-russian-kids-are-taught-world-war-ii-a57930
Congress of People's Deputies of the USSR. (1989). 'Postanovlieniie Siezda narodnykh dieputatov SSSR o paktie Molotova-Ribbentropa,' 24 September. https://doc20vek.ru/node/3261
Conquest, R. (1986). *The Harvest of Sorrow: Soviet Collectivization and the Terror-Famine*. London, New York: Oxford University Press.
Council of Europe. (2006). 'Need for International Condemnation of Crimes of Totalitarian Communist Regimes,' Parliamentary Assembly of the Council of Europe, Resolution 1481, 25 January. https://assembly.coe.int/nw/xml/XRef/Xref-XML2HTML-en.asp?fileid=17403&lang=En

Coynash, H. (2017). 'Jailed Historian of Stalin's Terror Declared a Political Prisoner in Putin's Russia,' *Kharkiv Human Rights Protection Group*, 4 August. http://khpg.org/en/index.php?id=1501022657

Czech Parliament. (2008). 'Prague Declaration on European Conscience and Communism,' Senate of the Parliament of the Czech Republic, 3 June. www.praguedeclaration.eu/; www.europarl.europa.eu/doceo/document/TA-9-2019-0021_EN.pdf

Domańska, M. (2019). 'The Myth of the Great Patriotic War as a Tool of the Kremlin's Great Power Policy', Centre for Eastern Studies, *OSW Commentary*, 316. 31 December. www.osw.waw.pl/en/publikacje/osw-commentary/2019-12-31/myth-great-patriotic-war-a-tool-kremlins-great-power-policy

Domańska, M., and Rogoża, J. (2021). *Forward, Into the Past! Russia's Politics of Memory in the Service of 'Eternal' Authoritarianism*, Centre for Eastern Studies, November. www.osw.waw.pl/sites/default/files/OSW-Report_Forward-into-the-past_net_0.pdf; www.osw.waw.pl/sites/default/files/OSW-Report_Forward-into-the-past_net_0.pdf

Dunlop, J. B. (1979). 'The Faces of Contemporary Russian Nationalism,' *Survey*, 24 (3): 18–35.

Epstein, M. (2022). 'Schizophrenic Fascism: On Russia's War in Ukraine,' *Studies in East European Thought*, 74: 475–481.

Etkind, A. (2023). *Russia against Modernity*. London: Polity Press.

European Parliament. (2008). 'European Day of Remembrance for Victims of Stalinism and Nazism,' Resolution P6_TA (2008)0439, 23 September. www.europarl.europa.eu/doceo/document/TA-6-2008-0439_EN.html

European Parliament. (2009). 'European Conscience and Totalitarianism', Resolution P6_TA (2009)0213, 2 April. www.europarl.europa.eu/doceo/document/TA-6-2009-0213_EN.html

European Parliament. (2010). 'On the Situation in Ukraine', Resolution, 25 February.

European Parliament. (2019). 'Importance of European Remembrance for the Future of Europe', Resolution 2019/2819(RSP), 19 September.

European Union. (2007). 'Reports and proceedings of the 8 April European public hearing on Crimes Committed by Totalitarian Regimes,' Slovenian Presidency of the EU, 8 April. https://web.archive.org/web/20111004145243/; www.mp.gov.si/fileadmin/mp.gov.si/pageuploads/2005/PDF/publikacije/Crimes_committed_by_Totalitarian_Regimes.pdf; www.europarl.europa.eu/doceo/document/TA-7-2010-0035_EN.html

Fedor, J., Kangaspuro, M., Lassila, J., and Zhurzhenko, T. (2017). Edited. *War and Memory in Russia, Ukraine, and Belarus*. New York: Palgrave Macmillan.

Felgenhauer, P. (2019). 'Victory Day 2019: Kremlin Envelops Itself in Militaristic Fervour,' *Eurasia Daily Monitor*, 16 (68). https://jamestown.org/program/victory-day-2019-kremlin-envelopes-itself-in-militaristic-fervor/

For Some Russians, Stalin 'Didn't Kill Enough People'. (2016). *Radio Free Europe/Radio Liberty*, 11 July.

Franchetti, M. (2014). 'Man of the Year (Alas),' *The Sunday Times*, 28 December. www.thetimes.co.uk/article/man-of-the-year-alas-zjkj3c3fsbx

Garner, I., and Kuzio, T. (2025). Edited. *Russia and Modern Fascism: New Perspectives on the Kremlin's War against Ukraine*. Stuttgart: Ibidem; New York: Columbia University Press.

Gaufman, E. (2015). 'Memory, Media, and Securitization: Russian Media Framing of the Ukraine Crisis,' *Journal of Soviet and Post-Soviet Politics and Society*, 1 (1): 141–174.

Grieff, P., de (2025). Commissioner of the Independent International Commission of Inquiry on Ukraine to United Nations Security Council Arria-Formula Meeting, New York, 13 January. www.ohchr.org/en/statements-and-speeches/2025/01/statement-pablo-de-greiff-commissioner-independent-international

Grove, T. (2025). '"Be Cruel": Inside Russia's Torture System for Ukrainian POWS,' *Wall Street Journal*, 10 February. www.wsj.com/world/russia/russia-prisons-ukranian-pow-torture-52df7908

Higgins, A. (2017). 'Putin Era Taboo: Telling Why Some Soviets Aided the Nazis,' *New York Times*, 21 June. www.nytimes.com/2017/06/21/world/europe/vladimir-putin-russia-vladimirmelikhov.html

Historical Revisionism: 'Polish imperialism against Ukraine and Belarus'. (2023). *EUvsDisinfo*, 6 May. https://euvsdisinfo.eu/historical-revisionism-polish-imperialism-against-ukraine-and-belarus/

Hrytsenko, O. (2017). *Prezydenty i Pamyat. Polityka pamyati prezydentiv Ukrayiny (1994–2014): pidhruntya, poslannya, realizatsiya, rezultaty*. Kyiv: K.I.S.

Ilyushina, M. (2023). 'Russia's New Historical Textbooks Teach Putin's Alternative Reality,' *The Washington Post*, 12 August. www.washingtonpost.com/world/2023/08/13/russia-history-textbook-revision-ukraine/

In New TV Spots, Ukraine Accuses Russia of 'Misappropriating' Victory Day. (2015). *Radio Free Europe/Radio Liberty*. www.rferl.org/a/new-tv-spots-ukraine-accuses-russia-misappropriate-victory-day/26983376.html

Istoricheskaja Pamjat. (2020). 'Istoricheskaja pamjat – eshhjo odno prostranstvo, gde reshajutsja politicheskie zadachi.' *Russia in Global Affairs*, 29 January. https://globalaffairs.ru/articles/istoricheskaya-pamyat-eshhe-odno-prostranstvo-gde-reshayutsya-politicheskie-zadachi-2/

Karmanau, Y. (2015). 'Ukraine's Rebel Centre in Limbo as Fighting Dies Down,' *Associated Press*, 5 November.

Khapaeva, D. (2009). 'Historical Memory in Post-Soviet Gothic Society,' *Social Research*, 76 (1): 359–394.

Khrushchev, N. S. (1976). *The Secret Speech*. Nottingham: Spokesman Books.

Khrushcheva, N. L. (2025). 'Putin Is Revving Up Russia's Nostalgia Machine,' *Globe and Mail*, 31 January. www.theglobeandmail.com/opinion/article-putin-is-revving-up-russias-nostalgia-machine/

Kiebuzinski, K., and Motyl, A. (2017). *The Great West Ukrainian Prison Massacre of 1941. A Sourcebook*. Amsterdam: Amsterdam University Press.

Kohut, A. (2015). 'Control over the Past: Russia's Archival Policy and Second World War Myths,' *Euromaidan Press*, 30 June. https://euromaidanpress.com/2015/06/30/control-over-the-past-russias-archival-policy-and-second-world-war-myths/

Kolesnikov, A. (2022). 'Putin's Stalin Phase. Isolated, Paranoid, and Ever More Like the Soviet Dictator.' *Foreign Affairs*, 8 November. www.foreignaffairs.com/russian-federation/putin-stalin-phase

Kryshtanovskaya, O., and White, S. (2003). 'Putin's Militocracy,' *Post-Soviet Affairs*, 19 (4): 289–306.

Kryshtanovskaya, O., and White, S. (2009). 'The Sovietization of Russian Politics,' *Post-Soviet Affairs*, 25 (4): 283–309.

Kuchma, L. (1999a). 'Pro Den sobornosti Ukrayiny,' Decree 42/99, 21 January. https://zakon.rada.gov.ua/laws/show/42/99#Text

Kuchma, L. (1999b). 'Pro vidznachennya 60-richchya vozzyednannya ukrayinskykh zemel v yedyniy Ukrayinskiy derzhavi,' Decree 437/99, 27 April. https://zakon.rada.gov.ua/laws/show/437/99/#Text

Kuchma, L. (2000). 'Pro vnesennya zmin do Ukazu Prezydenta Ukrayiny vid 26 lystopada 1998 roku', Decree 1181/2000, 31 October. https://zakon.rada.gov.ua/laws/show/1181/2000#Text

Kuchma, L. (2002a). 'Pro zakhody u zvyazku z 70-my rokovynam holodomoru v Ukrayini,' Decree 275/2002, 20 March. https://zakon.rada.gov.ua/laws/show/275/2002#Text

Kuchma, L. (2002b). 'Pro dodatkovi zakhody u zvyazku z 70-my rokovynamy holodomoru v Ukrayin', Instruction 393/2002, 6 December. https://zakon.rada.gov.ua/laws/show/393/2002-%D1%80%D0%BF#Text

Kuchma, L. (2002c). 'Pro vidznachennya 350-richchya Pereyaslavskoyi kozackoyi rady 1654 roku', Decree 238/2002, 13 March. https://zakon.rada.gov.ua/laws/show/238/2002#Text

Kuchma, L. (2023). *Ukrayina – Ne Rosiya. Dvatsyat Rokiv Potomu*. Kyiv: Adef-Ukrayina.

Kulchytskyy, S. (2002). Skilky nas Zahynulo Vid Holodomoru 1933 Roku?' *Dzerkalo Tyzhnya*, 23 November. http://gazeta.dt.ua/SOCIETY/skilki_nas_zaginulo_pid_golodomoru_1933_roku.html

Kuzio, T. (1998). *Ukraine. State and Nation Building*. London and New York: Routledge.

Kuzio, T. (2002). 'History, Memory and Nation Building in the Post-Soviet Colonial Space,' *Nationalities Papers*, 30 (2): 241–264.

Kuzio, T. (2005). 'Nation-State Building and the Re-Writing of History in Ukraine: The Legacy of Kyiv Rus,' *Nationalities Papers*, 33 (1): 30–58.

Kuzio, T. (2006). 'National Identity and History Writing in Ukraine,' *Nationalities Papers*, 34, (3): 407–427.

Kuzio, T. (2015). *Ukraine. Democratization, Corruption, and the New Russian Imperialism*. Santa Barbara, CA: Praeger.

Kyiv International Institute of Sociology. (2023). 'Dynamika Stavlennya Ukrayntsiv do Stalina', 9 November. www.kiis.com.ua/?lang=ukr&cat=reports&id=1326&page=1

Kyiv International Institute of Sociology. (2025). 'Stavlennya Ukrayinciv Do 9 Travnya (Den Peremohy) z 2013 do 2025 Roku', 7 May. www.kiis.com.ua/?lang=ukr&cat=reports&id=1516&page=1

Laqueur, W. (1993). *Black Hundred. The Rise of the Extreme Right in Russia*. New York: Harper Collins.

Laruelle, M. (2024). *Russia's Ideological Construction in the Context of the War in Ukraine*, Report 46. Paris: French Institute of International Relations. www.ifri.org/en/publications/etudes-de-lifri/russieeurasiereports/russias-ideological-construction-context-war

Levada Centre. (2017). 'Russia as a Great Power', 9 January. www.levada.ru/en/2017/01/09/russia-as-a-great-power/

Levada Centre. (2019). 'Perception of Stalin', 19 April. www.levada.ru/en/2019/04/19/dynamic-of-stalin-s-perception/

Levada Centre. (2021). 'Samyie vydaiushiiesia lichnosti v istorii', 21 June. www.levada.ru/2021/06/21/samye-vydayushhiesya-lichnosti-v-istorii/

Levada Centre. (2025). 'Samyie vydaiushiiesia lichnosti v istorii vseh vremjon i narodov', 17 June. www.levada.ru/2025/06/17/samye-vydayushhiesya-lyudi-vseh-vremyon-i-narodov/

Luhn, A. (2016). 'Stalin, Russia's New Hero,' *New York Times*, 11 March. www.nytimes.com/2016/03/13/opinion/sunday/stalinist-nostalgia-in-vladimir-putins-russia.html?_r=0

Luxmoore, M. (2020). '"It All Depends on the Body Count": Pandemic Threatens Putin's Spring of Political Pageantry,' *Radio Free Europe/Radio Liberty*, 10 April. www.rferl.org/a/russia-victory-day-coronavirus-putin-pandemic-political-pageantry/30546645.html

MacKinnon, M. (2015). 'Russia's Brief Shining Moment,' *Globe and Mail*, 15 August. www.theglobeandmail.com/news/world/russias-brief-shining-moment-the-city-of-perm-and-its-meandering-dance-withhistory/article25968031/

Manipulating Memory: Rewriting School History Books. (2024). *EUvsDisinfo*, 16 February. https://euvsdisinfo.eu/manipulating-memory-rewriting-school-history-books/

Martin, T. (2001). *The Affirmative Action Empire. Nations and Nationalism in the Soviet Union, 1923–1939*. Ithaca, NY: Cornell University Press.

McGlynn, J. (2023). 'Russia's History Textbook Rewrite Is a Bid to Control the Future,' *Moscow Times*, 15 August. www.themoscowtimes.com/2023/08/15/russias-history-textbook-rewrite-is-a-bid-to-control-the-future-a82146

Medvedev, D. (2009). 'Address to the President of Ukraine Viktor Yushchenko,' 11 August. http://kremlin.ru/events/president/news/5158

Medvedev, S. (2023). *A War Made in Russia*. London: Polity Press.

Musiał, F. (2023). 'Polityka historyczna a historia' In: J. Lubecka and M. Zakrzewski (eds.), *Polityka historyczna*. Kraków: Wydawnictwo Naukowe Uniwersytetu Ignatianum w Krakowie: 73–88.

Myers, S. L. (2007). 'Youth Groups Created by Kremlin Serve Putin's Cause,' 8 July, www.nytimes.com/2007/07/08/world/europe/08moscow.html

Naimark, N. (2010). *Stalin's Genocides*. Princeton, NJ: Princeton University Press.

Nazi east, Nazi west, Nazi over the cuckoo's nest. (2017). *EUvsDisinfo*, 27 February. https://euvsdisinfo.eu/nazi-east-nazi-west-nazi-over-the-cuckoos-nest/

Nelson, T. H. (2015). 'History as Ideology: The Portrayal of Stalinism and the Great Patriotic War in Contemporary Russian High School Textbooks,' *Post-Soviet Affairs*, 31 (1): 37–65.

Nougayrede, N. (2015). 'Heroes of 2014: Russian Human Rights Group Memorial,' *The Guardian*, 1 January. www.theguardian.com/commentisfree/2015/jan/01/heroes-2014-russian-human-rights-group-memorial

Oliinyk, A., and Kuzio, T. (2021). 'The Euromaidan Revolution of Dignity, Reforms and De-Communisation in Ukraine.' *Europe-Asia Studies*, 73 (5): 807–836.

Olszański, T. A. (2017). 'The Great De-communisation. Ukraine's Wartime Historical Policy,' Centre for Eastern Studies, *Point of View* 65. 13 September. www.osw.waw.pl/en/publikacje/point-view/2017-09-13/great-decommunisation-ukraines-wartime-historical-policy

Organisation for Security and Cooperation in Europe. (2009). 'Vilnius Declaration "Resolution on Divided Europe Reunited: Promoting Human Rights and Civil Liberties in the OSCE Region in the 21st Century",' Parliamentary Assembly of the OSCE, 29 June-3 July. www.oscepa.org/documents/annual-sessions/2009-vilnius/declaration-6/261-2009-vilnius-declaration-eng/file

Parfitt, T., (2017). 'Joseph Stalin Demonized by Russia's Enemies, Says Vladimir Putin in Oliver Stone Interviews,' *The Times*, 16 June.

Pastushenko, T. (2020). "The War of Memory" in Times of War. May 9 Celebrations in Kyiv in 2014–2015' In: A. Wylegala and M. Glowacka-Grajper (eds.), *The Burden of the Past. History, Memory, and Identity in Contemporary Ukraine*. Bloomington: Indiana Press: 77–90.

Paxton, R. (2004). *The Anatomy of Fascism*. London: Penguin.

Peter, L. (2015). 'Stalin Wiped from Soviet Gulag Prison Museum,' *BBC*, 3 March. www.bbc.co.uk/news/world-europe-31711287

Petrov, N. (2018). 'Don't Speak, Memory. How Russia Represses Its Past,' *Foreign Affairs*, 97 (1): 16–21.

Pomerantsev, P. (2014). *Nothing Is True and Everything Is Possible. The Surreal Heart of the New Russia*. New York: Public Affairs.

Pomerantsev, P. (2022). 'Ukraine is the Next Act in Putin's Empire of Humiliation,' *The New York Times*, 26 July. www.nytimes.com/2022/07/26/opinion/russia-ukraine-putin.html

Putin, V. (2009). 'Przemówienie premiera Putina na obchodach 70. rocznicy wybuchu II wojny światowej,' 1 September. https://dzieje.pl/aktualnosci/przemowienie-premiera-putina-na-obchodach-70-rocznicy-wybuchu-ii-wojny-swiatowej

Putin, V. (2020a). "This Crime Had Accomplices": Putin's World Holocaust Forum Speech,' 23 January. www.timesofisrael.com/this-crime-had-accomplices-full-text-of-vladimir-putin-holocaust-forum-speech/

Putin, V. (2020b). '75 liet vielikoi pobiedy: obshchaia otvetstviennost pieried istoriiei i budushchim,' 19 June. http://kremlin.ru/events/president/news/63527

Putin, V. (2021). 'On the Historical Unity of Russians and Ukrainians,' 12 July. http://en.kremlin.ru/events/president/news/66181

Putin, V. (2022a). 'Address by the President of the Russian Federation,' 24 February. http://en.kremlin.ru/events/president/news/67843
Putin, V. (2022b). 'Vladimir Putin Answered Journalists' Questions,' 29 June. http://kremlin.ru/events/president/news/68783
Putin, V. (2024). 'Speech on Victory Day,' 9 May. http://en.kremlin.ru/events/president/news/73995
Pynnöniemi, K. and Rácz, A. (2016). *Fog of Falsehood. Russian Strategy of Deception and the Conflict in Ukraine*. Helsinki: Finnish Institute of International Affairs, Report no. 45, 5 October. www.fiia.fi/en/publication/fog-of-falsehood
Revival of the Stalinist Sports Parades in Putin's Russia. (2025). *EUvsDisinfo*, 15 January. https://euvsdisinfo.eu/revival-of-the-stalinist-sport-parades-in-putins-russia/
Rumer, E. (2023). 'How Putin's War Became Russia's War. The Country Will Struggle to Reckon with Its Crimes in Ukraine.' *Foreign Affairs*, 9 June. www.foreignaffairs.com/russian-federation/how-putins-war-became-russias-war
Russkaia Pravoslavnaia Tserkov i Vielikaia Otiechestviennaia Voina. (2005). Moskva: Izdatelskij Sovet Russkoj Pravoslavnoj Cerkvi.
Satter, D. (2012). *It was a Long Time Ago, and It Never Happened Anyway*. New Haven, CT: Yale University Press.
Schneider-Deters, W. (2024). *Russia's War in Ukraine. Debates on Peace, Fascism, and War Crimes, 2022–2023*. Stuttgart: Ibidem; New York: Columbia University Press.
Shearlaw, M. (2016). 'Three Years after Euromaidan, How Young Ukrainians See the Future,' *The Guardian*, 22 November. www.theguardian.com/world/2016/nov/22/three-years-after-euromaidan-ukrainians-russia-future
Slovo Sviatieshevo. (2023). Slovo Sviatieishevo Patriarkha Kirilla na vstrieche s yunymi sportsmienami iz Donbassa. www.patriarchia.ru/db/text/6006766.html
Smith, H. (1976). *The Russians*. New York: Ballantine Books.
Snegovaya, M., Kimmage, M., and McGlynn, J. (2023). 'The Ideology of Putinism. Is it Sustainable?' *Centre for Strategic and International Studies*, 27 September. www.csis.org/analysis/ideology-putinism-it-sustainable
Snyder, T. (2010). *Bloodlands. Europe between Hitler and Stalin*. New York: Basic Books.
Snyder, T. (2022). 'We Should Say It. Russia is Fascist,' *New York Times*, 19 May. www.nytimes.com/2022/05/19/opinion/russia-fascism-ukraine-putin.html
Sovieshchaniie s Postoiannymi. (2024). 'Sovieshchaniie s postoiannymi chlenami Sovieta Biezopastnosti,' 20 September. www.kremlin.ru/events/president/news/by-date/20.09.2024
Sperling, V. (2016). 'Putin's Macho Personality Cult,' *Communist and Post-Communist Studies*, 49 (1): 13–23.
Stanovaya, T. (2024). 'Russia's Pro-Putin Elites. How the Dictator Recruited Them to His Anti-Western Agenda.' *Foreign Affairs*, 9 May. www.foreignaffairs.com/russia/russias-pro-putin-elites

Sviateieishiy. (2019), 'Sviatieishyi Patriarkh Kirill vstrietilsia c dietmi pogibshikh siriiskikh voiennykh,' 29 May. www.patriarchia.ru/db/text/5443720.html

Take care of Russia. (2016). *The Economist*, 22 October. www.economist.com/news/special-report/21708881-mr-putin-not-setting-about-it-best-way-take-care-russia

The battle for Russia's history. (2016). 'Remember, Remember,' *The Economist*, 5 November. www.economist.com/news/europe/21709557-memorial-was-founded-commemorate-victims-state-repression-now-human-rights-group-may

The making of a Neo-KGB state. (2007). *The Economist*, 23 August. www.economist.com/briefing/2007/08/23/the-making-of-a-neo-kgb-state

Tolz, V. (1988a). 'The Changing Official Line on Collectivisation,' *Radio Liberty*, RL 424/88, 20 September.

Tolz, V. (1988b). 'Controversy over Leninist Roots of Stalinism,' *Radio Liberty*, RL 446/88, 12 October.

Tolz, V., and Hutchings, S. (2023). 'Truth with a Z; Disinformation, War in Ukraine, and Russia's Contradictory Discourse of Imperial Identity.' *Post-Soviet Affairs*, 39 (5): 347–365.

Tumarkin, N. (1994). *The Living and the Dead: The Rise and Fall of the Cult of World War II in Russia*. New York: Basic Books.

Ukraine's Fragile Ceasefire. (2015). *BBC*, 17 April. www.bbc.co.uk/programmes/n3csy4jt

Ukrainian Government. (2002). 'Pro vidznachennya 85-richchya vid dnya narodzhennya V.V. Shcherbytskoho', Resolution, 11 July.

Ukrainian Parliament. (2002). 'Pro 70-ti rokovyny holodomoru v Ukrayini', Resolution, 28 November. https://zakon.rada.gov.ua/laws/show/258-15#Text

Ukrainian Parliament. (2003). 'Pro Zvernennya do Ukrayinskoho narodu uchasnykiv specialnoho zasidannya Verkhovnoyi Rady Ukrayiny 14 travnya 2003 roku shhodo vshanuvannya pamyati zhertv holodomoru 1932-1933 rokiv', Resolution, 15 May. https://zakon.rada.gov.ua/laws/show/789-15#Text

Ukrainian Parliament. (2004). 'Pro 85-richchya LKSMU ta posylennya roli molodizhnykh hromadskykh orhanizatsii u vykhovnii roboti z moloddyu', Resolution, 2 March. https://zakon.rada.gov.ua/laws/show/1559-IV#Text

Victory Day, 9 May in the Past in the USSR and Russia Today. (2023). *EUvsDisinfo*, 8 May. https://euvsdisinfo.eu/victory-day-9-may-in-the-past-in-the-ussr-and-russia/

Victory Day, 9 May in the Past in the USSR and Russia Today. (2024). *EUvsDisinfo*, 8 May. https://euvsdisinfo.eu/victory-day-9-may-in-the-past-in-the-ussr-and-russia-today-update-8-may-2024

Volkov, D. (2024). 'Mifologirizovannoie predstavlieniie o riepriessiiakh,' www.levada.ru/2024/12/23/mifologizirovannoe-predstavlenie-o-repressiyah/

Walker, S. (2015). 'Russia's Gulag Camps Cast in Forgiving Light of Putin Nationalism,' *The Guardian*, 29 October. www.theguardian.com/world/2015/oct/29/russia-gulag-camps-putin-nationalism-soviet-history

Wanner, C. (1998). *Burden of Dreams. History and Identity in Post-Soviet Ukraine.* University Park: Pennsylvania State University.
Wishnevsky, J. (1985). 'Neo-Nazis in the Soviet Union,' *Radio Liberty*, RL 226/85, 11 July.
Wishnevsky, J. (1986). 'Soviet Neo-Nazis in the Official Press,' *Radio Liberty*, RL 40/86, 23 January.
Yekelchyk, S. (2004). *Stalin's Empire of Memory. Russian-Ukrainian Relations in the Soviet Historical Imagination.* Toronto: University of Toronto Press.
Yermolenko, Y. (2019). *Re-Vision of History. Russian Historical Propaganda and Ukraine.* Kyiv: K.I.S., Internews, Ukraine World. https://ukraineworld.org/storage/app/media/Re_vision_2019_block%20eng.pdf
Young, C. (2015). 'Russia Denies Stalin's Killer Famine,' *The Daily Beast*, 31 October. www.thedailybeast.com/articles/2015/10/31/russia-denies-stalin-s-killer-famine.html
Yurchuk, Y. (2017). 'Global Symbols and Local Meanings: The "Day of Victory" after Euromaidan' In: T. Beichelt and S. Worschech (eds.), *Transnational Ukraine? Networks and Ties that Influence(d) Contemporary Ukraine.* Stuttgart: Ibidem; New York: Cambridge University Press: 89–114.
Yushchenko, V. (2007). 'Pro vidznachennya 100-richchya vid dnya narodzhennya Romana Shukhevycha,' Decree 420/2007, 16 May. www.president.gov.ua/documents/4202007-5885
Yushchenko, V. (2010). 'Pro prysvoyennya S. Banderi zvannya Heroy Ukrayiny,ik' Decree 46/2010, 20 January. https://zakon.rada.gov.ua/laws/show/46/2010#Text
Zaslavsky, V. (1982). *The Neo-Stalinist State. Class, Ethnicity, and Consensus in Soviet Society.* Armonk, NY: M. E. Sharpe.
Zygar, M. (2016). *All the Kremlin's Men. Inside the Court of Vladimir Putin.* New York: Public Affairs.
Zygar, M. (2023). 'Meet Putin's Ghostwriter,' *The New York Times*, 19 September. www.nytimes.com/2023/09/19/opinion/putin-russia-medinsky.html
Zygar, M. (2025). 'Red History Month. Putin's Recipe for Making a Country Great Again,' *Substack*, 4 February. https://zygaro.substack.com/p/red-history-month?utm_source=post-email-title&publication_id=2396897&post_id=156422708&utm_campaign=email-post-title&isFreemail=true&r=rzpsg&triedRedirect=true&utm_medium=email

5

Ukrainian 'Nationalists/Fascists/Nazis'

> Nazi Germany is ideological predecessor of modern Nazi Ukraine.[1]
> When a doctor is deworming a cat, for the doctor, it's a special operation. For the worms, it's a war, and for the cat, it's a cleansing.
> *Russian TV Presenter Vladimir Solovyov* (Hook, 2022).

The *tryzub* (trident) was the ancestral symbol of the Rurik dynasty who ruled Kyiv Rus from the tenth to twelfth century. In the tenth century, during the reign of Grand Prince Volodymyr the Great, coins bore his portrait on one side and the *tryzub* on the other. Russia has uncovered the trident (*tryzub*) is a 'Nazi symbol;'[2] presumably Ukrainian Nazis inhabited the medieval Kyiv Rus. The Russian principality of Vladimir-Suzdal and Grand Duchy of Muscovy never used the *tryzub*.

Russian propaganda campaigns against Ukrainian nationalism stretch as far back as Kyiv Rus, if we are to believe Russian propaganda, and especially since the 1709 Battle of Poltava, where Ukrainian Cossack forces led by Hetman Ivan Mazepa and their Swedish allies were defeated by Muscovy. Mazepa became the most hated figure in Russian nationalism – at least until OUN (Organisation of Ukrainian Nationalist) leader Stepan Bandera appeared two centuries later (Plokhy, 2023, p. 73). Ukrainian nationalists have been viewed by the Tsarist Empire, Soviet regime and contemporary Russia as 'traitors', 'treacherous', and 'reactionary' who were trying to turn Ukrainians against Russia (Erlacher, 2013, pp. 296– 297). Ukrainian nationalists were the 'enemy' of the Ukrainian people (Velychenko, 1993). Trials of members of the 1940s underground OUN, dissidents and nationalists continued until the late 1980s.[3] The Soviet

---

[1] https://euvsdisinfo.eu/report/nazi-germany-is-ideological-predecessor-of-modern-nazi-ukraine/
[2] https://euvsdisinfo.eu/report/the-ukrainian-trident-is-a-nazi-symbol/
[3] *Focus on Ukraine. Digest of the Soviet Press* (hereafter *FOUDSP*), September 1958, February 1960.

Ukrainian media attacked nationalists and Nazis in the USSR and in the Ukrainian diaspora until as late as 1990.[4] Indeed, some of the most vociferous propaganda tirades against the Ukrainian diaspora took place in the 1980s with the search for Nazi 'war criminals' in Canada, the UK and US.

During the last three centuries the myths of Ukrainian 'betrayal' and Western conspiracies to weaken Russia by encouraging Little Russians to believe they are Ukrainians have been at the centre of Ukrainian-Russian relations (Tolz, 2001, pp. 216, 218). Russian imperial nationalistic discourse has portrayed Ukrainians positively if they have supported their designation as a Little Russian branch of a pan-Russian people and negatively if they view themselves as Ukrainians who believe they have an identity distinct to Russian. The latter have been castigated as 'agents of Austria' by the Tsarist Empire, 'bourgeois nationalists', 'Nazi collaborators', and 'agents of Western secret services' by the Soviet Union and 'Nazis', 'nationalists' and 'Russophobes' by contemporary Russia. Russian imperial nationalists in the Tsarist Empire, Soviet Union and Russia have viewed Ukrainians as without agency and pawns used in conspiracies by the Austrians (Wolkonsky, 1920; Bregy and Obolensky, 1940), Nazi Germany, Western and Israeli intelligence agencies during the Cold War, and since 1991, the US, NATO and the EU. US and European democracy promoting foundations have allegedly orchestrated colour revolutions to weaken Russia (Ambrosio, 2007; Silitski, 2005). The *Project Russia* book series as early as 2005 denounced Western liberal democracy as decadent and infused with Nazism (Corum, 2018). Western dissident 'terrorists'[5] in the Soviet Union, and colour revolutions in the post-Soviet era allegedly had no local support and were funded and manipulated by Western intelligence agencies. Putin told the UN that the Euromaidan Revolution capitalised on 'discontent of the population with the current authorities' and 'the military coup was orchestrated from outside', which then 'triggered a civil war as a result.' Western governments, not Russia, were allegedly to blame for the ensuing conflict in eastern Ukraine, a similar Kremlin disinformation meme that blames the West for giving it no choice but to launch a 'special military operation' (see Karaganov, 2025).

There has therefore been a continuity of Russian imperial nationalist thinking from the Tsarist Empire and Soviet Union to Putin's Russia that Ukrainian nationalists have been Western puppets intent on weakening

---

[4] On Taras Kuzio, see 'Ostorozhno Falshyvka, ili kak ani "pomogaiut" nam v perestroike,' *Pravda Ukrainy*, 24 April 1988.

[5] FOUDSP, January 1985.

and harming Russia (Barbashin and Thoburn, 2015). Putin (2021b) claimed 'Since the Middle Ages, efforts have always been made to divide and break up the Russian people' ('Russian' understood as encompassing the three eastern Slavs).[6] Russians cannot comprehend why Ukrainians do not want to live within the Soviet Union or Pan-Russian World, believing this is due to Western machinations to quarrel both nations (McGlynn, 2023a, pp. 101–102).

In Putin's Russia, conspiratorial and imperial nationalistic views of Ukrainians grew from the mid 2000s when White Russian émigré writings began to be promoted by the Russian president and state apparatus. Not coincidentally, Soviet discourse of Ukrainians as nationalists/fascists/nazis was revived at the same time (Baekken, 2023). Putin's favourite author Ivan Ilyin believed, like all White Russian émigrés, 'There is no doubt as to the Austro-German origin of the legend of the existence of a separate Ukrainian nation' (Alexander Wolkonsky, 1920, p. 160; Barbashin and Thoburn, 2015). White Russian émigrés never considered Ukrainians to be a separate people and their attempts to build an independent state were a Western conspiracy against Russia.

As the Introduction to the book shows, there has been a continuity of Russian imperial nationalist demands towards Ukrainians from Russian President Dmitri Medvedev to Putin. David Satter (2017, pp. 133–134) pointed out it was misplaced, as US and other Western countries had believed, to describe Medvedev as a 'liberal'. In 2009–2012, Medvedev headed a Presidential Commission of the Russian Federation to Counter Attempts to Falsify History to the Detriment of Russia's Interests. In August 2009, Medvedev (2009) sent an 'address' (a form of demand and threat, rather than a friendlier open letter) to Ukrainian President Viktor Yushchenko which claimed that:

'Russian-Ukrainian relations have been further tested as a result of your administration's willingness to engage in historical revisionism, its heroisation of Nazi collaborators, exaltation of the role played by radical nationalists, and imposition among the international community of a nationalistic interpretation of the mass famine of 1932–1933 in the USSR, calling it the "genocide of the Ukrainian people"'.

Moscow was claiming it had the right, as in the Soviet Union, to demand how history would be written in Ukraine. Similar demands to reverse Ukraine's memory politics, language and education policies were made

---

[6] https://euvsdisinfo.eu/report/ukraine-and-russia-will-reunite-despite-natos-anti-russian-project-in-ukraine/

by the Russian delegation, led by Putin's ghost writer Vladimir Medinsky, during spring 2022 and 2025 peace talks and have remained in place as part of Russia's goal of the 'de-nazification' of Ukraine.

The term 'fascism' used in this chapter has nothing in common with Western political science definitions of the term (Davis, 2024, p. 153). Ukraine has the lowest electoral support for extreme right political parties of any European democracy. For the Kremlin, a 'fascist' is simply someone who opposes him [Putin]' (Schneider-Deters, 2024, p. 127). The term Nazi has been similarly applied to all shades of Ukrainian political opinions, ranging from Slavophiles and federalists to nationalists in the Tsarist Empire, national communists through to liberal democrats and nationalists in Soviet Ukraine, and since 1991, any Ukrainian who holds an identity distinct from Russians. Accusations against Ukrainians of 'nationalism' in the Soviet Union, Ivan Dzyuba wrote, was used to 'intimidate and subdue offhandedly all those who expressed concern about the state of national culture and the fate of the Ukrainian language' (Nahaylo, 1988). Chapter 7 analyses how Dzyuba's (1974, p. 99) well-known text *Internationalism or Russification?* showed how the Soviet regime abused the term 'nationalist' by applying it to 'any Ukrainian who has preserved the least trace of his nationality'. The Soviet regime viewed 'Ukrainian nationalists' as 'anyone possessing an elementary sense of national dignity, anyone concerned with the fate of Ukrainian culture and language and someone who failed to please Russian chauvinists, Great Russian bully' (Birch, 1971, p. 5). *Internationalism or Russification?* cited the officially published compilation *Lenin on Ukraine*; subsequent editions removed the texts that Dzyuba had cited showing how Lenin in the wrong hands could also constitute a threat to the Soviet regime. Dzyuba (1974) and dissidents were claiming the Soviet Union had strayed from 'Lenin's nationality policy'[7] in the 1920s, when indigenisation (Ukrainisation) policies were permitted, and were instead promoting Russian chauvinism and nationalism (see Chapter 9).

'Fascism' and 'Nazism' were misused and abused terms in the Soviet Union, and this continues to be the case in Putin's Russia. Vladimir Socor (2024) writes, 'As a political accompaniment to this war – and following Soviet practice – Russia designates resistance to itself as 'fascism' or 'Nazism', conflated with 'nationalism' and liable for political suppression. Draft peace agreements submitted by Russia in spring 2022 included a demand for Ukraine to ban 'aggressive nationalism' alongside 'fascism', 'Nazism', and 'neo-Nazism' (Socor, 2024).

[7] *FOUDSP*, August 1968.

A strong commitment to Ukrainian identity was equated with Nazism in the Soviet Union, and this continues to be the case in Putin's Russia (The Idea of Ukraine is Based on a Mythologised Lie, 2019; An Independent Legal Analysis of the Russian Federation's Breaches of the Geneva Convention in Ukraine and the Duty to Prevent, 2022; The Russian Federation's Escalating Commission of Genocide in Ukraine: A Legal Analysis, 2023; Hate speech and Russian calls for genocide in Putin's Russia, 2024). Anne Applebaum notes that both Joseph Stalin and Putin spoke obsessively about 'losing' Ukraine. The Soviet pathological hatred and fear of 'Ukrainian nationalism' within the Soviet secret police and KPSS (Communist Party of the Soviet Union) 'helped mould the thinking of the post-Soviet elite, long after the USSR ceased to exist' (Applebaum, 2017, p. 161). The former Soviet *siloviki* do after all, rule Russia.

In this chapter, Soviet and Russian anti-Ukrainian nationalist campaigns are analysed in three sections. The first section investigates the roots of Soviet propaganda campaigns against Ukrainian nationalism which took place from the mid 1930s and were coupled with repression of Ukrainian national communists, *Holodomor*, and *Rostrilyane Vidrodzhennya* (Executed Renaissance – the murder of Ukrainian cultural elites in the 1930s) (Lawrinenko, 1959). Chapter 7 analyses the interrelationship between the Executed Renaissance and post-communism in Ukraine. Changes in Soviet nationalities policies and mass repression took place alongside a return to Tsarist Russian historiography and a nationalities policy which designated Russians as the 'elder brother' and the eastern Slavs as forever united (see Chapter 9). The second section investigates campaigns against Ukrainian nationalism in Putin's Russia. The third section explores misuse of the Ukrainian 'Other' as 'nationalist/fascist/Nazi' since Russia's military invasions of Ukraine in 2014 and 2022.

Soviet Propaganda Campaigns against Ukrainian Nationalism

Soviet propaganda campaigns against Ukrainian nationalism began in the late 1920s-early 1930s (Shkandrij, 2015, p. 274; Wilson, 2014, p. 126). Stalin had come to view national communism as a threat to the Soviet regime amid rising fear of Ukrainian separatism working in cahoots with Poland. From 1934, Stalin's regime began to rehabilitate the Russian Empire, Russian nationalists, Russian imperial military leaders and Russian historians (Brandenberger, 2001, p. 280). The Soviet regime increasingly pursued the blurring of Soviet and Russian identities *and* Russian nationalism with Soviet patriotism. The Russian people were defined as the 'leading people' of the Soviet Union through the 'wartime restoration of an ethnic hierarchy' (Brandenberger, 2001, p. 287). Russians – who have a younger history than Ukrainians- were in effect designated as the 'elder brother' of the three eastern Slavs. In May 1945, Stalin's famous toast completed the rehabilitation of Russian imperial nationalism.[8]

After the Second World War the Soviet authorities fought a long security campaign against the tenacious Ukrainian nationalist underground until the early 1950s. Alexander Statiev (2010, p. 44) points to the OUN as the only nationalist movement in eastern Europe possessing a 'distinctive ideology and a widespread underground network'. The Bandera wing of OUN 'was a deeply rooted underground network enjoying popular support' and 'Ukrainian guerrillas fought with a resolution that no resistance in western Europe could have imagined' (Statiev, 2010, pp. 106, 108). The Stalinist regime responded to the security campaign with media and ideological campaigns against 'fascist nationalists' (Yekelchyk, 2004, p. 39). Anti-nationalist tirades increasingly targeted Ukrainian historians and political leaders, military formations from the Cossacks to the present that had fought for independence, the Ukrainian Autocephalous and Greek-Catholic Churches and Ukrainians who celebrated 'the struggle for independence' (Yekelchyk, 2004, pp. 31, 50, 54, 56–57).

With the incorporation of seven Western regions into Soviet Ukraine during the Second World War, Soviet attacks on Ukrainian nationalism also targeted Western Ukrainians who were seen as especially dangerous, nationalists and Russophobes. Galician Ukrainians who had travelled to Soviet Ukraine to work for the indigenisation campaign in the 1920s were repressed (Bertelsen and Shkandrij, 2014). Followers and supporters of OUN were labelled as 'Banderites' – a new term which replaced older derogatory depictions of Ukrainian nationalists as 'Mazepintsy' (supporters of Hetman Mazepa) and 'Petliurites' (supporters of UNR [Ukrainian Peoples Republic] military commander Symon Petlura). During the Stalin era, Andrei Zhdanov and Lazar Kaganovich sought 'To carry through the liquidation of bourgeois nationalist distortions in the history of Ukraine' and the 'cleansing' of Ukrainian culture and educational institutions (Yekelchyk, 2004, p. 78). Putin's ideological adviser Medinsky likes to

---

[8] https://soviethistory.msu.edu/1947-2/eight-hundred-years-of-moscow/eight-hundred-years-of-moscow-texts/toast-to-the-great-russian-people/

compare himself to conservative intellectuals in the Russian Empire like 'the infamous ideologue of Nicholas II's reign' Konstantin Pobedonostsev. Mikhail Zygar (2023b) though believes that closer models befitting Medinsky 'are Andrei Zhdanov, Stalin's right-hand man after the Second World War, and Mikhail Suslov, Leonid Brezhnev's chief ideologue, who advocated the persecution of dissidents'.

A brief respite from anti-nationalist campaigns followed Soviet leader Khrushchev's secret speech in 1956 and during Communist Party leader and Petro Shelest's leadership of Soviet Ukraine from 1963 to 1972. In the mid 1950s to late 1960s, when ethnic Ukrainians became a majority in the Soviet Ukrainian Communist Party for the first time, Soviet Ukrainian elites pushed the limits of the possible in language and culture. Ukrainian history experienced a brief renaissance whereby 'National history helped promote a neat, sanitised vision of Ukraine as a Ukrainian nation-space. Slowly but surely, the national paradigm overshadowed the international in Soviet Ukraine's politics of memory' (Wojnowski, 2017, p. 84). This teleological vision of history was promoted by the newly established *Ukrayinskyy Istorychnyy Zhurnal* (*Ukrainian Historical Journal*) which portrayed western Ukrainian territories as always having been Ukrainian. This ended in 1970 when Shelest was removed because of his book *Ukrayina nasha Radyanska* (Our Soviet Ukraine) which was condemned for 'national deviationism' in *Komunist Ukrainy*, the main theoretical journal of the Communist Party in Ukraine (Za Shcho Usunuly Shelesta? 1973). His removal was accompanied by what was described as a '*pohrom*' (pogrom) of Ukrainian dissent, culture and scholarship in the biggest purge in any Soviet republic since the Stalin era (Kupchinsky, 1980; Alexeyeva, 1980, pp. 21–59).

In 1972–1989, Soviet Ukraine was ruled by Communist Party leader Volodymyr Shcherbytsky who was fiercely loyal to Moscow, implemented harsh repression of dissidents and pursued an intense Russification policy. Shcherbytsky was the quintessential Little Russian the Kremlin and Communist Party preferred as their governor of Soviet Ukraine. Shcherbytsky possessed the correct ideological characteristics that were required for the pro-Russian puppet leader the Kremlin planned to install in Kyiv if its 'special military operation' had gone as planned. Political repression during Shcherbytsky's seventeen-year rule of Soviet Ukraine meant, 'Ethnic Ukrainians were thus pressed into the task of exorcising Ukrainian separatist nationalism' on behalf of Moscow (Beissinger, 1988, p. 84). Shcherbytskyy supported a natural bond and common history of the three eastern Slavs and equated Soviet loyalty with eternal Russian-Ukrainian friendship. Ukraine was always, and would always be, 'within the Russian cultural and political sphere of influence' (Wojnowski, 2017, p. 142) because Russians and Ukrainians are 'brotherly peoples'.

The Shcherbytsky era was a dark period for Ukrainian identity, culture, language, and dissent. After visiting Soviet Ukraine in the late 1960s and early 1970s, Ukrainian-Canadian John Kolasky (1968, 1970) returned to Canada as a disillusioned communist and wrote a number of highly critical books about his experience.[9] Kolasky (1968, p. XIII) wrote, 'Russians are everywhere with their arrogant overbearing attitude; their contempt, sometimes veiled but often overt, for the Ukrainian language, their open display of a feeling of Russian superiority'. Leftist Ukrainian-Canadians, who were especially prominent in the prairie provinces of Alberta, Manitoba and Saskatchewan where the Association of United Ukrainian-Canadians had many branches, represented a sizeable component of Canada's Communist Party. Its more mainstream competitor, KUK (Congress of Ukrainians in Canada) published and circulated Kolasky's (1968, 1970) highly critical books of Soviet Ukraine.

From the 1960s to the late 1980s, Soviet anti-nationalist tirades viciously and frequently attacked dissidents in Soviet Ukraine as 'bourgeois nationalists', Ukrainian émigré groups as 'Nazi collaborators', and both as agents of Western imperialism and Western secret services (Wilson, 2014, p. 126). Zbigniew Wojnowski (2017, p. 123) writes that 'bourgeois nationalism' as a 'term was fluid and open to interpretation' and usually was understood as somebody 'who articulated an understanding of what it meant to be Ukrainian that differed from the official Soviet script.' In other words, a 'bourgeois nationalist' was any Ukrainian who held an identity he/she believed was distinct from Russian. Putin calls 'someone who opposes him' a fascist' (Schneider-Deters, 2024, p. 127).

The Shcherbytsky era was an intense period of anti-Soviet propaganda which took place at the same time as Soviet nationalities policies increasingly supported Russification and the fusion of Soviet peoples into a Russian-speaking *Homo Sovieticus*. Putin's Russia has been able to draw upon these Soviet concepts because a Russian-speaking Soviet people is similar to the Tsarist and White Russian émigré concept of a Russian-speaking pan-Russian people. Indeed, as Chapter 4 analyses, Putin's Russia has fused Tsarist and White Russian émigré imperial nationalism with Soviet nostalgia (Kuzio, 2022).

[9] *FOUDSP*, August 1969.

In 1947, a new Stalinist thesis defined the eastern Slavs as constituting one people; de facto, the pre-Soviet pan-Russian people was reframed as a Soviet *Homo Sovieticus*. Ukrainians were treated as part of Russian history (Klid, 1991, p. 42). The thesis was codified in 1954 when the Soviet Union celebrated the three hundredth anniversary of the 1654 Treaty of Pereyaslav as the 're-union' of Russians and Ukrainians. These myths, combining 'some elements of the old pre-Soviet Russian nationalism with Soviet era recognition of the existence of a separate Ukrainian nation', have continued to remain influential in Putin's Russia (Plokhy, 2001, pp. 492–493). In the long essay penned by Putin (2021a) eight months before the full-scale invasion he wrote that the 'Russian state' 'decided to support their brothers in faith and take them under patronage', when Ukrainians 'swore allegiance to the Russian tsar' and 'referred to and defined themselves as Russian Orthodox people'. Ukrainian dissidents in the Soviet Union, histories of Ukraine published in the West, and history writing in Ukraine since 1991 have referred to the Treaty of Pereyaslav as a Ukrainian-Muscovite military alliance of equal partners – not as a 're-union' (Magocsi, 2010, pp. 226–230).

The USSR myth of the 'friendship of peoples' propagandised the Soviet people as 'a kind of supranational imagined community for the multiethnic Soviet people' (Martin, 2001, p. 81) that had been forged by Russia, and which had existed for centuries. This myth is one of a number which continues to buttress Russia's military aggression to 'liberate' Little Russians in 'Nazi-ruled' Ukraine. Such mythology ruled out objective appraisals of Russian-Ukrainian relations because it could not adequately analyse Russian and Soviet policies, such as the banning of the Ukrainian language, de-nationalisation and *Holodomor*. Putin's (2021a) positive appraisal of Russian-Ukrainian relations ignores these areas of conflict because he draws on a Soviet legacy whereby hostile relations between Ukrainians and Russians 'were downplayed, ignored or distorted' (von Hagen, 1995, p. 663).

Throughout the post-Soviet era, the Kremlin – as seen in Medvedev's (2009) 'address' to Yushchenko – has complained about the writing of history, school textbooks, and official anniversaries in Ukraine. Three days before Russia's full-scale invasion of Ukraine, Putin (2022) said: 'You want de-communisation? Very well, this suits us just fine. But why stop halfway? We are ready to show what real de-communisations would mean for Ukraine'. The Russian occupation authorities are reversing Ukraine's de-communisation by re-Sovietising and Russifying southeast Ukraine and Crimea (Oliinyk and Kuzio, 2021; The Kremlin's Occupation Playbook, 2024).

5 UKRAINIAN 'NATIONALISTS/FASCISTS/NAZIS'

In Soviet Ukraine, history writing was strongly policed to ensure it conformed to Soviet historiography. Kaganovich and Zhdanov 'liquidated' 'bourgeois nationalist distortions in the history of Ukraine' (Yekelchyk, 2004, p. 78). Ukrainians were re-educated by the Soviet regime to 'identify with the Soviet present and the Russian imperial past' (Yekelchyk, 2004, p. 71). From the mid 1930s to the mid 1980s, the Soviet regime promoted Russification and the Little Russianisation of Ukrainians. Soviet nationalities policies decreed there always had been, and always would be, an eternal union of Ukrainian and Russian 'fraternal peoples'. The history of Kyiv Rus was monopolised by Moscow as a 'Russian' state and Russians as having primacy among eastern Slavs from the thirteenth century (Velychenko, 1993, pp. 23–25). Soviet historiography portrayed Kyiv Rus as the birthplace of the 'fraternal' Russian, Ukrainian and Belarusian peoples and after its demise in 1240 its legacy was transferred to Vladimir-Suzdal, Muscovy, Imperial Russia, and the Soviet Union.

Ukrainian national historiography, which was banned in the Soviet Union but became dominant in Ukraine after 1991, described Kyiv Rus as the first Ukrainian state (Magocsi, 2010, pp. 55–130). After 1240, its legacy was transferred to the Galician-Volhynian Kingdom which existed from 1199 to 1349 and had ties to Europe. Hrushevsky, whose historical writings were banned from the mid 1930s to the late 1980s in the Soviet Union, continues to be denounced in Putin's Russia for developing a framework of separate Ukrainian and Russian histories (see Chapters 1 and 9).

The roots of claims by Putin's Russia's of a 'thousand years of Russian statehood' are to be found in the Soviet Union providing Russians with a monopoly over Kyiv Rus while marginalising Ukrainians as an accident of history brought about by foreign invaders and intrigue breaking apart 'Russian' unity. Medinsky has popularised the concept of a 'thousand-year Russian statehood' and succession of Russian history from Kyiv Rus to the present. For example, former director of the Carnegie Moscow Centre Dmitri Trenin (2020) writes that Kyiv Rus was the 'birthplace of the Russian state' (Zygar, 2023b).

School textbooks in Russia no longer refer to Kyiv Rus but only to 'Rus', the removal of Kyiv aimed at reducing its association with Ukraine (Finkel, 2024, p. 35). Indeed, the very term 'Ukraine' has been removed from new Russian school textbooks (Finkel, 2024, pp. 230–231). Grand Prince Vladimir (Volodymyr) was baptised in 'ancient Rus'. In 2016, Putin unveiled a huge monument to Grand Prince Vladimir (Volodymyr) next to the Kremlin. Volodymyr, who brought Christianity to Kyiv Rus, ruled from 978 to 1015; that is, over a century before Moscow was founded; in 1982, the Soviet Union celebrated Kyiv's 1,500-year anniversary, making Kyiv 600 years older than Moscow (Pritsak, 1981). Natalya Solzhenitsyn, widow of the well-known Russian nationalist dissident, Alexander Solzhenitsyn, attended the opening of the monument alongside Putin and Russian Orthodox Patriarch Kirill. This was intended to show that Russia's occupation of Crimea 'is building on the cultural tradition expressed by Solzhenitsyn himself in his 1990 article "Rebuilding Russia" in which he wrote that Ukraine is an ancestral part of Russia' (Zygar, 2023a, p. 331; Michel, 2024).

The religious question was so sensitive to the Soviet regime that the celebration of a millennium of Christianity was held in Moscow, a city that did not exist in 988, rather than Kyiv (Sorokowski, 1988). Instructions how to celebrate the 1035th anniversary of the baptism of Rus in 2023 included reference to the 'special military operation' goal of 'liberating' Kyiv from the 'Nazi satanists' who are allegedly occupying the city (Nazi Satanists are entrenched in the Holy Russian city of Kyiv, 2023). United Russia Party, State Duma deputy Valentina Tereshkova called on Patriarch Kirill to designate Zelenskyy as the 'anti-Christ'.[10]

In Soviet Russian and Russian historiography, Ukrainians have no separate history and having been artificially separated after the demise of Kyiv Rus, they sought 'reunion' with Russia (a yearning allegedly demonstrated by the 1654 Treaty of Pereyaslav). 'Good' Ukrainians were content in the Soviet Union, Putin adamantly believes, and since 1991 have yearned to be part of the Pan-Russian World and Russian-led Eurasia (Kuzio, 2005a; Wawrzonek, 2014).

Ukrainians who claimed to possess an identity distinct to Russians, upheld a history separate to Russians, and believed the future of their country lay outside the Pan-Russian World have always been castigated as 'Nazis' and 'fascists'. During the two decades prior to the Gorbachev era, the Soviet regime and KGB viewed support for the Ukrainian language and culture as manifestations of 'Ukrainian nationalism'. Being publicly proud of speaking Ukrainian would lead the KGB to view that person as ideologically subversive and a sign of 'bourgeois nationalism'. Ukrainian nationalist activist Anatoliy Lupynis recalled how the KGB

---

[10] https://infonavigator.com.ua/novosti/massovaya-shizofreniya-tereshkova-prosit-rpc-priznat-prezidenta-ukrainy-antihristom/; and https://news.telegraf.com.ua/novosti-rossii/2024-11-21/5887175-v-ee-chest-byli-nazvany-ulitsy-v-ukraine-kak-seychas-vyglyadit-pervaya-zhenshchina-kosmonavt-tereshkova-i-chto-govorit-o-voyne

5 UKRAINIAN 'NATIONALISTS/FASCISTS/NAZIS' 183

had asked him during an interrogation, 'Why do you converse exclusively in Ukrainian? What prompted you, one who had been speaking Russian during the first three years at the institute, to start speaking Ukrainian? Are you not aware that the official language of our country is Russian and that in the future all nations will speak Russian? Why did you grow a moustache?' (Jones and Yasen, 1977, p. 129). For the Soviet KGB, not only speaking Ukrainian but also sporting a Cossack moustache was a sign of 'bourgeois nationalism'.

The roots of contemporary Russian imperialist nationalist thinking about the Ukrainian language are to be found in the Soviet Union where the Ukrainian language came to be viewed as a 'Bandera-ite tongue' (Szporluk, 1976, p. 84). The KGB, and its successor organisations which rule Putin's Russia, witnessed how Ukrainian dissidents and writers in the Soviet Union and pro-Western Ukrainians have defended and promoted the Ukrainian language against Tsarist and Soviet policies of Russification. Alexander J. Motyl (2011) pointed out that 'a frequent refrain in Ukrainian dissident writings were the complaint that fellow citizens would sneer at them when they spoke Ukrainian and tell them to speak "human" [i.e., Russian]'. Soviet internationalism was understood by Russians as Ukrainians no longer speaking Ukrainian and switching to being a Russian speaker (Plyushch, 1979, p. 180). Dissident Leonid Plyushch (1979, p. 114) recalled asking somebody in Ukrainian in a bookshop to pass him a book. The person snarled back 'Can't you speak human [Russian]?' In the contemporary era, a Luhansk resident told of his preference for joining Russia over 'fascist Kyiv', one reason being that 'I don't speak the *telyacha mova* (calf's language);' that is, Ukrainian (Rudenko, 2014). Two decades into Ukrainian independent statehood, Anna Fournier (2012) found that Kyiv school students remained reluctant to speak Ukrainian in class for fear of appearing to be too 'nationalistic'. Ukrainian migrant workers in Russia were viewed with suspicion by Russians they came across because they viewed 'the men as simply Ukrainian extremists because they speak Ukrainian to one another' (Kurkov, 2014, p. 210) (Zygar, 2023b).

Olesya Khromeychuk (2015) estimated that 400,000 Russians and 250,000 Ukrainians out of 900,000 people from the USSR and central-eastern Europe served in German military, security and police formations during the Second World War. Although a larger number of Russians volunteered for military service in Nazi military and security forces, the Soviet regime and KGB did not conduct ideological tirades against émigré Russians. In 1941, White Russian émigrés and Soviet POWs set up the Russian Protective Corps[11] and Russian Cadet Corps, which collaborated with the Nazis. Up to 100,000 Russian Cossacks fought for the Nazis (McGlynn, 2023b; Szymanowicz, 2020, pp. 89–98). Russian Cossack collaboration with the Nazis does not deter Putin's Russia from supporting the revival of Cossack traditions, sending 43,000 Cossacks to fight against 'Ukrainian Nazis' and inviting the Great Don, Kuban, and Terek Cossack *voiskas* (armies) to participate in the 80th anniversary of the Great Patriotic War parade on Moscow's Red Square (Arnold, 2025). The émigré NTS (People's Labour Alliance) had grown out of the ROA (Russian Liberation Army) led by General Andrey Vlasov which at its peak included 300,000 troops. In comparison, an estimated 25,000 Ukrainians served in the Galician Division out of 250,000 Ukrainians who served in different German military and security formations. Émigré Russians and Russian nationalists were never targeted by Soviet propaganda regime because they never demanded the secession of the Russian SFSR from the Soviet Union (Motyl, 1990). The privileged status of the Russian language and culture meant Russian dissidents and anti-communist émigrés had few grounds to complain about national discrimination. This made Solzhenitsyn's (1980) claim that the Russian people had suffered the most in the Soviet Union to be untrue and a myth.

The Soviet regime spent huge resources condemning 'bourgeois nationalism' at home and abroad. From 1960, the KGB-controlled Society for Cultural Relations with Ukrainians Abroad, commonly known as *Tovarystvo Ukrayiny* (The Ukrainian Society), specialised in attacks against Ukrainian 'nationalist' émigrés. Similar societies were established for Lithuanians, Latvians, and Estonians – but not for Russians. *Tovarystvo Ukrayiny*'s two weekly newspapers, *Visti z Ukrayiny* (*News from Ukraine*) and its English-language equivalent *News from Ukraine*, both only available outside the Soviet Union, became major sources of disinformation and accusations against members of the Ukrainian diaspora. The newspapers contained information about trials of Ukrainian 'nationalists' in the USSR and analysis of the allegedly perfidious ways in which Ukrainian émigré organisations were seeking to undermine Soviet power with the support of Western and Israeli secret services.

The KGB and *Tovarystvo Ukrayiny* linked 'nationalist' émigrés with Ukrainian dissidents and cultural activists to buttress their claim they were not authentic homegrown movements but funded and controlled by outside 'Nazi war criminals' and Western and Israeli secret services. In

---

[11] www.kommersant.ru/doc/4801707

1958–1959, Soviet legislation expanded article 7 of the Soviet criminal code with the inclusion of the catch-all 'anti-Soviet agitation and propaganda'. This criminal charge entered the criminal code of the Ukrainian SSR in 1961 as article 62. The KGB's fifth directorate included departments combatting 'ideological diversion' in the trade unions, and among students, foreign journalists, unofficial groups, Jews, and émigrés. Ukraine's 1991 law 'On the Rehabilitation of Victims of Political Repression in Ukraine' initially investigated 307,000 victims of Soviet repression and in its final report rehabilitated 440,000 Ukrainians (Vyedyenyeyev, 2012). In the Soviet Union, Ukrainian 'nationalists' were imprisoned for 'ordinary criminal offenses' (Bilinsky, 1983, p. 10) and this tradition has continued in contemporary Russia and Russian-occupied Ukraine with the imprisonment, deportation, torture and sentencing of Ukrainians on false charges (Coynash, 2015a, 2015b). The soul and spirit of the KGB's fifth directorate was resurrected in Russian legislation combatting 'extremism' and 'terrorism' (Soldatov and Borogan, 2010, p. 73) and linking homegrown groups to Western-funded centres and intelligence services in the 2012 Russian law that defines foreign funded NGO's as 'performing the functions of a foreign agent'. The KGB obsessively tracked 'bourgeois nationalism' in the Ukrainian Helsinki Group, underground Ukrainian Greek Catholic Church and other dissident groups until the end of the Soviet Union (Wawrzonek, 2023, pp. 63–67).

Soviet Anti-Ukrainian Nationalist Propaganda

This section surveys ten areas targeted by Soviet anti-nationalist propaganda.

1) *Soviet Ideological Struggle:* The Communist Party of the Soviet Union and the Communist Party in Ukraine remained vigilant over the threat of ideological subversion. Through speeches at Communist Party congresses, the holding of special sessions devoted to combatting subversion, and ideological counter-offensives they called upon the KGB to conduct 'preventative work' 'against manifestations of hostile ideologies, particularly Ukrainian bourgeois nationalism'.[12] The Soviet Union published countless media articles, books, and pamphlets and produced numerous documentaries and films on the ideological struggle.[13]

---

[12] *FOUDSUP*, February 1963, April, August 1965, October 1969, October 1985.
[13] *FOUDSUP*, April 1968, February, November 1969, February, November 1970, January, May 1971, October 1973, January, April, November 1974, April 1975.

2) *Soviet Nationalities Policies:* The Communist Party was sensitive to Western criticism of Soviet nationalities policies.[14] Soviet propaganda outlets denied there was Russification in the USSR,[15] condemned claims the Soviet regime was undertaking colonial policies,[16] claimed Western analyses aimed to sow discord between Russians and Ukrainians and undermine the friendship of peoples.[17] Ukrainian émigré denunciations of Ukraine's colonial status in the Soviet Union were countered by the claim Ukraine was a sovereign republic. Of particular concern was Western criticism of the Soviet policy of the merging of the Soviet peoples into a Russian-speaking *Homo Sovieticus*.[18]

Ukrainian émigré re-publication of dissident *samvydav* (in Russian, *samizdat*) literature was viewed as a threat to the Soviet regime as it would be smuggled into the Soviet Union and read out in radio broadcasts beamed to the USSR.[19] Western radio stations transmitting into the Soviet Union, such as Radio Liberty, were of considerable irritation to the KGB and often jammed.

Soviet Ukrainian leaders and the KGB feared contagion from the 1956 and 1968 revolutions in Hungary and Czechoslovakia respectively and Solidarity movement in Poland in the 1980s. Day-to-day interaction between Ukrainians and eastern Europeans was also a concern because of smuggling of contraband, tourism, and supply of anti-Soviet and Ukrainian nationalist literature. The depiction of Hungary as a 'fascist' revolt in the Soviet Union was fanned by conservative Soviet leaders and the KGB, who clamoured for repression of the uprising. Russia's new school textbooks have come full circle and revive the description of 1956 as a Hungarian 'fascist revolt' (Zygar, 2023b). The Soviet Communist Party and KGB were alarmed by the 1968 'Prague Spring' (Do Podiy u Chekhoslovachchyni, 1968; Hodnett and Potichnyj, 1970; Teague, 1988).[20] 1968 witnessed the beginning of Soviet conservative campaigns against Communist reformers and

---

[14] *FOUDSP* February 1966, *DSUP*, April, December 1970, February 1971, May 1973, February, March 1975.
[15] *FOUDSUP*, October 1970, August, November 1971, March, November, December 1972, November 1974, January 1975.
[16] *FOUDSUP*, July 1967, *FOUDSUP*, November, December 1970, October 1971.
[17] *FOUDSP*, April, December 1970, March 1971.
[18] *FOUDSP*, November 1971, June, October 1972, February 1973.
[19] *FOUDSP*, November, October, December 1976.
[20] 'The Ideological Struggle Continues: Fighting Solidarity,' *Soviet Nationality Survey*, September-October 1984, 1 (9–10); *FOUDSUP*, March, July, August, September, October 1968.

Shelest, and dissidents and nationalists. The Kremlin feared contagion from Cardinal Karol Wojtyla (Pope John Paul II), the Polish Solidarity movement and Poland's large anti-communist underground which cooperated with Ukrainian émigrés, dissidents, and nationalists (Kuzio, 2012). In July 1989, a KGB secret bulletin reported on threats to Lviv *oblast* shaped by 'the influx of ethnic tourism from the US, Canada, and Germany' and 'the proximity of neighbouring Poland, where many emigrants from Ukraine lived, sharing the views of the leaders of "Solidarity" and supporting the clerical plans of the Vatican' (Wawrzonek, 2023, p. 63).

3) *Historiography*: History writing in Soviet Ukraine was kept closely under Communist and KGB control to ensure a Ukrainian historical identity separate to Russian was prevented from emerging (as seen in the condemnation of Shelest's 1970 book). Ukrainian history had to be written from the perspective of age-old and unbreakable unity with the Russian people. Soviet and Russian monopolisation of Kyiv Rus had two goals. The first was to emphasise the joint roots of Russians, Ukrainians, and Belarusians which was forever set in stone. The second was to emphasise Russia's leadership of the eastern Slavs. The struggle between Ukraine and Russia over the legacy of Kyiv Rus has existed throughout the post-Soviet era (Kuzio, 2005a).

Komunist Ukrayiny wrote that Ukrainian nationalists were 'cursed and condemned by the people for their attempts to separate Ukrainians from Russians'.[21] The Soviet media called on the Communist Party and KGB to combat 'nationalist and anti-communist myths' and 'nationalist theories' about Cossacks. Western histories of Ukraine, which provided the Ukrainian people with a history separate to Russian, were condemned as 'Nazi falsification'.[22] Mykhaylo Hrushevsky's writings showed the 'hostile essence of bourgeois nationalist concepts' found in 'reactionary historiography' published in the West.[23]

Soviet Ukrainian propaganda occasionally compared Tsarist and White Russian émigré denial of the existence of a Ukrainian people with the Soviet recognition of Ukrainians. 'Ukrainian bourgeois nationalists' were denounced for their (fictitious) alliance with Russian White émigrés who 'considered Ukraine as part of Russia, and the Ukrainian language as corrupted Russian'.[24] (In fact, it is Putin's

---

[21] *FOUDSUP*, 2, 1957.
[22] *FOUDSUP*, September 1970, October 1971, September, October 1975.
[23] *FOUDSUP*, June 1964.
[24] *FOUDSUP*, April 1958.

Russia which promotes White Russian émigré denials of a Ukrainian people). Russian nationalist dissident Solzhenitsyn, who became an ally of Putin in the 2000s, was denounced by the Soviet Ukrainian media as a Russian nationalist.[25] The Soviet media described Ukraine as an 'independent state' within the Soviet Union which had been liberated from the yoke of 'Muscovite tsars'. Soviet Ukraine was a sovereign 'Soviet, workers, and peasants, socialist Ukrainian nation'.[26] As the 'richest colony of Russian imperialism' Ukraine had been plundered by 'colonisers' and 'Even the language of the Ukrainian people was suppressed by tsarist decrees', the Soviet Ukrainian writer and publicist Ivan Mykytenko wrote.[27] Putin's (2021a) selective nostalgia for the USSR ignores even Soviet criticism of the Tsarist Empires repression of the Ukrainian language and culture.

4) *Poland as the Other:* A benefit of Soviet rule touted by the Soviet Communist Party was the unification of Ukrainian lands in the Second World War. Kuchma (2023, p.65) wrote that the Soviet regime unintentionally Ukrainised Lviv (see Chapter 4). The Nazi Holocaust of Jews and Soviet ethnic cleansing of Poles transformed Western Ukraine into a homogenic Ukrainian territory and, a centre of anti-Soviet opposition. In 1991–2013, Ukrainian identity gradually spread eastwards from western Ukraine, picking up speed from 2014 and especially 2022 (Kuzio, 2019b).

Soviet Ukrainian media promoted negativity towards Poles as historic oppressors of Ukrainians to deflect attention away from Russians. Anti-Russian poems by Ukraine's bard, Taras Shevchenko, were censored by the Soviet authorities, while anti-Polish poems remained in his published work. The Soviet regime tapped into anti-Polish sentiment to show western Ukraine 'as part of a wider East Slavic community' (Wojnowski, 2017, p. 173). Wojnowski (2017, p. 17) describes this Soviet Ukrainian identity as 'deeply xenophobic' with Poland portrayed as a 'mortal threat' to Ukraine and Ukrainians.

5) *Ukrainian Émigrés:* Of all the émigrés from the Soviet Union living in the West the Ukrainian diaspora was by far the biggest focus of Soviet propaganda.[28] Ukrainian émigrés were attacked for allegedly being Nazi collaborators during the Second World War, cooperating with

---

[25] *FOUDSUP*, May 1974.
[26] *FOUDSUP*, June 1958.
[27] *FOUDSUP*, December 1957.
[28] *FOUDSUP*, February 1975.

Western and Israeli intelligence services, smuggling anti-communist and Zionist literature into the Soviet Union,[29] establishing underground political and religious groups, funding and supplying dissidents,[30] fanning anti-Soviet and anti-Russian sentiments in Western governments,[31] and cooperating with Western radio stations beaming into Soviet Ukraine. *Samvydav* texts by writers and historians in Soviet Ukraine were smuggled to the West where they were re-published by Ukrainian émigré publishing houses and then smuggled back into the USSR. These publications were targeted by Soviet propaganda campaigns and the KGB, with occasionally couriers caught and forced to recant at press conferences.[32] The Soviet media and KGB failed to understand the irony of claiming 'fascist' and 'Nazi' Ukrainian émigrés allegedly cooperated with Zionists.[33]

6) *Ukrainian Nationalists/Fascists/Nazis:* Soviet propaganda targeted Ukrainians to a greater degree than other Soviet nationalities.[34] Following the Second World War, denouncing the collaboration of 'Ukrainian bourgeois nationalists' with Nazi Germany became a staple of Soviet propaganda and since the mid 2000s, this has become a staple of Russian propaganda and disinformation.[35] The Soviet regime used, and Putin's Russia continues to use, the term 'Banderite' to designate any Ukrainian 'nationalist/fascist/Nazi'. The Soviets and Putin's Russia ignore the historical fact Bandera was incarcerated in the Sachsenhausen Nazi concentration camp during the Second World War and his two brothers, Oleksandr and Vasyl, were murdered in the notorious Nazi death camp Auschwitz in 1942.

'Ukrainian bourgeois nationalism'[36] was a 'threat' and 'ideological enemy' of the Soviet system.[37] The Communist Party's counter-propaganda campaigns and films unmasked 'Ukrainian bourgeois nationalists' as 'traitors, agents for Western imperialism and enemies

---

[29] *FOUDSUP*, April, December 1966, *FOUDSUP*, May, June, September 1969, April 1971, April, September 1973, July 1975.
[30] *FOUDSUP*, July 1970.
[31] *FOUDSUP*, July 1970.
[32] *FOUDSUP*, June 1966.
[33] *FOUDSUP*, February 1976.
[34] *FOUDSUP*, June, November, December 1969, May, July, September, October 1970, April, December 1971, February 1973, March, June, August 1974, February, May, December 1975.
[35] *FOUDSUP*, December 1972, April 1974.
[36] *FOUDSUP*, December 1974.
[37] *FOUDSUP*, January, October 1972.

of the Ukrainian people'.[38] Communist Party propaganda especially targeted collusion between 'Ukrainian bourgeois nationalists' and banned Ukrainian national Churches.[39] 'Ukrainian bourgeois nationalists' were 'anti-democratic', a strange claim made by a regime that had nothing in common with a liberal democracy.[40]

Like contemporary Russian propaganda, the Soviet media depicted 'Ukrainian bourgeois nationalists' as agents of foreign powers and 'imperial masters'.[41] The Soviet media condemned Ukrainian émigré organisations, governments in exile, Ukrainian diaspora media, and publications and claimed they were funded by Western secret services (Kuzio, 2012).[42] 'Ukrainian bourgeois nationalists' were accused of being funded by the CIA.[43] The Soviet media wrote that Ukrainian 'bourgeois nationalists' always had 'foreign masters' paid by the Austrians, Kaiser and Nazi Germany, Poles, Romanians, Czechoslovaks, and by the 1960s, the Vatican and 'overseas bosses' and were 'traitors' and 'rabid enemies' who were 'spreading slander about the country of their birth.'[44] Ukrainian émigrés sought to build an 'independent state' as a 'colony of overseas imperialists'.[45] Then Russian National Security Council, Nikolai Patrushev (2016), with his long roots in the KGB and one of its successors the FSB, continues to use similar language many decades later when claiming Ukrainian leaders 'are doing their masters bidding to pull away from Russia'.

The Soviet media countered 'Ukrainian bourgeois nationalists' by claiming Ukrainians and Russians had a common origin, their languages and cultures were close, and they had inherited a common fate and 'desire for friendship and unity'.[46] Allegedly Ukrainians held a 'warm and sincere love for the culture of the Russian people, and they learn the rich Russian language'.[47] This is a similar discourse to that found in Putin's (2021a) long essay published ahead of the full-scale invasion.

---

[38] *FOUDSUP*, April 1958. See also *FOUDSUP*, December 1967, February 1972, January, February, May 1985.
[39] *FOUDSUP*, March 1972, February 1974.
[40] *FOUDSUP*, January 1977.
[41] *FOUDSUP*, February 1959.
[42] *FOUDSUP*, April 1958, March 1963, April 1964, April 1966, August 1968.
[43] *FOUDSUP*, September 1975, January 1977.
[44] *FOUDSUP*, September 1961, September 1962.
[45] *FOUDSUP*, November 1960.
[46] *FOUDSUP*, April 1958.
[47] *FOUDSUP*, April 1958.

7) *Ukrainian Autocephalous Orthodox and Ukrainian Greek-Catholic Churches*: The Ukrainian Autocephalous Orthodox Church[48] and Greek Catholic Church were banned in the late 1920s and after the Second World War respectively. The Russian Orthodox Church was re-legalised in 1943, and the parishes of Ukraine's two banned Churches were transferred to it (see Chapter 3). Soviet patriotism among the Ukrainian laity in the Russian Orthodox Church was acceptable if lip service was paid to the official view of the Ukrainian Greek-Catholic Church as a product of Austrian and Polish intrigue and Ukrainians having always wanted to return to the bosom of the Russian Orthodox Church (Wojnowski, 2017, p. 121). The Russian Orthodox Church was legalised not as a Russian national Church, as is common in the Orthodox world, but as a confession uniting 'Holy Rus' (Russia-Ukraine-Belarus) (see Chapter 3). The term 'Holy Rus' continues to be used by the Russian Orthodox Church placing it into direct conflict with the Orthodox Church of Ukraine which since 2018 is part of the canonical territory of the Patriarch of Constantinople.

Of the two banned Ukrainian Churches, the Soviet regime devoted most attention to the Greek Catholic Church which maintained a large underground structure in western Ukraine. The Soviet authorities were especially fearful of (Polish-born) Pope John Paul II because of his anti-communism and support for the Ukrainian Greek-Catholic Church (Hvat, 1983; Sysyn, 1983). The Ukrainian Greek Catholic Church was attacked for collaborating with the Nazis, being allies of Ukrainian 'bourgeois nationalists', 'fascist' and 'serving the interests of forces hostile to the Ukrainian people'.[49] The Communist Party called for increased religious propaganda[50] and the criminal convictions of members of the underground Ukrainian Greek-Catholic Church.[51] Nikolai Kolesnik, Chair of the Ukrainian Council for Religious Affairs, claimed Ukrainian Greek Catholic clergy 'do not enjoy popularity among the people' because Ukrainians 'do not approve of their alliance with outspoken supporters of the idea of Ukrainian bourgeois nationalism'.[52] Metropolitan Andrey Sheptytsky,[53] who passed away

---

[48] *FOUDSUP*, February 1971.
[49] *FOUDSUP*, September 1959, June, November 1970, January, February, December 1971, February 1972, December 1973, December 1975.
[50] *FOUDSUP*, April 1958, July 1959, June 1964.
[51] *FOUDSUP*, October 1964.
[52] *Izvestiia*, 1 February 1989.
[53] *FOUDSUP*, February 1969, October 1972.

in 1944, and his successor Cardinal Joseph Slipyy[54] who was released to the West in 1963 after eighteen years imprisonment in the Gulag, were often targeted by Soviet propaganda.

A flavour of anti-Ukrainian religious propaganda can be found in Soviet Ukrainian publications until only a year before the USSR disintegrated.[55] In 1990, *Ukrayinskyy Istorychnyy Zhurnal* claimed the Ukrainian Greek-Catholic Church was composed of 'former servants of the Hitlerites, and participants in Banderite gangs who have fled to the West' where they are being used by the Vatican and Western intelligence services to 'carry political and ideological subversive acts against the Soviet Union'.[56] This was published in the same year the Ukrainian Greek-Catholic Church was re-legalised after the democratic opposition took power in western Ukraine following Supreme Soviet of Ukraine and local elections in March 1990 (Wawrzonek, 2023).

8) *Youth:* The Soviet regime feared Soviet Ukrainian youth would be contaminated by Western ideas, books, journals, music, and fashions through smuggled contraband, listening to Western radio stations and receiving Ukrainian émigré and Western publications and music. Soviet media published articles warning about the threat from 'anti-communist propaganda, subversion of young Ukrainians', and the 'ideological instability' of Soviet Ukrainian youth.[57]

9) *Zionists*: For three decades from the 1960s-1980s, the Soviet Union promoted 'anti-Zionism' which to all intents and purposes was camouflaged anti-Semitism (Kuzio, 2017, pp. 117–139; Wojnowski, 2017). 'Ethnicity was a key marker of loyalty in Soviet Ukraine at the height of the 1956 crisis' and Jews and the Polish minority were viewed as living outside the Ukrainian nation (Wojnowski, 2017, p. 66). Soviet conservatives feared Ukrainians and Russians were threatened by foreigners in the West and 'ethnic minorities at home' (Wojnowski,

---

[54] *FOUDSUP*, October 1971, October 1972.
[55] See *Lyudyna i Svit*, no. 4, 1985, no.6, 1986, nos.2, 3, 5, 1988; *Robitnycha Hazeta*, 24 September 1985, 21 March 1986; *Pid Praporom Leninismu*, no.17, 18, 19, 1985; *Radyanska Ukayina*, 18 October 1985; *Raduga*, no.6, 1985; *Izvestia*, 23 December 1987; *Vilna Ukrayina*, 23 February 1988; and *Silski Visti*, 1 March 1989.
[56] O. L. Vovk, 'Nespromozhnist falsyfikatsiy Lvivskoho soboru uniatskoii tserkvy,' *Ukrayinskyy Istorychnyy Zhurnal*, no.10, 1982, pp. 117-129. http://resource.history.org.ua/cgi-bin/eiu/history.exe?&I21DBN=EJRN&P21DBN=EJRN&S21STN=1&S21REF=10&S21FMT=ASP_meta&C21COM=S&S21CNR=20&S21P01=0&S21P02=0&S21COLORTERMS=0&S21P03=IDP=&S21STR=journal_1982_10_117
[57] *FOUDSUP*, February and May 1972, November 1973.

2017, p. 214). Zionist circles give 'considerable financial help to many nationalist organisations and societies' because 'billionaires' have a 'covetous eye on the uncounted riches of Ukraine.'[58] Ukrainian Communist Party First Secretary Shcherbytsky demanded internationalists should wage an 'uncompromising struggle' against two of the 'fiercest enemies of the Ukrainian people' – 'Ukrainian bourgeois nationalists' and 'international Zionism' because they had established an anti-Soviet alliance (Sahaydak, 1976, p. 80).[59] Sheptytsky was allegedly linked to Zionists.[60] Ukrainian-Jewish collusion was described as a 'racist alliance', 'alliance of reactionaries' and 'toadies' in the service of [Western] imperialism.[61]

Similar anti-Zionist Soviet discourse that often is anti-Semitic is used by Russian leaders about President Zelenskyy whose Jewish-Ukrainian family in Kryvyy Rih was nearly all murdered by the Nazis. Semyon Zelenskyy managed to evade the Holocaust because he served in the Soviet army; the Ukrainian president is his grandson. 'Hitler wanted to kill me because I am Jewish. Now Putin is trying to kill me because I am Ukrainian', said eighty-nine-year-old Odessa resident Roman Shvartsman in the *Bundestag* (German parliament) on 29 January 2025 in a speech dedicated to the memory of the victims of the Holocaust.[62]

Zelenskyy's family's Holocaust history is irrelevant for the Kremlin's propaganda alleging Zelenskyy is in cahoots with Nazis ruling Ukraine. Sergei Naryshkin (2020), director of Russia's Foreign Intelligence Service (SVR) and Chairman of the Russian Historical Society, commented on Zelenskyy's visit to Poland: 'It is clear that Mr. Zelenskyy is more and more immersed in the ideas of Ukrainian nationalism'. Russia accused Zelenskyy of being an 'heir of German Nazism'.[63] Russian Foreign Minister Sergei Lavrov ridiculed the notion that Ukraine could not be a Nazi-led country if it had a Jewish president by saying, 'I could be wrong, but Hitler also had Jewish blood. [That Zelensky is Jewish] means absolutely nothing. Wise Jewish people say that the most ardent anti-Semites are usually Jews'.[64]

---

[58] *FOUDSP*, January 1966.
[59] *FOUDSUP*, March 1969, January, April, August 1970, July, December 1971, March 1972, June, October 1973, February, September, October 1974, April, December 1975, *FOUDSP*, October 1985.
[60] *FOUDSUP*, February 1970.
[61] *FOUDSUP*, April, November 1971, September 1976.
[62] www.bundestag.de/en/documents/textarchive/kw05-remembrance-1039942
[63] https://euvsdisinfo.eu/report/zelenskyy-is-the-heir-of-german-nazism
[64] www.bbc.co.uk/news/world-middle-east-61296682

Medvedev (2021) repeated a similar anti-Semitic slur against Zelenskyy, saying: 'He began to fervently serve the most rabid nationalist forces of Ukraine'. This 'is reminiscent of the insane situation in which representatives of the Jewish intelligentsia in Nazi Germany would have asked to serve in the SS for ideological reasons' (Medvedev, 2021). Zelenskyy's alleged collusion with Nazis was because:

> He needed to integrate into the 'pantheon of heroes' of this part of Ukrainian society. To shout with them: 'Glory to the heroes!' To accept the unconditional authority of such scoundrels as 'great Ukrainians.' To pray for the blessed memory of the terrorists and Judeophobes Bandera and [Roman] Shukhevych, who a significant part of Ukraine's political elite follows today (Medvedev, 2021).

10) *China*: Following a short border war in 1969, the Soviet Union and China experienced poor relations through to the disintegration of the USSR. From 1991 to 2021, Chinese-Russian relations were warm but not very good which changed after Russia's full-scale invasion of Ukraine, when China became the main foreign enabler of Russia's war machine (Kuzio, 2024).

Ironically, Soviet propaganda attacked 'Ukrainian bourgeois nationalists' for collusion with 'Red Chinese'.[65] Ukrainian nationalists were allegedly undertaking a 'Peking orientation'.[66] Soviet propaganda bizarrely claimed Maoism and Zionism were 'identical'.[67] In contrast to allegedly harmonious Soviet nationality policies, the Chinese Communist Party was attacked for 'cultural genocide' against national minorities (see Chapter 9).[68] The Soviet Union and China had both undertaken genocide against non-Russian and non-Han Chinese people's respectively and yet were accusing each other of genocidal crimes.

Soviet ideological and propaganda campaigns against Ukrainian nationalism continued until the Gorbachev era, when the policy of *glasnost* allowed greater criticism of past Soviet policies and the republication of previously banned works in the official and independent media. Under pressure from national communists and large

---

[65] *FOUDSUP*, April, May 1972.
[66] *FOUDSUP*, August 1972.
[67] *FOUDSUP*, July 1975.
[68] *FOUDSUP*, May 1970.

opposition movements, such as *Rukh* (Ukrainian Popular Movement for Restructuring) in Ukraine, the KPSS and media discussed reforms to nationalities policies.[69] With popular fronts, dissidents, writers, and nationalists becoming increasingly emboldened, the KPSS continued to discuss how to maintain its ideological vigilance in the face of the popular tide moving against it.[70]

By the late 1980s, Ukrainian independent media had grown from a small number of re-typed copies of *samvydav* to being mass printed in the three Baltic states and transported to Soviet Ukraine or printed by the Polish underground and smuggled into the Soviet Union (Kuzio, 1990, 2012). The proliferation of video recorders led to the circulation of smuggled videocassettes, including the 1985 documentary *Harvest of Despair* produced by the Ukrainian Canadian Research and Documentation Centre about the *Holodomor*.[71] The arrival of fax machines in the late 1980s revolutionised the way information could be moved back and forth between Soviet Ukraine and the West. The election of opposition politicians in the March 1990 Supreme Soviet of Ukraine and local elections provided them with access to official media. *Vilna Ukrayina (Free Ukraine)*, the Lviv *oblast* Ukrainian Communist Party newspaper, was renamed by dissident and *oblast* council chairman Vyacheslav Chornovil as *Za Vilnu Ukrayinu (For a Free Ukraine)*. In its heyday in the first half of the 1990s, *Za Vilnu Ukrayinu* had a circulation of up to half a million (Kuzio, 2000, p. 196).

With Shcherbytsky continuing to rule Soviet Ukraine until 1989, Ukrainians were afforded comparatively less space than Russians to use *glasnost* to its fullest. Nevertheless, Ukrainians pushed for evaluation of 'blank pages' of Ukrainian history: the *Holodomor, Rostrilyane Vidrodzhennya*, repression of Ukrainian Autocephalous Orthodox and Greek-Catholic Churches, 'distortions' in Soviet nationality policies, Russification and the status of the Ukrainian language (Kuzio, 1985, 1987, 1988, 1989).[72]

---

[69] 'The New Party Programme: The Withering Away of the Nationalities Question?', 'Nationalities Policy Under Gorbachev,' 'Union of Unequal's: The Nationality Question in the USSR,' 'The Ideological Struggle Continues: The Soviet People,' 'Nationalities Policy Under Review,' 'Constitutional Reforms and the Nationalities,' *Soviet Nationality Survey*, January 1986, 3 (1), March 1986, 3 (3), February 1987, 4 (2), March 1988, 5 (3), October 1989, 6 (10), November-December 1988, 5 (11–12).
[70] 'The Ideological Struggle Continues: Anti-Communism,' *Soviet Nationality Survey*, April 1984, 1(4).
[71] Taras Kuzio, 'Video Subversion in the USSR,' *Soviet Nationality Survey*, November-December 1986, 3 (11–12).
[72] 'The Language Question in Ukraine,' *Soviet Nationality Survey*, May 1987, 4 (5).

Shcherbytsky resigned in September 1989 and died a year later.[73] Kravchuk, who had held senior positions in the ideological and propaganda department of the Soviet Ukrainian Communist Party, became chairman of the Supreme Soviet of Ukraine in 1990. He oversaw three referendums in March 1990 providing an entire range of options: Gorbachev's 'renewed Soviet federation', Kravchuk's greater sovereignty for Soviet Ukraine in a Soviet confederation; and democratic opposition-led Ukrainian independence held in three Galician *oblasts*. Kravchuk proceeded to oversee the July 1990 Declaration of Sovereignty, August 1991 Declaration of Independence, and December 1991 referendum on independence (Kuzio, 2000, pp. 28-157). On 7-8 December 1991, Kravchuk initiated negotiations with Russian and Belarusian leaders in the Belarusian hunting lodge of Belovezhskaya Pushcha where the Soviet Union was replaced with the CIS (Commonwealth of Independent States) (Kuzio, 2000, pp. 179-213). In a sign of a stronger Ukrainian identity distinct from Russian, of the three eastern Slavs, only Ukraine adopted a Declaration of Independence (24 August 1991) and held a referendum on independence (1 December 1991). Russia undertook neither of these two steps while Belarus only adopted a Declaration of Independence but did not hold a referendum.

Putin's Russia

Since the 2003-2004 Orange Revolution, Russian media and state officials have portrayed Ukraine as run by 'nationalists/fascists/Nazis'. 'Russia's obsession with framing Ukraine as a Nazi state serves to justify the ongoing invasion and to distract from Russia's own historical baggage. This manipulative narrative, a cornerstone of Kremlin disinformation, relies on historical revisionism to falsely depict Ukraine as a haven for fascists (The Kremlin's misuse of Nazism as a weapon of information manipulation, 2025). The Kremlin's disinformation and propaganda has served two purposes. Firstly, it demonises Ukraine's leaders, including Jewish-Ukrainian President Zelenskyy. Secondly, it mobilises Russian public support by portraying the 'special military operation' as a second Great Patriotic War, and 'de-nazification' as 'a tool to justify violent repression and war crimes' by stirring 'up nationalistic fervour' to 'instigate violence and legitimise war' (The Kremlin's misuse of

---

[73] 'Shcherbytsky Soldiers On,' *Soviet Nationality Survey*, October 1988, 5 (10).

Nazism as a weapon of information manipulation, 2025). Since 2022, the Kremlin has cast the entire West as Nazi because it supports Ukraine and is seeking a 'final solution' of the Russian question, 'a grotesque insult to the memory of the six million Jewish people and countless other victims who were systematically murdered during the Holocaust' (The Kremlin's misuse of Nazism as a weapon of information manipulation, 2025). Anti-Semitism and 'Russophobia' are claimed to be similar (The Kremlin's misuse of Nazism as a weapon of information manipulation, 2025; on Russophobia see Darczewska and Żochowski, 2015).

Soviet style campaigns against 'Ukrainian nationalism/fascism/Nazis' were revived during the 2004 presidential elections by Party of Regions presidential candidate and Prime Minister Viktor Yanukovych's election campaign working together with Russian political technologists (Kuzio, 2005b). In October 2003, when Yushchenko's Our Ukraine electoral bloc was slated to hold a congress in Donetsk, billboards were put up in the city showing him giving a Nazi salute. The Party of Regions and pro-Russian presidential candidate Yanukovych, depicted Yushchenko as a 'nationalist monster', 'fascist' and 'Nazi' (see Tabachnyk, 2012). Andriy Yushchenko, Victor's father, served in the Soviet army in the Second World War, and he was captured and imprisoned as a POW in Nazi concentration camps, including Auschwitz-Birkenau.

The most common element of Russian anti-nationalist propaganda against Ukraine is the claim Ukraine is a Nazi state and, in turning away from the Pan-Russian World, Ukrainians are Nazis. This discourse dehumanises Ukrainians and, together with a cult of war in Putin's Russia, prepared the Russian population to back military aggression against Ukraine and undertake and accept war crimes against the Ukrainian people. As the EU Centre to Combat Disinformation pointed out:

> But this myth does more than justify Russia's illegal invasion. It also serves as the basis for Russia's would-be genocide against the Ukrainian language, culture, state and even the Ukrainian people, as we have noted before. In the imagination of radical Russian nationalists, Ukraine is an 'Anti-Russia' countering Russia, as anti-matter counters matter, and its mere existence is a mortal threat (Thirteen myths about Russia's war against Ukraine exposed 2024).

In addition, to shield Russia against charges of war crimes and genocide, Kremlin propagandists engage in 'projection of their own crimes onto their victims or even just slinging completely baseless accusations' (Thirteen myths about Russia's war against Ukraine exposed, 2024).

De-Humanisation of Ukrainians

From the mid 2000s, that is for nearly two decades before Russia's full-scale invasion, the Russian authorities and state-controlled media outlets promoted 'nationalists/fascists/Nazis' in Ukraine. Although the Kremlin no longer used the term 'bourgeois nationalists' two similarities to the Soviet Union remained.

First, a Ukrainian identity distinct to Russian was again portrayed as a conspiracy by Western security services to divide the 'Russian people'. Although describing Ukraine as a puppet state was a new approach, at the same time it built on the Russian imperial nationalist patronising of Ukrainians as being inherently incapable of building an independent state.

Second, Ukrainians who held an identity distinct to Russians continued to be described as a minority with most of the population allegedly subscribing to a Little Russian identity. Russian imperial nationalists remain adamant most of the Ukrainian population have been simply deluded into believing Ukrainians are different to Russians. Ukrainians were simply 'confused Russians' who needed to be indoctrinated to again become Little Russians. Moscow Spartak 'ultra' fan Ivan Katanaev said, 'Ukrainians are just Russians who've become like cattle' (Garner, 2023, p. 111). Putin (2024) claimed there are Ukrainians with whom Russia can talk 'who are dreaming together with us, about liberating their country from the neo-Nazi regime'. Russian Foreign Minister Sergei Lavrov (2024) differentiated between 'most' Ukrainians who 'are our brothers' and those 'whom the West brought to power through an anti-constitutional state coup' and 'are following the Western order to turn away the country into a Nazi threat to the Russian Federation'. *RT* head Margarita Simonyan denies Russia has invaded Ukraine, claiming what is taking place is a 'civil war' between (bad) 'fascist' Russophobes who are fighting against (good) Ukrainians whom Russia is supporting (Davis, 2024, p. 201). Medvedev (2021) described Nazis ruling Ukraine as accounting for only 5–7 per cent of the population. Patrushev (2025) accused 'Kyiv propagandists obsessed with "Ukrainianism"' for undermining Russian relations with Ukrainians who 'remain close to us, fraternally connected by centuries-old ties with Russia'.

The Kremlin never learnt lessons from 2014 when most Ukrainians did not support pro-Russian separatism (Kuzio, 2019a). The Kremlin's claim Euromaidan Revolution 'Nazis' represented a minority of the population ignored pre-term presidential and parliamentary election results in May and October 2014 respectively. In 2022, the Kremlin therefore repeated the same mistake by believing Ukrainians would – as Little Russians – greet the Russian army as 'liberators'.[74] The 'special military operation' used only 175,000 troops, a paltry number for the large size of Ukraine's territory and far larger Ukrainian armed and security forces. What was supposed to be a 'surgical' and quick intervention to occupy Ukraine and install a pro-Russian puppet leader turned into the bloodiest full-scale war in Europe since the Second World War with global ramifications (see Chapter 8).

Four years prior to Russia's first invasion in 2014, the Ukrainian library in Moscow was raided and closed by the Ministry of Interior who took away fifty books for 'psychological-linguistic expertise'. Natalia Sharina, head of the Ukrainian library in Moscow was arrested in October 2015 for allegedly stocking 'extremist' books and magazines, she was charged with inciting ethnic hatred and received a four-year suspended sentence.[75] In Russian-occupied territories, Ukrainian books are removed and destroyed from schools, museums and libraries (McGlynn, 2023c).

The revival of 'nationalist/fascist/Nazi' depictions of Ukrainians from the mid 2000s grew during the Euromaidan Revolution and Russia's first military invasion. After 2014, Russian writers in Moscow severed ties with Andrey Kurkov, a well-known Russian writer living in Kyiv (Kurkov, 2014, p. 132). The victory of the Euromaidan Revolution undermined the Kremlin's plans for Yanukovych to reject Ukraine's integration into the EU and become part of the Pan-Russian World and Eurasia. Like with all colour revolutions, the Euromaidan Revolution was viewed in Moscow as a Western-backed conspiracy against Russia. Since 2014, Russia has repeatedly blamed the West for launching an 'illegal putsch' against Yanukovych that brought to power 'nationalists/fascists/Nazis' who proceeded to transform Ukraine into an 'Anti-Russia' outpost. Russian propaganda and disinformation claiming the bulk of Ukraine's population were suffering under a 'Nazi' yoke, the Russian language was being discriminated against, and the 'Kyiv regime' was committing 'genocide' against Russian speakers had of course, nothing to do with reality.

Nevertheless, Vitaly Sych (2015), editor of the then Kyiv-based Russian-language *Novoye Vremya* magazine,[76] noted that although Russian

---

[74] https://euvsdisinfo.eu/report/russias-special-military-operation-in-ukraine-has-a-character-of-liberation/
[75] www.rferl.org/a/russia-sharina-ukrainian-literature-library-sentencing/28529055.html
[76] The Russian-language *Novoye Vremya* changed into the Ukrainian-language *Novi Chasy* magazine in 2022.

propaganda looked 'ridiculous' in Kyiv it was 'extremely effective' in parts of Russian-speaking Ukraine and Russia in describing the Euromaidan Revolution as 'an illegal rebellion of neo-Nazis financed and managed by Americans.' The Euromaidan 'anti-criminal revolution' was 'shown as an aggressive offense against anything that is Russian: culture, language, and identity' (Sych, 2015).

Putin (2014) described the leaders of the Euromaidan Revolution as having: 'resorted to terror, murder, and riots. Nationalists, neo-Nazis, Russophobes, and anti-Semites executed this coup'. International organisations such as the Council of Europe found no evidence of discrimination, let alone 'genocide', of Russian speakers in Crimea or southeast Ukraine. The coming to power of Euromaidan Revolutionaries in February 2014, after Yanukovych fled from Kyiv, was undertaken under articles 109–112 of the Ukrainian constitution where, in the absence of the president, power is transferred to the chairman of Ukraine's parliament, in this case Oleksandr Turchynov. This was therefore never a 'putsch' as the Kremlin alleges.

Putin's stark language drew on Soviet communist and KGB propaganda where Ukrainian 'nationalists' are a 'group defined as irredeemable by nature' that 'allows for the construction of conspiracy narratives and excluded alternative ways of thinking' (Bertelsen and Shkandrij, 2014, p. 53). The use of terror against such opponents in the Soviet Union 'required no evidence of crimes' (Bertelsen and Shkandrij, 2014, p. 53); similarly, Russian war crimes towards the 'special military operation' goal of 'de-nazification' are justified (Sergeytsev, 2022). Rabid Ukrainophobia and equating of the Euromaidan Revolution with the coming to power of 'nationalists/fascists/Nazis' encouraged violent conflict in eastern and southern Ukraine in spring 2014 and war crimes from 2022. Jakob Hauter (2023, p. 243) documents how Russian intervention in the Donbas escalated low-level conflict into full-scale and violent war. Pro-Russian activists guarding the large monument of Lenin in Kharkiv held signs saying 'Don't test Kharkiv's patience' and warning Kyiv not to unleash repression of Ukraine's Russian speakers (Sneider, 2014). Russian television's promotion of anti-Ukrainian hate-crime propaganda became so intense that those protecting Kharkiv's Lenin monument told CBC (Shprintsen, 2015) 'How can I support a state which has declared war against me?' Peaceful pro-Ukrainian protesters and supporters of the Euromaidan Revolution were violently attacked in Donetsk, Luhansk, Kharkiv and Odesa in spring 2014 when 'opponents of separatism were automatically branded as 'fascist', '*Banderovtsi*', and subhuman. *Berkut* riot police officers who had participated in the murder of unarmed Euromaidan Revolution protesters were applauded when they returned to Donetsk and Crimea (Crimea welcomes riot cops after murdering Euromaidan protesters, 2014). The Russian secret services trained and paid local *Oplot* (Bulwark) paramilitaries to beat up 'fascists;' that is, Euromaidan revolutionaries. They were dragged out of official buildings in Kharkiv and savagely beaten by a crowd with others applauding (Battle for Ukraine, 2014). As one observer wrote, even if you had never been a fascist, did not support the Euromaidan Revolution protests, and were not a Bandera follower, it was all the same to the Kremlin and its pro-Russian forces, who described you as an 'enemy' (Letters From Donbas, 2015).

Propaganda promoted by Russian state officials, political technologists and journalists in the state-controlled electronic, paper, and social media mobilised anti-Ukrainian hysteria within Russia and in the Donbas and Crimea (Ennis, 2013). Russian speakers were described as allegedly being threatened and needing Russia's protection, a lie that was repeated during the full-scale invasion. The Euromaidan Revolution was supposedly not supported by most Ukrainians and led by Russophobes, traitors, and fascists. The Kremlin claimed the Ukrainian state had disintegrated and there was anarchy and lawlessness. Putin and other Russian imperial nationalists increasingly demanded the return of 'historical Russian lands' wrongly included in Soviet Ukraine that were inherited by the independent Ukrainian state.

The Euromaidan government, which *Pravyy Sektor* (Right Sector) had allegedly brought to power, was an illegal junta that had proclaimed a 'holy war' against Russia (Osipian, 2014). The Russian population and Russian speakers in Ukraine were wrongly led to believe *Pravyy Sektor*, which had only been created during the Euromaidan Revolution, was a very popular political force, had many members and possessed a large arsenal of weapons. Russia hacked into the May 2014 Ukrainian presidential election results and changed them to give *Pravyy Sektor* leader Dmytro Yarosh first place with 37 per cent of the vote and Poroshenko 29 per cent. In fact, Poroshenko, who prior to 2014 had business interests in Russia, won the election in the first round with 55.46 per cent and Yarosh won less than 1 per cent. In the October 2014 pre-term parliamentary elections, *Pravyy Sektor* won only 1.8 per cent of the vote thereby not crossing the 5 per cent threshold to enter parliament (Coynash, 2015c).

The Euromaidan Revolution was led by 'barbarians, true fascists' and provoked by Americans, while Ukraine's army are 'tyrants' and 'worse than fascists' (Russian TV News, 2015). Ukrainian soldiers were called *karateli* (punishers), a term from the Great Patriotic War to describe the Nazis (Olszański, 2015). A lady in Crimea was adamant that after Euromaidan Revolutionaries had removed the Black Sea Fleet, NATO would establish bases in Sevastopol and 'Crimea would have been wiped from the face of the earth' (Rosenberg, 2017). Russia's propaganda and disinformation spread deliberate lies to inflame bloodshed. The most well-known examples were claims of a three-year old boy crucified by Ukrainian armed forces and a mother tied to a Ukrainian tank and dragged through the streets until she was dead (Walker, 2015). The Ukrainian soldiers who had allegedly undertaken these atrocities in the Donbas were 'beasts and fascists' (Ash, 2015). A third brazen lie alleged a 'mass grave' existed in Komunar with eighty victims, which included a decapitated pregnant woman killed by 'Ukrainian fascists', who had their ears chopped off (Walker, 2015). All these were brazen lies.

The 'Russian spring' of 2014 is an 'offshoot of political technology' where 'information warfare' plays a central role in the operation (Wilson, 2014). 'Lies are part of the coin of the intelligence operative, and facts are fungible' with Putin spending 'a great deal of time in his professional life bending the truth, manipulating facts, and playing with fictions' (Gaddy and Hill, 2015, p. 391). Lies and propaganda mobilised Russian imperial nationalists and European extremists to travel to the Donbas to fight against 'fascists', NATO and 'American mercenaries', although these were never found.

During the full-scale invasion, Russian soldiers told stunned Ukrainians they had come to liberate them from Nazis. Russia's invading army searched for 'nationalists/fascists/Nazis' and NATO troops. An invading Russian soldier explained to a stunned Ukrainian civilian in Mykolayiv 'We're here to liberate you. To protect you' from 'Fascists, Zelenskyy, and his Nazis' (Harding, 2023, p. 3). A Russian Orthodox priest in the Urals blessed volunteers heading for Ukraine to fight 'fascist scum' (Franchetti, 2015). Meanwhile, other Russian Orthodox priests assisted in the torturing of Ukrainian prisoners of war, beating them with crosses over their heads (Tereshchuk and Coalson, 2015). The level of indoctrination of Russians was so great that few of them turned their anger against Putin's regime when they found no 'Nazi' regime and NATO troops in Ukraine.

Russian troll factories targeted US and European leaders and Ukrainian 'nationalists/fascists/Nazis' by inserting derogatory comments in online media outlets about Russia's occupation of Crimea, the shooting down of the MH17 Malaysian airliner, killing 298 passengers and crew, Western sanctions and Euromaidan Revolution politicians. These often-repeated churlish claims, such as NATO troops were embedded in Ukrainian armed forces, were spread by Russia's state-controlled television (Stewart, 2015). Residents of the Donbas were quoted on Russian television saying outrageous comments such as 'They (Kyiv fascists) want to exterminate us' (Antelava, 2014).

Since 2016, the EU Centre to Combat Disinformation database on Russian disinformation has been collecting Russian propaganda in paper and electronic media. Half of these reports and articles are about Ukraine and Ukrainians, or 9,527 out of 18,132, as of December 2024 (see Narratives of Pro-Kremlin Disinformation: Nazis, 2022).[77] The ten main areas of Russian propaganda, with the number of disinformation stories indicted, are as follows:

1. The Euromaidan Revolutionaries came to power in 2014 in an illegal coup – 661.
2. Ukraine is a Nazi, neo-Nazi, and fascist country – 1,149.
3. The 'Kyiv regime' – 819.
4. Ukraine is an artificial and puppet entity and Ukraine does not exist – 1,534.
5. Ukraine is Little Russia and 'Historical Russia' – 967.
6. Ukrainians are Nazis – 210.
7. Ukrainians and Russians are one people – 1,218.
8. Southeast Ukraine is New Russia – 2,334.
9. Kyiv, Kharkiv, and Odesa are Russian cities – 312.
10. Ukraine is a terrorist state – 471.

The volume and breadth of Russian propaganda far surpasses that produced by the Soviet Union. Indeed, most of these ten propaganda tropes would have been impossible in the Soviet Union. For example, Ukraine could not have been depicted as an artificial entity as it was described as a 'sovereign republic' in the USSR. It would have been impossible for the Soviet media to call Soviet Ukraine Little Russia or 'Historical Russia'. Southeast Ukraine was never described in the Soviet Union as New Russia, a Tsarist imperial term only revived by Putin in 2014 but alluded to six years earlier in a speech to the NATO-Russia Council (Putin, 2008). In the Soviet Union, Ukrainians were not described as satanists or terrorists. Meanwhile, the roots of the Orange and Euromaidan Revolutions, described as having been orchestrated by Western secret services lie in Soviet propaganda about the ties of Ukrainian dissidents to 'Nazi

---

[77] See https://euvsdisinfo.eu/disinformation-cases/

collaborators' in the Ukrainian diaspora who were funded by Western and Israeli intelligence services. Nevertheless, although the Soviet regime recognised Ukrainians as a people separate to Russians, and therefore both peoples were not as in contemporary Kremlin discourse 'one people', Soviet propaganda hammered home that Russians and Ukrainians will always remain united.

Conclusion

Tsarist, Soviet and Russian campaigns against Ukrainian nationalism have taken place since the early eighteenth century and have become more pronounced and vociferous when the Russian and Soviet state were in crisis. There are four components to Tsarist imperial, Soviet and Russian anti-Ukrainian nationalist campaigns.

Firstly, they intensify during counter-revolutionary periods, such as the Russian civil war, Great Patriotic War, height of the Cold War, and Orange and Euromaidan Revolutions. Propaganda campaigns against Ukrainian nationalism have taken place during security operations against OUN in the 1940s and early 1950s, against Ukrainian dissidents and nationalist opposition during the 1970s and early 1980s, during Yushchenko's presidency in 2005–2010, and especially since Russia's first invasion of Ukraine in 2014.

Secondly, Ukrainians and Russians have viewed Soviet history very differently. Ukrainians have positively viewed liberalisation in the Soviet Union in the 1920s, mid 1950s to early 1970s, and second half of the 1980s to 1991 where they had the opportunity to raise cultural, linguistic, economic and political demands. Putin and Russian imperial nationalists negatively view Soviet liberalisation, preferring instead Stalin's totalitarianism (1924–1953) and conservative Soviet leaders Leonid Brezhnev, Yurii Andropov and Konstantin Chernenko (1964–1985). Gorbachev is an object of antipathy for Putin and Russian imperial nationalists. Liberalisation covered less of Soviet history, which was dominated by Stalinism and conservatism for 50 out of the USSR's 69 years of existence. Putin has himself presided over a quarter of a century of Russian imperial nationalism and Russia's re-Sovietisation and cult of Stalin.

Wojnowski (2017) differentiates between conservative and reformist Soviet Ukrainian leaders. Conservatives, as seen in Shcherbytsky, were anti-reform, feared instability, contagion from eastern Europe, war and Western intrigue, and supported repression of dissent in Ukraine and Russification. Reformers, as seen in Shelest, supported reforms in eastern Europe and within the Soviet Union through national roads to socialism. Reformist national communists called for a return to Leninist internationalism, defended Ukrainian language and culture against Russification, supported de-Stalinisation, condemned anti-Zionist campaigns as anti-Semitism and criticised Soviet repression. The limits to the power of reformers and short period of de-Stalinisation were evident in Khrushchev's replacement by Brezhnev in 1964 and Shelest's replacement by Shcherbytsky in 1972.

Thirdly, Tsarist, Soviet and Russian imperial nationalists divide the population of Ukraine into 'good' Ukrainians who understand they are Little Russians and 'bad' Ukrainian 'nationalists/fascists/Nazis' who believe they have an identity distinct from Russians. The myth of Ukrainians divided into 'good' and 'bad' types continue to dominate Russian imperial nationalist myths. That this was a myth was already evident in 2014, and with most Ukrainians coming to hold negative views of Russia and the Russian people, this has become even more of a myth since 2022 (Kyiv International Institute of Sociology, 2024). Three years of full-scale war and over one million Russian casualties have failed to change the Russian imperial nationalist myth of Ukrainians divided between 'good' Little Russians and 'bad' Ukrainian 'Nazis' in the pay of the West.

Fourthly, the Kremlin will remain frustrated by its deep-seated inability to comprehend why their military aggression and war crimes have turned most Ukrainians away from Russia and the Russian people (Stavlennya Ukrayintsiv do Rosii i Rosiyan, 2024). Irrespective of how much the Kremlin spreads propaganda and myths, it is Russia's military aggression and war crimes which have led to the marginalisation of pan-Russian identity and most Ukrainians holding negative views of Russia and the Russian people. Until 2013, most Ukrainians, including in western Ukraine, held positive views of Russia and the Russian people. Following Russia's annexation of Crimea and first invasion of Ukraine in 2014, most Ukrainians came to hold negative views of Russian leaders while most maintained a positive views of the Russian people. In late 2024, nearly three years into Russia's full-scale war against Ukraine, 93 per cent of Ukrainians had come to hold negative views of Russia and 84 per cent a negative view of the Russian people, with only 3 and 8 per cent respectively holding positive views (Stavlennya Ukrayintsiv do Rosii i Rosiyan, 2024). Between 88 and 96 per cent of Ukrainians in the East, South, Centre, and West of Ukraine hold a negative view of the Russian state, with only an 8 per cent difference in attitudes between the East (88 per cent) and the West (96 per cent) (Stavlennya Ukrayintsiv do Rosii i Rosiyan, 2024). Between 75 and 90 per cent of Ukrainians in the East, South, Centre, and West of

Ukraine hold negative views of the Russian people, with only a 15 per cent difference between attitudes in the East (75 per cent) and the West (90 per cent) (Stavlennya Ukrayintsiv do Rosii i Rosiyan, 2024).

Russia's two invasions have increased Ukraine's national integration, promoted public acceptance of controversial aspects of Ukrainian history, such as views of OUN, eviscerated the influence of the Russian Orthodox Church and created a high majority of Ukrainians who support NATO and EU membership. The annexation of Crimea and two Russian invasions destroyed Soviet myths of 'fraternal Russian-Ukrainian brotherhood' among Russophone Ukrainians and made them impervious to Russian propaganda and disinformation. Three centuries of Tsarist, Soviet and Russian propaganda against Ukrainian nationalism indoctrinated Russians into an intense dislike of 'bad' Ukrainians who refuse to accept they are Little Russians, an attitude which has underpinned Russia's military aggression against Ukraine and war crimes against Ukrainians. The growth of patriotism and nationalism in Ukraine and widespread negative views of Russia and the Russian people point to the Kremlin's policies having disastrously backfired and failed. Ukraine is now inhabited by what the Kremlin defines as 'bad' Ukrainians who hold an identity distinct from Russians, while 'good' Ukrainians who believe they are Little Russians, who were always in a small number, barely exists. Putin, in seeking to bring Ukraine into the Pan-Russian World, has in fact pushed Ukraine further away and closer to Europe. This reality will be impossible to change, as most Ukrainians have come to believe the real 'nationalists/fascists/nazis' are in fact, Russia and the Russian people (see Laruelle, 2016; Garner and Kuzio, 2025).

References

Alexeyeva, L. (1980). *Soviet Dissent. Contemporary Movements for National, Religious, and Human Rights*. Middletown, CO: Wesleyan University Press.

Ambrosio, T. (2007). 'Insulating Russia from a Colour Revolution: How the Kremlin Resists Regional Democratic Trends,' *Democratization*, 14 (2): 232–252.

An Independent Legal Analysis of the Russian Federation's Breaches of the Genocide Convention in Ukraine and the Duty to Prevent. (2022). New Lines Institute for Strategy and Policy and Raoul Wallenberg Centre for Human Rights, May. https://newlinesinstitute.org/an-independent-legal-analysis-of-the-russian-federations-breaches-of-the-genocide-convention-in-ukraine-and-the-duty-to-prevent/

Antelava, N. (2014). 'Russia's Invasion Uncorks Ethnic Strife in Crimea,' *The New Yorker*, 3 March.

Applebaum, A. (2017). *Red Famine. Stalin's War on Ukraine*. London: Allen Lane.

Arnold, R. (2025). 'Russia Prepares for 80th Anniversary of the End of World War Two,' *Eurasia Daily Monitor*, 22 (13), 4 February. https://jamestown.org/program/russia-prepares-for-80th-anniversary-of-the-end-of-world-war-two/

Ash, L. (2015). 'How Russia Outfoxes its Enemies,' *BBC Magazine*, 29 January. www.bbc.com/news/blogs-news-from-elsewhere-24383550.

Bækken, H. (2023). 'Merging the Great Patriotic War and Russian Warfare in Ukraine. A Case-Study of Russian Military Patriotic Clubs in 2022,' *Political Research Exchange*, 5 (1). https://doi.org/10.1080/2474736X.2023.2265135

Barbashin, A., and Thoburn, H. (2015). 'Putin's Philosopher. Ivan Ilyin and the Ideology of Moscow's Rule.' *Foreign Affairs*, 20 September. www.foreignaffairs.com/articles/ukraine/2015-09-20/putins-philosopher

Battle for Ukraine. (2014). *PBS Frontline*, 27 May. www.pbs.org/wgbh/pages/frontline/battle-for-ukraine/.

Beissinger, M. (1988). 'Ethnicity, the Personnel Weapon, and Neo-Imperial Integration: Ukrainian and RSFSR Provincial Party Officials Compared,' *Studies in Comparative Communism*, XXI (1): 71–85.

Bertelsen, O., and Shkandrij, M. (2014). 'The Secret Police and the Campaign against Galicians in Soviet Ukraine, 1929–1934,' *Nationalities Papers*, 42 (1): 37–62.

Bilinsky, Y. (1983). 'Shcherbytskyi, Ukraine and Kremlin Politics,' *Problems of Communism*, 32 (4): 1–20.

Birch, J. (1971). *The Ukrainian Nationalist Movement in the USSR since 1956*. London: Ukrainian Information Service.

Brandenberger, D. (2001). 'It Is Imperative to Advance Russian Nationalism as the First Priority: Debates Within the Stalinist Ideological Establishment, 1941–1945' In: R.G. Suny, and T. Martin, (eds.), *A State of Nations. Empire and Nation-making in the Age of Lenin and Stalin*. Oxford: Oxford University Press: 275–300.

Bregy, P., and Obolensky, S. (1940). *The Ukraine. A Russian Land*. London: Selwyn and Blount.

Corum, L. (2018). 'Project Russia: The Bestselling Book Series of Putin's Russia,' *South Central Review*, 35 (1): 74–100.

Coynash, H. (2015a). 'Russia's Sentsov – Kolchenko Case – "An absolutely Stalinist Trial".' Kharkiv Human Rights Protection Group, 21 August. http://khpg.org/en/index.php?id1440076117.

Coynash, H. (2015b). 'Nadiya Savchenko: "You Can Call Me the Artillery Spotter",' Kharkiv Human Rights Protection Group. 30 September. http://khpg.org/en/1443558682.

Coynash, H. (2015c). 'Russia's Right Sector Fever and Its Victims,' Kharkiv Human Rights Protection Group, 29 October. https://khpg.org/en/1414532707

Crimea welcomes riot cops after murdering Euromaidan protesters. (2014). www.youtube.com/watch?v=efii3FK9W7A

Darczewska, J., and Żochowski, P. (2015). *Russophobia in the Kremlin's Strategy. A Weapon of Mass Destruction*. Warszawa: Ośrodek Studiów Wschodnich im. Marka Karpia.

Davis, J. (2024). *In Their Own Words. How Russia Propagandists Reveal Putin's Intentions*. Stuttgart: Ibidem; New York: Columbia University Press.

Do Podiy u Chekhoslovachchyni. (1968). *Fakty, dokumenty, svidchennya presy i ochevydtsiv*. Kyiv: Pres-Hrupa Radyanskykh Zhurnalistiv.

Dzyuba, I. (1974). *Internationalism or Russification?* New York: Pathfinder Press.

Erlacher, T. (2013). 'Denationalizing Treachery: The Ukrainian Insurgent Army and the Organization of Ukrainian Nationalists in Late Soviet Discourse, 1945–1985,' *REGION: Regional Studies of Russia, Eastern Europe and Central Asia* 2 (2): 289–316.

Ennis, S. (2013). 'Russia: Kremlin's 'Hate TV' Compares West to Nazis', BBC, 3 October. www.bbc.com/news/blogs-news-from-elsewhere-24383550.

Finkel, E. (2024). *Intent to Destroy. Russia's Two-Hundred-Year Quest to Dominate Ukraine*. London: Basic Books.

Fournier, A. (2012). *Forging Rights in a New Democracy. Ukrainian Students between Freedom and Justice*. Philadelphia: University of Pennsylvania Press.

Franchetti, M. (2015). 'Putin Boosted by Orthodox "Inquisition,"' *The Sunday Times*, 5 April. www.thesundaytimes.co.uk/sto/news/world_news/Europe/.

Franchetti, M., Harnden, T., and Hookham, M. (2015). 'Ukraine Licks Wounds as Guns Go Quiet,' *The Sunday Times*, 7 September. www.thesundaytimes.co.uk/sto/news/world_news/Ukraine/article1455859.ece.

Gaddy, C. G., and Hill, F. (2015). *Mr. Putin. Operative in the Kremlin*. Washington, DC: Brookings Institution Press.

Garner, I. (2023). *Generation Z. Into the Heart of Russia's Fascist Youth*. London: Hurst.

Garner, I. and Kuzio, T. (2025). Edited. *Russia and Modern Fascism: New Perspectives on the Kremlin's War against Ukraine*. Stuttgart: Ibidem; New York: Columbia University Press.

Harding, A. (2023). *A Small Stubborn Town. Life, Death, and Defiance in Ukraine*. London: Ithaka Press.

Hate Speech and Russian Calls for Genocide in Putin's Russia. (2024). *EUvsDisinfo*, 19 February. https://euvsdisinfo.eu/hate-speech-and-calls-for-genocide-in-putins-russia/

Hauter, J. (2023). *Russia's Overlooked Invasion. The Causes of the 2014 Outbreak of War in Ukraine's Donbas*. Stuttgart: Ibidem; New York: Columbia University Press.

Hodnett, G., and Potichnyj, P. J. (1970). *The Ukraine and the Czechoslovak Crisis, Occasional Paper 6*. Canberra: Australian National University.

Hook, K. (2022). 'Why Russia's War in Ukraine Is a Genocide. Not Just a Land Grab, but a Bid to Expunge a Nation.' *Foreign Affairs*, 28 July. www.foreignaffairs.com/ukraine/why-russias-war-ukraine-genocide

Hvat, I. (1983). 'The Ukrainian Catholic Church, the Vatican and the Soviet Union during the Pontificate of Pope John Paul II,' *Religion in Communist Lands* 11 (3): 264–294.

Jones, L., and Yasen, B. (1977). Edited. *Dissent in Ukraine. The Ukrainian Herald, Issue 6. An Underground Journal from Soviet Ukraine*. Baltimore: Smoloskyp Publishers.

Karaganov, S. (2025). 'Breaking the Back of Europe: What Should Russia's Policy Be towards the West.' *Russia in Global Affairs*, 22 January. https://globalaffairs.ru/articles/slomat-hrebet-evrope-karaganov/

Khromeychuk, O. (2015). 'Ukrainians in the German Armed Forces during the Second World War,' *History*, 100 (5): 704–724.

Klid, B. W. (1991). 'The Struggle Over Mykhailo Hrushevsky: Recent Soviet Polemics,' *Canadian Slavonic Papers*, XXXIII (1): 32–45.

Kolasky, J. (1968). *Education in Soviet Ukraine. A Study in Discrimination and Russification*. Toronto: Peter Martins Association.

Kolasky, J. (1970). *Two Years in Soviet Ukraine: A Canadian's Personal Account of Russian Oppression and the Growing Opposition*. Toronto: Peter Martins Association.

Kuchma, L. (2023). *Ukrayina – Ne Rosiya. Dvatsyat Rokiv Potomu*. Kyiv: Adef-Ukrayina.

Kurkov, A. (2014). *Ukraine Diaries. Dispatches from Kyiv*. London: Harvill-Secker.

Kupchinsky, R. (1980). *Pohrom v Ukrayini: 1972–1979*. Munich: Suchasnist.

Kuzio, T. (1985). 'A Nationality Problem in the USSR?' *Soviet Analyst*, 14 (1), 9 January.

Kuzio, T. (1987). 'The Ukrainian Famine: Still a Blank Spot,' *Soviet Analyst*, 16 (24, 25), 9, 23 December.

Kuzio, T. (1988). 'The Ukrainian Famine and Terror under Discussion,' *Soviet Analyst*, 17 (10, 12), 1 May, 15 June.

Kuzio, T. (1989). 'Nationality Problems, Nationalism and State Policy in the USSR, 1985–1990,' *Soviet Nationality Survey*, 6 (11–12), November–December.

Kuzio, T. (1990). 'Independent (Samizdat) Press in Ukraine Under Gorbachev,' *Soviet Analyst*, 19 (17,18), 29 August, 12 September.

Kuzio, T. (2000). *Ukraine. Perestroika to Independence*, 2nd ed. London: Macmillan, New York: St. Martin's Press.

Kuzio, T. (2005a). 'Nation-State Building and the Re-writing of History in Ukraine: The Legacy of Kyiv Rus,' *Nationalities Papers*, 33 (1): 30–58.

Kuzio, T. (2005b). 'Russian Policy to Ukraine During Elections', *Demokratizatsiya*, 13 (4): 491–517.

Kuzio, T. (2012). 'The U.S. Support for Ukraine's Liberation during the Cold War: A Study of Prolog Research and Publishing Corporation,' *Communist and Post-Communist Studies*, 45 (1–2): 51–64.

Kuzio, T. (2017). *Putin's War against Ukraine: Revolution, Nationalism, and Crime*. Toronto: Chair of Ukrainian Studies, University of Toronto.

Kuzio, T. (2019a). 'Russian Stereotypes and Myths of Ukraine and Ukrainians and Why Novorossiya Failed,' *Communist and Post-Communist Studies*, 52 (4): 297–309.

Kuzio, T. (2019b). 'Three Revolutions, One War and Ukraine's West Moves East' In: P. Kowal, G. Mink, and I. Reichardt (eds.), *Three Revolutions: Mobilization and Change in Contemporary Ukraine I. Theoretical Aspects and Analyses on Religion, Memory, and Identity*. Stuttgart: Ibidem; Warsaw: College of Europe: 91–120.

Kuzio, T. (2022). *Russian Nationalism and the Russian-Ukrainian War: Autocracy-Orthodoxy-Nationality*. London: Routledge.

Kuzio, T. (2024). 'China Consistently Enables Russia's War of Aggression against Ukraine,' *Eurasia Daily Monitor*, 21 (128), 10 September. https://jamestown.org/program/china-enables-russias-war-of-aggression-against-ukraine/

Kyiv International Institute of Sociology. (2024). 'Stavlennya Ukrayintsiv do Rosii i Rosiyan', 7 November. https://kiis.com.ua/?lang=ukr&cat=reports&id=1446&page=1

Laruelle, M. (2016). 'The Three Colors of Novorossiya, or the Russian Nationalist Mythmaking of the Ukrainian Crisis,' *Post-Soviet Affairs*, 32 (1): 55–74.

Lavrov, S. (2024). 'Minister of Foreign Affairs of the Russian Federation S.V. Lavrov Interviewed by the TV Programme 'Moscow. Kremlin. Putin,' 8 September. www.mid.ru/ru/press_service/video/posledniye_dobavlnenniye/1968487/

Lawrinenko, J. (ed.), (1959). *Rostrilyane Vidrodzhennya. Antologia 1917–1939*. Paris: Instytut Literackie.

Letters From Donbas. (2015). Part 3: 'Dirt, Tears, and Blood', *Radio Free Europe-Radio Liberty*, 8 February. www.rferl.org/content/ukraine-letters-from-donbas-situation-fighting-day-to-day-life/26836295.html.

Magocsi, P. R. (2010). *A History of Ukraine. The Land and Its People*. 2nd ed. Toronto: University of Toronto Press.

Martin, T. (2001). 'An Affirmative Action Empire: The Soviet Union as the Highest Form of Imperialism' In: R. G. Suny, and T. Martin (eds.), *A State of Nations. Empire and Nation-making in the Age of Lenin and Stalin*. Oxford: Oxford University Press: 67–92.

McGlynn, J. (2023a). *Russia's War*. Cambridge: Polity Press.

McGlynn, J. (2023b). 'Russia Doesn't Care About the Fight against Fascism,' *Moscow Times*, 6 October. www.themoscowtimes.com/2023/10/06/russia-doesnt-care-about-the-fight-fgainst-fascism-a82684

McGlynn, J. (2023c). We Can't Condemn the People of Occupied Ukraine to the Reality of Russian Occupation,' *Moscow Times*, 17 January. www.themoscowtimes.com/2025/01/17/we-cant-condemn-the-people-of-occupied-ukraine-to-the-reality-of-russian-occupation-a87629

Medvedev, D. (2009). 'Address to the President of Ukraine Viktor Yushchenko,' 11 August. http://archive.kremlin.ru/eng/text/docs/2009/08/220759.shtml.

Medvedev, D. (2021). 'Pochemu bessmyslenny kontakty s nyneshnim ukrainskim rukovodstvom,' *Komersant*, 11 October. www.kommersant.ru/doc/5028300?tg#id2123320

Michel, C. (2024). 'How Aleksandr Solzhenitsyn Became Putin's Spiritual Guru. The Strange Story of a Global Literary Hero Who Went on to Inspire Russia's War on Ukraine.' *Foreign Policy*, 7 April. https://foreignpolicy.com/2024/04/07/putin-russia-nationalism-solzhenitsyn-became-putins-spiritual-guru-ukraine/

Motyl, A. J. (1990). 'The Myth of Russian Nationalism' In: *Sovietology, Rationality, Nationality. Coming to Grips with Nationalism in the USSR.* New York: Columbia University Press.
Motyl, A. J. (2011). 'Do Animals Speak Ukrainian?' *World Affairs Blog*, 11 February. http://worldaffairsjournal.org/blog/alexander-j-motyl/do-animals-speak-ukrainian.
Nahaylo, B. (1988). 'Disgraced Ukrainian Party Leader Petro Shelest Reappears After Fifteen Years – A Slap in the Face for Shcherbytsky?' *Radio Liberty*, RL 293/88, 29 July.
Narratives of Pro-Kremlin Disinformation: Nazis. (2022). *EUvs Disinfo*, 20 September. https://euvsdisinfo.eu/key-narratives-in-pro-kremlin-disinformation-nazis/
Naryshkin, S. (2020). 'Zelensky vse glubzhe pogruzhayetsia v ideyu ukrainskogo natsionalyzma,' *Tass*, 28 January. https://tass.ru/politika/7621843?fbclid=IwAR3SzRh-y9k2FBIRkY1sJv-PdmblCMx4ajG7VRnMkvEFtTHMBBRP3fJgWww
Nazi Satanists are entrenched in the Holy Russian city of Kyiv. (2023). *Meduza*, 27 July. https://meduza.io/en/feature/2023/07/27/nazi-satanists-are-entrenched-in-the-holy-russian-city-of-kyiv
Oliinyk, A., and Kuzio, T. (2021). 'The Euromaidan Revolution of Dignity, Reforms and De-Communisation in Ukraine,' *Europe-Asia Studies*, 73 (5): 807–836.
Olszański, T. A. (2015). 'Ukraine's Wartime Nationalism,' Centre for Eastern Studies, OSW Commentary, 179, 28 August. www.osw.waw.pl/en/publikacje/osw-commentary/2015-08-19/ukraines-wartime-nationalism
Osipian, A. (2014). 'Historical Myths, Enemy Images and Regional Identity in the Donbas Insurgency,' *Journal of Soviet and Post-Soviet Politics and Society*, 1(1): 109–140.
Patrushev, N. (2016). Interview, *Moskovski Komsomolets*, 26 November. www.mk.ru/politics/2016/01/26/nikolay-patrushev-mirovoe-soobshhestvo-dolzhno-skazat-nam-spasibo-za-krym.html
Patrushev, N. (2025). Interview, *Komsomolskaya Pravda*, 14 January. www.kp.ru/daily/27651/5036217/
Plyushch, L. (1979). *History's Carnival. A Dissidents Autobiography.* New York and London: Harcourt Bracer Jovanovich.
Plokhy, S. (2001). 'The Ghosts of Pereyaslav: Russo-Ukrainian Historical Debates in the Post-Soviet Era,' *Europe-Asia Studies*, 53 (3): 489–505.
Plokhy, S. (2023). *The Frontline. Essays on Ukraine's Past and Present.* Cambridge, MA: Harvard University.
Pritsak, O. (1981). 'Za kulisamy proholoshennya 1500-littya Kyeva.' *Suchasnist*, 9: 46–54. https://shron2.chtyvo.org.ua/Suchasnist/1981_N09_249.pdf?
Putin, V. (2008). 'Speech to the NATO Summit in Bucharest,' *UNIAN*, 18 April. www.unian.info/world/111033-text-of-putins-speech-at-nato-summit-bucharest-april-2-2008.html
Putin, V. (2014). 'Vladimir Putin Answered Journalists' Questions on the Situation in Ukraine,' 4 March. http://en.kremlin.ru/events/president/news/20366

Putin, V. (2021a). 'On the Historical Unity of Russians and Ukrainians,' 12 July. http://en.kremlin.ru/events/president/news/66181

Putin, V. (2021b). 'Direct Line with V. Putin,' 30 June. http://en.kremlin.ru/events/president/news/65973

Putin, V. (2022). 'Address by the President of the Russian Federation,' 21 February. http://en.kremlin.ru/events/president/news/67828

Putin, V. (2024). 'Results of the Year with Vladimir Putin,' 19 December. http://en.kremlin.ru/events/president/news/75909

Rosenberg, S. (2017). 'Crimea: The Place That's Rather Difficult to Get Into,' *BBC News*, 21 March. www.bbc.co.uk/news/world-europe-39329284

Rudenko, O. (2014). 'Ethnic Russians in Ukraine's Luhansk Also Want Closer Ties with Moscow,' *Kyiv Post*, 16 March. www.kyivpost.com/content/ukraine/ethnic-russians-in-ukraines-luhansk-also-want-closer-ties-with-moscow-339683.html

Russian TV News. (2015). 'Anti-Maydan vs "Fascists"; "Peace Returning" to Debaltseve, *BBC Monitoring*, 23 December.

Sahaydak, M. (1976). *The Ukrainian Herald 7-8. Ethnocide of Ukrainians in the USSR*. Baltimore: Smoloskyp.

Satter, D. (2017). *The Less You Know, the Better You Sleep. Russia's Road to Dictatorship Under Yeltsin and Putin*. London and New Haven, CT: Yale University Press.

Schneider-Deters, W. (2024). *Russia's War in Ukraine. Debates on Peace, Fascism, and War Crimes, 2022–2023*. Stuttgart: Ibidem; New York: Columbia University Press.

Sergeytsev, T. (2022). 'What should Russia Do with Ukraine?' *RIA Novosti*, 3 April. https://ria.ru/20220403/ukraina-1781469605.html

Shkandrij, M. (2015). *Ukrainian Nationalism. Politics, Ideology, and Literature, 1929–1956*. New Haven, CT: Yale University Press.

Shprintsen, A. (2015). 'CBC Producer Revisits Ukraine to Explore Conflict,' *CBC*, 22 February. www.cbc.ca/player/News/TV%20Shows/The%20National/ID/2487330867/

Sneider, N. (2014). 'The Empire Strikes Back. A Journey through Russia and Ukraine, where the Deep Past Shapes the Future,' *Open Rehearsal Project with the Big Roundtable*, 6 November. https://medium.com/the-empire-strikes-back/the-empire-strikes-back-c6e51efe9973

Socor, V. (2024). 'The Kremlin Spells Out the Terms of Ukraine's Surrender,' *Eurasia Daily Monitor*, 21 (82), 29 May. https://jamestown.org/program/the-kremlin-spells-out-the-terms-of-ukraines-surrender-part-one/

Soldatov, A., and Borogan, I. (2010). *The New Nobility. The Restoration of Russia's Secret State and the Enduring Legacy of the KGB*. New York: Public Affairs.

Solzhenitsyn, A. (1980). 'Misconceptions about Russia Are a Threat to America,' *Foreign Affairs*, 58 (4): 797–834.

Sorokowski, A. (1988). 'The Millennium a Ukrainian Perspective,' *Religion in Communist Lands*, 15 (3): 257–263.

Statiev, A. (2010). *The Soviet Counterinsurgency in the Western Borderlands*. Cambridge and New York: Cambridge University Press.
Stewart, W. (2015). 'Inside Putin's Secret 'Troll Factory:' How Mother Turned Whistleblower to Reveal the Secrets of Shadowy Propaganda Unit where Staff Were Told to Call Obama a 'Monkey' and Ukraine 'Nazis' Online,' *The Daily Mail*, 26 June. www.dailymail.co.uk/news/article-3138847/Putins-secret-.
Sych, V. (2015). 'The Moment of Truth,' *Novoye Vremya*, 4 April. http://nv.ua/opinion/sych/the-moment-of-truth-42442.html
Sysyn, F. (1983). 'The Ukrainian Orthodox Question in the USSR,' *Religion in Communist Lands*, 11 (3): 251–263.
Szporluk, R. (1976). 'Valentyn Moroz: His Political Ideas in Historical Perspective,' *Canadian Slavonic Papers*, 18 (1): 80–90.
Szymanowicz, A. (2020). 'Cossacks in the Service of the Third Reich,' *Scientific Journal of the Military University of Land Forces*, 52 (1): 87–102.
Tabachnyk, D. (2012). 'Kakim dolzhen byt uchebnyk istorii.' www.partyofregions.org.ua/pr-east-west/4c08a20a530d1
Teague, E. (1988). *Solidarity and the Soviet Worker: The Impact of the Polish Events of 1980 on Soviet Internal Politics*. London and New York: Croom Helm.
Tereshchuk, H., and Coalson, R. (2015). 'Ukrainian 'Cyborg': 'They Tried to Break Me, but It Didn't Work,' *Radio Free Europe/Radio Liberty*, 19 August. www.rferl.org/a/ukrainian-cyborg-prisoner-of-war-torture-beating-donetsk/27197605.html
The Idea of Ukraine is Based on a Mythologised Lie. (2019). *EUvsDisinfo*, 17 June. https://euvsdisinfo.eu/report/the-idea-of-ukraine-is-based-on-a-mythologised-lie
The Kremlin's misuse of Nazism as a weapon of information manipulation. (2025). *EUvsDisinfo*, 27 January. https://euvsdisinfo.eu/the-kremlins-misuse-of-nazism-as-a-weapon-of-information-manipulation/
The Kremlin's Occupation Playbook. (2024). Coerced Russification and Ethnic Cleansing in Occupied Ukraine, Institute for the Study of War, 8 February. www.understandingwar.org/backgrounder/kremlins-occupation-playbook-coerced-russification-and-ethnic-cleansing-occupied
The Russian Federation's Escalating Commission of Genocide in Ukraine: A Legal Analysis. (2023). New Lines Institute for Strategy and Policy and Raoul Wallenberg Centre for Human Rights, July. https://newlinesinstitute.org/rules-based-international-order/genocide/the-russian-federations-escalating-commission-of-genocide-in-ukraine-a-legal-analysis/
Thirteen myths about Russia's war against Ukraine exposed. (2024). *EUvsDisinfo*, 21 February. https://euvsdisinfo.eu/thirteen-myths-about-russias-war-against-ukraine-exposed/
Tolz, V. (2001). *Russia. Inventing the Nation*. London: Arnold and Hodder.
Trenin, D. (2020). 'Moscow's New Rules,' Carnegie Russia Eurasia Center Commentary, 12 November. https://carnegieendowment.org/posts/2020/10/moscows-new-rules?lang=en

Velychenko, S. (1993). *Shaping Identity in Eastern Europe and Russia. Soviet Russian and Polish Accounts of Ukrainian History, 1914–1991*. New York: St. Martin's Press.

Von Hagen, M. (1995). 'Does Ukraine Have a History?' *Slavic Review*, 54 (3): 658–673.

Vyedyenyeyev, D. (2012). 'Politychni represii 1920-1980-x ta problem formuvannya natsionalnoyi pamyati,' *Istorychna Pravda*, 26 December. www.istpravda.com.ua/research/50db659307b77/

Walker, S. (2015). 'Komunar, East Ukraine: "Nothing to Eat, Nothing to Do, No Point in Life",' *The Guardian*, 6 February. www.theguardian.com/world/

Wawrzonek, M. (2014). 'Ukraine in the "Gray Zone": between the "Russkiy Mir" and Europe,' *East European Politics and Society*, 28 (4): 758–780.

Wawrzonek, M. (2023). *Memory, Politics, and Legacy of Metropolitan Andrey Sheptytsky*. Krakow: Ignatianum University Press.

Wilson, A., 2014. *Ukraine Crisis. What It Means for the West*. New Haven, CT: Yale University Press.

Wojnowski, W. (2017). *The Near Abroad. Eastern Europe and Soviet Patriotism in Ukraine, 1956–1985*. Toronto: University of Toronto Press.

Wolkonsky, A. (1920). *The Ukrainian Question. The Historic Truth versus the Separatist Propaganda*. Rome: Ditta E Armani.

Yekelchyk, S., (2004). *Stalin's Empire of Memory. Russian-Ukrainian Relations in the Soviet Historical Imagination*. Toronto: University of Toronto Press.

Za Shcho Usunuly Shelesta? (1983). Munich: Suchasnist.

Zygar, M. (2023a). *War and Punishment. The Story of Russian Oppression and Ukrainian Resistance*. London: Weidenfeld and Nicolson.

Zygar, M. (2023b). 'The Man behind Putin's Warped View of History,' *New York Times*, 19 September. www.nytimes.com/2023/09/19/opinion/putin-russia-medinsky.html

PART III

Divergence

6

Diverging Identities in Russia and Ukraine

Excessive attention was given to Ukraine's linguistic divisions, which presented an image of Ukraine as a regionally divided state (Kuzyk, 2019). Meanwhile, Russian leaders' obsession with Ukraine as a renegade Little Russian province was given insufficient attention by scholars (Sharafutdinova, 2020; Kolstø and Blakkisrud, 2016; Laruelle, 2019; Kuzio, 2020, pp. 1, 8, 60, 72, 83, 86, 88–89), while denying the existence of ideology and downplaying nationalism in Russia made it difficult to understand how Russian imperial nationalism was, and remains, the driver behind Putin's full-scale invasion (Gorodnichenko, Sologoub, and Deryugina, 2023; Deryugina, Gorodnichenko, and Sologoub, 2023; Kuzio, 2020, pp. 82–105, 2022b, Kuzio, 2023). Few scholars analysed the nearly two-decade de-humanisation of Ukraine and Ukrainians, which is important in understanding the barbarity and war crimes that has accompanied Russian military aggression against Ukraine (an exception is Minchenia, Tornquist-Plewa, and Yurchuk, 2018; McGlynn, 2023b; Garner, 2023, pp. 83, 88, 124, 177).

Scholars have mistakenly divided Ukrainian politics between a 'nationalist west' and 'pro-Russian' east of Ukraine or civic and ethnic leaders (Shevel, 2024). In fact, nationalists were to be found in both Ukrainian and pan-Russian identities. Ukrainian politics was more complicated than a simple contest between 'Ukrainian nationalists' (grouping a wide array of centrist, centre-right and far right parties) and 'pro-Russian forces' (referring to the far left and the Party of Regions). Centrist and centre-right (also called national democratic) patriotic and far right nationalist political forces supported a Ukrainian identity distinct from Russian. Centrist parties were primarily found in the southeast of Ukraine, were ideologically weak and often had ties to oligarchs: the most recent example is Volodymyr Zelenskyy's Servant of the People Party. Centre-right patriots, with strongholds in the west of Ukraine and capital city of Kyiv, included the Ukrainian Popular Movement for Restructuring (*Rukh*), Ukrainian Republican Party, Yulia Tymoshenko Bloc and Fatherland Party, Our

Ukraine, UDAR (Ukrainian Democratic Alliance for Reform), and the Petro Poroshenko Bloc and European Solidarity Party. Ukraine's far right nationalists were the Social National Party of Ukraine and *Svoboda* (Freedom) Party, KUK (Congress of Ukrainian Nationalists), *Pravyy Sektor* (Right Sector) and National Corps. Russian and Soviet nationalists who supported a pan-Russian identity had strong bases of support in Crimea and the Donbas and included the KPU (Communist Party of Ukraine), other extreme left wing parties like the Progressive Socialist Party of Ukraine, and Party of Regions. Nikolay Mitrokhin (2024, p. 32) writes that KPU support for reviving the USSR 'coincided with the neo-imperial goals of Russian nationalists and made both forces reliable allies'. After Russia's full-scale invasion of Ukraine in March 2022 and June 2024, twelve political parties with ties to Russia were banned.[1] These included two successors to the Party of Regions (Opposition Bloc, Opposition Platform-For Life), Shariy Party, *Nashi* (Ours), *Derzhava* (The State), Volodymyr Saldo Bloc, Our Land Party, Left Opposition, Union of Left Forces, Progressive Socialist Party of Ukraine, Socialist Party of Ukraine,[2] and Socialists. The KPU was already de facto banned because it had refused to remove communist and Soviet symbols as required by the 2015 de-communisation laws.

Chapters 6 and 7 analyse how Russia and Ukraine have significantly diverged since 1991 in their identities and political systems. The Kremlin and Russian imperial nationalists never accepted Ukraine could be a fully independent state with the right to pursue memory politics, language, cultural, educational, and religious policies that reinforced a Ukrainian identity distinct from Russian and become part of Europe and the West by joining NATO and the EU. Instead, the Kremlin and Russian leaders demanded, lobbied, cajoled, and aggressively pursued a Ukraine that, to all intents and purposes would have a semi-sovereign relationship akin to what had existed between Moscow and the Soviet Ukrainian republic and that which exists between the Russian Federation and Belarus. After he was first elected president in 1994, Alexander Lukashenka overturned all the policies associated with Belarusian national identity and returned Belarus to Soviet and pan-Russian identity (Leshchenko, 2004; see also

---

[1] www.ukrinform.net/rubric-polytics/3434673-nsdc-bans-prorussian-parties-in-ukraine.html

[2] The Socialist Party of Ukraine had supported the Orange Revolution and legislation on the *Holodomor* but in summer 2006 joined a parliamentary coalition with the Party of Regions and KPU and was subsequently taken over by pro-Russian forces.

Bekus, 2023). Lukashenka's Soviet and pan-Russian identity policies are those promoted by pro-Russian forces in Ukraine and what the Kremlin expects to be implemented in its two 'younger brothers' – Ukraine and Belarus. Lukashenka has had at times a difficult relationship with Putin who proposed Belarus merge with Russia in 2002, two decades before the full-scale invasion of Ukraine (Bigg, 2005). Putin's imperial nationalist objective of merging Russia and Belarus; that is, returning White Russia to that of a Tsarist *guberni*a, undermines the legitimacy of Lukashenka's Soviet Belarusian identity that lies in what he views as a Belarusian SSR with semi-sovereignty within the Soviet Union. On the other hand, the growth of imperial nationalism in Russia and plans for ever-closer Russian-Belarusian unity undermined attempts by Lukashenka to pursue a nation-building strategy that merged national and Soviet identities because this was ultimately unacceptable to the Kremlin (Leshchenko, 2008). Mass protest rallies against fraud in the 2020 elections were followed by the Kremlin assisting Lukashenka's regime in mass repression. 1,265 political prisoners were incarcerated in Belarus, far more than the number of Belarusian political prisoners imprisoned in the USSR.[3]

Self-designated Belarusian President Lukashenka is the kind of leader Russia sought to install in Kyiv if its 'special military operation' had gone as planned as a quickly executed occupation followed by regime change. A Ukrainian puppet leader, such as Lukashenka, would fawn over Russia's primacy among the three eastern Slavic peoples and within Eurasia, implement pan-Russian memory politics, language, cultural, educational, and religious policies, be xenophobically hostile to NATO and the 'collective West' and disinterested in membership in the EU. In January 2025, Lukashenka was re-elected president with the support of the *Belaya Rus* (White Rus [sian]) political party in a fraudulent 87.71 per cent vote, a figure just under the 88.48 per cent Putin also received in a fraudulent re-election in March of the previous year. Although Russia has not held free elections for over two decades, Putin (2025) has the audacity to describe Zelenskyy as an 'illegitimate' president.

Tension has always existed between the Kremlin's goal of a semi-sovereign Ukraine (i.e., Little Russia) akin to Belarus (i.e., White Russia), and the desire of Ukrainians to build a fully independent state. Competition between Ukrainian identity distinct from Russian and pan-Russian identity was a major influence on Ukrainian politics between 1991 and 2013, with the fiercest struggle taking place between the 2003–2004

---

[3] https://spring96.org/en/news/117068

Orange and 2013–2014 Euromaidan Revolutions. The Kremlin's goal of ensuring the dominance of pan-Russian identity in Ukraine was too ambitious and impossible to achieve. Of Ukraine's six presidents only, Viktor Yanukovych was pro-Russian. Although Moscow viewed Ukraine in a similar way to Belarus, as one of three branches of a pan-Russian people, this ignored their different histories and how a Ukrainian identity distinct from Russia was more popular and widespread across Ukraine. A Belarusian identity distinct from Russian was not sufficiently powerful to constitute a threat to Lukashenka until 2020, when mass protests erupted against election fraud that were brutally repressed with Russia's assistance.

The roots of Russia's decision to launch a full-scale invasion in 2022 lie in the dominance of Ukrainian identity after the marginalisation from 2014 of pan-Russian identity, as epitomised in the disintegration of the Party of Regions and disbarring of the KPU from participating in elections. Centre-right and centrist political forces supporting a Ukrainian identity asserted their dominance through the adoption of legislation in memory politics, language, education, and media, and included the goals of NATO and EU membership in the constitution. Russia's first invasion in 2014 marginalised pro-Russian political forces who supported a pan-Russian identity, and Russia's full-scale invasion in 2022 eviscerated them. In 2014–2021, Russian television and radio media broadcasting into Ukraine and Russian social media were banned. On the eve of Russia's full-scale invasion, five pro-Russian TV channels in Ukraine were closed. Constantinople Patriarch Bartholomew I removed Ukraine from the canonical territory of the Russian Orthodox Church, which it had usurped since 1686,[4] and granted a *Tomos* (autocephaly) for the Orthodox Church of Ukraine; both steps were the equivalent of earthquakes for the Russian Orthodox Church and Kremlin as they removed Ukraine from 'Holy Rus' and the Pan-Russian World. New legislation has curtailed ties between the Russian Orthodox Church and its Ukrainian Orthodox Church branch.

This chapter is divided into three sections. The first section discusses the confusion surrounding the use of political science terms in Ukrainian politics. This section critically engages with the description of Ukraine as divided between nationalist and pro-Russian (this book uses pan-Russian) political forces and identities and between ethnic and civic presidents. The second section analyses Ukrainian politics as a struggle between Ukrainian identity distinct to Russian and Little Russian identity belonging within a pan-Russian identity. Since 1991, Russia has

[4] www.istpravda.com.ua/short/2018/10/2/153018/

intervened in Ukrainian affairs in support of Ukrainians viewing themselves as belonging within a pan-Russian identity. The second section explains how following the Euromaidan Revolution and Russian military aggression in 2014 pan-Russian identity was marginalised and Ukrainian identity became dominant. After 2014, pro-Russian political forces disintegrated (Party of Regions) or were not allowed to participate in elections (KPU). A key factor contributing to declining support was the loss of 16 per cent of Ukrainian voters in Russian-occupied Crimea and the Donbas, many of whom traditionally voted for pro-Russian political forces (D'Anieri, 2019b).

The third section analyses three factors that lay behind Putin's fateful decision. The first of these factors was the transformation of Russia from an authoritarian system with a collective leadership into a fascist dictatorship (Motyl, 2016; Garner, 2023; Garner and Kuzio, 2025). The second factor was the marginalisation of pan-Russian political forces and the growing dominance of Ukrainian identity following the Euromaidan Revolution. The third factor was the Kremlin's failure to impose its version of the 2014–2015 Minsk accords upon Presidents Petro Poroshenko and Zelenskyy. By 2020, the Kremlin had given up on the Minsk accords and a year later made the decision to launch its 'special military operation' to destroy Ukrainian identity (i.e., 'de-nazification') and replace it with a pan-Russian identity. Ukraine would lose Crimea and New Russia (southeast Ukraine) and become a truncated Little Russian puppet state (i.e., 'de-militarisation').

Understanding Nation-States and Ukraine

Scholars have defined Ukrainian presidents as ethnic and civic. This could reflect Hans Kohn's artificial division between civic Western European and ethnic eastern European states (Kuzio, 2002; Shevel, 2024). Some scholars apply the term civic subjectively towards politicians they view positively, although often without placing the term within the theoretical literature and use the term ethnic for political leaders and forces they dislike.

Olga Onuch and Henry Hale (2022) defines Zelenskyy as civic and Poroshenko as an ethnic president. Tamta Gelashvili (2023, p. 5) describes 'Ukrainian nationalists' as nativist and authoritarian in contrast to Zelenskyy, who is a liberal. Onuch and Hale (2022, pp. 8, 10, 23–24) write that Zelenskyy's emphasis on citizenship was different to earlier presidents by promoting 'civic national belonging', a 'strong sense of civic duty' and Ukraine's 'diversity'. Maria Popova and Oxana Shevel (2023, p. 189) describe Zelenskyy's 2019 election as the victory of 'civic' Ukrainian identity.

In fact, there is little to differentiate between Poroshenko and Zelenskyy on their domestic and foreign policies and Zelenskyy did not change any of his predecessors' policies. Yanukovych, in contrast, cancelled Viktor Yushchenko's decrees honouring nationalist leaders and upgraded the status of Russian to an official language. After being elected, Zelenskyy became in some areas more radical than his predecessor on ethnocultural policies. Poroshenko largely ignored the Russian occupation of Crimea, while Zelenskyy insisted the Minsk accords be revised to include Crimea, launching the Crimean Platform in 2020 to lobby the international community to not recognise its occupation. During Zelenskyy's presidency there have been greater restrictions on the Russian Orthodox Church, five pro-Russian television channels were closed, and twelve pro-Russian political parties banned. The Ukrainian Parliament (2021) defined Ukrainians as the indigenous peoples of Ukraine and Tatars, Karaites and Krymchaks as the indigenous people of Crimea. Russia effuses to agree to a ceasefire until what it calls the 'roots of the war' are resolved (see Kuzio, 2025).[5] In spring 2022 and 2025 peace talks, the Russian delegation headed by Vladimir Medinsky (Zygar, 2023b), author of Putin's (2021) ideological treatise underpinning the 'special military operation', revealed what Russia understands by the need to remove the 'roots of the war.' The goal of 'de-militarisation' is seen through the Russian demand that Ukraine become a permanently neutral state, never join NATO and end military cooperation with the West. The goal of 'de-Nazification' is seen through the demand for Ukraine to recognise as de jure Russian, occupied Crimea and four Ukrainian *oblasts* and to rescind legislative acts enacted throughout Ukraine's existence as an independent state, dealing with Veterans (1993, 2015), TV and Radio (1994), Culture (2011), Lustration (2014), four De-Communisation laws (2015), State Service (2016), Judiciary (2016), Education and Higher Education (2017, 2019), Language (2019), and Titular Nation (2021). Russia's goal of removing the 'roots of the war' are a demand for regime change to a Little Russian puppet state.

Scholars have also divided Ukraine into those upholding a nationalist Ukrainian and those with a pro-Russian (this book uses pan-Russian) identity. Nationalist and ethnic Ukrainian presidents are, for example,

---

[5] See pages 13–15 of the Russian draft treaty at: https://static01.nyt.com/newsgraphics/documenttools/17f655b584276917/07ec81ce-full.pdf

described as promoting 'nationalising policies' which are unpopular with Russian speakers (Eras, 2023, p. 118). Gelashvili (2023) continues a common misnomer of conflating nationalists and the centre-right in Ukrainian politics. Serhii Plokhy (XII–XIII, pp. 264, 270, 279) describes divisions in Ukraine over history between 'pro-Soviet' and 'pro-nationalist' forces and Zelenskyy having created a 'new majority' composed of 'nationalists and liberals' (Ukrainian nationalists have only been present in the 2012–2014 parliament). Popova and Shevel (2023, pp. 58) similarly describe Ukraine's centre-right as a 'nationalist faction' aligned with the reformist camp in Ukraine. Ukraine is led by 'Ukrainian nationalists' since the Euromaidan Revolution and President Poroshenko 'adopted an increasingly nationalist stance' after taking 'over the nationalist discourse' used by Yushchenko (Gelashvili, 2023).

It is never explained by these scholars why only the Ukrainian side is nationalist while pan-Russian identity is not nationalist. This confusing use of political science terms sends a signal that Ukrainian identity is undemocratic and intolerant (i.e., because it is nationalist) while its pan-Russian alternative is somehow less intolerant (because it is not nationalist). The intolerance of pro-Russian forces is evident in their support for Soviet era-style marginalisation of the Ukrainian language in Ukraine and no longer teaching the Ukrainian language in Russian-occupied Ukraine (Popova and Shevel, 2023, p. 109; Lewis, 2025). In Belarus, Lukashenka's pan-Russian nationality policies continued Soviet era Russification and the marginalisation of the Belarusian language. In fact, *both* Ukrainian and pan-Russian identities include ethnocultural attributes with the former supporting one state language (Ukrainian) while the latter supports two state languages (Ukrainian and Russian). Supporting two state languages does not make pan-Russian identity less nationalist. Zbigniew Wojnowski (2017, p. 16) reminds us that eastern Slavic (i.e., pan-Russian) nationalism was a key component of Soviet culture because the USSR was a 'nationalist state'.

Civic attributes in a nation-state traditionally refer to state institutions, the constitution, political system, and legislation. Ukrainian identity is therefore far more civic than its pan-Russian alternative. Ukrainian identity is more supportive of democratisation and other similar demands made by the EU than its pan-Russian alternative which is unenthusiastic towards European integration and more supportive of authoritarianism, as seen during Yanukovych's presidency. Russia and Belarus are both dictatorships. Ethnic factors in a nation-state encompasses the designated official (sometimes referred to as state) language, culture, historical myths, and national symbols. Stephen Shulman (2005, p. 82) writes that Ukrainian identity has not hindered democratisation in Ukraine, 'as scholars and commentators who promote "good" civic national identity over "bad" ethnic identity seem to believe'.

The proportion between civic and ethnic attributes in nation-states is a dynamic process that has changed throughout history (Kuzio, 2009). In the twentieth century, the civic component became proportionally larger as Western nation-states became more inclusive of previously marginalised groups and more tolerant of different views on traumatic periods of history. Western nation-states, for example, did not grant the vote to women until after the First and the Second World Wars; France and Italy expanded their franchise to women as late as 1944–1946, a decade later than Türkiye and nearly three decades later than Poland.

Using the terms ethnic and nationalist to describe centre-right political parties and presidents in Ukraine is confusing for four reasons. Firstly, it has little in common with the theoretical literature and provides a negative 'Other' for one wing of Ukrainian politics. Centre-right parties in Europe and North America are not defined as nationalist and yet some of these parties, for example in France and the US, incorporate policies from the far right. Secondly, conflating Ukraine's centre-right and far right makes it difficult to explain why the latter failed to win votes in elections held during a war with Russia; traditionally, support for ethnic nationalism tends to grow during a bloody conflict. Thirdly, every Ukrainian region, except Lviv, voted for Jewish-Ukrainian candidate Zelenskyy in the 2019 presidential elections, including many national democratic voters in western and central Ukraine. It is never explained why nationalists, traditionally described as anti-Semitic, would vote for a Jewish candidate? Fourthly, if the centre-right are understood as nationalists they should be opposed to Ukraine's membership of the EU, as is the case with populist nationalists and the far right throughout Europe. In fact, national democrats have always been the country's most strident supporters of returning Ukraine to Europe (Wolczuk, 2000).

Conflicts, wars, and bloodshed have always speeded up the crystallisation of national identities. Ukrainian identity became dominant after 2014 and especially following the full-scale invasion. Several scholars, including Onuch and Hale (2018) in an earlier study, have written about how Ukraine became more civic after 2014 (Kulyk, 2014, 2016; Chupyra, 2015; Käihkö, 2018; Pop-Eleches and Robertson, 2018; Aliyev, 2021; Bureiko and Moga, 2019). Decentralisation reforms boosted local civil society groups and political activism (Brik and Murtazashvili, 2022). The Euromaidan

Revolution did indeed lead to a major growth in civic activism, volunteer groups supporting the army and volunteer battalions (Poznyak-Khomenko, 2020). But there was also, from 2014 a strengthening of ethnic attributes of Ukrainian identity, such as language, culture and attitudes to history. Ukraine did not become a 100 per cent civic state after 2014 because such states only exist in theory, but not in practice.

A majority of Ukraine's Russophones expressed a loyalty to Ukrainian over pan-Russian identity (Bureiko and Moga, 2019, p. 138). Volodymyr Kulyk (2014, pp. 120–121) writes that 'modern Ukrainian anti-imperial nationalism' has a 'deeply inclusive' nature and is supported by Russophones and Jews in Ukraine. Russian speakers have been prominent in Ukrainian forces fighting in 2014–2021 (Aliyev, 2021) and since 2022. Changes in the identity of Russian speakers in Ukraine's southeast were especially pronounced in Zelenskyy's home region of Dnipropetrovsk, where the most radical de-communisation process took place (Oliinyk and Kuzio, 2021, p. 814; Kuzio, Zhuk, and D'Anieri, 2022).

Ukrainian versus Pan-Russian Identities

Since 1991, Ukrainian leaders could build their country around a Ukrainian nation distinct from Russia or a Ukrainian (Little Russian) identity ensconced within a pan-Russian identity (Shulman, 2005). Shulman (2005) described Ukraine as facing competition between what he called 'ethnic Ukrainian' and 'east Slavic' identities. Tatyana Zhurzhenko (2021, p. 1447) writes that until 2014, Ukraine was faced by political competition between the Party of Regions and KPU on the one side, supporting east Slavic identity, and national democrats and nationalists on the other, backing ethnic Ukrainian identity. Popova and Shevel (2023, pp. 47–48, 81, 86, 88) divide Ukrainian politics between those supporting a distinct Ukrainian nation and backers of a pan-Russian identity. Natalia Leshchenko (2004, 2008) used a similar framework of two nation-building strategies in Belarus, which she defined as national and Soviet. This chapter uses a framework of competition between Ukrainian ('ethnic Ukrainian' [Shulman, 2005]) versus pan-Russian ('east Slavic' [Shulman, 2005; Zhurzhenko, 2021]) identities. Table 6.1 shows policies pursued in Belarus, which Leshchenko (2004) described as national versus Soviet identities, and policies in Ukraine, which Shulman (2005) defined as ethnic Ukrainian versus east Slavic identities.

Throughout the post-Soviet era, Russia supported and interfered through soft power and military aggression in favour of east Slavic and pan-Russian identity. In Belarus, where a Belarusian identity distinct from Russian was weaker than in Ukraine, Russia was successful with Lukashenka. The Kremlin believed in the 2004 elections and during Yanukovych's presidency that he would be the Ukrainian leader who would bring Ukraine into the Pan-Russian World. Competition between the pro-Russian Party of Regions supporting Yanukovych's candidacy and pro-European forces backing Yushchenko's candidacy during and after the 2004 presidential elections and Orange Revolution was drawn upon by Shulman (2005) to create a framework for understanding these competing identities in Ukrainian politics.

This chapter argues that five Ukrainian presidents (Leonid Kravchuk, Leonid Kuchma, Yushchenko, Poroshenko, and Zelenskyy) pursued a Ukrainian identity distinct from Russian. Only one Ukrainian president (Yanukovych) 'embraced the Russian-Soviet-East Slavic identity' (Popova and Shevel, 2023, pp. 99). Language policies changed very little between Kuchma and Yushchenko, and only Yanukovych attempted to introduce two state languages (Popova and Shevel 2023, p. 110). A Ukrainian identity distinct from Russian is different in many key areas from a pan-Russian identity (see Table 6.1).

The Soviet Legacy

Eastern Slavic identity was a central element of Soviet political culture where Ukrainian loyalty to the USSR 'was tantamount to a close Ukrainian-Russian political union' (Wojnowski, 2017, p. 115); that is, the Soviet Union promoted a camouflaged form of the pan-Russian nation that had been fashioned in the Tsarist Empire. As other chapters have argued, fusion of Russians, Ukrainians and Belarusians into a Russian-speaking *Homo Sovieticus* was in effect fusion into a pan-Russian people. Soviet identity was 'a composite East Slavic identity' at the heart of which were joint accomplishments, such as victory in the Great Patriotic War (Wojnowski, 2017, p. 16). Belarus and Russia have maintained and revived elements of the Soviet system, fanned Soviet nostalgia and maintained their Soviet era allegiance to a pan-Russian nation (see Kryshtanovskaya and White, 2009). Russians, Ukrainians, and Belarusians are 'fraternal brothers' who were born together, never experienced conflict in their historical relationship and are forever united. President Putin and Russian imperial nationalists believe Ukrainians separated from Russians not by choice but through external invasions and foreign conspiracies (Koposov, 2022, 160; McGlynn, 2023a, p. 29).

Table 6.1 Ukrainian and Belarusian national versus Pan-Russian identities

	Ukrainian identity	Belarusian identity	Pan-Russian identities in Ukraine and Belarus
Policies	Centrist and centre-right parties	Belarusian Popular Front and centre-right parties	Communist Party of Ukraine, Party of Regions, Crimean Russian nationalist separatists in Ukraine. Belarus has no ruling party.
Defining the Ukrainian people	Ukrainians are the titular nation. Ukrainians are a distinct people separate to Russians.	Belarusians are the titular nation.	Ukrainians, Belarusians and Russians are co-members of a *triune* pan-Russian people.
Reforms	As in Europe, a culture of individualism and love of freedom. Support for political, legal, and economic reforms and to move Ukraine away from the Soviet legacy and Pan-Russian World and closer to Europe.	Reforms required to enter the EU.	As in Russia, a collectivist and authoritarian political culture. Weaker support for liberal and political views and democratisation. Opposition to, or disinterest in, reforms.
Religion	An inclusive understanding of the Eastern Christian tradition as including Ukrainian Orthodox and Ukrainian Greek Catholic Churches, as well as tolerance of Ukrainian Protestant and Evangelical denominations. Support for autocephaly of the Orthodox Church of Ukraine.	Leshchenko (2004) does not mention religion, but a Belarusian identity is tolerant towards Catholics and supports autocephaly for the Orthodox Church in Belarus.	An exclusive understanding of the Eastern Christian tradition with a dominant Russian Orthodox Church and intolerance towards 'non-traditional' confessions (i.e., Protestants, Evangelicals, Ukrainian and Belarusian Orthodox and Greek Catholic Churches).

(continued)

Table 6.1 (cont.)

Language	Support only Ukrainian as the state language and oppose Russian as a second state language.	Support only Belarusian as the only state language.	As in the USSR, the Russian language is superior to Ukrainian and Belarusian. Support for Russian to be constitutionally elevated to a second state language. Or legislatively made into an official language in regions with a high percentage of Russian-speakers. Lukashenka organised a referendum in 1995 to raise Russian to a second state language.
Attitudes to history	Ukrainian history is independent of Russia's. *Holodomor* was a genocide against the Ukrainian people. Official recognition of the (OUN) and Ukrainian Insurgent Army (UPA). De-communisation led to the Great Patriotic War being replaced by the Second World War and the banning of Communist, Soviet, and Nazi symbols. From 2022, support for Ukraine's de-Russification.	Belarusian history is independent of Russian history. Belarus emerged from the Polotsk Principality and Grand Duchy of Lithuania. Russia has been historically an enemy of Belarus. Independence Day for Ukraine is 24 August, and for Belarus it was the 27 July 1990 Declaration of Sovereignty and 25 August 1991 Declaration of Independence.	Ukraine and Belarus are part of eastern Slavic history, where Russians, Ukrainians, and Belarusians were born together in 'Kievan Russia' (Kyiv Rus) and would remain forever united. In Ukraine, they uphold the Soviet view of the 1654 Treaty of Pereyaslav as the 'reunification' of Ukraine and Russia. There was no *Holodomor*, only a Soviet-wide famine that equally affected Russians, Ukrainians and Belarusians. Russians, Ukrainians and Belarusians jointly celebrate victory in the Great Patriotic War. Russia did not declare independence in 1991 and celebrates 'Russia Day' based on its 12 June 1990 Declaration of Sovereignty. In a 1996 referendum, Lukashenka changed Belarusian 'Independence Day' to 3 July, the day Minsk was liberated from the Nazis in 1944.

Soviet nostalgia	No nostalgia for the USSR.	No Soviet nostalgia.	Strong sentiments of Soviet nostalgia. Lukashenka replaced the white and red national flag and *Pahonia* symbol with reformed Soviet Belarusian symbols.
Foreign and security policies	*Centrists until 2004*: Ukraine joined only economic bodies in the Commonwealth of Independent States (CIS) and opposed joining CIS political and security structures. Supported NATO and EU membership.	*Centre-right*: Withdrawal from CIS structures, return to Europe, and EU and NATO membership.	Belarus seeks to join the EU. Leshchenko (2004) does not mention Belarusian national identity supporting NATO membership.	Ukraine as part of the Pan-Russian World and a member of the Eurasian Economic Union. Ambivalent or hostile towards Europe and disbelief in Ukraine surviving a reduction of economic and trade ties with Russia. Strongly opposed to NATO membership. In 2006, Yanukovych rejected a MAP (Membership Action Plan) towards NATO membership and in 2013, Yanukovych refused to sign an Association Agreement with the EU. Belarus has sought to build a union with Russia since 1996 and is a founding member of the CSTO (Collective Security Treaty Organisation) and Eurasian Economic Union.

Sources and Notes: Ukrainian Identity and Pan-Russian Identity columns are compiled by the authors. The Belarusian column is taken from Leshchenko (2004, p. 339).

Serhii Plokhy (2023, p. 295) writes the promotion of a Soviet people and the eastern Slavs as 'fraternal' and united through the 'friendship of peoples', bore fruit in Ukraine and Belarus where it 'produced lasting effects among the east Slavic peoples of the Soviet Union'. The three eastern Slavs constituted about two-thirds of the Soviet population and represented the core of the USSR. The three eastern Slavic republics and the Transcaucasian republic (Georgia, Azerbaijan and Armenia) were founding members of the Soviet Union. Unlike other regions of the USSR the three eastern Slavic republics had seats at the UN – USSR (representing 'Historic Russia'), Ukrainian and Belarusian SSR's. Russian, Ukrainian, and Belarusian leaders met on 7–8 December 1991 to dismantle the USSR and only after they had accomplished their goal did and they advise the other republics the Soviet Union would cease to exist on 31 December 1991.

'Little Russian nationalism' was promoted by Soviet nationalities policies through historiography where Russians, Ukrainians, and Belarusians were described as born together in 'Kievan Russia' (Kievan Rus) and 're-united' in the 1654 Treaty of Pereyaslav (see Chapter 8). Plokhy (2023, pp. 284–286) describes Kyiv Rus as the 'foundation myth' for Russian imperial nationalists when a 'big Russian nation' (i.e., pan-Russian people) was divided by the Mongol invasion into three parts - Great Russians (Russians), Little Russians (Ukrainians), and White Russians (Belarusians). A Russian history that traced the origins of the Russian people to Novgorod, rather than Kyiv and with a separate trajectory to Ukrainian history, emerged in the 1990s, but this view was incompatible with Russian imperial nationalism under Putin (see Tolz, 2002).

Pan-Russian Identity

In 1991–1993, Belarus began state and nation-building around a Belarusian identity distinct from Russian. The election of Lukashenka in 1994 changed identity politics and memory policies to that of Belarusians as part of a Soviet past and pan-Russian nation. A pan-Russian identity also places Ukraine within the Pan-Russian World. Ukraine does not possess a history independent of Russia but is part of a common eastern Slavic history stretching from Kyiv Rus to the present day. Russian history for Putin (2023a) goes back a thousand years to Kyiv Rus which after its destruction in 1240 transferred its legacy to the Vladimir-Suzdal principality, Muscovite Kingdom, Tsarist Empire, Soviet Union, and the Russian Federation.

Pan-Russian unity is set in stone and cannot be broken, ruling out a Ukrainian identity distinct from Russia, with Ukraine not possessing independent agency to decide its domestic and foreign policies. A pan-Russian identity is never critical of Ukraine's experience within the Tsarist Empire and Soviet Union. It views the *Holodomor* as a common Soviet tragedy that affected Russians and Ukrainians in a similar way. A pan-Russian identity includes Ukraine within the Soviet and Russian narrative of the Great Patriotic War (Plokhy, 2023, p. 255). From 1995, Russia annually held Great Patriotic War parades on Victory Day (9 May) which became 'sacralised and canonised' with the addition of heavy military equipment from 2008 (Aron, 2023, p. 57). From 2015, Ukraine's commemorationn of the Second World War (1939–1945) challenged not only Russia's quasi-religious cult of the Great Patriotic War (1941–1945) but also its status as a great power which emerged from the Soviet victory over Nazism (McGlynn, 2020, 2023a, p. 15). In Russia, the quasi-religious cult of the Great Patriotic War has been accompanied by the rehabilitation of Soviet dictator Stalin (see Kuzio, 2017; Khapaeva, 2024 and Chapter 4).

The Ukrainian description of the *Holodomor* as a genocide has always been a bugbear for Russian imperial nationalists. Russian President Dmitri Medvedev's (2009) 'address' to Ukrainian President Viktor Yushchenko demanded the next elected Ukrainian president end the description of the *Holodomor* as a genocide (Kuzio, 2015, pp. 438–439) and instead describe the 1933 famine as a tragedy felt by all peoples in the USSR. Medvedev's demand, which was implemented by Yanukovych, was hypocritical. Putin's Russia has never put-up monuments to the famine, supported a cult of Stalin (see Kuzio, 2017) (see Chapter 4), and closed Memorial and other independent organisations which had been collecting data on mass repressions under Stalinism.

Returning to the presidency in 2012, President Putin set as his goal the 'gathering of Russian lands' (see Kuzio, 2022a, pp. 156–176) by preventing Ukraine from signing an Association Agreement with the EU and joining the Eurasian Economic Union. Russian pressure was successful on Yerevan to not sign the EU Association Agreement and Armenia joined the Eurasian Economic Union. Putin's attendance in Kyiv at the 1015th anniversary of the Baptism of Kyiv Rus in summer 2013 was a 'mystical experience' that led him to believe in the need to fight for Ukraine (Zygar, 2023a, p. 276). Claiming a thousand years of Russian history is only possible by laying claim to 'Kievan Russia' (Kyiv Rus) and Grand Prince Vladimir (Volodymyr) the Great, who brought Byzantine Christianity in 988. According to legend, Kyiv Rus received Christianity in Chersonese,

Crimea (McGlynn, 2023a, p. 13). After the annexation of Crimea, a cult of Volodymyr (in Russian, Vladimir) in Russia led to the proliferation of his monuments (Koposov, 2022, p. 160).

In 2012, political technologist Kirill Frolov, who was working for the Russian presidential administration, outlined an exhaustive list of goals in support of a pan-Russian identity in Ukraine. Many of these policies were implemented during Yanukovych's presidency, included in the Minsk accords, and implemented in Russian-occupied Crimea and the Donbas after 2014 and Russian-occupied southeastern Ukraine after 2022 (Frolov Leaks, 2018):

1. Ukraine to join the Eurasian Economic Union.
2. Elevation of Russian to a second state language.
3. The federalisation of Ukraine with the goal of 'maximum weakening of the Ukrainian state'.
4. Legalisation of the canonical status of the Russian Orthodox Church and removal of the legal registration of Ukrainian Orthodox Churches supporting autocephaly.
5. Changing the 'temporary' status of the Black Sea Fleet to a permanent base in Sevastopol.
6. Discontinuing the falsification of history and 'Banderite trends in education and upbringing'.
7. Restoration of the 'all-Russian self-identity of the *triune* (tripartite) pan-Russian nation' (i.e., Ukraine recognising itself as a Little Russian wing of the pan-Russian people).
8. Russia establishing control over Ukrainian gas transportation and key industries.
9. Creation of a Russian-Ukrainian military union and removal of 'Banderite trends' in the army and SBU (Security Service of Ukraine).

In November 2013, Yanukovych declared his intention to not sign the Association Agreement with the EU, a step that provoked the Euromaidan Revolution and a major political crisis, forcing him to flee from Ukraine four months later. Putin's goal had been for Yanukovych to not sign the EU Association Agreement and instead Ukraine joining the Eurasian Economic Union following his re-election in 2015; countries can only be in one customs union. Putin was less fortunate in Ukraine than he was in Armenia. Having lost the opportunity to bring Ukraine into Russian-dominated Eurasia, Russia invaded and annexed Crimea and financed, organised and led separatist movements in southeastern Ukraine (see Hauter, 2023).

Yanukovych did not support Ukraine's religious autocephaly and his presidency is synonymous with intolerance towards the Greek-Catholic, Ukrainian Orthodox Church-Kyiv Patriarch and Ukrainian Autocephalous Orthodox Churches. Pan-Russian identity upholds the Russian Orthodox Church as the canonical Church uniting eastern Slavs, a status it has possessed since 1943, when Stalin legalised the Russian Orthodox Church as the sole religious confession for Russians, Ukrainians and Belarusians. As Chapter 3 shows, the domestic and émigré branches of the Russian Orthodox Church became more imperial nationalist from 2007, when they reunited in the same year the Pan-Russian World Foundation was launched (Kuzio, 2022a, pp. 204–227). Prior to the two Russian invasions in 2014 and 2022, and the Orthodox Church of Ukraine receiving autocephalous status in 2018–2019, the Russian Orthodox Church and Pan-Russian World were important avenues for Russian soft power in Ukraine (see Chapter 2).

Ukrainian and Pan-Russian Identities and the Language Question in Ukraine

The Soviet regime recognised the Ukrainian language. Nevertheless, at the same time the Soviet Union promoted Russian as the dominant language in the USSR through Russification and policies to impede the growth of Ukrainian. The future *Homo Sovieticus*, created from the fusion of Russians, Ukrainians and Belarusians, would be Russian speaking. With Lukashenka supporting a Soviet and pan-Russian identity, Russification has continued in Belarus. As Zhurzhenko (2021) has written, the Russian language continued to dominate Ukraine until the Euromaidan Revolution which upholders of a Ukrainian identity believed was a product of centuries of Russification, state repression and discrimination. State affirmative action for the Ukrainian language was implemented by five Ukrainian presidents; the one exception was Yanukovych. Greater public support for the Ukrainian language also came in response to Russia's weaponisation of culture and language (see Ryazanova-Clarke, 2017) as reflected in its justification for intervening and 're-uniting' Crimea with Russia to 'protect' Russian speakers from 'Nazi genocide'.

Since the early 1990s, Russia has claimed the right to protect compatriots (Russian speakers) in the former USSR. Half of the Russian speakers outside the Russian Federation and inside the former USSR were to be found in Ukraine and therefore Russia's long-term foreign policy goal of protecting Russian speaking compatriots and elevating

Russian to a state language inevitably was a long running source of conflict with Ukraine.

Proponents of a pan-Russian identity do not view the continued domination of the Russian language as problematical, as they buy into the Soviet promotion of Russian as the language of universality, modernity, and urban life. In the Soviet Union, the Ukrainian language was recognised but at the same time derided as an uncouth peasant language slated to disappear.

The language question is important to *both* Ukrainian and pan-Russian identities; it is therefore mistaken for Onuch and Hale (2022, p. 104) to write it is not a priority for most Ukrainians or is only important for Ukrainian nationalists. Differences in language usage in Ukraine became less important (Onuch and Hale, 2022, pp. 105–106) not because Zelenskyy was espousing a civic identity but because Russian speaking Ukrainians, appalled by Russia's military aggression, began to psychologically move away from Russia and move closer to Ukrainian speakers and switch from being Russian to Ukrainian speakers (see Kulyk, 2023). This trend dramatically increased after Russia's full-scale invasion when millions of primarily Russian speaking Ukrainians from the country's southeast were killed, deported, became internally displaced persons in western and central Ukraine or fled abroad as refugees.

Proponents of a pan-Russian identity in Ukraine proposed Russian be elevated to a second state language, as in Belarus, a step which required two-thirds of parliamentary deputies voting to change the constitution. This was an impossibility because the Party of Regions and KPU possessed an insufficient number of deputies in the parliament elected in 2012. They therefore adopted legislation that upgraded Russian and other minority languages to official status in areas of Ukraine where it was used by more than 10 per cent of inhabitants. Proponents of a Ukrainian identity always strongly opposed the elevation of Russian to a second state language and the 2012 language law was met with large protests. If, as the Kremlin had planned, Yanukovych had remained in power and he had been re-elected in 2015, probably through election fraud, it is likely the planned 2017 parliamentary elections would have been engineered so that pan-Russian forces would have commanded a constitutional majority. The Ukrainian parliament would have then been able to change the constitution to upgrade Russian to a state language, placing Ukraine on the same path Belarus had taken since 1994.

Radical changes in Ukrainian identity after 2014 did not automatically lead to the growth of the number of Ukrainian speakers because changing one's daily language use is a longer process than changing a person's ethnicity. The growth of Ukrainian identity and patriotism after 2014, therefore, led to public support for Ukrainisation with a gradual increase in the use of Ukrainian. The number of Ukrainians declaring themselves to be ethnic Russians declined from 22 per cent in the 1989 Soviet census and 17 per cent in the 2001 Ukrainian census to only between 2-5 per cent in surveys conducted after 2014. Ninety-two per cent of the population of Ukraine consider themselves to be ethnic Ukrainian (Rating Sociological Group, 2022), making Ukraine the fourth most nationally homogenous country in Europe. By 2023, 69 per cent of Ukrainians could speak Ukrainian fluently and 78 per cent declared Ukrainian to be their native language (an increase from 68 per cent in 2015 and 52 per cent in 2006). Only 5 per cent of Ukrainians declared Russian to be their native language (down from 14 per cent in 2017 and 31 per cent in 2006). (Razumkov Centre, 2023).

From 2014, language was no longer viewed as a marker of loyalty to Ukraine because Ukrainians came to understand identity as more multifaceted (see Bureiko and Moga, 2019). Only 24–25 per cent in Ukraine's southeast linked patriotism to speaking Ukrainian while a higher 64–71 per cent believed the Ukrainian language to be an important attribute of the country's independence (Democratic Initiatives Foundation, 2020). Civic nationalism and patriotism, which are not very dissimilar in the theoretical literature, were becoming dominant in Ukraine, increasing its divergence from Russia which was experiencing a growth of imperial nationalism (see Kuzio, 2022a). Plokhy (2023, p. 296) described Russia as returning to 'outdated ways of thinking about nations and their relationship to language and culture'. Russian imperial nationalism was the driver behind the Kremlin's 'special military operation' (see Kuzio, 2023).

Ukrainian Identity

Left wing, centrist and centre-right parties' approach ethnocultural policies differently in Western democracies. Ukraine's centre-right (national democrats), in a similar manner to the centre right in European and North American democracies, have emphasised both ethnic and civic aspects of Ukrainian identity. Ukraine's liberal (centrists), like left wing and centrist parties in Western democracies, support multiculturalism and greater inclusivity. Although there have been differences, these have been relatively small between the ethnocultural policies pursued by centrist (i.e., Kuchma and Zelenskyy) and national democratic (i.e., Kravchuk, Yushchenko and Poroshenko) presidents.

Centrists and national democrats have supported Ukrainian as the only state language, autocephaly (independence) for the Orthodox Church of Ukraine from the Russian Orthodox Church, a Ukrainian history separate to that of Russian, condemned anti-Ukrainian policies undertaken by the Tsarist Empire and Soviet Union, defined the 1933 *Holodomor* as a genocide against Ukrainians, and supported the rehabilitation of Ukrainian nationalist groups. Ukrainian identity supports Ukrainian membership of NATO and the EU and opposes Ukraine's incorporation into the Pan-Russian World.

During Poroshenko's presidency, the Ukrainian language was given greater support, Ukraine's education system was Ukrainised, the Orthodox Church of Ukraine received autocephaly, de-communisation laws were implemented (see Oliinyk and Kuzio, 2021), electronic and social media from Russia were banned, and the goals of NATO and EU membership were enshrined in the Ukrainian constitution.

During the first two years of Zelenskyy's presidency, Ukraine banned five pro-Russian television channels and treason charges were instituted against Viktor Medvedchuk, leader of the pro-Kremlin Opposition Platform-For Truth party, and de facto Putin's political representative in Ukraine. Zelenskyy lobbied for the 2014–2015 Minsk accords to be revised to include Crimea (and not just the Donbas). After Russia's full-scale invasion, twelve pro-Russian political parties were banned and parliament adopted legislation which sought to break the Russian Orthodox Church's control over its Ukrainian branch, the Ukrainian Orthodox Church.

The Ukrainian parliament adopted four laws on the de-Russification and decolonisation of Ukraine. The first, adopted in April 2022, de-Sovietised Ukrainian legislation (Ukrainian Parliament, 2022b). The second, two laws adopted in May and July of the same year, decolonised toponyms and geographic placenames (Ukrainian Parliament, 2022c, 2022d). The third, adopted in May 2023, was the most ambitious and entitled 'On the condemnation and banning of the propaganda of Russian imperial policies in Ukraine and the de-colonisation of toponyms', which prohibited 'publicly honouring and promoting names with symbols of Russian imperial policy, its landmarks, memorable, historical, and cultural places, settlements, dates, events, and representatives'. The law specified that by January 2024, all Russian imperial, Soviet and Russian Federation toponyms had to be removed from public areas in Ukraine (Ukrainian Parliament, 2023b). The fourth, adopted in September 2024, decolonised the humanities sphere in

Ukraine's education system (Ukrainian Parliament, 2024). Russian literature, which had remained in Ukrainian school curriculums after 2014, was removed after 2022. Mykola Hohol (Nikolai Gogol) was reclassified from a Russian to a Ukrainian writer.

Russian Military Support for Pan-Russian Identity

Divergence between Russian and Ukrainian identities and political systems accelerated after 2014 because of the shock of Russian military aggression and imperialism towards Crimea, marginalisation of pan-Russian identity and loss of 16 per cent of voters in occupied territories, many of whom would have traditionally voted for pro-Russian political forces (see D'Anieri (2019b)). Policies in support of a Ukrainian identity therefore faced little resistance to becoming dominant under Presidents Poroshenko and Zelenskyy. By 2020–2021, the Kremlin's fear of Ukraine's trajectory becoming impossible to curtail brought about the fateful decision to launch a 'special military operation' to swiftly correct the 'abnormal' situation by destroying 'Anti-Russia' Ukraine and Ukrainian identity and replace them with a truncated Little Russian puppet state and population returned to its (Little) Russian roots. The failure of the 'special military operation' to bring Ukraine to heel instead placed Russia and Ukraine's divergence on steroids and destroyed relations between both peoples. Ninety-three per cent of Ukrainians hold negative views of Russia (with only 3 per cent holding positive views) and 84 per cent hold negative views of the Russian people (with only 8 per cent holding positive views), (Kyiv International Institute of Sociology, 2024). Three quarters of Ukrainians in eastern and southern Ukraine have come to hold negative views of the Russian people; that is, they now hold a similar antipathy as Western Ukrainians (Kyiv International Institute of Sociology, 2024). The 'special military operation' that had been ostensibly launched to 'protect' Russian speakers in Ukraine had instead made them enemies of Russia.

Paul D'Anieri (2019a, p. 94) writes in his detailed study of Russian-Ukrainian relations that most Russians have always viewed Ukraine as 'fundamentally Russian'. In 1991, Russia was ready to jettison the non-Slavic peoples of the USSR but not Belarus and Ukraine (Kuzio, 2022a, pp. 137–139; Plokhy, 2023, p. 295). This is coupled with a Russian imperial nationalist mindset that 'seeks an order based on the dominance of great powers that was widely accepted in the era prior to World War I' (D'Anieri, 2019a, p. 276; Kuzio, 2022a, pp. 137–139).

Since 1991, Russia has supported political forces who upheld a pan-Russian identity in Ukraine and the same domestic and foreign policies implemented by Lukashenka in Belarus. Putin twice visited Ukraine in 2004 to support Yanukovych's election as president, strongly backed his candidacy in the 2010 elections and intervened extensively during his 2010–2014 presidency. Russia opposed every aspect of identity, language, and memory politics policies introduced by Ukraine's five other presidents.

Although Russian leaders' obsession with Ukraine became more vocal after Putin returned to the presidency in 2012, as D'Anieri (2019a) writes, it had dominated Russia's relations with Ukraine ever since 1991. The first edition of Kuchma's book *Ukraine Is Not Russia* was given a frosty reception from the Russian public and politicians as long ago as in 2003. Kuchma described Putin's obsession with Ukraine as 'a kind of mania or mental disorder and believes that Putin's goal is the destruction of Ukraine' as a 'competitive alternative to Russia' (Harding, 2023). Mikhail Zygar (2016, p. 258) wrote that Putin has always been obsessed and frustrated with Ukraine from the first day of his 2000–2004 presidency saying, 'We must do something, or we'll lose it' (see also Belton, 2020, p. 385; Zygar, 2022, 2023a, p. 217). When somebody mentions Ukraine in front of Putin, 'he flies into a fury; the words at the end of his sentences are replaced by Russian expletives. For him, everything the Ukrainian government does is a crime' (Zygar, 2016, p. 4). Patrushev, who was chairman of the FSB when Putin was first elected in 2000, was closely involved in the decision-making process and planning of Russia's full-scale invasion of Ukraine.

From De-Humanisation to Genocide

For nearly two decades since the Orange Revolution, the Kremlin prepared its full-scale invasion and plans for the genocidal destruction of Ukraine and Ukrainians through two means. The first, analysed in Chapter 4, was a cult of war that infused how Putin's Russia changed its approach to the Great Patriotic War from commemoration and the slogan 'Never Again!' to celebration under the banner of 'We Can Do It Again!' The new approach ignored human suffering and was coupled with a cult of the tyrant and dictator Stalin guilty of the murder of millions of Soviet people, including Russians. A domestic cult of war was fanned externally, which we analyse in Chapter 9, in the de-humanisation of Ukrainians, which is discussed in the next section, and increasingly vitriolic xenophobia against the 'collective West'.

A cult of war, the de-humanisation of Ukraine and Ukrainians and anti-Western xenophobia are interrelated in Putin's Russia. De-humanisation has usually taken place before genocide was committed, as for example, in the *Holodomor* and Holocaust. Together they prepared the ground for Russia's full-scale war and goals of 'de-nazification' and 'de-militarisation;' that is, destruction of the Ukrainian state and genocide of 'bad' Ukrainians. Russian imperial nationalists hold contradictory attitudes towards 'bad' Ukrainians and 'good' Little Russians. Ukrainians are looked upon in Russian popular culture from a vantage point of chauvinistic condescension towards 'good' Ukrainians while bad Ukrainians are 'bloodthirsty racists' (McGlynn, 2023b, p. 149).

Violence towards subordinates has deep roots in the Tsarist and Soviet armies. Russian military reforms never removed the cruelty towards its own soldiers, disregard for high casualty rates, and penchant for bombing civilians, looting, raping, torturing, and conducting extrajudicial killings. Accountability for these criminal actions has never existed. Added to this, Putin arrived in the Kremlin in 1999–2000 during bombings of four Russian apartment buildings in Moscow, Buinaksk and Volgodonsk, killing 307 and wounding 1,700 and suspected to be the work of the FSB, and extreme destruction of Chechnya and violence and war crimes against the Chechen people (see Satter, 2017, pp. 10, 15, 17, 28). Then FSB Chairman Patrushev, over two decades later, was chairman of the Russian Security Council when Russia launched its full-scale invasion of Ukraine. This was followed by Russian military aggression against Syria, and Ukraine. The destruction of the Chechen capital city of Grozny was followed by the destruction of the Syrian city of Aleppo and Ukrainian port of Mariupol (Garner and Kuzio, 2025). Russia's full-scale invasion created a 'fusion of Putin's regime and citizens around violence', as reflected in a comment by an older Russian woman: 'You need to kill them [Ukrainians] all, and their children too' (Stephenson, 2023).

De-humanisation of Ukraine and Ukrainians has been taking place in Russia since the Orange Revolution; that is, for practically two decades before Russia launched its full-scale invasion[6] (see The Idea of Ukraine

---

[6] See Sergej Sumlenny on the growth of the Russian imperial nationalist, Stalinist, and anti-Ukrainian book market since the mid 2000s. https://twitter.com/sumlenny/status/1707407873603428717

is Based on a Mythologised Lie, 2019; When Words Kill – From Moscow to Mariupol, 2022; Into the Heart of Darkness-What Russia Wants in Ukraine, 2022; Kremlin Hate Speech Incites War Crimes in Ukraine, 2022). The *EUvsDisinfo* project has amassed a large database of nearly 20,000 cases of disinformation in the Russian media. The Kremlin's obsession with Ukraine and Ukrainians is evident in nearly two thirds of these disinformation articles and reports being about Ukraine, a figure which is higher in number than those on the US, EU, and NATO.[7]

The European Parliament (2025) denounced Putin's Russia for denying, 'Ukraine's distinct national identity, falsely claiming it as part of the Pan-Russian World, a narrative rooted in imperialistic ideology'. The European Parliament (2025) described Russia's disinformation campaign as:

> historical revisionism for the purpose of denying Ukraine its national identity, statehood and very existence, and with the aim of justifying its claims to exclusive spheres of influence, which is reminiscent of how the Soviet Union agreed with Nazi Germany to invade and occupy parts of Poland and Romania as well as Estonia, Latvia, Lithuania and Ukraine in the Molotov-Ribbentrop Pact…

The Ukrainian parliament issued resolutions condemning the Kremlin's war against Ukraine and Ukrainians as genocidal, describing Russia as a terrorist state and defining the Kremlin's ideology as *Rashism* (or *Ruscism*), a term combining Russian imperial nationalism and fascism (Ukrainian Parliament, 2022a, 2022e, 2023a). The Ukrainian parliament banned the propagation of Russian 'totalitarian Nazi' symbols used by the Russian army invading Ukraine (Ukrainian Parliament, 2022d). Eighty-nine per cent of Ukrainians believe Russia is committing genocide against Ukrainians, including 85–86 per cent in the East and South and 91–92 per cent in the West-Centre of Ukraine. Eighty and 92 per cent of Russians and Ukrainians in Ukraine respectively believed Russia is committing genocide (Rating Sociological Group, 2022).

De-humanising propaganda has been promoted by three 'mouthpieces' – education system, state-controlled media, and Russian Orthodox Church – which feed off one another and brainwash Russians into becoming supporters and unquestioning adherents of official views (Langdon and Tismaneanu, 2020, p. 177). From the mid 2000s, Putin's Russia republished and widely circulated White Russian émigré writers

---

[7] https://euvsdisinfo.eu/disinformation-cases/

and thinkers and officers who had been defeated by the Bolsheviks and fled to Europe, such as Ivan Ilyin, supported pan-Russian imperial nationalism and denied the existence of Ukrainians and Belarusians (see Barbashin and Thoburn, 2015). Putin personally oversaw the transfer and reburial in Russia of the remains of Ilyin and White Russian General Anton Denikin (see Kuzio, 2022a, pp. 99–128; Kuzio, 2024). State media 'has played a central part in prompting, encouraging, rationalising and normalising the Kremlin's massacre of its next-door neighbours' (Davis, 2024, p. 292). Well-known Russian TV presenter Vladimir Solovyov asked if the Ukrainian nation should continue to exist to which he replied 'in its current state, it should not. A nation whose ideology poses a danger to us cannot exist next to us' (Davis, 2024, p. 374). Meanwhile, Russian academics 'are happy to explain the logic of Kremlin-directed violence and to provide an intellectual gloss' (Davis, 2024, p. 294). Russian youth have been educated to be contemptuous of Ukraine and Ukrainians. Since 2014, this had spread to television and film (McGlynn, 2023b, p. 87). In the nearly two decades prior to Russia's full-scale invasion, 'demonising discourse was a staple of talk shows and serious analytical articles' that 'created an environment in which killing Ukrainians became a laudable act' (Harding, 2022, p. 106; see Garner, 2023, pp. 83, 124, 177, 189; McGlynn, 2023b, p. 153; Davis, 2024). With the enemy de-humanised, Russian soldiers do not see themselves fighting other human beings but 'rather a lower ranking group' (When Words Kill – From Moscow to Mariupol, 2022; see Minchenia, Tornquist-Plewa and Yurchuk, 2018; Kremlin Hate Speech Incites War Crimes in Ukraine, 2022; Applebaum, 2022; Young, 2022).

Jade McGlynn (2023a, p. 75) writes that after years of propaganda and disinformation on Ukraine, 'de-nazification' of Ukraine 'did not sound obscene – it sounded overdue'. The Institute for the Study of War, a Washington-based think tank that has provided a daily analysis of the Russian-Ukrainian war, wrote:

> Russian President Putin and many Kremlin officials have driven deep into the Russian political consciousness the ideas that Ukraine has no independent identity and no basis to continue to exist as an independent state; that any Ukrainian government not totally subservient to Moscow is a pawn of the West and a threat to Russia; that Ukrainian opponents of Russian rule are Nazis intent on conducting genocide against Russians in Ukraine; and that Russia has a legal, moral, and religious obligation to extirpate these supposed threats and restore Ukraine to its rightful place as a historically Russian land. Putin has made these arguments part of his 2024

presidential election platform. Russian administrators are inserting them in curricula throughout Russia and occupied Ukraine. Kremlin mouthpieces speak to the Russian domestic audience with one voice along these lines. Putin is training Russians to commit themselves to the task of subjugating Ukraine, and that training will neither stop nor vanish following some negotiated ceasefire. It will, in fact, shape the thoughts and likely policies of Putin's successors for years or decades (Kagan, Barros, Mikkelsen, and Mealie, 2023).

Seven Myths That Prepared Russian Military Aggression

The seven myths discussed below were promoted in Putin's Russia for nearly two decades prior to the launching of the full-scale invasion. After Putin returned to the presidency in 2012, de-humanising discourse moved from the fringes to the Russian mainstream on Russian state-controlled television which 'conditioned people to see Ukraine as inferior' (Key Narratives in Pro-Kremlin Disinformation: "Nazis", 2022; Scarr, 2022).

1. *Ukraine Does Not Exist:* Like many colonial powers, for example, the British about the Irish, the Soviet regime promoted an inability of Ukrainians to build their own state and therefore, by default Ukraine must be overseen by a paternalistic Russian 'elder brother'. Indeed, denying Ukrainian statehood has been a Kremlin staple for many years (The Idea of Ukraine is Based on a Mythologised Lie, 2019). 'President Putin himself has often perverted the historical record to claim that Ukraine did not exist until the Bolsheviks created it' and 'In sum, the Kremlin has done everything it can to undermine Ukrainian statehood' (Thirteen myths about Russia's war against Ukraine exposed, 2024). Ukraine was portrayed as never having had stable statehood, is illegitimate, and occupies Russian lands (McGlynn, 2023b, p. 141). A Ukrainian volunteer who was detained by Russian forces in Berdyansk said 'I told them I was not a protest organiser, just a patriot of my country, Ukraine. They said, there is no such country' (Ukraine: Torture, Disappearances in Occupied South, 2022).

2. *Ukraine's Independence from Russia Is an Aberration* (see D'Anieri, 2019a): Ukrainians are repeatedly told 'true sovereignty of Ukraine' is only possible in 'partnership with Russia' (Lewis, 2023, p. 383); that is, for example, when Ukraine was a loyal Soviet republic in the USSR or the example of Lukashenka's Belarus. Ukraine can only exist as a Little Russian puppet state (McGlynn, 2023b, p. 145). Ukraine requires

a suzerain because Ukrainians are incapable of forming and running their own state (Apt, 2024). A Ukraine that refuses to become a Little Russian puppet state must be destroyed the former Russian Ambassador to NATO, Dmitri Rogozin said because it is 'an existential threat to the Russian people, Russian history, Russian language and Russian civilisation' (When Words Kill – From Moscow to Mariupol, 2022). Popova and Shevel (2023, p. 117) describe this 'is unadulterated imperialism'.

3. *Ukraine Is an Artificial State*: Putin (2008) first claimed Ukraine was an artificial country and failed state in a speech to the NATO-Russia Council at the Bucharest NATO summit. Ukraine depicted as a backward and failed state are common themes in Russian disinformation (Martin, 2001, p. 112; Zolotukhin, 2018, pp. 302–358). The Kremlin claimed Ukraine's alleged political crisis and no longer functioning state required Russia's intervention in 2014. Ukraine is allegedly a land of perennial instability and revolution where extremists run amok, Russian speakers are persecuted, and pro-Russian politicians and media are repressed or closed. Other tropes include Ukrainian authorities are incapable of dealing with their problems, and Ukraine could not survive without trade with Russia.

Ukraine was artificially created with 'historically Russian' lands. Crimea and Ukraine's southeast are described using the Tsarist imperial term 'New Russia' with Russian leaders claiming the Bolsheviks were mistaken to have included these Russian lands within Soviet Ukraine. Only central Ukraine, encompassing the western and eastern regions of the Dnipro River and centred on Kyiv, should exist as a Little Russian puppet state. Western Ukraine, which Russian imperial nationalists have never believed is part of the Pan-Russian World, would return to Poland, Hungary, and Romania (see Goble, 2024). A Russian Ministry of Defence document[8] from late 2024 advocated partitioning Ukraine into three different parts: (a) New Russia (Luhansk, Donetsk, Zaporizhzhya, and Kherson *oblasts*) and occupied Crimea; (b) Pro-Russian puppet state centred in Kyiv under Russian military occupation; and (c) Designating Ukraine's western regions as 'disputed territories' which Russia would offer to Ukraine's western neighbours. Karaganov (2025) predicts after Ukraine will be destroyed: 'Its east and south will go to Russia. In the centre and west

---

[8] https://interfax.com.ua/news/general/1028868.html

of today's Ukraine, a de-militarised, neutral state with a no-fly zone over it should be formed, where all those who do not want to live in Russia and obey our laws can come'.

4. *Russians and Ukrainians Are 'One People'*: Although Ukrainians were recognised as a different people to Russians, Soviet propaganda repeatedly instilled they had always been and would always remain united. Building on this Soviet legacy, Putin (2017) told the Valdai Discussion Club that Russia and Ukraine's re-unification will inevitably take place. 'Kremlin propagandists, including Putin himself, repeatedly promoted the mythical claim that Ukrainians and Russians are one people who should be united. In the Kremlin's dystopia, Ukrainians are suffering from a false consciousness instilled by the West that has separated them from their true Russian selves' (Thirteen myths about Russia's war against Ukraine exposed 2024). Russians and Ukrainians constituting 'one people' was the main theme in Putin's (2021) long essay published eight months before the full-scale invasion and the ideological treatise underpinning the 'special military operation'.

   Russian propaganda portrays Ukraine as a place without its own history and identity. Russians and Ukrainians are 'one people' with a single language, culture and common history (Zolotukhin, 2018, pp. 67–85). Ukrainians are a 'brotherly nation'. 'One people inhabit Ukraine and the Russian Federation, for the time being, divided (by the border)' former Russian Security Council Secretary Patrushev (2016) said.

5. *The Ukrainian Language Is a Dialect of Russian*: Although the Soviet Union promoted Russification, it nevertheless recognised the existence of a Ukrainian language. Putin's Russia denies the existence of a Ukrainian language, claiming what is spoken in Ukraine are dialects of Russian. The Russian information agency *Rex* published an article claiming the 'Ukrainian language is a weapon in the hybrid war' because the Ukrainian language is 'artificial'. The Ukrainian language is a form of hybrid 'brain programming' political technology (Yermolenko, 2019). Deputy head of the Russian Security Council Medvedev (2023) described the Ukrainian language as a 'dialect' of Russian and, like other Russian leaders (see Putin, 2008), derogatorily depicts Ukraine as 'not a country but an artificial collection of territories'. Medvedev called Ukrainians 'bastards and freaks' and promised 'For as long as I live, I'll do everything I can to make sure they disappear' (Garner, 2023, p. 13).

6. *Ukraine Is a US Puppet State:* Viacheslav Volodin and Mariia Zakharova said Ukraine had sold its sovereignty to Washington, which controls its domestic and foreign policies since the Orange Revolution (Apt, 2024). Leonid Slutsky claimed Ukraine has been 'under the supervision of the collective West' since 2014 (Apt, 2024). Ukraine is a puppet state without real sovereignty which only exists because it is propped up by the West who have kept Russophobic 'nationalists/fascists/Nazis' in power since launching an un-constitutional 'putsch' in the Euromaidan Revolution (Laruelle, 2019). Most Ukrainians want to be part of the Pan-Russian World but are being prevented from doing so by a small clique of Nazis. Russian propaganda depicts Ukrainian Presidents Poroshenko and Zelenskyy as puppets of Ukrainian nationalists and the West. Sergei Glazyev (2019), one of Putin's presidential advisers on Ukraine, wrote: 'By itself, the election of a new president of Ukraine does not change the situation' because 'It is obvious that in the top three candidates who won most votes in the first round of the presidential "election," there was not a single candidate who did not swear allegiance to the American occupation authorities'. Russophile scholars in the West, such as Stephen Cohen (2019, p. 145), also described then US Vice President Joe Biden as Ukraine's 'pro-consul overseeing the increasingly colonised Kyiv'. President Poroshenko was not a Ukrainian leader but 'a compliant representative of domestic and foreign political forces' who 'resembles a pro-consul of a faraway great power' running a 'failed state' (Cohen, 2019, p. 36). *The Nation*, where Cohen was a contributing editor, described Ukraine in 2014 as the closest thing Europe has to a failed state.[9]

7. *Ukraine Is 'Anti- Russia':* Ukraine as an anti-Russian conspiracy was promoted by Russian imperial nationalists in the late nineteenth century when the Tsarist Russian and Austrian-Hungarian empires competed over control of western Ukraine. A Ukrainian people distinct from Russians was dreamt up by Austrians and other Western powers to divide the 'All-Russian People' (Weeks, 1996). Putin blames Soviet leader Vladimir Lenin for granting Ukrainians their own Soviet republic and thus encouraging them to view themselves as distinct from Russians. Putin's (2020a, 2020b) denunciations of the Soviet recognition of Ukrainians is coupled with the revival of Tsarist imperial nationalist myths about how 'The Ukrainian factor was specifically played out on the eve of World War I by the Austrian special service.

---

[9] www.thenation.com/article/world/a-path-out-of-the-ukraine-crisis/

Why? This is well-known – to divide and rule (the Russian people)'. The West transformed Ukraine (see Ennis, 2013) against the wishes of most of its population into an 'Anti-Russia' outpost on the Russian border. Allegedly, policies implemented by Presidents Poroshenko and Zelenskyy after 2014 to strengthen Ukrainian identity and reduce Russian influence were undertaken at the behest of the West, the US in particular, and against the wishes of most Ukrainians. Russian imperial nationalists repeatedly claim to know more about how Ukrainians feel than they do themselves.

War Crimes and Genocide

Together, a cult of war, de-humanisation of Ukraine and Ukrainians and anti-Western xenophobia mobilised the Russian people to provide their backing for Russia's full-scale invasion of Ukraine (see McGlynn, 2023c) and the Russian army and security services to commit war crimes against the Ukrainian people. Ukrainians had sold their souls to the West and were 'traitors' to the pan-Russian nation; they had to be forcibly returned to Russian identity through 'de-nazification'. Lies and deception emanating from Russian media served to reinforce hatred and divisions.

State-controlled Russian media encouraged and sanctified war crimes against Ukrainians and the destruction of Ukraine (see Sergeytsev, 2022; Young, 2022; Kovalev, 2022; Kremlin Hate Speech Incites War Crimes in Ukraine, 2022). Medvedev has called for the disappearance of Ukrainian 'bastards' and 'geeks', the erasure of Ukraine from the map, and the 'annihilation of all signs of [Ukrainian] statehood' (Apt, 2024). Rabble rouser TV journalist Solovyov calls Ukrainian identity a 'cancerous tumour' that should no longer exist after Russia's military victory (Apt, 2024). Medvedev, always providing the most colourful of discourse, said Ukrainians are led by 'dim-witted *mankurts*:[10] corrupt hucksters and stoned clowns, who worship their overseas markets' (Apt, 2024). Rostislav Ishchenko believes Russia will 'make sure that there is not even a memory left of it [Ukraine]', Oleg Yasinsky said the 'complete destruction of Ukraine' would 'eliminate the memory of that time [Ukraine] and its names', while Sergei Mardan called for Ukraine 'to be dismantled brick by brick, so that nothing at all is left' (Apt, 2024).

---

[10] *Mankurts* are slaves who are unable to think for themselves. See Aitmatov, C. (1980). *The Day Lasts More Than a Hundred Years*. Moscow: *Novyj Mir*.

Director of Broadcasting at *RT* Anton Krasivsky called upon Russia to drown or burn alive Ukrainian children so that 'Ukraine is not supposed to exist at all' (Apt, 2024). Russian political leaders, state officials, political technologists, journalists, historians, and think tank experts openly talk of Ukraine's destruction as Russia's military goal (see Davis, 2024). The goal of Russia's 'special military operation' is to destroy 'Anti-Russia' and Ukrainian identity (An Independent Legal Analysis of the Russian Federation's Breaches of the Genocide Convention in Ukraine and the Duty to Prevent, 2022; Hook, 2022; The Russian Federation's Escalating Commission of Genocide in Ukraine: A Legal Analysis, 2023). Russian academic Andrei Sidorov (2024) called for the 'liquidation of the Ukrainian state' and return to: 'a common faith, a common language and culture, and our shared historical fate will promote Russification of Little Russia and New Russia, heal the wounds of the civil war, and reconcile various branches of the Russian people'.

Medvedev said the 'special military operation' would 'completely eliminate Ukrainian statehood' (Apt, 2024) and Russia would 'crush the scum' by driving 'a long steel nail into the coffin lid of the [Ukrainian nationalist leader] Banderite quasi-state' which would return Ukraine 'to the bosom of the Russian land'.[11] Medvedev described Ukraine as having a 'mythical past, a sad present, and no future' (Apt, 2024). Head of *RT* Margarita Simonyan said 'Ukraine as it exists cannot continue. There'll be no Ukraine as we've known it for many years' (Apt, 2024).

The goals of Russia's 'special military operation' were 'de-nazification' and 'de-militarisation'. The goal of 'de-nazification' was to destroy Ukrainian national identity and annex Ukrainian territory. 'De-militarisation' would limit the size of the Ukrainian army to a pitifully small size and transform a truncated Ukraine into a neutral entity; that is, a Little Russian puppet state (see An Independent Legal Analysis of the Russian Federation's Breaches of the Genocide Convention in Ukraine and the Duty to Prevent, 2022; Hook, 2022; The Russian Federation's Escalating Commission of Genocide in Ukraine: A Legal Analysis, 2023).

Mass deportations, including up to 35,000 Ukrainian children and over two million Ukrainians to Russia has been accompanied by the influx of Russian settlers in Mariupol and other towns and cities in southeastern Ukraine ('"We Had No Choice." "Filtration" and the Crime of Forcibly Transferring Ukrainian Civilians to Russia',

---

[11] D. Medvedev, *Telegram*, 10 July 2024. https://t.me/medvedev_telegram/515

2022). Russia is implementing re-Sovietisation, Russification, and de-Ukrainisation in occupied southeastern Ukraine using policies introduced earlier in 2014–2021 in Crimea and Donbas (see McGlynn, 2023b; Oliinyk, 2023).[12] Russia has a long history of seeking to prevent the growth of Ukrainian identity and destroying and looting Ukrainian historical antiquities and cultural treasures. A Ukrainian study of two leading Russian museums found 110,000 items from Ukraine (The stolen treasures, 2023). 38 museums have been damaged or destroyed by Russian artillery and missiles, with an estimated $2.6 billion in damage to Ukraine's cultural heritage. 480,000 artworks 'have fallen into Russian hands' since the launch of the invasion (Inside the hunt for Ukraine's stolen art, 2024). Ukrainian-language books are being burnt. Monuments to Ukrainian literati and history, such as the *Holodomor*, are being destroyed and in their place monuments of Lenin are being returned (see Higgins, 2023; Kurin, 2023; Shydlovsky, Kuijt, Skorokhod, Zotsenko, Ivakin, Donaruma, and Field, 2023; Small, 2023; Whitacker, 2023; Garner, 2023, p. 124).

Conclusion

Nationalist versus pro-Russian and civic versus ethnic frameworks have little relation to the theoretical literature on nationalism and provide a weak understanding of Ukrainian politics and the roots of Russia's full-scale invasion of Ukraine. Ukrainian and pan-Russian identities both encompass civic *and* ethnocultural attributes. Ukrainian identity distinct from Russian incorporates greater civic factors because it is more supportive of democratisation while pan-Russian identity is more supportive of authoritarianism, as visibly seen in the Party of Regions and KPU in Ukraine, and in the Russian and Belarusian dictatorships. Dividing Ukrainian presidents into civic and ethnic leaders has little in common with reality, as the policies implemented by Poroshenko and Zelenskyy are not radically different from one another.

This chapter has analysed competition between a Ukrainian identity distinct from Russian and a pan-Russian identity where Ukrainians are forever united with Russians and Belarusians in the Pan-Russian World. A compromise between the two identities was impossible because supporters of both sought to dominate Ukraine. Meanwhile, the only outcome acceptable to Putin and Russian imperial nationalists was Ukraine

---

[12] https://almenda.org/en/category/pub/monitoringi/

accepting its Little Russian place within a pan-Russian people. Five presidents (Kravchuk, Kuchma, Yushchenko, Poroshenko, and Zelenskyy) upheld a Ukrainian identity distinct from Russian and only one president (Yanukovych) supported a pan-Russian identity. This showed to what degree Ukraine was very different to Belarus and why the Kremlin made its decision to launch a 'special military operation' to destroy Ukrainian identity and transform Ukraine into a truncated Little Russian puppet state.

Competition for dominance between Ukrainian and pan-Russian identities produced political crises, violence, and two popular uprisings, the Orange and Euromaidan Revolutions. Conflict was especially acute between the 2003–2004 Orange and 2013–2014 Euromaidan Revolutions when the Party of Regions was a formidable political force and Ukraine's only political machine (see Kudelia and Kuzio, 2015). Together with its KPU ally, the Party of Regions won plurality in the 2006, 2007, and 2012 parliamentary elections and won the 2010 presidential election. Russia pinned its hopes on Yanukovych imposing a dominant pan-Russian identity, pressuring him to abandon the EU Association Agreement and take Ukraine into the Eurasian Economic Union. When this strategy failed, Russia took revenge by annexing Crimea, supporting separatist movements in southeastern Ukraine, and pressuring Poroshenko and Zelenskyy to implement the Russian understanding of the Minsk accords.

The marginalisation of pro-Russian forces and loss of voters in Russian-occupied Crimea and Donbas undermined political support for a pan-Russian identity in Ukraine. By 2020–2021, the Kremlin had concluded that Ukrainian leaders would not implement the Russian interpretation of the Minsk Accords. In addition, Russian soft power and other forms of non-military intervention would be unable to bring about the dominance of a pan-Russian identity. Putin's thesis on Russian-Ukrainian unity provided the ideological justification for the Kremlin's 'special military operation'. The Kremlin's invasion goals of 'de-nazification' and 'de-militarisation' remain in place.

Although Russia had never reconciled itself to accepting Ukraine as an independent state, it was Putin that ultimately made the fatal decision to launch a full-scale war, the first in Europe since the Second World War. Outdated historical myths of Ukraine as an artificial construct and Ukrainians as Little Russians led to the mistaken belief that Russia's 'special military operation' would be quickly won, rather than lead to a long-drawn out war that would become global. Russian military aggression in 2014 and full-scale invasion in 2022 failed to achieve its goal of destroying Ukrainian identity; instead, empowering Ukrainian identity to become dominant in Ukraine and relegating pan-Russian identity to the historic past.

References

Aliyev, H. (2021). 'When Neighbourhood Goes to War. Exploring the Effect of Belonging on Violent Mobilization in Ukraine,' *Eurasian Geography and Economics*, 62 (1): 21–45.

An Independent Legal Analysis of the Russian Federation's Breaches of the Genocide Convention in Ukraine and the Duty to Prevent. (2022). New Lines Institute for Strategy and Policy and Raoul Wallenberg Centre for Human Rights, May. https://newlinesinstitute.org/an-independent-legal-analysis-of-the-russian-federations-breaches-of-the-genocide-convention-in-ukraine-and-the-duty-to-prevent/

Applebaum, A. (2022). 'Ukraine and the Words That Lead to Mass Murder. First Comes the Dehumanization. Then Comes the Killing,' *The Atlantic*, 25 April. www.theatlantic.com/magazine/archive/2022/06/ukraine-mass-murder-hate-speech-soviet/629629/

Apt, C. (2024). 'Russia's Eliminationist Rhetoric against Ukraine: A Collection', Just Security, 18 April. www.justsecurity.org/81789/russias-eliminationist-rhetoric-against-ukraine-a-collection/

Aron, L. (2023). *Riding the Tiger. Vladimir Putin's Russia and the Uses of War*. Washington, DC: American Enterprise Institute.

Ash, L. (2024). *The Baton and Cross. Russia's Church from Pagans to Putin*. London: Icon Books.

Barbashin, A. and Thoburn, H. (2015). 'Putin's Philosopher. Ivan Ilyin and the Ideology of Moscow's Rule,' *Foreign Affairs*, 20 September. www.foreignaffairs.com/articles/ukraine/2015-09-20/putins-philosopher

Bekus N. (2023). 'Reassembling Society in a Nation-State: History, Language, and Identity Discourses of Belarus,' *Nationalities Papers*, 51 (1): 98–113.

Belton, C. (2020). *Putin's People. How the KGB Took Back Russia and Then Turned on the West*. New York: William Collins.

Bigg, C. (2005). 'Russia/Belarus: Putin, Lukashenka Press Ahead with Unification,' *Radio Free Europe/Radio Liberty*, 22 April. www.rferl.org/a/1058613.html

Brik, T. and Murtazashvili, J. B. (2022). 'The Source of Ukraine's Resilience. How Decentralized Government Brought the Country Together,' *Foreign Affairs*, 28 June. www.foreignaffairs.com/articles/ukraine/2022-06-28/source-ukraines-resilience

Bureiko, N. and Moga, T. L. (2019). 'The Ukrainian–Russian Linguistic Dyad and Its Impact on National Identity in Ukraine,' *Europe-Asia Studies*, 71 (1): 137–155.

Chupyra, O. (2015). 'Civic Protest. Version 2.0. Maidan 2013–2014 as a Catalyst of Russian Speaking Ukrainian Patriotism,' *Russian Politics and Law*, 53 (3): 86–96.
Cohen, S. F. (2019). *War with Russia?: From Putin & Ukraine to Trump and Russiagate*. New York: Skyhorse Publishing.
D'Anieri, P. (2019a). *Ukraine and Russia: From Civilized Divorce to Uncivil War*. Cambridge: Cambridge University Press.
D'Anieri, P. (2019b). 'Gerrymandering Ukraine? Electoral Consequences of Occupation,' *East European Politics and Societies*, 33 (1): 89–108.
Davis, J. (2024). *In Their Own Words. How Russian Propagandists Reveal Putin's Intentions*. Stuttgart: Ibidem; New York: Columbia University Press.
Democratic Initiatives Foundation. (2020). 'Patriotyzm, mova ta zovnishnopolitychni priorytety - hromadska dumka,' 21 January. https://dif.org.ua/article/%20patriotyzm_mova%20%20
Deryugina, T., Gorodnichenko, Y. and Sologoub, I. (2023). 'Russian Studies in the West: Time for a Critical Review,' *Vox Ukraine*, 17 October. https://voxukraine.org/en/russian-studies-in-the-west-time-for-a-critical-review
Ennis, S. (2013). 'Russia: Kremlin's 'Hate TV' Compares West to Nazis', *BBC*, 3 October. http://www.bbc.com/news/blogs-news-from-elsewhere-24383550.
Eras, L. (2023). 'War, Identity Politics, and Attitudes toward a Linguistic Minority: Prejudice against Russian-speaking Ukrainians in Ukraine between 1995–2018,' *Nationalities Papers*, 51 (1): 114–135.
European Parliament. (2025). 'Russia's Disinformation and Historical Falsification to Justify Its War of Aggression against Ukraine,' Resolution 2024/2988(RSP), 23 January. www.europarl.europa.eu/doceo/document/TA-10-2025-0006_EN.pdf
Frolov Leaks. (2018). 'Hounding of Pussy Riot and Patriarch's "Dusty Case",' *Inform Napalm*, 5, 16 October. https://informnapalm.org/en/frolovleaks-hounding-of-pussy-riot-and-patriarchs-dusty-case-episode-5/
Garner, I. (2023). *Generation Z. Into the Hart of Russia's Fascist Youth*. London: Hurst.
Garner, I. and Kuzio, T. (2025). Edited. *Russia and Modern Fascism: New Perspectives on the Kremlin's War against Ukraine*. Stuttgart: Ibidem; New York: Columbia University Press.
Goble, P. (2024). 'Moscow Opens Pandora's Box with New Talk About Changing Ukraine's Western Borders,' *Eurasian Daily Monitor* 21 (162), 7 November. https://jamestown.org/program/moscow-opens-pandoras-box-with-new-talk-about-changing-ukraines-western-borders/
Gelashvili, T. (2023). 'Political Opportunities and Mobilisation on the Far Right in Ukraine,' *East European Politics*. https://doi.org/10.1080/21599165.2023.2268000
Gorodnichenko, Y., Sologoub, I. and Deryugina, T. (2023). 'Why Russian Studies in the West Failed to Provide a Clue about Russia and Ukraine,' *Vox Ukraine*, 21 June. https://voxukraine.org/en/why-russian-studies-in-the-west-failed-to-provide-a-clue-about-russia-and-ukraine

Harding, L. (2022). *Invasion: Russia's Bloody War and Ukraine's Fight for Survival*. London: Guardian and Faber.
Harding, L. (2023). 'US Will "Lose Face before World" If It Abandons Kyiv, Says ex-Ukrainian President,' *The Guardian*, 11 December. www.theguardian.com/world/2023/dec/11/us-will-lose-face-before-world-if-it-abandons-kyiv-says-ex-ukraine-president#:~:text=Ukraine's%20former%20president%20Leonid%20Kuchma,all%2Dout%20invasion%20last%20year.
Hauter, J. (2023). *Russia's Overlooked Invasion. The Causes of the 2014 Outbreak of War in Ukraine's Donbas*. Stuttgart: Ibidem; New York: Columbia University Press.
Higgins, C. (2023). 'Battle for the Past: The Ukrainians Trying to Save Their Archaeological Treasure Amid War,' *The Guardian*, 26 December. www.theguardian.com/science/2023/dec/26/battle-for-the-past-the-ukrainians-trying-to-save-their-archaeological-treasure-amid-war
Hook, K. (2022). 'Why Russia's War in Ukraine Is a Genocide. Not Just a Land Grab, but a Bid to Expunge a Nation,' *Foreign Affairs*, 28 July. www.foreignaffairs.com/ukraine/why-russias-war-ukraine-genocide
Into the Heart of Darkness-What Russia Wants in Ukraine. (2022). *EUvsDisinfo*, 6 April. https://euvsdisinfo.eu/into-the-heart-of-darkness-what-russia-wants-in-ukraine/?highlight=darkness
Inside the hunt for Ukraine's Stolen Art. (2024). *The Economist*, 5 January. www.economist.com/culture/2024/01/05/inside-the-hunt-for-ukraines-stolen-art
Kagan, F. W., Barros, G., Mikkelsen, N. and Mealie, D. (2023). *The Lands Ukraine Must Liberate*, Institute for the Study of War, 31 December. www.understandingwar.org/backgrounder/lands-ukraine-must-liberate
Käihkö, I. (2018). 'A Nation-in-the-Making, in Arms: Control of Force, Strategy and the Ukrainian Volunteer Battalions,' *Defence Studies*, 18 (2): 147–166.
Karaganov, S. (2025). 'Breaking the Back of Europe: What Should Russia's Policy Be towards the West.' *Russia in Global Affairs*, 22 January. https://globalaffairs.ru/articles/slomat-hrebet-evrope-karaganov/
Key Narratives in Pro-Kremlin Disinformation: "Nazis". (2022). *EUvsDisinfo*, 20 September. https://euvsdisinfo.eu/key-narratives-in-pro-kremlin-disinformation-nazis/
Khapaeva, D. (2024). *Putin's Dark Ages. Political Neo-Medievalism and Re-Stalinisation in Russia*. London: Routledge.
Kolstø, P. and Blakkisrud H. (2016). Edited. *The New Russian Nationalism. Imperialism, Ethnicity, and Authoritarianism*. Edinburgh: Edinburgh University Press.
Koposov, N. (2022). 'Holocaust Remembrance, the Cult of War, and Memory Laws in Putin's Russia' In: E. Barkan and A. Lang (eds.), *Memory Laws and Historical Justice*. Cham: Springer Nature Switzerland and New York: Palgrave Macmillan: 131–166.
Kovalev, A. (2022). 'Russia's Ukraine Propaganda Has Turned Fully Genocidal,' *Foreign Policy*, 9 April. https://foreignpolicy.com/2022/04/09/russia-putin-propaganda-ukraine-war-crimes-atrocities/

Kremlin Hate Speech Incites War Crimes in Ukraine. (2022). *EUvsDisinfo*, 9 June. https://euvsdisinfo.eu/kremlin-hate-speech-incites-war-crimes-in-ukraine/

Kryshtanovskaya, O. and White, S. (2009). 'The Sovietization of Russian Politics,' *Post-Soviet Affairs*, 25 (4): 283–309.

Kudelia, S. and Kuzio, T. (2015). 'Nothing Personal: Explaining the Rise and Decline of Political Machines in Ukraine,' *Post-Soviet Affairs*, 31 (3): 250–278.

Kulyk, V. (2014). 'Ukrainian Nationalism Since the Outbreak of Euromaidan,' *Ab Imperio*, 3: 94–122.

Kulyk, V. (2016). 'National Identity in Ukraine: Impact of Euromaidan and War,' *Europe-Asia Studies*, 68 (4): 588–608.

Kulyk, V. (2023). 'Mova ta identychnist v Ukrayini na kinets 2022-ho,' *Zbruch*, 7 January. https://zbruc.eu/node/114247?fbclid=IwAR399VVX7y4EDXgVedqvA2o1BlnIEUGylLtBIEBotJ16hxjItDQ0L-cOvJM

Kurin, R. (2023). 'How Ukrainians Are Defending Their Cultural Heritage from Russian Destruction,' *Smithsonian Magazine*, February. www.smithsonianmag.com/smithsonian-institution/ukrainians-defend-their-cultural-heritage-russian-destruction-180981661/

Kuzio, T. (2002). 'The Myth of the Civic State: A Critical Survey of Hans Kohn's Framework for Understanding Nationalism,' *Ethnic and Racial Studies*, 25 (1): 20–39.

Kuzio, T. (2009). 'Civic Nationalism and the Nation-State: Towards a Dynamic Model of Convergence' In: I. P. Ireneusz and A. M. Suszycki (eds.), *Multiplicity of Nationalism in Contemporary Europe*. New York: Lexington Books: 9–30.

Kuzio, T. (2015). *Ukraine: Democratization, Corruption, and the New Russian Imperialism*. Santa Barbara, CA: Praeger.

Kuzio, T. (2017). 'Stalinism and Russian and Ukrainian National Identities,' *Communist and Post-Communist Studies*, 50 (4): 289–302.

Kuzio, T. (2020). *Crisis in Russian Studies? Nationalism (Imperialism), Racism, and War*. Bristol: E-International Relations. www.e-ir.info/publication/crisis-in-russian-studies-nationalism-imperialism-racism-and-war/

Kuzio, T. (2022a). *Russian Nationalism and the Russian-Ukrainian War: Autocracy-Orthodoxy-Nationality*. London: Routledge.

Kuzio, T. (2022b). 'The Nationalism in Putin's Russia That Scholars Could Not Find but Which Invaded Ukraine,' *Ideology, Theory, Practice, Journal of Political Ideologies*, 4 April. www.ideology-theory-practice.org/blog/the-nationalism-in-putins-russia-that-scholars-could-not-find-but-which-invaded-ukraine

Kuzio, T. (2023). 'Imperial Nationalism as the Driver behind Russia's Invasion of Ukraine,' *Nations and Nationalism*, 29 (1): 30–38.

Kuzio, T. (2024). 'Historical Preparation and Ideological Legitimisation of the Russian Invasion of Ukraine: A Critical Discourse,' *Journal of Contemporary European Studies*, 32 (3): 850–869.

Kuzio, T. (2025). 'Putin's Demands Mean Trump Can Never Truly End the War. Here's Why?' *Moscow Times*, 17 April. www.themoscowtimes

.com/2025/04/17/putins-demands-mean-trump-can-never-truly-end-the-war-heres-why-a88753

Kuzio, T., Zhuk, S., and D'Anieri, P. (2022). Edited. *Ukraine's Outpost: Dnipropetrovsk and the Russian-Ukrainian War*. Bristol: E-International Relations. www.e-ir.info/publication/ukraines-outpost-dnipropetrovsk-and-the-russian-ukrainian-war/

Kuzyk, P. (2019). 'Ukraine's National Integration before and after 2014. Shifting "East–West" Polarization Line and Strengthening Political Community,' *Eurasian Geography and Economics*, 60 (6): 709–735.

Kyiv International Institute of Sociology. (2024). 'Stavlennya Ukrayintsiv do Rosii i Rosiyan', 7 November. https://kiis.com.ua/?lang=ukr&cat=reports&id=1446&page=1

Langdon, K. C. and Tismaneanu, V. (2020). *Putin's Totalitarian Democracy. Ideology, Myth, and Violence in the Twenty-First Century*. Cham: Imprint Springer International Publishing.

Laruelle, M. (2019). *Russian Nationalism. Imaginaries, Doctrines, and Political Battlefields*. London: Routledge.

Leshchenko, N. (2004). 'A Fine Instrument: Two Nation-building Strategies in Post-Soviet Belarus,' *Nations and Nationalism*, 10 (3): 333–352.

Leshchenko, N. (2008). 'The National Ideology and the Basis of the Lukashenka Regime in Belarus,' *Europe-Asia Studies*, 60 (8): 1419–1433.

Lewis, D. (2023). 'The Role of Ideology in Russian Foreign Policy' In: J. M. Leader and M. L. Haas (eds.), *The Routledge Handbook of Ideology and International Relations*. London: Routledge: 374–390.

Lewis, D. (2025). *Occupation. Russian Rule in South-Eastern Ukraine*. London: Hurst.

Martin, T. (2001). *The Affirmative Action Empire. Nations and Nationalism in the Soviet Union, 1923-1939*. Ithaca: Cornell University Press.

Medvedev, D. (2009). 'Message to the President of Ukraine Viktor Yushchenko,' 11 August. kremlin.ru/events/president/news/5158

Medvedev, D. (2023). 12 November. https://t.me/medvedev_telegram/411

McGlynn, J. (2020). 'Historical Framing of the Ukraine Crisis through the Great Patriotic War: Performativity, Cultural Consciousness and Shared Remembering,' *Memory Studies*, 13 (6): 1058–1080.

McGlynn, J. (2023a). *Memory Makers: The Politics of the Past in Putin's Russia*. London: Bloomsbury Press.

McGlynn, J. (2023b). 'Russian Propaganda Tactics in Wartime Ukraine,' The Russia Program at George Washington University, 10 November. https://drive.google.com/file/d/1xdmk4Mn2G-jNSWhljjuv7sCqMbE-LT3Y/view

McGlynn, J. (2023c). *Russia's War*. London: Bloomsbury Publishing.

Minchenia, A., Tornquist-Plewa, B. and Yurchuk, Y. (2018). 'Humour as a Mode of Hegemonic Control: Comic Representations of Belarusian and Ukrainian Leaders in Official Russian Media' In: N. Bernsand and B. Tornquist-Plewa (eds.), *Cultural and Political Imaginaries in Putin's Russia*. Leiden: Brill Academic Publishers: 211–231.

Mitrokhin, N. (2024). 'Organizations of Russian Nationalists in the Russia-Ukraine Conflict' In: A. Heinemann-Gruder (ed.), *Who Are the Fighters? Irregular Armed Groups in the Russian-Ukrainian War since 2014*. Stuttgart: Ibidem; New York: Columbia University Press: 15–46.

Motyl, A. J. (2016). 'Putin's Russia as a Fascist Political System,' *Communist and Post-Communist Studies*, 49 (1): 25–36.

Oliinyk, A. and Kuzio, T. (2021). 'The Euromaidan Revolution of Dignity, Reforms and De-Communisation in Ukraine,' *Europe-Asia Studies*, 73 (5): 807–836.

Oliinyk, A. (2023). *The Military-Patriotic Infrastructure in Eastern Ukraine: Russian Proxy Republics (2014–2022)*. Norwegian Defence University College. https://fhs.brage.unit.no/fhs-xmlui/handle/11250/3101161

Onuch, O. and Hale, H. E. (2018). 'Capturing Ethnicity: The Case of Ukraine,' *Post-Soviet Affairs*, 34 (2–3): 84–106.

Onuch, O. and Hale, H. E. (2022). *The Zelenskyy Effect*. London: Hurst and Co.

Plokhy, S. (2023). *The Frontline. Essays on Ukraine's Past and Present*. Cambridge, MA: Harvard University Press.

Pop-Eleches, G. and Robertson, G. B. (2018). 'Identity and Political Preferences in Ukraine – before and after the Euromaidan,' *Post-Soviet Affairs*, 34 (2–3): 107–118.

Popova, M. and Shevel, O. (2023). *Russia and Ukraine. Entangled Histories. Diverging States*. Cambridge and Hoboken, NJ: Polity Press.

Poznyak-Khomenko, N. (ed.), (2020). *Volontery: Syla nebayduzhykh*. Kyiv: Ukrainian Institute for National Remembrance and Ternopil: Dzhura. https://uinp.gov.ua/elektronni-vydannya/volontery-syla-nebayduzhyh

Putin, V. (2008). 'Putin's Speech to the NATO-Russia Council,' 2 April. www.unian.info/world/111033-text-of-putins-speech-at-nato-summit-bucharest-april-2-2008.html

Putin, V. (2017). 'Speech to the Valdai Discussion Club', http://en.kremlin.ru/events/president/news/55882

Putin, V. (2020a). 'Vladimir Putin rasskazal o "podarkakh" russkogo naroda respublykam, vyshedshym iz sostava Sovetskogo Soyuza,' *Nika TV*, 22 June. https://nikatv.ru/news/obshestvo/vladimir-putin-rasskazal-opodarkah-russkogo-naroda-respublikam-vyshedshim-izsostava-sovetskogo-soyuza

Putin, V. (2020b). 'Twenty questions with Vladimir Putin. Putin on Ukraine', *Tass*, 18 March. https://putin.tass.ru/en

Putin, V. (2021). 'On the Historical Unity of Russians and Ukrainians,' 12 July. http://en.kremlin.ru/events/president/news/66181

Putin, V. (2023a). 'Speech to the World Russian Peoples Council,' 28 November. http://en.kremlin.ru/events/president/news/72863

Putin, V. (2023b). 'Direct Line Forum,' 14 December. http://en.kremlin.ru/events/president/transcripts/72994

Putin, V. (2023c). 'Expanded Meeting of the Ministry of Defence Ministry Board,' 19 December. http://en.kremlin.ru/events/president/news/73035

Putin, V. (2025). 'Interview with TV channel *Rossiya 1*,' 28 January. www.1tv.ru/news/2025-01-28/499557-ob_uregulirovanii_ukrainskogo_krizisa_govoril_prezident_v_intervyu_pavlu_zarubinu

Rating Sociological Organisation. (2022). 'The Tenth National Survey: Ideological Markers of the War', 27 April. https://ratinggroup.ua/en/research/ukraine/desyatyy_obschenacionalnyy_opros_ideologicheskie_markery_voyny_27_aprelya_2022.html

Razumkov Centre. (2023). 'Efficiency of Implementation of the State Policy in the field of Ukrainian Nation-and Civil Identity-Building: Sociological Indicator,' May. https://razumkov.org.ua/en/component/k2/efficiency-of-implementation-of-the-state-policy-in-the-field-of-ukrainian-nation-and-civil-identity-building-sociological-indicators-may-2023

Ryazanova-Clarke, L. (2017) 'From Commodification to Weaponization: The Russian Language as "pride" and "profit" in Russia's Transnational Discourses,' *International Journal of Bilingual Education and Bilingualism*, 20 (4): 443–456.

Satter, D. (2017). *The Less You Know, the Better You Sleep. Russia's Road to Dictatorship Under Yeltsin and Putin*. London and New Haven, CT: Yale University Press.

Scarr, F. (2022). 'I Monitor Russian State TV for a Living – Here's How Putin's Propaganda Is Changing,' *The Telegraph*, 30 April. www.telegraph.co.uk/world-news/2022/04/30/monitor-russian-state-tv-living-putins-propaganda-changing/

Sergeytsev, T. (2022). 'What should Russia Do with Ukraine?' *RIA Novosti*, 3 April. https://ria.ru/20220403/ukraina-1781469605.html

Sharafutdinova, G. (2020). *The Red Mirror. Putin's Leadership and Russia's Insecure Identity*. Oxford: Oxford University Press.

Shevel, O. (2024). 'Some Lessons from the Post-Soviet Era and the Russo-Ukrainian War for the Study of Nationalism,' *Ethics & International Affairs*, 38 (3): 333–353.

Shydlovsky, P., Kuijt, I., Skorokhod, V., Zotsenko, I., Ivakin, I., Donaruma, W. and Field, S. (2023). 'The Tools of War: Conflict and the Destruction of Ukrainian Cultural Heritage,' *Antiquity*, 97 (396) 36: 1–7.

Small, Z. (2023). 'Met Museum Trains "Monuments Men" to Save Ukrainian Cultural Heritage,' *New York Times*, 13 June. www.nytimes.com/2023/06/13/arts/design/met-museum-trains-monuments-men-ukraine.html?campaign_id=51&emc=edit_mbe_20230616&instance_id=%E2%80%A6

Shulman, S. (2005). 'National Identity and Public Support for Political and Economic Reform in Ukraine,' *Slavic Review*, 64 (1): 59–87.

Sidorov, A. (2024). 'Russia and the West after the SMO: A New Level of Confrontation,' *International Affairs (Moscow)*, 3 July. https://en.interaffairs.ru/article/russia-and-the-west-after-the-smo-a-new-level-of-confrontation/

Stephenson, S. (2023). 'How Criminal Culture Has Led Russian Society towards Miltaristic Madness,' *Moscow Times*, 28 March. www.themoscowtimes

.com/2023/03/28/how-criminal-culture-has-led-russian-society-toward-militaristic-madness-a80635

The Idea of Ukraine is Based on a Mythologised Lie. (2019). *EUvsDisinfo*, 17 June. https://euvsdisinfo.eu/report/the-idea-of-ukraine-is-based-on-a-mythologised-lie

The Stolen Treasures. (2023). 'The 110,000 Artifacts from Ukraine Found in Two Russian Museums,' *Texty*, 19 September. https://texty.org.ua/d/2023/stolen_heritage/en/ and https://texty.org.ua/d/2023/stolen_heritage/

The Russian Federation's Escalating Commission of Genocide in Ukraine: A Legal Analysis. (2023). 'New Lines Institute for Strategy and Policy and Raoul Wallenberg Centre for Human Rights,' July. https://newlinesinstitute.org/rules-based-international-order/genocide/the-russian-federations-escalating-commission-of-genocide-in-ukraine-a-legal-analysis/

Tolz, V. (2002). 'Rethinking Russian–Ukrainian Relations: A New Trend in Nation-building in Post-communist Russia?' *Nations and Nationalism*, 8 (2): 235–253.

Ukrainian Parliament. (2021). 'Pro korinni narody Ukrayiny,' Law, 1 July with amendments on 13 December 2022. https://zakon.rada.gov.ua/laws/show/1616-20#Text

Ukrainian Parliament. (2022a). 'Declaration on the Genocide Committed by the Russian Federation in Ukraine,' 14 April. https://itd.rada.gov.ua/billinfo/%D0%94%D0%BE%D0%B4%D0%B0%D1%82%D0%BE%D0%BA (eng).pdf

Ukrainian Parliament. (2022b). 'Pro deradyanizatsiyu zakonodavstva Ukrayiny,' Law, 21 April. https://zakon.rada.gov.ua/laws/show/2215-20#Text

Ukrainian Parliament. (2022c). 'Pro zaboronu propahandy rosiyskoho nacystskoho totalitarnoho rezhymu, zbroynoyi ahresiyi Rosiyskoyi Federaciyi yak derzhavy-terorysta proty Ukrayiny, symvoliky voyennoho vtorhnennya rosiyskoho nacystskoho totalitarnoho rezhymu v Ukrayinu,' Law, 22 May. https://zakon.rada.gov.ua/laws/show/2265-20#Text

Ukrainian Parliament. (2022d). 'Zakonu pro vnesennya zmin do Zakonu Ukrayiny "Pro heohrafichni nazvy" shhodo dekolonizaciyi toponimiyi ta vporyadkuvannya vykorystannya heohrafichnykh nazv u naselenykh punktakh Ukrayiny,' Law, 18 July. https://zakon.rada.gov.ua/laws/show/2601-20#Text

Ukrainian Parliament. (2022e). 'Postanova. Pro Zayavu Verkhovnoyi Rady Ukrayiny shhodo vyznannya rosiykhskoho rezhymu terorystychnym, nelehitymnosti perebuvannya rosiyskoyi federaciyi v Orhanizaciyi Obyednanyx Naciy i yiyi reformuvannya, vidpovidalnosti chleniv rosiyskykh politychnykh partiy, shho pidtrymuyut ahresiyu, Resolution, 1 December. https://zakon.rada.gov.ua/laws/show/2787-IX#Text

Ukrainian Parliament. (2023a). 'Postanovy pro Zayavu Verkhovnoyi Rady Ukrayiny "Pro vyznachennya isnuyuchoho v Rosiyskiy Federaciyi politychnoho rezhymu yak rashyzmu ta zasudzhennya yoho ideolohichnykh zasad i suspilnykh praktyk yak totalitarnykh ta lyudonenavysnyckykh",' Resolution, 2 May. https://itd.rada.gov.ua/billInfo/Bills/Card/41531

Ukrainian Parliament. (2023b). 'Pro zasudzhennya ta zaboronu propahandy rosiyskoyi imperskoyi polityky v Ukrayini i dekolonizaciyu toponimiyi,' Law, 3 May. https://zakon.rada.gov.ua/laws/show/3005-20#Text

Ukrainian Parliament. (2024). 'Zakonu pro dekolonizaciyu humanitarnoyi sfery Ukrayiny,' Law, 20 June. https://itd.rada.gov.ua/BILLINFO/Bills/Card/40350

Ukraine: Torture, Disappearances in Occupied South. (2022). Human Rights Watch, 21 July. www.hrw.org/news/2022/07/22/ukraine-torture-disappearances-occupied-south

Weeks, T. R. (1996). *Nation and State in Late Imperial Russia. Nationalism and Russification on the Western Frontier, 1863-1914.* De Kalb: Northern Illinois University Press.

"We Had No Choice." "Filtration" and the Crime of Forcibly Transferring Ukrainian Civilians to Russia. (2022). Human Rights Watch. 1 September. www.hrw.org/report/2022/09/01/we-had-no-choice/filtration-and-crime-forcibly-transferring-ukrainian-civilians

When Words Kill – From Moscow to Mariupol. (2022). *EUvsDisinfo*, 17 June. https://euvsdisinfo.eu/when-words-kill-from-moscow-to-mariupol/

Whitacker, B. (2023). 'Ukraine Accuses Russia of Looting Museums, Destroying Churches as Part of Looting Heritage,' *CBC News*, 12 November. www.cbsnews.com/news/ukraine-accuses-russia-museum-looting-church-destruction-60-minutes-transcript/

Wojnowski, Z. (2017). *The Near Abroad. Eastern Europe and Soviet Patriotism in Ukraine, 1956–1985.* Toronto: University of Toronto Press.

Wolczuk, K. (2000). 'History, Europe and the "National Idea." The "Official" Narrative of National Identity in Ukraine.' *Nationalities Papers*, 28 (4): 671–694.

Yermolenko, Y. (ed.), (2019). *Re-Vision of History. Russian Historical Propaganda and Ukraine.* Kyiv: K.I.S., Internews, Ukraine World. https://ukraineworld.org/storage/app/media/Re_vision_2019_block%20eng.pdf

Young, C. (2022). 'Russians Accuse Ukraine of Nazism – but Look at How Russian Propagandists Talk. The Gruesome Rhetoric of Putin's Talking Heads,' *The Bulwark*, 27 October. www.thebulwark.com/russians-accuse-ukraine-of-nazism-but-look-at-how-russian-propagandists-talk/27

Zhurzhenko, T. (2021). 'Fighting Empire, Weaponising Culture: The Conflict with Russia and the Restrictions on Russian Mass Culture in Post-Maidan Ukraine.' *Europe-Asia Studies*, 73 (8): 1441–1466.

Zolotukhin, Y. D. (2018). *Bila Knyha. Spetsialnykh Informatsiynykh Operatsiy Proty Ukrayiny 2014–2018.* Kyiv: Mega-Press Hrup. http://mip.gov.ua/files/pdf/white_book_2018_mip.pdf?fbclid=IwAR1oloK5UbxY5fyxRJLbnnd7FxcBPs6zEiNdqG89Rx7c23uLqriJ-ZVAYLY

Zygar, M. (2016). *All the Kremlin's Men. Inside the Court of Vladimir Putin.* New York: Public Affairs.

Zygar, M. (2022). 'How Vladimir Putin Lost Interest in the Present,' *New York Times*, 10 March. www.nytimes.com/2022/03/10/opinion/putin-russia-ukraine.html

Zygar, M. (2023a). *War and Punishment. The Story of Russian Opposition and Ukrainian Resistance*. London: Weidenfeld and Nicolson.

Zygar, M. (2023b). 'The Man behind Putin's Warped View of History,' *The New York Times*, 19 September. www.nytimes.com/2023/09/19/opinion/putin-russia-medinsky.html

7

Diverging Political Systems in Russia and Ukraine

At first glance, at the time of the disintegration of the USSR, Russia and Ukraine's political systems and societies began their post-Soviet transitions from the same point. In the case of Russia, the socio-political transformation led to a dictatorship. During the same period, a political system and a broadly understood social order were formed in Ukraine, based on pluralism, freedom, democratic mechanisms of exercising and changing power, and a dynamic civil society. Why did this happen, and where do these differences come from? Paul D'Anieri (2023a), among others, has tried to answer this question, as have Maria Popova and Oxana Shevel (2024). This chapter will build on their analyses.

In order to properly understand these differences, it is necessary to take into account the fact that in the case of both Russia and Ukraine, the transformation of the political and social system took place on four interconnected levels: (1) political (regime change); (2) economic (adoption of elements of a market economy); (3) identity (redefinition of the political community); and (4) institutional (creation of state structures that would implement the interests of this community). Therefore, in relation to the post-Soviet space in general, and to Russia and Ukraine in particular, we can speak of a 'quadruple transition', that is, parallel processes of democratisation, marketisation, state-building and nation-building (see Kuzio, 2001).

Due to the framework of the research question, the economic transition will not be included in this analysis. This chapter consists of two parts. The first analyses the key question related to nation-building in Ukraine: What are the sources of Ukrainian identity? Of course, these sources are anchored deeply in the past, but a contemporary form of Ukrainian identity must have been determined to a greater extent by post-communism. This includes basic concepts and political mechanisms, as well as the ways in which various cumulative elements of identity from the near past (i.e., the Soviet period) and the general past (i.e., the romanticism of the nineteenth century) were adapted to the realities that began to form after the collapse of communism. The second part of the chapter analyses the process of state building and political transition in Ukraine. It will investigate how the institutional framework for political transformation in Ukraine was shaped, and the reasons for the fundamental differences between Ukraine's and Russia's political transformation.

Post-Communism and Diverging Identities in Russia and Ukraine

To gain a better understanding of the specificity of the Russian and Ukrainian paths of post-communism, one must consider the wide cultural context of the changes which took place 'after communism'. As Jadwiga Staniszkis (2005, p. 228) claims, their shape and development depend on 'the premises of the form of existence'. On this basis, two types of post-communism can be distinguished: Russian and Central European. The former grows out of the culture, which Staniszkis (2005) calls 'Orthodox' and which is 'a culture of antinomy'. Its essence is the fact that 'the meaning of a given element (institution) is mediated by its opposite (...) and by the formula for interpreting this antinomical whole' (Staniszkis, 2005, p. 229).

The point of reference for Russia, which is the subject of 'mediation', is the West. Its relations with the West have been interpreted, depending on the period, as either a 'contradiction' (confrontational) or mutual 'complementation' (see Chapter 8). For most of the Soviet period, the former, a confrontational version of the interpretation of the essence of Russia's relations with the West, was in force. This can be found in the 'Leninist interpretation of the idea of exporting revolution', which after the Second World War was adapted to the conditions of the 'Cold War'. In the second half of the 1980s, Soviet leader Mikhail Gorbachev carried out a 'revolution from above' and decreed a new paradigm of the USSR (Russia) versus the West antinomy whose essence would be 'complementation'. This conciliatory version was implemented into political discourse in the form of the idea of a 'common European home', laid out by Gorbachev in 1989 (Staniszkis, 2005, p. 229). Russia as part of a 'common European home' lasted until 1996, when Yevgeny Primakov was appointed Russian foreign minister, and since when Russia has defined itself as lying at the centre of Eurasia.

The transformations in Russia after 1991 can be interpreted as an attempt to shape a new 'conciliatory' formula for complementing two opposites (Russia and the West). However, this led to chaos and a permanent institutional crisis in the 1990s, with two hardline coup attempts in 1991 and 1993. The transformation itself was contested as a disastrous policy of imposing Western cultural patterns upon Russia through its Westernisation. This is discussed, for example, in Chapter 2, which is devoted to the genesis of the ideology of the Pan-Russian World.

Central European post-communism, in contrast, was shaped based on a culture which was originally deeply rooted in bivalent logic, where 'the concept of identity is closely intertwined with the category of difference' (Staniszkis, 2005, p. 228). Consequently, Central European cultural diversity would result from the fact that, in principle, identities and geopolitical and civilisational orientations always differed and never generally ruled each other out within one country or region.

The differences between these types of post-communism are culturally conditioned and result from processes that took place within the communist elites throughout the duration of the Soviet Union. They can be captured within Staniszkis's (2005) concept of 'the mechanism of *three beginnings*', which assumes a close link 'between the first split within communist elites', which then influences the fledgling pluralisation of society on the bottom level, that Staniszkis (2005) called the 'audience', or it influences the ruling elites 'on the top', who are already in the twilight of communism' (Staniszkis, 2005, p. 231).

For the Russian version of post-communism, this 'founding' dispute was the problem of 'the formula for interpreting the antinomical "whole": communism – capitalism' (Staniszkis, 2005, p. 232.) The controversial issue was whether the only kind of interaction between these systems is conflict, or whether 'interdependence' and mutual 'complementarity' are possible. The roots of this dispute are to be found among the Bolshevik elites of Russia – Vladimir Lenin, Joseph Stalin, Leon Trotsky and Nikolai Bukharin. A similar conflict within Russian elites transpired during the disintegration of the USSR and changed during discussions over Gorbachev's concept of 'a common European home' (Staniszkis, 2005, p. 232.). From 1991, the core problem of this founding dispute was transformed into the Russia versus the West antinomy. In the Central European model of post-communism, the determining 'first dispute' which 'returned' at the end of the 1980s concerned 'the relationship: *the country – the people of Moscow*' (Staniszkis, 2005, p. 232.). This 'first dispute' took place before the Soviet Union was founded, on the eve of the October Revolution.

Bolsheviks did not have a large support base in Ukraine, and they focused primarily on the industrial urban proletariat. At the beginning of the twentieth century, just ahead of the Bolshevik Revolution, 93 per cent of Ukrainians in the Russian Empire were peasants (Hrycak, 2000, p. 79). By 1917, there were only 273 Ukrainians in the ranks of the Bolsheviks (Doroshko, 2008, p. 64). Until April 1918, there was no separate Ukrainian Bolshevik structure, and only after the first unsuccessful attempts to seize power in Ukraine did the Leninist leadership decide to establish the Communist Party (Bolshevik) of Ukraine KP(b)U. Its main initiator was one of the most prominent Ukrainian Bolsheviks, Mykola Skrypnyk (Stryjek, 2000, pp. 332–397), who postulated that a new independent party would enter the Comintern as a separate and equal entity. However, only the name was used from Skrypnyk's proposal, which was intended to suggest the distinctiveness of the Ukrainian Bolshevik Party. Meanwhile, the KP(b)U was only a differently named regional organisation of the Russian Communist Party (Kulchytskyy, 2004, p. 14).

The ethnic make-up of the Bolshevik organisational structure in Ukraine is very significant. Out of 4,364 Bolsheviks who were active on Ukrainian territory in July 1918, only 130 called themselves 'Ukrainians', while the Ukrainian Socialist-Revolutionary Party had 300,000 members (Subtelny, 1992, p. 304). At that time, among the 15 members of the Central Committee of the Communist Party of Ukraine, there were only 3 Ukrainians (Doroshko, 2008, p. 64). In 1922, Ukrainians comprised merely 23.3 per cent of Communist Party of Ukraine members (Hrycak, 2000, p. 173).

The Bolsheviks were faced with competition in Ukraine not only from the UNR (Ukrainian Peoples' Republic), but also from local Ukrainian communists who possessed their own organisation, the Ukrainian Communist Party (UCP) (*Borotbists*), which had about 15,000 members (three times more than local Bolshevik structures). In 1920, the *Borotbists* sent a memorandum to the Comintern in which they defined themselves as the authentic representation of Ukrainian communists, in contrast to the Communist Party of Ukraine, which in their opinion was completely alien in Ukraine and was not even able to recognise the need for a separate Ukrainian centre (Mace, 1983, p. 55). They also emphasised that Ukraine was fundamentally different from Russia: it had its own structure of economic life. The *Borotbists* noted that the communist movement in Ukraine had so far ignored the rural proletariat, yet it was the main revolutionary force there. In their opinion, to gain support in the countryside it was necessary to adapt the slogans and methods of building a new society to the mentality of Ukrainian peasants, one of whose basic characteristics was a deeply rooted sense of ownership (Mace, 1983, p. 55–56). The *Borotbists* also expressed the belief that after a long period of Russification during the Tsarist period, Ukrainians were very suspicious of everything Russian. The Bolshevik version of communism also seemed suspicious of them. They predicted that if Russianness was not removed from the communist idea in Ukraine, most of the local proletariat would turn away from the Bolsheviks (Mace, 1983, p. 55).

Ultimately, the *Borotbists* party was liquidated, and some of its members (about 4,000) joined the branch of the Communist Party of Ukraine (Kulchytskyy, 2004, p. 24). They should have become a catalyst for the Ukrainisation of the Communist Party of Ukraine from within (Shkandrii, 2006, p. 32). However, it very quickly turned out that the whole operation was aimed at eliminating the *Borotbists*, and in the Communist Party of Ukraine there was only room for the Russian interpretation of the Marxist-Leninist doctrine on the nationality question. In 1923, only 118 of the former *Borotbists* remained in the Bolshevik ranks, and their leaders were murdered in the 1930s (Kulchytskyy, 2004, p. 24).

Today, Stalin is an authority for Putin, among other things, in the field of nationality policy. Therefore, it is worth recalling what one of the aforementioned *Borotbists*, Mykhaylo Poloz,[1] wrote to Stalin in 1919: 'As a result of your party dictatorship, which is being implemented in the almost complete absence of properly trained party workers in Ukraine who know local conditions, the idea of Soviet power is being discredited even in the eyes of the workers' (Kulchytskyy, 2004, p. 16). Poloz showed that the conflict between the Ukrainian revolutionary elites and the 'people of Moscow' had been taking place since the Bolshevik Revolution.

At about the same time, in 1920, another group of left wing Ukrainian activists, the *Ukapists*, formed another political party that was independent of the Russian Bolshevik Party and its Ukrainian division. Representatives of this group emphasised in December 1918 that the KP(b)U was an anti-Ukrainian organisation: instead of the dictatorship of the proletariat in Ukraine, a 'dictatorship of the KP(b)U' had been introduced, and the new government was 'obsessively' attached to violence as a way 'to resolve every possible problem' (Mace, 1983, p. 74). The 'Ukrainian Communist

---

[1] Mykhailo Poloz (1890–1938?) took part in the attempt to overthrow the Central Rada and establish Soviet power independent of the Bolsheviks, was a member of the government of the Ukrainian SSR in 1919, one of the leaders of the Ukrainian Communist Party (*Borotbists*), an opponent of its liquidation through merging with the KP(b)U, but eventually he himself joined the KP(b)U and was twice a member of its Central Committee. Arrested in 1933 for activities in a 'nationalist organisation', imprisoned in Solovki from 1934, and executed in 1938. *Encyclopedia of Ukrainian Science*. Lviv: 1996, 6, p. 2197.

Party' accepted the Soviet model of power, but at the same time they were against the domination of the KP(b)U as perpetuating the colonial relationship of Ukraine's dependence on Russia (Mace, 1983, p. 74). The UCP survived as a legal opposition party until 1925, when it 'self-dissolved' and some of its activists joined the KP(b)U. Again, most of its leading representatives were murdered in the 1930s. Russian Bolsheviks and Ukrainian supporters of communism and socialism were not only divided by conflict over power, but above all, by a mental and cultural abyss. *Borotbists* and *Ukapists* were representatives who are traditionally referred to as national communists in Ukraine.

In the 1920s, the conflict in the bosom of the Soviet elites between 'the country' and 'the people of Moscow' moved to the sphere of culture and science. The focus of the dispute became the so-called theory of 'two cultures', formulated in 1923 by the second secretary of the KP(B)U Dmytro Lebed, which presented Russian culture as revolutionary and progressive, and Ukrainian culture as counter-revolutionary, backward, and doomed to fail and disappear (Hrycak, 2000, p. 173). Lebed's 'Theory of Two Cultures' represented a new Bolshevik version of Russian imperialism and the 'people of Moscow's' challenge to the nationally conscious Ukrainian intelligentsia. The Bolsheviks assumed that the free development of national cultures would lead to them losing their differences. As a result, the previously oppressed nations should voluntarily unite under the rule of the Bolsheviks, who 'gave' them cultural independence (Mace, 1983, p. 13). This was the genesis of the indigenisation (Ukrainisation) policy which Ukrainian intellectual elites used to fight for the full and equal status of Russian and Ukrainian cultures.

It very quickly became apparent that the Bolshevik authorities were losing control over the process they had implemented. Contrary to Lenin's expectations, Ukrainisation led to a growing divergence of the mental and cultural differences between Ukraine and Russia. These were most clearly formulated by Mykola Khvylovy, a Ukrainian national communist of Russian descent, who wrote about the destructive influence of Russian culture and the need for Ukraine's reorientation towards 'psychological Europe' (Shkandrii, 2006, pp. 89–90). Khvylovy accused Moscow of not appreciating the value of the Ukrainian national revival, treating Ukrainians as simpletons and denying the intellectual independence of the Ukrainian intelligentsia. Meanwhile, he argued that Ukrainian culture was emancipated from Russian tutelage and was becoming directly acquainted with new Western European trends and ideas (Khvylovy, 1996, p. 639).

Khvylovy represented the continuation of national communism and the tension between Ukrainian communist elites and the 'people from Moscow', not only in politics but also in culture. Not surprisingly, Khvylovy's concepts were met with strong criticism from the leaders of the KP(b)U. Khvylovy, author of the slogan 'Away from Moscow! Closer to Europe!' had to publicly withdraw his concepts and apologise for them. His suicide in 1933 symbolised an end to the illusion of the possibility of competition between local Ukrainian communist elites and the 'people of Moscow'.

In the heat of the debate sparked by Khvylovy's political pamphlets, a new formula for the dispute between the 'country' and the 'people of Moscow' crystallised in Ukraine: Ukrainians as Europeans versus Moscow outside Europe. Khvylovy clearly placed Ukrainian culture in the general trend of European civilisation. Meanwhile, his opponents described the supporters of so-called Khvylovism as 'Westernised intellectuals who lack faith in their own people' (Shkandrii, 2006, p. 87). Critics of Khvylovy negated the universal value of the Western European cultural legacy and claimed that Europe was synonymous with 'decay and rot' (Shkandrii, 2006, p. 87). As seen in Chapters 8 and 9, this defacement of the West has deep roots in Russian imperial nationalism and Soviet Russian communism.

The question of attitudes towards Europe understood as a system of values became the main element that would distinguish Ukrainian national communists from the Bolshevik 'people of Moscow'. Although they both referred to Marxist achievements, Marxism in Russia and Ukraine developed under different conditions. In Russia, Marxism appeared before 'the problems raised by Russian nationalism were fully discussed' (Szporluk, 2003, p. 310).

Such a fundamental 'undiscussed' problem was the distinction between Russian and imperial identity. As a result, 'Marxism in Russia did not undergo the same process of nationalisation that it experienced elsewhere in Europe' (Szporluk, 2003, p. 310). The emergence of the trend of national communism in Ukraine and its strength testify to the fact that this 'nationalisation of Marxism' had taken place in the Ukrainian lands in the Russian and Austro-Hungarian Empires. Thus, the development of the Marxist left in Ukraine was subject to pan-European influences. Meanwhile, Marxism in Russia was a kind of pathology – or at least an anomaly – compared to these pan-European features. Ukrainian national communists and Bolsheviks used the same concepts: both spoke of social liberation, democracy, the dictatorship of the proletariat, class struggle, and internationalism. However, the similarities ended when it came to implementing these slogans and, in practice, both versions of communism turned out to be incompatible. Only if we take this fact into account will we be able to fully and properly understand the meaning of Khvylovy's slogan 'Away from Moscow. Closer to Europe'.

Khvylovy also symbolises another fundamental difference between Ukrainian national communists and Bolsheviks: the former used arguments from the intellectual sphere, while the latter never considered any compromise in their calculations regarding Ukraine and always ended with exclusion from the party, repression and physical liquidation. New intellectual elites emerged in Soviet Ukraine, which, contrary to Lenin's predictions, demanded autonomy from Moscow and the redefinition of what is Ukrainian and what is supposedly internationalist but, in reality, is Russian in nature.

When Ukrainisation began to spin out of control, the Bolshevik authorities decided to launch repressions from the late 1920s. The Ukrainian national and cultural revival is described as having been 'exterminated' (Mokry, 1993). It is estimated that 200 out of 240 Ukrainian writers and 62 out of 85 linguists disappeared in various ways (one of the basic assumptions of Ukrainisation was the promotion of the Ukrainian language) (Subtelny, 1992, p. 364). In 1933, Stalin's personal representative in Ukraine, Pavlo Postyshev, who held prominent positions in the KP(b)U throughout the period of Ukrainisation,[2] proudly reported, 'A great deal of work has been done. Suffice it to say that we cleansed only one People's Commissariat of Education of two thousand people who belonged to nationalist elements, including about 300 scholars and writers' (Subtelny, 1992, p. 364). It is estimated that because of repressions in Soviet Ukraine at that time, about four-fifths of the Ukrainian intelligentsia were murdered (Hrycak, 2000, p. 181). The Sovietisation of Ukraine was accomplished with the aid of mass terror and Russification.

The Ukrainian renaissance of the 1920s was literally executed. Its history, as well as the history of Ukrainian national communism, were meticulously erased from the official Soviet narrative of the past. Nevertheless, their erasure was never complete, and the ideas and questions posed to 'the people from Moscow' in the 1920s returned in the 1960s and the second half of the 1980s. The *Shestydesiatnyky* (Sixtiers [generation of

---

[2] Pavel Postyshev (1887–1940), among others, secretary of the Kyiv district committee of the KP(b)U, member of the Politburo and the Central Committee. Encyclopedia of Ukrainian Science, Lviv 1996, vol. 6, p. 2275

the 1960s]) were national communists, intellectuals, and dissidents who emerged in Ukraine after Soviet leader Nikita Khrushchev's thaw and de-Stalinisation. This was a movement of 'a semi-autonomous space of cultural expression that was tolerated by the authorities and defined, developed, and inhabited by young Ukrainian intellectuals' (Yekelchyk, 2015, p. 46). It should be underlined that representatives of this dissident movement 'were a typical product of the Soviet education system'. (Subtelny, 1992, p. 445). As Serhii Yekelchyk (2015, p. 45) pointed out, 'The cultural terrain inhabited by young Ukrainian intellectuals was not fully separate from mainstream Soviet Ukrainian culture or in opposition to it, although their vibrant cultural space also reached into a world of non-conformist culture unregulated by the state'. Although the dissident movement in Ukraine was not numerous, it had a distinct Ukrainian national character and was the largest found in the Soviet republics (Subtelny, 1992, p. 445). One of the most important manifestations of *Shestydesiatnyky* nonconformism was a struggle with Russification and defence of freedom of artistic creativity. Many *Shestydesiatnyky* were repressed during political purges in the mid 1960s, and especially during the 1972 *pohrom*.

As a result, controversies over the differences between Ukrainian and Russian understandings of communism, which had bedevilled the Soviet Union from its inception, again appeared in the 1960s. Ivan Dzyuba, who was a young Ukrainian communist and party intellectual, decided to admonish the leaders of the Communist Party about their victimisation of the *Shestydesiatnyky*, which he believed was at variance with the fundamental ideological premises of the party, that were formulated when Soviet Ukraine was founded and Ukrainisation took place. Dzyuba wrote a paper for the Communist Party which circulated in *samvydav* and was republished in the West as *Internationalism or Russification?* (Dzyuba, 2005). He was arrested and sentenced to 5 years in prison and 5 years in exile, which was commuted after he recanted. The work of Dzyuba, who revised and updated memories of the original conflict between 'the country' and 'the people of Moscow', can be treated as a symbol of 'the second beginning' of Staniszkis' (2005) concept.

The third, decisive split in the bosom of Soviet Ukrainian elites occurred in the late 1980s during Gorbachev's *perestroika* (restructuring) and *glasnost* (openness), which again revived discussions about problems raised at the very beginning of Soviet rule in the 1920s (Hnatiuk, 2003, p. 126). On this occasion, it was coloured by Gorbachev's slogan of 'returning to roots', that is, to Lenin's original principles, and imposed a particular way of narrating the history of the USSR, whereby the building of communism was carried out in accordance with Lenin's principles before Stalin took power and compromised them through mass repressions. Ukrainian intellectual elites eagerly reacted to the appeal to return to Lenin's roots (Hnatiuk, 2003, p. 92) as a signal towards the modernisation and rebuilding of the Soviet Empire (Hnatiuk, 2003, p. 92). This, in turn, inevitably led to the rediscovery of discussions, disputes and dilemmas faced by supporters of national communism in Ukraine in the 1920s and 1960s. The problem Gorbachev faced was that national communism had been extinguished in the first half of the 1970s during the removal of Shelest, the criminal sentencing of Dzyuba, and the *pohrom* of Ukrainian elites and dissidents. Shcherbytsky ran Ukraine as a Little Russian Soviet republic, Ukrainian in name only, for the next seventeen years.

Gorbachev's *glasnost* brought top-down permission to discuss topics in public that were previously forbidden to be spoken or written about, along with the discovery of so-called 'blank spots', the *Holodomor*, memory of the Executed Renaissance and national communists. As Aleksandra Hnatiuk (2003, p. 94) writes, the next 'Ukrainian revolution', or 'the third beginning' according to Staniszkis' (2005) concept, in the late 1980s was to be realised through 'updating the 1920s project and returning to the roots of Soviet identity' (Hnatiuk, 2003, p. 94). This meant updating the Ukrainian variety of this identity, which centred upon the tension between 'the country' and the 'people of Moscow'.

When the 'third beginning' emerged in the late 1980s, the relationship between the 'country' and the 'people of Moscow' was taking shape in relatively new conditions. First, the 'people of Moscow' were no longer 'obsessed with violence as a way to resolve every possible problem'. Gorbachev's *perestroika* and *glasnost* contributed to this. Second, the 'people of Moscow' were divided into two main camps. The first was headed by Gorbachev, who pushed for maintaining the Soviet Union as a 'renewed federation', while the second option was symbolised by Yeltsin, who focused on Russia's emancipation from the Soviet Union. The same goal was also pursued by a wing of the Communist Party elites in Soviet Ukraine. Consequently, 'Yeltsin's Russia became their important ally, as it was in the case of the other non-Russian republics which pressed for the USSR to be transformed into a confederation, in contrast to Gorbachev's agenda of 'renewed federation'. Russia signed bilateral agreements with the other republics which recognised existing borders, including with Ukraine in November 1990' (Kuzio, 2000, p. 158). The third, the Moscow centre, showed its weakness in the face of centrifugal tendencies in the three Baltic republics in 1990–1991. In these conditions, the 'embryonic national communism' within the ranks of the Communist Party in Ukraine began to surface, led by Leonid Kravchuk (Kuzio, 2000, p. 166).

Throughout most of the Soviet period, social, economic, political and cultural life in Ukraine had been controlled by the 'people of Moscow' through Communist Party structures and the KGB; however, in the conditions of the late 1980s, their previous monopoly on power was disintegrating. In a sense, Gorbachev himself contributed to this by allowing relatively competitive republican elections to the *Verkhovna Rada* (Supreme Soviet) quasi-parliament of Soviet Ukraine in March 1990 and a referendum on the future of the Union in March 1991 (to which were added two further referendums: one on Ukraine's sovereignty, organised by Kravchuk based on Ukraine's 16 July 1990 Declaration of Sovereignty, and another on independence, organised by the democratic opposition in the three Galician *oblast* councils).

Being simply 'people of Moscow' was insufficient for Ukrainian communists to remain in power. In addition, an ideological vacuum emerged when Marxism-Leninism could not offer reasonable prospects for overcoming the crisis in which Ukraine found itself as part of the Soviet Union. Therefore, 'Authority-seeking republican elites had to ground their appeals in the new set of myths and symbols' (Kuzio, 2000, p. 173). In turn, the non-communist opposition – dominated by the cultural intelligentsia, including veterans of the *Shestydesiatnyky* – lacked structures, organisational support, and broader support in society, thus it was too weak to come to power in the December 1991 presidential election (Kuzio, 2000, pp. 18–42).

The representatives of this opposition, however, had symbolic capital that could re-establish credibility for the discredited *nomenklatura* in the changing circumstances. This included the legacy of the struggle for national liberty (patriotism and nationalism), the Executed Renaissance and national communism. In these conditions, there was a revival of national communism within the ranks of the Communist Party in Ukraine, led by a western Ukrainian, Kravchuk, from the Volyn region, where the KPZU (Communist Party of Western Ukraine) had been powerful in the 1920s but had been eclipsed in the 1930s by Ukrainian nationalist groups. The national communism notion, however, 'no longer implied a commitment to the building of utopian goals in a national context. It simply referred to those members of the KPSS (Communist Party of the Soviet Union) who chose to pursue their goals in a specifically national context, and whose politics were based primarily in the defence of national interests, despite whatever ideological baggage they still carried with them' (Kuzio, 2000, p. 23). In other words, national communism – or 'sovereign communism' as it was called in the late 1980s – was a kind of survival strategy of a wing of the Soviet Ukrainian elites who jumped 'onto the opposition bandwagon' and 'created sufficient momentum towards independence' (Kuzio, 2000, p. 216).

Meanwhile, the ideas of Ukrainian sovereignty and independence were tempered in the discussions over the place of Ukraine and its culture between the 'Asian' space (i.e., Moscow) and 'psychological Europe'. It is no accident that Mykola Riabchuk (1991, p. 99) expressed the view that the democratic and freedom movement in Ukraine fought 'Russian etatism', which was the negation of 'civil society'. This is the reason why the well-known writer Ivan Drach strongly emphasised that 'we must follow the European path' (Riabczuk 1991, p. 101). It is worth noting that 'civil society' is just one of the basic conceptual categories of 'psychological Europe'. The intellectual climate of the Ukrainian national revival in the late 1980s and 1990s and its European context is well illustrated by Riabchuk's conclusion: 'it is difficult to imagine an educated Ukrainian who is in favour of independence and self-determination and against Europe and European democratic institutions' (Riabczuk, 1991, p. 103).

Obviously, the idea of 'Europeanness', which in the 1990s achieved popularity in Ukrainian discourse on Ukrainian identity, was ambiguous at a time when the EU had not yet begun enlargement to former communist countries and when Brussels was itself unclear whether Ukraine was European. The popular meaning of Europe that perpetuated itself in the general awareness has become a synonym for 'whatever is civilised, democratic, full of dignity and filled with the spirit of cooperation' with the West 'in political, economic and cultural matters' (Protsyk, 2004, p. 150). 'On a more thought-out, scientific level', Europeanness was understood as everything that is directly or indirectly connected with the roots of the civilisation of the Old Continent; that is, with 'Greek philosophy, Roman law, Christian morality, the Renaissance, Reformation, Enlightenment, and the ideology of the Risorgimento' (Protsyk, 2004, p. 150).

Post-Soviet Ukrainian *nomenklatura* elites understood the idea of 'Europe' in their own way. It was both a means to keep a resurgent Russia at a distance and a sphere of development, stability and tolerance rather than an assembly of sovereign national states (Wolczuk, 2000, pp. 687–688). The reasons for referring to national symbolism and mythology, including those connected with the conflict of 'the country' versus 'the people of Moscow', were purely pragmatic (Wolczuk, 2000, p. 689). This does not, however, change the fact that this 'founding' dispute between Ukrainian and Russian identities did not lose its significance and relevance.

Importantly, in Ukraine the 'we' versus the West antinomy never took root. Of Ukraine's six presidents, only Yanukovych could be classified as pro-Russian, and even he played with EU integration until the Kremlin convinced him otherwise. This permitted, on the one hand, an attitude of openness for Occidental influences and cultural inspirations in Ukrainian identity. It is worth recalling that even the Ukrainian version of Marxism-Leninism, as espoused by Khvylovy, was characteristically pro-European.

The tension between the 'country' and 'the people of Moscow' that dominated Russian-Ukrainian relations throughout the twentieth century became acutely apparent during the Orange Revolution, when the national democratic opposition achieved what they were unable to do in earlier presidential elections. Putin gave all round support to Yanukovych, leader of the powerful and rising Party of Regions, during the election campaign. As Peter Dickinson (2024) aptly noted, Putin's 'open and unapologetic attempt to interfere in Ukraine's internal affairs was widely interpreted as a grave insult and an indication of his contempt for Ukrainian statehood. This electrified public opinion and helped mobilise millions of previously apolitical Ukrainians'.

Scholars have debated whether the Orange or Euromaidan Revolutions signified the end of 'post-communism' and the 'post-Soviet era' in Ukraine, or whether, as Kuzio (2019) writes, it was the election of Volodymyr Zelenskyy in 2019. Whereas Kravchuk and Leonid Kuchma, who ruled Ukraine in 1991–2004, were clearly from the Soviet *nomenklatura*, Viktor Yushchenko, Petro Poroshenko and Zelenskyy, who were elected after the Orange Revolution in 2004, were not. The manifestation of the end of post-communism could be proscribed to the mass dismantling of Lenin monuments in Ukraine, but, alas, this took place at different times in Ukrainian regions. Then, the 2015 de-communisation laws, one of which decreed the removal of Soviet and communist monuments, plaques and toponyms, had the greatest impact, firstly in southeastern Ukraine, and secondly in some central areas (see Oliinyk and Kuzio, 2021). De-communisation after the Euromaidan Revolution was the culmination of a process of de-Sovietisation and de-Stalinisation that had been taking place since the late 1980s.

The best example of this is the KPU (Communist Party of Ukraine), which was revived and re-registered as a new party in 1993. The KPU programme advocated the restoration of the 'Soviet community' and appealed to some Ukrainians' Soviet nostalgia. For over a decade, the KPU was one of the main forces in Ukraine's political arena, until becoming eclipsed by, and a satellite of, the Party of Regions. In the 2002 parliamentary elections, almost a fifth of Ukrainians voted for the KPU, giving it the third largest faction in the 2002–2006 parliament. However, throughout the 2000s the KPU progressively lost voters to the Party of Regions, receiving only 3.66 per cent in 2006, 5.39 per cent a year later, and 13.18 per cent in 2012. However, after the Euromaidan Revolution, when anti-Russian sentiments were growing against pro-Russian forces, the KPU failed to cross the threshold to enter parliament and a year later was banned from participating in elections after refusing to remove its communist and Soviet symbols, which (together with Nazi symbols) are banned under Ukraine's de-communisation laws.

Russia's post-communism, on the other hand, never ended and, in fact, went into reverse during its re-Sovietisation and re-Stalinisation from the 2000s. There are two versions of Russia's post-communism. The first, which could be described as 'cavernicolous', is led by the Communist Party of the Russian Federation (KPRF) and its eternal leader, Gennadiy Zyuganov. The KPRF's discourse mixes traditional Marxist phraseology with Russian imperialist and Eurasianist myths. The KPRF stands together with Putin and the Kremlin on the cult of Stalin, the quasi-religious Great Patriotic War, and the necessity of war against 'Nazi' Ukraine. With such a programme and discourse, the Kremlin guarantees the KPRF a permanent place in the Russian political arena as a systemic opposition party with the stable support of a fifth of the electorate (alongside the Liberal Democratic Party of the Russian Federation, Just Russia Party, and New People Party). The former *Rodina* (Motherland) Party played a similar role in the 2000s (see Dollbaum and Kim, 2024).

The second version of Russian post-communism can be described as 'modernised' and is symbolised by Putin and his circle, whose post-communist discourse is built upon selected elements of contemporary concepts and theories, taken out of a broader context, such as Samuel P. Huntington's clash of civilisations, globalisation, and multiple modernities. History dominates this discourse. Putin and pro-Kremlin intellectuals, journalists and political technologists abuse history in a manner like how Stalin's USSR and the Nazis compiled dogmatic justifications for the physical annihilation of domestic (liberal opposition, anti-war activists) and external (Ukrainians who hold an identity distinct to Russians) enemies. The Kremlin's 'modernised' post-communism is built on historical determinism and anti-Westernism that eclectically synthesises Tsarist and White Russian émigré imperial nationalism with Soviet symbolic capital.

The consolidation of Putin's regime came about at a time when the share of intellectuals with academic degrees within the state's elites was in decline. During Yeltsin's presidency, they represented a little over half of the higher political elite, while this has declined to just a fifth during Putin's quarter of a century of direct and indirect rule (Koczetkow, 2015, p. 125). Characterising the political mentality of the Russian ruling elite, Oksana Gaman-Golutvina emphasised that 'the cult of force remains the dominant feature of the attitude of both the central and regional authorities, as well as society' (Koczetkow, 2015, p. 125).

The 'people of Moscow', personified by Putin and the post-communist Kremlin, began to resemble their earlier archetypes from the 1930s, when the Ukrainian cultural 'renaissance' was executed and the 'national communists' repressed. In fact, Putin was not so different to his predecessor Yeltsin, and communism was followed by imperial nationalism in Russia, with democratisation rather limited in its time frame to the first half of the 1990s. Russia and Ukraine diverged politically from the mid 1990s, and especially after 2000 under Putin. From 1990 to 1991, on the eve of the disintegration of the Soviet Union, most Russians (including Gorbachev and Yeltsin, as well as, of course, Putin) had difficulty accepting a fully independent Ukraine that was promoting a Ukrainian identity distinct from Russian and was seeking to leave the Kremlin's sphere of influence (whether the CIS, Russian World, or Eurasia) (see Chapter 6). Following the Orange Revolution, which we define as the first critical juncture in Russia's trajectory, 'Ukraine became Vladimir Putin's personal project' (Shevtsova, 2020, p. 139) and the growth of imperial nationalism over the next two decades especially targeted Ukraine as the 'lost younger brother' that needed to be returned to the Russian World. Putin's (2021) article 'On the Historical Unity of Russians and Ukrainians' is a programmatic manifesto of this Russian imperial nationalism.

Moreover, Russian post-communism, regardless of its version, is strongly attached to the myth of NATO as an existential threat to Russia; that this is a myth can be seen in the Kremlin's ignoring of Finland and Sweden joining NATO after the full-scale invasion. As Igor Gretskiy (2021) pointed out, 'Russian society entered the post-Soviet era with an outlook firmly fixed on the past and with a hardening anti-Western mood. As then Foreign Minister Andrey Kozyrev wrote in spring 1992, 'NATO is not Russia's adversary, but this view is not shared by Russian society and is totally alien to political and security elites'. Primakov, a former senior KGB officer and head of the SVR (Foreign Intelligence Service), wrote as Russian Foreign Minister that 'Public opinion in the Russian Federation has long been formed in the anti-NATO spirit, and it cannot change in an hour' (Erlanger, 1993). The questions scholars rarely ask is why Ukrainians, who were also brought up with anti-NATO propaganda, do not view the organisation in a negative manner and why Russia is so adamantly against Ukraine joining but not Finland, with whom it has a far longer border. NATO-phobia was a problem of 'public opinion' not only inherited from the Soviet Union but also framed and continued by Russia's post-Soviet leaders, who believed 'the West launched its war against Russian interests as long ago as the late 1990s, when NATO and the US orchestrated a democratic revolution in Serbia and supported an independent Kosovo' (Kuzio, 2017, pp. 2–3). As early as Putin's first year in office, the 'National Security Concept of the Russian Federation' defined NATO as a threat to Russia and its position in the world (Putin, 2000). All parties important for the Russian political system as well as public opinion agree in their hostility to NATO (see Levada Centre, 2022)

Five out of six Ukrainian presidents have supported NATO membership: Yanukovych was the only exception. Although NATO has promised Ukraine will 'one day' become a member since 2008, in fact two of its biggest members, the US (since 2009) and Germany, have blocked this. Popova and Shevel (2024, p. 140) wrote that 'Ukrainians themselves did not believe in the benefits of NATO membership in the 1990s and 2000s. While Kravchuk may have wanted a US nuclear umbrella and Yushchenko's administration actively sought NATO membership and advocated it abroad, at home barely a fifth of Ukrainians shared the goal throughout the 1990s and 2000s'. At the same time, however, opinion polls showed that respondents who saw NATO as a threat to Ukraine were in a minority, and their numbers had been declining long before the Euromaidan Revolution. In 2012, only a fifth of Ukrainians viewed NATO as a threat, while over half did not (Razumkov Centre, 2012, p. 75).

In July 2010, after the election of Yanukovych as president, the Ukrainian parliament adopted a new foreign policy doctrine that was one of several steps in line with pan-Russian identity demanded by Russian President Dmitri Medvedev a year earlier in his 'address' to President Yushchenko (see Kuzio, 2015, pp. 438–439): NATO membership was no longer a goal, and Ukraine's foreign policy was described as 'non-bloc'. NATO-Ukrainian cooperation nevertheless continued, but at a lower level than under Kuchma and Yushchenko. It is worth recalling that Ukraine's 'non-bloc' status did not prevent Russia's military aggression in 2014.

Russia's two invasions in 2014 and 2022 boosted Ukrainian support for NATO membership. Pro-Russian political forces were marginalised after 2014 and banned after 2022. This growth of pro-NATO sentiment did not push against NATO-phobia, which had never been widespread in Ukraine but had always influenced most Russians. The biggest remarkable change is how most Ukrainians living in the southeast of the country came to support NATO membership.

Diverging States and Political Systems: Democratic Ukraine and Authoritarian Russia

Popova and Shevel (2024, p. 58) assert that 'Russia and Ukraine started their journeys as independent states with nearly identical state institutions'. It seems, however, that this is not an entirely accurate diagnosis, as Russia and Ukraine did not assume independence from identical starting points. The Russian SFSR (Soviet Federative Socialist Republic) never declared independence from the USSR and was the only one of the fifteen Soviet republics to not possess republican institutions; the Soviet Union was, therefore, a 'Russocentric empire' (Brudny and Finkel, 2011, p. 818). The Soviet institutional order encouraged 'ethnic Russians to view the entire Soviet Union as their own nation-state. The policy was to deliberately blur Russian and Soviet identity' (Brudny and Finkel, 2011, p. 818).

Paradoxically, although Russians were the largest ethnic group in the Soviet Union, 'they could not claim any of the union republics as their own national home. Contrary to all other union republics, the RSFSR was not a republic *of* and *for* Russians, even though ethnic Russians constituted approximately 82 per cent of the republican population' (Brudny and Finkel, 2011, p. 818). Chapter 1 discusses how the Russian homeland was the Soviet Union, not the Russian SFSR. In late 1991, Yeltsin captured Soviet institutions in Moscow for the post-Soviet Russian state, and in subsequent years their imperial character was reconciled with the imperial nationalist identity of the Russian Federation.

Ukraine's Declaration of Independence on 24 August 1991 marked the beginning of a long process of state and nation-building, during which a kind of limbo existed between the 'non-state' that was the Ukrainian Soviet Socialist Republic and the new post-Soviet state per se, but the very definition of the latter requires, of course, clarification. According to Max Weber (1946, p. 2), a human community is one that successfully claims the monopoly of the legitimate use of physical force within a given territory. This conceptualisation of the state should be enriched with the historical sociology espoused by Charles Tilly to add the constitutive features of the state's 'centralisation and mutual coordination of organisational units'

(Wołek, 2012, p. 37). Only in such conditions can 'rulers make use of their power' (Wołek, 2012, p. 37). Moreover, according to institutional theory, the state 'is not only an order of public authority, depersonalised, different from the rulers and the ruled, but also relatively independent of society, having a certain amount of autonomy in action, not reducible to the interests occurring in society' (Wołek, 2012, p. 37).

The model of the state that emerged in post-Soviet Ukraine after 1991 was largely inadequate for the above definition of the state. It would indeed be difficult to reach any positive conclusions about the progress of state-building in post-Soviet Ukraine if it were assessed using criteria such as management efficiency, the ability to act for the common good, competence of the bureaucratic apparatus, rationality of structures, and broadly understood governability (see Kudelia, 2012; Gil, 2015; Olejarz and Stępniewski, 2016).

The Ukrainian state was 'weak', 'incomplete', 'failed', 'dysfunctional', and above all it seemed 'immobile'. That is, it gave the impression that no crisis, change on the political scene, or other stimulus could move the Ukrainian state towards positive change. 'Immobility' was 'a product of the many domestic constraints arising from Ukraine's path dependency following the centuries of Russian and decades of Soviet rule that produced the post-Soviet political culture that exists in independent Ukraine' (Kuzio, 2011, p. 89). As Artur Wołek (2012, p. 81) aptly noted, 'the uniqueness of creating a democratic state after communism' resulted from the fact that it was built on the ruins of the 'party-state'. Therefore, 'the process of separating the party and the state was long-lasting, and thanks to the communist apparatus, it left a permanent mark on the institutions of post-communist states' (Wołek, 2012, p. 81).

The moment the multidimensional transformation of the political system, social life, economy and state structures began can be described as the 'new political opening'. This new beginning was interrelated with a real consensus among the elites who initiated the process of change. Where 'democratic pacts of elites' arose (Fisun, 2010, p. 160), 'velvet revolutions' took place and the process of democratisation and building effective state structures began. The measure of effectiveness in this system was the ability to 'support the rule of law' and the resistance of these structures to pressure from various interest groups, such as oligarchs.

In the 1990s, the Russian and Ukrainian political systems became stuck in hybrid regimes lying between non-democracy and democracy, and between a lack of state structures and a strong, efficient state. At first glance in these countries, the 'initial political opening' after the fall of communism 'failed' (Herbut and Baluk, 2010, p. 12); in fact, however, it simply followed a different logic in Russia and Ukraine, where it was imposed by a consensus within the mainly *nomenklatura* elites.

Its aim was to appropriate the structures of the emerging post-communist state and to shape a regime that would provide a monopoly on access to 'rent-seeking', a consensus that was a 'neo-patrimonial elite pact' which sanctioned the use of administrative resources to achieve the political or economic goals of certain interest groups. In a neo-patrimonial elite pact, the efficiency of the state is largely focused on effectively securing 'rent-seeking' for informal, *nomenklatura*-backed oligarchic clans – not on the ability to formulate and implement public policy for the common good. This was clearly visible in the fact that privatisation created oligarchic clans. In the case of Ukraine, the problem of the effectiveness of the state and the way in which it did not function has dramatically revealed itself since the outbreak of the first armed conflict with Russia. The Ukrainian armed forces had been infiltrated by Russia and asset-stripped by the Party of Regions' Donetsk clan.

Efficiency, strength, and weakness at the state level can be assessed using three 'interdependent, irreducible elements'. First, this concerns 'the ability to manage resources in such a way that conscious collective choices regarding strategic directions of realisation of public goals are possible'. Second, 'effective management of human and material resources necessary for state activities' enables the achievement of public goals. Finally, the third criterion would be 'the ability to mobilise the consent of social forces in favour of achieving public goals' (Wołek, 2012, p. 16).

The Ukrainian state proved to be remarkably resistant to various crises. The Orange and Euromaidan Revolutions should have disrupted at least part of its structure, but this did not happen. It was only Russia's first invasion that proved to be a catalyst for changes in state-building in Ukraine, finally forcing the immobile Ukrainian state to implement the most basic assumptions of the Weberian definition of the state as 'a compulsory organisation with a territorial basis' that 'upholds the claim to the monopoly of the legitimate use of physical force in the enforcement of its order' (Weber, 1978, pp. 54–56).

The first and most important effect of the new stage in Ukrainian state-building was the reconstruction of its armed forces. The first months of the war in Donbas in 2014 'highlighted the Ukrainian army's weaknesses, as well as its total inability to implement its constitutional duties. This forced the government in Kyiv to take real action to clean up the country's armed forces' (Wilk, 2017, p. 5). Andrzej Wilk (2017, p. 6) noted that 'within a period of two years, in the relatively difficult situation in which the Ukrainian state found itself (economic collapse, entanglement in long-lasting positional warfare in the east of Ukraine), significant changes were made to the Ukrainian army to improve its condition and to make it better suited to current challenges', representing 'the first structural and organisational changes' in the Ukrainian army since 1992 (Wilk, 2017, p. 6). Military spending as a share of GDP doubled to 4 per cent (The Ukrainian Army, 2021). *The Economist* commented that 'Ukraine has 250,000 troops and a further 900,000 reserves. Some 300,000 of them have experience on the front line. The new soldiers are better trained. The West, at first reluctant to send Ukraine weaponry, is changing tack' (The Ukrainian army has got better at fighting Russian-backed separatists, 2021).

The state-building process is about not only the creation of institutional structures but also shaping relations between them and society. First, it is about public trust in state institutions, which has always been low in Ukraine, even following the Orange and Euromaidan Revolutions. Ukrainians traditionally declared a dramatically low level of trust in their state institutions. It was not until 2017 that the armed forces overtook the Church in public trust in Ukrainian state institutions (Razumkov Centre, 2022).

After Russia's full-scale invasion, there was another exception in positive public trust, namely the president. In 2019, Zelenskyy enjoyed the trust of about four-fifths of Ukrainians, a record for this institution (Kyiv International Institute of Sociological Studies, 2024). On the eve of Russia's full-scale invasion, most respondents declared they did not trust the head of state, but this had changed to 90 per cent expressing positive trust in him by summer 2022. All previous presidents of Ukraine had negative ratings. This example clearly shows that the state is not only structures; it is also patterns of behaviour within these structures. Zelenskyy's attitudes would become a certain turning point in the process of the transformation of the Ukrainian state.

The Kremlin's full-scale invasion and the way it is being conducted clearly show that the Russian state-building process has gone in a completely different direction. Russian state-building is neither directed at 'conscious collective choices regarding strategic directions for achieving public goals' nor striving for 'effective management of human resources' (Domanska, 2023, p.4). In Putin's Russia, 'the ability to mobilise the consent of social forces in order to achieve public goals' has replaced the ability to enforce obedience through terror while the 'glorification of violence as an attribute of state sovereignty' is boosted by a 'cult of death, combined with elements of the cult of personality of Putin' (Domańska, 2023, p. 4). The process of 'criminalisation' of the Russian state has led to 'the intensified erosion of the state's institutional system and the semblance of legalism', which have been replaced by 'the growing privatisation of the state by the ruling elite' (Domańska, 2023, p. 4).

Relations between the Russian state and society transitioned 'from an authoritarian "social contract" based on passive support for the authorities to a dictatorship that implies mobilisation for, and complicity in, military aggression and war crimes' (Domańska, 2023, p. 3). Monthly mobilisations of cannon fodder for the war against Ukraine – reaching over one million casualties by May 2025 – and Yevgeny Prigozhin's June 2023 mutiny have not shaken the stability of the regime, with public support for Putin remaining high.

Russia and Ukraine: Political Transition

The differences between the political systems in Russia and Ukraine have been growing since the 1990s. Popova and Shevel (2024) highlighted the key moments that show these differences. Both Yeltsin in Russia and Kravchuk in Ukraine experienced conflict with their parliaments over the division of power. However, the outcomes of these conflicts were completely different. In Russia, 'at Yeltsin's orders, the Army dispersed protesters by force and opened fire on the parliament building' (Popova and Shevel, 2024, p. 61). The leaders of the parliamentary anti-presidential opposition were arrested and imprisoned, whereas in Ukraine a similar clash between president and parliament led to 'all sides making compromises', with an agreement to hold preterm presidential and parliamentary elections in 1994. Kravchuk accepted his defeat to Kuchma in presidential elections (Popova and Shevel, 2024, p. 62). Ukraine continued to change its president after holding competitive elections, which 'Russia has not had happen to this day' (Popova and Shevel, 2024, p. 63). At the same time, however, it would be an exaggeration to say, as do Popova and Shevel (2024), that the presidential elections in 1994 led to a 'turnover in power'. Competition between Kravchuk and Kuchma primarily took place during the election campaign, and after the elections they largely cooperated, albeit through different political forces. Thus, it is difficult to speak of a real 'turnover in power'.

To understand the political and social transformation in Ukraine, as well as the differences between the political systems and social orders that have been formed since 1991 in Ukraine and Russia, we should consider their specificity by going beyond a liberal democratic framework. Such a framework 'implicitly assumes the structure and logic of Western-type polities, that is, that the regimes the language is used for do share the essential features, the pattern of elements and internal dynamics, of liberal democracies' (Magyar and Madlovics, 2020, p. 1). Indeed, in 'Western-type polities' the defeat of an incumbent president means a turnover in power; however, in the case of Ukraine, this is not so obvious because it represents a different 'post-Soviet type of polity' that is best understood through the concept of 'patronalism'.

Henry Hale (2015, p. 61) describes patronalism as 'a social equilibrium whereby individuals organise their political and economic pursuits more around the personalised exchange of concrete rewards and punishments than around abstract impersonal principles', upon which the liberal democratic order is based. Under patronalism this

> can be conceived of as a kind of collective action problem, a vicious cycle whereby individuals understand politics as an arena of personal wealth redistribution and targeted coercion and therefore reproduce these very practices themselves for fear of being the "sucker," the feckless soul who acts on principle but only succeeds in impoverishing their family, marginalising themself, and accomplishing nothing (Hale, 2015, p. 61).

Formal institutions and rules – like elections and constitutions, as well as political crises including 'revolutions' in countries with patronalism – 'are different than they are widely assumed to be in the West' because politics in societies with patronalism 'revolves chiefly around personalised relationships joining extended networks of patrons and clients, and political struggle tends to take the form of competition among different patron client networks' (Hale, 2015, p. 21). Thus, although concepts and institutions known from liberal democratic systems are imported into the reality of societies with patronalism, they are rather a reflection of the changing relations between patronal networks and their 'power-related activities', rather than what is usually attributed to them in the West (Hale, 2015, p. 64).

In light of these assumptions, it becomes clear that when analysing transformations in 'post-Soviet type polities', we need to go beyond the common and overly simplified model of autocracy-democracy. Much more useful for this purpose is 'the conceptual space of regimes' proposed by Bálint Magyar and Bálint Madlovics (2020, p. 15). In this approach, the evolution of the political system takes place in a trajectory between 'patronal autocracy' – 'patronal democracy' – 'liberal democracy'.

Vladimir Dubrovskiy (2023, p. 55) pointed out that 'patronalism is one of the forms of a limited-access social order'. Within such a kind of social order, 'the problem of violence' is solved 'by granting political elites privileged control over parts of the economy, each getting some share of the rents'. At the opposite pole is an open access social order that 'control[s] the problem of violence through open access and competition' (Dubrovskiy, 2023, p. 55).

A major transformative change in Ukraine took place during the Orange Revolution (Popova and Shevel, 2024, p. 57), when Ukraine's increasingly democratic political system came to diverge from the growing authoritarianism and imperial nationalism in Russia's regime. From 2004, Ukraine's presidents were post-communist and arguably from 2019 post-Soviet (Kuzio, 2019). The Orange Revolution showed that even in a hybrid political system with patronalism, or Steven Levitsky and Lucan Way's (2020) competitive authoritarianism, presidents can lose control over the results of elections, which retain real competition and lead to a 'turnover in power'.

Importantly, for the purposes of the analysis of the four roots of Russia's full-scale invasion, the Orange Revolution also showed that the status of the 'people of Moscow' was no longer a factor that decided important questions in the Ukrainian political system. In the 2004 elections, Putin took patronage over Yanukovych's candidacy, providing him with political technologists and manipulation of voters' consciousness, and playing on anti-American phobias and stereotypes about 'anti-Russian, nationalist' Western Ukrainians. However, the dirty tactics which worked in Russia failed to work in Ukraine, proving the correctness of the title of Kuchma's book *Russia is Not Ukraine*, which had been published a year earlier. After his defeat in the 2004 presidential elections, Yanukovych's oligarch supporters in the Party of Regions agreed with Kuchma and exchanged Russian political technologists for Americans. In preparation for the 2006 parliamentary elections, the Party of Regions hired the American lobbyist and political consultant Paul Manafort, who modernised and Westernised Yanukovych's image from that of looking like a discotheque bouncer to a businessperson and professional political leader. The Orange Revolution was the first signal the Kremlin was losing the influence of Russian soft power within the Ukrainian political system. Indeed, the Orange Revolution 'triggered fears in Putin's Russia, which accelerated the descent into authoritarianism and consolidation of Russia's imperial vision', with their political systems increasingly becoming different (Popova and Shevel, 2024, p. 57).

Did the election of Yushchenko 'put Ukraine on a democratic and pro-European path'? Popova and Shevel (2024, p. 73) believe that after the Orange Revolution, 'Ukraine made strides toward democratic consolidation'. The Orange Revolution was an example of 'deliberative democracy', namely 'a public debate about the common good, dialogue and compromise shaping both the actions and preferences of political actors' (Popova and Shevel, 2024, p. 74). Despite the differences, Ukraine's political system was like Russia's in that the political elites remained alienated from their societies. As noted earlier, public trust in Ukrainian leaders and state institutions only took shape from 2019; perhaps frameworks discussing Ukraine's political system should differentiate between the end of post-communism in 2004 and the finale of post-Sovietism fifteen years later?

In 2004, Tatiana Zaslavskaya (2004, pp. 294–295), when writing about the Russian political system, concluded that ruling elites created the rules of the game, which ensured a lack of scrutiny from society and lack of responsibility towards it. The result was a deepening mutual alienation between the authorities and society that was manifested, on the one hand, in the indifference of the authorities to the misfortunes of the nation, and, on the other, in the near complete distrust of the nation towards the representatives and institutions of power. The situation in Ukraine was similar, and the Orange Revolution by itself did not fundamentally change this. Popova and Shevel (2024, p. 76) write that the events of 2004–2005 'entrenched' basic democratic institutions like 'free elections, free media, civil society participation'. However, these liberal-democratic concepts are based on 'formal legal and constitutional norms, rational-legal actions, and the language of bureaucratic rationality' (Fisun, 2022, p. VIII). These concepts change slightly when applied to post-Soviet patronalist regimes, which are determined not by the will and expectations of voters but by their relations with patronal networks.

After the Orange Revolution, Ukraine held free elections within a system of 'feckless pluralism'. As Thomas Carothers (2002, p. 10) pointed out, there are 'significant amounts of political freedom, regular elections, and alternation of power between genuinely different political groupings' under such conditions. However, at the same time 'democracy remains shallow and troubled' because 'the alternation of power seems only to trade the country's problems back and forth from one hapless side to the other. Political elites from all the major parties are widely perceived as corrupt, self-interested, dishonest, and not serious about working for their country' (Carothers, 2002, p. 10).

Carothers' (2002) analysis fits Ukraine's case perfectly, both before and after the Orange Revolution. The fundamental difference in elections between Ukraine after 2004 and Russia was that, in the case of the former their outcome was not predetermined, as they were in Russia. At the same time, the outcome in Ukraine was primarily about a victory or defeat of oligarchic networks (or groups of such networks), not of the Ukrainians who cast their votes. Popova and Shevel (2024, p. 76) noted that 'the main achievement of the Orange Revolution was the systemic transformation of the rules of the game and, thus, the political regime'. It should be remembered, however, that the formal rules were the most important change that resulted from the compromise of constitutional reform reached during the Orange Revolution, which changed the political regime from presidential to parliamentary. As a result, parliament, rather than the president himself, gained a decisive influence on the process of forming the government through a majority coalition. This compromise undoubtedly protected the Ukrainian political system from drifting towards authoritarianism; it is no coincidence that post-communist states with democracies have parliamentary systems and are members of the EU, while Russian and Eurasian authoritarian regimes are presidential regimes. In 2006, 2007 and 2019, Ukraine's parliamentary elections were held using a proportional system, while in 2012, 2014 and 2019 a mixed system was used where half of the seats were elected proportionally by party lists, and half through first-past-the-post single mandate constituencies.

Between the Orange and Euromaidan Revolutions, parliamentary elections in Russia were also held according to a proportional system. However, unlike in Ukraine, the *Yedinaia Rossiia* (United Russia) Party, Putin's party of power, won majorities which created conditions for the consolidation of Putin's patronal authoritarian regime. Thus, similar formal election rules in Russia and Ukraine led to completely different outcomes because of different patronal networks throughout the post-Soviet era. After the Orange Revolution in Ukraine, competitive authoritarianism (Levitsky and Way, 2020) provided for a pluralistic parliamentary arena and the evolution of Ukraine's political system towards patronal democracy. In Russia, on the other hand, the consolidation of a patronal authoritarian regime took place where the chief patron – Putin – controlled the structures of state power and the single pyramid of oligarchic networks.

Another turning point in the transformation of the Ukrainian political system was the Euromaidan Revolution. Mass protests were a public response to four years of democratic backsliding, high levels of corruption, and attempts to reverse democratisation and European integration in 2013 (Popova and Shevel, 2024, p. 80). Three factors shaped the Euromaidan Revolution. The first was Yanukovych, who began to act in a manner similar to that found in Putin's Russia. After the Orange Revolution, this way of behaving was 'considered rather alien' in Ukraine (Dubrovskiy, 2023, p. 76). Secondly, using the political power he had gained, Yanukovych attempted to build a patronal network independent of the Donetsk clan, but this would prove to be difficult in the relatively weak Ukrainian state. Moreover, as Vladimir Dubrovskiy (2023, p. 77) noted, 'unlike in Russia, where drillable hydrocarbons strongly dominate the economy over all other rent sources, rents of mutually comparable magnitudes can be found in many different sectors in Ukraine, including but not limited to power generation and distribution, natural gas drilling and trading, ferrous ore mining and processing, agriculture (which itself is diverse), and more'. Thus, relatively favourable conditions remained in Ukraine for oligarchic pluralism.

The third factor shaping the Euromaidan Revolution could be considered the beginning of the process of transition from limited access towards an open access social order. Orange Revolution protests in defence of free and fair presidential elections 'served as a national awakening, establishing Ukraine's democratic credentials and setting the country on a path that diverged sharply from the increasing authoritarianism of Vladimir Putin's Russia' (Dickinson, 2020). As a result, a new agent appeared in the game of Ukrainian power politics: civil society. Yanukovych unintentionally reactivated Ukraine's civil society when he refused to sign an Association Agreement with the EU in November 2013, and two months later the Party of Regions-KPU parliamentary coalition adopted anti-protest laws that became known as the 'dictatorship laws', or what Timothy Snyder (2014) aptly classified as 'a rather sad imitation of Russia'.

The Orange and Euromaidan Revolutions were the first real 'turnovers in power'. Paul D'Anieri (2023b, p. 6) aptly pointed out that participants in these transformative revolutions adopted 'procedures that were entirely improvised', and which were 'deviations from established rules'. The outcomes of these activities (repeat of the second round of the presidential elections in 2004, ousting of Yanukovych in 2014) 'were widely seen as legitimate, while the formal procedures that had previously been enacted were not' (D'Anieri, 2023b, p. 6). Trying to explain this peculiar paradox, D'Anieri (2023b, p. 8) came to the conclusion that 'people have substantive notions of democracy along with procedural notions, and that when democratic procedures appear to be subverted (…) substantive notions of democracy, which can be attributed to intuitive or commonsensical notions of fairness, and which focus on outcomes as well as processes, can outweigh procedural notions'.

During the Orange Revolution, 'Ukrainians appeared to believe' that if the rules are technically followed but their intent is subverted, the results are not fully legitimate and do not have to be followed' (D'Anieri, 2023b, p. 7). Subsequently in Ukraine, 'intuitive or commonsensical notions of fairness' gained systemic significance. The case of the Orange and Euromaidan Revolutions 'shows that for elections to convey legitimacy, they must be seen as free and fair, not as shams' (D'Anieri, 2023b, p. 23). But for this to become possible, civil society had to take on the same systemic significance that it did in Ukraine. This was an important step on the way to an open-access social order and liberal democracy. Of course, the resistance of patronal elites remained an obstacle to the further evolution of Ukraine's political system. As Yuriy Matsiyevsky (2018, p. 354) noted, 'the circulation of elites in Ukraine has never produced a genuine renewal: neither in 1991, nor in 2004, nor in 2014, when entrenched rent-seekers were replaced by true reformers'.

One of the key challenges on the way to an open-access social order and a liberal model of democracy was reform of electoral law. In 2012 and 2014, parliamentary elections were held using a mixed system where half of the seats were elected proportionally with closed electoral lists, and half by voting in single-member constituencies. These rules effectively preserved the dominance of patronal networks over the Ukrainian parliament. In 2012, the election system had been designed by the Party of Regions and its communist allies to preserve their dominance in parliament. In 2014, preterm elections were held quickly during Russia's first invasion, after which Ukrainian democratic forces became aware of the need to change the election law to a fully proportional electoral law with open party lists. This electoral reform was adopted only after the 2019 parliamentary elections (Opora, 2021). Unfortunately, the introduction of martial law after Russia's full-scale invasion has prevented the holding of elections using the new electoral legislation.

Meanwhile, in Russia, especially after Putin's return to the presidency in 2012, the consolidation of patronal authoritarianism continued to consolidate. As we have argued elsewhere in this book, a fundamental transformation took place after 2020, when the Russian constitution was changed to permit the president to remain in power until 2036, in effect indefinitely. With extensive political repression, including the growth of the number of political prisoners to numbers greater than in post-Stalin USSR (see Reznikova and Korostelev, 2024), the murder of opposition leader Alexei

Navalny in prison, and closure of all independent media outlets, Russia transitioned from collective leadership in a patronal authoritarian system to one-man rule in a dictatorship. After nearly two decades of a cult of war in Russia, Putin's regime's war against internal and external enemies has targeted all those opposed to the Kremlin's imperial nationalism at home, in Ukraine and in the West.

Meanwhile, full-scale war has placed Ukraine on a trajectory that diverges even further from Putin's Russia. The war has greatly expanded Ukraine's volunteer, civil society, and small business sector. The full-scale war is continuing the de-oligarchisation of Ukraine that began in 2014, when the Party of Regions, Ukraine's only political machine, imploded. Oligarchs are no longer as powerful, and most have divested their media assets (see Skorkin, 2022; Siedin, 2024). Igor Kolomoysky, who was key to bringing Zelenskyy to power in 2019, is awaiting trial from a jail cell. Rinat Akhmetov has lost billions of dollars from the devastation in his home region of the Donbas, while other oligarchs, such as Viktor Pinchuk, have gone AWOL. In June 2023, the European Commission recommended the European Council grant Ukraine candidate status for accession to the EU,[3] a step strongly backed by the European Parliament. Ukraine's path to EU membership will be long and difficult.

Conclusions

The social and political changes in both Russia and Ukraine since the disintegration of the Soviet Union can be reconstructed using the quadruple transition framework. In Russia, an important component of the state-building process was the capture of the central Soviet structures that provided the institutional background for the development of an eclectic post-Soviet form of Russian imperial nationalism from the very beginning of its transition. As discussed in Chapter 1, Russia's post-Soviet nation-building process inherited an identity bigger than the Russian Federation, which – depending on the purpose and situation – viewed 'Russia' either as the former Soviet Union, the Tsarist Empire, the CIS, Eurasia, Alexander Solzhenitsyn's Russian Union, or Putin's and Patriarch Kirill's Russian World. The post-imperial civic *Rossiiskii* (Russian) identity proved to be weak as the new Russia was dominated far more by imperial nationalism than by democratic impulses. *Russkii* (which is also translated as 'Russian')

---

[3] https://neighbourhood-enlargement.ec.europa.eu/european-neighbourhood-policy/countries-region/ukraine_en

was used, albeit in different ways, as either referring to ethnic Russians or the pan-Russian people of Great, Little, and White Russians; indeed, since the revival of the use of *triune* (tripartite), *the term Russkii* has been in vogue. The Kremlin promoted a third identity from 2012 of Russia lying at the centre of a 'state-civilisation'. Both the pan-Russian *triune* and 'state-civilisation' identities had none of the fixed borders commonly found with nation-states. Russia's eclectic imperial nationalism combines the symbolic capital of Soviet totalitarianism with the imperial legacy of pre-revolutionary Russia. The latter was kept alive by White Russian émigrés, whose legacies were brought back to Russia from the mid-2000s and promoted by the state. Under Putin, as Chapter 9 shows, Russian imperial nationalism has expanded its core belief of Russia possessing a 'special historical mission' (Panov, 2010, p. 92). Imperial nationalism came to increasingly dominate Russia as it transitioned from authoritarianism to a dictatorship at war with the Russian people, Ukraine, and the West.

In the case of Ukraine, state-building was bottom up rather than – as in Russia – top down, aiming to transform the inherited quasi-state structures of Soviet Ukraine into institutions required for an independent state. Ukraine inherited Ukrainian and pan-Russian identities, which competed, at times ferociously, until the Euromaidan Revolution, after which the former became hegemonic and the latter became marginalised (see Kuzio, 2024). Ukrainian identity was strongest in western Ukraine and Kyiv, and after 2014 and especially since 2022 – it has spread to and has come to dominate southeast Ukraine.

The identity of Ukrainians after the beginning of the nation-building process in the nineteenth century was most developed in western Ukraine, which was the least Russified and Sovietised, and which possesses deep traditions of fighting for an independent Ukrainian state. This was one major reason why Russian imperial nationalists never included western Ukraine within the Russian World. If the Kremlin had been able to influence western Ukraine, it could have 'set the framework of Ukrainian identity, language, and memory politics as well as controlled its geopolitical orientation and foreign economic policy' (Popova and Shevel, 2024, p. 81). However, this was a myth believed by Russian imperial nationalists, namely that Ukrainian patriots and nationalists only existed in western Ukraine, when in fact Presidents Kuchma, Yushchenko, and Zelenskyy, acting head of state Oleksandr Turchynov, and Prime Minister Yulia Tymoshenko were from Dnipropetrovsk and Sumy *oblasts* in eastern Ukraine. Ukrainian identity was espoused by five of Ukraine's six presidents, with four of the five from southeastern Ukraine – two from

Dnipropetrovsk (Kuchma, Zelenskyy), one from Sumy (Yushchenko) and one from Odesa (Poroshenko). Ukraine has only elected one president from western Ukraine – Kravchuk.

The Kremlin never could accept that Ukraine was not Russia, as Kuchma wrote, but was also not Belarus. Lukashenka has ruled Belarus since 1994, and his Soviet Belarusian identity was dominant until 2020, when fraudulent presidential elections mobilised mass protests. Ukraine's pro-Russian camp was weaker and influential mainly in Crimea and the Donbas. Russia's 'special military operation' failed because Ukrainians from all parts of the country, and perhaps especially those from central and southeastern Ukraine, viewed the Russian army as occupiers, not liberators. Ukrainian identity had been growing since the Orange Revolution in conditions of pluralism, free elections, free media, and vibrant civil society values. The language spoken by Ukrainians was not central in deciding whether they were patriots of Ukraine or Little Russian supporters of the Russian World.

The introduction of elements of Western political culture in Russia and Ukraine's post-Soviet transition, such as elections, free media, a market economy, and private property, brought different results in Russia and Ukraine. Initially, in both cases they served as a facade under the cover of which a similar model of a patronal society emerged. In Russia, however, from the beginning, its transition moved towards patronal authoritarianism and imperial nationalism. Putin's re-Sovietisation and re-Stalinisation of Russia have maintained Russians as Soviet subjects. Ukraine's transition has proved to be very different, with the Orange and Euromaidan Revolutions, de-Sovietisation, de-Stalinisation, and de-communisation transforming Ukrainians from Soviet subjects into Ukrainian and European citizens and making Ukrainian identity hegemonic. In the absence of elections that are not permitted under martial law, Russia's full-scale invasion has deepened Ukraine's democratisation (see Nations in Transit Ukraine, 2024), improved Ukrainian trust in state institutions, led to de-oligarchisation, and placed Ukraine on the path to EU membership.

References

D'Anieri, P. (2023a). *Ukraine and Russia: From Civilized Divorce to Uncivil War.* Cambridge: Cambridge University Press.

D'Anieri, P. (2023b), 'Elections, Succession, and Legitimacy in Ukraine', *Communist and Post-Communist Studies*, 57 (4): 6–27.

Brudny, Y. and Finkel, E. (2011). 'Why Ukraine Is Not Russia: Hegemonic National Identity and Democracy in Russia and Ukraine', *East European Politics and Societies*, 25 (4): 813–833.

Carothers, T. (2002). 'The End of The Transition Paradigm', *Journal of Democracy*, 13 (1): 5–21.

Dickinson, P. (2020). 'How Ukraine's Orange Revolution Shaped Twenty-First Century Geopolitics', *Atlantic Council of the US*, 22 November. www.atlanticcouncil.org/blogs/ukrainealert/how-ukraines-orange-revolution-shaped-twenty-first-century-geopolitics/

Dickinson, P. (2024). 'Putin's Ukraine Obsession Began 20 Years Ago with the Orange Revolution', *Atlantic Council of the US*, 26 November. www.atlanticcouncil.org/blogs/ukrainealert/putins-ukraine-obsession-began-20-years-ago-with-the-orange-revolution/

Dollbaum, J. and Kim, S. (2024). 'Going Jingo: A Classification of the Wartime Positions of Russia's "systemic opposition" Parties', *Post-Soviet Affairs*, 40 (3): 222–241.

Domańska, M. (2023). 'Putin's Neo-totalitarian Project: The Current Political Situation in Russia', Centre for Eastern Studies, 17 February. www.osw.waw.pl/en/publikacje/osw-commentary/2023-02-17/putins-neo-totalitarian-project-current-political-situation

Doroshko, M. (2008). *Nomenklatura: kerivna verkhivka Radianskoii Ukraiiny (1918–1938)*. Kyiv: Nika-Tsentr.

Dubrovskiy, V. (2023). 'Patronalism and Limited Access Social Order: The Case of Ukraine' In: B. Madlovics and B. Magyar (eds.), *Ukraine's Patronal Democracy and the Russian Invasion*. Budapest-Vienna-New York: CEU Press: 55–90.

Dzyuba, I. (2005). *Internatsionalizm chy rusyfikatsiia?* Kyiv: Vydavnychyi Dim 'KM Akademiia'.

Erlanger, S. (1993). 'Russia Warns NATO on Expanding East', *New York Times*, 26 November. www.nytimes.com/1993/11/26/world/russia-warns-nato-on-expanding-east.html

Fisun, O. (2010). 'K pieriesmyslieniiu postosovietskoi politiki: nieopatrimonialnaia interprietatsiia', *Politicheskaia kontsieptologiia*, 4: 158–187.

Fisun, O. (2022), 'Foreword' In: B. Magyar and B. Madlovics (eds.), *A Concise Field Guide to Post-Communist Regimes*. Budapest-Vienna-New York: VII-IX.

Gil, G. (2015). 'Doubletake: Is Ukraine a Failed State?', *New Eastern Europe*, 3–4: 97–103.

Gretskiy, I. (2021). 'Could the West Have Saved Russia from Itself?' *Riddle Russia*, 12 May. https://ridl.io/could-the-west-have-saved-russia-from-itself/

Hale, H. (2015). *Patronal Politics: Eurasian Regime Dynamics in Comparative Perspective*. New York: Cambridge University Press.

Herbut, R. and Baluk, W. (2010). *Transformacja systemów politycznych państw obszaru byłego Związku Sowieckiego*. Wrocław: Wydawnictwo Uniwersytetu Wrocławskiego.

Hnatiuk, A. (2003). *Pożegnanie z imperium. Ukraińskie dyskusje o tożsamości*. Lublin: UMCS.

Hrycak, J. (2000). *Historia Ukrainy: 1772–1999*. Lublin: Instytut Europy Środkowo-Wschodniej.
Khvylovy, M. (1996). 'Ukraiyna chy Malorosiia?' In: O. I. Semkiv (ed.), *Politologiia: Kinets XIX-persha polovyna XX st. Khrestomatiia*. Lviv: Vydavnytstvo Svit: 637–649.
Koczetkow, A. (2015). 'Rosyjska elita: historia i współczesność', *Politeja*, 7 (34/2): 117–129.
Kudelia, S. (2012). 'The Sources of Continuity and Change of Ukraine's Incomplete State', *Communist and Post-Communist Studies*, 45 (3–4): 417–428.
Kulchytskyy, S. V. (2004). 'Narodzhennia radianskoho ladu' In: V. A. Hrynevych, V. M. Danylenko, S. V. Kulchytskyy and O. E. Lysenko (eds.), *Ukraina i Rosiia v istorychnii retrospektyvi: Radianskyi projekt dlia Ukraiiny*. Kyiv: Naukowa Dumka: 72–122.
Kuzio, T. (2000). *Ukraine: Perestroika to Independence*, 2nd edn. London: Macmillan Press.
Kuzio, T. (2001). 'Transition in Post-Communist States: Triple or Quadruple?' *Politics*, 21 (3): 168–177.
Kuzio, T. (2011). 'Political Culture and Democracy. Ukraine as an Immobile State', *East European Politics and Societies*, 25 (1): 88–113.
Kuzio, T. (2015). *Ukraine: Democratization, Corruption, and the New Russian Imperialism*. Santa Barbara, CA: Praeger.
Kuzio, T. (2017). *Putin's War Against Ukraine: Revolution, Nationalism, and Crime*. Toronto: Chair of Ukrainian Studies.
Kuzio, T. (2019). 'The End of Ukraine's Post-Soviet Era', *New Eastern Europe*, 13 August. https://neweasterneurope.eu/2019/08/13/the-end-of-ukraines-post-soviet-era/
Kuzio, T. (2024). 'Ukrainian versus Pan-Russian Identities: The Roots of Russia's Invasion of Ukraine', *Studies in Ethnicities and Nationalism*, 24 (3): 233–402.
Kyiv International Institute of Sociological Studies. (2024). '5-richchia prezydentstva Volodymyra Zelenskoho', 7 June. www.kiis.com.ua/?lang=ukr&cat=reports&id=1413&page=1
Levada Centre. (2022). 'Rossiia i NATO', 6 June. www.levada.ru/2022/06/06/rossiya-i-nato-2/
Levitsky, S. and Way, L. (2020). 'The New Competitive Authoritarianism', *Journal of Democracy*, 31 (1): 51–65.
Mace, J. (1983). *Communism and the Dilemmas of National Liberation: National Communism in Soviet Ukraine 1918–1933*. Cambridge, MA: Harvard University Press.
Magyar, B. and Madlovics, B. (2020). *The Anatomy of Post-Communist Regimes: A Conceptual Framework*. Budapest-New York: CEU Press.
Matsiyevsky, Y. (2018). 'Revolution without Regime Change: The Evidence from the Post-Euromaidan Ukraine', *Communist and Post-Communist Studies*, 51 (4): 349–359.
Mokry, W. (1993). 'Polityczny wymiar "Rozstrzelanego Odrodzenia" na Ukrainie' In: M. Pułaski (ed.), *Ukraińska myśl polityczna w XX wieku*. Kraków: Wydawnictwo Uniwersytetu Jagiellońskiego: 105–113.

Nations in Transit Ukraine. (2024). Washington, DC: Freedom House. https://freedomhouse.org/country/ukraine/nations-transit/2024

Olejarz, T. and Stępniewski, T. (2016). 'Zjawisko dysfunkcji państwa na przykładzie Ukrainy– analiza problemowa', *Politeja*, 41: 353–377.

Oliinyk, A. and Kuzio, T. (2021). 'The Euromaidan Revolution of Dignity, Reforms and De-Communisation in Ukraine', *Europe-Asia Studies*, 73 (5): 807–836.

Opora. (2021). 'Vyborcha reforma: shliakh dovzhynoiu v desiatylittia', 23 April. www.oporaua.org/vybory/viborcha-reforma-shliakh-dovzhinoiu-v-desiatilittia-23025

Panov, P. (2010). 'Nation-building in Post-Soviet Russia: What Kind of Nationalism Is Produced by the Kremlin?' *Journal of Eurasian Studies*, 1: 85–94.

Popova, M. and Shevel, O. (2024). *Russia and Ukraine: Entangled Histories, Diverging States*. Cambridge: Polity Press.

Protsyk, A. (2004). '"Yevropeiskist" yak chynnyk identychnosti' In: V. Isaiiv (ed.), *Ukraiinske suspilstvo na shliakhu peretvoren: zakhidna interpretatsiia*. Kyiv: KM Akademiia: 149–154.

Putin, V. (2000). 'O Kontseptsii natsionanoi bezopasnosti Rossiiskoi Fiedeieratsii', Decree 24, 10 January. www.consultant.ru/document/cons_doc_LAW_25677/0841190fb523698c7094446612ad818ef663d032/

Putin, V. (2021). 'Pro istorychnu yednist rosiyan ta ukrayinciv', 12 July. http://en.kremlin.ru/events/president/news/66181

Razumkov Centre. (2012). *Natsionalna Bezpeka i Oborona*, 2–3. https://razumkov.org.ua/uploads/journal/ukr/NSD131-132_2012_ukr.pdf

Razumkov Centre. (2022). 'Otsinka Hromadianamy Sytuatsii v Krayini,' 28 October. https://razumkov.org.ua/napriamky/sotsiologichni-doslidzhennia/otsinka-gromadianamy-sytuatsii-v-kraini-dovira-do-sotsialnykh-instytutiv-politykoideologichni-oriientatsii-gromadian-ukrainy-v-umovakh-rosiiskoi-agresii-veresen-zhovten-2022r

Reznikova, E. and Korostelev, A. (2024). 'A Study into Repression under Putin', *Proiekt*, 22 February. www.proekt.media/en/guide-en/repressions-in-russia-study/

Riabchuk, M. (1991). 'Społeczeństwo obywatelskie i emancypacja narodowa', *Zustriczi*, 1 (7): 96–106.

Shevtsova, L. (2020). 'Russia's Ukraine Obsession', *Journal of Democracy*, 31 (1): 138–147.

Shkandrii, M. (2006). *Modernisty, marksysty i natsiia: Ukraiinska literatura dyskusiia 1920–kh rokiv*. Kyiv: Nika-Tsentr.

Siedin, O. (2024). 'The Collapse of Ukraine's Oligarchy in Ten Years of War', *Focus Ukraine, Kennan Institute*, 14 March. www.wilsoncenter.org/blog-post/collapse-ukraines-oligarchy-ten-years-war

Skorkin, K. (2022). 'Ukraine's Oligarchs Are a Dying Breed. The Country Will Never Be the Same', *Carnegie Politika*, 14 September. https://carnegieendowment.org/russia-eurasia/politika/2022/09/ukraines-oligarchs-are-a-dying-breed-the-country-will-never-be-the-same?lang=en

Snyder, T. (2014), 'Ukraine: The New Dictatorship', *New York Review of Books*, 18 January. www.nybooks.com/online/2014/01/18/ukraine-new-dictatorship/?insrc=wbll

Staniszkis, J. (2005). *Postkomunizm. Próba opisu*. Gdańsk: słowo/obraz/ terytoria.

Stryjek, T. (2000). *Ukraińska idea narodowa okresu międzywojennego*. Wrocław: Funna.

Subtelny, O. (1992). *Ukrayina. Istoriya*. Kyiv: Lybid.

Szporluk, R. (2003). *Imperium, komunizm, narody: Wybór esejów*. Kraków: Arcana.

The Ukrainian Army has Got Better at Fighting Russian-backed Separatists. (2021). *The Economist*, 23 November. www.economist.com/europe/the-ukrainian-army-has-got-better-at-fighting-russian-backed-separatists/21806546

Weber, M. (1946). *Politics as Vocation*. New York: Oxford University Press. https://archive.org/details/weber_max_1864_1920_politics_as_a_vocation/page/n1/mode/2up?view=theater

Weber, M. (1978). *Economy and Society*. Berkeley: University of California Press. https://archive.org/details/weber_max_1864_1920_politics_as_a_vocation/page/n1/mode/2up?view=theater

Wilk, A. (2017). The Best Army Ukraine Has Ever Had: Changes in Ukraine's Armed Forces Since the Russian Aggression, Centre for Eastern Policy, 7 July. www.osw.waw.pl/en/publikacje/osw-studies/2017-07-07/best-army-ukraine-has-ever-had-changes-ukraines-armed-forces

Wolczuk, K. (2000). 'History, Europe and the 'National Idea': The 'Official' Narrative of National Identity in Ukraine', *Nationalities Papers*, 28 (4): 671–694.

Wołek, A. (2012), *Słabe państwo*. Kraków-Warszawa, Ośrodek Myśli Politycznej, ISP PAN.

Yekelchyk, S. (2015). 'The Early 1960s as a Cultural Space: A Microhistory of Ukraine's Generation of Cultural Rebels', *Nationalities Papers*, 43 (1): 45–62.

Zaslavskaya, T. (2004). *Sovriemiennoie rossiiskoie obshchestvo. Sotsialnyi mekhanizm transformatsii*. Moscow: Dielo.

PART IV

International Dimension

8

Messianism, Imperialism and Anti-Colonialism

> Every nation has an inalienable sovereign right to determine its own development path, choose allies and political regimes, create an economy and ensure its security. Russia has always respected these rights and always will. This fully applies to Ukraine and the Ukrainian people.
>
> *Vladimir Putin's Address to the Federal Assembly on 4 December 2014 (From Accepting NATO Aspirations to 'Denazifying': 20+ Years of Putin's Changing Views on Ukraine, 2022).*

Messianism and imperialism permeate the schizophrenic Russian state built by Vladimir Putin. The Kremlin accuses other countries of the very crimes undertaken by Russia. The Kremlin falsely accuses other countries of promoting 'nationalist/fascist/Nazi' ideologies that are more prominent in Russia's fascist dictatorship and in its far-right allies in Europe (Garner and Kuzio, 2025). Russian schizophrenia harbours, on the one hand, an imperial innocence about how its interventions in other countries were made by invitation, while, on the other hand, being proud of expanding its territory and becoming an empire. Russian nationalists in the Soviet Union had, and in the post-Soviet era, they continue to hold, a contemptuous racist arrogance towards peoples in the Caucasus and Central Asia, while at the same time demanding they remain together in a bigger union. A messianic view of Russia as a 'state-civilisation' borrows 'heavily from fascist theories' and 'even racial aspects of Russian identity' (Snegovaya, Kimmage, and McGlynn, 2023).

Russia's schizophrenic identity is especially visible in its relationship with Ukraine and the West, where it is exhibited in an angry, xenophobic and militarily aggressive manner. A lack of borders is praised as an attribute of Russia's schizophrenic 'state-civilisation' identity. Russian imperial nationalists hold a deep, historical inferiority complex vis-à-vis the West, while at the same time they sent their children to private schools, bought luxury properties and stashed their stolen loot in Western countries. Russia's 'state-civilisation' is touted as superior to the West, despite the fact social data disproves this claim. Russians claim that they are more spiritual than the public in Western countries, and yet Church attendance in Russia, which stands at 17 per cent, is like that found in the EU and is half that in Ukraine (35 per cent) and the United States (32 per cent) (Pew Research Centre, 2017). Most NATO armies have chaplains, and the Ukrainian armed forces officially introduced them in 2021 (see Kapelany. Na sluzhbi Bohu i Ukrayni, 2019). There is no legislation for chaplains in the Russian armed forces.[1]

As Chapter 1 shows, Russians have traditionally viewed 'Russia' as bigger than the Russian SFSR and Russian Federation. Putin described the USSR as 'Historic Russia'. The multiplicity of definitions of what constitutes 'Russia' forges alliances between the extreme left and right, as seen in violent hard-line coup d'états in 1991 and 1993. A Russia without borders is imperialistic, fuelled by a cult of war, a war economy and a subject population so thoroughly indoctrinated that they are willing to die in 'meat assaults', which lead to an astonishingly high average of 1,500 daily casualties.

Russians are schizophrenic about the origins of the state they live in. The Russian description of 12 June as 'Independence Day' is untrue, as the Russian SFSR never declared 'independence' from the USSR. Russia's anniversary is based on the 12 June 1990 Declaration of Sovereignty. In contrast, Ukrainians are not schizophrenic about their identity. Ukraine overwhelmingly voted for a Declaration of Sovereignty on 16 July 1990 (355 voted for and 4 voted against) and a Declaration of Independence on 24 August 1991 (321 voted for and 2 voted against) and supported their country's independence in a referendum held on 1 December 1991 (92.3 per cent voted for and 7.74 per cent voted against). Ukrainian independence from 'Historic Russia' (USSR) was supported by majorities in every region, including Crimea and the Donbas.

Russian messianism, imperialism and schizophrenia should be understood and analysed in five ways.

Firstly, although Putin's Russia has promoted nostalgia for the Soviet Union, the Kremlin holds a schizophrenic attitude towards the Soviet legacy. Putin blames Vladimir Lenin, the first Soviet leader, for cultivating an 'artificial' Ukrainian identity by allocating Little Russians their own republic. Ukraine possessed its own republic in the USSR, its language and separate identity were recognised by the Soviet regime, and it was a

---

[1] https://eanews.ru/rossiya/20250131115422/svyaschenniki-v-zone-svo-poluchat-osobyy-status and https://nachfin.info/SMF/index.php?topic=3967.435

founding member of the UN in 1945 (where the USSR ['Historic Russia'], Ukraine and Belarus held three seats).

Secondly, Russia is, as Timothy Snyder and other experts have described, a schizophrenic fascist state where the Kremlin accuses Ukraine and the West of being 'nationalist/fascist/Nazi' while itself being a fascist dictatorship (see Chapter 5) (Garner and Kuzio, 2025). Another term, *Ruscism*, combines the words Russian and fascism and is to be found in a 2023 Ukrainian parliamentary resolution that described Putin's regime as *Ruscism*, which it condemned as totalitarian and misanthropic (*lyudonenavysnyckykh*) (see Ukrainian Parliament, 2023). Snyder writes: 'Fascists calling other people "fascists" is fascism taken to its illogical extreme as a cult of unreason. It is a final point where hate speech inverts reality and propaganda is pure insistence. It is the apogee of will over thought.'[2] Russia denounces Ukrainians as 'nationalists/fascists/Nazis', while the Kremlin's discourse and financial resources politically and financially support fascists, Nazis and populist nationalists in the EU and United States. In the Kremlin's dystopian world, it is the liberal West which is Nazi while fascist Russia and its far-right allies in Europe are true Europeans. The European Parliament (2025) gave its backing to the Ukrainian Parliament (2023) by denouncing *Ruscism* as a 'nationalist imperialist ideology, policy and practices of the current Russian regime' and pointing to the 'incompatibility of this ideology and policy and these practices with international law and European values'.

Thirdly, Russia claims it is a country suffused with patriotism while 'nationalism/fascism/Nazism' dominates Ukraine. In fact, far-right parties have received the lowest electoral support in Ukrainian elections of any European country, and were only elected to one of eight parliaments in 2012. Opinion polls show Russian speakers in Ukraine do not believe they have been discriminated against and therefore the Kremlin's claim of genocide of Russian speakers is blatantly bogus. Russian and Ukrainian speakers can both be found in the Ukrainian army and security forces fighting Russian military aggression. In fact, as discussed later in this chapter, Russian imperial innocence prevents recognising the Russian and Soviet Empires had a history of committing genocide against minority peoples (Ukrainian Parliament, 2025). The Soviets and Russians have a history of committing genocide against Ukrainians. The second largest national minority in Russia, Ukrainians, have been exposed to Russification and

---

[2] https://euromaidanpress.com/2022/07/06/timothy-snyder-on-ukraine-russian-fascism-german-ostpolitik-the-american-left-and-ukraines-agency/

denationalisation by being denied access to educational, cultural, religious and media facilities (Zelenskyy, 2024). Russia's denial of any form of minority rights to Ukrainians was contrasted with Ukraine's exemplary law on national minorities (Ukrainian Parliament, 2022b). 92 per cent of Ukrainians believe Joseph Stalin's *Holodomor* was an act of genocide against the Ukrainian people (Rating Sociological Organisation, 2023). 89 per cent of Ukrainians believe Putin's Russia's full-scale war since 2022 is genocide against Ukrainians (Rating Sociological Organisation, 2022). As Anne Applebaum (2017) wrote, Stalin and Putin have a common fear and paranoia of Ukrainians who hold an identity distinct from Russians.

The Kremlin claimed it launched its 'special military operation' to protect Russian speakers in southeast Ukraine from a 'genocide' being perpetrated against them. Nevertheless, Russian-speaking Ukrainians in southeast Ukraine have suffered the greatest from Russian bombardment and war crimes. Former Ukrainian President Leonid Kuchma (2023, pp. 11–12), who had been a Russian speaker when he was director of the *Pivdenmash* (*Yuzhmash*) plant in the Soviet Union, came to understand: 'They [Russians] very much hate our statehood and will do everything to destroy it', adding 'they don't know the country, don't understand the people, and don't understand the society'. After Russia's full-scale invasion in 2022, 'Their idiocy finally spilled over into hatred' (Kuchma, 2023, pp. 11–12).

Fourthly, drawing on Soviet anti-colonialist propaganda, the Kremlin alleges Russia is defending the Global South and the 'Global Majority' by fighting Western colonialism. This falsehood obfuscates Russia's own colonial history of genocide and the imperial nature of the Soviet Union. Russian accusations and anti-colonialist discourse conveniently ignore ongoing, brutal, and criminal Russian colonialism undertaken by the Wagner Group and Africa Corps in African countries (see Koena, Zivanovic, and Eckel, 2025). Andreas Heinemann-Gruder (2024, p. 334) described the Wagner Group as a 'state-terrorist group' who could be compared to the 'Einsatzgruppen of the SS Secret Service and Security Police'.

The Russian Federation, where ethnic Russians account for only 70 per cent of the population, is the world's last remaining empire. Russia's imperial innocence, or schizo-imperialism, denies that Russian rule was negative while accusing the West of harbouring a brutal colonial past and continuing its colonialism through the United States-dominated world order. Imperial innocence, the myth of Russia never having attacked anybody, the peacefulness of Russian culture, and the belief that Russia has always won wars and has never surrendered are products of what Andrey Kuraev (2024) describes as *The Mythology of Russian Wars*. As Alexander J. Motyl (1999, p. 148) pointed out, 'democratic elites have been perfectly capable of genocide, war, and gross interference', but this does not translate into Russians not having undertaken the same, if not worse, and possessing a more positive record of colonialism.

Soviet historiography claimed, and Russia's post-1991 historiography continues to falsely write, that non-Russian peoples voluntarily joined the Tsarist Empire, where they benefitted from a more advanced Russian civilisation. Ukrainians allegedly always yearned to 'reunite' with Russia. Because Russia has never undertaken an introspection of crimes committed by Russian and Soviet colonialism, they have never understood these are historical untruths. Instead, they become angry at changes in the way history has been rewritten since 1991 in Ukraine and other former non-Russian Soviet republics (see Kuzio, 2002, 2005, 2006).

Post-Soviet Ukrainian history has publicised and condemned crimes committed by the Tsarist and Soviet empires, which Putin and his imperial nationalist accolades refuse to acknowledge. Putin's Russia's cult of brutal Russian leaders – Ivan the Terrible, Peter I, Catherine I and Stalin – denies, excuses or ignores their crimes against humanity. Book series and school billboards portray Putin as following these historical leaders into Russian history by expanding Russian territory and reviving Russia as a great power.[3]

Fourthly, Russia is schizo-European. The Kremlin claims that Russia's superior civilisation is the guardian of true European values, which have been lost in the EU and 'collective West'. A belief in the superiority of Russia and its 'state-civilisation' over Western civilisation compensates for Russian feelings of dependence, poverty and humiliation, Lev Gudkov of the Levada Centre believes (Matthews, 2023, p. 67). Putin has never sought Russian membership of the EU; instead, the Kremlin created a weak and corrupt alternative – the Eurasian Economic Union (EAEU) – uniting, apart from democratic Armenia, Russia's fascist dictatorship with Eurasian authoritarian regimes. In the early 1990s, the Kremlin launched the Collective Security Treaty Organisation (CSTO) as the successor to the Warsaw Pact and a weak counterweight to NATO. The Kremlin's vague concept of 'Eurasian security architecture' is supposedly being created by

---

[3] https://rvio.histrf.ru/activities/news/knigu-o-vladimire-putine-predstavili-chitatelyam-i-zhurnalistam; and www.ozon.ru/category/sobirateli-zemli-russkoy/?__rr=1&abt_att=1

adding countries to the Shanghai Cooperation Organisation and seeking to (unsuccessfully) transform BRICS into an anti-Western alliance.[4] In fact, Russia has few real military allies except for Iran, North Korea and China united in the Axis of Upheaval (see Chapter 9).

Putin has constructed a schizophrenic Russian state without borders, with unfounded claims of a 'state-civilisation' superior to the West and built on lies and falsehoods that promote a dystopian claim that its 'special military operation' is a defensive action forced upon it by Ukrainian 'Nazis' and Western nefariousness (Garner and Kuzio, 2025). Putin's fascist dictatorship incorporates some aspects of twentieth-century fascism but also has new components only found in the twenty-first century, such as mobilisation through the Internet and social media. Although Putin's Russia claims to be upholding 'traditional European values', this has nothing to do with reality.

This chapter is divided into four sections. The first analyses the roots of Russian imperial innocence, Soviet and Russian historical myths and how Russian nationalists have incorporated these into their ideologies, outlook on the world and contemptuous attitude towards Ukraine. The second section analyses how Putin's Russia has sought to draw on Soviet anti-colonialist discourse. This section also investigates how Ukraine is promoting a counter-narrative of Russia having a brutal legacy of colonialism and genocide. The third section analyses Russian messianism and imperialism through the portrayal of Russia as a *Katechon* (Restrainer) and leader of the 'Global Majority', with the goal of defeating the United States-led unipolar world and 'collective West' and on its ruins build a new multipolar world order. The fourth section investigates Russian imperialism towards Ukraine within the context of Russia's imperial innocence and historical myths.

Russian Imperial Innocence

Russian historian Yury Afanasev complained, 'there is not, nor has there ever been a people and country with a history as falsified as ours is…' (Velychenko, 1994a, p. 327). Chapter 6 on Russian-Ukrainian divergence outlines how from the late 1980s and 1990s, during Mikhail Gorbachev's *glasnost* and Boris Yeltsin's presidency, Russia and Ukraine began to

---

[4] https://meduza.io/en/feature/2024/10/24/kremlin-tells-propagandists-to-promote-anti-dollar-brics-payment-system-and-push-u-s-election-conspiracy-theories-in-latest-media-guidelines

diverge in their treatment of history. Russia revived pre-Soviet writers, historians and military leaders who had been published in the Tsarist Empire and by White Russian émigrés in the interwar era, such as Ivan Ilyin. Much of the groundwork for the rehabilitation of Russian imperialists and Tsarist generals had already been undertaken by the Soviet Union from the mid 1930s.

Ukraine began de-Sovietising its history in the late 1980s and has never really stopped, even under pro-Russian President Viktor Yanukovych. De-Sovietisation was accompanied by the condemnation of Stalin's crimes against humanity, particularly the *Holodomor*. In 2015, Ukraine's approach to history diverged even further after the adoption of four de-communisation laws (see Oliinyk and Kuzio, 2021). These four laws condemned in equal fashion Nazi and communist totalitarianism, changed Ukraine's approach from the celebration of the Great Patriotic War (1941–1945) on 9 May to the commemoration of World War II (1939–1945) on 8 May, rehabilitated Ukrainian patriotic and nationalist groups and movements that had fought for Ukrainian rights and independence and opened security service archives.

The key divergence between Ukraine and Russia lay in their attitudes towards their past. Ukraine's condemnation of Tsarist colonialism, Soviet genocide and Russian imperial rule clashed throughout the post-Soviet era with Soviet Russian imperial nationalist myths and history writing. A deeply held view of Russian imperial innocence coupled with a belief Russia had always brought benefits towards peoples it had ruled over left little room for critical introspection (Langdon and Tismaneanu, 2020, p. 127). Sergei Karaganov (2025), who was once a respected academic, calls for escalating Russia's genocidal war against Ukraine while writing, 'Europe is the source of all the main ills of humanity, two world wars, genocides, anti-human ideologies, colonialism, racism, Nazism and so on down the list'.

After all, Tsarist, Soviet and contemporary Russian colonialist claims have little in common with historical facts. In the seventeenth century, on the eve of Ukraine and Muscovy signing the Treaty of Pereyaslav, the former was more socially and politically advanced. Muscovy had introduced serfdom in 1597. Ukraine had free Cossack peasants until the Cossack Hetmanate was destroyed by Russia in 1775, only eight years before Moscow's colonial conquest of Crimea. Not surprisingly, Ukrainians associate serfdom with Russian rule because it was imposed by the Tsarist Empire (Shkandrij, 2001, pp. 82–83). Ukrainian cultural, educational and political life stagnated in the Tsarist Empire in the nineteenth century.

During Leonid Kravchuk's (1991–1994) and Kuchma's (1994–2004) presidencies, both of whom had belonged to the higher levels of the Soviet *nomenklatura*, criticism of Russia and the USSR was tempered by occasional positive references to Soviet rule, such as the unification of Ukrainian lands during World War II and the benefits of modernisation, industrialisation and urbanisation in the USSR. Nevertheless, both Kravchuk and Kuchma defined the *Holodomor* as a genocide against the Ukrainian people, and few Ukrainian historians and policymakers had anything positive to say about Tsarist imperial rule over Ukraine.

From the mid 2000s, three presidents – Viktor Yushchenko, Petro Poroshenko and Volodymyr Zelenskyy – have been more critical of both Tsarist imperial and Soviet rule over Ukraine. De-communisation began under Yushchenko and was completed by Poroshenko. Meanwhile, de-russification (sometimes referred to as de-colonisation) began under Zelenskyy. Yanukovych was an aberration among Ukraine's six presidents and at the same time the Kremlin's favourite because of his Soviet nostalgia and willingness to pursue memory politics according to ideological parameters outlined by the Kremlin. Kuchma understood Ukraine is not Russia, but Yanukovych never comprehended Ukraine is not the Donbas.

The Roots of Imperial Innocence

The 1920s were a period of relative liberalisation in the Soviet Union. The New Economic Policy and indigenisation (Ukrainisation) policies provided national communists with the freedom to promote Ukrainian identity, culture and language. Urbanisation and Ukrainisation proceeded simultaneously; indeed, if this had been allowed to continue, southeastern Ukrainian cities would have become Ukrainian speaking (see Kuzio, 1998). During this period, Russian nationalism was viewed by historians and Communist Party functionaries as the main threat to the Soviet regime and a greater evil than non-Russian nationalisms.

Indigenisation abruptly ended in 1933 with the *Holodomor*. From the mid 1930s, the Soviet Union rehabilitated Russian imperialists and Tsarist generals. For five decades through to the mid 1980s, non-Russian nationalisms – especially Ukrainian – were regarded as the greatest threat to the Soviet regime and greater evil. A Sovietised form of Russian nationalism flourished (see Kuzio, 2022, pp. 99–128). Soviet national Bolshevism resembled White Russian émigré Eurasianism shorn of its communist ideology. Alexander Dugin, a leading Eurasianist ideologist, was also a member of the National Bolshevik Party. An insignificant number of

8 MESSIANISM, IMPERIALISM & ANTI-COLONIALISM

Russian nationalists challenged the Soviet regime although they never clamoured for the independence of the Russian SFSR. There were fewer Russian nationalist political prisoners than Ukrainians. Russian – unlike Ukrainian – nationalists were never considered threats to the Soviet regime because they called for the Soviet Union to transform into a new Russian Empire.

From the mid 1930s, Soviet history writing incorporated Tsarist Russian imperial nationalist historiography, and 'could, for the most part, be read with approval by the tsars themselves', Lowett Tillett wrote (1969, p. 4; see also Tillett, 1964, 1967). Historiography served the goals of the Communist Party of the Soviet Union's nationalities policies in the elaboration and inculcation of new myths. Russians were lauded as the leading nation of the Soviet Union and the 'elder brother' of the three eastern Slavs. Ukrainians and Russians were recognised as different peoples, but they were at the same time very close, were born together, always strived to live together and were slated to always be united. As Tillett (1969, p. 4) wrote, Soviet historiography 'which ran counter to those of other historians (especially the first generation of Bolshevik historians) can only be described as an elaborate historical myth'. These myths are not myths for Putin and Russian imperial nationalists, but they are hardbound truths that underpinned his decision to launch a 'special military operation'.

Putin was socialised into Soviet myths of imperial innocence and Russian and Stalinist imperial glory. In the late 1950s and 1960s, when Putin attended Soviet schools, history teaching in the USSR emphasised the struggle of Russian tsars and the Orthodox Church against foreign domination, not class struggle (Brudny, 2000, p. 72). Fighting foreign domination of Russia is a major component of Putinism. The myth of proletarian internationalism was replaced by Russian patrimony and prerogative to rule stretching back to 'Kievan Russia' (Kyiv Rus) (Farmer, 1980, p. 30). During this period, the Soviet Union promoted a history of the eastern Slavs, which was a refashioned version of that found in the Tsarist era. In contrast, Ukrainian national historians such as Mykhaylo Hrushevsky were banned from the mid 1930s to the late 1980s.

Contemporary Russian chauvinism, imperial nationalism and anti-Western xenophobia are rooted in Soviet history writing that was propagated in official Russian nationalist literary journals such as *Rossiia (Russia)*, *Oktiabr (October)*, *Rodina (Motherland)*, *Molodaia Gvardiia (Young Guard)* and *Nash Sovremennik (Our Contemporary)*. Russian nationalist dissidents espoused a common pan-Russian identity for eastern Slavs, were nostalgic for a Great Russia and an idyllic Russian past, and they adamantly believed in Russia's superiority and the uniqueness of its mission (Joo, 2008, pp. 223, 233; see Kuzio, 2022, pp. 99–128). After 1991, when Russia exchanged communism for imperial nationalism, 'the old ideas of hatred and bigotry continued with new mouthpieces' (Joo, 2008, p. 237).

Little wonder Putin described the USSR as 'Historic Russia' because the *History of the USSR* was, in fact, the same as that of the '*History of Russia*'. The Russian SFSR did not have a separate history to that of the USSR, just as the Russian SFSR did not possess its own republican institutions. In the Soviet Union, the histories of the non-Russian peoples were treated as regional histories of 'Russia'. Official Ukrainian history writing in the post-Stalin era became marginalised and in 'a state of deep crisis' (Wynar, 1979, p. 19). Soviet historiography restricted the collective memory and identity of each nation within the former USSR to that of an *ethnie* and geographical unit. Within southeastern Ukraine, Tsarist and Soviet historiography reinforced a strong 'all-Russian' national component already part of popular consciousness. This channelled collective historical memory and national awareness generated by modernisation into an ethnographic regionalism 'compatible with Soviet loyalty' (Velychenko, 1993, pp. 140, 160, 167, 210; Velychenko, 1994b, p. 28). During periods of Soviet liberalisation, Ukrainian dissidents and national communists challenged official Soviet history and attempted to carve out a Ukrainian history separate from that of Russian.

Only in the late 1980s, did we witness the beginning of a revival of Ukrainian national history. Since 1991, Ukrainian national history has returned to the espousal of a Ukrainian history separate from Russian. A Ukrainian history separate from Russia is unacceptable for most Russians because they cannot accept Ukrainians are a separate people, and Ukraine is a fully sovereign country.

The myths and legends formulated within Soviet historiography had gone full circle by the early 1950s. By the time of Stalin's death in 1953, further revisions of Soviet historiography made the Soviet interpretation of Ukrainian–Russian relations into a replica of that found in the Tsarist Russian Empire. The 1954 'Thesis on Re-Union' marking the 300th anniversary of the 1654 Pereyaslav Treaty replicated and updated much of the schema originally formulated within Tsar Nicholas I's 1833 'Official Nationality' policy of 'Orthodoxy, Autocracy, Nationality'. The Tsarist, White Russian émigré and Soviet ideology of pan-Russian unity and imperial nationalism lies at the heart of Putin's regime and drives the Kremlin's war against Ukraine.

Russian historiography tailored the past to fit the present by justifying Russian rule over Ukrainian territories not in terms of conquered territories but as beneficial rule over a people with allegedly similar history, language and culture. There could not be therefore any repression of Ukrainian lands because there was allegedly cultural unity of Russians and Ukrainians. By 1991, after six years of glasnost, only one Russian historian had summoned up the courage to reject the 1954 'Thesis'. Mark von Hagen believes, even under Yeltsin, there was 'very little attempt on the part of Russian historians to reject the imperial scheme of Russian history'.[5]

Since the early to mid 1990s, publishing houses in Moscow and St Petersburg have re-published Tsarist surveys of 'Russian' history and White Russian émigré writers. These histories and writings increased imperial nationalistic attitudes and the denial of Ukraine and a separate Ukrainian people. New histories of 'Russia' do not limit themselves to only surveying Muscovy, 'Great Russians' or the Russian Federation because they are replicas of the histories of the USSR repeating notions of the 'old Russian nation' and treating 1654 as a 'reunion'.

The propagation and circulation of these myths and legends reinforced a Russian tendency to identify not with the Russian SFSR or from 1991 with the Russian Federation but instead with empire and union. Additionally, they reinforced a widespread view that Ukrainian independence is 'temporary'[6] and out of step with the preordained destiny of eastern Slavic unity.

Soviet and Russian Historical Myths

Soviet historiography accepted that Ukrainians were a separate people with their own republican homeland. But this was a temporary phenomenon because the 'natural' course of history would lead to the merger of eastern Slavs into a Russian-speaking *Homo Sovieticus*. As David G. Rowley (2000) pointed out, Tsarist imperial nationalist universalism was recast as Soviet internationalism – with the result being the same. The Tsarist Empire aimed to mould a Russian people from the three wings of

---

[5] Interview with Professor Mark von Hagen, Director of the Harriman Institute, Columbia University, 19 November 1996.
[6] A Ukrainian diplomat told Taras Kuzio that in the 1990's negotiations with Russians always ended with them asking 'When will you stop playing with this independence and return to us.'

the pan-Russian nation, while the Soviet regime sought to fashion a Soviet people with its inner core from the three eastern Slavs.

There were eight key elements of the Soviet 'elaborate historical myth' (Tillett, 1969, p. 4; see Mazour, 1975):

1. *Nostalgia:* Rehabilitation of the Tsarist past, Russian imperial innocence and lack of critical introspection deepened a nostalgic view of Russian rule coupled with an inability to comprehend criticism, especially from Ukrainians. Russian state archives have remained closed, while Moscow has never embraced the type of de-communisation policies that were introduced in Ukraine, the three Baltic states, and central-eastern Europe. Instead, post-Soviet Russia has rehabilitated the Russian ideologues of imperialism who glorified the Tsarist and Soviet empires. A steady stream of films, TV serials, literature, and school textbooks celebrate and reinforce Russia's imperial nationalist identity. Meanwhile, crimes against the non-Russian peoples of the empire, such as the 1933 *Holodomor*, have been removed from official histories or rewritten to deny or downplay Stalinist crimes.
2. *Paternalism:* Great Russians are the natural leading people of the USSR reinforcing Russia's arrogant disdain towards the former Soviet republics and an inability to accept them as fully sovereign states.
3. *Harmony:* Denial there had been ethnic hostility between Russians and Ukrainians in the past. Differences between Russians and Ukrainians were obfuscated (see Velychenko, 1993). Putin's (2021) elaboration of Russian-Ukrainian history ignores past conflicts, Russification of the Ukrainian language and repression of Ukrainian culture and political leaders. Most Russians, including members of the opposition, maintain their imperial innocence by never acknowledging Russian imperial violence and the denigration and destruction of non-Russian cultures and by denying most Russians are influenced by Russian chauvinism and imperialism (Eristavi, 2023).[7]
4. *Russians were never imperialists:* A belief Russia never conquered territories but had been invited by non-Russians to intervene or negotiate 'unions' and 'reunions'. Communist theorists Friedrich Engels and Karl Marx, Soviet leader Lenin and Bolshevik historians in the 1920s, such as Mikhail Pokrovskyj, had been wrong to condemn Tsarist Russian 'expansionism'.

---

[7] See Interview with Vladimir Kara-Murza, *BBC Hardtalk*, 15 January 2025. www.bbc.co.uk/iplayer/episode/m0027ll9/hardtalk-vladimir-karamurza-russian-opposition-politician

8 MESSIANISM, IMPERIALISM & ANTI-COLONIALISM

5. *Lesser of two evils:* 'Unions' and 'reunions' brought only positive benefits or, at a minimum, were the 'lesser of two evils'. The incorporation of territories into Russia was either a beneficial act or it had been better for these peoples to be ruled by Russians rather than Poles, Austrians or Ottomans (Brandenberger and Dubrovsky, 1998, p. 878). Russian rule, integration, centralisation and uniformity were 'good' and 'progressive' for non-Russian peoples (see Velychenko, 1993). Russian rule provided modernity to backward non-Russian peoples (Kassymbekova, 2022). Meanwhile, Ukrainian historians and political leaders condemned Tsarist imperial rule as 'disastrous, while in Russia, Ukraine constituted an inalienable part of the national self-image' (Velychenko, 2004, p. 21).
6. *Russia's right to rule Ukraine:* Russian control over Ukraine and Belarus was never perceived as 'annexation', but merely the recovery of the Tsar's patrimony from Kyiv Rus. The annexation of seven regions in western Ukraine was depicted in a similar manner as the 'reunification' of Ukrainian lands. In 1947 and 1954, new theses codified the eastern Slavs as historically belonging to one pan-Russian people, and the use of the terms Russian, Rus'ian and eastern Slavic became interchangeable.
7. *Beneficial rule:* Unlike European empires, which accumulated their wealth by robbing colonies over many centuries (Putin, 2023a, 2023b), the Russian *mission civilisatrice* was allegedly beneficial to the non-Russian peoples. Mikhail Zygar (2023a, p. 79) writes that the messianic discourse of the Tsarist Empire and Soviet Union promoted the equivalent of Rudyard Kipling's concept of the 'White Man's Burden' bringing civilisation to backward peoples. This discourse continues to dominate Putin's Russia. Palestinians are 'victims of Western neocolonial policies' by a West only interested in bringing 'chaos', 'destabilisation' and 'instability in the pursuit of global dominance' (Putin, 2023c). Putin describes Russia as never having been 'self-interested' because the Russian state was altruistic and concerned for non-Russian peoples. Colonialism, in the mind of the Kremlin, is a term that should only be used for Western empires, ignoring the violent colonial policies of the Tsarist Empire, Soviet Union, and Russian state-controlled mercenaries in Africa (see Koena, Zivanovic and Eckel, 2025).

Western colonialism 'exterminated entire ethnicities', a claim that is true, but which ignores the equally violent legacy of past Russian imperialism and Soviet colonialism (Ukrainian Parliament, 2022a, 2022b, 2022c, 2023, 2025) and ongoing violent and exploitative Russian colonialism in

Africa (see Koena, Zivanovic, and Eckel, 2025). After three years of ferocious Russian attacks on Ukrainian civilians and over 160,000 war crimes, Russian Foreign Minister Sergei Lavrov (2024a) said – without a hint of irony – that Russia has no goal to 'exterminate' Ukrainians because 'they are brothers and sisters to the Russian people'. The Ukrainian Parliament (2022a) disagreed, accusing Russia of committing genocide against the Ukrainian people. So did Ukrainians, 89 per cent of whom believed Russia is committing genocide against them (Rating Sociological Organisation, 2022).

8. *Evil Ukrainian nationalism:* Being 'ungrateful' for not acknowledging the allegedly positive aspects of the Soviet Union made 'bad' Ukrainians into 'traitors' who could not be negotiated with and had to be destroyed (Davis, 2024, p. 137). Russians could not comprehend, and became angry at, why Ukrainians and other non-Russians in the Tsarist Empire and Soviet Union were not grateful for allegedly prospering under Russian and Soviet rule. Nationalist agitation for independence was against the wishes of the people who have always sought to remain united with Russia. Ukrainian nationalists, whether Cossack Hetman Ivan Mazepa to socialist Symon Petlura and integral nationalist Stepan Bandera, were 'bad', 'reactionary' and financed by the West. Russians viewed Ukrainians and other non-Russians as politically disloyal if they rejected Russian cultural domination and pursued a pro-Western foreign policy (Kassymbekova, 2022). The celebration, commemoration and promotion of patriots and nationalists who demanded and fought for Ukrainian independence, as in the 2015 de-communisation laws, would never be accepted by Putin's Russia and Russian imperial nationalists because they were 'nationalists/fascists/Nazis' and Russophobes.

Russian Nationalist Myths

Soviet historiography and nationalities policies influenced Russian nationalist dissidents such as Alexander Solzhenitsyn. As Robert Horvath (2011) and Casey Michel (2024) convincingly show, in the 2000s, Solzhenitsyn became ideologically closer to Putin. Solzhenitsyn's proposal for a Russian Union of the three eastern Slavs to replace the Soviet Union is remarkably like Putin's Pan-Russian World and the Russian Orthodox Church's 'Holy Rus'. Solzhenitsyn, ahead of Putin's Russia, questioned Ukrainian sovereignty over its southeast region and was critical of Ukrainians seeking a future for their country outside Russia's sphere of influence.

8 MESSIANISM, IMPERIALISM & ANTI-COLONIALISM

Living in exile in the United States, Solzhenitsyn (1980) wrote a damning article for the well-known *Foreign Affairs magazine*, which was imbued with Russian imperial innocence. Solzhenitsyn (1980) claimed:

1. *Russia and Communism:* There is no link between communism and Russia, and it was wrong to use the USSR and Russia interchangeably. Most Russians would disagree. Putin, who believes the Soviet Union was 'Historic Russia', would certainly disagree even though he became friends with Solzhenitsyn in the 2000s.
2. *Oppression of Russians:* Russians were an oppressed people in the USSR whose national consciousness, religion and culture were suppressed. The Russian past was 'outlawed' and Russian 'history reviled'. In fact, as analysed earlier and in Chapter 5, Russian historians had far greater freedom than Ukrainian historians, and they monopolised research and publishing on Kyiv Rus. Solzhenitsyn – like current Russian leaders – described Russia as having existed for a thousand years, thus monopolising 'Kievan Russia' (Kyiv Rus) as the first Russian state. Russian dissidents, nationalist or liberal, never complained about the decline of the Russian language or denationalisation. The Russian Orthodox Church was legalised in 1943 and occupied Ukrainian parishes which once had belonged to the banned Ukrainian Autocephalous Orthodox and Greek-Catholic Churches. Irrespective of Solzhenitsyn's myths, Russian history, language, culture and identity flourished in the Soviet Union.
3. *Stalin and Russia:* Stalinism was not a form of Russian nationalism or a reversion to Tsarism. Earlier in this chapter, we analysed how Stalin returned Soviet historiography to many tenets of Tsarist imperialism and nationalism. Putin has promoted a cult of Stalin (see Kuzio, 2017).
4. *Russians suffered:* Russian suffered most of the peoples in the USSR. Millions of Russians did suffer during Stalinism; nevertheless, this has been ignored during the cult of Stalin in Putin's Russia (see Kuzio, 2017). The Kremlin has been hostile to Ukraine's de-Stalinisation and commemoration of the *Holodomor* as a genocide. Memorial, which documented Stalinist crimes in Russia, was banned in December 2021.
5. *Russian rulers:* Russian people were not the 'ruling nationality' of the Soviet Union. As discussed earlier, from the late 1930s, the Soviet regime promoted Russians as the 'elder brother' of the Soviet peoples. The USSR planned to merge the three eastern Slavic peoples into a Russian-speaking *Homo Sovieticus*.
6. *Western academia:* American scholars provided a 'distorted portrayal of old Russia'. In fact, most Western historians of Russia used, and

many continue to use, nineteenth-century Russian imperial historiographical frameworks. White Russian émigré historians like Nicholas V. Riasanovsky influenced the writing of Western histories of Russia using a pan-Russian and imperial nationalist framework. In Western histories of Russia, Ukraine is a marginal actor within a Russian and eastern Slavic historical framework (see Kuzio, 2020, pp. 9–35). Mirosław Filipowicz's (2007, pp. 346–347) analysis of American historiography on Russia concluded that 'Ukraine in America was perceived for decades as a province deeply integrated with Russia'. An alternative viewpoint to this pan-Russian paradigm of the history of Eastern Europe and Russia only appeared in the second half of the twentieth century with publications by historians Richard Pipes, Adam Ulam and Piotr Wandycz and the establishment of the Harvard Ukrainian Research Institute in 1973, Canadian Institute of Ukrainian Studies in 1976 and Chair of Ukrainian Studies at the University of Toronto in 1980.

Soviet and Russian Anti-colonialism

The Soviet Union was a Russian-led empire with a core and controlled peripheries (see Motyl, 1999, 2001; Velychenko, 1995, 2002, 2004). Alexander Motyl (1999, p. 124) writes that in imperial arrangements 'core elites' rule, peripheral elites govern. Empires can be formal with direct control (e.g., the former USSR) or informal with indirect control exercised (such as the US sphere of influence in Central and Latin America during the Cold War). Motyl (1999) predicted that Russia would attempt to recreate an informal empire modelled along the lines of US relations with Latin America or the Soviet Union with central-eastern Europe in the Cold War. Ultimately, Russia's 're-imperialisation will in all likelihood produce an imperial system suffering from extreme decay, one especially prone to both further disintegration and to collapse' (Motyl, 1999, p. 161; see Motyl, 2001). Russia's full-scale invasion and war against Ukraine has shown it to be a stagnating great power, whose armed forces were never the 'second best army in the world'.

The Soviet Union expanded at the end of World War II by annexing Moldova, western Ukraine, western Belarus and the three Baltic states of Lithuania, Latvia and Estonia and creating an empire in central-eastern Europe. The myth of the all-wise Lenin was promoted throughout the Soviet empire. In communist Poland, for example, pupils and students were taught that the Polish people received independence in 1918 because of Lenin's declaration on the right to self-determination for the nations of the Tsarist Empire (and in Europe in general). The Soviet Union under Stalin was a champion of the principle of self-determination, but not of its own republics. Johannes Socher (2021, p. 26) writes: 'The successful introduction of the formula of self-determination as one of the principles of the United Nations in the Charter may therefore rightly be called a distinctive Soviet contribution.' The Soviet Union under Stalin included the principle of self-determination as the basis for respect for human rights in not only the United Nations Charter but also the International Covenants on Civil and Political Rights and Economic, Social, and Cultural Rights adopted in 1966 and going into effect a decade later (Socher, 2021, p. 27). In the decade following World War II, the Soviet Union 'acted as a strong supporter of self-determination in the drafting process of all important international legal instruments that led to the juridification of the principle' (Socher, 2021, p. 54).

Johannes Socher (2021, p. 35) writes that the Soviet Union was 'one of the strongest and most aggressive supporters of self-determination outside its own sphere of influence in the context of decolonisation…'. Nevertheless, both Stalin and Putin have displayed double standards on this question. Stalin promoted the principle of self-determination in Western colonies – but not in the Soviet empire. Yeltsin manufactured frozen conflicts in Moldova, Azerbaijan and Georgia by supporting separatist movements. Putin falsely applied the principle of self-determination to South Ossetia, Abkhazia, Crimea and four Ukrainian *oblasts* while denying the right to Chechnya.

Drawing on this Soviet legacy, Russia champions itself as the leader of the anti-colonialist movement in the world, while at the same time undertaking an imperialist war against Ukraine. Russia's allies in the Anti-Western Axis of Upheaval have a similar duplicitous adherence to anti-colonialism, and Iran seeks to destroy Israel's statehood. Aside from North Korea, three other members of the Anti-Western Axis of Upheaval have pursued assimilationist and discriminatory policies towards their national minorities, and their poor colonial records make them ineligible to be moral leaders of the 'Global Majority' and anti-colonialist movement. In the Russian Federation, national minorities account for 30 per cent of the population; in Iran, Persians account for only 61 per cent of the population, while Han Chinese account for 92 per cent of China's population; Russia, Iran and China would never allow their national minorities to secede. China is denationalising both Tibet and Xinjiang (see French, 2021), and Beijing's treatment of the Muslim population of Xinjiang has been condemned as genocide (see Pompeo, 2021).

Russian Anti-colonialism

Putin's understanding of anti-colonialism echoes Soviet narratives that first emerged in the aftermath of the Bolshevik Revolution and evolved further after World War II. The advent of the Cold War led to a major revival in Soviet anti-colonial propaganda, with the Soviet Union actively supporting liberation movements which swept Africa and Asia in the 1950s and 1960s. Putin has made much of this Soviet backing for countries seeking to shake off Western colonial rule and has repeatedly referenced this when addressing African leaders.

Putin's bid to position Russia as the leading anti-colonial power is more than just geopolitical opportunism brought on by the necessity of frayed relations with the West. It is the culmination of decades of Tsarist, Soviet and post-Soviet indoctrination that has excused Russian colonialism towards Ukrainians and other non-Russian peoples, while conflating Russia's own anti-Western xenophobia with the broader global struggle against the liberal world order (which is derided as continued 'Western imperialism'). The countries of the Global South may have many good reasons for pursuing closer ties with Putin's Russia, but a shared opposition to imperialism is most certainly not one of them. On the contrary, if anti-imperial sentiment in the Global South has any impact on attitudes towards the Russian invasion of Ukraine, it should logically fuel support for Ukraine's fight back against Russian imperialism.

The Kremlin deploys anti-colonialist discourse whenever Ukraine receives military support from its Western partners or when Russia is losing its hold on temporarily occupied territories in Ukraine.[8] The EU, United States and NATO member states have provided Ukraine with military assistance to help repel Russia's unprovoked aggression, but they are not involved in any fighting.[9] The West does not seek to destroy Russia; it wants Russia to stop trying to destroy Ukraine. Former Ukrainian President Kuchma (2023, p. 497) wrote: Ukrainians and Russians are fighting different wars: 'Ukraine is fighting to continue to exist as a nation which decides itself how it wishes to live; Russia is fighting to continue to exist as an empire, which uses force against others to decide how they live.'

While the West is accused of always seeking enemies in its eternal quest for expansion, Russia's invasions of foreign countries are downplayed or excused. It is, in fact, Putin's Russia, as Chapter 9 shows, that cannot exist

---

[8] https://euvsdisinfo.eu/report/russia-fighting-collective-west-and-nato-in-ukraine-war/
[9] https://euvsdisinfo.eu/report/russia-fights-the-collective-west-not-just-ukraine/

without a cult of war and internal and external enemies. Russia has a long tradition of blaming outsiders (the United States, Western Europeans, Western secret services, 'collective West', and Anglo-Saxons) for Russian difficulties, thus ignoring their domestic roots. The Soviet Union allegedly disintegrated because of Western machinations and conspiracies. Russia was forced to launch a 'special military operation' because the West has transformed Ukraine into an 'Anti-Russia' security threat. Ivan Grek (2023) writes:

> A blend of Orthodox pan-Slavism and right-wing post-colonialism helps to make sense of Russia's invasion of Ukraine: Western racist attempts to destroy Russianness by means of cultural colonialisation have failed with the collapse of the liberal course in Russia, but the Orthodox Slavic brothers (an extension of Russians) in Ukraine lost in a colonial war in 2014. Starting with the 30 September 2022 speech on annexation of Ukrainian lands, Putin explicitly addresses Russia's war on Ukraine as a colonial struggle against the West.

Grek (2023) continues:

> Despite its essentialist premise, the pan-Slavic paradigm acknowledges constructivism when it comes to political discontent among Slavic peoples. Just as the Poles were fooled by Germans who forced Catholicism on them, the Slavs of Ukraine were duped by ideas of nationalism, delivered by the colonisers. Removal of this cultural construct will return Ukrainians to their primordial condition as a part of the Pan-Russian World. As Putin (2022c) put it in his address to the conference of Russian historians on 4 November 2022, the West has 'raped the consciousness of Ukrainians and stolen their history', turning Ukraine into an 'Anti-Russia', and Poland has always been in the vanguard of this process. Putin noted that Russians and Ukrainians will reunite once historical truth will be resorted. Hence, Ukrainian Slavic Orthodox brothers lost their brotherly status until Russia reconstructs the cultural framework of Ukrainianess.

Ukrainian Anti-colonialism

As Paul Goble (2022, 2023a, 2023b, 2024a, 2024b, 2024c, 2024d, 2025) has analysed, Ukraine has taken the anti-colonial fight against and inside Russia. Ukrainians are the second largest national minority in Russia, but they are invisible to both Russian officials *and* Western scholars. Since 1991, Western academics have often raised the question of Russian speakers in Ukraine while ignoring the rights of Ukrainians in Russia (see Prina, 2016). Ukrainians in Russia have not been given cultural, educational and religious rights for most of the twentieth and twenty-first centuries. Discrimination against Ukrainians in Putin's Russia has grown during his quarter of a century of direct and indirect rule. The treatment of Ukrainians in Russia makes a mockery of Russian accusations about the poor treatment of Russian speakers in Ukraine, one of the Kremlin's justifications for the full-scale invasion. From being the second largest national minority in Russia in the 2000s, Ukrainians became on the eve of the full-scale invasion, the eighth in size national minority (see Shtohrin, 2021).[10]

Russia's territorial claims towards Ukraine based on 'historical injustice' have been upended by Ukrainian claims to historical areas of Russia that were settled by Ukrainians, and which have long historical ties to Ukraine (see Zelenskyy, 2024). The Ukrainian–Russian border is artificial and was adjusted in the 1920s in Russia's favour; using Putin's discourse, Lenin wrongly included 'historical Ukrainian lands' inside Russia (see Kuzio, 2009; Rindlisbacher, 2018).[11] Indeed, when Ukrainian forces intervened into the Russian *oblast* of Kursk, which borders the Ukrainian *oblast* of Sumy, they found locals speaking Ukrainian or a *surzhyk* (Ukrainian–Russian) dialect. A similar Ukrainian dialect is spoken in Belgorod, which borders Kharkiv.

In addition to expressing concern about the discrimination of Ukrainians in Russia, the Ukrainian Parliament and president have adopted resolutions and appeals about the Russian genocide of the Chechen, Circassian and other non-Russian peoples living in the Tsarist Empire, Soviet Union and Russian Federation. Publicising the Russian genocide has two goals. Firstly, it undermines the myth of Russian imperial innocence that claims its rule over non-Russians was beneficial and harmonious and therefore different to the brutality of Western colonialism. Secondly, Ukraine seeks to deter non-Russian peoples, who live in economically depressed regions, from fighting in the Russian army against Ukraine. During the first two years of Russia's full-scale invasion, non-Russians constituted a higher proportion of Russian soldiers fighting in Ukraine than their numbers in the population of the Russian Federation (see MacKinnon, 2022).

President Zelenskyy (2022) appealed in the first year of the full-scale invasion to peoples in the Caucasus and other regions of Russia to not be 'among those many who still serve the one who wants this war. You must not die in Ukraine. Your sons should not die in Ukraine'. Zelenskyy

---

[10] https://meduza.io/en/feature/2023/01/26/it-s-not-safe-to-admit-you-re-ukrainian?utm_source=email&utm_medium=briefly&utm_campaign=2023-01-26&s=03

[11] See a very good presentation in December 2016 by Pavlo Hrytsenko in a hearing on the Sergei Kivalov-Vadym Kolesnichenko 2012 language law in the Constitutional Court of Ukraine. www.youtube.com/watch?v=Wspvva4YqX0

(2022) called upon non-Russian peoples in the Russian Federation to not join the Kremlin's mobilisation and fight against Ukraine but instead: 'Fight not to die! Defend your freedom now in the streets and squares, so that you don't have to fight later in the mountains and forests simply for your right to live, when the Russian authorities begin the next waves of mobilisation.' Dagestanis, Chechens, Ingush, Ossetians, Circassians and other peoples under Russian occupation 'should not die in Ukraine'. The Ukrainian Parliament (2025) stated that, 'Unfortunately, Russia is actively recruiting representatives of enslaved peoples (including the Circassian) for their use as "cannon fodder" in the war with Ukraine.'

Just a year after Zelenskyy's election and preterm parliamentary elections that elected a large majority for his *Sluha Narodu* (Servant of the People) Party, the Ukrainian Parliament (2020) appealed to the United Nations, parliaments of foreign states and parliamentary assemblies of international organisations:

1. To condemn Russia's violations and restriction of the 'political, civil, national, religious and cultural rights' of representatives of Indigenous peoples in the Russian Federation and in Russian-occupied Ukraine, which are 'contrary to generally recognised principles and norms of international law'.
2. To increase 'political and diplomatic pressure' on Russia to halt its assimilationist policy of Indigenous peoples, 'violation of the sovereignty of the autonomous republics of the Russian Federation as a form of national statehood of Indigenous peoples', and provide 'full and real equality of persons belonging to Indigenous peoples in Russia and Russian-occupied Ukraine'.
3. To pay 'special attention to the need to protect the languages of Indigenous peoples' in Russia and Russian-occupied Ukraine, demand the restoration of teaching in their native language and study of their native language in education institutions and 'use all possible international political, diplomatic and sanction mechanisms against the Russian Federation in order to stop its violations of human rights and freedoms and de-occupy the Autonomous Republic of Crimea and the city of Sevastopol'.
4. To apply sanctions to Russian state officials involved in the persecution of Indigenous peoples for their beliefs and activities in defence of their rights and 'support the efforts of representatives of Indigenous peoples aimed at protecting the rights of Indigenous peoples and preserving their identity, languages, culture and traditions'.

A second Ukrainian parliamentary (2022a, 2022b, 2022c) resolution condemned 'armed aggression' against Chechnya, 'the occupation of its territory and the crime of genocide of the Chechen people'. This Ukrainian parliamentary (2022a, 2022b, 2022c) resolution supported the Declaration of State Sovereignty of the Chechen Republic and the adoption of a constitution by its parliament on 12 March 1992, which established 'a sovereign, independent, democratic and legal state'. Russian 'armed aggression' led to the temporary occupation of its entire territory during which 'its armed forces committed numerous international crimes', which 'included the genocide of the Chechen people'.

Consequently, the Ukrainian Parliament (2022c)

1. does not recognise Russia's occupation of Chechnya 'and considers the regime existing there to be an occupation and illegitimate';
2. condemns Russian 'crimes' committed 'during the first (1994–1996) and second (1999–2009) wars against the Chechen Republic of Ichkeria, the policy of genocide against the Chechen people, imitating the criminal actions of the Tsarist regime of 1817–1864 and the Soviet government of 1944';
3. 'calls on the UN and international organisations to ensure an independent and impartial investigation of international crimes committed on the territory of the temporarily occupied Chechen Republic of Ichkeria and to bring the perpetrators to justice'; and
4. calls on the UN and international organisations 'to recognise the Chechen Republic of Ichkeria as temporarily occupied by the Russian Federation and to condemn the crime of genocide against the Chechen people'.

Zelenskyy (2024) issued a presidential decree defending the rights of Ukrainians in the Russian Federation. Russia should 'ensure that Ukrainians living in its territories, including those historically inhabited by ethnic Ukrainians, have the right to education in the Ukrainian language and its free use, civil, social, cultural and religious rights, access to Ukrainian-language media, and the right of peaceful assembly'. The Ukrainian government, in consultation with 'international experts, the Ukrainian World Congress, and scholars', should produce and submit to the National Security and Defence Council of Ukraine an 'action plan to preserve the national identity of Ukrainians living in the Russian Federation'. This particularly relates to the historical Ukrainian lands of Kuban, *Starodubshchyna*, Northern and Eastern *Slobozhanshchyna*

(Krasnodar Krai), Belgorod, Bryansk, Voronezh, Kursk and Rostov *oblasts*. The 'action plan' should collect and examine 'evidence and testimonies about crimes committed against Ukrainians who live, or have lived, in Ukrainian historical territories in Russia, especially relating to Russification, political repression and deportation of Ukrainians'.

Zelenskyy's (2024a, 2024b) decree called for an intensification of counter-disinformation and propaganda 'regarding the history and present-day conditions of Ukrainians in Russia and all the peoples enslaved by it'. The purpose would be to hold events 'aimed at debunking Russian myths about Ukraine', dissemination of materials on Ukraine's more than one-thousand-year history of statehood and Ukrainian historical ties to lands 'inhabited by ethnic Ukrainians'.

The Ukrainian Parliament (2025) expressed its solidarity 'with all enslaved peoples of the Russian Empire and the USSR, who, along with the Ukrainian people, have suffered significant sacrifices and suffering because of being in a common "prison of peoples"'. The Ukrainian Parliament (2025) adopted a further resolution calling upon the UN and other international organisations to condemn Russian policies towards the Circassian people in the eighteenth and nineteenth centuries as genocide. 'Ethnic cleansing of the Circassian territories during the Russian-Caucasian War of 1763–1864', which led to 'more than ninety percent of the Circassians being physically destroyed or expelled from their homeland, was a series of pre-planned and cruel actions with the intention of oppressing the Circassian people, suppressing their identity, and deliberately creating living conditions for this ethnic group aimed at their complete or partial physical destruction'. The Russian authorities and army 'created artificial famine and epidemics among the civilian population with the aim of physically destroying the Circassians'.

The Ukrainian Parliament (2025) recognises Kabardians, Circassians, Adyghe and Shapsugs 'as the only Circassian (Adyghe) people' and 'heirs of historical Circassia' who survived genocide and 'were divided by artificial administrative borders'. These crimes against the Circassian and other peoples 'have not yet received proper legal and moral assessment'. The Ukrainian Parliament (2025) believes that Russia's justification 'of the crimes of previous ruling regimes' lies at the roots of Russia's state sponsorship of 'terrorism and a state that uses terrorist means to commit terrible crimes against Ukrainian and other peoples'.

The Ukrainian Parliament (2025) resolved to restore historical justice towards these peoples by

1. recognising that 'mass extermination of the Circassians (Adyghe)' and their ethnic cleansing 'bears all the hallmarks of genocide' 'in accordance with the UN Convention of 9 December 1948';
2. 'honouring the memory of all victims of this crime and express our solidarity with the Circassian (Adyghe) people';
3. calling on all countries and international organisations to recognise 'the mass extermination of the Circassians as genocide' and call upon Russia 'to officially recognise this crime and apologise for it';
4. condemning Russian attempts 'to distort historical facts in order to support an ideology of oppression and aggression'; and
5. recognising the right to national self-determination of Circassia 'on their historical territory'.

Messianism and Imperialism in Putin's Russia

Russian imperial innocence continues to be convinced of its generosity towards peoples Russia ruled over. This colonial narrative of empires being benign is a product of 'imperial amnesia' that was promoted by all imperialist powers. But only in Russia does it continue to shape attitudes towards Ukraine and other former Soviet republics in Eurasia.

European imperialists exhibited similar traits until World War II when Western historiographies were 'nationalistic', and they 'equalled the pan-Germans in their excess by the turn of the century…' (Kennedy, 1973, p. 82). Since World War II, intellectuals, scholars and policymakers in Western Europe, the United States, Australia and New Zealand have criticised imperialism, colonialism and empires. These have become negatively associated with crimes committed against conquered peoples, exploitation and destruction of their territories and condescension towards their cultures and identities (see Kennedy, 1973).

Times have changed in the West but not in Russia where a similar decolonisation of the mind has never taken place. In Putin's Russia, the continued prevalence of imperial nationalist narratives guides Russian foreign and security policies towards Ukraine, other former Soviet republics in Eurasia and the broader world. Russian state television promotes the colonialist narrative of Russia having paid a heavy burden and toll to develop its neighbours (Laruelle 2024, p. 328).

Except for brief periods during the 1920s, under Gorbachev and the first half of Yeltsin's presidency, Russia has not undertaken a critical introspection of its imperial and colonial legacies. A critical introspection of Russian imperialism and colonialism would have been only possible if Russia had moved towards a post-imperial, civic identity after 1991. Unfortunately, as Chapter 1 shows, this did not happen, and Russia exchanged communism for imperial nationalism, with only a brief democratic interlude in the first half of the 1990s. A Russian leader in the manner of Mustafa Kemal Atatürk, who built a Turkish nation-state on the ruins of the Ottoman Empire, never emerged to guide Russia from empire to post-imperial nation-state.

History is falsified in the service of glorifying Russian conquest and imperialism and denying the existence of Ukraine and a separate Ukrainian people. Indeed, as Kate C. Langdon and Vladimir Tismaneanu (2020, p. 1980) pointed out before the full-scale invasion, Russian chauvinistic attitudes towards Ukraine are 'a form of modern colonialism that pits Russia into a civilized "Us" (which also claims the right to geopolitical conquest) and Ukraine into a barbaric "Them"'. Russia's disparaging of non-Russian successor states of the USSR as not possessing full sovereignty, coupled with Moscow's abrogation to itself of the right to make decisions on their behalf, is especially true regarding Ukraine. An arrogant chauvinism is coupled with a messianic belief 'that Russia is saving Ukraine from the United States and the rest of the West' (Langdon and Tismaneanu, 2020, p. 206).

Anti-Americanism has deep roots in Russian identity since the Stalin era, with short breaks under Gorbachev and Yeltsin. Russian national identity in the Soviet Union and among White Russian émigrés was shaped in opposition to the West (see Kolesnikov, 2023). Putin and Russian imperial nationalists view NATO as not only a military but a civilisation adversary – which Ukraine cannot be allowed to join. The world is supposedly divided into 'cultural-civilisation spaces', with NATO one of these 'military-civilisation' blocs, which are competing with one another (see Sherr and Gretskiy, 2023; Lewis, 2023). Russia's 'state-civilisation', which includes Ukraine, is one of the poles in a multi-polar world (Lewis, 2023).

The Kremlin portrays the war against Ukraine as one of 'good Russia' versus an 'evil collective West'. State Duma Deputy Viacheslav Nikonov, grandson of Stalin's Foreign Minister Viacheslav Molotov, claimed Russia is a force for good, the war in Ukraine is a clash between good and evil and Russia is defending traditional values in a holy war against the 'satanic' West. Well-known TV host Vladimir Solovyov and Chechen warlord Ramzan Kadyrov agreed (Davis, 2024, pp. 301–302, 309).

The Kremlin's justification for its 'special military operation' against Ukraine is rooted in Russian messianism and Russian culture, as found in

Russia's 2013 foreign policy concept (Engstrom, 2014). Andrei Kolesnikov (2023) writes that Putin is obsessed with his mission to revive Russia as a great power, respected by and an equal to the United States. Putin and other Russian imperial nationalists believe Russia can only be revived as a great power if Ukraine is reunited. Putin's other obsessions are returning Ukraine to the Pan-Russian World and reunifying the *triune* (tripartite) 'fraternal peoples' – Russians, Ukrainians and Belarusians (Kolsto and Kolov, 2024).

Russia is fighting to restore its rightful place in the world by guaranteeing its great power status and protecting Russian traditional values and ways of life (Snegovaya, Kimmage, and McGlynn, 2023). Fixated on the past, Russia is seeking to regain its imperial glory and, in a similar manner to the Soviet Union, again become a *Katechon* (Restrainer) in a multipolar world. The 'ideologisation' of Russian foreign and security policy returned a sense of messianism and exceptionalism which would be accomplished through the spiritual mobilisation of Russians (Garner and Kuzio, 2025).

Chapter 2 analyses Russia's 2000 national security concept, which introduced 'spiritual security' defined as the protection of the 'historical, spiritual, cultural, and ethnic heritage of all Russia' (Putin, 2020; see Stoeckl, 2022). In January 2022, a long list of Russian spiritual and moral values was outlined in a decree, and the following year, new fundamental principles on culture and education were adopted (Snegovaya, Kimmage, and McGlynn, 2023).

Russian messianism and 'orthodox imperialism' assert hegemony over its neighbours by blurring the distinction between the Russian Federation and Russia as a 'state-civilisation' (Lewis, 2023; Kolsto and Kolo, 2024). 'Historic Russia', Putin said, is the equivalent of the former Soviet Union, a territory where Russia has a God-given mission (Kolsto and Kolov, 2024).

Lying at the centre of the Russian 'state-civilisation' is the Pan-Russian World uniting great, little and white Russians. Belarus has been successfully transformed into a White Russian puppet state, and the Kremlin's 'special military operation' was launched to transform Ukraine into a Little Russian puppet state. Russians, Ukrainians and Belarusians hold the same 'Russian' cultural and spiritual values, and Ukraine breaking away from the Russian 'state-civilisation' cannot be allowed to happen as it 'thrives as a single spiritually and culturally rich entity', Putin (2023b) told the Valdai Discussion Club. Ukrainians are forever bonded with Russians. No one 'should betray their civilisation', as this 'is unnatural' and 'I would say disgusting' (Putin, 2023b).

Russia's concept of 'spiritual security' has important ramifications for Ukrainians building an identity distinct from Russians, for example, possessing an autocephalous Orthodox Church of Ukraine. As the Spring 2022 and 2025 peace talks showed, and Russian leaders' comments since have reiterated, Putin and Russian imperial nationalists believe they have a God-given right to make demands towards Ukraine over which domestic and foreign policies it can pursue (see Domańska, 2021). 'They [Russians] very much hate our statehood and will do everything to destroy it', Kuchma (2023, p. 11) wrote.

As Chapter 6 shows, President Dmitri Medvedev's 'address' to President Yushchenko condemned Ukrainian President Yushchenko for pursuing policies that continued to be condemned by the Kremlin to this day (Kuzio, 2015, pp. 438–439). Thirteen years later, similar complaints were presented in the form of demands to Ukraine by Russia's team during the Spring 2022 peace talks headed by Putin's nationalist intellectual adviser Vladimir Medinsky (see Zygar, 2023b; Kuzio, 2025). Medvedev in 2009 and Medinsky, acting on behalf of Putin, in 2022 and 2025 made similar demands to revise Ukraine's memory politics, language, cultural and religious policies. These have always been the 'de-Nazification' goals of the 'special military operation'.

Russia as a Katechon

Adopting the discourse of Eurasianists, Putin claims Russia is the 'original "state-civilisation"'. This discourse is a sign of Russia's embrace of imperialism and the rehabilitation of empire as a positive phenomenon (Laruelle, 2024, p. 15). Russian-Ukrainian unity, state and empire, expansion and reunification, and imperialist irredentism and revanchism are closely integrated into Russian identity (Kolsto and Kolov, 2024). Putin's (2023b) definition of Russia as a 'state-civilisation' negates an understanding of itself as a nation-state. 'Russia has no borders', Putin (2023b) said, 'just like other civilisations have no borders either'. The Kremlin's claim of 'Russian [state-]civilisation' transcending the Russian Federation is 'central to Putin's conception of the state' (Sherr and Gretskiy, 2023).

Russia's 'state-civilisation' allegedly united different nationalities under benevolent Russian leadership and cultural superiority, a false claim we analysed earlier. Russians are God's chosen people to lead 'Holy Rus' (Kolsto and Kolov, 2024). Russia's 'state-civilisation' rests on the rejection of Western models and Russia' pursuit of its own unique path based on a 'thousand-year' tradition of statehood, greatness and national unity. The West has liberal democracy, and Russia has 'sovereign democracy'.

The Russian *Katechon* challenges the hegemony of the 'collective West' and opposes its spread of Godless, 'satanic' Western colonialism and liberal values. Although the colonies of European empires received their independence after World War II, the Kremlin claims that the 'collective West' continues to control their fate. Russia is the world's shield against the West's promotion of apocalyptic chaos, mobilising Russians and other peoples to fight for 'justice' against Western colonialism. Drawing on the imperialistic credo of 'Moscow as the Third Rome' (see Kolsto and Kolov, 2024), Russians are the chosen people and *Katechon* protecting the World from the Western Anti-Christ. The enemies of the Russian *Katechon* are the pro-Western opposition, Ukrainian 'nationalists/fascists/Nazis' and the 'collective West'. Russia has acted as a *Katechon* in Georgia, Ukraine and Syria; by revealing Western lies and duplicity in Kosovo and Iraq; and in opposing the 'collective West's' colonial policies towards the Global South. In fact, 'insecurity', 'imperial expansion' and 'autocratic exploitation of its own people' are the 'repeated hallmarks of Russian history', Dmitri Levitin (2024) writes.

The Russian Orthodox Church justifies its support for Russia's war against Ukraine in such terms as a 'holy war' (see Chapter 3). Putin's Russia and the Russian Orthodox Church are waging a 'national liberation struggle' against the 'criminal regime in Kyiv' and the United States-led unipolar order. Russia's 'holy war' is defending the single spiritual space of 'Holy Rus', uniting great, little and white Russians (Russians, Ukrainians and Belarusians) (see Stoyanov, 2024). In Russia's dystopian worldview, Ukrainians are 'at war with God' and are 'servants of the Prince of Darkness', where Zelenskyy is the 'devils spawn', while Russia is fighting 'ghouls' and 'the undead who rose from the grave' (Apt, 2024).

The West, having fallen into satanism, is being restrained by the Russian *Katechon*. The Russian army is 'liberating' Ukrainian land from 'absolute evil', Medvedev said, because the 'Kyiv regime' is led by an 'anti-Christian force', which unites 'satanists, Nazis, paganists and occult worshippers' (Apt, 2024). The war is between 'good versus evil, light versus darkness' (Apt, 2024); of course, Russia is understood to be 'good' and the 'light' and Ukraine and the West 'evil'.

Satanists have captured Kyiv, warned well-known Russian TV presenter Vladimir Solovyov, adding Ukrainian Nazis are 'Satanists and followers of misanthropic cults who make sacrifices and commit ritual murders'. 'Ukrainian satanists filmed a culinary show in Church during the [nativity] fast',[12] one report claimed. Ukrainians are really 'Russian people, possessed by the devil', former governor of the Donetsk Peoples Republic Pavel Gubarev said. Ukraine is a *Moloch* (pagan deity), which is why, Medvedev wrote, it should be destroyed (Apt, 2024).

The Russian *Katechon* is hard at work fighting to 'liberate' Ukraine, so it can reunite with 'Holy Rus' and destroy the anti-Christ 'collective West'. 'Russian' holy sites in Kyiv need to be liberated from Ukrainian Nazi satanists who are practising 'bloody paganism' and are suffering from 'demonic possession' (Apt, 2024). Ukraine's 'occupation' of 'Russian' cities and lands is anti-Russian, anti-Christian and anti-human, Medvedev wrote.

Russia and the New World Order

Russian opposition outlet *Meduza* reported that the Kremlin had issued a manual to state-controlled media with instructions to highlight the special role Russia plays in bringing about a proposed 'new world order'.[13] These instructions portray Putin as the 'world's greatest leader', whose deep thinking, 'breadth of political thought' and role as the 'voice of the global majority and new world order' distinguish him from Western political leaders. *Meduza* noted that, by contrast, the instructions do not discuss future negotiations with the United States about ending the war in Ukraine, even though Putin largely aimed his 2023 Discussion Club statements at shaping US President Donald Trump's foreign policy and achieving another reset in US–Russian relations on Russia's terms.

The Kremlin's media guidelines present Putin as 'the voice of the world's majority – and at the same time, the voice of the ordinary man'. Russia has a supposed special role in 'building the new world order', which includes the protection of 'the rights and freedoms of humanity', a hyperbolic claim considering Russia is a fascist dictatorship with no human rights or rule of law and imprisoning more political prisoners than in post-Stalin USSR (Garner and Kuzio, 2025).

Putin's proposed 'new world order' emphasises an interconnected international system without great powers or security blocs, a claim that

---

[12] https://euvsdisinfo.eu/report/culinary-show-filmed-at-church-during-fasting-period-is-worse-than-satanism/
[13] https://meduza.io/en/feature/2024/11/09/with-new-media-guidelines-the-kremlin-seeks-to-make-putin-s-valdai-club-speech-into-the-foundation-of-a-russian-defended-new-world-order

contradicts and undermines his claims. The instructions divided Putin's 'new world order' into six areas:

1. *Openness between states:* This is impossible because Russia is not a democracy and has no free media.
2. *The absence of 'universal dogmas':* This is obviously a rebuke against the United States allegedly promoting 'global [liberal] totalitarianism' around the world. Sergei Karaganov (2025), in another one of his bizarre commentaries, writes that 'A totalitarian liberal ideology is essentially being imposed' by Western countries that 'forget about their pretensions to democracy, although they continue to squeal about it'.
3. *Considering each country's voice in making 'global decisions':* Russia, as a great power, seeks to sit at the high table with the United States to make global decisions over the heads of countries with no real sovereignty, such as Ukraine.
4. *Rejection of certain international blocs:* NATO should be downsized and not invite Ukraine and Georgia to join. CSTO, BRICS and the Shanghai Cooperation Organisation can continue to grow.
5. *Closing the developmental gap between nations:* This is a worthwhile goal, but Russia does not have the financial resources to provide foreign aid to the Global South. China has shown that it is in a far better position to provide security *and* financial assistance.
6. *Pursuing equality for all peoples:* Russia falsely claims that 'The West sticks to racial attitudes and treats others as barbarians. The Russian civilisation is unique because it is the only one which treats all people, irrespective of their origin, as equal.' (1000 and 4000 days of hate speech in support of Russia's war against Ukraine, 2024).[14] 'Equality' for peoples is not reflective of Russia's approach towards Ukraine; indeed, there is no sign of equality in Russia's derogatory attitude towards former non-Russian Soviet republics whom the Kremlin views as not possessing real sovereignty. Russia's view of the world is shaped by an outdated nineteenth-century imperial and Cold War division between empires, spheres of influence and great powers on the one hand and less important countries who should obey them on the other. At one time, this was described as the division between historical and non-historical peoples with Ukrainians, the Irish and others included in the latter.

---

[14] https://euvsdisinfo.eu/report/the-russian-civilisation-is-unique-in-treating-all-people-equally/

Russia and the 'Global Majority'

Russia's full-scale invasion of Ukraine has transformed the geopolitical landscape and led to a near-complete rupture in the often-rocky relationship between Russia and the West. The Kremlin has sought to compensate for this loss by strengthening economic, security and diplomatic ties with the Global South. In an apparent bid to provide an ideological basis for this pivot, Putin has sought to promote Russia as the leader of a global anti-colonial movement. This cynical move echoes earlier Soviet propaganda, positioning the USSR as an enemy of Western imperialism.

Ironically, Putin (2022b) first championed Russia's anti-colonial credentials (at the same time as quoting imperial nationalist Ilyin) during a September 2022 ceremony, marking the imperialist annexation of the four Ukrainian *oblasts* of Donetsk, Luhansk, Kherson and Zaporizhzhya. At one point in his address, Putin spoke of ending US hegemony through an 'anti-colonial movement' led by Russia. Russian leaders have continued to promote a narrative of Moscow at the centre of an anti-colonial movement of the 'world majority'.

At a September 2023 forum in Vladivostok, Putin (2023b) stated that Russia had 'never been a coloniser anywhere'. One month later, he told an international audience at the annual Valdai Discussion Club that 'the era of colonial rule' was long over, before accusing the West of robbing the entire planet. 'The history of the West is essentially a chronicle of endless expansion', he declared without a hint of irony ruling over a country that became the largest in the world because of centuries of imperial expansion.

A basic knowledge of Russian history will recognise the absurdity of Putin's efforts to portray his country as an ideological opponent of imperialism. Modern Russia includes vast territories, including Ukraine, conquered from the fifteenth century onwards. Muscovy and the Tsarist Empire swallowed up numerous non-Russian nations and incorporated much of the northern Eurasian landmass, eventually reaching the Pacific Ocean. Russian imperial expansion into Siberia and the Caucasus region provided generations of Russian rulers with access to valuable resources, including oil, gas, gold, diamonds, timber and much more. These natural treasures have been a primary source of Russia's wealth for hundreds of years, representing a textbook example of colonial exploitation. The USSR earned huge dividends from exporting these valuable commodities. In the post-Soviet era, oligarchs have become billionaires from exploiting these riches, depositing this wealth in Western Europe while leaving the regions where these riches come from, and national minorities live, in an impoverished state. Indeed, these non-Russian regions remain among the poorest and most deprived areas of today's Russian Federation and are often a source of troops for Russia's war machine.

Russian Imperialism and Colonialism towards Ukraine

Putin has described the 'reunification' of four Ukrainian *oblasts* (Donetsk, Luhansk, Zaporizhzhya and Kherson) as 'returning' to Russia. Putin's Russia demands Ukraine, and the West recognise these territories as Russian, which Ukraine has rejected. Putin (2024) and other Russian leaders insist that peace talks need to go ahead based on Ukraine 'recognising realities on the ground', a euphemism that Ukraine must recognise annexed territories as now belonging de jure to Russia, which is nothing but old-fashioned imperialism. In addition, the Kremlin is demanding Ukraine transfer the parts of the four *oblasts* of Donetsk, Luhansk, Zaporizhzhya and Kherson that Ukraine continues to control.

In June 2022, Putin compared his conquest of Ukrainian territories as following in the manner of Peter I. On the 350th anniversary of the emperor's birth, Putin said Peter I did not take anything from Sweden; instead 'he returned [what was Russia's]'. Putin, who has viewed himself since 2012 as the 'gatherer of Russian lands' (with 'Russian' understood here as the three eastern Slavs), said 'Apparently, it also fell to us to return [what is Russia's] and strengthen [the country]'.[15] Putin seeks to enter the hallowed ground of Russian history by following in the footsteps of Peter I, Catherine I and Stalin.

Russian imperial nationalist attitudes towards Ukraine can be comprehended in four ways:

1. *Ukraine never existed:* They claim that Ukraine never existed or was artificially created by the Soviet regime. In fact, Ukraine is an older name than Russia. In May 2022, Putin pored over a 400-year-old map as proof that Ukraine did not then exist. Unfortunately, Putin ignored 'UKRAINE' written on the map over contemporary Ukrainian territory. No maps prior to the early eighteenth century used the term 'RUSSIA', which only came into usage in 1721 when Muscovy became the Russian Empire. Serhii Plokhy (2023, p. 17) explains that 'UKRAINE' has medieval origins and was first used by twelfth-century

---

[15] www.theguardian.com/world/2022/jun/10/putin-compares-himself-to-peter-the-great-in-quest-to-take-back-russian-lands

chroniclers. In the seventeenth century, 'UKRAINE' 'entered the international vocabulary' as one of the names of the Cossack state created after Hetman Bohdan Khmelnytsky's uprising in 1648–1657.

Crimea was 'always Russian': This racist view of Crimean history claims that its history began in 1783 when the Russian Empire conquered the peninsula. This patently ignores 600 earlier years when a Tatar khanate existed in Crimea. Reputable historians would never claim Australia's history begins with the arrival of Great Britain's Captain Cook in 1770 because to do so would be a racist denial of the history of the native peoples who already lived there. Indigenous peoples in Australia describe 26 January not as 'Australia Day' but as 'Invasion Day' (An angry culture war surrounds Australia Day, 2024). For Crimean Tatars, 19 April 1783 could also be called 'Invasion Day'. Meanwhile, 19 May is commemorated by Ukraine – but not Russia – as the day of genocide of the Crimean Tatars, 200,000 of whom were ethnically cleansed in 1944 in the *Sürgünlik* (Exile) by Stalin's Soviet Union (see Ukrainian Parliament, 2020).

2. *'Russian historical lands'*: Southeast Ukraine is 'historically Russian land' that was wrongly included in Soviet Ukraine. Putin (2023b) described New Russia (i.e., southeastern Ukraine) as 'historically Russian territory' and neither Crimea nor the Black Sea region has any connections to Ukraine. Putin and other Russian leaders have claimed Odesa, Mykolayiv, Kherson, Kharkiv, Dnipro, Kyiv and other Ukrainian cities are 'Russian' cities.

The myth of southeastern Ukraine being New Russia is debunked by Olivia I. Durand (2022) who writes that Tsarist, Soviet and Ukrainian censuses never showed any region of Ukraine, except Crimea, with an ethnic Russian majority. Durand (2022) shows that southern Ukraine had a history prior to its conquest by the Russian Empire in 1783 when it was called *Khanska Ukrayina* or *Tombasar Mukataasi*. Scholarly work on the region written in the late nineteenth century called it 'Southern Ukraine' and 'Steppe Ukraine'. Cossack Ukraine (*Zaporozhzhyan Sich*), the Nogai Hord, the Crimean Khanate and the Ottoman Empire coexisted and clashed in Southern Ukraine for centuries before the Russian Empire conquered the region.

In the nineteenth century, foreigners made up a large component of the inhabitants of Odesa, Mariupol, Mykolayiv and Kherson. Odesa was inhabited by many Italians and French while Greeks were prominent in Mariupol. In addition, Ukrainian settlers had been migrating and settling in southern Ukraine since the seventeenth century.

Durand shows that Ukrainians constituted a 54 per cent majority in the Kherson governate, which included Odesa; 69 per cent of the Yekaterinoslav governate, which covered Luhansk, Donetsk, Dnipropetrovsk and Zaporizhzhya; and 42 per cent, or nearly half of the inhabitants of Taurida governate, which encompassed Crimea.

The only manner the Kremlin stakes its claim that Russians constituted the largest group of inhabitants in New Russia is by defining 'Russians' as encompassing great, little and white Russians. Ethnic (or great) Russians never constituted majorities in any of the governates of New Russia when it was part of the Tsarist Empire. Durand (2022) writes that prior to the formation of Soviet Ukraine in 1922, southeast Ukraine was mainly inhabited by both Ukrainians and foreigners. Putin's revival of the term New Russia in 2014 to justify Russian territorial claims to southeast Ukraine is 'not only factually inaccurate', Durand (2022) writes, 'it is a completely modern assertion that serves recolonising purposes'. Putin is using bogus history to deny the existence of Ukraine and of the Ukrainian people who have lived on the territory of contemporary Ukraine, including its southeastern region, for centuries before their territory was colonised by Russia.

3. *Little Russia:* Central Ukraine, with both banks of the Dnipro River and the city of Kyiv, is Little Russia. Originally holding no negative connotations, the term Little Russia came to be used by Russian imperial nationalists since the nineteenth and twentieth centuries to denote a branch of the pan-Russian people alongside Great Russia (Russians) and White Russia (Belarusians). The term Little Russia, denoting central Ukraine, is derogatory and unacceptable to Ukrainians, as it is used by Russian imperial nationalists who deny the existence of Ukraine and a separate Ukrainian people.

Putin's (2022a) speech on the first day of the 'special military operation' 'was seeped in disinformation narratives' in order 'to mobilise support for armed aggression against a democratic and peaceful country'. *EUversusDisinfo* analysed Putin's (2022a) disinformation and what his words really meant:[16]

1. 'Self-defence of Russia': Attack and invasion of a sovereign state which does not pose any threat.
2. 'Limited military operation': All-out attack. Missile strikes, air and land invasion. Civilian targets, cities and infrastructure included.

---

[16] https://euvsdisinfo.eu/what-he-said-and-what-it-really-means/

3. 'No occupation': Intent to occupy as much as possible, as long as necessary. Place Ukraine under Moscow's control. Indefinitely.
4. 'De-Nazification of Ukraine': Stalinist-type repression of elected, legitimate officials of a sovereign country.
5. 'Holding election for a new government': Gun-point fake-democracy to place Kremlin-loyal puppets in power.

The European Parliament (2025) rejected claims by Putin's Russia:

> to justify an illegal war of aggression that constitutes a blatant violation of the UN Charter and of the responsibility of the Russian Federation as a permanent member of the UN Security Council to maintain peace and stability and that was immediately recognised as such by the other permanent members of the UN Security Council, along with an overwhelming majority of the UN General Assembly; recalls that no consideration of whatever nature, whether political, economic, military, historic or otherwise, may serve as a justification for Russia's aggression against Ukraine.

Written on billboards during Russia's occupation of parts of Kharkiv *oblast* in 2022 was the slogan 'Russia Never Attacks Anyone!' An unwillingness to critically condemn Russian imperialism lies at the root of Russian imperial innocence. Only four days before Russia's full-scale invasion, Kremlin press spokesman Dmitri Peskov said, 'But we remind you that Russia has never attacked anyone throughout its history', adding, 'Russia has no plans to invade anyone'.[17] Russian imperial innocence is evident in the Kremlin's claims that it did not begin the Russian-Ukrainian war because the 'special military operation' was a response to Western perfidy. Putin described the 'special military operation' as Russia's attempt to 'stop this war' as Russia 'did not start this war in 2022' (Davis, 2024, p. 398; Putin, 2024).[18] NATO is, of course, to blame for the war,[19] as are 'Anglo-Saxons', the 'collective West' and the United States. In 2008, Putin made a similar claim that Russia had not attacked Georgia and was not a party to the conflict, while de facto annexing the two territories of South Ossetia and Abkhazia (From Accepting NATO Aspirations to 'Denazifying': 20+ Years of Putin's Changing Views on Ukraine, 2022). After Russia's full-scale invasion, Lavrov (2024b) told the UN that Russia was not attacking anybody,

---

[17] https://sputnikglobe.com/20220220/moscow-has-no-plans-for-aggression-has-never-attacked-anyone-in-its-history-kremlin-spox-says-1093201581.html
[18] See https://euvsdisinfo.eu/report/russia-did-not-invade-ukraine/; https://euvsdisinfo.eu/report/ukraine-itself-is-to-blame-for-the-russian-invasion-of-ukraine/; https://euvsdisinfo.eu/report/russia-never-attacked-ukraine/
[19] https://euvsdisinfo.eu/report/nato-is-responsible-for-russias-war-against-ukraine/

in fact: 'The United States has attacked us using the Ukrainian regime as a proxy. It is waging a war against us using Ukrainian neo-Nazis, arming them, and helping them shell our territory with long-range weapons, as they directly participate in preparing such attacks. This is not something we chose.' The Kremlin's diatribe reflected the angry parallel universe it lived in which had nothing in common with reality or international law.

Conclusion

Russia's messianism and discourse on anti-colonialism reflect those of a schizophrenic state where contradictions, duplicity and untruths abound. The colonial legacies of Muscovy, the Tsarist Empire and the Soviet Union are as bad as those of Western empires; both imperialisms committed genocides. But since World War II, only Western scholars, intellectuals and policymakers have undertaken critical introspections of colonialism, imperialism and empires. From 1991, Ukrainians and other non-Russian peoples of the former Soviet Union also began to undertake critical introspections (see Kuzio, 2002, 2005, 2006), much to the annoyance of the Kremlin. The Soviet Union and Russia have never undertaken critical introspections of their colonial pasts. A brief interlude in the late 1980s and the first half of the 1990s, which uncovered 'blank spots' in history, was overshadowed by decades, if not centuries, before and decades after of Russian imperial innocence.

Ukrainian and Russian histories are incompatible, the former critical of the Tsarist Empire and Soviet Union and the latter rejecting anything critical in these two periods of history. The Soviet regime and Russia have poured scorn on Ukrainian history writing being separate from Russian. Over a century ago, Hrushevsky wrote *The Traditional Scheme of 'Russian' History and the Problem of a Rational Organization of the History of the East Slavs* (Wynar, 1979, pp. 55–64) to provide a framework for separate Ukrainian and Russian histories that is incompatible with Russian imperial nationalist history and the Kremlin's claim of 'one thousand years of Russian statehood' (Snegovaya, Kimmage, and McGlynn, 2023). Russian imperial nationalist history cannot accept the concept of Ukraine 'as a state unrelated to Russia'.[20]

Russia's imperial innocence is a game of smoke and mirrors used to obscure its colonial past and distract from historical truth. The Kremlin's

---

[20] https://tass.kribrum.ru/nazism and https://rvio.histrf.ru/activities/news/eksperty-obsudili-korni-ukrainskogo-nacizma

8 MESSIANISM, IMPERIALISM & ANTI-COLONIALISM

anti-colonialist discourse draws on Soviet anti-colonialism and an unwillingness to critically examine the many 'blank spots' in a 'thousand years of Russian statehood'. Putin's conflating of the USSR and 'Historic Russia' is an example of how the roots of his understanding of history lie in Soviet history writing from the mid 1930s to the mid 1980s when Russian imperialists and imperial generals were rehabilitated and glorified. While Ukrainian national historians like Hrushevsky were banned, Russian historians monopolised the history of 'Kievan Russia (Kyivan Rus) and Sovietised the Tsarist Empire's imperial historical framework. A historical trajectory of 'Kievan Russia' (Kyiv Rus)–Vladimir–Suzdal–Muscovy–Russian Empire–Soviet Union sidelined Ukrainians within a pan-Russian historical framework, made them out to be illegal squatters on 'historical Russian land' and marginalised them as pawns of foreign powers. Irrespective of Solzhenitsyn's (1980) complaints about North American historians, practically all Western historians of Russia used, and have continued to use since 1991, similar pan-Russian and Russian imperial nationalist frameworks (see Kuzio, 2020, pp. 9–35).

Russia's imperial innocence prevents most Russians from comprehending or accepting criticism of their treatment of Ukrainians and Ukraine's desire to distance itself from the Pan-Russian World. Soviet and Russian historical myths present only positive appraisals of imperial and communist rule over Ukrainians and other non-Russian peoples, denouncing, for example, the portrayal of the *Holodomor* as a genocide. In August 2009, Russian President Medvedev sent an 'address' to Ukrainian President Yushchenko infused with imperial innocence, which blamed Ukraine for the deterioration of Russian-Ukrainian relations.

Russia's schizophrenia is also apparent in how the Kremlin denies the existence of the name 'UKRAINE' and ignores its older age than that of 'RUSSIA'. Muscovy only became the Russian Empire in 1721. Kyiv, which celebrated its 1,500th year anniversary in 1982, is 600 years older than Moscow, a city that did not exist when Kyiv Rus was Christianised in 988. Describing Crimea as 'always Russian', which is common among Russian and Western historians of Russia (see Kuzio, 2022, pp. 36–55), is racist as it denies 600 years of Crimean Tatar history prior to 1783.

Durand (2022) shows how the Russian imperial nationalist concept of New Russia is a myth as ethnic Russians never constituted a majority in southeast Ukraine. The continued use of Little Russia to denote central Ukraine is derogatory with its roots in Russian imperial nationalist dismissal of Ukrainian identity. Similarly, Russian rule over Crimea should be understood as a Tsarist colonial conquest, not as a territory that 'was always Russian'.

Russia's posturing as a *Katechon*, leader of the new world order and 'Global Majority' has little to do with reality. A Russian *Katechon* fuses Soviet, Russian imperial nationalist and Russian Orthodox xenophobia against the 'collective West', United States, NATO, 'totalitarian liberalism', and the Ukrainian puppet state. The European Parliament (2025) 'Condemns Moscow's exploitation of Orthodox religion for geopolitical purposes, notably through the instrumentalisation of the Russian Orthodox Church (Moscow Patriarchate) as a tool to influence and exert control over Orthodox populations in Ukraine, Georgia, Moldova, Serbia and other countries'.

Russia was a declining great power before launching its 'special military operation', and this trend has accelerated since 2022. Poor social and weak economic factors show that Russia is not a great power: Russia's economy is the same size as the Netherlands, Belgium and Luxembourg combined, and the economies of the US states of California, Texas and New York are each bigger than Russia's. Russia's claim to be a great power rests on its possession of nuclear weapons, although we would never call Israel or Pakistan great powers.

Russia's inept and criminal war against Ukraine has shown it never possessed the second-best army in the world. Russia had to turn to Iran, China and North Korea for military equipment, dual-use technology and troops after its 'special military operation', resting on false myths and stereotypes of a country populated by Little Russians eagerly awaiting their liberation from 'nationalists/fascists/Nazis', failed to conquer Ukraine in a few days. The Kremlin's 'special military operation' became a full-scale war, which in its first three years produced very high military casualties of over one million and the loss of over 30,000 tanks and armoured fighting vehicles, and other military equipment.[21] Russia has lobbied support from the 'Global Majority' for its anti-Western Axis of Upheaval. Ukraine has countered by exposing how Russia's anti-colonialism rests on a schizophrenic view of history and imperial innocence that ignores a long history of brutal Russian colonialism and genocide of Ukrainians and other non-Russian peoples, a legacy that is being continued in Africa.

---

[21] www.oryxspioenkop.com/2022/02/attack-on-europe-documenting-equipment.html and https://ukdefencejournal.org.uk/russia-estimated-to-have-lost-almost-10000-tanks-in-ukraine/

The Kremlin's war against Ukraine has brought international isolation, as seen in only four countries voting with Russia at the UN. Russia's isolation cannot be compensated by an anti-Western axis that includes one rising power (China) and two pariah states (North Korea and Iran), with the latter severely weakened by Israeli attacks and the removal of the pro-Russian Assad regime in Syria. Russia's lacklustre military performance in Ukraine and lack of financial resources for foreign aid undermine the Kremlin's projection of itself as a leader of the new world order.

References

1000 and 4000 Days of Hate Speech in Support of Russia's War against Ukraine. (2024). *EUvsDisinfo*, 27 November. https://euvsdisinfo.eu/1000-and-4000-days-of-hate-speech-in-support-of-russias-war-against-ukraine/

An Angry Culture War Surrounds Australia Day. (2024). *The Economist*, 23 January. www.economist.com/asia/2025/01/23/an-angry-culture-war-surrounds-australia-day?utm_content=ed-picks-image-link-6&etear=nl_today_6&utm_campa%E2%80%A6

Applebaum, A. (2017). *Red Famine: Stalin's War on Ukraine*. London: Allen Lane.

Apt, C. (2024). Russia's Eliminationist Rhetoric against Ukraine: A Collection, Just Security, 18 April. www.justsecurity.org/81789/russias-eliminationist-rhetoric-against-ukraine-a-collection/

Brandenberger, D. L. and Dubrovsky, A. M. (1998). '"The People Needs a Tsar": The Emergence of National Bolshevism in Stalinist Ideology, 1931–1941', *Europe-Asia Studies*, 50 (5): 873–892.

Brudny, Y. M. (2000). *Reinventing Russia. Russian Nationalism and the Soviet State, 1953–1991*. Cambridge, MA: Harvard University Press.

Davis, J. (2024). *In Their Own Words. How Russian Propagandists Reveal Putin's Intentions*. Stuttgart: Ibidem; New York: Columbia University Press.

Domańska, M. (2021). 'Putin's article: 'On the historical unity of Russians and Ukrainians', Centre for Eastern Studies, *OSW Analyses*, 13 July. www.osw.waw.pl/en/publikacje/analyses/2021-07-13/putins-article-historical-unity-russians-and-ukrainians

Durand, I. O. (2022). 'New Russia' and the Legacies of Settler Colonialism in Southern Ukraine', *Journal of Applied History*, 4 (1–2): 58–75.

Engstrom, M. (2014). 'Contemporary Russian Messianism and New Russian Foreign Policy', *Contemporary Security Policy*, 35 (3): 356–379.

Eristavi, M. (2023). 'Five Myths That Helped Russian Colonialism Remain Hidden in Plain Sight', *EUvsDisinfo*, 10 November. https://euvsdisinfo.eu/five-myths-that-helped-russian-colonialism-remain-hidden-in-plain-sight/

European Parliament. (2025). 'Russia's Disinformation and Historical Falsification to Justify Its War of Aggression against Ukraine', Resolution 2024/2988(RSP), 23 January. www.europarl.europa.eu/doceo/document/TA-10-2025-0006_EN.pdf

Farmer, K. C. (1980). *Ukrainian Nationalism in the Post-Stalin Era. Myth, Symbols and Ideology in Soviet Nationality Policy*. The Hague: Martinus Nijhoff Publishers.

Filipowicz M. (2007). *Emigranci i Jankesi. O amerykańskich historykach Rosji*. Lublin: Wydawnictwo KUL.

French, H. W. (2021). 'A Prison Called Tibet. How China Controls Its Restive Regions', *Foreign Affairs*, 100 (3): 179–184.

From Accepting NATO Aspirations to 'Denazifying': 20+ Years of Putin's Changing Views on Ukraine. (2022). *Russia Matters* 16 June. www.russiamatters.org/analysis/accepting-nato-aspirations-denazifying-20-years-putins-changing-views-ukraine

Garner, I. and Kuzio, T. (2025). Edited. *Russia and Modern Fascism: New Perspectives on the Kremlin's War against Ukraine*. Stuttgart: Ibidem; New York: Columbia University Press.

Goble, P. (2022). 'Moscow Alarmed by Growing Non-Russian Nationalism and Ukraine's Role in It', *Eurasia Daily Monitor*, 19 (160), 27 October. https://jamestown.org/program/moscow-alarmed-by-growing-non-russian-nationalism-and-ukraines-role-in-it/

Goble, P. (2023a). 'Moscow Alarmed by Kyiv's Interest in Russian Far East – and with Good Reason', *Eurasia Daily Monitor*, 20 (93), 8 June. https://jamestown.org/program/moscow-alarmed-by-kyivs-interest-in-russian-far-east-and-with-good-reason/

Goble, P. (2023b). 'Kyiv Expands Efforts to Attract Non-Russians in Russia', *Eurasia Daily Monitor*, 20 (158), 13 October. https://jamestown.org/program/kyiv-expands-efforts-to-attract-non-russians-in-russia/

Goble, P. (2024a). 'Kyiv Raises Stakes by Expanding Appeals to Ukrainian 'Wedges' Inside Russia', *Eurasia Daily Monitor*, 21 (12), 25 January. https://jamestown.org/program/kyiv-raises-stakes-by-expanding-appeals-to-ukrainian-wedges-inside-russia/

Goble, P. (2024b). 'Moscow Alarmed by Kyiv's Increased Interest in Ethnic Ukrainians Across Russia', *Eurasia Daily Monitor*, 21 (16), 1 February. https://jamestown.org/program/moscow-alarmed-by-kyivs-increased-interest-in-ethnic-ukrainians-across-russia/

Goble, P. (2024c). 'Moscow Worried about Ukrainian 'Wedges' in Russia and Their Growing Support from Abroad', *Eurasia Daily Monitor*, 21 (115), 30 July. https://jamestown.org/program/moscow-worried-about-ukrainian-wedges-in-russia-and-their-growing-support-from-abroad/

Goble, P. (2024d), 'Kyiv Set to Expand Support for Non-Russians in Russia', *Eurasia Daily Monitor*, 21 (121), 8 August. https://jamestown.org/program/kyiv-set-to-expand-support-for-non-russians-in-russia/

Goble, P. (2025). 'Circassian National Movement Energized by Kyiv's Recognition of Russian Genocide', *Eurasia Daily Monitor*, 22 (2), 14 January. https://jamestown.org/program/circassian-national-movement-energized-by-kyivs-recognition-of-russian-genocide/

Grek, I. (2023). 'The Grassroots of Putin's Ideology: Civil Origins of an Uncivil Regime', *East European Politics*, 39 (2): 220–239.

Heinemann-Gruder, A. (2024). 'Russia's Corporate Warriors' In: A. Heinemann-Gruder (ed.), *Who Are the Fighters? Irregular Armed Groups in the Russian-Ukrainian War Since 2014*. Stuttgart: Ibidem; New York: Columbia University Press: 333–354.
Horvath, R. (2011). 'Apologist of Putinism? Solzhenitsyn, the Oligarchs, and the Specter of Orange Revolution', *The Russian Review*, 70 (2): 300–318.
Joo, H-min. (2008). 'The Soviet Origin of Russian Chauvinism: Voices from below', *Communist and Post-Communist Studies*, 41 (2): 217–242.
Kapelany. Na sluzhbi Bohu i Ukrayni. (2019). Kyiv: Ukrainian Institute of National Memory. https://uinp.gov.ua/elektronni-vydannya/kapelany-na-sluzhbi-bogu-i-ukrayini
Karaganov, S. (2025). 'Breaking the Back of Europe: What Should Russia's Policy Be towards the West', *Russia in Global Affairs*, 22 January. https://globalaffairs.ru/articles/slomat-hrebet-evrope-karaganov/
Kassymbekova, B. (2022). 'Time to Question Russia's Imperial Innocence', *Ponars Eurasia*, Policy Memo 771, April. www.ponarseurasia.org/time-to-question-russias-imperial-innocence/
Kennedy, P.M. (1973). 'The Decline in Nationalistic History in the West: 1900–1970', *Journal of Contemporary History*, 8 (11): 77–100.
Koena, J-F. Zivanovic, M. and Eckel, M. (2025). 'Wagner's Successors Wage Campaign of Terror in Central African Republic', *Radio Free Europe/Radio Liberty*, 9 February. www.rferl.org/a/russia-wagner-mercenaries-central-african-republic-crimes/33306858.html
Kolesnikov, A. (2023). 'The Plot against Russia. How Putin Revived Stalinist Anti-Americanism to Justify a Botched War', *Foreign Affairs* 25 March. www.foreignaffairs.com/russian-federation/plot-against-russia
Kolsto, P. and Kolov, B. (2024). 'The Religious Component in Contemporary Russian Imperialism', *Religions*, 15 (9): https://doi.org/10.3390/rel15091138
Kuchma, L. (2023). *Ukrayina – Ne Rosiya. Dvatsyat Rokiv Potomu*. Kyiv: Adef-Ukrayina.
Kuraev, A. (2024). *Myfologiia Russkyh Vojn*. Moscow: BABooks Publishing House.
Kuzio, T. (1998). 'Ukraine: Coming to Terms with the Soviet Legacy', *The Journal of Communist Studies and Transition Politics*, 14 (4): 1–27.
Kuzio, T. (2002). 'History, Memory and Nation Building in the Post-Soviet Colonial Space', *Nationalities Papers*, 30 (2): 241–264.
Kuzio, T. (2005). 'Nation-State Building and the Re-Writing of History in Ukraine: The Legacy of Kyiv Rus', *Nationalities Papers*, 33 (1): 30–58.
Kuzio, T. (2006). 'National Identity and History Writing in Ukraine', *Nationalities Papers*, 34 (3): 407–427.
Kuzio, T. (2009). 'Commentary – Territorial Claims Can Work Two Ways: Russia and Ukraine', *Eurasia Daily Monitor*, 6 (18), 28 January. https://jamestown.org/program/commentary-territorial-claims-can-work-two-ways-russia-and-ukraine/
Kuzio, T. (2015). *Ukraine: Democratization, Corruption, and the New Russian Imperialism*. Santa Barbara, CA: Praeger.

Kuzio, T. (2017). 'Stalinism and Russian and Ukrainian National Identities', *Communist and Post-Communist Studies*, 50 (4): 289–302.
Kuzio, T. (2020). *Crisis in Russian Studies? Nationalism (Imperialism), Racism, and War.* Bristol: E-International Relations. www.e-ir.info/publication/crisis-in-russian-studies-nationalism-imperialism-racism-and-war/
Kuzio, T. (2022). *Russian Nationalism and the Russian-Ukrainian War: Autocracy-Orthodoxy-Nationality.* London: Routledge.
Kuzio, T. (2025). 'Putin's Demands Mean Trump Can Never Truly End the War. Here's Why?' *Moscow Times*, 17 April. www.themoscowtimes.com/2025/04/17/putins-demands-mean-trump-can-never-truly-end-the-war-heres-why-a88753
Langdon, K. C. and Tismaneanu, V. (2020). *Putin's Totalitarian Democracy. Ideology, Myth and Violence in the Twentieth Century.* Cham: Palgrave Macmillan and Springer Nature.
Laruelle, M. (2024). 'Russia's Ideological Construction in the Context of the War in Ukraine', *Russia. Eurasie Reports* 46, March. Paris: French Institute of International Relations. www.ifri.org/en/studies/russias-ideological-construction-context-war-ukraine
Lavrov, S. (2024a). 'Interview with Tucker Carlson', 6 December. https://mid.ru/en/foreign_policy/news/1985783/
Lavrov, S. (2024b). 'Remarks and Answers to Media Questions Following the Meeting of the OSCE Council of Foreign Ministers, Valletta', 5 December. https://mid.ru/en/foreign_policy/news/1985743/
Levitin, D. (2024). 'The Ongoing Reality of Russian Imperialism', *The Critic*, 18 March. https://thecritic.co.uk/the-ongoing-reality-of-russian-imperialism/
Lewis, D. (2023). 'The Role of Ideology in Russian Foreign Policy' In: J. M. Leader and M. L. Haas (eds.), *The Routledge Handbook of Ideology and International Relations.* London: Routledge: 374–390.
MacKinnon, A. (2022). 'Russia Is Sending Its Ethnic Minorities to the Meat Grinder', *Foreign Policy*, 23 September. https://foreignpolicy.com/2022/09/23/russia-partial-military-mobilization-ethnic-minorities/
Matthews, O. (2023). *Overreach. The Inside Story of Putin's War against Ukraine.* London: Mudlark.
Mazour, A.G. (1975). *Modern Russian Historiography.* Westport, CO and London: Greenwood Press.
Michel, C. (2024). 'How Aleksandr Solzhenitsyn Became Putin's Spiritual Guru', *Foreign Policy*, 7 April. https://foreignpolicy.com/2024/04/07/putin-russia-nationalism-solzhenitsyn-became-putins-spiritual-guru-ukraine/
Motyl, A. J. (1999). *Revolutions, nations, empires: conceptual limits and theoretical possibilities.* New York: Columbia University Press.
Motyl, A. J. (2001). *Imperial Ends: The Decay, Collapse, and Revival of Empires.* New York: Columbia University Press.
Oliinyk, A. and Kuzio, T. (2021). 'The Euromaidan Revolution of Dignity, Reforms and De-Communisation in Ukraine', *Europe-Asia Studies*, 73 (5): 807–836.

Pew Research Centre. (2017). 'Religious Belief and National Belonging in Central and Eastern Europe,' 10 May. www.pewresearch.org/religion/2017/05/10/religious-belief-and-national-belonging-in-central-and-eastern-europe/
Plokhy, S. (2023). *The Frontline. Essays on Ukraine's Past and Present*. Cambridge, MA: Harvard University Press.
Pompeo, M. R. (2021). 'Determination of the Secretary of State on Atrocities in Xinjiang', US Department of State, 19 January. https://2017-2021.state.gov/determination-of-the-secretary-of-state-on-atrocities-in-xinjiang/
Prina, F. (2016). *National Minorities in Putin's Russia. Diversity and assimilation*. London and New York: Routledge.
Putin, V. (2020). 'On the Concept of the National Security of the Russian Federation', 10 January. www.prlib.ru/item/352298
Putin, V. (2021). 'On the Historical Unity of Russians and Ukrainians', 12 July. http://en.kremlin.ru/events/president/news/66181
Putin, V. (2022a). 'Vladimir Putin Announced the Start of a Special Military Operation in Connection with the Situation in Donbas', 24 February. www.1tv.ru/news/2022-02-24/421583-vladimir_putin_ob_yavil_o_nachale_spetsialnoy_voennoy_operatsii_v_svyazi_s_situatsiey_v_donbasse
Putin, V. (2022b). 'Signing of Treaties on Accession of Donetsk and Lugansk People's Republics and Zaporozhye and Kherson Regions to Russia', 30 September. http://en.kremlin.ru/events/president/news/69465
Putin, V. (2022c). 'Meeting with Historians and Representatives of Russia's Traditional Religions', 4 November. http://en.kremlin.ru/events/president/transcripts/69781
Putin, V. (2023a). 'Russia Has Never Acted as Coloniser, Unlike West', *Tass*, 12 September https://tass.com/economy/1673569
Putin, V. (2023b). 'Speech to Valdai Discussion Club', 5 October. http://en.kremlin.ru/events/president/news/72444
Putin, V. (2023c). 'Meeting with Members of the Security Council, and Government, and Heads of Security Agencies', 30 October. http://en.kremlin.ru/events/president/news/72618
Putin, V. (2024). 'Results of the Year with Vladimir Putin', 19 December. www.en.kremlin.ru/events/president/transcripts/75909
Rating Sociological Organisation. (2022). 'The Tenth National Survey: Ideological Markers of the War,' 27 April. https://ratinggroup.ua/en/research/ukraine/desyatyy_obschenacionalnyy_opros_ideologicheskie_markery_voyny_27_aprelya_2022.html
Rating Sociological Group. (2023). 'The Dynamics of Attitudes Towards the 1932–1933 Holodomor,' 23 November. https://ratinggroup.ua/en/research/ukraine/92_ukraincsv_vvazhayut_golodomor_genocidom_ukrainskogo_narodu.html
Rindlisbacher, S. (2018). 'From Space to Territory: Negotiating the Russo-Ukrainian Border, 1919–1928', *Revolutionary Russia*, 31 (1): 86–106.

Rowley, D. G. (2000). 'Imperial versus national discourse: the case of Russia', *Nations and Nationalism*, 6 (1): 23–42.

Sherr, J. and Gretskiy, I. (2023). 'Why Russia Went to War. A Three-Dimensional Perspective', International Centre for Defence and Security, 30 January. https://icds.ee/en/why-russia-went-to-war-a-three-dimensional-perspective/

Shkandrij, M. (2001). *Russia and Ukraine. Literature and the Discourse of Empire from Napoleonic to Post-Colonial Times*. Montreal and Kingston.: McGill-Queens University Press.

Shtohrin, I. (2021). 'Rosiya "planomirno zachyshhaye" Ukrayinski Orhanizaciyi: Shhoza Cym Stoyit?' *Radio Svoboda*, 4 November. www.radiosvoboda.org/a/rosiya-planomirno-zachyshchaye-ukrayinski-orhanizatsiyi/31544435.html

Snegovaya, M., Kimmage, M. and McGlynn, J. (2023). 'Putin the Ideologue. The Kremlin's Potent Mix of Nationalism, Grievance, and Mythmaking', *Foreign Affairs* 16 November. www.foreignaffairs.com/russian-federation/putin-ideologue

Socher, J. (2021). *Russia and the Right to Self-Determination in the Post-Soviet Space*. Oxford: Oxford University Press.

Solzhenitsyn, A. (1980). 'Misconceptions about Russia Are a Threat to America', *Foreign Affairs*, 58 (4): 797–834.

Stoeckl, K. (2022). 'Russia's Spiritual Security Doctrine as a Challenge to European Comprehensive Security Approaches', *The Review of Faith and International Affairs*, 20 (4): 37–44.

Stoyanov, Y. (2024). 'The War in Ukraine: Challenges to Just War Doctrines in Eastern Orthodoxy', *Studies in Christian Ethics*, 37 (3): 669–692.

Tillett, L.R. (1964). 'Soviet Second Thoughts on Tsarist Colonialism', *Foreign Affairs*, 42 (2): 309–319.

Tillett, L.R. (1967). 'Nationalism and History', *Problems of Communism*, XVI (5): 36–45.

Tillett, L.R. (1969). *The Great Friendship. Soviet Historians on the Non-Russian Nationalities*. Chapel Hill, NC: University of North Carolina Press.

Ukrainian Parliament. (2020). 'Pro Zvernennya Verxovnoyi Rady Ukrayiny do Orhanizaciyi Obyednanykh Nacii, Yevropejskoho Parlamentu, Parlamentskoyi Asambleyi Rady Yevropy, Parlamentskoyi Asambleyi OBSYe, Parlamentskoyi Asambleyi NATO, Parlamentskoyi Asambleyi OChES, uryadiv i parlamentiv derzhav svitu shhodo vshanuvannya zhertv henocydu krymskotatarskoho narodu ta zasudzhennya porushen Rosijskoyu Federaciyeyu yak derzhavoyu-ahresorom prav i svobod krymskotatarskoho narodu', Appeal, 2 June. https://zakon.rada.gov.ua/laws/show/639-IX

Ukrainian Parliament. (2022a). 'Declaration on the Genocide Committed by the Russian Federation in Ukraine', 14 April. https://itd.rada.gov.ua/billinfo/%D0%94%D0%BE%D0%B4%D0%B0%D1%82%D0%BE%D0%BA (eng).pdf

Ukrainian Parliament. (2022b). 'Pro natsionalni menshyny (spilnoty) Ukrayiny', Law, 13 December with amendments 21 September and 8 December 2023. https://zakon.rada.gov.ua/laws/show/2827-20#Text

Ukrainian Parliament. (2022c). 'Zayavu Verxovnoyi Rady Ukrayiny pro zasudzhennya zbrojnoyi ahresiyi rosijskoyi federaciyi proty Chechenskoyi Respubliky Ichkeriya, okupaciyi yiyi terytoriyi ta zlochynu henocydu Chechenskoho narodu', Appeal, 18 October. https://zakon.rada.gov.ua/laws/show/2672-20#Text

Ukrainian Parliament. (2023). 'Postanovy pro Zayavu Verkhovnoyi Rady Ukrayiny "Pro vyznachennya isnuyuchoho v Rosiyskiy Federaciyi politychnoho rezhymu yak rashyzmu ta zasudzhennya yoho ideolohichnykh zasad i suspilnykh praktyk yak totalitarnykh ta lyudonenavysnyckykh"', Resolution, 2 May. https://itd.rada.gov.ua/billInfo/Bills/Card/41531

Ukrainian Parliament. (2025). 'Postanovy Pro Vyznannya Henocydu Cherkeskoho Narodu, Vchynenoho Rosijskoyu Imperiyeyu', Resolution, 9 January. https://itd.rada.gov.ua/billInfo/Bills/Card/44400

Velychenko, S. (1993). *Shaping Identity in Eastern Europe and Russia*. New York: St Martin's Press.

Velychenko, S. (1994a). 'Restructuring and the Non-Russian Past', *Nationalities Papers*, 22 (2): 325–335.

Velychenko, S. (1994b). 'National History and the "History of the USSR": The Persistence and Impact of Categories' In: D.V. Schwartz and R. Panosian (eds.), *Nationalism and History. The Politics of Nation-Building in Post-Soviet Armenia, Azerbaidzhan and Georgia*. Toronto: University of Toronto: 23–47.

Velychenko, S. (1995). 'Identities, Loyalties and Service in Imperial Russia: Who Administered the Borderlands?' *Russian Review*, 54 (2): 188–208.

Velychenko, S. (2002). 'The Issue of Russian Colonialism in Ukrainian Thought', *Ab Imperio*, 2002 (1): 323–367.

Velychenko, S. (2004). 'Post-Colonialism and Ukrainian History', *Ab Imperio*, (1): 391–404.

Wynar, L. R. (1979). 'The Present State of Ukrainian History in Soviet Ukraine: A Brief Overview', *Nationalities Papers*, VII (1): 1–24.

Zelenskyy, V. (2022). 'Address by the President of Ukraine to the Indigenous Peoples of Russia: Fight to Avoid Death, Defend Your Freedom in the Streets and Squares', 29 September. www.president.gov.ua/en/news/zvernennya-prezidenta-ukrayini-do-korinnih-narodiv-rosiyi-bo-78137

Zelenskyy, V. (2024a). 'Volodymyr Zelenskyy Instructed to Draw up an Action Plan to Preserve the National Identity of Ukrainians in Russia', 22 January. www.president.gov.ua/en/news/volodimir-zelenskij-doruchiv-rozrobiti-plan-dij-shodo-zberez-88469

Zelenskyy, V. (2024b). 'Pro Istorychno Naseleni Ukrayintsyamy Terytorii Rosiyskoyi Federatsii', Decree 17/2024, 22 January. www.president.gov.ua/documents/172024-49513

Zygar, M. (2023a). *War and Punishment. The Story of Russian Oppression and Ukrainian Resistance*. London: Weidenfeld and Nicholson.

Zygar, M. (2023b). 'The Man Behind Putin's Warped View of History', *New York Times*, 19 September. www.nytimes.com/2023/09/19/opinion/putin-russia-medinsky.html

9

Xenophobia

> Russia isn't fighting for territories or Ukraine's resources. Russia is fighting for God, for God's sake, and for God's world, for the world as God intended it to be, where all people are different but equal, where everyone is original in their own way, where there is not this stupid satanic melting pot.
>
> *Russia Channel 1, 12 December 2024.*[1]

Russia's war against Ukraine is not only about revanchist designs towards Ukrainian territory but about attempts to destroy Ukrainian independent statehood and national identity. Important issues are also at stake in the war that have strategic ramifications for the world order and international law. To what extent will the world order be based on a set of universal values defined by the UN Charter? To what extent will international relations depend on the sovereign interests of individual countries as opposed to being decided over their heads by great powers? To what extent will xenophobic obsessions, prejudices, conspiracy theories and primitive stereotypes become the driving force of the world order in the future? Indeed, will international law continue to have any relevance? This chapter discusses these questions.

For centuries, Russia has fluctuated between, on the one hand, seeking to catch up with the West and, on the other, viewing the West in a xenophobically negative manner. The latter dominated most of the Soviet era and post-Soviet Russia. Kate Langdon and Vladimir Tismaneanu (2020, pp. 139–141) write that Putin is a survivor and a remnant of *Homo Sovieticus*, the term coined by Aleksandr Zinoviev in 1984. *Homo Sovieticus* are xenophobic towards the West, imperialist, and believe in the superiority of Russia's civilisation. Maintaining Russians as *Homo Sovieticus*, rather than allowing them to emerge as citizens with agency as in Ukraine (see Chapter 8), has provided Vladimir Putin with the cannon

---

[1] https://x.com/Gerashchenko_en/status/1866924756810760426

fodder he needs for Russia's full-scale war with Ukraine and the West. President Volodymyr Zelenskyy (2024) said, 'They [Russians] are afraid of freedom. They were born under Putin, went to school under Putin, joined the army under Putin and are dying for his sick ideas.'

As early as Russia's first invasion of Ukraine in 2014, between 70 and 80 per cent of Russians harboured xenophobic feelings towards the West (Laruelle, 2014). Nearly a decade later, three-quarters of Russians held negative attitudes towards the United States, NATO, the EU and, of course, Ukraine. Russians hold positive attitudes towards China, Iran and Türkiye, although this is unlikely to remain the case for the latter country after it assisted in the overthrow of the pro-Russian Bashar al-Assad regime in Syria (Levada Centre, 2023a; Levada Centre, 2023b). Most Russians agree with their leaders and media personalities, such as the well-known TV host Vladimir Solovyov (Davis, 2024, p. 110) in blaming the United States and NATO for the Kremlin's full-scale war against Ukraine. Nearly two-thirds (65 per cent) of Russians blame the United States and NATO, an increase from 57 per cent in 2022 (Levada Centre, 2024). Less than 10 per cent of the Russian people blame Russia. Russian academic Andrey Sidorov (2024) wrote that the West, because of its 'hatred of Russians and Historical Russia', declared war on Russia with the goal of capturing its resources, dismembering Russia and liquidating the Russian state and civilisation'.

Mikhail Gorbachev's Soviet Union and the first half of Boris Yeltsin's Russia adopted liberalising policies and pursued good relations with the West. But this period was an aberration in Russian and Soviet history: Gorbachev was preceded by conservative leaders Leonid Brezhnev, Yuri Andropov and Konstantin Chernenko, while Yeltsin was succeeded by anti-Western xenophobe Putin. Yevgeny Primakov, Russian foreign minister from 1996–1998, redefined Russia from belonging within the 'common European home' to that of Russia lying at the centre of Eurasia, thus preparing the ground for Putin's imperial nationalism from 2000. As Owen Matthews (2023, p. 368) points out, it is misplaced to believe Russia exchanged communism for Western liberalism in 1991; in fact, since the mid 1990s, imperial nationalism has been more powerful in Russian politics and popular opinion.

In Russian history, the West has acted as a positive and, to a far greater extent, a negative 'Other'. In both cases, Russia's deep-seated inferiority complex plays an influential role in how the country relates to the West (see Matthews, 2023, p. 79; McGlynn, 2023, p. 131). Russia's inferiority complex towards the West is compensated for by adopting a superiority complex, which alleges that Russian civilisation is spiritually superior to the West, and Russia is a defender of 'traditional family values' and morally upright (McGlynn, 2023, p. 131). Public opinion has risen to a peak belief that Russia is a great power, which they – like Putin – understand as a return to the respected status the Soviet Union possessed.

Lev Gudkov (2023), of the Levada Centre, Russia's last remaining independent polling organisation, writes of an inner Russian conflict between pride in Russia being a great power and nuclear state and shame in the country's eternal poverty and backwardness. Russians fail to comprehend how Russia is not a great power when looking at its extensive poverty and backwardness, low average life expectancy, Russia as a 'mafia state' (Spain Details Its Strategy to Combat the Russian Mafia, 2010), poor capabilities and quality of military equipment in the Russian army (clearly the war has shown that it is not the 'second best in the world' but the second best in Ukraine), lack of technological exports (compared to China's Huawei and electric cars), declining demand for Russian arms exports and loss of its biggest energy market in Europe. Russian soldiers, told they were superior to their Little Russian 'younger brothers', were stunned – and visibly angered – at the higher standard of living they found in Ukrainian villages and towns, leading to widespread looting of literally everything that could be stolen (Horycheva, 2022). A Ukrainian soldier returned to his home in the Kyiv region to find that the contents of his laundry basket had been looted. Some Russian soldiers had never seen indoor plumbing, toilets, showers and baths. 'People saw them simply loading everything on to Ural trucks, everything they could get their hands on', said Natalia Samson after returning to her liberated village of Novyy Bykiv in the Kyiv region.[2] Russian soldiers with looted Ukrainian washing machines became a ubiquitous image of the first year of the full-scale invasion.[3]

For liberalising Russian and Soviet leaders, seeking to catch up with the West is a means to modernise the country and improve its economic and military potential. For them, the West is a positive 'Other' to provide reforms, foreign investment and technology to overcome Russia's relative backwardness. For conservatives and imperial nationalists, the West has always been a negative 'Other'. Wendy Slater (1998, p. 79) writes the West was a constant opponent and the antithesis of the 'imagined Russia'. Accusations that the West is imposing alien values on Russia have a deep

---

[2] www.theguardian.com/world/2022/apr/11/ukrainian-homes-looted-by-russian-soldiers?
[3] https://archive.kyivpost.com/article/opinion/op-ed/if-russia-is-rich-and-powerful-why-are-their-soldiers-looting-ukrainian-villages.html

history going back to the Slavophiles, Eurasianists, Russian nationalist dissidents and Soviet anti-imperialist and anti-American discourse (Laruelle, 2014). Alexander Solzhenitsyn and Ivan Ilyin, Putin's favourite writer, both expounded on the question of the West's antagonism towards Russia. During his exile in the US during the Cold War, Solzhenitsyn derided the West for its alleged loss of spiritual values.

Putin's Russia attacks the West for promoting LGBTQ, destroying family values, imposing multiculturalism and losing national sovereignty because of globalisation. Putin's Russia is described as the bastion of cultural conservativism and family values and a defender of national sovereignty in the face of an aggressive American promotion of liberal values (see Etkind, 2023, p. 11). Russia is protecting itself from 'filth' and 'destructive ideas and values' exported by the West to Russia, which are 'alien' to the Russian people (Apt, 2024). The West attempted to destroy Russian values in the 1990s and continues to try and do so by imposing its 'pseudo-values' and alien ideals and in so doing threaten Russia's cultural sovereignty (Aron, 2023, pp. 41–42).

Anti-Western xenophobia has grown exponentially in Putin's Russia since the mid 2000s. Leon Aron (2023, p. 36) writes that Putin's xenophobic 'war rhetoric' is 'crude and raw' and worse than that used by Soviet leaders, including Joseph Stalin (Aron, 2023, p. 39). The United States has no allies, dominates vassals and acts in an imperialist and neo-colonial manner towards Russia, China, Iran and the Global South (Kimmage and Shapiro, 2024). The Kremlin believes US support for liberal internationalism is a smokescreen hiding US self-interest and American hegemony, as seen in its naked military aggression against Yugoslavia and Iraq, which were undertaken without UN mandates, and recognition of the independence of Kosovo. The West has promoted regime change in Eurasia and the Middle East and has imposed its will upon those who disagreed with it. The West is described by Putin's Russia as 'insolent', 'uncultured', 'arrogant', a 'swindler', 'shameless', a 'deceiver' and 'disgusting' (Aron, 2023, p. 40).

The United States and West are attacked by Putin's Russia in four ways. The first is the West's interference in Eurasia. Both Yeltsin and Putin view the former Soviet Union as Russia's exclusive sphere of influence and de facto, an extension of 'Russia'; Putin has described the USSR as 'Historical Russia'. Russia does not respect the Soviet successor states, especially Ukraine and Belarus, as countries possessing full sovereignty. Russia's demand for a 'new world order' with equality of states does not therefore apply to Ukraine and other former Soviet republics. Speaking in Kyiv on the eve of Russia's first invasion of Ukraine and annexation of Crimea, Putin (2013) said, 'we will respect whatever choice our Ukrainian partners, friends, and brothers make'. In fact, he meant to say Ukraine's 'choice' would be only acceptable to Russia if it entailed turning its back on the EU and becoming part of the Pan-Russian World and joining the Eurasia Economic Union. Nearly a decade later, the World Russian Peoples Council (2024a) described the multipolar ('polycentric') world, which they are supporting to replace the US-led unipolar world, as 'compliance with the generally recognised principles of international law, sovereignty, equal cooperation, and the right of each country to its own development, culture, and religion'. Russia obviously does not grant Ukraine these rights.

Russian leaders believe they have a right to decide Ukraine's foreign and security policy, claiming that Ukraine and Russia can only have good relations if Ukraine becomes a 'neutral' state, ignoring the fact that Ukraine was a neutral state in 2014 when Russia launched its first invasion. Putin (2024a) asks, 'Why this is the case is because it means that Ukraine will be constantly used as a tool in the hands of others and to the detriment of the interests of the Russian Federation. Thus, the basic conditions for normalising relations will not be created and the situation will develop according to an unpredictable scenario. We would very much like to avoid this.' Russia's understanding of 'neutrality' is very different from dictionary definitions with the Kremlin believing, as it laid out in its peace proposals in Spring 2022 and 2025, it had the right to dictate Ukraine's 'correct' language, cultural and memory politics (i.e., 'de-Nazification'), limit the size of the Ukrainian army (i.e., 'demilitarisation') and decide which international organisations Ukraine could join (Surnacheva, 2024). In other words, the Kremlin's understanding of 'neutrality' is that of a Little Russian puppet state (Barros, 2025).

The World Russian Peoples Council (2024a) placed Russia at the 'centre of the international anti-colonial movement', a hyperbolic claim which is obviously contradicted by Russian imperialist military aggression against Ukraine. 'The way other states run their lives is none of our business', Putin (2023a) told the Valdai Discussion Club, unless of course when Russia is referring to Ukraine.

The second is that Russia's ruling elites are former Soviet security and military officers (*siloviki*) with a xenophobic view of the West. *Siloviki* inherited a conspiracy mindset from the Soviet Union, which has remained in place in the Kremlin (see Soldatov and Borogan, 2022). The *siloviki* leading Russia believe the West had been at war with Russia ever since they had conspired to destroy the Soviet Union, a country they still possess deep levels of nostalgia for (Corum, 2018). This conspiratorial mindset, Andrei Soldatov and Irina Borogan (2022) remind us, has deep roots in the senior *siloviki* whose formative careers were in the KGB (Committee for State Security), GRU (Soviet military intelligence) and Soviet military and who became Russia's ruling elites. Russia's full-scale invasion of Ukraine was decided by Putin and his former KGB comrades – Nikolai Patrushev, Alexander Bortnikov, Sergei Naryshkin, Sergei Ivanov, Igor Sechin, Sergei Beseda and Dmitry Kozak (Matthews, 2023, p. 161). When Putin was appointed as prime minister in 1999, he recommended Patrushev replace him as chairman of the FSB (Federal Security Service) (Grove, Cullison, and Pancevski, 2023). Patrushev assisted Putin's rise to power by stoking a cult of war and anti-Caucasus xenophobia through the bombing of four apartment buildings, which killed 307 and wounded 1,700 and were blamed on Chechens and used as the excuse to restart the war against Chechen separatism (see Satter, 2017, pp. 10, 15, 17, 28). Patrushev's FSB undertook assassinations at home and abroad of those Putin's Russia deemed to be terrorists or extremists. Journalists who investigated the apartment bombings and blamed the Russian authorities were assassinated – Yuri Shchekochikhin, Natalia Esemirova, Sergei Yushenkov, Anna Politkovskaya and Alexander Litvinenko (see Satter, 2017, pp. 97–132). The first assassinations abroad were Ukrainian opposition presidential candidate Yushchenko in Kyiv in September 2004, who survived a dioxin poisoning, and FSB defector Litvinenko, who was murdered in London with radiation poisoning in November 2006. As secretary of the Russian Security Council, Patrushev played a key role in Putin's decision to launch a 'special military operation' against Ukraine and oversaw the assassination of Yevgeny Prigozhin in August 2023, three months after the Wagner Group's rebellion (see Grove, Cullison and Pancevski, 2023).

Ukraine and the West as negative 'Others' are closely intertwined in the minds of the former *siloviki* running Russia. The Kremlin conjures up a Ukrainian hand in practically every unpleasant event for Russia and its allies – the Crocus City Hall terrorist attack in March 2024, the assassination attempt on pro-Russian Slovak Prime Minister Robert Fico in May 2024, terrorist attacks in Dagestan in June 2024 and Ukrainian training for insurgents who overthrew the Assad Syrian regime in late 2024.[4] Ukraine's

---

[4] https://euvsdisinfo.eu/report/the-attack-on-crocus-city-hall-was-prepared-by-the-ukrainian-secret-services-using-tajiki-terrorists/; https://euvsdisinfo.eu/report/crocus-hall-terrorists-confess-to-carrying-out-the-attack-with-the-help-of-ukrainian-special-services/; https://euvsdisinfo.eu/report/ukrainian-intelligence-and-nato-countries-masterminded-terror-attacks-in-dagestan/;

assassination of Lieutenant General Igor Kirillov, head of Russia's chemical and biological defence troops, in Moscow in December 2024 was blamed on his exposure of (non-existent) US bio labs in Ukraine.[5] The suspect who blew up a truck outside the Donald Trump hotel in Las Vegas on 1 January 2025 had allegedly posted pictures of himself on social media wearing a *Slava Ukrayini!* (Glory to Ukraine!) tee shirt.[6]

The third is that anti-Western xenophobia is an essential component of the cult of war and search for internal (liberal opposition) and external (Ukraine and the West) enemies in Putin's Russia. Unveiled in June 2020, the Main Cathedral of the Russian Armed Forces is a 'pagan temple to the God of War' (Ash, 2024, p. 245). The Russian Orthodox Church promotes anti-Western xenophobia, and its clergy have supported Russia's 'holy war' against 'satanic' and 'Nazi' Ukraine (Ash, 2024, pp. 302–306). A close relationship exists between growing authoritarianism and political repression at home and military aggression abroad. Russia's war with the West, which is 'inevitable' according to Margarita Simonyan, head of the Kremlin propaganda mouthpiece *RT*, began in Ukraine (Davis, 2024, p. 82).

The fourth factor is Putin's and Russian imperial nationalist obsession with Ukraine. On 24 February 2022, the day Russia launched its 'special military operation', Putin accused NATO of establishing a 'military foothold' on 'territories adjacent to Russia, which I have to note is our historical land' (i.e., Ukraine), where it is building a 'hostile' 'Anti-Russia' (Putin, 2022a). The World Russian Peoples Council (2024b) adopted a resolution requesting the Russian government adopt legislation legally defining a *triune* (tripartite) pan-Russian people, which would deny the existence of a separate Ukrainian people. Deputy Head of the Russian Security Council Medvedev (2022) said that Ukraine would no longer exist within two years, while Patrushev (2025) predicted Ukraine's demise by the end of 2025.

This chapter has six sections. The first analyses authoritarianism, dictatorship, fascism and war from a theoretical and comparative perspective. The second section investigates the cult of war in Putin's Russia. The third

---

https://euvsdisinfo.eu/report/the-attack-on-robert-fico-linked-to-nato-and-ukraine-sponsored-terrorism/; https://euvsdisinfo.eu/report/escalation-in-syria-has-a-ukrainian-trace/; https://euvsdisinfo.eu/report/ukrainian-instructors-train-jihadists-in-syria/; https://euvsdisinfo.eu/report/zelenskyys-regime-is-training-terrorists-in-syria/

[5] https://euvsdisinfo.eu/report/the-west-killed-general-kirillov-to-cover-up-its-crimes-in-syria-and-ukraine/; https://euvsdisinfo.eu/report/the-murder-of-general-kirillov-is-an-attempt-by-biden-and-the-us-deep-state-to-provoke-russia-into-a-tough-response/

[6] https://euvsdisinfo.eu/report/suicidal-cybertruck-explosion-trump-hotel-may-be-ukrainian-operation/

section analyses how Putin's Russia believes international law does not apply to Russia. Russia's full-scale invasion of Ukraine and committing of over 160,000 war crimes has infringed countless international laws.[7] As a great power, Putin believes Russia has a right to define international laws as it chooses; the annexation of Crimea in 2014 was allegedly in accordance with the right to 'self-determination' under the UN Charter, as was the annexation of four Ukrainian regions in 2022. While defending the annexation of Crimea, Russian Foreign Minister Sergei Lavrov (2024a) called for a multipolar world 'based on the UN Charter', which recognised the 'principle of sovereign equality of states'. Russia does not apply its 'new world order' to Ukraine, which the Kremlin deems has no right to choose its domestic, foreign and security policies. In Summer 2025, permanent member of the UN Security Council Russia – in a blatant example of double standards - condemned Israeli and US attacks on Iran as infringing the UN Charter after repeatedly violating the same document and many other international laws for over three years during its military campaign against Ukraine:

This reckless decision to launch missile and aerial strikes on the territory of a sovereign state, regardless of the justifications offered, constitutes a blatant violation of international law, the UN Charter, and relevant resolutions by the UN Security Council, which has consistently and unequivocally deemed such actions unacceptable. Particularly concerning is the fact that the strikes were executed by a permanent member of the UN Security Council (Russian Ministry of Foreign Affairs, 2025).

The fourth and fifth sections analyse Russia's hybrid war against the West and how Russia defines itself as a counter-revolutionary power. To end the West's geopolitical games and disrespect for Russia, Ukraine and its master – the US-led unipolar world – need to be destroyed and replaced by Little Russia and a multipolar world, respectively. The sixth section investigates why the failure of the 'special military operation' to quickly subdue Ukraine led to the creation of an Axis of Upheaval uniting Russia, Iran, China and North Korea (see Kendall-Taylor and Fontaine, 2024). The Axis of Upheaval believes it is at war with the United States and West in Israel and Ukraine, and the defeat of both countries will lead to the collapse of the US-led unipolar world. A new era of multipolarity would lead to the United States and Russia, following a second Yalta-type summit, recognising Russia's right to an exclusive sphere of influence over Ukraine and Eurasia (Cole and Feng, 2024; Trofimov, 2024). Putin's

---

[7] https://kyivindependent.com/zelensky-137-000-war-crimes/

'restorative nostalgia' would overcome Russia's humiliation by the West through the rebuilding of 'Historic Russia' and returning to the multipolar world that existed prior to 1991 when the United States treated the Soviet Union ('Historic Russia') as an equal (see Nicolosi, 2022).

Authoritarianism, Fascism and Dictatorship

During Putin's quarter of a century of direct and indirect rule of Russia, the country evolved from authoritarianism into a dictatorship and, following the change in Russia's constitution in 2020 and the full-scale invasion of Ukraine in 2022, into a fascist dictatorship (see Garner and Kuzio, 2025). Authoritarian states prefer their populations to remain demobilised and passive, as in Russia prior to 2020, while fascist regimes, such as Russia since 2020–2022, 'want to engage and excite the public' (Paxton, 2005, p. 217). Russia has mobilised pro-war Z activism and turbocharged nationalism for young Russians through a cult of war and genocidal rhetoric on state-controlled TV and radio, school curriculums, textbooks and compulsory military training in Soviet-style youth groups (Dixon, 2024). In Putin's Russia, 'War has captured the population's imagination; it has become attractive, even sexy' (Medvedev, 2023, p. 13). Putin (2024b) said: 'You know, when all is calm and life is measured and stable, we get bored. This amounts to stagnation, so we crave action. When action begins, time starts whistling by – or bullets do, for that matter. Unfortunately, bullets are what is zipping past our heads these days. We are scared, yes – but not as "all get out" kind of scared.'

Constitutional changes in 2020 de facto made Putin president for life (de jure until 2036 when, if he remains alive, the constitution would be again changed). Putin's fascist dictatorship replaced authoritarian collective leadership. A cult of Putin extolled him as the embodiment of the Russian state and its military might, as well as the defender of Russian interests against a nefarious West. Without any form of accountability in place, a self-reinforcing cycle of military aggression feeds a personality cult, leading to repression at home and military aggression abroad (1000 and 4000 days of personality cult in support of Russia's war against Ukraine, 2024).

Published a year after the Orange Revolution, the five-volume *Project Russia*, viewed by many in Russia's elites as Putin's 'official ideology', became a bestseller and sold millions of copies (Corum, 2018, p. 75). The *Project Russia* book series already described Putin as early as the mid 2000s as Russia's salvation, who was linking contemporary Russia with the Soviet Union (Corum, 2018). In that same year, Putin (2005) said in a state of the nation speech to the Russian Federal Assembly:

> Above all, we should acknowledge that the collapse of the Soviet Union was a major geopolitical disaster of the century. As for the Russian nation, it became a genuine drama. Tens of millions of our co-citizens and compatriots found themselves outside Russian territory. Moreover, the epidemic of disintegration infected Russia itself.

Only five years into his second term, Putin's nostalgia for the Soviet Union, which he conflates with 'Historic Russia', was very evident. In less than two years, Putin (2007) made his first major anti-Western xenophobic speech.

After his re-election in 2024, Putin was described by Russian politicians as Russia's new tsar. Putin compared himself to 'Jesus Christ' in his struggle to save Russia from the poisonous viruses of Western liberalism and decadence (Grylls, 2024). Archbishop Pitirim of Syktyvkar and Komi-Zyryansk published a poem about Putin, writing 'There is no better president' who is 'the Chosen One'. The archbishop expressed confidence God would 'save the whole world' through Putin to ensure 'Holy Rus' 'will not fall'.[8]

Putin's Russia portrays the West as degenerate, Godless and weak (McGlynn, 2023, pp. 133–134). Putin said, 'we must defend our traditional values, our culture, our traditions and our history' (Grylls, 2024). Ironically, Church attendance in Russia is low at only 17 per cent, which is half that found in Ukraine (35 per cent). The Kremlin's claim that Russia is spiritually superior to the West is bogus if we use its Church attendance, which is like that found in most European countries (see Pew Religious Centre, 2017).

Domestic repression, authoritarianism, dictatorship and external military aggression are interrelated (Matthews, 2023, p. 167). Internal cleansing and external expansion through 'redemptive violence' and 'without ethical or legal restraints' are typical of fascist regimes like that found in Russia (Paxton, 2005, p. 218). Fascist regimes implement and prioritise economic policies for the preparation and waging of war (Paxton, 2005, p. 145).

The roots linking internal and external threats to the state go back as far as the Stalin era and 'would remain a high priority for the duration of the Soviet period' (Brandenberger and Dubrovsky, 1998, p. 875). Putin's Russia is fighting the 'collective West'[9] and Anglo-Saxons, who together

---

[8] https://spzh.eu/ru/news/78429-ierarkh-rpts-poobeshchal-chto-boh-spaset-mir-cherez-putina
[9] https://euvsdisinfo.eu/report/russia-fights-the-collective-west-not-just-ukraine/

are the country's number one enemy. The 'collective West' and Anglo-Saxons control the world through 'global liberalism' and 'global totalitarianism'. Ukrainian President Zelenskyy is 'fighting against Russia for the Anglo-Saxon domination over the unipolar world'.[10] The 'collective West does not want to see a strong, sovereign Russia pursuing its own national interests'. Russia is surrounded by enemies, a theme with deep roots in Soviet political culture, and is a besieged fortress (Efimov, Vasilchenko, and Lyapin, 2024). These xenophobic views ignore the fact global anti-Russian feelings were largely absent prior to 2014 and only began to grow after Russia launched its first invasion of Ukraine and especially following the full-scale invasion (Efimov, Vasilchenko, and Lyapin, 2024).

Fascist regimes 'need a demonised enemy against which to mobilise followers' (Paxton, 2005, p. 37). Putin is in thrall to a distinctive brand of Russian fascism (see Medvedev, 2023, p. 17; Pomerantsev, 2022). The West is seeking the subjugation of Russia by sowing instability and supporting fifth columnists with the goal of imposing its external rule over the Russian Federation (Aron, 2023, p. 73). The 'cleansing' of Russia from 'scum' and 'traitors' would leave only 'true patriots' in Russia (Dixon, 2024). Russia's 'special military operation' would 'cleanse' Russia 'from the dirt and mould' and 'from aggressive parasites that poisoned the social body' (Apt, 2024) Putin's Russia has combined internal repression with external military aggression and war crimes on an industrial scale in Ukraine and Syria. Putin's Russia's represses domestic opponents and externally seeks to destroy Ukrainian identity (Bondarev, 2022).

Ukraine is both an internal enemy, being a 'traitor' to the pan-Russian people and Pan-Russian World, and an external threat, which has been artificially constructed by the United States and NATO, who seek to weaken and divide the 'Russian people'. As an instrument of the West, Ukrainians are therefore both an internal and external threat to Russia. Ukrainian leaders, and Euromaidan 'putschists', are 'satanists' and 'terrorists' who are a threat to Russia (Apt, 2024). Medvedev describes Ukrainians who hold an identity distinct from Russians as 'cockroaches' and 'pseudo-Ukrainian rabid mongrels' (Apt, 2024; Bondarev, 2022). Chapter 5 analyses how Russia's de-humanisation rhetoric defines Russians as 'humans' and Ukrainians as 'non-humans'. Ukrainians and

---

[10] https://euvsdisinfo.eu/report/zelenskyy-is-fighting-against-russia-for-the-anglo-saxon-domination-over-the-unipolar-world/

the 'anti-Christian [Ukrainian] state' must be destroyed because to not do so 'would be a compromise with the devil' (Apt, 2024)

For fascists, war provides the 'clearest radicalising impulse'. The exaltation of war and 'war making proved essential to the cohesion, discipline, and explosive energy of fascist regimes' (Paxton, 2005, p. 155). War hardens society, conquers land and fulfils imperialistic dreams. Putin's Russia cannot exist without wars and internal and external enemies (see Shevtsova, 2014). Fascist regimes, such as Putin's Russia, seek the expansion of their territory through war and conquest.

The idealisation of the 'master race', another common attribute of fascism, is to be found in Russian imperial nationalist denial of a separate Ukrainian people, disrespect for the sovereignty of former non-Russian Soviet republics and demand Russia be treated as a great power. Chosen people, whether Germans and Japanese in the 1930s or Russians today, believe they have an inherent right to dominate 'inferior peoples' (i.e., Ukrainians) without being restrained by international or divine law (Paxton, 2005, p. 219).

Robert O. Paxton (2005, p. 142) writes that 'A fascist regime could imprison, despoil, and even kill its inhabitants at will and without limitation.' Prime Minister Putin launched his rule in 1999 with the deaths of 307 Russians in terrorist attacks in apartment buildings in Moscow and two other cities that were blamed on 'Chechen terrorists' but were in fact an FSB false flag operation. As Russian president, 132 Russians died during the freeing of a theatre in Moscow in October 2022 and a further 334 Russians, including 186 children, died during the freeing of a school in Beslan in September 2004. Estimates of up to 100,000 Chechens died and disappeared during the first and second Chechen wars in the 1990s and 2000s with an additional approximately 20,000 Russian military casualties. In July 2014, 298 crew and passengers, including 80 children, were killed when a Russian BUK system downed the MH17 civilian airliner over eastern Ukraine. Putin's war against Ukraine has damaged Russia's economy and finances and in just over three years led to over one million casualties, twenty times more than the Soviet Union suffered after a decade of occupying Afghanistan. Putin's obsession with destroying Ukraine and taking revenge on the West for destroying the Soviet Union and disrespecting Russia in the 1990s points to the difficulty of negotiating an end to the war (see Rumer, 2022). Putin cannot retreat, as to do so would lead to his political demise. Importantly, without a military victory over 'Nazi Ukraine', Putin would not enter Russian history on a par with Peter I, Catherine I and Stalin. Fascists, Paxton (2005, p. 171) reminds us, have a 'fanatical preference to destroy everything in a final paroxysm, even their own country, rather than admit defeat'.

Militarism and Xenophobia

Chapter 4 analyses how a cult of war has been fanned in Putin's Russia for nearly two decades prior to the full-scale invasion of Ukraine. War has 'become the language of everyday life in Russia', Sergei Medvedev (2023, p. 12) writes, and 'militaristic rituals have become a part of state propaganda and daily routine'. 'Violence has become part of the flesh and blood of Russian society', Medvedev (2023, p. 133) added. Russia has become a 'main exporter of war' (Medvedev, 2023, p. 25) inside Russia against the renegade Chechen province and the Russian people and externally against Georgia, Ukraine and Syria.

When exported abroad the Russian state's 'culture of cruelty' and disrespect for Russian human rights and dignity at home transforms into sadism towards Ukrainians, Syrians and others. Riccardo Nicolosi (2022) writes how Russian propaganda has cultivated Russia as a victim who has been humiliated, suffered repeated injustices and insults and was deceived by the West. Peter Pomerantsev (2022) describes humiliation and aggression as a cycle in the Russian psyche and identity. Russians are subjected to humiliation at home by corrupt officials, oligarchs, police and Russian Orthodox clergy, which creates a desire to humiliate foreign 'Others' so they can also experience it. The Russian victim masochistically accepts his/her fate in Russia and then applies his/her sadistic anger verbally against the West and physically as a Russian soldier against Ukrainians and others. Instead of taking responsibility and blaming their poverty, backwardness and humiliation on Putin, who after all has been in power directly and indirectly for a quarter of a century, most Russians blame Ukrainian 'traitors' and 'nationalists/Nazis/fascists' and the 'collective West'. Seventy-seven per cent of Russians blame Ukrainians for poor relations between their countries, ignoring Russia's culpability for launching two illegal invasions and stealing Ukrainian territories (Levada Centre, 2023c). A high 86 per cent of Russians support the annexation of Crimea, a figure that has not fluctuated greatly since 2014 (Levada Centre, 2021; Kuzio, 2022, p. 181).

Russia believes it is fighting the 'collective West' in Chechnya, Georgia, Ukraine and Syria. Russian xenophobia towards the West rests on its alleged support for Islamic terrorism in Chechnya, backing for NATO membership and military bases in Georgia and Ukraine and instigation of colour revolutions in Serbia, Georgia, Ukraine, Russia and the Arab Spring. Putin (2023b) said that Russia is fighting an existential war against 'the official ideology of the Western ruling elites', which consists of 'Russophobia' racism and neo-Nazism. Karaganov (2025) claimed that 'NATO and Brussels anti-Russian propaganda already surpasses Hitler's' and 'A totalitarian liberal ideology is essentially being imposed' by the West.

The 'collective West' had for centuries entertained the goal of the 'disintegration and weakening of Russia'. Russia therefore had to mobilise its resources for the struggle against Western aggression (Troianovski, 2022). The Kremlin's manual for state officials and propagandists played up the West's long record of invading Russia through the Teutonic Knights, Polish-Lithuanian Commonwealth, Sweden, Napoleon, Nazis and NATO. The manual claimed that the age-old goals of the 'collective West' were to divide the 'Russian people', seize Russian resources and destroy the Russian Orthodox Church (Pertsev, 2022). Ukraine is propped up by the West to be used as a springboard to attack Russia.

The West attempted to impose its alien values in the 1990s when Russia was weak. United Russia Party deputy Vitaly Milonov believed the Gorbachev era was therefore worse for Russia than the Nazi occupation during the Great Patriotic War (Ramani, 2023, p. 223). Fortunately, under Putin's leadership, Russia has fought back domestically and externally (Garner, 2023, p. 33; McGlynn, 2023, pp. 79–85). Russia was described as a colony of the West in the 1990s 'but managed to break free' (Davis, 2024, p. 189) and is now defending itself from Western colonialism, alien values, militant secularism and lack of respect for traditions (Snegovaya, Kimmage, McGlynn, 2023). The West is also allegedly seeking to exploit Ukraine's raw materials and mineral resources, a claim that was also made by Soviet propaganda campaigns (see Chapter 5).[11] Such views help to justify the Kremlin's disrespect for the sovereignty of its neighbours while reinforcing demands they accept Russia as the dominant and leading power in Eurasia.

Russian imperial nationalists define the 'special military operation' as Russia's 'liberation' of Ukraine from Western colonialism and status as a US puppet state. (Ukraine, of course, has no agency to decide if it wishes to be liberated.) The United States, at the helm of an 'aggressive minority' and pursuing 'colonial practices', is fighting to preserve its hegemony

---

[11] https://euvsdisinfo.eu/report/ukraine-is-a-sort-of-colony-to-extract-resources-for-the-us/; and https://euvsdisinfo.eu/report/western-masters-are-continuing-the-war-for-ukraines-natural-resources/

by maintaining Ukraine as a 'tool in the hands of its American puppet masters' (Lavrov, 2024a). Russia's 'special military operation' is bringing freedom to Ukrainians who are occupied since 2014 by the United States. Russia's description of its invasions of Ukraine as 'liberations' is rooted in Soviet and Russian myths of imperial innocence (see Chapter 9).

Drawing on centuries of Russian messianism, Russia's anti-colonial struggle against the West is supposedly on behalf of itself and the 'world majority' and is of a 'national liberation nature', Putin (2023b) told the World Russian Peoples Council. The Kremlin and the Pan-Russian World 'are now fighting for the freedom of not only Russia but the whole world' against the 'dictatorship of the one hegemon' (Putin, 2023b). Russia is at 'the forefront of creating a more equitable world order' (Putin, 2023b) – which, as pointed out earlier, does not apply to Ukraine and other former Soviet non-Russian republics.

Russia has a 'historical right to be Russian – a strong, independent power, a "state-civilisation"' (Putin, 2023b), which the West seeks to prevent. This widespread view, which feeds into historically imbedded grievances in Russian identity, is built on a Russian refusal to take responsibility for Russia's backwardness by investigating why there is such a wide gulf between claims to be a great power and the lack of evidence to show this to be reality (possessing nuclear weapons is not a sign of a great power unless we also define Israel, North Korea and Pakistan in such a manner). Nearly two-thirds of Russians feel the West is not treating Russia fairly and Western sanctions are seen as unjust and not as punishment for invading a sovereign country and illegally annexing its territory (Volkov, 2021).

Nearly two-thirds of Russians view the war with Ukraine in terms of a civilisation struggle with the West. The 'special military operation' is therefore a justified response to mythical threats to Russia (New Survey Finds Most Russians See Ukrainian War as Defence Against West, 2024). The Kremlin claimed seven falsehoods about Ukraine on the eve of Russia's full-scale invasion:

1. *Defensive war*: Russia had no choice but to undertake 'defensive' measures by launching a 'special military operation' because NATO was transforming Ukraine into a 'military foothold against Russia' (Lavrov, 2021). NATO and the United States have never planned to open military bases in Ukraine.
2. *Western missiles*: The West had installed missiles and were deploying 'attack missiles' in Ukraine. The United States, the UK and France only sent missiles to Ukraine *after* Russia launched its full-scale invasion.

3. *Ukraine–NATO*: Ukraine is 'de facto already a NATO member' (Gordon, 2022). In fact, Ukraine has never received a NATO membership offer. The last US president to support Ukraine joining NATO was George W. Bush (2000–2008). Three US presidents since 2009 have opposed Ukraine joining NATO.
4. *Western military aid:* The Kremlin claimed that Ukraine had always lied about wanting peace when in fact Kyiv was preparing for military aggression, as shown by the United States increasing its military aid to Ukraine (Putin, 2022b; Lavrov, 2022). In 2014–2021, the Barack Obama and Joe Biden administrations vetoed the sending of military assistance to Ukraine, while the Trump administration sent low-level military aid. US and European policymakers believed the Russian army would quickly defeat Ukraine and therefore prior to the full-scale invasion had only sent weapons that would be useful in guerrilla warfare, such as javelins, stingers and NLAWS (see Kuzio, 2024c). The US and Europe only began sending heavier weapons to Ukraine from Spring 2022 after the Russian army had been forced to withdraw from the Kyiv region.
5. *Ukrainian threat against Russian speakers*: Ukraine was shelling and threatening to launch an attack against Russian-controlled Donbas. During the eight years between Russia's two invasions, Russia and its Donbas proxies' broke countless ceasefires and launched unprovoked attacks on Ukrainian-controlled territory.
6. *US mercenaries:* US private contractors were training special forces and the far-right in Ukraine, while the EU was training the Ukrainian military and 'anti-Russian units'. NATO–Ukrainian military exercises have been held for over two decades during and after Kuchma's two presidential terms (1994–2004). US private contractors have never operated, and the EU has not undertaken military training in Ukraine.
7. *Chemical warfare:* The United States had delivered 'unidentified chemical agents' to Ukraine (Putin, 2021). A common Russian disinformation theme which has no bearing on the truth. In fact, Russia collaborated with Syria's Assad regime in using banned chemical weapons against civilians. Russia has itself committed numerous war crimes by using banned chemical and biological agents in 10, 000 documented cases during its war against Ukraine.[12]

---

[12] https://ssu.gov.ua/novyny/sbu-zadokumentuvala-ponad-10-tysiach-khimatak-rf-proty-syl-oborony-ukrainy-z-pochatku-povnomasshtabnoi-viiny-video.

International Law Does Not Apply to Russia

By illegally annexing Crimea and invading Eastern Ukraine in 2014 and launching a full-scale invasion in 2022, Russia has grossly violated international law and the UN Charter and is threatening world peace, global security and stability. United Nations resolutions condemned Russia for its sham referendum in March 2014, which annexed Crimea. Nevertheless, the Kremlin continues to claim that the 'reunification' of Crimea with Russia was legitimate having been undertaken according to international law and 'after a referendum on the basis of self-determination of its people'.[13] On 2 March 2022, the United Nations General Assembly voted by an overwhelming majority for a resolution condemning Russia's full-scale invasion of Ukraine and demanding Russia immediately withdraw its forces and abide by international law (United Nations, 2022a). In October 2022, the UN General Assembly again voted overwhelmingly to condemn Russia's annexation of four Ukrainian *oblasts* following sham referendums (United Nations, 2022b). These resolutions have little importance for Putin's Russia because it is convinced 'brute strength is more important than morality' (Medvedev, 2023, p. 135).

There is little question Russia is breaking many international laws and the UN Charter and undermining Western sanctions against Iran and North Korea. Russia is violating UN Security Council Resolution 2397 (United Nations, 2017) in response to North Korea's intercontinental ballistic missile tests. The resolution prohibits North Korea from sending its citizens abroad for work and mandated all UN member states expel North Koreans working and earning income abroad by December 2019. Russia is importing both North Korean workers and military personnel are fighting against Ukraine.

This, though, is not how the Kremlin views international law. Russian Foreign Minister Sergei Lavrov (2024b) answered criticism at the UN in the following manner:

> Let's face it: not all countries represented in this chamber recognise the key principle of the UN Charter which is the sovereign equality of all states. Speaking through its presidents, the United States has long declared its exceptionalism. This applies to Washington's attitude towards its allies, whom it demands to be unquestioningly obedient even to the detriment of their national interests.

---

[13] https://euvsdisinfo.eu/report/crimeans-voted-to-join-russia-in-a-democratic-manner-and-according-to-international-laws/ and https://euvsdisinfo.eu/report/crimea-became-part-of-russia-after-a-referendum-on-the-basis-of-self-determination-of-its-people/

Rule, America! This is the thrust of the notorious 'rules-based order' which presents a direct threat to multilateralism and international peace.

The most important components of international law – the UN Charter and the resolutions of our Council – are interpreted by the collective West in a perverse and selective manner, depending on the instructions coming from the White House.

Lavrov (2025) defends the UN Charter as the main source of international law and explains that 'Russia, like the majority of the world community, has never had any difficulty' in respecting this. This, not surprisingly, contrasts with the West, which 'was never cured of its syndrome of exceptionalism and retains its neocolonial habits, i.e. living at the expense of others. Interstate relations based on respect for international law were, from the very beginning, not to the West's liking.' Lavrov (2025) complained about 'U.S. dominance in the international arena' and 'Washington's policy of geopolitically absorbing Eastern Europe. Meanwhile, Lavrov (2025) could not resist bringing up Nazis, attacking Trump's' 'America First' slogan as 'alarmingly like' the Hitlerite slogan 'Germany above all'.

Lavrov (2025) travels into the depths of newspeak in George Orwell's *1984* novel when claiming that Russia supports the UN Charter's 'principles of sovereign equality of states' and 'non-interference in their internal affairs' without mentioning how these two principles are upheld at the same time as Russia is pursuing a war of aggression against Ukraine. Lavrov (2025) explains this dichotomy by making the absurd claim 'a state's territorial integrity must be respected [only] if its government represents its entire population' and 'It goes without saying that, since the February 2014 coup, the Kyiv regime does not represent the people of Crimea, Donbas, or New Russia any more than the Western powers represented the peoples of the colonial territories that they exploited.' Thus, Crimea and four Ukrainian *oblasts* had a 'right', Lavrov (2025) claimed to 'self-determination'. If Lavrov's definitions of international law were used by other countries, the world would descend into chaos with the Russian Federation itself – as in the 1990s – experiencing multiple claims to sovereignty and 'self-determination'. Of course, this has nothing to do with the UN definition of 'self-determination', as these territories are not independent states but have been annexed by Russia in a traditional imperialist manner.

Medvedev (2024) told a Russian newspaper that Russia was justified in launching the 'special military operation' because 'in the event of a threat to our security, independence and sovereignty, we had the right to use force in self-defence, including acting pre-emptively. Which was done in full accordance with the UN Charter. In any case, Russia will act in strict accordance with the UN Charter and key documents, and generally accepted norms of international law.'

Patrushev (2025) used similar, legally incoherent arguments when he said Russia would never agree to returning four Ukrainian *oblasts*, Crimea and Sevastopol because they are defined as Russian territory in Russia's constitution. Patrushev (2025), like other Russian leaders, demanded Ukraine and the West recognise these territories as legally Russian. These territories, Patrushev (2025) claimed, became part of Russia based 'on the will of citizens in accordance with international law, the laws of the Russian Federation and the legislation of these regions'.

Russian leaders often use Kosovo's independence from Serbia to justify the 'self-determination' of Crimea and four Ukrainian *oblasts*. Like Russia, Ukraine does not recognise Kosovo's independence. Importantly, Russia's comparison of Kosovo and Crimea is a false analogy as Russia annexed Crimea, and it is therefore not an independent state, unlike Kosovo. Moreover, if the analogy is allowed to run its course, the potential number of regions which could obtain 'self-determination' would be very many. If we, for example, applied the Kremlin's definition of 'self-determination' to the Russian Federation, twenty-one autonomous republics would presumably have this right. The Kremlin's claim of 'self-determination' is as legally incoherent as its claim to possess the right to annex 'historical Russian land' that could presumably also be used by Japan, Finland and Germany towards the Kurile islands, Karelia and Kaliningrad, respectively, or as a matter of fact, Germany towards the French region of Alsace Lorrain and Silesian region of Poland. China and Iran hold grievances towards Russia over what they consider to be their 'historical lands' in eastern Siberia and the South Caucasus, respectively, being occupied by Russia in the nineteenth century.

Putin (2024a) claimed that the annexation of Crimea and four Ukrainian *oblasts* is in accordance with the UN Charter, which states 'every nation has the right to self-determination, then the people who live in Crimea and the people who live in the southeast of Ukraine, who did not agree with the coup d'etat, and this is an illegal, unconstitutional act, have the right to self-determination, right? Right'. According to the Kremlin, what was good for Kosovo is good for Crimea:

> The International Court of Justice ruled regarding Kosovo, analysing the situation around Kosovo, that any territory, declaring its independence, should not, is not obliged to ask the opinion and permission of the central authorities of the country to which this territory is currently part, at the

time of the decision, right? Of course, that's true, because this is the decision of the International Court of Justice. So, these territories, including New Russia and Donbas, had the right to decide about their sovereignty, right? Of course, yes. This is fully consistent with today's international law and the UN Charter. If this is so, then we had the right to conclude corresponding interstate agreements with these new states, right? Of course, yes. Did we, do it? We did. (Putin, 2024)

Irrespective of the Kremlin's legally incoherent definitions of the UN Charter, Russia's lack of support at the UN shows it is isolated. In all UN votes dealing with Russian military aggression against Ukraine, only four countries have typically supported Russia – Belarus, North Korea, Nicaragua and (until 2024) Syria. Except for Belarus, Russia's allies in the Collective Security Treaty Organisation and Eurasian Economic Union have abstained. China has usually abstained. Iran refused to recognise Crimea and other Russian-occupied territories in Ukraine as part of the Russian Federation in its strategic partnership treaty with Russia signed in January 2025.

Russia does though have military partners – China, Iran and North Korea – as well as economic partners such as India. Russia's energy, the bulk of which was exported to Europe until 2022–2024, is now largely imported by China and India. Not all countries have followed the West's lead on imposing sanctions against Russia, especially in Africa and Latin America. In southeast Asia, pro-Western Taiwan, South Korea, Japan, Australia and New Zealand have imposed sanctions, while other countries have not. Meanwhile, the UAE, Türkiye, Armenia, Georgia, Kyrgyzstan and Kazakhstan are profiting from the re-export of sanctioned Western goods to Russia. Until new US sanctions in January 2025, the UAE was a major hub for Russian oil exports via its shadow fleet.

Russia's Nostalgia for a Multipolar World

Putin's nostalgia for the pre-1991 multipolar world has two components.

The first is during the Cold War, the United States treated the Soviet Union as an equal. Russia does not respect the EU, while the Kremlin is convinced NATO is fully controlled by the United States. The Kremlin describes the EU and NATO as US puppet structures, whereas it was pointless to talk to Ukraine as it was a puppet state (Medvedev, 2021).[14] Russia is seeking respect and equal status from the EU or NATO's US

---

[14] https://euvsdisinfo.eu/report/eu-ukraine-are-us-puppets-in-ukraine-war/

puppet master. As Patrushev (2025) said, 'I believe that negotiations on Ukraine should be conducted between Russia and the United States without the participation of other Western countries. There is nothing to talk about with London and Brussels.'

The second is the US and West recognised spheres of influence in the 1945 Yalta agreement. Putin seeks to negotiate a second Yalta-style agreement with US President Trump over Ukraine's and Europe's heads. Five months before the 'special military operation', Medvedev (2021) described Ukraine as 'under direct foreign control' and asked, 'what to do in this situation?' He answered his own question: Russia needed to wait for the emergence of a sane leadership in Ukraine, which is not aimed at a total confrontation with Russia' and interested in 'building equal and mutually beneficial relations with Russia. Only with such a leadership of Ukraine is it worth dealing.'

Russia's seeking of a second Yalta agreement was seen in the two draft Russian treaties submitted in December 2021 as ultimatums to the West (Russian Ministry of Foreign Affairs, 2021a, 2021b; see The Kremlin's security demands mean insecurity for the rest of us, 2021). These US–Russian agreements consigned Ukraine and other countries to the Russian sphere of influence – as in 1945 when the first Yalta agreement consigned the three Baltic states and central-eastern Europe to the Soviet empire. Today, Putin is demanding the United States recognise Ukraine (and the remainder of Eurasia) as lying within Russia's exclusive sphere of influence.

Putin's War against the West

Russian opposition leader Garry Kasparov (2023) writes that the Biden administration did not wish to admit that the United States is at war with the Anti-Western Axis of Upheaval. This is also true of European states. NATO Secretary General Mark Rutte is more realistic, saying:

> Russia, China, but also North Korea and Iran, are hard at work to try to weaken North America and Europe. To chip away at our freedom. They want to reshape the global order. Not to create a fairer one, but to secure their own spheres of influence. They are testing us. And the rest of the world is watching. No, we are not at war. But we are certainly not at peace either.[15]

The four members of the Axis of Upheaval *do believe* that they are at war with the West. Putin's Russia, for example, believes it is fighting the 'collective West' and saving the world from 'fascism' (Dixon and Abbakumova, 2024).

---

[15] www.nato.int/cps/en/natohq/opinions_231348.htm

Putin believes the 'special military operation' is 'the beginning of a cardinal breakdown of the American-led world order' (Belton, 2022).

Since the mid-2000s, the very popular *Project Russia* book series had been describing the West as decadent and democracy not working (Corum, 2018, p. 75). 'For decades now, the Russian people have been spoon-fed disinformation portraying liberal democracies as weak, perverse or dying'[16] (Why is the Kremlin so hung up on smearing Zelenskyy? 2025). The coming collapse of the West was 'central to the ideas in *Project Russia*' (Corum, 2018, p. 85). Two decades later, the Kremlin welcomed the election of Trump in 2024 believing it signalled the beginning of the end for the United States and the death of liberal internationalism and the unipolar world (Zygar, 2024). Patrushev, whose KGB mindset is dominated by United States and Western conspiracies, 'told Russia's *Izvestia* newspaper that the U.S. is plotting to take over Russia because a massive volcanic eruption in Wyoming could soon make it uninhabitable' (Grove, Cullison, and Pancevski, 2023). Trump, the Kremlin hoped, would preside over the disintegration of the United States in a similar manner to Gorbachev having presided over the disintegration of the Soviet Union. Sergei Karaganov (2022), head of the Council for Foreign and Defence Policy and dean of the Faculty of World Economy and International Affairs at Moscow's Higher School of Economics, traces the decline of the United States as far back as 1999, believing the war against Ukraine will be the final nail in the coffin of the old-world order and leading to the creation of a 'free' and 'more just, more politically and culturally pluralistic and multicoloured world'. The Global South would no longer be 'suppressed, robbed, and culturally humiliated' by the West (Karaganov, 2022). That Russia is suppressing, robbing and culturally humiliating Ukraine is presumably irrelevant.

A Russian victory in the war against the US-led unipolar world would also be an Iranian victory. Russia and Iran fought together in Syria – and were both defeated when the Assad regime was overthrown in late 2024. Russia and Iran militarily assisted the Assad regime to crush the opposition with the use of barbaric carpet bombing, war crimes and chemical weapons. Russia provides high-level military technology to Iran

---

[16] https://euvsdisinfo.eu/report/western-civilisation-is-corrupt-and-is-dying-the-barbarians-that-it-welcomes-will-inherit-its-ruins/; https://euvsdisinfo.eu/report/there-is-no-democracy-in-europe/; https://euvsdisinfo.eu/report/only-authoritarian-states-and-closed-societies-will-be-able-to-protect-their-populations-from-the-coronavirus-and-from-future-pandemics/

and North Korea, possibly including nuclear weapons technology (see Weiniger and Grylls, 2025). Iran provides drones since August 2022 for Russia's war against Ukraine. North Korea provides artillery shells, missiles and combat troops since 2024. Russia shares captured US and NATO weapons with Iran for them to be reverse engineered (see Kagan, Jhaveri, Ganzeveld, Carl, Barros, 2024).

The Hamas terrorist attack against Israel in October 2023 ended Russia's balancing act between Israel and Iran; henceforth, Russia is aligned with Iran and Iranian proxies in the Greater Middle East. Russia and Iran view Israel and Ukraine, respectively, as artificial interlopers on Russian and Palestinian lands. Iran seeks the eradication of the state of Israel and Russia seeks the destruction of the Ukrainian state.

Russia's Hybrid Warfare against the West

Putin's Russia did not invent hybrid warfare; the Soviet Union practised what was called active measures for decades (Kuzio and D'Anieri, 2018, pp. 25–60; Rid, 2021). Soviet assassinations of leaders go back over a century to 1926 when Ukrainian nationalist and military leader Symon Petlura was assassinated in Paris. Three more Ukrainian nationalist leaders were assassinated: Yevhen Konovalets in Rotterdam in 1938, and Lev Rebet and Stepan Bandera in 1957 and 1959 respectfully in Munich. The first example of Russia returning to the Soviet policy of assassinations was the attempted poisoning with dioxin of opposition presidential candidate Yushchenko in the 2004 Ukrainian presidential elections. The second example was the murder of Litvinenko in London in 2006 using polonium-210. Dioxin and radioactive polonium are produced in former Soviet and, since 1991, Russian laboratories, which have always been tightly controlled by the Soviet and Russian secret services. Tens of Chechen nationalists have also been murdered in Europe, Türkiye and the Middle East since Ramzan Kadyrov was installed by the Kremlin as its Chechen warlord.

It is no coincidence Russia's first use of hybrid warfare against the West took place in 2007 during the same year Putin gave a xenophobic speech to the Munich Security Conference. The Kremlin orchestrated violent riots and a month-long massive cyberattack against Estonia, which targeted computer networks, banks and the media. A year after the attacks, NATO opened a Cooperative Cyber Defence Centre in Tallinn.[17]

---

[17] https://ccdcoe.org/

Different types of hybrid warfare attacks have grown in number and brazenness since then. In 2024, there were one hundred 'suspicious incidents' in Europe, which were attributed to Russia, according to the Czech Foreign Ministry.[18] These hybrid warfare attacks have included the following:

1. Arson attack on a Ukrainian-linked business in London.
2. Disruption of Czech rail-signalling system.
3. Cutting of underwater cables in the Baltic Sea.
4. Planned sabotage against military installations in Germany.
5. Reconnaissance at Rzeszow airport, the main hub for the transportation of Western military equipment to Ukraine.
6. Fire at the Diehl Metall plant, Germany.
7. Plot to assassinate the CEO of Rheinmetall, Armin Papperger.
8. Preparations for sabotage in Western Norway.
9. Fire at a Warsaw shopping centre.
10. Plot to bomb a store in northern Paris.

NATO General Secretary Mark Rutte outlined how:

> Malicious cyber-attacks on both sides of the Atlantic. Assassination attempts on British and German soil. Explosions at an ammunition warehouse in Czechia. The weaponisation of migrants crossing illegally into, Latvia, Lithuania and Finland. Jamming to disrupt civil aviation in the Baltic region. These attacks are not just isolated incidents. They are the result of a coordinated campaign to destabilise our societies and discourage us from supporting Ukraine. They circumvent our deterrence and bring the front line to our front doors. Even into our homes. Putin believes that 'a serious, irreconcilable struggle is unfolding for the formation of a new world order'. These are his own words. Others share his belief.[19]

Russia's hybrid warfare campaign since 2007 was largely ignored by NATO and Western governments. In a similar manner so were the Russian invasion of Georgia and Russia's de facto annexation of South Ossetia and Abkhazia. A year after the invasion, US President Obama launched a 'reset' of US–Russian relations and imposed no sanctions on Russia for its invasion of Georgia and imperial conquest of two of its territories. The year 2014 should have been a wake-up call after Russia annexed Crimea and launched its first invasion of Ukraine (see Kuzio, 2024d). But the Western response

---

[18] www.theguardian.com/world/2024/dec/04/up-to-100-suspicious-incidents-in-europe-can-be-attributed-to-russia-czech-minister-says
[19] www.nato.int/cps/en/natohq/opinions_231348.htm

was again pitifully weak, sanctions were symbolic and Europe continued business as usual with Russia; Germany, for example, continued building Nord Stream II. Then Dutch Prime Minister, and since 2024 Secretary General of NATO, Mark Rutte asserted in his 'Message on the inauguration of Nord Stream II' in October 2012 of 'how proud' he was of participating in the project and of 'the excellent working relationship' between Russia and the West in constructing the pipeline.[20] US President Biden cancelled US President Trump's sanctions on Nord Stream II. Ignoring the 1994 Budapest Memorandum that had provided Ukraine with security assurances in exchange for nuclear disarmament, its two signatories, United States and UK, and other Western leaders opposed providing Ukraine with military assistance, claiming that such a step would be 'escalatory'.

Ukraine's then Defence Minister Oleksii Reznikov (2023) believed Russia's impunity for its invasion of Georgia in 2008 led to Russia believing it would get away with annexing Crimea in 2014. Meanwhile, the West's 'inattention to events in Crimea and Donbas' led to Russia's intervention in Syria and full-scale invasion of Ukraine in 2022.

NATO General Secretary Rutte recalled how NATO members had only come to fully comprehend Russia's anti-Western objectives after Russia's full-scale invasion of Ukraine in 2022:

> Over 1 million casualties since February 2022. Putin is trying to wipe Ukraine off the map. He is trying to fundamentally change the security architecture that has kept Europe safe for decades. And he is trying to crush our freedom and way of life. His pattern of aggression is not new. But for too long, we did not act. Georgia in 2008. Crimea in 2014. And many did not want to believe he would launch all-out war on Ukraine in February 2022. How many more wake-up calls do we need? We should be profoundly concerned. I know I am.

Rutte continued:

> Russia's economy is on a war footing. In 2025, the total military spending will be 7 to 8 percent of GDP, if not more. That's a third of Russia's state budget – and the highest level since the Cold War. And Russia's defence industry is producing huge numbers of tanks, armoured vehicles, and ammunition. What Russia lacks in quality, it makes up for in quantity – with the help of China, Iran and North Korea. This all points in one clear direction: Russia is preparing for long-term confrontation. With Ukraine. And with us.[21]

---

[20] www.nord-stream.com/media/documents/pdf/en/2012/10/speech-rutte.pdf
[21] www.nato.int/cps/en/natohq/opinions_231348.htm

The Soviet Union had also undertaken propaganda campaigns and active measures against the West, but this was in the Cold War before 24-hour news, the Internet and social media and when Western and Eastern political systems were sealed off from one another. Russia has weaponised all manner of activities and thus broadened what hybrid warfare encompasses. After Russia's major use of disinformation against Ukraine in 2014 (see Chapter 5), recognition of the threat from Russian disinformation began to grow among Western policymakers; in January 2016, the EU launched the Centre to Combat Disinformation and the *EUvsDisnfo* website to counter Russian disinformation. Nevertheless, Russian outlets, such as *RT* and *Sputnik*, were only banned following Russia's full-scale invasion of Ukraine.

From the 2010s, there was a recognition of the growing threat from Russian espionage. Expulsions of Russian agents increased from the 2010s. On 29 December 2016, in a move not seen since the 1962 Cuban Missile Crisis, the United States expelled thirty-five Russian diplomats and intelligence agents. It would take another attempted poisoning two years later using the chemical agent Novichok in Salisbury, England, of Russian GRU officer Sergei Skripal for 342 Russian agents to be expelled with the highest numbers from the United States (120) and UK (96). The West's reaction to the attempted assassination of Skripal was far more robust than the West's feeble response to the murder of Litvinenko.

After 2014, US think tanks began investigating Russia as the source of the hacking and other hybrid warfare activities (Looking Glass Cyber Solutions, 2015). A report published by the FBI and the US Department of Homeland Security (DHS) said that there had been 'spear phishing, campaigns targeting government organisations, critical infrastructure, think-tanks, universities, political organisations, and corporations; theft of information from these organisations; and the recent public release of some of this stolen information' (Department of Homeland Security/ Federal Bureau of Investigation, 2016). These expulsions and the FBI–DHS report described a 'decade-long campaign' of Russian 'behaviour unprecedented in the post-Cold War era'.

Putin's Anger against the West

After the end of the Cold War in 1991, Europe and the United States believed in the 'peace dividend', and all NATO members, with the notable exception of the United States, had reduced their defence spending. In 2014, only five out of the then twenty-eight NATO members spent the recommended 2 per cent of GDP on defence. NATO's members defence spending only began to increase following Russia's first invasion of Ukraine and Trump's haranguing of NATO members to spend more, eventually agreeing at the June 2025 NATO summit to spend 3.5 per cent on their militaries and another 1.5 per cent on related areas. By 2025, twenty-three out of thirty-two members of NATO were spending 2 per cent of GDP on defence.

In contrast, Putin never believed the Cold War had ended, and he was angry at how Western conspiracies and machinations had brought down the Soviet Union. Typically, blame was laid on foreign actors ignoring domestic factors such as the economic crisis and nationalism in Ukraine and the other non-Russian republics. Aron (2023) portrays Putin as bemoaning the loss of the USSR and believing it was destroyed by treachery, incompetence and Western conspiracies. On 1 August 1991, President George H. W. Bush advised, in what would come to be derided as his 'chicken-Kyiv' speech, the Ukrainian parliament to not support independence.[22]

Putin (2007) has cultivated the West as an external enemy for nearly two decades since his well-known speech at the Munich Security Conference. The Russian public has come to agree with Russian leaders that the outside world is a hostile environment, and Russia is threatened by the West. Russian leaders believe the onus for an improvement of relations with the United States has always laid with Washington because Russia is, as always innocent of wrongdoings, and its actions are merely in self-defence. Opinion polls show that most Russians are convinced the West is an enemy which poses a threat to Russia. This image of Ukraine and the West as enemies of Russia has been fanned by the state-controlled Russian media since the mid 2000s.

Russian information, cyber and hybrid war are viewed by the Kremlin as strategic tools to respond to what they view as long-term Western nefarious activities, especially of the colour revolution type which took place in the Balkans, Ukraine and Eurasia. The Kremlin believes colour revolutions are orchestrated by the CIA, Western democracy-promoting foundations and the EU to foment regime change. The Kremlin views colour revolutions as the West's use of soft power, which it implements to complement hard power through NATO enlargement and military intervention. The Euromaidan Revolution, Russian leaders claimed, was

---

[22] www.youtube.com/watch?v=Vkjxf76xRTw

merely cover for the Black Sea Fleet bases becoming NATO and US naval bases after Ukraine joined NATO.

When the Eastern Partnership was launched by the EU in 2009 for post-Soviet countries, such as Ukraine and Georgia, Russia launched a competing CIS Customs Union that became the Eurasian Economic Union in 2015. Armenia and Ukraine were pressured by Russia to reject EU Association Agreements and instead join the Eurasian Economic Union. Armenian leaders succumbed to the Kremlin's pressure after facing no public protests. In contrast, Ukrainians rose up in protest in the Euromaidan Revolution against President Yanukovych's refusal to sign an Association Agreement with the EU. Russia has continued similar tactics with partial success in Moldova and with greater success in Georgia.

The EU never took Putin's plans for a competing Eurasian Economic Union seriously, and in the 2014 crisis, Brussels was therefore stunned to realise that Russia had come to view the EU in the same way as it had always viewed NATO, that is, as an expansionist Western project intruding into Russia's 'privileged zone of interests' in Eurasia (see Kuzio, 2017). European leaders were even more shocked to find that since returning to the presidency in 2012, Putin had developed a broader strategy of undermining the EU by supporting populist-nationalist and neo-fascist, anti-European political forces. Russia has cultivated a long-term financial relationship with French populist-nationalist leader Marine Le Pen, leader of the National Rally Party. In 2016, the United Russia Party, Putin's party of power, signed a cooperation agreement with the far-right Austrian Freedom Party. Russia has also backed far-right parties in Germany, the Netherlands, Bulgaria, Romania and elsewhere in Europe. While attacking mythical Ukrainian 'nationalists/fascists/Nazis' in Ukraine, the Kremlin is financing and cooperating with real 'nationalists/fascists/Nazis' in Europe.

Putin seemed to hold a personal grudge against US Secretary of State Hilary Clinton because she had supported Russian protests in 2011–2012. Putin's revenge, the hacking of the 2016 US presidential elections and support for Trump's candidacy, shed a spotlight on Russian hybrid warfare that had been developed and improved over the previous decade. It remains unclear if Russia's intervention in the 2016 US elections was decisive in Trump's victory, as he won the electoral college votes but lost the popular vote. In the 2024 Romanian elections, far-right candidate Calin Georgescu's campaign was backed by Russia through social media. Romania's Constitutional Court annulled the results of the first round of the election, where Georgescu had come in first place, after the country's intelligence agencies provided evidence of widespread Russian interference.

Russia backed the 'Leave' campaign during the June 2016 UK referendum on EU membership, which won the Brexit vote by a small 4 per cent margin. Russia supported the 'No' campaign in the April 2016 Dutch referendum on the EU–Ukraine Association Agreement. The Kremlin has also supported separatism when it intervened in support of Scottish and Catalonian independence during their holding of legal and illegal referendums, respectively. Putin's Russia has always had a Janis-faced policy towards separatism: on the one hand, brutally suppressing aspirations for independence in Chechnya, while, on the other, promoting separatism in Moldova, Georgia, Azerbaijan, Ukraine and inside the EU.

Putin's Russia has undertaken countless cyberattacks and disinformation against the United States, the European Parliament, the national parliaments of EU members, the OSCE (Organisation for Security and Cooperation in Europe) and NATO.[23] Russia launched a major hacking and disinformation campaign against Germany's February 2025 federal elections (Nothing new from the east, 2025). The Kremlin has disseminated disinformation to sow public protests and spread negative propaganda against politicians deemed to be hostile to Russian interests and supportive of Ukraine. In January 2016, Russia was behind a fake story alleging a 13-year-old Russian–German girl had been raped by migrants, fuelling support for the far-right and leading to condemnations of mainstream German politicians for permitting high levels of immigration. As Chapter 5 shows, Russian disinformation has especially targeted Ukraine, the EU, NATO and the United States.

Russia as a Revolutionary Power

Russia is now a 'revolutionary power', Dmitri Trenin (2024) argued. Robyn Dixon (2024) described Russian foreign policy as 'revolutionary' and agrees with Trenin (2024) that Russia is a 'revolutionary power'. Trenin (2024) explains that Russia is no longer attempting to adapt itself to the US-led unipolar world. Russia's new militarised elite supports the Kremlin's war against its 'mortal enemy', the West and the US puppet state of Ukraine. As a 'revolutionary power', the Kremlin is asserting its sovereignty by claiming that Russian legislation is supreme over international laws and treaties.

---

[23] https://theins.ru/en/news/278159

With Russia defined as a 'state-civilisation' since 2012, Russia's war with the West is viewed as a civilisation struggle. Russia's 2021 National Security Strategy outlined the importance of defending 'traditional Russian spiritual and moral values, culture, and historical memory' against existential threats from Western puppet states, such as Ukraine, Western hypocrisy and anti-Russian machinations (McGlynn, 2023, p. 135). Russia's ultra-conservative model, traditional Orthodox values and 'turbo-patriotic youth' are pitted against domestic and Ukrainian 'traitors' and Western liberalism (see Dixon, 2024).

Russia's emergence as a 'revolutionary power' can be traced to the mid-2000s, following what it regarded as three US-backed colour revolutions in Serbia, Georgia and Ukraine and Putin's (2007) speech at the Munich Security Conference. In that same year, the Russian World Foundation was created with the goal of supporting Russians and Russian speakers and reuniting the three eastern Slavs as a pan-Russian nation. Although touted as analogous to the British Council and Goethe Institute, the Russian World Foundation was always different because of its close ties to the Russian secret services. The Pan-Russian World, for example, provided financial support and ideological indoctrination for pro-Russian extremist groups in Ukraine, Eurasia and central-eastern Europe. Ukraine's relations with Russia sharply deteriorated in 2009 after two Russian diplomats were expelled for supporting Crimean separatists and Russian extreme nationalists in Odesa (see Chapter 2 on the Pan-Russian World).

Cyber and information warfare have been combined with the use of GRU and FSB special forces, paramilitaries, private contractors and mercenaries. Veterans with combat experience in Bosnia, such as Igor Girkin, who led Russian special forces in Crimea and the Donbas in 2014, Chechnya, Georgia and Ukraine, have been drawn upon by Russia's GRU to camouflage official Russian involvement in hybrid warfare activities.

Russia's intervention in the Balkans sought to halt Serbia from joining the EU and Montenegro from joining NATO. The most egregious example of Russian interference was the Kremlin's organisation of a coup attempt in Montenegro and an assassination plot against Montenegrin Prime Minister Milo Djukanovic using Serbian nationalists and Russian Cossacks, who had fought for pro-Russian separatists in the Donbas. Russian Cossack General Viktor Zaplatin told a rally in Montenegro 'The Orthodox world is one world. Here we see Serbs, Montenegrins, Russians, and Belarusians.' Twenty Serbs and Russians were imprisoned in Montenegro and an international warrant was issued for a further two Russians and three Serbs. Nemanja Ristic, one of the Serbs sought by Montenegro, was photographed next to Russian Minister of Foreign Affairs Lavrov during his December 2016 visit to Belgrade.

Putin's Goals

In the last quarter of a century, the United States has failed on three occasions to reset relations with Russia. President George W. Bush sought an alliance with Putin against Islamic terrorism following the 9/11 attacks on the United States, but this failed because both countries held different understandings of terrorism, and they fundamentally disagreed over Iraq. Obama and Clinton pinned high hopes upon the supposedly 'liberal' Russian President Medvedev but became disillusioned when Russian domestic and foreign policies failed to fundamentally change. Medvedev has become one of the most hawkish Russian leaders in the war against Ukraine. In his first term as president, Trump believed he could improve US relations with Putin but failed to do so.

Russia's imperial innocence in international affairs and the Kremlin's long-term hybrid warfare activities make successful US–Russian resets impossible to achieve. Russian imperial innocence will always claim that it is the innocent party in the deterioration of relations with the United States and therefore place the onus upon Washington to reset relations. The Kremlin believes Russia is in an existential conflict with the West that it did not begin but has been forced to respond to. Russia's actions, such as the 'special military operation' against Ukraine, are therefore purely defensive to protect Russia's 'state-civilisation'. Russian imperial innocence casts Russia as the victim of Western aggression in Ukraine and the West as having always mistreated, not treated with respect and snubbed Russia. 'The Kremlin has weaponised victimhood for years to justify its outward aggression against perceived threats' (The sins of their forefathers, 2023). Russian imperial nationalist claims of Russia's 'thousand-year' glorious past and superior civilisation are at odds with perennial complaints the West has repeatedly and successfully hoodwinked Russians.

Believing Russian imperial nationalist myths and stereotypes about Ukraine as an artificial construct and Ukrainians as Little Russians hoodwinked by the West led the Kremlin to feel confident the 'second best army in the world' would decisively and quickly defeat Ukrainians. Russian forces sent to Kyiv were given parade uniforms to hold a victory parade on Kyiv's main thoroughfare the *Khreshchatyk*. But the Kremlin's 'special military operation' did not go as planned. Russian forces withdrew from the Kyiv region in late March 2022, they were routed in Kharkiv in September and withdrew from Kherson, which was liberated by Ukraine in November 2022.

Following these defeats, Putin undertook three steps.

The first step was to launch a mobilisation of troops to increase the number of occupation forces in Ukraine from 175,000 to half a million. Although the Kremlin still uses the term 'special military operation', and punishes Russians with years of imprisonment for calling it a 'war', the reality is that mobilisation, a war economy, very high military casualties and daily Ukrainian strikes inside Russia point to what is taking place as constituting a full-scale war.

The second step taken by Putin was to increase xenophobic attacks against the 'collective West' (especially the United States and NATO) who are blamed for Russia's inability to secure a quick victory. Russia could not blame Ukrainians for their resilience and putting up a tough resistance, as that would mean recognising they are a separate people. Four months before Russia's full-scale invasion of Ukraine, Alexei Levinson (2021) of the Levada Centre wrote that for Russians 'To imagine that the Ukrainian army is at war with the Russian [army] is beyond the imagination of Russians.' Because most Russians believe the Kremlin's myths, stereotypes and propaganda about Russians and Ukrainians being 'one people', any Russian military action would be not 'perceived by them as war'. Russians believed they would find 'no resistance to us there [in Ukraine]'. Ukrainian resilience and resistance have upended these Russian imperial nationalist myths, but it would take Russia's military defeat, or the non-fulfilment of the Kremlin's 'special military operation' objectives, for Russians to fully comprehend what they have been told about Ukraine and Ukrainians is a pack of lies.

The third step taken by Putin was to seek external allies who could supply military equipment lacking in Russia and who also condemned the US-led unipolar order. Long-standing anti-Americanism, support for replacing the US-dominated unipolar order with a multipolar system and goal of ending Western sanctions united Russia, Iran, North Korea and China in the Anti-Western Axis of Upheaval and some countries in the Global South, particularly in Africa (see Kendall-Taylor and Fontaine, 2024; Cole and Feng, 2024; Trofimov, 2024). Türkiye refused to sell *Bayraktar* drones to Russia, which therefore gave the Kremlin no choice but to turn to Iran. China, initially taken aback by Russia's invasion, which had made it cautious in 2022, became the main external enabler of Russia's military machine from 2023 (Kuzio, 2024a). Finally, North Korea used the window of opportunity to establish military cooperation with Russia, break out of international isolation and receive financial income from supplying artillery shells and cannon fodder for the front lines (Kuzio, 2024a, 2024b, 2024c, 2024d). In January 2025, nearly three years into the full-scale war, Ukraine captured the first North Korean POWs thousands of miles from home who fought for Russia in a full-scale war in Europe.

Conclusion

This chapter has discussed six different aspects of xenophobia in Russia and how this has intertwined with Russia's imperial nationalist obsession with Ukraine. Anti-Western xenophobia and distrust of the West as a threat to Russia have dominated Tsarist, Soviet and Russian history, while attempts at emulating and catching up with the West during periods of liberalisation have been brief. Russia evolved from an authoritarian into a fascist dictatorship after the constitution was changed to de facto extend Putin's rule indefinitely. There is a close link between political repression in Russia and the Kremlin launching a full-scale invasion of Ukraine. Unlike an authoritarian system which does not need to mobilise the population, a fascist dictatorship requires mobilisation of the population for Russia's full-scale war against Ukraine. Putinism was born in a brutal war in Chechnya, where the capital city of Grozny was destroyed, a harbinger to come for the Syrian city of Aleppo and the Ukrainian port of Mariupol (Garner and Kuzio, 2025). A cult of war in Putin's Russia translated into military aggression against Georgia, Ukraine and Syria, hybrid warfare attacks against Europe and North America and acceptance of very high Russian casualties. This cult of war was accompanied by nearly two decades of de-humanisation of Ukrainians, which prepared the ground for the perpetrating of war crimes against the Ukrainian people, primarily Russian speakers who the 'special military operation' was ostensibly protecting. As a great power, Putin's Russia believes it can ignore international laws or interpret them differently to meet its imperialist goals. Russia justifies its annexation of Crimea by pointing to the West's support for the independence of Kosovo, irrespective of the fact that Ukraine has never diplomatically recognised Kosovo; the analogy with Crimea would be more comparable if Albania had annexed Kosovo. Russia's actions do not comply with international law and are simply old-fashioned nineteenth-century imperialism.

The origins of Russia's leaders in the Soviet *siloviki* created a permissive environment for the flowering of conspiracy theories. Russia's *siloviki* rulers are convinced that the USSR was brought down by

Western conspiracies and machinations while colour revolutions were orchestrated by Western secret services for regime change, pulling Ukraine into the West, and dividing the 'Russian people'. Soviet *siloviki* believed dissidents in the Soviet Union were puppets of Western secret services. Meanwhile, former Soviet *siloviki* ruling Russia are convinced that participants in colour revolutions are pawns in the hands of the CIA and other Western secret services. With roots in Soviet anti-Ukrainian nationalist propaganda, which we discussed in Chapter 5, Russian leaders believe Ukrainians are incapable of creating their own state and, therefore, because Ukraine is a US puppet state and the West's 'Anti-Russia' bridgehead, it must be destroyed and its people returned to their Little Russian identity.

Finally, anti-Western xenophobic discourse and hybrid warfare against the West have worked in parallel since 2007. Russia views its military aggression against Ukraine as part of its hybrid war against the West. Since 2022, the emergence of Russia as a 'revolutionary power' has placed it on a full-blown collision course with the West. The failure of the 'special military operation' to quickly conquer Ukraine and install a pro-Russian puppet regime led to Russia seeking military and other forms of assistance from its allies in the Anti-Western Axis of Upheaval – Iran, North Korea and China. The four members of the Axis of Upheaval believe they are at war with the US-led unipolar world in Ukraine and Israel – two Western puppet states which should be wiped from the map.

References

1000 and 4000 Days of Personality Cult in Support of Russia's War against Ukraine. (2024). *EUvsDisinfo*, 4 December. https://euvsdisinfo.eu/1000-and-4000-days-of-personality-cult-in-support-of-russias-war-against-ukraine/

Apt, C. (2024). 'Russia's Elimination Rhetoric against Ukraine: A Collection', *Just Security*, 26 August. www.justsecurity.org/81789/russias-eliminationist-rhetoric-against-ukraine-a-collection/

Aron, L. (2023). *Riding the Tiger. Vladimir Putin's Russia and the Uses of War*. Washington DC: American Enterprise Institute.

Ash, L. (2024). *The Baton and Cross. Russia's Church from Pagans to Putin*. London: Icon Books.

Barros, G. (2025). *Russia's Quiet Conquest: Belarus*, Institute for the Study of War, 14 January. www.understandingwar.org/sites/default/files/Russia%27s%20Quiet%20Conquest%20Belarus.pdf

Belton, C. (2022). 'The Man Who Has Putin's Ear – and May Want His Job', *The Washington Post*, 13 July. www.washingtonpost.com/world/2022/07/13/nikolai-patrushev-russia-security-council-putin/

Brandenberger, D. L. and Dubrovsky, A. M. (1998). 'The People Need a Tsar: The Emergence of National Bolshevism as Stalinist Ideology, 1931–1941', *Europe-Asia Studies*, 50 (5): 873–892.

Bondarev, B. (2022). 'The Source of Russian Misconduct. A Diplomat Defects from the Kremlin', *Foreign Affairs*, 101 (6): 36–55.

Cole, B. and Feng, J. (2024). 'Map Shows Possible WWIII Frontlines If Russia Invaded Europe', *Newsweek*, 14 December. www.newsweek.com/map-russia-invades-europe-1999747

Corum, L. (2018). 'Project Russia: The Bestselling Book Series of Putin's Russia', *South Central Review*, 35 (1): 74–100.

Davis, J. (2024). *In Their Own Words. How Russian Propagandists Reveal Putin's Intentions*. Stuttgart: Ibidem; New York: Columbia University Press.

Department of Homeland Security/Federal Bureau of Investigation. (2016). *GRIZZLY STEPPE – Russian Malicious Cyber Activity (Report)*. www.us-cert.gov/sites/default/files/publications/JAR_16-20296.pdf

Dixon, R. and Abbakumova, N. (2024). 'Confident of Victory over Ukraine, Russia Exhibits Western Trophies', *The Washington Post*, 4 May. www.washingtonpost.com/world/2024/05/04/russia-war-trophies-ukraine-moscow/

Dixon, R. (2024). 'Under Putin, a Militarized New Russia Rises to Challenge US and the West', *The Washington Post*, 6 May, www.washingtonpost.com/world/interactive/2024/putin-values-russian-society-conservatism/

Efimov, A., Vasilchenko, V. and Lyapin, I. (2024). 'The Collective West. What Is Putin Really Talking about When He Rails against the West?' *Meduza*, 20 February. https://meduza.io/en/feature/2024/02/20/the-collective-west

Etkind, A. (2023). *Russia against Modernity*. London: Polity Press.

Garner, I. (2023). *Generation Z. into the Heart of Russia's Fascist Youth*. London: Hurst.

Garner, I. and Kuzio, T. (2025). Edited. *Russia and Modern Fascism: New Perspectives on the Kremlin's War against Ukraine*. Stuttgart: Ibidem; New York: Columbia University Press.

Gordon, M. R. (2022) 'Russia's Demands on Ukraine Must Be Addressed Urgently', *Wall Street Journal*, 6 January. www.wsj.com/articles/russias-demands-on-ukraine-must-be-addressed-urgently-russian-official-says-11641470402

Grove, T., Cullison, A. and Pancevski, B. (2023). 'How Putin's Right-Hand Man Took Out Prigozhin', *The Wall Street Journal*, 22 December. www.wsj.com/world/russia/putin-patrushev-plan-prigozhin-assassination-428d5ed8

Grylls, G. (2024). 'Putin Compares Himself to Jesus in His Battle to Uphold Tradition', *The Times*, 9 April. www.thetimes.com/world/article/vladimir-putin-jesus-christ-comparison-russia-7720bgz7w?t=1737639786670

Gudkov, L. (2023). 'Longing for the "Great Power"', *Levada Centre*, 25 December. www.levada.ru/2023/12/25/toska-po-velikoj-derzhave/

Horycheva, Y. (2022). 'Ukrainians Describe Russian Troops Astonished by Basic Amenities', *Radio Free Europe/Radio Liberty*, 26 July. www.rferl.org/a/ukraine-villagers-describe-russian-troops-/31960860.html

Kagan, F. W., Jhaveri, A., Ganzeveld, A., Carl, N. and Barros, G. (2024). 'Why You Can't Be an Iran Hawk and a Russian Dove', *Institute for the Study of*

War, 18 April. www.understandingwar.org/backgrounder/why-you-cant-be-iran-hawk-and-russia-dove

Kasparov, G. (2023). 'Biden Needs a New Foreign Policy Team', *Wall Street Journal*, 2 November. www.wsj.com/articles/biden-needs-a-new-foreign-policy-team-israel-ukraine-d6b8c151

Karaganov, S. (2022). 'We Are Witnessing a New World in the Making', *Rossiiskaia Gazeta*, 26 October. https://karaganov.ru/en/sergei-karaganov-we-are-witnessing-a-new-world-in-the-making/

Karaganov, S. (2025). 'Breaking the Back of Europe: What Should Russia's Policy Be Towards the West', *Russia in Global Affairs*, 22 January. https://globalaffairs.ru/articles/slomat-hrebet-evrope-karaganov/

Kimmage, M. and Shapiro, J. (2024). 'The Myths That Warp How America Sees Russia – And Vice Versa', *Foreign Affairs*, 25 January. www.foreignaffairs.com/united-states/myths-warp-how-america-sees-russia-and-vice-versa

Kendall-Taylor, A. and Fontaine, R. (2024). 'How America's Adversaries Are Uniting to Overturn the Global Order', *Foreign Affairs*, 103 (3): 50–63.

Kuzio, T. and D'Anieri, P. (2018). *The Sources of Russia's Great Power Politics: Ukraine and the Challenge to the European Order*. Bristol: E-International Relations. www.e-ir.info/publication/the-sources-of-russias-great-power-politics-ukraine-and-the-challenge-to-the-european-order/

Kuzio, T. (2017). 'Ukraine between a Constrained EU and Assertive Russia', *Journal of Common Market Studies*, 55 (1): 103–120.

Kuzio, T. (2022). *Russian Nationalism and the Russian-Ukrainian War: Autocracy-Orthodoxy-Nationality*. London: Routledge.

Kuzio, T. (2024a). 'China Consistently Enables Russia's War of Aggression against Ukraine', *Eurasia Daily Monitor*, 21 (128), 10 September.

Kuzio, T. (2024b). 'Russia Escalates Its War against Ukraine into Global War against the West', *Eurasia Daily Monitor*, 21 (158), 30 October.

Kuzio, T. (2024c). 'Nine Things Western Analysts Got Wrong about Russia and Its Invasion of Ukraine', *Eurasia Daily Monitor*, 21 (33), 4 March. https://jamestown.org/program/nine-things-western-experts-got-wrong-about-russia-and-its-invasion-of-ukraine/

Kuzio, T. (2024d). *Crimea 2014–2024: Where Russia's War Started and Where Ukraine Will Win*. Jamestown Foundation, 8 July. https://jamestown.org/program/crimea-where-russias-war-started-and-where-ukraine-will-win/

Langdon, K. C. and Tismaneanu, V. (2020). *Putin's Totalitarian Democracy. Ideology, Myth and Violence in the Twenty-First Century*. Cham: Imprint Springer International Publishing.

Laruelle, M. (2014). 'The "Russian Idea" on the Small Screen: Staging National Identity on Russia's TV', *Demokratizatsiya*, 22 (2): 313–333.

Lavrov, S. (2021). 'Grazhdanskaia voina na Ukraine daleka ot zavershennia', *RIA Novosti*, 31 December. https://ria.ru/20211231/lavrov-1766234596.html

Lavrov, S. (2022). 'Foreign Minister Sergey Lavrov's Remarks and Answers to Media Questions at a News Conference on Russia's Foreign Policy Performance in 2021', 14 January. https://mid.ru/pt/press_service/minister_speeches/1794396/?lang=en

Lavrov, S. (2024a). '"For the Freedom of Nations" Forum of Supporters of the Struggle against Modern Practices of Neocolonialism', 16 February. https://mid.ru/en/foreign_policy/news/1932745/

Lavrov, S. (2024b). 'Statement to the UN Security Council', 6 July. www.mid.ru/en/press_service/minister_speeches/1962040/

Lavrov, S. (2025). 'The UN Charter Should Become the Legal Foundation of a Multipolar World', *Russia in Global Affairs*, 4 February. https://eng.globalaffairs.ru/articles/un-charter-lavrov/

Levada Centre. (2021). 'Crimea,' 19 May. www.levada.ru/en/2021/05/19/crimea-3/

Levada Centre. (2023a). 'Attitude to countries', 5 April. www.levada.ru/en/2023/04/05/attitude-to-countries-february-2023/

Levada Centre. (2023b). 'International Relations', 6 August. www.levada.ru/2023/06/08/mezhdunarodnye-otnosheniya-otsenki-maya-2023-goda/

Levada Centre. (2023c). 'Velikie strany, otnoshenie k SShA, ES, Kitaju i Ukraine, grazhdanam etykh stran', 9 December. www.levada.ru/2023/09/12/velikie-strany-otnoshenie-k-ssha-es-kitayu-i-ukraine-grazhdanam-etih-stran/

Levada Centre. (2024). 'Conflict with Ukraine: Key Indicators, Responsibilities, Concerns, Threat of Clash with NATO and Use of Nuclear Weapons', 7 July. www.levada.ru/2024/07/04/konflikt-s-ukrainoj-osnovnye-indikatory-otvetstvennost-povody-dlya-bespokojstva-ugroza-stolknoveniya-s-nato-i-primeneniya-yadernogo-oruzhiya/

Levinson, A. (2021). '"Yesli zavtra voina". Kak Vlyiaiet Nan as Novostnoi Shum Provtorzhenie', *Levada Centre*, 24 November. www.levada.ru/2021/11/24/esli-zavtra-vojna-kak-vliyaet-na-nas-novostnoj-shum-pro-vtorzhenie/

Looking Glass Cyber Solutions. (2015). *Operation Armageddon: Cyber Espionage as a Strategic Component of Russian Modern Warfare (Report)*. www.lookingglasscyber.com/webinar-operation-armageddon

Matthews, O. (2023). *Overeach. The Inside Story of Putin's War against Ukraine*. London: Mudlark.

McGlynn, J. (2023). *Russia's War*. Cambridge: Polity.

Medvedev, D. (2021). 'Pochemu Bessmyslenny Kontakty S Nyneshnim Ukrainskim Rukovodstvom', *Komersant*, 11 October. www.kommersant.ru/doc/5028300?tg#id2123320

Medvedev, D. (2022). 15 June. https://t.me/medvedev_telegram/111

Medvedev, D. (2024). Interview, *Argumenty i Fakty*, 17 July. https://aif.ru/politics/russia/dmitriy-medvedev-poryadok-zapada-eto-kidalovo

Medvedev, S. (2023). *A War Made in Russia*. London: Polity Press.

New Survey Finds Most Russians See Ukrainian War as Defence against West. (2024). NORC, University of Chicago, 9 January. www.norc.org/research/library/new-survey-finds-most-russians-see-ukrainian-war-as-defense-against-west.html

Nicolosi, R. (2022). 'Paranoia, Resentment, and Reenactment: The Russian Political Discourse on the War in Ukraine', *Ab Imperio*, 2002 (3): 247–261.

Nothing New from the East. (2025). *EUvsDisinfo*, 4 February. https://euvsdisinfo.eu/nothing-new-from-the-east/

Patrushev, N. (2025). Interview, *Komsomolskaya Pravda*, 14 January. www.kp.ru/daily/27651/5036217/
Paxton, R. O. (2005). *The Anatomy of Fascism*. London: Penguin.
Pertsev, A. (2022). 'Compassion, Tolerance, and Love for Others'. What the Kremlin's Latest Propaganda Guides Tell Pro-Government Media Outlets to Say about the War', *Meduza*, 2 August. https://meduza.io/en/feature/2022/08/02/compassion-tolerance-and-love-for-others
Pew Research Centre. (2017). 'Religious Belief and National Belonging in Central and Eastern Europe', 10 May. www.pewresearch.org/religion/2017/05/10/religious-belief-and-national-belonging-in-central-and-eastern-europe/
Pomerantsev, P. (2022). 'Ukraine Is the Next Act in Putin's Empire of Humiliation', *New York Times*, 26 July. www.nytimes.com/2022/07/26/opinion/russia-ukraine-putin.html
Putin, V. (2005). 'Annual Address to the Federal Assembly of the Russian Federation', 25 April. http://en.kremlin.ru/events/president/transcripts/22931
Putin, V. (2007). 'Speech and the Following Discussion at the Munich Conference on Security Policy', 10 February. www.en.kremlin.ru/events/president/transcripts/statements/24034
Putin, V. (2013). 'Orthodox-Slavic Values: The Foundation of Ukraine's Civilisational Choice conference', 27 July. www.en.kremlin.ru/events/president/news/18961
Putin, V. (2021). 'On the Historical Unity of Russians and Ukrainians', 12 July. http://en.kremlin.ru/events/president/news/66181
Putin, V. (2022a). 'Address by the President of the Russian Federation', 24 February. http://en.kremlin.ru/events/president/news/67843
Putin, V. (2022b). 'New Year Address to the Nation', 31 December, http://en.kremlin.ru/events/president/transcripts/speeches/70315
Putin, V. (2023a). 'Valdai Discussion Club meeting', 5 October. http://en.kremlin.ru/events/president/news/72444
Putin, V. (2023b). 'Speech to the World Russian Peoples Council', 28 November. http://en.kremlin.ru/events/president/news/72863
Putin, V. (2024a). 'President of Russia, Meeting of the Valdai Discussion Club', 7 November. http://en.kremlin.ru/events/president/news/75521
Putin, V. (2024b). 'Results of the Year with Vladimir Putin', 19 December. www.en.kremlin.ru/events/president/transcripts/75909
Ramani, S. (2023). *Putin's War on Ukraine. Russia's Campaign for Global Counter-Revolution*. London: Hurst.
Reznikov. O. (2023). 'I was Ukraine's Defence Minister. Here's My Message for our Allies: We Must not Lose Sight of Victory', *The Guardian*, 8 September. www.theguardian.com/commentisfree/2023/sep/08/ukraine-defence-minister-allies-victory-military-oleksii-reznikov
Rid, T. (2021). *Active Measures. The Secret History of Disinformation and Political Warfare*. London: Profile Books.
Rumer, E. (2022). 'Putin's Long War', *Carnegie Endowment for International Peace*, 9 December. https://carnegieendowment.org/research/2022/12/putins-long-war?lang=en

Russian Ministry of Foreign Affairs. (2021a). 'Treaty between the United States of America and the Russian Federation on Security Guarantees', 17 December. https://mid.ru/ru/foreign_policy/rso/nato/1790818/?lang=en

Russian Ministry of Foreign Affairs. (2021b). 'Agreement on Measures to Ensure the Security of the Russian Federation and Member States of the North Atlantic Treaty Organization', 17 December. https://mid.ru/ru/foreign_policy/rso/nato/1790803/?lang=en&clear_cache=Y

Russian Ministry of Foreign Affairs. (2025). 'Foreign Ministry statement in connection with the US strikes on Iran', 22 June. https://mid.ru/en/foreign_policy/news/2029109/

Satter, D. (2017). *The Less You Know, the Better You Sleep. Russia's Road to Dictatorship under Yeltsin and Putin.* London and New Haven, CT: Yale University Press.

Shevtsova, L. (2014). 'The Putin Doctrine: Myth, Provocation, Blackmail, or the Real Deal', *The American Interest*, 14 April. www.the-american-interest.com/2014/04/14/the-putin-doctrine-myth-provocation-blackmail-or-the-real-deal/

Sidorov, A. (2024). 'Russia and the West After the SMO: A New Level of Confrontation.' *International Affairs (Moscow)* 3 July. https://en.interaffairs.ru/article/russia-and-the-west-after-the-smo-a-new-level-of-confrontation/

Slater, W. (1998). 'Russia's Imagined History: Visions of the Soviet Past and the New 'Russia Idea', *Journal of Communist Studies and Transition Politics*, 14 (4): 69–86.

Snegovaya, M., Kimmage, M. and McGlynn, J. (2023). 'The Ideology of Putinism. Is It Sustainable?' 27 September. www.csis.org/analysis/ideology-putinism-it-sustainable

Soldatov, A. and Borogan, I. (2022). 'Dead Water: How the Russian Security Services' Paranoid Mindset Justifies the War', *SCEEUS Guest Report* 5. https://sceeus.se/en/publications/dead-water-how-the-russian-security-services-paranoid-mindset-justifies-the-war/

Spain Details Its Strategy to Combat the Russian Mafia. (2010). *US Diplomatic Cable*, Madrid, 8 February. https://wikileaks.org/plusd/cables/10MADRID154_a.html

Surnacheva, E. (2024). 'What Is Putin's "SVO goals": a 2022 Document Reveals Russia's Plans for the Post-War Structure of Ukraine', *Nastoiashcheie Vremia*, 4 November. www.currenttime.tv/a/dogovor-project-systema/33185521.html

The Kremlin's Security Demands Mean Insecurity for the Rest of Us. (2021). *EUvsDisinfo*, 26 December. https://euvsdisinfo.eu/the-kremlins-security-demands-mean-insecurity-for-the-rest-of-us/

The Sins of Their Forefathers. (2023). *EUvsDisinfo*, 26 January. https://euvsdisinfo.eu/the-sins-of-their-forefathers/

Trofimov, Y. (2024). 'Has World War III Already Begun? An Axis of Autocracies Led by Russia, China, Iran and North Korea Is Challenging the Democratic World Order', *Wall Street Journal*, 14 December. www.wsj.com/world/has-world-war-iii-already-begun-16fb94c9?mod=Searchresults_pos3&page=1

Troianovski, A. (2022). 'Putin Concedes Military Failings, but Insists Russia Will Win', *New York Times*, 21 December. www.nytimes.com/2022/12/21/world/europe/vladimir-putin-russia-ukraine.html

Trenin, D. (2024). 'Russia Is Undergoing a New, Invisible Revolution', *RT*, 2 April. www.rt.com/russia/595266-ukraine-west-pushed-russia/

United Nations. (2017). UN Security Council Resolution 2397, 22 December. https://main.un.org/securitycouncil/en/s/res/2397-%282017%29

United Nations. (2022a). 'UN General Assembly Demands Russia Reverse Course on 'Attempted Illegal Annexation',' 10 October. https://news.un.org/en/story/2022/10/1129492

United Nations. (2022b). 'UN General Assembly Demands Russian Federation Withdraw All Military Forces from the Territory of Ukraine', 2 March. www.eeas.europa.eu/eeas/un-general-assembly-demands-russian-federation-withdraw-all-military-forces-territory-ukraine_und_en

Vladimir Putin Is in Thrall to a Distinctive Brand of Russian Fascism. (2002). *The Economist*, 28 July. www.economist.com/briefing/2022/07/28/vladimir-putin-is-in-thrall-to-a-distinctive-brand-of-russian-fascism

Volkov, D. (2021). 'General Attitude of Russians to Sanctions – The West Is against Us. Interview with Levada Centre Director Denis Volkov', 10 June. www.levada.ru/2021/06/10/glava-levada-tsentra-obshhee-otnoshenie-rossiyan-k-sanktsiyam-zapad-protiv-nas/

Weiniger, G. and Grylls, G. (2025). 'Iran in Secret Talks with Russia to Bolster Nuclear Ambition', *The Times*, 12 January. www.thetimes.com/article/d651f344-2e44-4c2e-afbc-e45df740a92e?shareToken=d9ece98d721f156c04057762da63bfe4

Why Is the Kremlin so Hung up on Smearing Zelenskyy? (2025). *EUvsDisinfo*, 19 February 2025. https://euvsdisinfo.eu/why-is-the-kremlin-so-hung-up-on-smearing-zelenskyy/

World Russian Peoples Council. (2024a). 'Resolution of the 11th All-Russian Forum of the World Russian Peoples Council "Pan-Russian World" in Sevastopol', 29 July. https://vrns.ru/forumy/rezolyutsiya-ii-vserossiyskogo-foruma-vrns-russkiy-mir-v-sevastopole/

World Russian Peoples Council. (2024b). 'At the WRC "Pan-Russian World" Forum in Sevastopol, They Proposed to Adopt a Law on the Tripatrite Russian people', *Sevastopol*, 29 July. https://vrns.ru/forumy/na-forume-vrns-russkiy-mir-v-sevastopole-predlozhili-prinyat-zakon-o-triedinstve-russkogo-naroda/

Zelenskyy, V. (2024). 'New Year's Greetings from President of Ukraine Volodymyr Zelenskyy', 31 December. www.president.gov.ua/en/news/novorichne-privitannya-prezidenta-ukrayini-volodimira-zelens-95297

Zygar, M. (2024). 'Putin Sees America Hurtling to Disaster, with Trump at the Wheel', *New York Times*, 19 November. www.nytimes.com/2024/11/19/opinion/putin-trump-russia-america.html

INDEX

Adamski, Łukasz, 158, 162
Afanasev, Yury, 302
Aitmatov, Chinghiz, 246
Akhmetov, Rinat, 287
al-Assad, Bashar, 335, 343, 347, 357, 363
Alexander I, Emperor of Russia, 13
Alexander II, Emperor of Russia, 6
Alexander III, Emperor of Russia, 13
Alexander Nevsky, 13, 131, 147
Alexei I, Patriarch of Moscow, 95
Alexei II, Patriarch of Moscow, 79, 98, 100, 102, 105, 114–115, 130, 145
Alexeyeva, Ludmilla, 178
Aliyev, Huseyn, 224–225
Amalrik, Andrei, 137
Ambrosio, Thomas, 173
Andropov, Yuri, 127, 136, 143, 204, 343
Antelava, Natalia, 203
anti-colonialism, 76, 297, 312–313, 332
    Russian, 314, 334
    Soviet, 333
    Ukrainian, 315
anti-Russia Ukraine, 40–41, 43, 78, 152, 161–162, 197, 199, 237, 315, 348
anti-Western
    agenda, 149
    alliance, 302
    Axis of Upheaval, 16, 313, 334, 362, 373
    mood, 274
    xenophobia, 5, 12, 33, 38–39, 128, 144, 151, 239, 246, 305, 314, 345, 348
anti-Zionism, 192
Antonii, metropolitan, 116
Applebaum, Anne, 25, 47, 150–151, 153, 176, 241, 300
Apryshchenko, Victor, 132, 161

Apt, Clara, 36–38, 43, 46, 84, 243, 245–247, 324–325, 345, 352–353
Arahcheev, Vladimir, 37
Arel, Dominique, 1
Arnold, Richard, 184
Aron, Leon, 33, 39, 130, 143, 231, 345, 352, 368
Artyzov, Andrei, 68
Arutunyan, Anna, 3
Ash, Lucy, 3, 27–28, 35, 91, 202, 348
Atatürk, Mustafa Kemal, 321
autocephaly, of the Orthodox Church of Ukraine, 12, 78, 91, 94–95, 97, 99, 103, 110, 112, 114, 121, 131, 145, 220, 227, 232, 236

Baburin, Sergei, 77
Baekken, Havard, 128–129, 174
Baltic states, 25, 127, 138, 140, 159, 161, 195, 308, 312, 362
Baluk, Walenty, 278
Bandera, Stepan, 157, 160, 172, 177, 183, 189, 194, 201, 310, 364
Banderites, 177, 189, 192, 232
Barash, R., 72
Barbashin, Anton, 174, 241
Barros, George, 11, 16, 33, 242–243, 346, 364
Barroso, Manuel, 21
Bartholomew I, Patriarch of Constantinople, 95, 110, 131, 220
Beissinger, Mark, 178
Bekus, Nelly, 219
Belarusians, 5–8, 11, 25, 29, 31, 66, 93, 106, 187, 226–228, 230, 233, 241, 248, 322, 324, 330
Belton, Catherine, 39, 41, 238, 363

INDEX

beneficial rule of Russia, 307, 309
Berdyaev, Nikolai, 38
Bertelsen, Olga, 177, 200
Beseda, Sergei, 347
Bezborodov, Aleksandr, 64
Bezyev, Dmitrii, 37
Biden, Joe, 245, 357, 362, 366
Bigg, Claire, 219
Bilinsky, Yaroslav, 155, 185
Birch, Julian, 175
Blakkisrud, Helge, 217
Bogumił, Zuzanna, 145–146
Bohlen, Celestine, 29
Bolotov, Sergei, 112–113
Bolton, John, 34, 238
Bondarev, Boris, 352
Bordachev, T., 41
Borogan, Irina, 22, 25, 185, 346–347
Bortnikov, Alexander, 347
Bourdieu, Pierre, 62
Bovt, Georgii, 70
Brandenberger, D. L., 176–177, 309, 351
Brands Kehris, Ilze, 117
Bregy, Pierre, 173
Brezhnev, Leonid, 127, 136–137, 178, 204–205, 343
Brik, Tymofii, 224
Brudny, Yitzhak, 137, 276, 305
Brzezinski, Zbigniew, 5
Bukharin, Nikolai, 262
Bureiko, Nadiia, 224–225, 235
Bush, George W., 2, 357, 368, 372

canonical territory, 12, 99–100, 106, 113, 121, 191, 220
capital, symbolic, 58, 62–63, 66, 70, 84–85, 93, 103, 108, 119, 270, 273, 288
Carl, Nicholas, 75, 364
Carlson, Tucker, 37
Carothers, Thomas, 283–284
Catherine I, Empress of Russia, 13, 47, 127, 301, 328, 353
Catherine II, Empress of Russia, 151
Chaffin, Joshua, 44
Chaplin, Vsevolod, 109
Chawryło, Katarzyna, 80
Chernenko, Konstantin, 127, 136, 204, 343

Chernomyrdin, Viktor, 59
Chernyshenko, Dmitry, 68
China, 15, 114, 194, 302, 313, 326, 334–335, 343–345, 349, 360–362, 366, 373, 375
Chornovil, Vyacheslav, 195
Chovgan, Vadym, 25
Chupyra, Olga, 224
Cichowlas, Ola, 151
Clinton, Bill, 44, 372
Clinton, Hillary, 369
Clover, Charles, 29
Coalson, Robert, 203
Cohen, Eliot A., 2
Cohen, Roger, 27, 35
Cohen, Stephen, 245
Cole, Brendan, 349, 373
colonialism, 301–303, 309, 320–321, 332
  Russian, 143, 300, 309, 314, 320, 328, 334
  Soviet, 301, 309
  Tsarist, 303
  Western, 300, 309, 316, 324, 355
Commonwealth of Independent States, 28, 72, 116, 196, 229
Communist Party of Ukraine, 7, 221, 225, 227, 234, 249, 263–264, 272
compatriots, 30, 58, 60–62, 69, 85, 115, 233, 351
Conquest, Robert, 154, 160
Cook, James, 333
Corum, Lynn, 173, 347, 350–351, 363
Cossacks, 177, 184, 187, 371
Coynash, Halya, 147, 185, 201
Crimea
  annexation of (2014), 9, 11, 24, 28, 38, 45–46, 109, 127, 205–206, 232, 249, 346, 349, 354, 358, 360, 365–366, 374
Crimean Tatars, 176, 333
crimes against humanity, 13, 127–128, 130, 134, 141, 143–144, 147, 301, 303
Cullison, Allan, 34, 238, 347, 363
Curanović, Alicja, 74, 86, 99, 113–116, 121

D'Anieri, Paul, 3, 8, 22, 221, 225, 237–238, 242, 260, 285–286, 364
Darczewska, Jolanta, 197

Davis, Julia, 3, 37, 175, 198, 241, 247, 310, 321, 331, 343, 348, 355
de Grieff, Pablo, 153–154
de Rivière, Nicolas, 117
de-communisation, 8, 14, 128, 130, 133, 141, 153, 157, 159–160, 180, 218, 225, 228, 236, 272, 289, 303–304, 308, 310
de-humanisation, 3, 13, 26, 46–47, 66, 198, 217, 238–239, 246, 352, 374
de-militarisation, 10, 16, 22, 40, 221, 239, 247, 249, 346
democratisation, 15, 78, 163, 223–224, 227, 248, 260, 274, 277, 285, 289
de-nazification, 9, 14, 16, 22, 40, 43, 68, 81, 153, 175, 197, 200, 221, 239, 241, 246–247, 249, 323, 331, 346
Denikin, Anton, 69, 241
Deryugina, Tatyana, 217
Destivelle, Hyacinthe, 92
Dickinson, Anna, 92–93, 112, 272, 285
Dixon, Robyn, 28, 47, 350, 352, 362, 370–371
Djukanovic, Milo, 371
Dmitri Donskoy, 131
Dmitriev, Yury, 147
Dollbaum, Jan, 273
Domańska, Maria, 129, 144, 146, 159, 280, 323
Donaruma, William, 248
Donetsk Peoples Republic, 2, 40, 111, 325
Dontsov, Dmytro, 7
Doroshko, M., 263
Drach, Ivan, 271
Driscoll, Jesse, 1
Dubrovskiy, Vladimir, 282, 285
Dubrovsky, A. M., 351
Dugin, Alexander, 29, 37, 64–65, 75, 83, 138, 304
Dunlop, John B., 137
Durand, Olivia I., 45, 329–330, 333
Dzyuba, Ivan, 134, 175, 268–269

Eckel, Mike, 300, 309–310
Ecumenical Patriarch, 91, 106, 159
Edenborg, Emil, 21
Efimov, Artem, 352
Ellis, Jane, 97
Empire

Austro-Hungarian, 6, 245, 266
British, 136
Ottoman, 321, 329
Russian, 5, 29, 34, 46, 133, 176, 178, 263, 299, 305, 319, 329
Soviet, 120, 127, 269, 299, 301, 308, 312–313, 362
Tsarist, 5–6, 8, 22, 25, 28, 30, 132, 150, 157, 172–173, 175, 188, 226, 230–231, 236, 287, 301, 303, 306–307, 309–310, 313, 316, 330, 332–333
Engels, Friedrich, 308
Engström, Maria, 75–76
Ennis, Stephen, 246
Epstein, Mikhail, 127
Eras, Laura, 223
Eristavi, Maksym, 308
Erlacher, Trevor, 41, 172
Erlanger, Steven, 275
Esemirova, Natalia, 347
Etkind, Alexander, 127, 345
Euromaidan Revolution, 3, 9, 10–12, 14, 22, 26, 30, 40–41, 47, 80–81, 91, 109–110, 130, 140, 157, 159–162, 173, 198–202, 220–221, 223, 225, 232–233, 245, 272–273, 275, 278–279, 284–286, 288, 352, 368–369
European Parliament, 141–143, 157, 240, 287, 299, 331, 334, 370
European Union (EU), 8, 22, 38, 78, 80, 103–105, 109, 116, 140–141, 161, 173, 197, 199, 203, 206, 218–220, 223–224, 227, 229, 231–232, 236, 240, 249, 271–272, 284–285, 287, 289, 298–299, 301, 314, 343, 346, 357, 361, 367–371
exclusivist, 109

Farmer, Kenneth C., 25, 305
fascists, 14, 29, 43, 128, 135, 162, 172, 174, 182, 189, 196, 198–203, 205–206, 245, 299, 310, 324, 334, 353–354, 369
Fedor, Julie, 134–135
Feifer, Gregory, 39
Felgenhauer, Pavel, 41, 143
Feng, John, 349, 373
Fico, Robert, 347
Field, Sean, 248

INDEX 385

Filaret (Denysenko), metropolitan, 97–99
Filatov, Sergei, 105–106
Filevska, Tetyana, 3
Filipowicz, Mirosław, 312
Filonova, Svetlana, 100
Finkel, Eugene, 3, 22–23, 27, 37, 181, 276
Firsov, S., 110
Fisun, Oleksandr, 277, 283
Fokht, Elizaveta, 34, 238
Fontaine, Richard, 349, 373
Fournier, Anna, 183
Franchetti, Mark, 150, 202
Francis, Pope, 114, 118–119
Freedman, Lawrence, 34
French, Howard W., 313
Frolov, Kirill, 232
Fursov, Andrey, 132

Gaddy, Clifford G., 202
Gagarin, Yuri, 136
Gaidar, Yegor, 59
Galuzin, Mikhail, 40
Gaman-Golutvina, Oksana, 274
Ganzeveld, Annika, 364
Garner, Ian, 3, 33, 35, 198, 217, 221, 241, 244, 248, 350, 355
Gaufman, Elizaveta, 159
Gelashvili, Tamta, 221, 223
genocide, 13, 22, 31, 37, 65, 82, 128, 153–156, 159–160, 174, 176, 194, 197, 199–200, 228, 231, 233, 236, 238–241, 246, 299–304, 310–311, 313, 316, 318–320, 332–334
Georgescu, Calin, 369
Gil, Grzegorz, 277
Glazyev, Sergei, 245
Goble, Paul, 94, 243, 315
Gogol, Nikolai, 237
Gorbachev, Mikhail, 7, 23, 29, 97, 127–129, 133–137, 139, 143, 182, 194–196, 204, 261–262, 268–270, 274, 302, 320–321, 343, 355, 363
Gordon, Michael R., 357
Gorodnichenko, Yuriy, 217
Goryashko, Sergey, 34, 238
Great Patriotic War, 12–13, 15, 23, 30, 64, 71, 85, 127–139, 141, 143–144, 146, 149–152, 155, 157–158, 160–162, 184, 197, 202, 204, 226, 228, 231, 238, 273, 303, 355
great power, 5, 32–33, 44, 57, 85, 127, 129, 132–133, 144, 151, 162, 231, 237, 245, 301, 312, 322, 325–326, 334, 344, 349, 353, 356, 372, 374
Greene, Taylor Marjorie, 118
Grek, Ivan, 315
Gretskiy, Igor, 33, 37, 274, 321, 323
Griffin, Roger, 129
Grove, Thomas, 34, 154, 238, 347, 363
Grylls, George, 33, 351, 364
Gubarev, Pavel, 325
Gudkov, Lev, 301, 344
Gumenyuk, Nataliya, 25

Hale, Henry, 1, 221, 224, 234, 281
Harding, Luke, 25, 34, 43, 202, 238, 241
Hauter, Jakob, 1–3, 200, 232
Hedrick, Hedrick, 44, 136
Heinemann-Gruder, Andreas, 300
Higgins, Andrew, 129
Higgins, Charlotte, 248
Hill, Fiona, 202
Hird, Karolina, 82–83
historiography, 25, 187, 311
 American, 312
 Russian, 176, 182, 187, 305, 307
 Soviet, 137, 181, 230, 301, 306–307, 310
 Ukrainian, 43, 181
Hitler, Adolf, 154, 193, 197, 355
Hnatiuk, Aleksandra, 268–269
Hodnett, Grey, 186
Holodomor (death by hunger), 7, 65, 128, 154–157, 159–160, 176, 180, 195, 228, 231, 236, 239, 248, 269, 300, 303, 304, 311, 333
Holub, Oleksandr, 157
Holy Rus, 12, 28, 57, 76, 79, 83–85, 115, 135, 182, 191, 220, 310, 323–325, 351
holy war, 15, 33, 76, 82–83, 201, 321, 324, 348
Homo Sovieticus, 7, 110, 153, 179–180, 186, 226, 233, 307, 311, 342
Hook, Kristina, 172, 247
Horsfjord, Vebjørn, 83
Horvath, Robert, 310
Hosking, Geoffrey A., 26

386 INDEX

Hovorun, Cyril, 78
Hrushevsky, Mykhaylo, 6, 159, 181, 187, 305, 332–333
Hrycak, Jarosław, 263, 265, 267
Hrynevych, Ludmilla, 27
Hryshchenko, Konstantin, 80
Hrytsenko, O., 156
Hrytsenko, Pavlo, 316
Huntington, Samuel P., 273
Hutchings, Stephen, 132
Hvat, Ivan, 191

Ibrahim, Azeem, 246
identity, 8, 12, 14, 23, 26, 113, 162–163, 173, 175, 179, 182, 200, 230, 241, 244, 248, 260, 262, 287, 306, 311, 317–319, 323
    Belarusian, 218–220, 226–227, 229–230, 289
    civic, 31–32, 46, 234, 321
    imperial, 30
    invented, 83
    Little Russian, 30, 81, 198, 220, 225, 375
    Orthodox, 99, 103
    Pan-Russian, 6–7, 10, 30, 39–41, 57, 62, 79, 85, 102, 107, 115, 218–221, 223, 225, 229–230, 232–234, 237, 248–249, 305
    racial, 31–32, 297
    Russian, 23, 26, 30–32, 34, 39, 60, 84, 287, 297, 321, 323, 354, 356
    Slavic, 225–226
    Soviet, 218, 226, 269, 276
    state-civilisation, 64, 70, 297
    Ukrainian, 5–7, 10, 15–16, 35, 40, 78, 82–83, 112, 121, 136, 156, 176, 179, 187–188, 196, 198, 205–206, 217–223, 225–227, 229, 231, 233–237, 246, 248, 260, 271–272, 274, 288–289, 298, 304, 333, 352
Ilyin, Ivan, 11, 27, 32, 36–39, 64–65, 69, 174, 241, 303, 345
Ilyushina, Mary, 150
institutionalisation, symbolic, 57–59, 64–67, 85
invasion of Ukraine
    first of (2014), 3, 11, 38, 86, 130, 149–150, 199, 204–205, 220, 278, 286, 343, 346, 352, 365, 368
    full-scale of (2022), 1, 3, 5, 13–14, 16, 22, 25–27, 35–36, 39, 41, 46, 57, 63, 66, 74–76, 82, 95, 108, 110, 113, 117–118, 121, 128, 143, 145, 149–150, 152, 180, 190, 194, 201–202, 217–220, 224, 234, 236, 238–242, 246, 250, 274, 279, 282, 286, 289, 300, 312, 316, 321, 327, 331, 344, 347, 349–350, 352, 354, 356–358, 366–367, 373–374
Irysova, M., 61
Ishchenko, Rostislav, 246
Ivakin, Vsevolod, 248
Ivan III, Grand Prince of Moscow and all Russia, 13, 24
Ivan the Terrible, Tsar of all Russia, 147, 301
Ivanov, Sergei, 347
Iwański, Tadeusz, 80

Jesus Christ, 33, 102, 109, 351
Jhaveri, Ashka, 364
John Paul II, 91, 97, 100, 187, 191. *See also* Wojtyla, Karol
Jones, Lesya, 183
Joo, Hyung-min, 306

Kadyrov, Ramzan, 321, 364
Kagan, Frederick W., 33, 37, 242–243, 364
Kaganovich, Lazar, 177, 181
Kagarlitskii, Boris, 70
Käihkö, Ilmari, 224
Kangaspuro, Markku, 134–135
Karaganov, Sergei, 44, 243, 303, 326, 355, 363
Kara-Murza, Aleksei, 70, 308
Karatnycky, Adrian, 3
Karmanau, Yuras, 147
Karpov, Georgii, 93, 96
Kasianov, Georgiy, 66–67
Kasparov, Garry, 362
Kassymbekova, Botakoz, 309–310
Katanaev, Ivan, 198
Katechon, 75–76, 302, 322–325, 334
Katyn massacre, 128, 145–146, 160
Kaurov, Valerii, 78
Kazantsev, Andrei, 73
Kendall-Taylor, Andrea, 349, 373
Kennedy, Paul M., 320
Khapaeva, Dina, 144, 147, 231

INDEX 387

Khmelnytsky, Bohdan, 329
Kholmogorov, Yegor, 76
Khromeychuk, Olesya, 183
Khrushchev, Nikita, 127, 136, 153, 176, 178, 205, 268
Khrushcheva, Nina L., 136
Khvylovy, Mykola, 7, 265–267, 272
Kiebuzinski, Ksenya, 154
Kim, Seongcheol, 273
Kimmage, Michael, 27–28, 32, 35, 150, 297, 322, 332, 345, 355
Kinetz, Erika, 25
Kipling, Rudyard, 309
Kipshidze, Vakhtang, 117
Kirill, Patriarch of Moscow, 28, 36, 59, 73, 76, 79, 81–83, 91, 94, 105–110, 114, 116, 118, 129, 131, 145, 152, 182, 232, 287
Kirillov, Igor, 348
Kirillova, N. A., 37
Kivalov, Sergei, 316
Klid, Bohdan W., 180
Koczetkow, Aleksandr, 274
Koena, Jean-Fernand, 300, 309–310
Kohn, Hans, 1, 221
Kohut, Andriy, 128
Kolasky, John, 179
Kolesnichenko, Vadym, 316
Kolesnik, Nikolai, 191
Kolesnikov, Andrei, 27–28, 32–34, 135, 321–322
Kolomoysky, Igor, 287
Kolov, Bojidar, 322–324
Kolstø, Pål, 217
Kondrashyn, Viktor, 65
Konovalets, Yevhen, 364
Kopelev, Lev, 137
Koposov, Nikolay, 226, 232
Korostelev, Alexey, 286
Kosmodemiańska, Zoya, 131
Kostelnyk, Havryil, 95–96
Koval, N., 3, 27–28, 32, 61, 85
Kovalchuk, Yuri, 27
Kovalenko, Georgy, 109–110
Kovalev, Alexey, 246
Kozak, Dmitry, 347
Kozerova, Veronika, 25
Kozicki, Andrzej, 57–58, 84
Kozyrev, Alexei, 69, 274
Krasivsky, Anton, 247

Kravchuk, Leonid, 98–99, 154–156, 159, 196, 226, 236, 249, 270, 272, 275, 280, 304
Kryshtanovskaya, Olga, 128, 136, 226
Kuchma, Leonid, 21, 102, 154–157, 159, 188, 226, 236, 238, 249, 272, 275, 280, 282, 288–289, 300, 304, 314, 323, 357
Kudelia, Serhiy, 249, 277
Kuijt, Ian, 248
Kulakov, A., 44
Kulchytskyy, Stanislav, 154, 263–264
Kulyk, Volodymyr, 31, 224–225, 234
Kupchinsky, Roman, 178
Kuraev, Andrey, 301
Kurginyan, Sergei, 29
Kurin, Richard, 248
Kurkov, Andrey, 183, 199
Kuzio, Taras, 1, 3, 8–9, 21, 24–25, 31, 35, 40, 78–79, 98–99, 128, 130, 133, 141, 154, 156, 157, 159, 173, 179–180, 182, 187–188, 190, 192, 194–198, 217, 221, 224–225, 231, 233, 235–237, 241, 249, 260, 269–272, 275, 277, 288, 301, 303–304, 306–307, 311–312, 316, 323, 332–333, 350, 354, 357, 364–365, 369, 373–374
Kuzyk, Petro, 1, 217
Kwasniewski, Alexander, 47
Kyiv
  regime, 324, 359
  Rus (Kievan Russia), 6, 35, 45–46, 80, 94, 159, 172, 181–182, 187, 228, 230–231, 305, 309, 311, 333
Kyiv-Pechersk Monastery, 95, 107–108

Lahodych, M., 96
Langdon, Kate C., 28, 38, 240, 303, 321, 342
Laquer, Walter, 23, 143
Laruelle, Marlene, 29, 34, 68–69, 128, 217, 245, 320, 323, 343, 345
Larys, Martin, 1, 3
Lassila, Jussi, 134–135
Laurus (Škurla), metropolitan, 145
Lavrov, Sergei, 33–34, 43, 114–116, 193, 198, 310, 331, 349, 356–359, 372
Lawrinenko, Jurij, 176
Le Pen, Marine, 369
Lebed, Dmytro, 265

Lenin, Vladimir, 41, 127, 134, 136–137, 148, 175, 200, 245, 262, 265, 267–269, 272, 298, 308, 312, 316
Leshchenko, Natalia, 218–219, 225, 227, 229
Levinson, Alexei, 373
Levitin, Dmitri, 324
Levitsky, Steven, 282, 284
Lewis, David, 25, 32–33, 242, 321–322
Litvinenko, Alexander, 347, 364, 367
Luhansk Peoples Republic, 2, 40, 111
Luhn, Alec, 144
Lukashenka, Alexander, 9, 11, 22–23, 29, 42, 218–220, 223, 226, 228–230, 233, 238, 242, 289
Lunkin, Roman, 113–114
Lupynis, Anatoliy, 182
Luxmoore, Matthew, 159
Lyapin, Ilya, 352

Mace, James E., 263–265
MacKinnon, Mark, 144, 316
Madlovics, Bálint, 281
Magocsi, Paul R., 180–181
Magyar, Bálint, 281
Malakhov, Vladimir, 69–71
Malofeev, Konstantin, 39, 83–84
Manafort, Paul, 282
Manson, Katrina, 42
Mardan, Sergei, 46, 246
Marrow, Alexander, 42
Martin, Terry, 153, 180, 243
Marx, Karl, 308
Matrossov, Oleksandr, 131
Matsiyevsky, Yuriy, 286
Matthews, Owen, 301, 343, 347, 351
Mazepa, Ivan, 5, 34, 106, 159–160, 172, 177, 310
Mazour, Alexandr, 308
Mazyrin, Alexander, 92
McGlynn, Jade, 3, 24, 27–28, 32, 35, 38, 68, 150–151, 174, 184, 199, 217, 226, 231–232, 239, 241–242, 246, 248, 297, 322, 332, 343–344, 351, 355, 371
Mealie, Daniel, 33, 242–243
Medinsky, Vladimir, 12–14, 37, 40, 146, 152, 175, 177–178, 181, 323

Medvedchuk, Viktor, 10, 80, 108, 155, 236
Medvedev, Dmitri, 8–10, 32, 36, 38, 40, 43–44, 46, 78, 82, 115, 127, 133, 137, 154, 159, 174, 180, 194, 198, 231, 244, 246–247, 275, 323–325, 333, 348, 350, 352, 354, 358–359, 361–362, 372
Medvedev, Sergei, 28
Melnychuk, Vasyl, 25
memory politics
  Russian, 14, 23, 129, 131, 134, 140, 142, 145–146, 152, 158, 163, 219
  Ukrainian, 8, 14, 22, 78, 133, 156–157, 160–162, 174, 218, 323
messianism, Russian, 15, 32–33, 76, 84, 128–129, 131, 137, 297–298, 302, 320–322, 332
Michel, Casey, 182, 310
Mikkelsen, Noel, 33, 242–243
militarism, 32, 150, 354
millennium of Christianity, 182
Milonov, Vitaly, 355
Minchenia, Alena, 25, 217, 241
Mironowicz, Antoni, 112
Mitrokhin, Nikolay, 103, 218
model for Orthodoxy
  exclusivist for, 102, 106, 112, 120
  pluralistic for, 103, 105, 107, 109, 120
Moga, Teodor L., 224–225, 235
Mogilevskii, Konstantin, 64
Mokry, Włodzimierz, 267
Molotov, Viacheslav, 27, 62, 93, 129–130, 132, 138–140, 142–143, 145–146, 157, 160–161, 240, 321
Moore, Steven, 118
Moscow Patriarchate, 12, 69, 78–79, 91, 93, 97–101, 103, 105–107, 109–113, 115–121, 145, 334
Motyl, Alexander, 26, 28–29, 46, 154, 183–184, 221, 301, 312
Murtazashvili, Brick, 224
Musiał, Filip, 161
Myers, Steven L., 151
Mykytenko, Ivan, 188
myths, historical, 25, 93, 130, 138, 141, 144, 149–150, 152, 155, 173, 180, 187, 205–206, 224, 249, 302, 305–307, 310, 319, 333, 356

Nahaylo, Bohdan, 175
Naimark, Norman, 153–154
Narochnitskaya, Natalia, 74, 77
Naryshkin, Sergei, 65–67, 85, 193, 347
nationalism
  bourgeois, 179, 182–185, 189, 191
  civic, 1, 26–27, 235
  ethnic, 1, 224
  Russian, 5, 11–12, 15, 21, 24, 26–29, 34, 46, 58, 69, 73, 84, 106, 132, 135, 137, 151, 177, 204, 217, 219, 235, 240, 266, 273–274, 282, 287–289, 305–306, 321, 343
  Ukrainian, 30, 41, 172, 175–177, 182, 193–194, 197, 204, 206, 310, 315, 368
nationalists
  Chechen, 364
  Russian, 5–9, 16, 22–25, 28–29, 32–33, 37, 41, 43, 46, 76–77, 139, 143, 160, 173, 176, 184, 197–198, 201–202, 204–205, 218, 226, 230–231, 239, 243, 245–246, 248, 288, 297, 302, 305, 310, 321–323, 330, 355, 371
  Serbian, 371
  Ukrainian, 7, 13–14, 37, 41–42, 138, 156, 158, 160, 172–175, 177, 179, 184–185, 187, 189–191, 193–194, 196, 198–200, 202, 205–206, 217–218, 221, 223, 225, 228, 234, 245, 288, 299, 310, 324, 334, 354, 369
NATO (North Atlantic Treaty Organization), 8, 15, 23, 26, 32–34, 78, 118–119, 121, 140, 150, 173, 202–203, 206, 218–220, 229, 236, 243, 274–275, 297–298, 314, 321, 326, 331, 343, 348, 352, 354–357, 361, 364–368
Navalny, Alexei, 287
Nazis, 13, 32, 81, 84, 128, 131, 138–140, 150–151, 158, 173, 184, 193–194, 198, 202, 241, 273, 355
Nebenzia, Vasilii, 117
Nelson, Todd H., 150
neo-patrimonialism, 85, 120, 278
Never again! (Great Patriotic War's slogan), 13, 129, 133, 238
new world order, 302, 325–326, 334–335, 345, 349, 365

Nicholas I, Emperor of Russia, 306
Nicholas II, Emperor of Russia, 105, 178
Nicolosi, Riccardo, 350, 354
Nikiforov, Yevgienii, 84
Nikolskii, Sergei, 70–71
Nikonov, Viacheslav, 27, 62, 69, 132, 146, 321
Nizioł, Monika, 99
nostalgia, Soviet, 13–14, 27–30, 32, 57–58, 121, 133, 136, 150, 179, 188, 226, 229, 272, 298, 304, 347, 351
Nougayrede, Natalie, 144
Novorossiya (New Russia), 9, 15, 31, 45, 65

O'Brien, Philips, 2
Obama, Barack, 357, 365, 372
Obolensky, Serge, 173
Okara, Andrei, 106
Olejarz, Tomasz, 277
Oliinyk, Anna, 128, 130, 133, 141, 157, 180, 225, 236, 248, 272, 303
Olszański, Tadeusz, 136, 202
Omarova, Z., 60
Onuch, Olga, 1, 221, 224, 234
Onufrii (Berezovskyy), metropolitan, 110–111, 121
Orange Revolution, 1, 9, 78, 91, 101–103, 105–106, 110, 115, 120, 151, 196, 218, 226, 238–239, 245, 272, 274, 282–286, 289, 350
Organisation of Ukrainian Nationalists (OUN), 156–157, 172, 177, 204, 206, 228
orientalism, 3
Orthodox Church of Ukraine (OCU), 12, 91, 94–95, 97, 110, 114, 131, 145, 191, 220, 227, 232–233, 236, 323
Orwell, George, 359
Osborn, Andrew, 27, 30, 42
Osipian, Alexandr, 201
Østbø, Jardar, 73, 75
Ostroukh, Andrey, 27, 30

Pain, Emil, 72
Pakhaliuk, Konstantin, 149
Palotai, Mónika, 60
Pancevski, Bojan, 34, 238, 347, 363

Panov, Petr, 288
Pan-Russian
  civilisation, 83
  nation, 25, 29–30, 46–47, 71–73, 77,
    81, 85, 106, 120, 226, 230, 246, 308
  people, 11, 21–22, 24, 86, 94–95, 112, 119,
    121, 162, 173, 179, 220, 226–227, 230,
    232, 249, 288, 309, 330, 348, 352
  unity, 78, 160, 231, 306
Pan-Russian World, 7–14, 16, 21, 31–32,
    35–36, 46, 57–66, 68–71, 73–74, 76,
    78–86, 94–95, 103, 105–108, 110, 112,
    115, 120, 129–132, 135, 174, 182, 197,
    199, 206, 220, 226–227, 229–230,
    233, 236, 240, 243, 245, 248, 262,
    310, 315, 322, 333, 346, 352, 356, 371
pan-Slavism, 315
Parfitt, Tom, 153
Parolin, Pietro, 119
Party of Regions, 80, 102, 197, 217–218,
    220–221, 225–227, 233–234, 249,
    272–273, 278, 282, 285–287
Pastushenko, Tetiana, 158
paternalism, 150, 308
Patrushev, Nikolai, 34, 41–43, 190,
    198, 238–239, 244, 347–348, 360,
    362–363
Pavlo (Lebid), archbishop, 107–109
Pavlovsky, Gleb, 68
Paxton, Robert O., 129, 350–353
Pertsev, Andrey, 355
Peskov, Dmitri, 38, 331
Peter I, Emperor of Russia, 47, 91, 127,
    148, 151, 301, 328, 353. *See also* Peter
    the Great, Emperor of Russia
Peter the Great, Emperor of Russia, 12
Peter, Laurence, 144
Petlura, Symon, 160, 177, 310, 364
Petrov, Nikita, 131
Pimen (Izviekov), patriarch, 98
Pinchuk, Viktor, 287
Pipes, Richard, 312
Pitirim (Volochkov), archbishop,
    104, 351
Plokhy, Serhii, 3, 23–24, 172, 180, 223,
    230–231, 235, 237, 328
Plyushch, Leonid, 183
Pobedonostsev, Konstantin, 178

Pokrovskyj, Mikhail, 308
Poland, 9, 24, 68, 95, 112, 138, 140, 145,
    155, 161, 176, 186–188, 193, 224, 240,
    243, 312, 315, 360
Polish-Lithuanian Commonwealth, 355
Politkovskaya, Anna, 347
Poloz, Mykhaylo, 264
Pomerantsev, Peter, 147, 151, 352, 354
Pompeo, Mike R., 313
Pop-Eleches, Grigore, 224
Popova, Maria, 3, 40, 222–223,
    225–226, 243, 260, 275–276, 280,
    282–285, 288
Poroshenko, Petro, 9, 13, 22, 24, 40, 157,
    201, 218, 221–223, 226, 236–237,
    245–246, 248–249, 272, 304
Pospielovskii, Dmitry, 92
Postyshev, Pavlo, 267
Potichnyj, Peter J., 186
Poznyak-Khomenko, Natalka, 225
Prigozhin, Yevgeny, 280, 347
Primakov, Yevgeny, 61, 261, 274, 343
Prina, Federica, 315
Prince Vladimir, 35, 79, 181
Prince Volodymyr the Great, 159, 172,
    231. *See also* Prince Vladimir
Pritsak, Omelian, 23, 182
Prokhanov, Alexander, 29
propaganda
  nationalist/fascist/nazi, 43, 199, 297
  religious, 191–192
  Russian, 13, 45, 82, 128, 143, 152, 158–
    159, 162, 172, 189–190, 199–200,
    202–203, 206, 244–245, 354–355
  Soviet, 14, 113, 137–138, 157–158,
    176, 184–186, 188–189, 192, 194,
    203–204, 244, 327, 355
  Ukrainian, 187
Protsyk, Anna, 271
Pushkin, Alexandr, 39
Putin, Vladimir, 3–15, 21–38, 40–42,
    44–47, 57–62, 64–68, 71, 73–77,
    79–86, 91, 94, 102, 105–108,
    113–116, 118–120, 127–133, 135–151,
    153, 157–162, 173–177, 179–184,
    187–190, 193, 196–198, 200–204,
    206, 217, 219, 221, 226, 230–232,
    236, 238–245, 249, 264, 272–275,

279–280, 282, 284–289, 297–302,
305–306, 308–311, 313–316,
320–331, 333, 342–358, 360–374
Putinism, 28, 34, 143, 146, 305, 374
Pynnöniemi, Katri, 159

Rácz, András, 159
Ramani, Samuel, 3, 355
Rebet, Lev, 364
red-white-brown alliance, 29, 119, 135,
  137–138
re-Sovietisation, 85, 130, 143, 204, 248,
  273, 289
re-Stalinisation, 130, 143, 273, 289
revisionism, historical, 128–129,
  139–142, 146, 162, 174, 196, 240
Reznikov, Oleksii, 366
Reznikova, Ekaterina, 286
Riabchuk, Mykola, 271
Ribbentrop, Joachim, 129–130, 138–140,
  142–143, 145–146, 157, 160–161, 240
Rid, Thomas, 364
Rindlisbacher, Stephan, 316
Robertson, Graeme B., 224
Rogoża, Jadwiga, 144, 146
Rogozin, Dmitri, 243
Romanov, Mykhailo, 25
Rosenberg, Steve, 40, 202
Rowley, David G., 26, 28–29, 46, 307
Ruane, Joseph, 27
Rudenko, Olga, 183
Rumer, Eugene, 42, 150, 353
Russia
  Great, 132, 305, 330
  Little, 6, 22, 119, 203, 219, 247, 322,
    330, 333, 349
  Red, 39
  White, 39, 219, 330
Russian imperial innocence, 128, 140,
  152, 299, 302–303, 308, 311, 316,
  320, 331–332, 372
Russian Orthodox Church, 8, 12,
  14, 23, 28, 30, 36, 57, 59–61,
  64, 73, 77–79, 84–86, 91–117,
  119–121, 130, 132, 135, 145, 152,
  159, 191, 206, 220, 222, 227,
  232–233, 236, 240, 310–311, 324,
  334, 348, 355

Russian World Foundation, 8, 27–28,
  60–63, 65, 106, 132, 146, 371
Russianists, 2
Russians
  Great, 76, 93, 230, 307–308
  Little, 6, 9, 16, 21–22, 31, 37–38, 76, 82,
    93, 173, 180, 198–199, 205–206, 230,
    239, 249, 298, 334, 344, 372
  White, 11, 25, 76, 230, 288
  White émigré, 3, 9, 11, 25, 27, 32,
    36, 39, 77, 121, 135, 162, 174, 179,
    187–188, 240, 273, 304, 307
Russian-Ukrainian unity, 12, 24–25, 37,
  249, 323
Russification, 7, 134, 159, 175, 178–179,
  181, 183, 186, 195, 204–205, 223,
  228, 233, 244, 247–248, 263,
  267–268, 299, 308, 319
Russkij mir, 8, 57, 74, 94
Russophile, 3, 245
Rutte, Mark, 362, 365–366
Ryabkov, Sergei, 34, 238
Ryazanova-Clarke, Lara, 233
Rybkin, Ivan, 59

Sahaydak, Maksym, 193
Saldo, Volodymyr, 218
Samokhina, Sofia, 34, 238
Samoylyuk, Yekaterina, 79
Samson, Natalia, 344
Satter, David, 134, 174, 239, 347
Sauer, Pjotr, 37
Sava (Hrycuniak), metropolitan, 113
Scarr, Francis, 242
schizophrenia, 127, 297–299, 302,
  332–334
Schneider-Deters, Winfried, 32, 91, 129,
  175, 179
Sechin, Igor, 347
Seddon, Max, 42, 44
Sergeytsev, Timofey, 200, 246
Sergieiev, Nikolai, 77
Sergius (Stargoroskii),
  metropolitan, 92–93
Sergius of Radonezh, 114
Shakhovskoi, Dmitry, 39
Shapiro, Jeremy, 345
Sharafutdinova, Gulnaz, 217

Sharina, Natalia, 199
Shchedrovitsky, Petr, 68
Shchekochikhin, Yuri, 347
Shcherbytsky, Volodymyr, 7, 156, 178–179, 193, 195–196, 204–205, 269
Shearlaw, Maeve, 147
Shekhovtsov, Anton, 37
Shelest, Petro, 7, 178, 187, 204–205, 269
Sheptytsky, Andrey, metropolitan, 191, 193
Sheremetev, Boris, 39
Sherr, James, 33, 37, 321, 323
Shevchenko, Maksym, 69
Shevchenko, Taras, 63, 188
Shevel, Oxana, 1, 3, 40, 217, 221–223, 225–226, 243, 260, 275–276, 280, 282–285, 288
Shevtsova, Lilia, 274, 353
Shkandrij, Myroslav, 21, 176–177, 200, 303
Shlikhta, Natalia, 96–97
Shprintsen, Alex, 200
Shtohrin, Iryna, 316
Shukhevych, Roman, 157, 194
Shulman, Stephen, 30, 224–226
Shumeiko, Vladimir, 59
Shvartsman, Roman, 193
Shydlovsky, Pavlo, 248
Sidorov, Andrei, 247, 343
Siedin, Oleksandr, 287
Silitski, Vitali, 173
Simonyan, Margarita, 41, 198, 247, 348
Skorkin, Konstantin, 287
Skorokhod, Viacheslav, 248
Skripal, Sergei, 367
Skrypnyk, Mykola, 263
Slater, Wendy, 344
Slipyy, Joseph, 192
Slutsky, Leonid, 245
Small, Zachary, 248
Snegovaya, Maria, 27–28, 32, 35, 150, 297, 322, 332, 355
Sneider, Noah, 200
Snyder, Timothy, 39, 127, 154, 285, 299
Socher, Johannes, 313
Socor, Vladimir, 46, 175
Soldatov, Andrei, 22, 25, 185, 346–347
Sologoub, Ilona, 217

Solovey, Julia, 3
Solovyov, Vladimir, Russian philosopher and theologian, 38
Solovyov, Vladimir, Russian TV presenter, 36, 172, 241, 246, 321, 324, 343
Solzhenitsyn, Alexander, 30, 84, 182, 184, 188, 287, 310–311, 333, 345
Solzhenitsyn, Natalia, 182
Sorokowski, Andrew, 182
Soviet
  regime, 13, 24–25, 37, 41, 92, 112, 132, 154, 156, 160–161, 172, 175–176, 181–184, 186, 188–189, 191–192, 204, 233, 242, 298, 304–305, 308, 311, 328, 332
  Ukraine, 7, 95, 154, 175, 177–179, 181, 187–189, 192, 195–196, 201, 203, 243, 267–270, 277, 288, 329–330
  Union (USSR), 1–7, 12–13, 22–24, 27–30, 33, 35, 41–44, 46, 57, 60–61, 67–68, 77, 83, 84, 92, 95, 110, 113–114, 119, 127, 131–135, 138–140, 142, 149–150, 153, 157, 159, 161, 173–177, 180–186, 188–189, 192, 194–196, 198, 200, 203–204, 219, 226, 230–231, 233–234, 236, 240, 244, 262, 268–270, 274–276, 287, 297–298, 300, 303–306, 309–316, 321–322, 332–333, 342–346, 350–351, 353, 361, 363–364, 367–368, 375
Sovietisation, 91, 95, 267
special military operation, 2, 9–10, 15–16, 22, 24, 26, 31, 34, 40–42, 63, 81–82, 86, 140, 150, 173, 178, 182, 197, 199–200, 219, 221, 235, 237, 247, 249, 289, 300, 302, 305, 315, 321–323, 330–331, 334, 347–349, 352, 355–356, 359, 362–363, 372–375
Sperling, Valerie, 144
Stalin, Josef, 7, 13–16, 24–25, 27, 29–30, 33, 47, 57, 62, 70, 85, 93, 105, 112–113, 119, 121, 127–137, 139, 141, 143–151, 153–155, 176–178, 204, 231, 233, 239, 262, 264, 267, 269, 273, 286, 300–301, 303, 306, 311, 313, 321, 325, 328, 333, 345, 351, 353

Staniszkis, Jadwiga, 261–262, 268–269
Stankevich, Sergei, 99
Stanovaya, Tatiana, 149
statehood, 6, 21, 26, 33, 35–36, 45, 65, 71, 73, 130, 159, 181, 183, 240, 242, 246–247, 272, 300, 313, 317, 319, 323–324, 332–333
Statiev, Alexander, 177
Stepanenko, Kateryna, 37
Stephenson, Svetlana, 239
Stępniewski, Tomasz, 277
Stewart, Will, 203
Stoeckl, Kristina, 73, 116–117, 121, 322
Stoyanov, Yuri, 28, 324
Stricker, Gerd, 100
Stryjek, Tomasz, 263
Subtelny, Orest, 159, 263, 267–268
Sumlenny, Sergej, 240
Surkov, Vladislav, 38
Surnacheva, Yelizaveta, 346
Suslov, Mikhail, 178
Sych, Vitaly, 199–200
Sysyn, Frank, 191
Szporluk, Roman, 32, 183, 266
Szymanowicz, Adam, 184

Tataryn, Myroslaw, 99–100
Teague, Elizabeth, 186
Terelia, Yosyp, 97
Tereshchenko, Denys, 3, 27–28, 32, 61, 85
Tereshchuk, Halyna, 203
Tereshkova, Valentina, 182
Thoburn, Hannah, 174, 241
Tikhon (Shevkhunov), metropolitan, 35
Tillett, Lowett R., 305, 308
Tilly, Charles, 276
Tishkov, Valerii, 62
Tismaneanu, Vladimir, 28, 39, 240, 303, 321, 342
Tolochko, Petro, 66–67, 81
Tolstoy, Leo, 37, 39
Tolstoy, Pyotr, 37
Tolz, Vera, 24–25, 27, 29–31, 35, 84, 132, 134, 173, 230
Tornquist-Plewa, Barbara, 25, 217, 241
transition, 121, 157, 160, 163, 260–261, 280, 285, 287, 289

Treaty of Pereyaslav (1654), 24, 180, 182, 228, 230, 303
Trenin, Dmitri, 181, 370
trinity of the Russian people (Russians, Belarusians, and Ukrainians), 11, 227, 348
Trofimov, Yaroslav, 37, 349, 373
Trotsky, Leon, 262
Trump, Donald, 15, 44, 325, 348, 357, 359, 362–363, 366, 368–369, 372
Tsypin, Vladislav, 93
Tumarkin, Nina, 134
Turchynov, Oleksandr, 200, 288
Turii, Oleh, 101
Tymoshenko, Yulia, 217, 288
Tytiuk, Serhiy, 61

Ukraine
  as an artificial state, 26, 243
  as a puppet state, 9, 11, 15, 22–23, 34, 38, 40, 47, 198, 221, 237, 242–243, 245, 247, 249, 322, 334, 361, 370, 375
Ukrainian Greek Catholic Church (UGCC), 95, 97, 185, 191, 227
Ukrainian Insurgent Army (UPA), 154, 156, 228
Ukrainian Orthodox Church of the Moscow Patriarchate (UOC-MP), 111
Ukrainians
  de-humanisation of, 3, 13, 26, 46, 66, 198, 217, 238, 246, 374
  ethnic, 31, 178, 318–319
  Russian speaking, 31, 233–234, 300
  Western, 177, 183, 237, 282
Ulam, Adam, 312
United States of America (US), 15, 22, 26, 33, 43–44, 47, 60, 127, 129, 150, 173–174, 187, 202, 240, 246, 275, 298–299, 323, 326–327, 343, 345, 349–350, 352, 356–357, 361–364, 366–369, 372–373
Uzlaner, Dmitri, 116–117

values, spiritual-moral, 60, 71, 73–75
Valuev, Petr, 6
Vance, James D., 118
Vasilchenko, Vitaly, 352

Vasilyeva, Olga, 150
Vatican, 77, 97, 118–119, 131, 187, 190, 192
Velychenko, Stephen, 27, 30, 172, 181, 302, 306, 308–309, 312
Veres, Kristóf G., 60
Victory Day (9th May), 129, 132–133, 135–137, 146, 152, 158, 160–161, 231
Vlasov, Andrey, 184
Volkov, Denis, 149
Volodin, Viacheslav, 245
Volodymyr (Sabodan), metropolitan, 99, 101–105, 107–108, 110, 120
von Hagen, Mark, 180, 307
Voronina, Tatiana, 145–146
Vyedyenyeyev, Dmytro, 185
Vysotsky, Vladimir, 136

Walker, Shaun, 144, 202
Wandycz, Piotr, 312
Wanner, Catherine, 154
war, cult of, 15, 128–130, 133, 144, 151–152, 162, 197, 238–239, 246, 287, 298, 315, 347–348, 350, 354, 374
Wawrzonek, Michał, 8–10, 57, 61, 99, 182, 185, 187, 192
Way, Lucan A., 282, 284
We Can Do It Again! (Putin's slogan), 13, 129, 133, 136, 162, 238
Weber, Max, 146, 276, 278
Weiniger, Gabrielle, 364
Weiss, Andrew, 42
Whitacker, Bill, 248
White, Stephen, 128, 136, 226
Wilk, Andrzej, 278–279
Wilson, Andrew, 176, 179, 202
Wishnevsky, Julia, 147
Wojnowski, Zbigniew, 25, 178–179, 188, 191–192, 204, 223, 226
Wojtyla, Karol, 187. *See also* John Paul II
Wolczuk, Kataryna, 224, 271
Wołek, Artur, 277–278
Wolkonsky, Alexander, 173–174
Wołowski, Paweł, 79
World Russian People Council (WRPC), 130
World War II, 13, 24, 95, 112–113, 133, 138–140, 142–145, 151, 157–158, 160–162, 177, 183, 188–189, 191, 197, 199, 228, 231, 249, 261, 303–304, 312, 314, 320, 324, 332
Wynar, Lubomyr, 306, 332

xenophobia, 5, 15, 28, 85, 100, 334, 342, 347, 354, 374
anti Western, 5, 12, 33, 38–39, 128, 137, 144, 151, 239, 246, 305, 314, 345, 348, 354, 374
towards Ukraine, 151

Yanukovych, Viktor, 8–11, 14, 22–23, 36, 78–81, 101–102, 105, 108–109, 115, 153, 155, 157, 160, 197, 199–200, 220, 222–223, 226, 229, 231–234, 238, 249, 272, 275, 282, 285, 303–304, 369
Yarosh, Dmytro, 201
Yaroslav the Wise, Grand Prince of Kiev, 159
Yasen, Bohdan, 183
Yasinsky, Oleg, 246
Yefriemenko, Dmitri, 142
Yegorov, Yurii, 78
Yekelchyk, Serhy, 137, 177, 181, 268
Yelenskyi, Victor, 96–97, 100
Yeltsin, Boris, 7, 23, 29, 44, 99, 129, 133–135, 139, 269, 274, 276, 280, 302, 307, 313, 320–321, 343, 345
Yermolenko, Volodymyr, 244
Young, Cathy, 128, 154, 241, 246
Yunarmiia (Young Army, Russia), 151
Yurash, Andrii, 101
Yurchuk, Yuliya, 25, 158, 217, 241
Yushchenko, Victor, 8, 22, 40, 78, 101, 115, 133, 154, 156–157, 159–160, 174, 180, 197, 204, 222–223, 226, 231, 236, 249, 272, 275, 283, 288, 304, 323, 333, 347, 364
Yushenkov, Sergei, 347

Zakharova, Mariia, 245
Zaplatin, Viktor, 371
Zarycki, Tomasz, 58, 84
Zaslavskaya, Tatiana, 283
Zaslavsky, Victor, 137, 154
Zatulin, Konstantin, 77

Zelenskyy, Volodymyr, 8–9, 14, 22, 24, 35, 40, 117–118, 182, 193–194, 197, 202, 217, 219, 221–226, 234, 236–237, 245–246, 248–249, 272, 279, 287–288, 300, 304, 316–319, 324, 343, 352, 363
Zhdanov, Andrei, 177–178, 181
Zhegulev, Ilya, 36
Zhirinovskii, Vladimir, 77
Zhuchkovsky, Alexander, 24
Zhuk, Sergei, 225
Zhukov, Georgy, 131
Zhurzhenko, Tatiana, 134–135, 225, 233
Zinoviev, Aleksandr, 342
Zivanovic, Maja, 300, 309–310
Żochowski, Piotr, 197
Zolotukhin, Yuriy D., 243–244
Zotsenko, Ivan, 248
Zygar, Mikhail, 13, 14, 29, 34, 36–37, 41, 127, 132, 135, 143, 145–146, 150–151, 178, 181–182, 186, 231, 238, 309, 323, 363
Zyuganov, Gennadiy, 59, 73, 138, 273

For EU product safety concerns, contact us at Calle de José Abascal, 56–1°, 28003 Madrid, Spain or eugpsr@cambridge.org.

www.ingramcontent.com/pod-product-compliance
Ingram Content Group UK Ltd.
Pitfield, Milton Keynes, MK11 3LW, UK
UKHW020009021225
465586UK00015BA/461